# Thomas Jefferson and American Nationhood

This book emphasizes the centrality of nationhood to Thomas Jefferson's thought and politics, envisioning Jefferson as a cultural nationalist whose political project sought the alignment of the American state system with the will and character of the nation. Jefferson believed that America was the one nation on earth able to realize in practice universal ideals to which other peoples could only aspire. He appears in the book as the narrator of what he once called "American Story": as the historian, the sociologist, and the ethnographer; the political theorist of the nation; the most successful practitioner of its politics; and its most enthusiastic champion. The book argues that reorienting Jefferson around the concept of American nationhood recovers an otherwise easily missed coherence to his political career and helps make sense of a number of conundrums in his thought and practice.

Brian Steele is assistant professor of history at the University of Alabama, Birmingham. His work has appeared in the *Journal of American History* and the *Journal of Southern History*.

Endorsements for Brian Steele's *Thomas Jefferson and American Nationhood*

"In this important book Brian Steele interrogates the origins of Thomas Jefferson's thinking about the meaning and purpose of the United States. Steele delineates how Jefferson crafted an ideal of American nationhood through his politics as well as his study of the history and sociology of the new nation. He does so with verve and style. Steele makes an important and original contribution to our understanding of Jefferson and his time. This book will be a landmark in the literature."
Francis D. Cogliano, University of Edinburgh, Author of *Thomas Jefferson: Reputation and Legacy*

"Brian Steele's new book makes the most compelling case to date for Thomas Jefferson's central importance to American national mythology and history, offering fresh and crucially important insights to our understanding of his political thought and statecraft. Thomas Jefferson and American Nationhood is a major contribution to the rich literature on the author of the Declaration of Independence."
Peter S. Onuf, University of Virginia, Author of *Jefferson's Empire: The Language of American Nationhood*

"Steele brilliantly dissects Jefferson's complex relationship with America, portraying American nationhood not just as the intellectual product of a great mind, but as the love of Jefferson's life. Some of the enduring Jeffersonian paradoxes—his cosmopolitanism and his patriotism, his defense of local prerogative and his embrace of government power—are rendered newly intelligible in this elegant and forceful argument for nationhood as a defining obsession in Jefferson's thought."
Paul Quigley, University of Edinburgh

"Was Thomas Jefferson a localist or a nationalist? Did he give his first allegiance to Virginia or to the United States of America? How is he to be situated with regard to the nullificationists of 1832 and the secessionists of 1860? These have long been disputed questions, and in this volume Brian Steele addresses them in a manner not only forthright and eloquent, but also scrupulous and rigorous. He will no doubt be attacked, but his argument cannot be ignored."
Paul A. Rahe, Hillsdale College

"It would be hard to deny that Jefferson still matters to us today when we engage in our own acts of imagining America, and Steele's book, *Thomas Jefferson and American Nationhood,* helps us to see where that story begins. In his absorbing and informative study, Steele shows himself to be an expert interpreter of the Jefferson canon, familiar and unfamiliar alike. Readers will come away from this book with an enhanced appreciation of Jefferson's many ways of understanding America."
Herbert Sloan, Barnard College

CAMBRIDGE STUDIES ON THE AMERICAN SOUTH

Series Editors

Mark M. Smith, University of South Carolina, Columbia
David Moltke-Hansen, Center for the Study of the American South, University of
    North Carolina at Chapel Hill

Interdisciplinary in its scope and intent, this series builds on and extends Cambridge
University Press's long-standing commitment to studies on the American South. The
series not only will offer the best new work on the South's distinctive institutional,
social, economic, and cultural history but will also feature works in a national,
comparative, and transnational perspective.

Titles in the Series

Robert E. Bonner, *Mastering America: Southern Slaveholders and the Crisis of
    American Nationhood*
Christopher Michael Curtis, *Jefferson's Freeholders and the Politics of Ownership
    in the Old Dominion*
Peter McCandless, *Slavery, Disease, and Suffering in the Southern Lowcountry*
Jonathan Daniel Wells, *Women Writers and Journalists in the Nineteenth-Century
    South*

# Thomas Jefferson and American Nationhood

BRIAN STEELE

*University of Alabama, Birmingham*

CAMBRIDGE
UNIVERSITY PRESS

# CAMBRIDGE
## UNIVERSITY PRESS

32 Avenue of the Americas, New York NY 10013-2473, USA

Cambridge University Press is part of the University of Cambridge.

It furthers the University's mission by disseminating knowledge in the pursuit of education, learning and research at the highest international levels of excellence.

www.cambridge.org
Information on this title: www.cambridge.org/9781107635746

© Brian Steele 2012

This publication is in copyright. Subject to statutory exception and to the provisions of relevant collective licensing agreements, no reproduction of any part may take place without the written permission of Cambridge University Press.

First published 2012
First paperback edition 2015

*A catalogue record for this publication is available from the British Library*

*Library of Congress Cataloguing in Publication data*
Steele, Brian Douglas, 1970–
   Thomas Jefferson and American nationhood / Brian Steele,
   University of Alabama, Birmingham.
      pages cm. – (Cambridge studies on the American South)
   Includes bibliographical references and index.
   ISBN 978-1-107-02070-2
   1. Jefferson, Thomas, 1743–1826 – Political and social views.   2. Jefferson,
   Thomas, 1743–1826 – Philosophy.   3. United States – Politics and
   government – Philosophy.   I. Title.
   E332.2.S77   2012
   973.4´6092–dc23        2012013662

ISBN 978-1-107-02070-2 Hardback
ISBN 978-1-107-63574-6 Paperback

Cambridge University Press has no responsibility for the persistence or accuracy of URLs for external or third-party internet websites referred to in this publication, and does not guarantee that any content on such websites is, or will remain, accurate or appropriate.

# Contents

# Acknowledgments

"All this was given to you…"

This book has its earliest roots in a paper written for an inspired senior seminar with Lawrence Cress at the University of Tulsa and a dissertation written at the University of North Carolina under the direction of Don Higginbotham. Neither man lived to see the book; both shaped it in fundamental ways, and, I might add, altered the course of my life.

Among the other teachers who inspired me, I must, for the pleasure of mentioning them, single out Paul Dykes and Judith Kimrey at Booker T. Washington High School; Thomas Buckley at the University of Tulsa; and Harry Watson, Peter Coclanis, and Lloyd Kramer at Carolina. I understand even more today how much I owe to each of them. Harry, in particular, deserves a medal – and perhaps a therapist's license – for his open door and unfailing kindness.

My colleagues in the Department of History at the University of Alabama at Birmingham have been universally supportive and have provided a stimulating environment in which to think, teach, and write. I have benefited from knowing each of them. Andrew Keitt and Ray Mohl, extraordinary mentors in word and deed, each in his own way, has made this book possible and my life better. Neither has ever once disputed my childlike presumption that a closed door did not apply to me. Danny Siegel, Michele Forman, John Moore, and Mary Whall have also become valued friends – and mentors – here.

Dick Latner gave me my first job at Tulane University. I will always be grateful to him and the members of that department as well as the students I taught there and who taught me, in turn. Jim Tent, chair of the department my first few years at UAB, was generosity itself to me. I do not underestimate the value of his particular care or what it has meant to my family and to my ability to complete this project. Carolyn Conley, our current chair, has been supportive as the tenure clock ticked; I've learned much from her storehouse of knowledge. Tennant McWilliams, dean when I first arrived, understood the meaning of scholarship and its indispensability to good teaching; his enthusiasm infected me from the beginning. I am grateful for the UAB Advance grant that bought me a course release one semester and the laptop on which the majority of the manuscript was composed.

Andrew O'Shaughnessy at the International Center for Jefferson Studies gave me two months of uninterrupted time to write in the inspirational environs of Monticello. More, he offered consistently cheerful and enthusiastic support for my project. Endrina Tay, also at ICJS, offered me a "word fitly spoken" at just the right time. What a gift. Christa Dierksheide was extraordinarily generous with her time and knowledge and continues to be a trusted friend and adviser on all things Jefferson.

Conversations and various exchanges with Matthew Crow, Johann Neem, Rob McDonald, and Frank Cogliano – perhaps the finest Jefferson scholars of this generation – have been enormously challenging and exciting even as they have convinced me that I don't understand the half of it. Matt and Johann fundamentally shaped the way I read Jefferson; Johann read drafts of three of the chapters and offered invaluable suggestions for sharpening the argument. Rob and Frank both gave me opportunities to write through ideas that eventually made their way into the book, which is the stronger for their generosity and editorial guidance. Rob has been a valued friend for many years.

Kris Ray read portions of the manuscript and always challenged me to think bigger, as he does. Ruth Homrighaus stepped in at a crucial moment with her customary combination of ruthless editing and gentle guidance and affirmation. I am very grateful to John Boles for his support and encouragement at an early stage in the development of the argument.

Peter Onuf has surpassed his already extraordinary reputation for generosity. As he has with almost every scholar writing on Jefferson today, he has become a much appreciated surrogate mentor to me, and my debt to his scholarship will be clear in the pages that follow. My experience of his kindness and humor leaves fewer traces on the printed page; I acknowledge it here and thank him.

I owe an enormous debt, both intellectual and personal, to Paul Rahe, who read the entire manuscript in draft and offered invaluable guidance. His careful critique forced me to greater precision in many places and saved me from embarrassing errors in others. His support, in spite of certain fundamental disagreements with the argument, is a credit to his generosity.

I join a very long list of students and scholars grateful to William Leuchtenburg for an example, perhaps unattainable, of scholarship and integrity. Bill read the entire dissertation and portions of the draft manuscript, which might seem well outside his field of expertise were such limits applicable in his case. I appreciate him most for his fundamental decency, which I have experienced, in ways large and small, for many years now.

Chris and Mary Meyers, James and Joy Nelson, Margaret Myers, Susan Myers, and Mike Ross all transformed New Orleans into a city teeming with happy memories, much as David and Amelia O'Dell and Ben Huffman did for Chapel Hill.

With more space and ability, I would be justified in writing a volume on each of the following friends. As a substitute, I will simply affirm my love and admiration for Jonathan Weiler, Steve Keadey, Spencer Downing, Adam Tuchinsky, Karl and Elizabeth Davis, Bill Estes, and Mike Wilhoit: "I cannot tell how my ankles bend ... nor whence the cause of my faintest wish,/ Nor the cause of the friendship I emit ... nor the cause of the friendship I take again."

David Voelker read every word of the manuscript, some of them many times, and often at a moment's notice. If Emerson is right to say that a friend is "a person with whom I may be sincere" and who handles shortcomings with "tenderness," then David is surely the best of friends. He has long enlarged "the meaning of all my thoughts." One might search a lifetime for a more virtuous soul.

The book is much better for its time at Cambridge University Press. I had heard that Lewis Bateman sets the standard for professionalism and efficiency in academic editing. I heard correctly. Anne Lovering Rounds went beyond the call of duty in ways I very much appreciate. Both overlooked the numerous mistakes of a freshman author. The Press's anonymous readers clearly knew what they were about. I took every one of their invaluable suggestions as seriously as they engaged my manuscript; their work strengthened the thing immeasurably.

The portions of this work that have appeared in other forums are all the better for the careful attention of editors and anonymous readers. Chapter 2 is a slightly revised version of "Thomas Jefferson's Gender Frontier," *Journal of American History*, 95 (June 2008), 17–42. Chapter 3 is a revised and expanded version of "'The Yeomanry of the United States are not the *canaille* of Paris': Thomas Jefferson, American Exceptionalism, and the Spirit of Democracy," in Robert M. S. McDonald, ed., *Light and Liberty: Thomas Jefferson and the Politics of Knowledge* (Charlottesville: University of Virginia Press, 2012), 19–46. Portions of Chapter 6 first appeared in slightly different form as "Thomas Jefferson, Coercion, and the Limits of Harmonious Union," *Journal of Southern History*, LXXIV, No. 4 (November 2008), 823–854. And the Epilogue is a shortened and revised version of "Jefferson's Legacy: The Nation as Interpretative Community," in Francis D. Cogliano, ed., *The Blackwell Companion to Thomas Jefferson* (Malden, MA: Blackwell, 2012), 526–550. I am grateful to the publishers and editors of each, both for the original publications and for permission to reprint here.

Ruffin and Melissa Snow, in-laws from heaven, have made my way pleasant and have given me an extended family of incredible warmth and fun: Joel and Bradley, Daniel and Jenny, Lowell and Peggy have all enriched my life in ways too numerous to recount.

Brandon and Betsy, my life is irrevocably bound up with yours. I'm grateful to have such good and faithful siblings. And for new ones in Jen and Spencer.

Jennifer Snow and our four wonderful children, Gretchen, Cora, Christopher, and Graham, our pearls of great price, have endured the writing of this book and have given me a life apart from it. The very "earth is metamorphosed" in their hands.

I dedicate the book to Don Higginbotham, whose generosity, guiding hand, and fundamental goodness are deeply missed; to Sam Ramer, whose friendship buoyed me in dark times and light; and to my mother and father, who raised me to understand that there is something better than mammon. All of the above suggests that they were right. And to Jennifer, who reminds me every day.

"May I prove to be deserving of that high company."

# Key to Brief Citations

| | |
|---|---|
| *AHR* | *American Historical Review* |
| *AJL* | Lester J. Cappon, ed., *The Adams-Jefferson Letters: The Complete Correspondence Between Thomas Jefferson and Abigail and John Adams*, 2nd ed., (Chapel Hill, 1987) |
| *FE* | Paul Leicester Ford, ed., *The Works of Thomas Jefferson, Federal Edition*, 12 vols. (New York, 1904–1905) |
| *JAH* | *Journal of American History* |
| *JER* | *Journal of the Early Republic* |
| *JSH* | *Journal of Southern History* |
| *LC* | *Thomas Jefferson Papers*, Library of Congress |
| *L&B* | Andrew A. Lipscomb and Albert Ellery Bergh, eds., *The Writings of Thomas Jefferson*, 20 vols. (Washington, D.C., 1903–1904) |
| *Notes* | Thomas Jefferson, *Notes on the State of Virginia* (1784), ed. William Peden (Chapel Hill, 1954) |
| *PAH* | Harold C. Syrett, ed., *The Papers of Alexander Hamilton*, 25 vols. (New York, 1961–1977) |
| *PJM* | William T. Hutchinson et al., eds., *The Papers of James Madison* (Chicago and Charlottesville, 1962–) |
| *PTJ* | Julian P. Boyd, ed., *The Papers of Thomas Jefferson*, 34 vols. to date (Princeton, 1950–). |
| *PTJ, Retirement Series* | J. Jefferson Looney, ed., *The Papers of Thomas Jefferson, Retirement Series*, 8 vols. to date (Princeton, 2004–) |
| *ROL* | James Morton Smith, ed., *The Republic of Letters: The Correspondence Between Thomas Jefferson and James Madison, 1776–1826*, 3 vols. (New York, 1995) |
| *TJW* | Merrill D. Peterson, ed., *Thomas Jefferson: Writings* (New York, 1984). |
| *WJA* | Charles Francis Adams, ed., *Works of John Adams*, 10 vols. (Boston, 1850–1856). |
| *WMQ* | *William and Mary Quarterly*, Third Series |

# Introduction

## *Jefferson's America*

> My affections were first for my own country, and then generally for all mankind.
>
> Thomas Jefferson 1811[1]

Jefferson's most enduring love affair was with America. Onto it he projected some of his deepest longings, and he drew sustenance from its reciprocal affection. He neglected his family, his farm, and his books for it and at times seemed to abandon cherished principles and to forsake the world itself for its service. He must have been particularly gratified to hear John Adams admit that "the nation was with you," because his "yearning for" its "sympathy," as Henry Adams later suggested, "was almost feminine" and a "loss of popularity was his bitterest trial."[2] Jefferson long insisted that his principles were "unquestionably the principles of the great body of our fellow citizens," and, in point of fact, Henry Adams noted, "every one admitted that Jefferson's opinions, in one form or another, were shared by a majority of the American people." Jefferson's "visionary qualities seemed also to be a national trait," much to the dismay of the Federalists.[3] Jefferson had a palpable sense that his own life would always be bound up with America's, for good or ill – that his own fame and legacy depended to a large extent on America's future greatness. His relationship with America, then, was symbiotic, and his own assertions about America occasionally verged on the autobiographical. His claim to have expressed the sentiments

---

[1] Thomas Jefferson (hereinafter "TJ") to Thomas Law, January 15, 1811, *PTJ, Retirement Series*, 3:298–299.

[2] John Adams to TJ, May 1, 1812, in *AJL*, 301; Lester J. Cappon, ed., *The Adams-Jefferson Letters: The Complete Correspondence Between Thomas Jefferson and Abigail and John Adams*, (2nd ed., Chapel Hill, 1987); Henry Adams, *History of the United States of America in the Administrations of Thomas Jefferson* (New York, 1986), 100, 1239.

[3] To Elbridge Gerry, January 26, 1799, in *TJW*, 1058; Merrill D. Peterson, ed., *Thomas Jefferson: Writings* (New York, 1984); Adams, *History*, 117.

of all America in the Declaration of Independence looks very much like a way of saying that he spoke for America or, even more boldly, that America spoke through him. If the "sense of America" really did "approve" of Jefferson's views, as he once told Washington, he had merely to "acquiesce," in turn, for the identification to be complete.[4] In any case, he once told French political economist, Jean Baptiste Say, "I think for America."[5] Historians are sometimes frustrated by the tendency of Americans to take Jefferson as a kind of proxy for America, but Jefferson himself was probably the first to do so.[6] This book explores the story that Jefferson told about America and suggests that this narrative shaped his politics, his statecraft, and, ultimately, his – and our – identification of his own person with the nation. In short, it envisions Jefferson as the author of an American nationalism.

Nearly everything Jefferson did in public life (and much obliquely in private) he justified in the name of the American nation. Yet few historians have explored the centrality of nation as an organizing principle of Jefferson's thought, politics, and statesmanship.[7] Jefferson's nationalism manifested itself in a rhetorical discourse, a political and cultural project, and an evaluative assessment of American identity and experience as the universal ideal toward which all nations would one day aspire.[8]

There is no essential or exclusively authentic Jefferson, and I steer clear of any attempt to unveil one here. What I do suggest is that scrutinizing him through the lens of nationalism envisions some coherence to a career that others have characterized as a bundle of contradictions. Scholars have gleaned important insights by looking carefully at the sources of Jefferson's ideas. But Jefferson was not the defender of a preexisting Lockean or a classical republican tradition. These are scholarly paradigms – created to serve contemporary historiographical needs – that Jefferson might not have recognized as worth distinguishing in the way scholars have so carefully done.[9] Jefferson's thought was no doubt molded by his education and studies but was also crucially forged in the fires of experience and necessity. What if, instead of beginning with Jefferson's commitment to a tradition of thought, we begin with Jefferson's assumptions about national identity and try to understand the implications of those assumptions for his politics and statecraft? In other

---

[4] See TJ to Washington, September 9, 1792, in *TJW*, 996.

[5] TJ to Say, February 1, 1804, in *TJW*, 1144.

[6] See the reflections in Jan Ellen Lewis and Peter S. Onuf, "American Synecdoche: Thomas Jefferson as Image, Icon, Character, Self," in *AHR*, 103 (February 1998), 125–136.

[7] The major exception is Peter S. Onuf in *Jefferson's Empire: The Language of American Nationhood* (Charlottesville, 2000) and *The Mind of Thomas Jefferson* (Charlottesville, 2007).

[8] See Craig Calhoun, *Nationalism* (Minneapolis, 1997), 6.

[9] See Daniel Rogers, "Republicanism: The Career of a Concept," in *JAH*, 79 (June 1998), 11–38; Alan Gibson, *Understanding the Founding: The Crucial Questions* (Lawrence, 2007), 130–164.

words, what if we begin with Jefferson's conception of the "good people" whom he believed constituted the American nation in 1776, and with the stories he told about them?[10]

Nationhood was never a dispensable element in Jefferson's thought, never merely a means to an end. My emphasis on the significance of nationhood does not exclude the centrality of individual natural rights or federalism in his thought. To the contrary, Jefferson always imagined that when the American nation was truest to its character and purpose, individual rights and the deepest interests of its various communities would be fulfilled. Jefferson rarely had to prioritize rights or federalism over nationhood precisely because his highest universal principles were manifested, in historical time, in a particular nation, the only one on earth explicitly committed to them.

Jefferson's commitments to state, nation, and world overlapped. To the degree that scholars (or partisans) have emphasized one of these to the exclusion of others – Jefferson's Virginia provincialism, for example, over his enlightenment cosmopolitanism; his commitment to states' rights over his expansion of national power; his lifelong effort to enlarge the capabilities of individuals over his sense that such individuals were fully liberated only as members of something larger than the self – they have missed something crucial about the complexity of his thought.

Jefferson came of age – and grew old – among the Virginia gentry, and he remained throughout his long public career in national government a member of the planter class.[11] This fact, to be sure, informed his deepest values, but it did not limit (or exhaust) them. Likewise, his membership in the trans-Atlantic "republic of letters" was a fundamental aspect of his self-understanding, but he typically described in capacious or universal language characteristics he believed to be uniquely *American*. *Nationalism*, *cosmopolitanism*, and *provincialism* are not mutually exclusive, but are of necessity bound up with one another. Cosmopolitanism can be assimilated by provincial culture, nationalism is generally experienced locally, and cosmopolitan values can shape provincial perspectives. The tired and generally unexamined assertion that Jefferson meant *Virginia* when he said "my country," for example, is not only empirically false – Jefferson's "country" could mean Virginia, America, or Albemarle County, depending on the context – but is also analytically useless, telling us little about the way Jefferson's deepest values were an inseparable amalgamation of the cosmopolitan, nationalist, and provincial.

In this book, I make two broad suggestions that may appear to be in tension. First, I describe Jefferson as an American nationalist. American historians

---

[10] See "Original Rough Draught," in *PTJ*, 1:427.

[11] For two treatments that emphasize this aspect of Jefferson's public life, see, Herbert E. Sloan, *Principle and Interest: Thomas Jefferson and the Problem of Debt* (New York, 1995) and Ronald L. Hatzenbuehler, *"I Tremble for My Country": Thomas Jefferson and the Virginia Gentry* (Gainesville, FL, 2006).

have been reluctant to do this because they tend to juxtapose Hamilton's fiscal-military state with Jefferson's federalism. Now, to the extent that Jefferson understood the indispensability of a central state (and served in its offices for decades), he was a nationalist in this traditional sense, yes, and one of the aims of this book is, in fact, to recover this aspect of Jefferson's politics.[12] But when we drop the equation of nationalism with attachment to a particular form of the state, and focus instead on the claims Jefferson made about the nation, we can begin to see the multifarious nature of his nationalism.[13] If nations are the "imagined communities" that Benedict Anderson has suggested, then it might be fruitful to think of nationalism as the process of imagining.[14] And, indeed, Jefferson's imagining is a central subject of this book. If all nationalisms assume a collective homogeneity that renders internal differences superficial and external ones endemic and profound, Jefferson's was no exception.[15] He imagined a national unity deeply rooted in affection and in what he considered a peculiarly American set of characteristics: unified history, general prosperity, republican "spirit," and domestic happiness. Jefferson was, if not the first, then

[12] Also see the important insights in Colin Bonwick, "Jefferson as Nationalist," in Gary L. McDowell, Sharon L. Noble, eds., *Reason and Republicanism: Thomas Jefferson's Legacy of Liberty* (Lanham, MD, 1997), 149–168.

[13] Nationalism is less an "identification with the *state* than loyalty to the *nation*" (Walker Connor, "A Nation is a Nation, is a State, is an Ethnic Group is a ...," *Ethnic and Racial Studies* 1 [October 1978], 383; emphasis added). Among a multitude of studies, I have found particularly helpful two books by Craig Calhoun and two review essays by Lloyd Kramer. See Calhoun, *Nationalism* (Minneapolis, 1997) and *Nations Matter: Culture, History, and the Cosmopolitan Dream* (London and New York, 2007); Kramer, "Historical Narratives and the Meaning of Nationalism," *Journal of the History of Ideas*, 58 (1997), 525–545, and "Nations as Texts: Literary Theory and the History of Nationalism," in *The Maryland Historian*, 24 (1993), 71–82. I also gratefully acknowledge my debt to David Potter's classic essay, "The Historian's Use of Nationalism, and Vice Versa," in *AHR*, 67 (July 1962), 924–950, and to Peter Onuf, "Federalism, Republicanism, and the Origins of American Sectionalism," in Peter Onuf, Edward L. Ayers, Patricia Nelson Limerick, and Stephen Nissenbaum, *All Over the Map: Rethinking American Regions* (Baltimore and London, 1996), 11–37; 107–117. Also see the lucid introduction to the literature in Paul Quigley, *Shifting Grounds: Nationalism and the American South, 1848–1865* (New York, 2011), esp. 3–15.

[14] Anderson, *Imagined Communities: Reflections on the Origin and Spread of Nationalism* (London, 2006). Anderson is quick to point out that "imagined" does not mean "imaginary," a nice corrective to an assumption all too common in the literature on the "constructed" nature of nations (6). On the denaturalization of the nation, see Ernest Gellner, *Thought and Change* (Chicago, 1965), 150, 168, and Eric Hobsbawm, *Nations and Nationalism Since 1780: Programme, Myth, Reality* (Cambridge and New York, 1990), especially 1–15. For a brilliant defense of the viability and continued relevance of national history rooted in a vision of nations, not as assumptions to be taken for granted (naturalized), but as the results of historical processes, see Johann Neem, "American History in a Global Age," *History and Theory*, 50 (February 2011), 41–70, esp. 62–68. I also maintain a particular appreciation of David Hollinger, "The Historian's Use of the United States and Vice Versa," in Thomas Bender, ed., *Rethinking American History in a Global Age* (Berkeley, 2002), 381–395; and, from a different but not ultimately incompatible perspective, Louis A. Perez, Jr., "We Are the World: Internationalizing the National, Nationalizing the International," in *JAH*, 89 (September 2002), 558–566.

[15] See Liah Greenfeld, *Nationalism: Five Roads to Modernity* (Cambridge, MA, 1992), 7.

certainly the most prolific and articulate early exponent of a kind of American exceptionalism.

If my first contention dislodges nation (and nationalism) from an exclusive association with the state, my second turns our attention back to the state, though this time, I hope, with new eyes. Jefferson's conception of the state was both deeply intertwined with his nationalism and more complex and profound than a simple preference for limited government. Many of the most common spurious quotations attributed to Jefferson emphasize his hostility to state power, and many of Jefferson's actual phrases have been decontextualized and used for purposes he would not recognize as his own.[16] Thoreau, not Jefferson, asserted "that government is best which governs least," and Gerald Ford, not Jefferson, first warned Americans (in 1974) that "a government big enough to give you everything you want is a government big enough to take from you everything you have."[17] Misattribution of this sort is understandable because Jefferson did value limits on government power, and he eyed the state with an ambivalence rooted in traditional republican concerns about corruption: "Free government is founded in jealousy, and not in confidence," he wrote.[18] The point here is emphatically not to trade proof texts (we could certainly find genuine Jefferson quotes that approximate the spurious ones and others that undermine them, but that would do little to clarify matters) or to encourage a snide contempt for the public (hardly a Jeffersonian occupation, as we will see). But it is incumbent on the historian to seek to understand words in the context in which they were uttered. Ford's concern, for example, could not have been Jefferson's, precisely, rooted as it was in a critique of a twentieth-century welfare state that Jefferson could never have imagined. Jefferson can be neither a social democrat, a New Deal liberal, or a libertarian (or a Maoist, for that matter),[19] because he lived in a world that was not animated by the specific issues and institutions that gave rise to those later political ideologies. Indeed, one of my intentions is to recover the Jefferson of history from exclusive claims made by any twentieth-century political ideology. Jefferson's fear of consolidation and abuse of power was rooted in his democratic nationalism, and understanding this renders Jefferson's approach to government less sphinx-like and more coherent, if not always perfectly consistent or free from the gyrations of pragmatic flexibility that bewilder the ideologically rigid. What Jefferson feared about consolidation was its threat to disconnect the state from the only thing

---

[16] See the running list of lines misattributed to Jefferson compiled by the research staff at Monticello: http://www.monticello.org/site/jefferson/spurious-quotations, accessed August 13, 2011.

[17] Ford, Address to Joint Session of Congress, August 12, 1974. Text at John T. Woolley and Gerhard Peters, *The American Presidency Project*, Santa Barbara, CA: http://www.presidency.ucsb.edu/ws/?pid=4694, accessed June 11, 2010.

[18] Draft of the Kentucky Resolutions, October 1798, in *TJW*, 454.

[19] See Conor Cruise O'Brien, *The Long Affair: Thomas Jefferson and the French Revolution, 1785–1800* (Chicago, 1996), 150; Joseph Ellis, *American Sphinx: The Character of Thomas Jefferson* (New York, 1997), 127.

that could grant it legitimacy, the people. The goal of Jefferson's federalism, which diffused power, then, was, perhaps paradoxically, an intimacy between state and nation rather than an inflexible bulwark against state action.

Because, if "the nation" was, as Jefferson once told George Washington, "the source of authority with us," Jefferson also understood that the will of the nation enabled and required power.[20] The state could not rest content with proper ideology; it had an obligation to enact the nation's ends. As he once put it, "governments are republican only in proportion as they embody the will of the people *and* execute it."[21] Jefferson understood that threats to liberty could come from the state, certainly, and from private concentrations of power as well as distant empires. But the American federal system with its overlapping spheres of authority and separation of powers would limit state violence against citizens while also mobilizing government power for the fulfillment of the nation's purposes. This is why Jefferson could value the Bill of Rights precisely for setting "further guards to liberty without touching the energy of the government."[22]

Jefferson understood that the state could become powerful in ways that undermined liberty: He had seen this happen at home and abroad, even though he could never have anticipated all the resources the modern state has at its disposal to monitor and organize the most intimate details of the lives of citizens. But Jefferson's ambivalence became hostility only when the state failed to embody the will of the nation. By the mid-1790s, Jefferson believed that the Federalists were willing to take the power of the state as an end in itself rather than as a facilitator of the nation's purposes. So his political opposition was never about rendering government impotent. His end was always what he believed to be the only proper goal of the republican statesman: alignment of the state with the will of the nation. This commitment to nation offers a fundamental continuity between the politics he pursued in the 1790s and his statecraft as president. Despite the many apparent twists and turns in his career, the Ariadne's thread that follows them all is Jefferson's belief that government submission to what he called the "will of the nation" was sine qua non in a republic.[23] This book explores the ways in which that commitment played out over the various political battles of the era.

Jefferson envisioned a fairly intimate relationship between the state and the people, rooted in a democratic sensibility alien to the possessive individualism embraced by classic descriptions of modern American liberalism.[24] Jefferson

---

[20] TJ to George Washington, February 4, 1792, in *PTJ*, 23:100–101.

[21] TJ to Samuel Kercheval, July 12, 1816, in *TJW*, 1396, emphasis added. For important and compelling reflections on the relationship between executive energy and public approbation in Jefferson's thought, see Jeremy D. Bailey, *Thomas Jefferson and Executive Power* (Cambridge, 2007).

[22] TJ to John Paul Jones, March 23, 1789, in *PTJ*, 14:689.

[23] "Notes on the Legitimacy of Government," December 30 1792, in *PTJ*, 24: 802.

[24] For recent efforts to render American liberalism historically less individualistic and more democratic, see Adam-Max Tuchinsky, "'The Bourgeoisie Will Fall and Fall Forever': The *New-York*

never defended a radical individualism or imagined that democracy was possible in the absence of certain social conditions that made it viable. Without economic independence, education and access to information, and maximum popular participation in government, democracy would add up to nothing other than what all political thought to his day said it would: mob rule. In other words, democratic procedure was important to him, but it could never be efficacious in the absence of a substantive democratic culture – a culture that he believed existed uniquely in America.

I make no definitive claims here about American nationality, as distinct from Jefferson's assertions about it. In this sense, then, this study is both less and more than we typically get in studies of Jefferson. This is not a biography of Jefferson, nor is it an exhaustive history of his political thought, his statecraft, or his political career and achievements, much less an exploration of his personal life, though all of these are crucial to its theme. Neither do I tell the story of the nation itself (or even assume its unqualified existence) but, rather, identify and analyze the story Jefferson told about it. In doing so, I claim Jefferson as a progenitor of American nationalism, and I make suggestions about how his conception of the nation shaped his politics and statecraft. My goal is neither to find a definition for the nation nor to insist that Jefferson conforms to some predetermined theory of the nation, though many of those theories inform this work (and in crucial ways make it possible). Rather, I explore the process by which Jefferson himself imagined the nation and developed the claims he made on its behalf.

Because Jefferson believed that the nation was constituted by popular embrace of its existence and purpose, and that no state could be legitimate without embodying the people's will and aspirations, he never imagined that a nation could be understood entirely through a study of its intellectual elite. The people themselves (as several recent studies have demonstrated) created a national identity through their practices of nationhood and citizenship (including, but not limited to, participation in parades and national celebrations, absorption of civic texts, erection of memorials, voting, petitioning, writing, and imagining). Jefferson would be the first to – in fact *was* the first to – describe American nationhood as an embodiment of popular aspirations.[25]

But Jefferson's "American story" is worth thinking through if only because, like all discourse, it is an "event" in its own right, a "driving force ... of

---

*Tribune*, the 1848 French Revolution, and American Social Democratic Discourse," in *JAH*, 92 (September 2005), 470–497; James T. Kloppenberg, *The Virtues of Liberalism* (Oxford, 1998), esp. 21–37; and Kloppenberg, "In Retrospect: Louis Hartz's *The Liberal Tradition in America*," *Reviews in American History* 29.3 (2001), 460–476.

[25] Simon P. Newman, *Parades and the Politics of the Street: Festive Culture in the Early American Republic* (Philadelphia: University of Pennsylvania Press, 1997); Len Travers, *Celebrating the Fourth: Independence Day and the Rites of Nationalism in the Early Republic* (Amherst, 1997); David Waldstreicher, *In the Midst of Perpetual Fetes: The Making of American Nationalism, 1776–1820* (Chapel Hill, 1997); Francois Furstenberg, *In the Name of the Father: Washington's Legacy, Slavery, and the Making of a Nation* (New York, 2006).

history, and not merely [a] representation."[26] Arguments and assertions, David Hollinger reminds us, "are social acts" and, therefore, legitimate "objects of historical study."[27] If, like all national discourses, Jefferson's was congratulatory and often self-serving, ignoring, or papering over, the multiple contradictory realities and experiences that failed to align with it (or which might form the basis for an alternate narrative), such was, to some degree, the basis of its popular appeal.[28] The significance of Jefferson's narrative rests, in part, on its historical capacity to persuade large numbers of Americans (including historians), whose assent thereby constituted certain social realities in the early Republic and ultimately shaped the meaning of the nation for many.[29]

Jefferson also understood, as Thomas Bender put it, that "the nation cannot be its own context" but owes its existence to "a framework larger than itself."[30] From the beginning, Jefferson's assertions of American sovereignty assumed a "candid world" and a global system of states and national experiences and histories against which to define America's own. So the international or interstate system defined and legitimized the nation even as it threatened its existence.

Jefferson's national project was no mere exercise in political theory, and this exploration of his practices of nationalism remains separate from any discussion of whether Jefferson was a successful statesman. The sometimes crooked timbers of Jefferson's thought cannot be straightened without distorting the historical record. Though I make a case for the essential coherence of Jefferson's nationalism, I do not suggest that it remained unchanged or consistent throughout his life. We will witness plenty of contradictions and paradoxes – as we might very well expect of any pragmatic nationalism. The historian's task, it seems to me, is to describe, explain, and interrogate claims, not to force clarity on what is inherently irreconcilable. I hope to describe Jefferson's thought without necessarily embracing his as an absolutely trustworthy depiction of contemporary events (particularly when it comes to his assessment of Federalist motives and ideals). So, the book is not a defense or exoneration of Jefferson any more than it is an attack on him. Perhaps it should go without saying that what follows is not by any means the "whole truth" about Jefferson – everything we need to know. But if it is one truth

---

[26] Tzvetan Todorov, *On Human Diversity: Nationalism, Racism, and Exoticism in French Thought* (Cambridge, MA, 1993), xiii.

[27] David Hollinger, *In the American Province: Studies in the History and Historiography of Ideas* (Bloomington, 1985), x.

[28] For explorations of this theme, see Homi K. Bhabha, ed., *Nation and Narration* (New York, 1990), esp. 1–7, and the succinct statement in Jack P. Greene, "Empire and Identity from the Glorious Revolution to the American Revolution," in P.J. Marshall, ed., *The Oxford History of the British Empire*, 2: *The Eighteenth Century* (Oxford, 1998), 208.

[29] Fabián Alejandro Campagne, *Homo Catholicus. Homo Superstitiosus. El discurso antisupersticioso en la España de los siglos XV a XVIII* (Buenos Aires: Miño y Dávila, 2002), 21–25. I am grateful to Andrew Keitt for translating these pages and sharing them with me.

[30] Thomas Bender, *A Nation Among Nations: America's Place in World History* (New York, 2006), 7.

about him – and I believe it is – we will need to accommodate the other stories we tell about Jefferson to it.

In the chapters that follow, Jefferson will appear as the historian, the sociologist, the ethnographer, and the political theorist of America, as well as the most successful practitioner of its politics and its most enthusiastic champion. Chapter 1 describes Jefferson's narrative of American nationhood as it first emerged in his revolutionary writing in the 1770s. Jefferson's "American story" assumed and asserted the existence of a people, described the character of that people, and projected this people into nation-time past and future, as well as the obvious present.[31] I argue that the Declaration of Independence made cultural and historical claims about American character and identity even as it asserted American sovereignty in a world of states, or, rather that these two projects were intimately connected; the political claims could be legitimate, by the Declaration's logic, only if the cultural and historical ones were true. The legitimacy of the statehood project, Jefferson implied, rested on the existence of a people.

The second through fourth chapters explore some of the more complex and particularistic claims Jefferson made about the character of this American people. Chapter 2 explores Jefferson's description of American domestic life as a universal standard achieved fully only in the United States. Chapter 3 follows out this analysis by unpacking Jefferson's further elaboration of the American "spirit" and character that he believed made democratic politics possible in the United States and rendered European political theory inapplicable to its experience.[32] Chapter 4 examines the intimate relationship Jefferson envisioned between the public and the state, between citizens and republican leadership, a relationship that rendered Americans remarkably free but that also, somewhat paradoxically, sharply circumscribed the boundaries of the public. In this chapter, I also suggest that the democratic Jefferson we celebrate today is inseparable from the Jefferson who temporized on slavery, excluded African Americans from the national public, and included Indians on only the most rigidly assimilationist terms. Jefferson's nation, like all nations, gained coherence from its "others," abroad and at home, so that the same nationalism that welcomed participation among citizens also found it imperative to close off paths to citizenship for those not easily assimilated.

Chapter 5 explores the ramifications of all of these claims and assumptions about America for Jefferson's politics, or, rather, it suggests that Jefferson's politics in the 1790s might best be understood in light of his nationalism. Federalists, Jefferson came to believe, did not share his understanding of the ways in which the American experience had created a public uniquely suited

---

[31] See Stefan Berger, "The Power of National Pasts: Writing National History in Nineteenth- and Twentieth-Century Europe," in Berger, ed., *Writing the Nation: A Global Perspective* (New York, 2007), 36.

[32] On national character as causally sufficient explanation for behavior, see Joep Leerssen, "The Rhetoric of National Character: A Programmatic Survey," *Poetics Today*, 21 (Summer 2000), 267–292, esp. 272.

for democratic politics or the ways in which this experience could be indefinitely reinforced by a close connection between the public and the state. Eventually, he came to read the Federalist agenda as a counterrevolutionary and ultimately un-American effort to administer the national state according to its own rationale, disconnected except in the most superficial of ways to the will of the nation. His political opposition, I argue, was, at heart, a project designed to realign the state with the only thing that rendered it legitimate: the nation. Reading Jefferson's political project through the lens of nationhood, I suggest here, might contribute to new insights into his presidency, rendering his expansion of executive authority and aggressive uses of national power less a contradiction than a fulfillment of his opposition in the 1790s. Chapter 6 reads the Kentucky Resolutions as an episode in this larger project of reconnecting state and nation, reflects on the problem of coercion in his theory of union, and considers the inextricability of Jefferson's federalism from his nationalism.

While the body of the book strives to describe Jefferson's program as historically specific, unassimilable precisely to any of our own political ideologies, the Epilogue faces the reality that Jefferson always slips the bounds of historicism because he remains an icon of our public culture. What I hope to suggest here is that the continuing national project of renewing civic life and national purpose operates largely in the broad terms Jefferson laid out for the continuation of the national community. Insofar as the nation continues to link itself with that tradition, it remains Jefferson's America, even as its scale, scope, and structure have been transformed out of all recognition from the America Jefferson himself knew. Jefferson may have felt little sense of debt or obligation to the past, because he believed his generation had made the world anew. But he remained concerned that future generations maintain a sense of connection with that revolutionary and constitutive moment. Whenever we reverence the "founders," Jefferson included, as "our" ancestors, we are in some fundamental sense affirming Jefferson's original vision of a national community moving through time. In a sense, then, the Epilogue concedes the defeat of history by tradition and collective memory. And this takes us back to the founders' conception of history as a moral exercise rather than an effort to simply reconstruct the past as it really was.

Reading Jefferson as an American nationalist, then, may offer a way of envisioning him anew, of questioning our shibboleths not only about him but also about ourselves. The world may not need another book about Thomas Jefferson, but I hope that this one at least suggests that wrestling with Jefferson remains a fruitful exercise for both the scholar and the citizen.

# I

# American Story

> Few people have extended their enquiries after the foundation of any of their rights, beyond a charter from the crown. There are others who think when they have got back to old *Magna Charta*, that they are at the beginning of all things. They imagine themselves on the borders of Chaos (and so indeed in some respects they are) and see creation rising out of the unformed mass, or from nothing.... But liberty was better understood, and more fully enjoyed by our ancestors, before the coming in of the first Norman Tyrants.
>
> James Otis, 1764[1]

> I shall need, too, the favor of that Being in whose hands we are, who led our forefathers, as Israel of old, from their native land, and planted them in a country flowing with all the necessaries and comforts of life; who has covered our infancy with his providence, and our riper years with his wisdom and power.
>
> Thomas Jefferson, 1805[2]

Jefferson began what would prove his most enduring piece of writing with distinctions between peoples. It was a theme that would never be far from his thought and writing. "One people" (or as he put it in his initial draft, "a people") was deciding to sever its previous connection with another.[3] Americans would climb "the road to glory & happiness ... in a separate state."[4] "By our

---

[1] "The Rights of the British Colonies Asserted and Proved" (1764), in Merrill Jensen, *Tracts of the American Revolution* (Indianapolis, 1966), 20–21.

[2] Second Inaugural Address, March 4, 1805, in *TJW* 523.

[3] See Peter S. Onuf, "A Declaration of Independence for Diplomatic Historians," *Diplomatic History* 22 (1998), 71–83, to the insights of which this chapter is deeply indebted. Also see J.G.A. Pocock, "America's Foundations, Foundationalisms, and Fundamentalisms," *Orbis* (Winter 2004), 37–44, at 39; and Pocock, "States, Republics, and Empires: The American Founding in Early Modern Perspective," in Terence Ball, ed., *Conceptual Change and the Constitution* (Lawrence, KS, 1988), 55–77.

[4] Jefferson's "original rough draught" of the Declaration, in *PTJ* 1:427. In a later fragment, Jefferson changed the phrase to "apart from them." See "Fragment of the Composition Draft of the Declaration of Independence," in ibid., 421. Congress excised both.

separation from Great-Britain," he explained later, "British subjects became aliens" in America."[5] So the crisis that led to Revolution created two peoples, and there could be "no middle character" between them: "Natural subjects" of the crown could not be "American citizens" who had somehow become "aliens" to the English, free citizens of "a nation now separated from them."[6] In this reading, the Declaration of Independence was the genesis of American nationhood as well as the "fundamental act of union of these states," as Jefferson later characterized it.[7] The real question, Jefferson and other supporters of independence in the Congress argued, had not been whether a Declaration would "make ourselves what we are not; but whether we should declare a fact which already exists." The Declaration would simply describe "an existent truth."[8] The Declaration's logic – and Jefferson's later explanation that with that document he was simply expressing "the American mind" – assumed the existence of the nation already.[9] But two peoples cannot become two overnight, and the burden of much of Jefferson's most important writing from the Revolutionary era fell to explaining the origins and describing the unique character of the American people, a people with a past and a future as well as a present. For this explanation, Jefferson first turned to history. Americans, he argued, were connected through a common experience of expatriation and of alienation from Britain. If there was "a people" in North America, as the Declaration assumed, his 1774 pamphlet, *A Summary View of the Rights of British America*, described its history. If the Declaration was a birth, a "rupture in time," the *Summary View* described the long gestation of a nation. In the *Summary View*, Jefferson first began to spin what he there called "American story."[10] In becoming one of the first chroniclers of the nation's past, Jefferson became its first postcolonial theorist of the nation's present and projector of its indefinite future.

## A PEOPLE IN THE EMPIRE

The most compelling work written on the "first" British Empire suggests at least three conclusions: first, that the practice of empire was federal whatever it purported to be in theory; second, that intercolonial relations were tenuous at best and that whatever gave Britons in North America any semblance of unity was precisely their shared embrace of British identity; third, that the craving of the eighteenth-century colonial elite to emulate British cultural

---

5 *Notes*, 155.

6 *Notes on British and American Alienage* [1783], in *PTJ*, 6:433.

7 Minutes of the Board of Visitors, University of Virginia, 1822–1825, March 4, 1825, in *TJW*, 479.

8 Thomas Jefferson's "Notes of Proceedings in the Continental Congress" [June 7 to August 1, 1776], in *PTJ*, 1:311.

9 David Armitage, *The Declaration of Independence: A Global History* (Cambridge, 2007), 17.

10 See the reflections in Anderson, *Imagined Communities: Reflections on the Origin and Spread of Nationalism* (New York, 1991, rev. ed.), ch. 11.

standards – to measure up – was consistently thwarted by the knowledge of its provincial status vis-à-vis the real British aristocracy, a knowledge continually reinforced by traffic patterns of administration. Unlike Spanish Americans, British Americans had a good deal of experience running local affairs. But as among the former, it was only the extremely rare American Creole who could even imagine acquiring enough cultural and economic capital to ever parlay that into some kind of authoritative political power in the metropolis.[11] When American elites did show up in England, they were typically awestruck.[12] It speaks worlds that the artificially unifying term *American* emerged out of Britain as a nomenclature of difference.[13]

It was their very status as provincials that nevertheless freed Americans to make remarkable leaps in political creativity.[14] Moreover, British efforts to overadminister the colonies after the 1760s, as well as the print culture that reinforced America's distinct status as an outpost to be administered, gradually set into place a "grammar" of imagining that would awaken a kind of national consciousness in Americans vis-à-vis the "imperial" center. Such imagining rhetorically rendered the diverse "American" pasts a common heritage even as colonial political claims to statehood (and unity) were shockingly new. In other words, British practice of making "others" of American provincials helped wear a footpath toward American nationalism.[15]

Colonists who opposed the implementation of new British policies in the 1760s and 1770s – Jefferson included – rooted their initial resistance in their Britishness but ended, of necessity, making claims as Americans.[16] If their initial opposition was rooted in collective historical experiences they believed they shared with all Britons, their Revolution very quickly demanded that

---

[11] On the aspirations of one such rarity, see Gordon S. Wood, *The Americanization of Benjamin Franklin* (New York, 2004), esp. ch. 2.

[12] See a description of John Adams's (now an official representative of the United States) encounter with George III in Andrew Jackson O'Shaughnessy, "'If Others Will Not Be Active, I Must Drive': George III and the American Revolution," *Early American Studies* (Spring 2004), 1–46, at 1–4. Naturally, colonial self-loathing could manifest itself just as loudly as resentment or disgust at the luxurious self-indulgence of the British court. See H. Trevor Colbourn and Richard Peters, "A Pennsylvania Farmer at the Court of King George: John Dickinson's London Letters, 1754–1756," *The Pennsylvania Magazine of History and Biography* 86 (July 1962), 241–286 and (October 1962), 417–453. See also the complicated response(s) of Benjamin Franklin detailed in Wood, *The Americanization of Benjamin Franklin*.

[13] P.J. Marshall, "A Nation Defined by Empire, 1755–1776," in Alexander Grant and Keith J. Stringer, eds., *Uniting the Kingdom?: The Making of British History* (London and New York, 1995), 220.

[14] Bernard Bailyn, "Politics and the Creative Imagination," in *To Begin the World Anew: The Genius and Ambiguities of the American Founders* (New York, 2003), 3–36.

[15] My debt to Anderson, *Imagined Communities*, should be obvious here and throughout this chapter.

[16] Anthony Pagden and Nicholas Canny, "Afterword: From Identity to Independence," in Canny and Pagden, eds., *Colonial Identity in the Atlantic World, 1500–1800* (Princeton, 1987), 277–278. Also see Jack P. Greene, "Changing Identity in the British Caribbean: Barbados as a Case Study," in ibid., 214.

narratives of their past become localized and independent. Jefferson was one of the first Americans to make the leap from using history to make claims on the empire itself to describing that history as culminating in a new "American story." The history Jefferson wrote in the 1770s, and which he tried to incorporate into the Declaration of Independence itself, was transitional in the sense that it tried to do both the work of legitimizing the colonial position in the empire and serving as the protohistory of a new national community. From July of 1776, Jefferson's history of British America became a narrative of a new nation, no longer serving its original purpose of envisioning a British "commonwealth."

A lifelong student of history, Jefferson read, preserved, and collected rare manuscripts and documents for the use of future historians.[17] But as a producer of history, Jefferson became a weaver of the national tale, a project that predated his service in the Continental Congress and ran through his perhaps willful death on the very date he had begun to call "our nation's birthday."[18] Jefferson's historical investigations, far from merely antiquarian, would assist his compilation of a national narrative: "American story."

The difficulties of contemplating the approach of independence owed at least as much to the problematics of union among the colonies – each with its own history and links to London – as it did to the heartbreak of severing ties to the metropolis. This point – the tenuousness of union – contextualizes Jefferson's assertion in 1776 that Americans were "a people," sovereign and clearly distinguishable from "another," and returns to it something of the astonishing quality the claim must have held for contemporaries.[19] Until the First Continental Congress met at Philadelphia in the autumn of 1774, intercolonial cooperation,

---

[17] Francis D. Cogliano, *Thomas Jefferson: Reputation and Legacy* (Charlottesville, VA, 2006), esp., perhaps, ch. 1; and Matthew Crow, "Jefferson, Pocock, and the Temporality of Law in a Republic," *Republics of Letters: A Journal for the Study of Knowledge, Politics, and the Arts* 2, no. 1 (December 15, 2010), 55–81. Jefferson clearly had a reputation as a scholar familiar with sources and as a collector of manuscripts or at least someone familiar enough with the sources to direct others in their research. For an example, see Samuel Miller to TJ March 4, 1800, *PTJ*, 31: 411.

[18] Three witnesses to his death testify to Jefferson's apparent wish to live until the Fourth of July. See "Jefferson's Last Words," at http://www.monticello.org/site/research-and-collections/jeffersons-last-words. Accessed January 19, 2012. Also see Margaret P. Battin, "July 4, 1826: Explaining the Same-Day Deaths of John Adams and Thomas Jefferson (and What Could This Mean for Bioethics?)" in Battin, *Ending Life: Ethics and the Way We Die* (New York, 2005), 175–185. For Jefferson's identification of the Fourth as "our nation's birthday," see TJ to Ellen Randolph Coolidge, November 14, 1825, in Edwin Morris Betts and James Adam Bear, Jr., eds., *The Family Letters of Thomas Jefferson* (Charlottesville, VA, 1986. Originally published: Columbia, MO, 1966), 461–462.

[19] Garry Wills, *Inventing America: Jefferson's Declaration of Independence* (New York, 1978), 49–50. Note that Wills himself now says he has "repudiate[d]" such a view in light of later research (in particular, Richard B. Morris's "The Forging of the Union Reconsidered: A Historical Refutation of State Sovereignty Over Seabeds," *Columbia Law Review* 74 [1974], 1056–1093). See the Introduction to the Mariner edition of *Inventing America* (New York, 2002), ix.

much less political unity, had been all but unthinkable; even that Congress was, at least at first, more a diplomatic assembly than a national government.[20] Little precedent existed for intercolonial cooperation, and even at this relatively late juncture in the conflict with Britain, suspicion and even distrust of other colonies ran high among the delegates to Congress. The commercial, political, and cultural orientation of the colonies was toward London rather than to one another, and contemporary observers generally emphasized the differences between the colonies rather than any similarities they might have shared.[21] Although we tend to look back at the Continental Congress as the first national government, anticipating all future iterations of the U.S. state, the delegates themselves were in Philadelphia to assert the rights and interests of individual colonies against British encroachment.[22]

What the various colonies did share, in addition to their common grievances vis-à-vis Parliament, was perhaps less what made them uniquely American than their mutual emulation of British economic, cultural, and social practices.[23] In a very real sense, then, if the Americans were coming together, it was because they were aspiring to be and actually becoming more like the metropolitan English. Such "Anglicization" in the British colonies in the eighteenth century coincided with an intensification of patriotism in the British Isles – a celebration of British culture and legacy of political freedom, all of which the colonists

[20] See Jack N. Rakove, *The Beginnings of National Politics*, for a compelling contrary argument. For a rich complication, see Jerrilyn Greene Marston, *King and Congress: The Transfer of Political Legitimacy, 1774–1776* (Princeton, 1987). Also see J.R. Pole, "The Politics of the Word 'State' and its Relation to American Sovereignty," in *Parliaments, Estates and Representation* 8 (June 1988), 1–10, esp. 4.

[21] For contemporary assessments, see *Burnaby's Travels Through North America: Reprinted from the Third Edition of 1798* (New York, 1904), 152–153; and Benjamin Franklin, *The Interest of Great Britain Considered with Regard to Her Colonies and the Acquisition of Canada and Guadaloupe* (London, 1760) in Leonard W. Labaree, et al., ed., *The Papers of Benjamin Franklin*, 40 volumes to date (New Haven and London, 1959–2011), 9:90.

[22] Wills, *Inventing America*, 37–38; Neil York, "The First Continental Congress and the Problem of American Rights," *Pennsylvania Magazine of History and Biography* 122 (October 1998), 353–383.

[23] Jack P. Greene provides the most concise synthesis of this scholarship on cultural convergence in *Pursuits of Happiness: The Social Development of Early Modern British Colonies and the Formation of American Culture* (Chapel Hill, 1988). Also see Michael Zuckerman, "Identity in British America: Unease in Eden," in Canny and Pagden, eds., *Colonial Identity in the Atlantic World*, 115–157; T.H. Breen, "An Empire of Goods: The Anglicization of Colonial America, 1690–1776," in *Journal of British Studies* 25 (October 1988), 467–499; and P.J. Marshall, "Introduction," in Marshall, ed., *The Oxford History of the British Empire: Volume II: The Eighteenth Century* (Oxford, 1998), 12. On the other hand, Max Savelle, "Nationalism and Other Loyalties in the American Revolution," *AHR* 67 (July 1962), 901–923; Paul A. Varg, "The Advent of Nationalism, 1758–1776," *American Quarterly* 16 (Summer 1964), 178; and John Clive and Bernard Bailyn, "England's Cultural Provinces: Scotland and America," *WMQ* 11 (April 1954), 200–213, all emphasize that this pull toward emulation of metropolitan style was nevertheless mixed with a certain pride in a distinctly provincial identity that, Savelle suggests, was the seedbed of future American nationalism that flourished, he argues, during the Revolution.

embraced as their heritage and birthright.[24] When the New York Assembly proclaimed in 1768 that "We are *Englishmen,* and as such, presume ourselves intitled to the Rights and Liberties, which have rendered the Subjects of *England* the Envy of all Nations," it merely made explicit what most American colonists took for granted.[25]

Such assertions imply that it ought to have been a straightforward matter for the metropolitan British to embrace Americans as "British Brethren." And, in fact, English traveler Arthur Young described such an ideal in his 1772 *Political Essays Concerning the Present State of the British Empire.* "The British dominions," he wrote, "consist of Great Britain and Ireland, divers colonies and settlements in all parts of the world and there appears not any just reason for considering these countries in any other light than as a part of a whole." The best policy, Young suggested, would be "to consider all as forming one nation, united under one sovereign, speaking the same language and enjoying the same liberty, but living in different parts of the world."[26] John Foxcroft assumed with many Britons that "a Good Englishman and a good American" were "synonimous terms it being impossible to be one without being the other also."[27]

In certain key respects, of course, official British policy proceeded as if Americans were English subjects. Americans were considered Englishmen for purposes of the Acts of Trade, for example.[28] Nevertheless, the intensification of British national consciousness bore a dual-edged potential: Over time, its tendency to embrace the colonists as good Britons diminished as its sense of Americans as provincial grew. If Americans saw themselves as "societies of Britons overseas," many in Britain began to consider the colonies, rather, as little more than "outposts of British economic or strategic power," legally separate from the realm of England and woefully lacking in metropolitan cultural standards.[29] In this formulation, subordination of the peripheries became a

---

[24] Linda Colley, *Britons: Forging the Nation, 1707–1837* (New Haven, 1992); Jack P. Greene, *The British Revolution in America* (Austin, 1996), 9.

[25] Quoted in John Phillip Reid, *Constitutional History of the American Revolution, Volume I: The Authority of Rights* (Madison, 1986), 14. Also see Greene, *The British Revolution in America,* 8–15. Greene's focus on rule of law should be supplemented with Colley's highlighting of religion and ethnicity as well as Breen's emphasis on consumption (in various articles and culminating in *The Marketplace of Revolution: How Consumer Politics Shaped American Independence* [New York, 2004]).

[26] Arthur Young, quoted in Marshall, "A Nation Defined by Empire," 216.

[27] Foxcroft to Franklin, January 14, 1771, in Labaree, ed., *Papers of Benjamin Franklin,* 18:9; Marshall, "A Nation Defined by Empire," 216; Jack P. Greene, "Empire and Identity from the Glorious Revolution to the American Revolution," in Marshall, ed., *The Oxford History: Volume II,* 222.

[28] See John J. McCusker, "British Mercantilist Policies and the Colonies," in Stanley L. Engerman and Robert E. Gallman, ed., *The Cambridge Economic History of the United States,* vol. 1: *The Colonial Era* (Cambridge, 1996), 337–362. Also see Stephen Conway, "From Fellow-Nationals to Foreigners: British Perceptions of the Americans, circa 1739–1783," *WMQ* 59 (January 2002), 66.

[29] T.H. Breen, "Ideology and Nationalism in the American Revolution: Revisions Once More in Need of Revising," *JAH* 84 (June 1997), 13–39, at, 19; Marshall, "A Nation Defined by Empire,"

necessary concomitant of colonization itself.[30] Anglicization in the colonies, then, was on a collision course with a growing metropolitan sense of distinction from its colonial "possessions."

Some scholars suggest that long-standing efforts to keep the colonies dependent and economically subservient to the needs of the metropolis provided Americans with a new conception of their uniqueness and singularity that would translate seamlessly into a sense of separate destiny during the revolutionary crisis of the 1770s.[31] Other scholars note that the United States emerged as a political entity well before the development of any widespread popular embrace of an American character or national identity.[32] Even most colonial leaders who were developing theories of empire that logically entailed independence from Britain did so in the name of inherited English rights and remained adamantly proud of their British identity. For many Americans, the violence and suddenness of British rejection implied in the parliamentary edicts passed in the 1760s and 1770s came as a shock. British reduction of the colonists from their standing as fellow Britons to that of a different people gave many Americans a sudden, but effective, reason to define themselves as united: After all, the common denominator of British policy was its application to *American* patriots as rebels against the crown.[33] Richard Bland, as early as 1766, had

221; Michal J. Rozbicki, "The Curse of Provincialism: Negative Perceptions of Colonial American Plantation Gentry," *JSH* 63 (November 1997), 727–752; Varg, "The Advent of Nationalism," at 175–176; and Greene, "Empire and Identity," 223–227. But see also Conway, "From Fellow-Nationals to Foreigners," who cautions against reading every British assessment of colonials as "provincial" as an exclusion of Americans as "foreigners."

[30] Linda Colley, "Britishness and Otherness: An Argument," *Journal of British Studies* 31 (October 1992), 309–329. On the importance of American slavery to English conceptions of colonial difference, see Greene, "Empire and Identity," 226, and "*The* British *Revolution in America*," 15–16.

[31] See Breen, "Ideology and Nationalism," and John Shy, "Franklin, Washington, and a New Nation," *Proceedings of the American Philosophical Society* 131 (1987), 308–324.

[32] See, for example, John M. Murrin, "'A Roof Without Walls': The Dilemma of American National Identity," in Richard Beeman, Stephen Botein, and Edward C. Carter, eds., *Beyond Confederation: Origins of the Constitution and American National Identity* (Chapel Hill, 1987), 333–348. Savelle ("Nationalism and Other Loyalties") contends that an American nationalism emerged gradually during the Revolution as the colonists transferred their loyalties from Britain to some concept of an American nation. Varg ("Advent of Nationalism," 181), in contrast, suggests that "something that can appropriately be called nationalism" – rooted in an alienation from the metropolitan center – predated the Revolution. Again, however, see Conway, "From Fellow-Nationals to Foreigners," for a convincing picture of British perceptions (which may or may not have been accurately understood by Americans). Albert Harkness, Jr., "Americanism and Jenkins' Ear," *Mississippi Valley Historical Review* 37 (1950), 61–90, argued that Americans began to distinguish themselves in a significant way from Europeans, in general, as early as 1739. Richard L. Merritt analyzed the frequency of use of American symbols and place names in the popular press and suggests that by 1774 Americans had a high level of self-interest and self-awareness. See Merritt, "The Colonists Discover America: Attention Patterns in the Colonial Press, 1735–1775," *WMQ* 21 (April 1964), 270–287, and "The Emergence of American Nationalism: A Quantitative Approach," *American Quarterly* 17 (Summer 1965), 319–335.

[33] Breen, "Ideology and Nationalism," 25–26. Also see Anderson, *Imagined Communities*, 163–185.

noted that Parliament had long been treating Americans as if they were "a distinct People." By 1775, it required even less imagination for a Massachusetts man to argue for American rights on the basis of the Virginia charters and to suggest, as John Adams did, that "the ancestors of the Virginians are our ancestors, when we speak of ourselves as Americans."[34]

Americans may have revolted initially to preserve the "ancient constitution" of Britain from corruption, but they felt suddenly compelled to do so in the name of an America they believed uniquely suited to preserve it. Britain, not so long before, the palladium of liberty, was now assumed by many Americans to be corrupt beyond remedy; the torch of liberty, so the argument went, was passing to America.[35]

If some found this sudden transition psychologically difficult, Thomas Jefferson, by contrast – who, as a young law student in Williamsburg, turned twenty-two years old in April of 1765 just as news of the passage of the Stamp Act was beginning to reach the colonies – seemed to understand intuitively the new roles Britain and America were (he believed) destined to play in the project of world history. Jefferson came of age during the Revolutionary crisis and missed few opportunities to trumpet his confidence in America's uniqueness and future greatness. No ordinary provincial, Jefferson had made a point of traveling to Philadelphia and New York in the 1760s, and he remained deeply engaged with cosmopolitan currents in literature and thought. Certainly, his political outlook was shaped, of necessity, by events affecting the colonies as a whole; and his first public paper, written to articulate common American grievances, also made bold assertions about American character. Americans, he wrote in 1774, were not a people who flattered kings.[36]

NATION PAST

A couple of years before he died, Jefferson insisted that Americans of the Revolutionary generation had "had no occasion to search into musty records, to hunt up royal parchments, or to investigate the laws and institutions of a semi-barbarous ancestry" for their rights. Instead, "We appealed to those [laws] of nature, and found them engraved on our hearts."[37] This is a rousing sentiment, of course, but most American writers, including Jefferson, in the scramble to understand the nature of the empire they would soon leave, really did search carefully through the "musty records" of the past. In retrospect, Jefferson's own writing from this period did the work of sorting through and piecing together an American history in which the "one people" of the

---

[34] John Adams, *Novanglus*, VII, in *WJA* 4:110.

[35] Bernard Bailyn, *The Ideological Origins of the American Revolution* (Cambridge, MA, 1967), 138–143. Also see Jefferson's succinct statement of this view in *Notes*, 65.

[36] *Summary View*, in *TJW*, 121. Also see TJ to John Page, May 25, 1766, in *PTJ*, 1:18–20; and TJ to Francis Willis, July 23, 1766, in ibid., 21.

[37] TJ to Major John Cartwright, June 5, 1824, in *TJW*, 1491.

Declaration could become visible in the misty past. In his writing, disparate events that might otherwise be read as disconnected episodes of an imperial past are, through the alchemy of national history, lent an air of destiny and become the prehistory of a nation.[38]

Today, we largely take the nation – its existence, or what Benedict Anderson has called its "it-ness" – for granted. But the founding generation could not. Historians and political theorists have fairly convincingly suggested not only the precarious nature of the American Union throughout the founding era[39] but also all the ways in which the United States, even when it could manage to maintain union and a political-institutional structure, lacked most of the traditionally understood foundations of nationhood itself that would cultivate a national consciousness.[40] But events of the 1760s and 1770s forced many Americans to think through the implications of their allegiance, and contemporary assertions of American distinctiveness – whether they are objectively verifiable by social science – become significant for the historian of American nationalism as practice.

Nations – or at any rate national narratives – have a magisterial and mystical power to transform the past, incorporating centuries of change into a "seamless narrative of one realm, the territory of the modern state."[41] This is

[38] See Etienne Balibar, "The Nation Form: History and Ideology," in Balibar and Immanuel Wallerstein, *Race, Nation, Class: Ambiguous Identities* (London, 1991), 86–106, esp. 88.

[39] See, especially, Peter S. Onuf, "Anarchy and the Crisis of the Union," in Ronald Hoffman, Peter Albert, and Herman Belz, eds., *"To Form a More Perfect Union": The Critical Ideas of the Constitution* (Charlottesville, VA, 1992), 272–302; Onuf, "State Sovereignty and the Making of the Constitution," in Terence Ball and J.G.A. Pocock, eds., *Conceptual Change and the Constitution* (Lawrence, KS, 1988), 78–98; David C. Hendrickson, *Peace Pact: The Lost World of the American Founding* (Lawrence, KS, 2003); Kevin M. Gannon, "Calculating the Value of the Union: States' Rights, Nullification, and Secession in the North, 1800–1848" (Ph.D. dissertation, University of South Carolina, 2002); Jack P. Greene, *Peripheries and Center: Constitutional Development in the Extended Polities of the British Empire and the United States, 1607–1788* (Athens, GA, 1996), 157–165; and Kenneth Stampp, "The Concept of a Perpetual Union," *JAH* 65 (June 1978), 5–33, reprinted in Stampp, *The Imperiled Union: Essays on the Background of the Civil War* (New York, 1980), 3–36.

[40] See, among others, Murrin, "'A Roof Without Walls'"; Hans Kohn, *American Nationalism: An Interpretative Essay* (New York, 1957), ch. 1; Peter J. Parish, "An Exception to Most of the Rules: What Made American Nationalism Different in the Mid-Nineteenth Century?" *Prologue* 27 (Fall 1995), 222; Greene, *Peripheries and Center*, 162; Shy, "Franklin, Washington, and a New Nation;" David Potter, "The Historian's Use of Nationalism and Vice Versa," in Don E. Fehrenbacher, ed., *History and American Society: Essays of David M. Potter* (New York, 1973), 106; and Liah Greenfeld, "The Origins and Nature of American Nationalism in Comparative Perspective," in Knud Krakau, ed., *The American Nation – National Identity – Nationalism* (Lit Verlag, 1997), 19–52. For hints of a counterview, see J.M. Bumsted, "Things in the Womb of Time": Ideas of American Independence, 1633 to 1763, in *WMQ*, Third Series, 31 (Oct. 1974), 534–564; Savelle, "Nationalism and Other Loyalties;" Varg, "The Advent of Nationalism," 178; and, Greene, *Peripheries and Center*, 165–174. For a provocative argument that the colonies *were* becoming distinctly American before the Revolution, see Jon Butler, *Becoming America: The Revolution Before 1776* (Cambridge, MA, 2000).

[41] Partha Chaterjee, *The Nation and Its Fragments: Colonial and Post-Colonial Histories* (Princeton, 1993), 95.

why, to take one example, the world's antiquities, which fill the museums of
the former imperial powers of the West, are now demanded by the postcolonial
nation-states that emerged from that very process of imperialism as part of their
national heritage; the legitimacy of the demand is rooted in the plausibility of
the historical claim linking the sometimes quite distant past with the configu-
ration of the modern nation-state.[42] In such nationalist tales Mughal emperors
from the sixteenth through eighteenth centuries, for example, became part of
the story of an independent postcolonial India, an entity that existed only in
the minds of prominent twentieth-century nationalists who "discovered" it in
history[43]; Angkor Wat, built by Suryavarman II in the twelfth century became
the prominent symbol of Cambodian identity in the flags of the successive (and
diametrically antagonistic) regimes of the Kingdom of Cambodia, Lon Nol's
Khmer Republic, and Pol Pot's Democratic Kampuchea[44]; the recent imperial
acquisitions of the Qing empire (Tibet and Mongolia among them) became part
of the primordial Chinese "nation" as it was imagined by the Revolutionaries
of 1911[45]; and New England Puritans and Virginia "Cavaliers" planted the
seeds of American democracy, anticipating the United States. (Thus, John
Winthrop's assertion of a "city on a hill," originally exclusive to Calvinists in
Massachusetts Bay, later was appropriated effortlessly by the presidents and
statesmen of the twentieth-century American empire.[46]) However questionable
these particular claims, the point here is not that nations misappropriate the
past so much as that their very existence demands some sort of temporal and
spatial continuity. None of this is to say (although in some cases one would
be justified in so saying) that nations and their narrators are simply the gross
manipulators of the past, tossing inconvenient truths "down the memory hole"
like Winston Smith in Orwell's *1984*. Nor is it to suggest merely that national
interests, domestic and international, encourage an investment in historical
recovery, unifying disparate pasts. It is to say, rather, something much more

[42] For provocative reflections on this problem, see, Hugh Eakin, "Who Should Own the World's
Antiquities?" *New York Review* 56 (May 14, 2009); and Eakin, "The Affair of the Chinese
Bronzes," April 15, 2009, http://www.nybooks.com/articles/archives/2009/may/14/the-affair-of-
the-chinese-bronze-heads/, accessed November 19, 2010.
[43] See Immanuel Wallerstein, "Does India Exist?" in *The Essential Wallerstein* (New York, 2000),
310–314.
[44] See Anderson, *Imagined Communities*, 183.
[45] See Evelyn S. Rawski, "Presidential Address: Reenvisioning the Qing: The Significance of the
Qing Period in Chinese History," *The Journal of Asian Studies* 55 (Nov. 1996), 829–850, esp.
838–842.
[46] The typical college course on "The History of the United States to 1865" (or 1877) contains an
ending point with a clear rationale, but where should such a course begin? 1492? 1607? 1776?
1783? 1789? There is even a case to be made that the United States as the political entity we
know today really did not emerge until after the Civil War (which, if embraced, would considerably shorten the aforementioned course). In any case, the point is that "Colonial America"
(generally taken to mean "British" America, with the West Indies removed) becomes – in these
courses – part of the story of the United States. For reflections on the latter problem, see James
A. Hijiya, "Why the West is Lost," *WMQ* (1994), 276–292; and the responses in the October
issue of *WMQ* (1994), 717–754.

interesting: that nations, by their very existence, change the meaning of past events (when new meanings become salient to the ongoing national project) precisely because they possess a monopoly of legitimate narration, much in the same way that states, in Weber's definition, possess a monopoly of legitimate violence. But just as states possess such a monopoly only insofar as they have the power to maintain their legitimacy, so nations command narratives only when the discourse of nationalism corresponds in some meaningful way with the reality of people's everyday social experience of "nation-ness" or when the narrative is so hegemonic as to render all other ways of reading the past not simply obsolete but literally unthinkable.

In this light it seems worth thinking about Thomas Jefferson, here, as engaged in the process of narrating America. Jefferson's public career began with the effort to both create a common past for a "nation" that existed only from 1776 (if then) and to articulate a national character, embedded in a claim for a sovereign American state in a world of states. His public career ended with frequent reassertions of such a national character, reading its infancy as riven with strife, to be sure, but basically homogenous and unified to the end. It seems not unwarranted to see these bookends as part of a larger single project that preoccupied Jefferson: his narration of the national story. Jefferson is famous for his hopeful projection of the American nation into the indefinite future, but he was also attentive to the collective memory of its past. Jefferson's attention to the historical construction of American nationhood was a life-long project to stave off national decay (and death) by delimiting the nation in time (creating a myth of origins) and demarcating a kind of sacred space (endorsed by "Nature's God") within which the nation could legitimately act out its destiny.[47]

The point here, it should perhaps be noted, is not that Jefferson tells us the truth about America – its history or its character – though his version has without question shaped the story we tell about ourselves. The point is that Jefferson was compelled to tell the story at all, that his lifelong project was on one fundamental level, a practicing of nationalism.[48] In the 1770s, Jefferson crafted a history for the American people that was able to do the work of separation from its all-too-obvious British past and then, in turn, root the legitimacy of the new state in the claims of its sovereign people.

Jefferson wrote the essay that has come to be known as *A Summary View of the Rights of British America* in response to Parliament's Coercive Acts of

---

[47] With these phrases, I am explicitly noting my debt to Regis Debray, "Marxism and the National Question," *New Left Review* (September/October, 1977), 25–41.

[48] This, then, is a study not of Jefferson's philosophy of history but a description of his practice of nationalism. For a study of Jefferson's philosophy of history, see Hannah Spahn, "Visual History? Jefferson, Lord Kames, and the Crisis of Historical Aesthetics," *GRAAT Online*: Issue #4 (October 2008): http://www.graat.fr/backissuejefferson.htm. On nationalism as practice rather than ideology, see David Waldstreicher, *In the Midst of Perpetual Fetes: The Making of American Nationalism, 1776–1820* (Chapel Hill, 1997).

early 1774. The measures adopted by the British government in the aftermath of the Boston Tea Party of December 1773, were designed to isolate rebellious Massachusetts Bay and force it into submission. Instead, they galvanized colonial opposition. In a remarkable show of unity, all the colonies except for Georgia expressed support for Massachusetts and moved to appoint delegates to a Continental Congress in Philadelphia. Members of Virginia's House of Burgesses, recently dissolved by Governor Dunmore for declaring a day of fasting and prayer for Massachusetts, met at the Raleigh Tavern and expressed the sentiments of most Americans when they proclaimed that "an attack, made on one of our sister colonies, to compel submission to arbitrary taxes, is an attack made on all British America, and threatens ruin to the rights of all."[49]

Jefferson was elected to the convention that would choose Virginia's delegates to the First Continental Congress, but, as he later wrote, he was "stopped on the road by sickness." "Unable to proceed," Jefferson instead sent his proposed draft of instructions to the delegates in Williamsburg.[50] Although Jefferson later described his argument as "the only one orthodox or tenable," the convention rejected the paper as "too bold," Jefferson remembered. But many immediately recognized its importance and published it anonymously, without Jefferson's knowledge, under its most familiar title.[51]

As Jefferson later characterized it, the *Summary View*'s argument was twofold. First, he insisted that "the relation between Gr. Br. and these colonies was exactly the same as that of England & Scotland after the accession of James & until the Union, and the same as her present relations with Hanover, having the same Executive chief but no other necessary political connection." In some respects, this argument very much anticipated the direction of colonial protest, though it was perhaps prematurely provocative in its assertion that Parliament had "no right to exercise authority over us," the precise antithesis of Parliament's 1766 Declaratory Act. In substance, this argument was explicitly advanced only gingerly throughout the colonies prior to 1774, and then, only by Jefferson, John Adams, and James Wilson.[52]

It has often been suggested that Jefferson's *Summary View* indicted Parliament while the Declaration blamed the king. But strictly speaking, this is not quite right and part of what makes the *Summary View* unique is Jefferson's direct and pointed attack on George III and its less than respectful suggestion that the king was already deeply implicated in offenses against the British Constitution

49 "An Association, Signed by 89 Members of the Late House of Burgesses," May 27, 1774, in *PTJ* 1:108. David L. Ammerman, *In the Common Cause: American Response to the Coercive Acts* (New York, 1975).

50 TJ to John W. Campbell, September 3, 1809, in *TJW*, 1210; Jefferson, *Autobiography*, in ibid., 9.

51 Ibid., 9–10.

52 For context, see Edmund S. Morgan, "Colonial Ideas of Parliamentary Power, 1764–1766," in *WMQ* (July 1948), 311–341; Greene, *Peripheries and Center*, 87–93; Anthony Pagden, *Lords of All the World: Ideologies of Empire in Spain, Britain and France, c. 1500-c. 1800* (New Haven, 1995), 127–128, 135; Becker, *The Declaration of Independence*, 102.

that would justify independence.[53] To be sure, Jefferson seemed to encourage the king to muster the moral strength to veto the legislation of a Parliament that had "lost the confidence of their constituents," sold "their most valuable rights," and assumed undelegated powers.[54] "Let no act be passed by any one legislature," Jefferson insisted, "which may infringe on the rights and liberties of another." "Fortune" had placed the king in this "important post," "holding the balance of a great, if a well poised empire."[55] But Jefferson cannot have imagined that George III would, at the insistence of an unknown Virginian, exercise a monarchical prerogative not invoked since the time of Queen Anne (an idea Lord North thought would occur only to a Tory), and he seems to have intended to set it up as a kind of impossible task to highlight, by contrast, the frequency with which the crown exercised such prerogative in the colonies.[56] If the king would not dare exercise these prerogatives at home (dissolving parliaments at pleasure had been treasonous since the reign of Richard II, Jefferson noted, and never attempted since the glorious revolution), he certainly had no logical right to do so in the colonies – at least according to Jefferson's conception of the empire. In any case, whatever ostensible deference to monarchical authority exists in the paper seems progressively undermined by the directness, not to say irreverence, with which Jefferson addressed the king himself, asserting unequivocally that the king had acted unjustly in violation of the Americans' rights as Englishmen and insisting that the king's legitimate authority was "restrained in every part of the empire" by the consent of the legislatures of its various parts. "Can his majesty … put down all law under his feet? Can he erect a power superior to that which erected himself? He has done it indeed by force; but let him remember," Jefferson demanded, "that force cannot give right."

Looking back, Jefferson would later sardonically call George III the "American Messias" because it was he who labored "twenty long years … to drive us to our good."[57] From Jefferson's position in 1774, the *Summary View* appears to offer the king his last chance to do his duty, but it was a duty hardly compatible with the sovereignty of king-in-parliament. Jefferson's Americans would speak "with that freedom of language and sentiment which becomes a free people," demanding rights "as derived from the laws of nature, and not as the gift of their chief magistrate." Jefferson's king was "no more than the chief

---

[53] Ian R. Christie and Benjamin W. Labaree, *Empire or Independence, 1760–1776: A British-American Dialogue on the Coming of the American Revolution* (New York, 1977), 206.

[54] *Summary View*, in *PTJ* 1:133; O'Shaughnessy, "'If Others Will Not Be Active, I Must Drive,'" 17.

[55] *TJW*, 121.

[56] See J.G.A. Pocock, "1776: The Revolution Against Parliament," in *Virtue, Commerce, and History: Essays on Political Thought and History, Chiefly in the Eighteenth Century* (Cambridge, 1985), 281. Pocock outlines Jefferson's "strategy" as the offering to "the King a role in order to denounce him for refusing it." The suggestion should be read, nevertheless, in light of Brendan McConville, *The King's Three Faces: The Rise & Fall of Royal America, 1688–1776* (Chapel Hill, 2005).

[57] TJ to Abigail Adams, August 9, 1786, in *AJL*, 149.

officer of the people" and "subject to their superintendance." So Jefferson's language was "divested of [customary] expressions of servility," he said, precisely because such might confuse the king into assuming "that we are asking favors and not rights." Ultimately, Jefferson's paper demanded quite directly that the king do his duty: "Open your breast Sire, to liberal and expanded thought. Let not the name of George the third be a blot in the page of history."[58]

All of this was heady, indeed, for the time. Jefferson later suggested that it was considered too radical to actually affect congressional deliberations.[59] "If it had any merit," he reiterated, it was that "of first taking our true ground, & that which was afterwards assumed & maintained."[60] Indeed, as James Madison suggested years later, "the fundamental principle of the Revolution was, that the Colonies were coordinate members with each other and with Great Britain, of an empire united by a common executive sovereign, but not united by any common legislative sovereign," precisely Jefferson's description in the *Summary View*.[61]

But not everything Jefferson wrote in 1774 was "afterwards assumed & maintained" by the Congress. What made Jefferson's paper truly distinctive was not its rejection of parliamentary authority – others had come to that conclusion – but its historical argument about the experience that ultimately made Americans a distinct people: "our emigration from England to this country gave her no more rights over us, than the emigrations of the Danes and Saxons gave to the present authorities of the mother country over England." It was an argument that he could never get anyone to agree with, he recalled years later, other than his old law tutor and friend, George Wythe.[62] But he remained stubbornly wedded to it, and its traces remain in many of the documents he drafted for Congress, including the Declaration itself.[63] It was not particularly unique

---

[58] *Summary View, PTJ* 1:134, 121. The *Summary View* is the subject of a growing discussion in the historical literature. For a superb introduction to the historiography that adds an important argument of its own, see Kristofer Ray, "Thomas Jefferson and A Summary View of the Rights of British America," in Francis D. Cogliano, ed., *The Blackwell Companion to Thomas Jefferson* (Malden, MA, 2012), 32–43. Highlights in this literature include Garry Wills, *Inventing America: Jefferson's Declaration of Independence* (New York, 1979), 76–90; H. Trevor Colbourn, *The Lamp of Experience: Whig History and the Intellectual Origins of the American Revolution* (Chapel Hill, 1965), 158–184; Steven A. Conrad, "Putting Rights Talk in Its Place: *The Summary View* Revisited," in Peter S. Onuf, ed., *Jeffersonian Legacies* (Charlottesville, 1993), 254–280; Garrett Ward Sheldon, *The Political Philosophy of Thomas Jefferson* (Baltimore and London, 1991), 19–40; Anthony M. Lewis, "Jefferson's *Summary View* as a Chart of Political Union," *WMQ* (January 1948), 34–51; and Julian P. Boyd, "Jefferson's Expression of the American Mind," *Virginia Quarterly Review* (1974), 538–562. Also see Lee Ward, *The Politics of Liberty in England and America* (Cambridge, 2004), 351–374.

[59] Jefferson, *Autobiography, TJW*, 10.

[60] TJ to John Campbell, September 3, 1809, *PTJ, Retirement Series* 1:486.

[61] Madison, "Notes on the Resolutions," 1799–1800, in *The Writings of James Madison*, Gaillard Hunt, ed., 9 vols. (New York, 1900–1910), 6:373.

[62] Jefferson, *Autobiography, TJW*, 9.

[63] See, for example, Jefferson's Composition Draft of the Declaration of the Causes and Necessity of Taking up Arms [June 1775], in *PTJ*, 1: 193, an explicit assertion largely erased from the paper adopted by Congress [July 6, 1775], in ibid., 214.

that Jefferson looked to the past to substantiate American claims to present rights. Nearly every pamphleteer did the same, others with much greater precision. Nor did his embrace of the ancient constitution materially differentiate his pamphlet from the others. What distinguished Jefferson's argument was his description of the original colonization as an expatriation. Others also acknowledged the natural right of leaving, but Jefferson's description of the process and consequences of the migration was unique and problematic for most.[64] Jefferson essentially argued that the migration of the original settlers to America had made a clean break with Britain, establishing at least the potential foundation of a separate legal and political tradition, if not cultural identity.

Jefferson began with expatriation, reminding the king "that our ancestors" had migrated from Britain by the natural right of "departing from the country in which chance, not choice has placed them." The first thing to notice, perhaps, is the possessive pronoun: *our*. These were *American* ancestors, the "expatriated men" Jefferson would later describe.[65] This is a kind of distinctive historical claim, analogous to his argument that the Anglo-Saxons, who had "driven out the former inhabitants" of England, thereby "became aborigines" to the island, and, he told one English historian, "your lineal ancestors."[66] If contemporary Americans could trace their "lineal ancestors" back to the expatriation, as Jefferson believed they could, this made them, in a sense, "aboriginal" to North America (especially, perhaps, as they had "driven out the former inhabitants" of the continent).

Jefferson molded his argument from pieces left by his friend and early mentor in the Virginia House of Burgesses, Richard Bland, whose 1766 essay later earned Jefferson's praise as "the first pamphlet on the nature of the connection with Great Britain which had any pretension to accuracy of view on that subject."[67] And, indeed, Bland had there asserted a natural right of "men" in "Society" (opposed to a "State of Nature") "to retire from the Society, to renounce the Benefits of it, to enter into another Society, and to settle in another Country" if that society does not "conduce to their Happiness, which they have a natural Right to promote."[68] Staying implied consent to – even approval of – a society's laws and practices. But dissatisfaction had an outlet: "a natural Right to quit the Society of which they are Members, and to retire into another Country." When Jefferson said that Bland's pamphlet hit the target, he must have meant, in part, this argument about the right of expatriation (which fundamentally clashed with the British conception of subjectship).[69] But Bland

---

[64] John Philip Reid, *The Authority of Rights*, 114–123, 139–145.

[65] TJ to John Tyler, June 17, 1812, in *PTJ, Retirement Series* 5:135.

[66] TJ to Major John Cartwright, June 5, 1824, in Peterson, 1490.

[67] TJ to William Wirt, August 5, 1815, in *L&B* 13:338. On Bland, see Clinton Rossiter, *Six Characters in Search of a Republic: Studies in the Political Thought of the American Colonies* (New York, 1964), 150–205; and James E. Pate, "Richard Bland's Inquiry into the Rights of the British Colonies," *WMQ*, second series, 11 (January 1931), 20–28.

[68] Bland, *Inquiry into the Rights of British Colonies* [1766], in Charles S. Hyneman and Donald S. Lutz, eds., *American Political Writing During the Founding Era, 1760–1805*, 1:72.

[69] James H. Kettner, *The Development of American Citizenship, 1608–1870* (Chapel Hill, 1978), esp. ch. 1–6.

most closely approached Jefferson's later argument with his assertion that "when Men exercise this Right, and withdraw themselves from their Country, they recover their natural Freedom and Independence: The Jurisdiction and Sovereignty of the State they have quitted ceases; and if they unite, and by common Consent take Possession of a new Country, and form themselves into a political Society, they become a sovereign State, independent of the State from which they separated."[70]

What Bland described as theory, Jefferson took for history. Bland was saying that "Subjects of England" in fact have a "natural Right" to "form a new political Society and independent State." But when it came time to describe what actually had happened, he noted that the English who came to North America had made a "Compact with the Sovereign of the Nation, to remove into a new Country, and to form a civil Establishment upon the Terms of the Compact." Bland was saying that Englishmen who had a natural right to expatriate, could surely, by implication, migrate legitimately with the leave of their sovereign. Bland's actual history of the migration to North America began with the latter scenario. North America was settled, he wrote, "by Men who came over voluntarily, at their own Expense, and under Charters from the Crown, obtained for that Purpose, long before the first and great Act of Navigation."[71] Here, Bland became too conventional for Jefferson: Everyone argued from the charters. And here, presumably, was where Bland's pamphlet fell short of Jefferson's unqualified approval, precisely why he later described Bland's pamphlet as a kind of exercise in backpedaling from the logical outcome of the premises. Bland, Jefferson observed, certainly "set out on sound principles," but he soon discovered that they led to a "precipice" that he was loathe to "leap." So, Jefferson said, Bland would "start back alarmed, then resume his ground, go over it in another direction, be led again by the correctness of his reasoning to the same place, and again back about, and try other processes to reconcile right and wrong." Jefferson said that the whole "process" left Bland and his readers "bewildered between the steady index of the compass in their hand, and the phantasm to which it seemed to point."[72]

Jefferson exaggerated the confused quality of Bland's logic. In fact, all Bland asserted was that the first English migrants to America came out with charters from the crown and that this historical fact (which he very carefully described) proved that there was no original assumption that the colonists would remain subordinate to the authority of Parliament and that, therefore, any parliamentary imposition of "internal Taxes upon the Colonies is an Act of Power, and not of Right."[73] Bland's pamphlet was written to deny that the colonies owed any allegiance to Parliament – which was advanced enough a position in 1766. His conclusion followed from the premises of his history. But what

---

[70] Bland, *Inquiry*, 75.
[71] Ibid., 76.
[72] TJ to William Wirt, August 5, 1815, in *L&B* 13:338.
[73] Bland, *Inquiry*, 82.

may have dissatisfied Jefferson later was Bland's disappointing admission that "the Colonies are [nevertheless] subordinate to the Authority of Parliament: subordinate I mean in Degree, but not absolutely so."[74] The only way Bland could force this awkward concession into his earlier argument was by noting that the Colonies had "after the Restoration" submitted to parliamentary regulation over their "Commerce with foreign Nations," and by falling back on the authority of precedent to legitimize Parliament's superintending power over the trade of the empire.[75]

In any case, where Bland's pamphlet assumed that the monarch's granting a "licence to remove" entailed "obligatory and binding" allegiance of the settlers to the crown, Jefferson, on the other hand, went all the way over the precipice by insisting that the emigration to America had effected a complete (if temporary) separation from the mother country and severed all ties to its laws, its system of government, and its king. Jefferson took Bland's theory of expatriation as a simple description of what had in fact happened to the relationship between early American settlers and the mother country. Americans, in other words, upon leaving England, did not merely carry with them the common law rights of Englishmen; they had become independent of England altogether.[76]

Jefferson followed Bland in acknowledging the historical fact that the colonies had acquiesced in the Acts of Trade, but he described this as a concession to sentimental ties rather than anything rooted in right: "Some occasional assumptions of power by the parl. of Gr. Brit. however unacknoleged by the constitution of our governments, were finally acquiesced in thro' warmth of affectn."[77] Bland's central argument was a fairly straightforward denial that Parliament could tax the colonies without the consent of their legislatures. He argued this from a careful explication of the original charters. Because the charters were created by the crown rather than Parliament, arguing from them would not necessarily lead to conservative conclusions in the 1760s and 1770s. In fact, they led many theorists ultimately to the conclusions drawn by Adams, Franklin, Wilson, and, here, Bland: that Parliament's jurisdiction did not extend to North America, that the charters tied settlers to the Crown but

---

[74] Ibid., 83.

[75] Also see Bland, *The Colonel Dismounted: Or the Rector Vindicated* [Williamsburg, 1764], in Bailyn, ed., *Pamphlets*, 320; James Otis, Thomas Cushing, Samuel Adams, and Thomas Gray, Letter "To Dennys De Berdt," December 20, 1765, in Harry Alonzo Cushing, ed., *The Writings of Samuel Adams* [New York, 1904], 1:67; and Stephen Hopkins, *The Rights of Colonies Examined* [1764], in Jensen, ed., *Tracts of the American Revolution*, 49.

[76] See TJ to John Tyler, June 17, 1812, in *PTJ: Retirement Series* 5:135–136.

[77] Jefferson's composition draft of Congress's Declaration of the Causes and Necessity for Taking Up Arms, in *PTJ* 1:193. Also see "Answers to the Queries of M. Soules," September 13, 1786, in *FE*, 5: 187–189, where Jefferson went further, arguing that, in the absence of Parliamentary sovereignty over the colonies, even the navigation acts had to be "founded on compact or force." Unless Parliament was willing to "bottom their pretensions on force," the acts of trade, "therefore" would be "a proper subject of treaty between the two nations."

never "to a Subjection to the Supreme Authority of the English Parliament," as the Massachusetts House put it.[78]

The Massachusetts House of Delegates came to the same conclusion as Bland by following the same route some seven years later in its debate with Governor Hutchinson over the precise nature of the empire. Hutchinson asked the central question: "Does it follow that the government, by their removal from one part of the dominions to another, loses its authority over that part to which they remove, and that they are freed from the subjection they were under before; or do they expect that government should relinquish its authority?" The Massachusetts House answered that because the charters had been received from the Crown, not Parliament, "The parliament lost no Authority over" the settlers, "having never had such Authority." The emigrants undoubtedly had been subject to Parliament prior to "their Removal" to America. But now, as a result of migration, the Americans were "freed from th[at] Subjection" and had been for generations. "The Power and Authority of Parliament" was "constitutionally confined within the Limits of the Realm and the Nation collectively, of which alone it is the representing and legislative Assembly."[79] If the charters entitled settlers to their own representative bodies, then it followed that "to suppose a Parliamentary Authority over the Colonies under such Charters would necessarily induce that Solecism in Politics *Imperium in Imperio*."[80] (Here was a powerful turning of the tables on critics who argued that colonial refuge in the authority of their legislatures attempted the impossible task of dividing sovereignty.)

In short, many colonists, arguing from the charters, were coming to the same conclusion Jefferson would: that the empire was made up of separate corporate communities connected by one head.[81] So what did Jefferson mean when he said that only George Wythe agreed with his argument in the *Summary View*? For one thing, Jefferson dismissed out of hand several of the assertions the Massachusetts House made about Crown authority, particularly that "the Right of disposing of the Lands was in the Opinion of those Times vested solely in the Crown," or that the king held such a "prerogative of disposing of the American Territory by such Charters" at all.[82] His history allowed for no such equivocation. Essentially, Jefferson dismissed the authority of the king to dispose of American lands precisely because, he argued, America was not part of the king's realm. If the authority to leave and settle had come through a grant from the crown – something all other of the most forward American

---

[78] Reply of the House to Hutchinson's First Message, January 26, 1773, in Robert J. Taylor, Mary-Jo Kline, and Gregg L. Lint, eds., *Papers of John Adams*, 1:318–319.

[79] Ibid., 322.

[80] Ibid., 318–319.

[81] Also see, of course, James Wilson, "Considerations on the Nature and Extent of the Legislative Authority of the British Parliament" (1774, but originally written in 1768), in *Collected Works of James Wilson*, 2 vols., Kermit L. Hall and Mark David Hall, eds. (Indianapolis, 2007), 1:3–31.

[82] *Papers of Adams* 1:318–319.

theorists (Bland, Wilson, and Adams) admitted – the settlers came, on some level, as feudal vassals. Jefferson seemed eager to avoid the implications of such a dependency, and it was his particular distinction to deny explicitly that America was part of the royal demesne.[83]

On some fundamental level, the *Summary View* was an effort to educate King George, and Jefferson's fellow colonists, in a Whig history that began prior to the Norman Conquest, prior, indeed, to the Saxon migration. "In the earlier ages of the Saxon settlement," he wrote, "feudal holdings were certainly altogether unknown." "Our Saxon ancestors held their lands, as they did their personal property, in absolute dominion, disencumbered with any superior, answering nearly to the nature of those possessions which the Feudalists term Allodial."[84] John Adams had long ago rejected such a view, which, he argued, "would have constituted a government, too nearly like a commonwealth."[85] Adams believed that although the Saxons "shook off some part of the feudal fetters" of Europe after "intermingl[ing] with the ancient Britons," they were unable to fully abandon "the whole" system. Instead, "they retained a vast variety of the *regalia principis* of the feudal system, from whence most branches of the present prerogatives of our kings are derived."[86] The settlers, Adams asserted, "were contented therefore to hold their lands of their King, as their sovereign Lord, and to him they were willing to render homage."[87]

Jefferson, on the other hand, argued that feudalism was "first introduced" by William the Conqueror who parceled out to his Norman followers the lands owned by those killed at the Battle of Hastings. These lands were now technically owned by the king and "subject to feudal duties." But, Jefferson insisted, "still much was left in the hands of [William's] Saxon subjects, held of no superior, and not subject to feudal conditions." Even though these lands "were made liable to ... military duties," and even though "Norman lawyers soon found the means to saddle" them "with all the other feudal burthens ... as if they had been feuds," they "still ... had not been surrendered to the king, they were not derived from his grant, and therefore they were not holden of him." So the "general" Norman "principle" that all English lands were owned by the king derived, Jefferson maintained, "from those holdings which were truly feudal, and only applied to others for the purposes of illustration." In this view, then, it was the truly feudal holdings that were the exception to the rule of the "Saxon laws of possession, under which all lands were held in absolute right." The Saxon laws of property, "therefore still form the basis or

---

[83] See Pagden, *Lords of all the World*, 131–134.

[84] *Summary View*, in *PTJ* 1:132.

[85] Adams, "A Dissertation on the Canon and Feudal Law," No. 3, September 30, 1765, in Taylor, ed., *Papers of John Adams* 1:118.

[86] Adams, to the *Boston Gazette*, February 1, 1773, in C.F. Adams, *WJA* 3:545.

[87] Adams, "A Dissertation on the Canon and Feudal Law," No. 3, September 30, 1765, in Taylor, ed., *Papers of John Adams* 1:119. Also see Adams, *Novanglus*, VII, in *WJA* 4:124: "Scarcely any thing is involved in more systematical obscurity, than the rights of our ancestors, when they arrived in America."

groundwork of the Common law, to prevail wheresoever the exceptions have not taken place."[88]

Establishing that Saxon landholding patterns free from feudal obligation prevailed where no explicit surrender to the king had occurred was of crucial importance to Jefferson, precisely because its application to the English migration to the new world ratified his argument about the nature of the empire: "*America was not conquered by William the Norman*, nor it's lands surrendered to him or any of his successors." It followed, therefore, that American lands remained "undoubtedly of the Allodial nature," outside of the king's demesne.[89] Here was the embryo of Jefferson's republic of freeholders of land, disposable at their individual pleasure, but, much more significant, it also created a historical foundation for a degree of American independence from the empire that few, if any others, at the time were willing to countenance. If, as Jefferson had argued earlier, Parliament had no authority over the American colonies, which maintained a connection to the empire in the person of the king only, his argument that America was not naturally part of the king's dominion severed any legal or constitutional connection to the empire not rooted in American consent. The political link between the colonies and the king was founded, Jefferson suggested, not on the prerogative of the monarch, or even the tacit consent of the settlers, but on the free choice of independent Americans. In "the inhospitable wilds of America," the settlers "established civil societies with various forms of constitution but possessing all, what is inherent in all, the full & perfect powers of legislation."[90] Americans, in other words, moved from a kind of state of nature into civil society of their own making. Their migration had forced them to address the question: "By what law will we govern ourselves?"[91] Because they were "laborers, not lawyers," Jefferson later suggested, they decided on the simplest plan: to adopt "that system with which we were familiar."[92] "The [English] emigrants" to the "wilds of America," after a period of what can only be described as independent sovereignty, "had thought proper to adopt that system of laws under which they had hitherto lived in the mother country, and to continue their union with her by submitting themselves to the same common sovereign, who was *thereby made* the central link connecting the several parts of the empire thus newly multiplied."[93] Accordingly, they formed a reconnection with the king to establish

---

[88] *TJW*, 118–19. Also see Gilbert Chinard, ed., *The Commonplace Book of Thomas Jefferson: A Repertory of His Ideas on Government* (Baltimore, 1926), 186, entry 733; and 191, entry 740.

[89] *Summary View*, in *PTJ* 1:132–133, emphasis added.

[90] Jefferson's Composition Draft of the *Declaration of the Causes and Necessity of Taking up Arms* [June 1775], ibid., 193.

[91] TJ to Judge John Tyler, June 17, 1812, *L&B* 13:165.

[92] *Summary View*, in *PTJ* 1:133; TJ to Tyler, June 17, 1812, *L&B* 13: 165.

[93] Ibid., 122–123, emphasis added. The passive construction here suggests, by implication, the action of the settlers, vis-à-vis the crown, but also casts a mist of ambiguity over the precise nature of the asserted agreement or reconnection, no documentation of which Jefferson cites. Perhaps Jefferson's most explicit statement of this theory is in his Composition Draft of the *Declaration of the Causes and Necessity of Taking up Arms*, where Jefferson locates the origin of the "charters of compact under one common king" exclusively in the "arrange[ment]" of the

a union with him and adopted the common law of England, but henceforth to be modified and "adapted to our new situation."[94] Certainly these agreements would be binding, and the whole argument may therefore seem an exercise in hairsplitting. After all, the argument from the charters enabled Adams and others to break with a king who had been unfaithful to the terms of the grant – without bothering with the extra and somewhat dubious complexities of Jefferson's argument. But the key for Jefferson was that the link with the king, in his view, had been the result of deliberation among American settlers, contrived by their initiative out of affection and interest, not granted by the will of the crown. The Americans, in short, had chosen a union with the king and, by implication, were bound by it only so long as the king upheld his own contractual obligations. This understanding of the colonial connection to the crown forms the essential backdrop to Jefferson's later list of grievances against George III in the Declaration of Independence, in which the Americans justifiably, in Jefferson's logic, removed their consent, precisely because the crown had repeatedly proved unfaithful to the original terms.

Jefferson bolstered his position by arguing that America was settled by individuals, at their own expense, without assistance from the crown or people of Britain. In fact, Jefferson's entire argument in the *Summary View* (and elsewhere around this time) was underpinned with a confidence that the American colonies were colonies of settlement rather than conquest, a claim that had long been crucial to American self-conception and self-identification as Englishmen.[95] As Jefferson put it in his rough draft of the Declaration, the colonies "were effected at the expence of our own blood & treasure, unassisted by the wealth or the strength of Great Britain."[96] By contrast, the British had come to understand

settlers themselves. The King, "thus became the link of union between the several parts of the empire." What is clearest here is that the settlers are the constituent power. See ibid., 193.

94 TJ to Tyler, June 17, 1812, in *L&B* 13:165.

95 On the distinction, see Robert Young, *Postcolonialism: An Historical Introduction* (Malden, MA, 2001), chapters 2–3; Pagden, *Lords of All the World*, 63–102; Edwin G. Burrows and Mike Wallace, "The American Revolution: The Ideology and Psychology of National Liberation," in *Perspectives in American History* 6 (1972), 167–306, esp. 210–211. Richard Bland made such an argument explicit as early as 1763, noting that even the Indians had never been "fully conquered." See his *Colonel Dismounted* (1763), in *WMQ* 19 (July 1910), 31–41, esp. 32–33. See Jefferson's report on the same as well as the congressional statement of June 25, 1775, that "none of the twelve United Colonies were settled, or even discovered, at the expense of England," which had largely remained "indifferent" to the colonies throughout their infancy and youth. The colonies "had been planted and established without any expense to the State." The British had little interest in them until their "commerce became an object of revenue, or of advantage to British merchants," until which time "our own arms, with our poverty, and the care of a kind Providence, were all this time our only protection; while we were neglected by the *English* Government." See "Proposed Vindication and Offer to Parliament, Drawn up in a Committee of Congress, June 25, 1775," in Force, ed., *American Archives*, 4th ser., II, 1081–1084. Also see Jefferson's description of the prioritization of commercial self-interest in modern colonization "to the Swedish Ambassador at Paris," June 12, 1786, in *FE*, 5: 124.

96 Jefferson's "original Rough draught," *PTJ* 1:426. Also see Jefferson's "Composition Draft" of the Declaration of the Causes and Necessity of Taking up Arms, in ibid., 193.

the colonies as "possessions" that existed for British "convenience" rather than "provinces" or "genuine communities."[97] Charles Townshend confessed himself astonished at the ingratitude shown by Americans who, he said, were "children planted by our care, nourished up by our Indulgence until they are grown to a Degree of Strength & Opulence, and protected by our Arms."[98]

But for Jefferson, such assumptions betrayed a bewildering lack of historical understanding. Americans, he noted, held free title by historical analogy, descent, and actual practice: "America was conquered, and her settlements made and firmly established, at the expence of individuals, and not of the British public." The blood of these individuals "was spilt in acquiring lands for their settlement, their own fortunes expended in making that settlement effectual. For themselves they fought, for themselves they conquered, and for themselves alone they have right to hold."[99] Jefferson was so dismayed by the contrary assertion that he took time to prepare a historical essay to refute George III's claim that Britain "planted" the colonies "with great industry, nursed with great tenderness, encouraged with many commercial advantages, and protected and defended at much expence and treasure."[100] That the physical hardship and monetary expense of migration borne by the original settlers had purchased, in effect, certain of their rights, was a common enough American argument.[101] But Jefferson used it in tandem with his theory of emigration to suggest that the colonists, by their own efforts, purchased an initial independence from Britain, and that any pretensions the Parliament might have to governing Americans not founded on compact must be based "on force."[102]

Jefferson's reading in ancient history led him to much earlier precedent for the independence of settler colonies from their mother countries: "neither the Egyptians nor Phenicians," he observed, "ever pretended any right of dominion over the Greeks, their colonists."[103] But in the *Summary View*, Jefferson fixed

[97]  See Burrows and Wallace, "The American Revolution," 226.
[98]  See this claim and others in ibid., 228–229. See Whig disputes of such claims in ibid., 235–236.
[99]  *Summary View*, in *PTJ* 1:122.
[100]  Jefferson, "Refutation of the Argument that the Colonies Were Established at the Expense of the British Nation (After January 19, 1776), in *PTJ* 1:277–284. Quote from King George III on page 284.
[101]  John Phillip Reid, *The Authority of Rights*, 124–131; Michael Kammen, "The Meaning of Colonization in American Revolutionary Thought," 342.
[102]  "Answers to the Queries of M. Soules," September 13, 1786, in *FE*, 5: 188.
[103]  Jefferson's note on Pelloutier's *Historie des Celtes*, in Chinard, ed., *Commonplace Book*, 172, entry 701. Also see John Adams, *Novanglus*, VII, in *WJA* 4:102: "The Greeks planted colonies, and neither demanded nor pretended any authority over them but they became distinct independent commonwealths." It was precisely this distinction between Greek and Roman *imperia* that distinguished the British from the Spanish and French conceptions of empire, according to Anthony Pagden (which implies, of course, that British efforts to consolidate and centralize metropolitan authority over the colonies prior to and, especially after the Seven Years' War, were a renegotiation of the practice of empire and left the colonists properly bewildered). See Pagden, *Lords of All the World*.

on the migration of Saxons to the British Isles in the fifth and sixth centuries as his model analogy. These Saxons, Jefferson wrote, had embraced the right of expatriation and had "left their native wilds and woods in the North of Europe, had possessed themselves of the island of Britain ... and had established there that system of laws which has so long been the glory and protection of that country." After the Saxon migration, Jefferson pointed out, no one from the "mother country from which they had migrated" ever attempted to subject the migrants to a dependence on it or thought to assert a "claim of superiority" over them.[104]

If the modern Germans were to try anything of the kind, Jefferson assumed that the British "have too firm a feeling of the rights derived to them from their ancestors to bow down the sovereignty of their state before such *visionary pretensions*."[105] Absurd in the one case, such "pretensions" were equally preposterous in the other. "Our emigration from England to this country," Jefferson later recounted, "gave her no more rights over us, than the emigrations of the Danes and Saxons gave to the present authorities of the mother country over England."[106] "No circumstance has occurred," Jefferson insisted, "to distinguish materially the British from the Saxon emigration." The British migration to North America had created a new American society independent of the mother country and no longer subject to its authority.[107]

Jefferson's fondness for the Saxon analogy was not a passing one. His attachment to the idea of a "golden age" of liberty somewhere in the misty Saxon past in the centuries prior to the Norman Conquest was lifelong.[108] This "Saxon myth," which many American patriots embraced to one degree or another, emerged among seventeenth-century English Whig historians who elaborated on Tacitus's descriptions of the virtuous and freedom-loving Saxons in the *Germania*, postulating that the Saxon settlers of England had established representative government, an elective kingship, freehold tenure of land, and a degree of personal and political liberty to which the present age could only aspire. For the historians who "discovered" it, this "ancient constitution" provided the foundation of the common law and constitution of Britain, grounding

---

[104] Jefferson, *Summary View*, in *PTJ* 1:121–122. Jefferson here echoed a satirical piece of Benjamin Franklin's from the previous year, which had promulgated a fake edict by Frederick II of Prussia asserting Prussia's "Claims, antient and modern" over England. Franklin's Frederick reasoned that the current residents of England, as "Descendants of our antient [German] Subjects," "owe us due Obedience" and "should contribute to the replenishing of our Royal Coffers." "Frederick's" obviously absurd claim that the original migrants to England had "never been *emancipated*" from mother Prussia made a mockery of the current British position in the controversy with the American colonies and bolstered Jefferson's view. See Franklin, *An Edict By the King of Prussia* (1773), in Labaree, ed., *Papers of Benjamin Franklin*, 20:413–418, quotations from 415. Also see Franklin to William Franklin, October 6, 1773, ibid., 438–439.

[105] Jefferson, *Summary View*, in *PTJ* 1:122, emphasis added.

[106] Jefferson, *Autobiography*, in *TJW*, 9.

[107] Ibid., 122, 121.

[108] See Merrill D. Peterson, *Thomas Jefferson and the New Nation*, 56–65; and H. Trevor Colbourn, *The Lamp of Experience*, 158–184.

the rights of its citizens in antiquity rather than the prerogative of the Crown.[109] Plus, it had the virtue of accounting for the legal consequences of the Norman Conquest that, according to this view, eradicated the ancient Saxon law and introduced feudalism to England. From this perspective, the political history of England since the conquest had been a struggle to regain the rights lost in 1066. Magna Carta was one milestone in the reassertion of these rights, but the greatest advance had come with the Glorious Revolution of 1688, which established the authority of "the people" represented in Parliament against the pretentions of the Crown to absolutism. The *Summary View*'s description of the "glorious revolution" as the moment when the British constitution had been established "on its free and antient principles" was simply an endorsement of this particular reading of history, a reading he had imbibed in his youth. In his Commonplace Book, Jefferson had copied Blackstone's classic statement of this theory: "English liberties" were "not infringements merely of the king's prerogative, extorted from our princes by taking advantage of their weakness; but a restoration of that antient constitution, of which our ancestors had been defrauded by the art and finesse of the Norman Lawyers, rather than deprived by the force of the Norman arms."[110] While seventeenth-century Whigs used this history to advance the claims of Parliament against the authority of the king, eighteenth-century American patriots believed the constitution to be threatened yet again, this time "by the corruption of eighteenth-century politics" and turned their Whig reading of history into a defense of their rights against the pretensions of Parliament itself.[111]

If many Americans could accept some version of this history, Jefferson embraced it wholesale, longing, he said, for a full "restitution of the antient Saxon laws ... [a] return at once into that happy system of our ancestors, the wisest and most perfect ever yet devised by the wit of man, as it stood before the 8th century."[112] And his unique 1776 proposal for the official seal of the United States even pictured the more familiar image of "the children of Israel in the wilderness, led by a cloud by day and a pillar of fire by night" on the other side of an engraving of "Hengist and Horsa, the Saxon chiefs from whom we claim the honor of being descended, and whose political principles and

---

[109] J.G.A. Pocock, *The Ancient Constitution and the Feudal Law: A Study of English Historical Thought in the Seventeenth Century* (New York, 1967). Also helpful are Corinne C. Weston, "England: Ancient Constitution and Common Law," in J.H. Burns, ed., *The Cambridge History of Political Thought, 1450–1700* (Cambridge, 1991), 374–411; Christopher Hill, "The Norman Yoke," in *Puritanism and Revolution: The English Revolution of the 17th Century* (New York, 1958), 50–122; and Reginald Horsman, *Race and Manifest Destiny: The Origins of American Racial Anglo-Saxonism* (Cambridge, MA, 1981), 9–24.

[110] Chinard, ed., *Commonplace Book*, 192–193, entry 740.

[111] Bailyn, *Ideological Origins*, 82, n.26.

[112] TJ to Edmund Pendleton, August 13, 1776, in *PTJ* 1:492. John Adams recognized that finding the whole truth about the ancient Saxon system of government, veiled as it was "in much obscurity," was practically impossible. Jefferson acknowledged no such ambiguity. See Adams, *Boston Gazette*, February, 1, 1773, in *WJA* 3:543.

form of government we have assumed."[113] What seems significant here is that the Saxon migration – as well as the Hebrew – provided a model and historical analogy of precisely the kind of expatriation Jefferson was claiming for Americans. The implications seem clear: just as the Saxons and the Hebrews expatriated from Germany and Egypt, respectively, and thus became a people distinguishable from those who remained, so the Americans established peoplehood upon migration from the British Isles.

So Jefferson was right to see himself as moving well beyond Bland, even as he remained appreciative of Bland's efforts. When Jefferson remembered that Bland approached the truth about "the nature of the connection with Great Britain," he may have been thinking of Bland's suggestion that the British government had long treated Americans "as a distinct People" and Virginia "as a distinct State."[114] The *Summary View* and the Declaration both recounted the myriad ways in which the British marking of Americans had unfolded in history. Jefferson, praising Bland years later, compared his pamphlet favorably with John Dickinson's "celebrated Farmer's letters, which," he suggested, "were really but an *ignis fatuus*, misleading us from true principles."[115] Obviously, we can only speculate about what Jefferson had in mind here, but several hints are suggestive. Dickinson's *Letters from a Farmer in Pennsylvania* had disputed Parliament's right to raise revenue from the colonies (his definition of taxation) but went to great lengths to admit the colonies' "dependence on Great Britain" and Parliament's "parental right" to regulate the trade of the colonies, all of which Jefferson denied.[116] Moreover, Dickinson asserted that the Parliament did possess the power "to preside, and preserve the connection" of the colonies to one another and to the empire because the colonies were "but parts of a whole" and therefore "as much dependent on Great Britain, as a perfectly free people can be on another."[117] For Dickinson, then, there was "no privilege these colonies claim, which they ought in duty and prudence more earnestly to maintain and defend, than the authority of the

---

[113] John Adams to Abigail Adams, August 14, 1776, in Charles Francis Adams, ed., *Familiar Letters of John Adams and His Wife Abigail Adams, During the Revolution* (Boston and New York, 1875), 210–211. It is not clear from Adams's letter whether the description is in Jefferson's own words or Adams's, but note Adams's own reference to "our ancestors the Saxons" in his *Dissertation on the Canon and Feudal Law*, in *WJA* 3:545, as well as Otis's reference to the same in the epigraph to this chapter.

[114] TJ to William Wirt, August 5, 1815, in *L&B* 13:338; Bland, *Inquiry*, 74, 79.

[115] TJ to Wirt, August 5, 1815, in *L&B* 13:338.

[116] Dickinson, "Letter III," in *Empire and Nation*, 18; "Letter VI," in ibid., 34. In his *Autobiography*, Jefferson decried Dickinson's "half-way house" as admitting "that England had a right to regulate our commerce, and to lay duties on it for the purposes of regulation, but not of raising revenue." Jefferson denies that there was any "foundation" for such an admission in either "compact," the "acknowledged principles of colonization," or "in reason" itself. See *Autobiography*, in *TJW*, 9. Also see TJ's "Answers to the Queries of M. Soules," September 13, 1786, in *FE*, 5: 187–88, where he calls Dickinson "a lawyer of more ingenuity than sound judgment, and still more timid than ingenious," and identifies his "half-way house" a "mysterious system" that "took for a moment" until "sounder heads" prevailed.

[117] Dickinson, "Letter II," in *Empire and Nation*, 7.

British parliament to regulate the trade of all her dominions."[118] For Jefferson, conversely, Parliament was simply another legislature with no superintending rights over the others.

Perhaps the biggest difference between Dickinson and Jefferson was Dickinson's admission that the colonies had originally been sent out at the mother country's insistence and to serve its purposes.[119] By contrast, Jefferson insisted that Great Britain had become interested in the colonies only "of very late times, after the colonies had become established on a firm and permanent footing" – in other words, only once they had "become valuable to Great Britain for her commercial purposes."[120] Such recent and self-serving attention justified little in the way of the kind of affection and dependence Dickinson went out of his way to proclaim. After all, Jefferson pointed out, Britain had granted similar commercial assistance to Portugal without implying any submission on the part of the latter to the sovereignty of the former.[121] Dickinson contemplated with anguish a separation from "our mother country ... to which we are united by religion, liberty, laws, affections, relation, language and commerce." It would be a tearing from the body: "We must bleed at every vein," he lamented.[122] Jefferson, of course, thought such a separation had taken place long ago – the connection was no longer organic but contractual and therefore subject to termination.

It is often suggested that Dickinson and others reached to history to argue for the rights of Englishmen whereas Jefferson directly asserted natural rights antecedent to government. But what seems perhaps most striking about the *Summary View* is that Jefferson's appeal to the natural right of expatriation emerged from his history of the North American colonies. In other words, natural rights and historical experience were not separate genres in his writing as they were in Bland's. So it was less the assertion of a natural right of expatriation that made Jefferson's paper unique than Jefferson's historical claim that the migration to America was in fact an expatriation that effected the independence from Britain that Bland described as a right in theory. This is what John Quincy Adams later thought "too absurd" about Jefferson's paper and why no one but George Wythe would agree with it. Hard as it was to "draw the line where the authority of Parliament commenced and where it closed,"

---

[118] Dickinson, "Letter VI," in *Empire and Nation*, 37. Something Bland did not exactly deny, though he saw it as a declension from the colonies' original liberty: "It must be admitted that after the Restoration the Colonies lost that Liberty of Commerce with foreign Nations they had enjoyed before that Time," *Inquiry*, 81.

[119] Dickinson, "Letter V," in *Empire and Nation*, 27.

[120] *Summary View*, in *TJW*, 106. Adam Smith endorsed this view shortly thereafter. See *Wealth of Nations* [1776], 2:590: "England contributed ... little towards effectuating the establishment of some of its most important colonies in North America. When those establishments were effectuated, and had become so considerable as to attract the attention of the mother country, the first regulations which she made with regard to them had always in view to secure to herself the monopoly of their commerce."

[121] Jefferson, *Summary View*, in *PTJ* 1:122.

[122] Dickinson, "Letter III," in *Empire and Nation*, 18.

it would be difficult to conclude from the historical record that "the British Parliament never had any authority over the Colonies," Adams insisted.[123] But Jefferson went further, of course. If the migration was an expatriation, then, as Adams pointed out, it would mean the "dissolving [of] their allegiance" and the "constituting [of] them [as] independent sovereignties." This is precisely what Jefferson seems to have had in mind – and what distinguished him from even Bland. Such a claim, Adams noted "was doubtful in theory and unfounded in fact." The truth was – and most every Revolutionary pamphleteer agreed with Adams – that "the original colonists came out with charters from the King, with the rights and duties of British subjects. They were entitled to the protection of the British King, and owed him allegiance." Over time, "they had submitted to commercial legislation by parliament" but "never to taxation by a legislature in which they were not represented." So "when Parliament undertook to tax them for the benefit of the people of England, this was a violation of their rights, both by charter and by the common law, and it was resisted." No wonder the Virginia delegation politely put aside Jefferson's paper.[124]

NATION PRESENT

Jefferson's unique claim was not only unnecessary to the task of resisting Parliament's assertion of sovereignty but also difficult to reconcile with the historical record, as Adams noted. But Jefferson's history remains salient precisely because in a retrospective assessment of Jefferson's career it inaugurated a lifelong project of forging a narrative about America and its unique character. Surveying this larger context might prepare us to better understand the Declaration wherein the descendants of the *Summary View*'s "our ancestors" became the "one people" with a common experience of expatriation and alienation. Insofar as this continuity remains an important feature of his project, the critics of Jefferson's claims about the expatriation missed the point; we are not dealing with history here, strictly speaking, but with national mythos. Nor is this to deny that what the *Summary View* demanded at the time was essentially autonomy *within* the empire for the individual colonies or that its assertion of potentially conflicting arguments reflects the confused nature of the historical moment;[125] only that in retrospect, after independence, the *Summary View*'s description of the expatriation became part of a national story that justified or legitimized national autonomy *from* the empire. After the Declaration, there was simply no way for Jefferson to imagine (or desire) the United States's reincorporation into a "Greater Britain" along the lines later envisioned by

---

[123] Adams, Journal entry of January 17, 1831, in C.F. Adams, ed., *Memoirs* 8:282–283. Of course, Jefferson never denied that the colonists had in fact submitted to the general superintending power of Parliament over trade. What he denied was that such submission was rooted in parliamentary right rather than colonial forbearance and affection.

[124] Adams, Journal entry of January 15, 1831, in C.F. Adams, ed., *Memoirs* 8:278–279.

[125] On this, see Kristofer Ray, "Thomas Jefferson and *A Summary View*."

John Seeley or Cecil Rhodes, or even those suggested in the *Summary View* itself.[126] In the new post-Declaration world, the *Summary View*'s mythology was transformed into a history that could legitimize the Declaration's claims that Americans were one people. With the Declaration, Jefferson called the nation into being, but he also became its first historian and myth maker. With the Declaration, the *Summary View* retroactively took on a new significance as a record of the distant past in which the nation had first emerged.

To be sure, the document we celebrate as Jefferson's was really the assertion of the Continental Congress; Jefferson himself acknowledged that the Declaration was the act of a "public body" to which he had "no personal claim."[127] All Jefferson claimed to have done in the Declaration was express the "American mind."[128] They were words, he said, calculated to "command … assent." But only "a people" that already agreed with him could assent to the claims he made in the Declaration. So the assent itself calls into being a people whose "mind" the Declaration was merely expressing, assuming precisely what had yet to be established (and proven).[129] John Lind, pamphleteer for the North Ministry, zeroed in on this ambiguity in the text: "It is one thing for [Americans] to *say*, the connection, which bound them to us, is *dissolved*, another to *dissolve* it; that to *accomplish* their *independence* is not quite so easy as to *declare* it."[130] In other words, American claims of peoplehood were founded on nothing more than assertions. The Patriots did not need Lind to tell them that they could not achieve independence without war and diplomacy. But they also agreed that the Declaration would simply "declare a fact which already exists," not least because the king had declared Americans "out of his

---

[126] See Young, *Postcolonialism*, 34–41. "Independence," Jefferson told James Monroe in 1823, "made us a nation," an argument that potentially infuses the *Summary View* with new meaning. TJ to James Monroe, October 24, 1823, in *FE*, 12: 318.

[127] See TJ to John Campbell, September 30, 1809, in *PTJ, Retirement Series* 1:486–487. Campbell had proposed compiling a "complete Edition of [Jefferson's] different writings." See Campbell to TJ, July 29, 1809, in ibid., 385. Making Jefferson the draftsman rather than the author of the Declaration is the burden of Pauline Maier, *American Scripture: Making the Declaration of Independence* (New York, 1997). The original effort to diminish Jefferson's authorship was made by Timothy Pickering, *Col. Pickering's Observations Introductory to Reading the Declaration of Independence* (Salem, MA, 1823). Distinguishing Jefferson's draft from the congressional revisions is the central organizing principle of Wills, *Inventing America*. Also see John Phillip Reid, "The Irrelevance of the Declaration," in Hendrik Hartog, ed., *Law in the American Revolution and the Revolution in the Law* (New York, 1981), 46–89.

[128] TJ to Henry Lee, May 8, 1825, in *L&B* 16:118.

[129] Jacques Derrida, "Declarations of Independence," *New Political Science* 15 (1986), 7–15. Also see John Searle, *Making the Social World: The Structure of Human Civilization* (Oxford, 2010), 11–15. Declarations, in Searle's formulation, are a special form of speech act that changes the world "by declaring that a state of affairs exists and thus bringing that state of affairs into existence."

[130] John Lind, *An Answer to the Declaration of the American Congress* (London, 1776), 131. For Jeremy Bentham's influence on Lind and possible authorship of part of Lind's *Answer*, see Douglas G. Long, *Bentham on Liberty: Jeremy Bentham's Idea of Liberty in Relation to his Utilitarianism* (Toronto and Buffalo, 1977), 51–54.

protection."[131] Jefferson had already demonstrated, to his satisfaction, the existence of a people whose experience of expatriation and then of grievance had given them a kind of shared identity, whether Britain's power could compel them to stay within the empire or not.

If the Declaration renders Americans "one people" for certain purposes, it maintains their status as members of separate corporate communities for others, so that the document is always ambiguous about just what is becoming independent. But individual, state, and nation are mutually constitutive in the Declaration. Without the "consent" of the "people" there could be no legitimate state or "government" (says paragraph two), and this process of consent gives individuals an identity for the first time as citizens of a state that demands and acknowledges their consent (individually and collectively). We cannot easily separate all of these concepts as if they can exist apart from one another.

But their mutuality nevertheless partakes of certain logical difficulties. One fundamental paradox of the Declaration is that its assertions of human rights may, in theory, clash with its claims of sovereignty. If we focus on the Declaration's announcement that a new state is joining the international community of states, then the rights claims of paragraph two might seem peculiarly out of place, or, at best unnecessary.[132] Their presence certainly confused Lind: Americans did not seem to understand, he wrote in reference to their "self-evident" rights claims, "that nothing which can be called Government ever was, or ever could be, in any instance, exercised, but at the expense of one or other of those rights. – That, consequently, in as many instances as Government is ever exercised, some one or other of these rights, pretended to be unalienable, is actually alienated."[133] Interestingly, Abraham Lincoln and John C. Calhoun later agreed – with very different kinds of appreciation – that Jefferson's statement of human equality and his litany of rights in the second paragraph were unnecessary to Congress's immediate task, and perhaps at odds with the very concept of sovereignty. Calhoun also echoed Lind's ridicule of the assertion of human equality, calling it "the most false and dangerous of all political errors." The statement, he said, "was inserted in our Declaration of Independence without any necessity. It made no necessary part of our justification in separating from the parent country, and declaring ourselves independent."[134] For Lincoln, Jefferson had to have "coolness, forecast, and capacity to introduce into a merely revolutionary document an abstract truth, applicable to all men and all times."

---

[131] Jefferson, "Notes of Proceedings in the Continental Congress" (June 7 to August 1, 1776), in *PTJ* 1:311. Others, Jefferson later recalled, were not so sure. See TJ to William Gardner, February 19, 1813, in *FE* 11:281: Many in Congress had in fact doubted "whether we were provided sufficiently with the means of supporting" a claim to independence and "whether the minds of our constituents were yet prepared to receive it."

[132] David Armitage, "The Declaration of Independence and International Law," *WMQ* 59 (January 2002), 39–64; Armitage, *The Declaration of Independence: A Global History* (Cambridge, MA, 2007).

[133] Lind, *An Answer*, 120.

[134] "Speech on the Oregon Bill," June 27, 1848, in *Papers of Calhoun* 25:535.

But Lincoln understood something about Jefferson's argument that Lind and Calhoun did not; the Declaration, he noted, was the textual expression of "a struggle for national independence by a single people."[135] And this is what made the Declaration's rights claims so unique. The American war of independence was certainly not the first time a subjugated people had risen up in arms against its oppressor. But it was the first such anticolonial rebellion to assert its claims to sovereignty – and the independence of its nation – on the basis of natural rights. Such rights, embraced by the American "We," were, Americans believed (so said the Declaration), rooted in nature and endorsed by "Nature's God," but they could be protected only by sovereign states.[136] The legitimacy of a state, in turn, as we have seen, was rooted in the sovereignty of its people. American citizens, suggests the rationale of the Declaration, would be afforded rights legitimately claimed by all human beings but realized fully only here. In other words, the rights claims are themselves expressions of a national character that legitimizes the statehood of the entity that will have the charge – as its raison d'etre – of securing those rights and "effect[ing]" the "Safety and Happiness" of that "People" whose existence is asserted, yes, but whose beliefs and commitments also are described in the text.

Not unlike other anticolonial independence movements that followed, American post-revolutionary politics quickly became a site of contestation over the security, certainly, but especially over the essence of the nationality and the integrity of its character.[137] This latter is crucial for understanding Jefferson. Jefferson did not care solely about the sustainability of a state, but he also cared – no less than Lincoln – about the nation's becoming "worthy of the saving."[138] One has only to read the most famous lines of the Declaration to see that a people is claiming its sovereign statehood in a world of states not solely on the basis of its peoplehood but on the basis of what that people is committed to: government rooted in consent and dedicated to human rights. Any straying from these claims – as Lincoln would later argue – would be to soil

---

[135] Lincoln to H.L. Pierce, April 6, 1859, in *Complete Works of Abraham Lincoln*, John G. Nicolay and John Hay, ed. (New York, 1894), 5:126–127.

[136] Americans did not always make the fine distinctions favored by modern historians. James Otis very early argued that American rights came "by the common law, by their several charters, by the law of nature and nations, and by the law of God" (Otis, "Vindication of the Conduct of the House," quoted in Kettner, *The Development of American Citizenship*, 154). There is no sense here that these are in conflict or that they represent incompatible ideological traditions. See Congress's "Bill of Rights and List of Grievances" (October 1774), which claimed that the "RIGHTS" of Englishmen in the colonies of North America were rooted in "the immutable laws of nature, the principles of the English constitution, and the several charters or compacts" (James Hutson, ed., *A Decent Respect to the Opinions of Mankind: Congressional State Papers, 1774–1776* [Washington, DC, 1975], 53). Or, as John Adams put it simply: "English liberties are but certain rights of nature reserved to the citizen, by the English constitution, which rights cleaved to our ancestors when they crossed the Atlantic" (*Novanglus*, VIII, in *WJA* 4:124).

[137] See Douglas Bradburn, *The Citizenship Revolution: Politics and the Creation of the American Union, 1774–1804* (Charlottesville, 2009).

[138] Speech at Peoria, Illinois, October 16, 1854, in Roy P. Basler, ed., *Collected Works of Abraham Lincoln*, 8 vols. (New Brunswick, NJ, 1953), 2: 276.

the nation's garments and run backward against history. So what Jefferson was doing was truly unprecedented in modern history: making an original assertion of state sovereignty and rooting that sovereignty in a particular nation and nationality, the legitimacy of whose claims were rooted in both the consent of the people in question and in their adherence to certain natural rights. The second paragraph is less a deflection from than an explication of the character and significance of the "one people" announced by the first.[139]

So the Declaration asserts rights that it understands are realized or actualized only in and by states even as it is emphatic in its denial that those rights originate in states. Americans claimed their rights, as Jefferson put it in the *Summary View*, "as derived from the laws of nature, and not as the gift of their chief magistrate." So the Declaration defends rights that do not come from any state but recognizes that the American state is necessary to effect them. So Jefferson's nationalism is never in tension with his liberalism. To the contrary, his nationalism is what makes his liberalism work. For only "a people" can legitimately tell the state to change its course and uphold rights and check power. Otherwise, you have a state without a nation – precisely how he read the Federalist project in the 1790s, as we will see.

From a purely philosophical standpoint, such claims might seem preposterous, or at least provocative. As if echoing Lind, contemporary political theorist John Dunn notes that, "history offers us no licence at all for viewing [Americans'] possession of these rights as in any sense prior to the claims of political authority." But Jefferson did not quite assert that the truths were self-evident or defend such claims in the text. He simply told the world that Americans believed them to be so: "We hold these truths." Others should hold them, too, and one day would, Jefferson believed, but in 1776, all Jefferson claimed was that Americans assented to them and would act on them.[140] In other words, there is no generally applicable philosophical claim in the Declaration. There is, instead, a cultural claim, what Dunn calls a "cultural truth:" "that Americans are apt to regard their possession of rights as self-evident." What makes these real, then, is "not the nature of the universe or the properties of the human species as such," but precisely that Americans believe them to be true. The Declaration's assertions, then, are on one fundamental level the "political history of a culture."[141] And there is a strong sense in which this seems to be what Jefferson was after, the cultural fact underpinning the character of the emergent state, a state that, because it was animated by this particular people, would be committed to rights they understood to be antecedent to government, rights that the British state had failed to uphold but that this new state would recognize.[142]

---

[139] Onuf, "Declaration of Independence," 71.

[140] Zuckert, *The Natural Rights Republic: Studies in the Foundation of the American Political Tradition* (South Bend, IN, 1996), 42–46.

[141] Dunn, "What is Living and What is Dead in the Political Theory of John Locke?" in Dunn, *Interpreting Political Responsibility: Essays, 1981–1989* (Princeton, 1990), 15–17.

[142] Where British conceptions of political obligation, for example, had long imagined that subjectship was rooted in the "chance" Jefferson had described in the *Summary View*, Americans

In other words, there are cultural claims being made in the Declaration. This is why the second paragraph remains crucial to Jefferson's Revolutionary project. If the assertion of statehood in the Declaration could not be actualized without military success and diplomatic recognition, these victories would themselves have no larger meaning transcending independence in the absence of the cultural facts proclaimed in the Declaration. Without the second paragraph, the Revolution is reduced to an anticolonial independence movement and the creation of a new sovereign entity in the world of states. With the second paragraph, the Declaration becomes the assertion of a national character and identity oriented around the embrace of natural rights liberalism. It tells us who this "people" is – what they are like and what the world can expect from them – and this, in turn, legitimizes the state's claims to sovereignty. Without paragraph two, the state itself runs the risk of being "self-justifying."[143]

Jefferson was more interested than Congress in making the cultural claims – distinguishing the people from another – which may explain why Jefferson's draft points its finger most sharply not at the king but at the "unfeeling brethren" in England who had led Americans to assume their "equal & independant station ... among the powers of the earth."[144] Congress dropped most of Jefferson's lament, masking the anguished features of his draft that nevertheless offer a suggestion about what was most important to him in this moment. The king may have become "a tyrant ... unfit to be the ruler of a people who mean to be free," but it was "our British brethren" who had enabled the king's behavior and that of Parliament.[145] It was they who had been "deaf to the voice of justice & of consanguinity" – who had denied, in other words, descent from the same ancestors – and who had "by their free election re-established ... in power" those "disturbers of our harmony." Worse, perhaps, "they are permitting their chief magistrate to send over not only soldiers of our common blood, but Scotch & foreign mercenaries to invade & deluge us in blood." It was this betrayal of "our common blood" that had "given the last stab to agonizing

---

would honor "Choice" or volitional allegiance as a natural right. Jefferson believed "the right of expatriation" was "inherent in every man by the laws of nature, and incapable of being rightfully taken from him even by the united will of every other person in the nation" (TJ to Albert Gallatin, June 26, 1806, in *L&B*, 8: 454). No wonder that among the grievances in the Declaration was the king's obstruction of "laws for naturalization of foreigners" and his forcing "our fellow Citizens taken Captive on the high Seas to bear Arms against their Country, to become the executioners of their friends and Brethren." See Jefferson's "original Rough draught," in *PTJ* 1:424, and the text as adopted by the Congress (ibid., 431).

[143] See Charles Royster, "Founding a Nation in Blood: Military Conflict and American Nationality," in Ronald Hoffman and Peter J. Albert, eds., *Arms and Independence: The Military Character of the American Revolution* (Charlottesville, 1984), 25–49, at 31.

[144] Jefferson's "original Rough draught" of the Declaration, in *PTJ* 1:423; William Hedges, "Telling off the King: Jefferson's *Summary View* as American Fantasy," in *Early American Literature* 22 (Fall 1987), 166–174; Winthrop Jordan, "Familial Politics: Thomas Paine and the Killing of the King, 1776," *JAH* 60 (September 1973), 294–308.

[145] Jefferson's hatred of George III nevertheless remained palpable until the end of his life. See *TJW*, 57, and Charles Ritcheson, "The Fragile Memory: Thomas Jefferson at the Court of King George III," *Eighteenth Century Life* 7 (January–May 1981), 1–16.

affection." "We might have been a free & a great people together," but experience had severed the connection and rendered the one people two. Americans would "climb" the "road to glory & happiness ... in a separate state."[146]

The Declaration's passage through Congress was delayed, Jefferson remembered many years later, by "the pusillanimous idea that we had friends in England worth keeping terms with," and it was this very illusion – which "still haunted the minds of many" – that led Congress to strike out "those passages" in the document that "conveyed censure on the people of England."[147] But Jefferson included them precisely because they demonstrated to Americans just how different their own character had become from that of the "unfeeling brethren" they were leaving behind. These passages, then, illuminate or bolster the more positive claims about American character in paragraph two, and their exclusion from the final draft obscures the crucial place of that paragraph for the meaning of the whole in Jefferson's text.[148]

The point here is that the English nation, from which the American was separating, would continue on its path with a character strikingly different from that all true Americans shared. It turned out to be no surprise to Jefferson that the English would continue, through the years, to operate by "the principle that force is right," that "whatever power can make hers, is hers of right."[149] Americans, on the other hand, understood that right was antecedent to and transcended mere power. But they should never be surprised to hear the opposite from European leaders. Britain was "a nation of buccaneers,"[150] Jefferson said, and "nothing but views of interest can govern" it.[151] Its "governing principles" were "conquest, colonization, commerce, monopoly," and its government was "the most flagitious which has existed since the days of Philip of Macedon, whom they make their model."[152] And because "their spirit towards us is deeply hostile," reciprocity was not to be expected of the British, who would never "be content with equality" but demanded instead "a monopoly of commerce &

[146] Jefferson's "original Rough draught," in *PTJ* 1:426–427. These ties, which rendered their separation "agonizing," remained strong enough even after years of hostility to prompt this 1816 hope for reconciliation: "Were [the British nation] once under a government which should treat us with justice and equality I should myself feel with great strength the ties which bind us together, or origin, language, laws and manners: and I am persuaded the two people would become in future, as it was with the antient Greeks, among whom it was reproachful for Greek to be found fighting against Greek in a foreign army" (TJ to John Adams, November 25, 1816, in *AJL*, 498).

[147] *Autobiography*, in *TJW*, 18.

[148] See Wills's discussion of the Declaration as "a sentimental paper," in *Inventing America*, 259–319, esp. 307–319.

[149] TJ to Caesar Rodney, February 10, 1810, in *TJW*, 1217; TJ to John Adams, January 11, 1816, in *AJL*, 459; TJ to John Langdon, March 5, 1810, in *TJW*, 1220.

[150] TJ to Henry Middleton, January 1813, in *L&B* 13:203.

[151] TJ to James Madison, September 1, 1785, in *ROL* 1:381.

[152] "Outline of Policy on the Mississippi Question," August 2, 1790, in *PTJ* 17:115; TJ to John Adams, November 25, 1816, in *AJL*, 498. Also see TJ to John Adams, September 28, 1787, in ibid., 200.

influence with us."[153] The "warmest feeling of the king's heart" was "his hatred to us,"[154] but even the "death of George III" would not "restore order and safety on the ocean." The king and his ministers were "ephemeral." The "animosities of sovereigns are temporary but those which seize the whole body of a people … produce calamities of long duration." Their "nation" was "permanent, and it is that which is the tyrant of the ocean."[155] The "will of the nation" would not die with the persons administering it or even with the institutions through which it expressed its will.[156] This is why English "piratical principles and practices, have no fixed term of duration."[157] Unlike Americans, the British nation "never admitted a chapter of morality into her political code."[158] If Americans were going to treat the English no longer as brethren but as "enemies in war, in peace friends," the burden of the relationship fell on the English.[159] The problem here was that years of depredation had given Americans "more reason to hate [Great Britain] than any other nation on earth."[160]

These quotations address a wide range of circumstances, and my assemblage of them here, rather unattentive to chronology or context, is not meant to suggest that Jefferson had a fixed and unchanging mind on the matter of U.S. strategic relations with Britain, only to suggest that Jefferson's feeling that Americans were of a remarkably different character than other peoples on earth did remain constant throughout his life.[161]

To be sure, American "laws, language, religion, politics and manners" were "so deeply laid in English foundations, that we shall never cease to consider their history as a part of ours, and to study ours in that as its origin."[162] But

[153] TJ to David Humphreys, May 7, 1786, in *PTJ* 9:469; TJ to Elbridge Gerry, May 13, 1797, in *TJW*, 1042. Also see TJ to Madame de Stael, May 24, 1813, in ibid., 1272–1277.

[154] TJ to Madison, April 25, 1786, *PTJ* 9:433.

[155] TJ to Caesar Rodney, February 10, 1810, in *TJW*, 1217. Also see TJ to M. Dumas, May 6, 1786, in *The Diplomatic Correspondence of The United States of America, 1783–1789* (Washington, 1837), 1:730–731.

[156] TJ to Edmund Randolph, August 18, 1799, in *TJW*, 1067; TJ to Samuel Brown, July 14, 1813, in *PTJ, Retirement Series* 6:294.

[157] TJ to Madame de Stael, May 24, 1813, in *TJW*, 1272.

[158] TJ to John Langdon, March 5, 1810, in *TJW*, 1219. Beside these expressions of hostility, Jefferson was also capable of playful teasing about this issue. See TJ to Abigail Adams, September 25, 1785, in *AJL*, 70.

[159] Jefferson's "original Rough draught," in *PTJ* 1:427. Also see TJ to Caesar Rodney, March 16, 1815, in *L&B* 14:285; TJ to James Maury, March 1815, ibid., 14:313; TJ to James Maury, April 25, 1812, ibid., 13:146); TJ to John Adams, November 25, 1816, in *AJL*, 497; TJ to Henry Dearborn, June 14, 1809, *PTJ, Retirement Series* 1:279; TJ to Madison, August 17, 1809, in *ROL* 3:1600; TJ to William Duane, August 4, 1812, *FE* 11:266; TJ to John Sinclair, June 30, 1803, in *L&B* 10:397; TJ to Monroe, October 24, 1823, in *TJW*, 1481–1483.

[160] TJ to James Monroe, October 16, 1816, in *FE* 12:40. Also se TJ to William Carmichael, December 15, 1787, in *FE* 5:364: "I consider the British as our natural enemies, and as the only nation on earth who wish us ill from the bottom of their souls. And I am satisfied that, were our continent to be swallowed up by the ocean, Great Britain would be in a bonfire from one end to the other."

[161] For a complication of Jefferson's views of England, see Chapter 3, note 42, of this book.

[162] TJ to William Duane, August 12, 1810, in *TJW*, 1228.

Americans should never mistake the one for the other. "Sameness of language, of manners, of appearance" might render "it impossible to distinguish us from her subjects." But "free and independent men" – the distinguishing features of American character – would never submit "to their bondage" just because "we speak English, and look like them."[163] Americans, on the other hand, would recognize one another by their common adherence to the "principles of '76."[164]

It was understandable that America was "so hated" by Britain. After all, if "America was the great pillar on which British glory was raised," America was also "the instrument for leveling that glory with the dust."[165] No wonder "that nation hates us."[166] So, real Americans considered "a return under the dominion of Gr. Br." to be "the greatest of all possible miseries."[167] This, as we will see, was precisely why Jefferson found it utterly astonishing to later discover a British party in America working to "assimilat[e] ... us in all things to the rotten as well as the sound parts of the British model" and precisely why Jefferson could never understand the Federalists as true Americans, but rather, as "English in all their relations & Sentiments."[168] He simply took it for granted that "the toryism with which we struggled in '77 differed but in name from the federalism of '99" as well as "the Anglicism of 1808."[169] Americans had cast off the "unfeeling brethren" to join in a union of what Jefferson called in his First Inaugural Address "brethren of the same principle."[170]

What Jefferson was claiming in the Declaration's first sentence, then, was antecedent to the other claims about rights and sovereignty. For without the existence of the "one people," with a particular identity and character, the other claims make little sense. Only the people can have a character or express its sovereignty in the political institutions of statehood. As David Potter once put it so clearly, the historian's "attribution of nationality" – and here we must remember Jefferson as a chronicler of nationhood – "involves a sanction ... for the exercise of autonomy or self-determination."[171]

Jefferson thus dodged the conundrum that Lind exploited by transforming the natural rights claims of paragraph two into cultural facts about a particular people taking their place in history.

---

[163] TJ to Madame de Stael, May 24, 1813, in *TJW*, 1275.

[164] TJ to Fayetteville Republican Citizens, March 17, 1801, in *PTJ* 33:319.

[165] "Reply to the Representations of Affairs in America by British Newspapers," before November 20, 1784, in *TJW*, 574.

[166] TJ to John Page, May 4, 1786, in *TJW*, 854.

[167] "Reply to the Representations of Affairs in America by British Newspapers," before November 20, 1784, in *TJW*, 573. Also see TJ to G.K. van Hogendorp, October 13, 1785, in ibid., 835–836.

[168] TJ to Horatio Gates, May 30, 1797, *FE* 8:294.

[169] TJ to Phillip Mazzei, April 24, 1796, in *TJW*, 1037; TJ to John Langdon, March 5, 1810, in *TJW*, 1218.

[170] Jefferson, First Inaugural Address, March 4, 1801, in *FE* 9:195.

[171] Potter, "The Historian's Use of Nationalism and Vice Versa," in Fehrenbacher, ed., *History and American Society*, 72.

## NATION FUTURE

If Jefferson's American history began with the emergence of a people in history (rooted in both an obscured migration in centuries past as well as in a revolutionary break with a tyrannical parent), the living and future generations of the American people would remain united through continual affirmation of the political and cultural accomplishments of past generations.[172]

Few modes of thought, it would seem, could be more out of step with Thomas Jefferson's than the conservatism of Edmund Burke. But if what I have suggested here is at all persuasive – that a central theme of Jefferson's Revolutionary writing is an assertion of nationhood, the existence of a sociological entity moving through time – then we would expect to find precisely what we do find: that Jefferson, from at least 1776, assumed and projected a continuity between the Revolutionary generation of Americans and the latest one, down to our own. For Jefferson, American longevity would depend on posterity's remembrance of and adherence to the original Revolutionary tradition.[173]

The tensions between Burke and Jefferson's worldviews are obvious. Jefferson privileged the "sovereignty of the living generation," a point of view that Burke believed rendered each generation terrifyingly alone and even less than human. Men in such a state, Burke said, "would become little better than the flies of a summer."[174] Jefferson assumed progress and that advances in truth must transform human institutions to "keep pace with the times." "We might as well require a man to wear still the coat which fitted him when a boy," Jefferson asserted, "as civilized society to remain ever under the regimen of their *barbarous ancestors*."[175] Civilization was advancing, barbarism "receding before the steady step of amelioration."[176] A "bigotted veneration for the supposed superlative wisdom of their fathers, and the preposterous idea that they are to look backward for better things, and not forward" seemed to Jefferson little more than a "longing ... to return to the days of eating acorns and roots," binding men to a "present state of barbarism and wretchedness."[177]

For Burke, on the other hand, ancestors had entered a contract with the future, with society becoming "a partnership not only between those who are living, but between those who are living, those who are dead, and those who are to be born."[178] No generation could act as if it was the "entire master ..."

---

[172] See Jefferson's description of America's present contributions to world science, art, and culture, as well as his projections of its future ones: *Notes on the State of Virginia*, in *TJW*, 190–191.

[173] See Hannah Arendt, *Between Past and Future* (New York, 2006), 153–155.

[174] Burke, *Reflections on the Revolution in France*, ed., Conor Cruise O'Brien (London, 2004), 193.

[175] TJ to Samuel Kercheval, July 12, 1816, in *TJW*, 1401, emphasis added.

[176] TJ to William Ludlow, September 6, 1824, in *TJW*, 1497.

[177] "Report of the Commissioners for the University of Virginia," August 4, 1818, in *TJW*, 461–462.

[178] Burke, *Reflections*, 194–195.

but had a kind of obligation to past and future. For Jefferson, the "dead have neither power nor rights" that the living were obligated to sustain; "the earth belongs in usufruct to the living."[179]

Moreover, Jefferson praised Burke's most prolific and aggressive antagonist, Thomas Paine, whose critique of Burke rested on the assumption that "every age and generation must be free to act for itself, in all cases," just "as the ages and generations which preceded it." Paine's *Rights of Man* was, Jefferson said, "a refreshing shower," whereas Burke's book, he said, colored its author's earlier "virtue & patriotism," raising questions about his motives. "The Revolution of Mr. Burke," who had been a kind of champion for Americans during the crisis of their own revolution,[180] was more astonishing, Jefferson insisted, than "the Revolution of France" and considerably less "pure."[181] Real Americans, Jefferson suggested, loved Paine and read him "with delight," thus demonstrating their devotion to republicanism.[182]

But Jefferson's rejection of the idea that the dead could somehow bind the living as a matter of right was never in conflict with his sense that devotion inevitably bound the future to the Revolutionary generation that had secured that republicanism for the nation. Burke worried that if the present generation felt no obligation to the past it would ignore its duty to posterity, that eliminating entail (as Jefferson had worked to do in Virginia) would "leave to those who come after them a ruin instead of a habitation."[183] But if Jefferson's living generation was freed from crushing burdens piled by previous generations, it would leave future generations likewise free to maintain a continuity of affection so that the generations would be bound together by the kind of devotion to republican principles that Jefferson described to Paine.[184] It was this devotion that linked Americans present with the tradition established by the Declaration, a tradition that declares hostility to all binding tradition that would undermine rights.

[179] TJ to James Madison, September 6, 1789, in *ROL* 1:632.

[180] See *Select Works of Edmund Burke*, vol. 1 (Indianapolis, 1999). Burke could both support the American cause in Parliament and oppose the French Revolution because the first, he believed, had precedent and Constitution on its side while the other he read as invested in a radical rejection of both. The first was a concession to practical politics; his revulsion at the latter a check against hubris and utopia. See Russell Kirk, *Edmund Burke: A Genius Reconsidered* (Wilmington, DE, 1997), 165. And, esp. David Womersley, "Introduction: A Conservative Revolution," in Womersley, ed., *Liberty and American Experience in the Eighteenth Century* (Indianapolis, 2006), 6–10. Burke would have balked at Jefferson's expatriation or his idea that Americans had chosen their king. Even the English had not done so! See his description of the Glorious Revolution and a defense of the principle of hereditary succession in *Reflections on the Revolution in France*, 99–110.

[181] TJ to Benjamin Vaughan, May 11, 1791, in *FE* 6:260.

[182] TJ to Paine, June 19, 1792, in *FE* 7:121.

[183] Burke, *Reflections*, 192.

[184] For crucial reflections on Jefferson's sense of the interconnectedness of generations see Peter Onuf, *Jefferson's Empire*, 14–15, and *Mind of Jefferson*, 169–178.

If "nothing [was] unchangeable but the inherent and unalienable rights of man," as Jefferson asserted near the end of his life, then the only thing the nation was never free to do was cast aside the rights of man – the principles of the Revolution – for doing so would render the sociological entity moving through time un-American, an entity disconnected from its history and its nature.[185] Jefferson's principle that the earth belongs to the living is paradoxically more restrictive than it appears at first glance; the present generation is rendered a mere custodian, of sorts, of the tradition of the Revolutionary past.[186] The sovereign living are "but tenants for life." But, to square the circle, that Revolutionary "tradition" assumes that each generation will be "unencumbered by their predecessors," freed from the shackles of the past to pursue the Revolutionary ends in its own time, according to its own lights and in its own context.[187]

It is easy to overlook the dependence of Jefferson's project on the interconnectedness of generations – the sense that the future's prosperity depends on the behavior of the living and that the prospects for the present's ultimate glory rests with the future's willingness to remember and uphold the Revolutionary principles of the past. Every act was fraught with momentous significance for past, future, and present. If the Revolutionary generation had passively submitted "with folded arms to military butchery & depredation," Jefferson noted in 1775, "we should be wanting to ourselves, we should be perfidious to posterity, we should be unworthy that free ancestry from whom we derive our descent."[188]

Jefferson put great hope in future generations to fulfill, correct, and ameliorate defects in the fabric, and he was devastated by any indication that the next generation would dash those hopes.[189] If "predecessors" are "but tenants for life" handing down a world "unencumbered" by the previous generation, as Jefferson suggested to John Taylor, then it would be incumbent on the present generation to relinquish the earth to the next without any "burthen" on "its use."[190] The following generations would "administer the commonwealth with increased wisdom" precisely because the "progressive advance of science" would render them "wiser than we were" just as "their successors will be wiser than they."[191] If each generation makes "periodical repairs" to "the form of

---

[185] TJ to Major John Cartwright, June 5, 1824, in *TJW*, 1494.

[186] Noted in Sloan, *Principle and Interest*, 61.

[187] TJ to John Taylor, May 28, 1816, *TJW*, 1392.

[188] Jefferson's Composition Draft of the *Declaration of the Causes and Necessity of Taking up Arms* [June 1775], in *PTJ* 1: 197.

[189] Some scholars have perhaps overstated the differences between Jefferson and Madison on this point. See Drew McCoy, *The Last of the Fathers: James Madison and the Republican Legacy* (Cambridge, 1992), ch. 2. After all, Jefferson came to appreciate that it was "more convenient to suffer the laws of our predecessors to stand on our implied assent, as if positively reenacted, until the existing majority positively repeals them." What Jefferson wanted to be understood was that the tacit consent of the present generation did not in any way "lessen the right of that [new] majority to repeal whenever a change of circumstances or of will calls for it." See TJ to Thomas Earle, September 24, 1823, in *L&B* 15:471.

[190] TJ to John Taylor, May 28, 1816, in *FE* 11:528–529; TJ to Thomas Earle, September 24, 1823, *L&B* 15: 471.

[191] TJ to Lafayette, November 4, 1823, in *FE* 12:325; TJ to Spencer Roane, September 6, 1819, in *FE* 12:139.

government" and in this way is able "to accommodate to the circumstances in which it finds itself, that received from its predecessors," then constitutions "may be handed on ... from generation to generation, to the end of time, if anything human can so long endure."[192] In this sense, then, the "present generation['s] ... right to self-government" is not incompatible with a sense of continuity with the Revolutionary past even as it modifies institutions to fit its own time and circumstances.[193]

Jefferson's preoccupation with posterity partly explains his fear of slavery: "If something is not done, and soon done," he told St. George Tucker in the wake of the Haitian Revolution, "we shall be the murderers of our own children."[194] But just as the present generation could unjustly burden the next, the next could squander the gifts of the previous one. It was precisely this concern about posterity that elicited Jefferson's lament over the Missouri Compromise: "I regret that I am now to die in the belief that the useless sacrifice of themselves, by the generation of '76 to acquire self-government and happiness to their country, is to be thrown away by the unwise and unworthy passions of their sons." His "only consolation" at such an event, he said, was that he would not live "to weep over it."[195] Surely one reason Jefferson was so distraught over Missouri was this sense that the rising generation was undoing the work his had so carefully wrought. So continuities were ultimately as important to Jefferson as the right of each generation to begin afresh, for without remembrance, the Revolutionary achievements would be lost.

Jefferson grasped what Machiavelli had noted centuries earlier: Republics that have "longer life" are those that "by means of their orders can often be renewed." Moreover, "they do not last if they do not renew themselves," and the "mode of renewing them is ... to lead them back toward their beginnings."[196] In fact, there is something startlingly conservative about Jefferson's concept of nation. "A nation never dies," Jefferson told Madame de Stael, and precisely because the nation is the community – the partnership, Burke called it – that is connected by past and future, what the present generation does has relevance for the future (and for how the future will read its past).[197] What this generation should do is free up the future one to pursue its own happiness (this is the radical bit), but only in ways that are rooted firmly in the founding moment

---

[192] TJ to Samuel Kercheval, July 12, 1816, in *FE* 12:13.

[193] To John Pleasants, April 19, 1824, in *FE* 12:354. Also see the provocative reflections on Jefferson's uses of architectural "prototypes," not as models for slavish imitation, "but to provide a consistent and compatible theme capable of variation,'" in Buford Pickens, "Mr. Jefferson as Revolutionary Architect," *Journal of the Society of Architectural Historians*, 34 (December 1975), 257–79, quote at 259–60.

[194] TJ to Tucker, August 29, 1797, in *PTJ* 29:519.

[195] TJ to John Holmes, April 22, 1820, *TJP*. Jefferson also said here that such behavior by posterity would constitute "treason against the hopes of the world."

[196] *Discourses*, Book 3, ch. 1, in Niccolo Machiavelli, *Discourses on Livy*, ed. and trans., Harvey Mansfield and Nathan Tarcov (Chicago, 1996), 209.

[197] TJ to Madame de Stael, May 24, 1813, in *TJW*, 1272. Also see TJ to Caesar A. Rodney, February 10, 1810, in ibid., 1217.

and the American character. So the revolutionary becomes the inaugurator of a tradition – precisely why he eventually called July 4 "our nation's birthday" and hoped its relics would be preserved and venerated by each successive generation of Americans.

This concern for the preservation of the "relics" of the Revolution was not entirely new for Jefferson, who seemed to intuit the importance of symbols and icons to the cultivation of national devotion.[198] National myths, as Carleton Hayes noted long ago, resemble and even appropriate the mysteries of religions; faith in nation as transcendent seemed to promise the incorporation of ephemeral and otherwise disconnected generations into a living community. Symbols of nation, then, acquired real power to evoke unity, emotion, and sacrifice.[199] Jefferson was never unaware of the cultural work that monuments, statutes, and even uniform systems of coinage and measurements could do in reinforcing national community.[200] Jefferson's lifelong interest in the cartography of the West also did the work of projecting the nation into an indefinite future space. "The work we are now doing" – exploration, surveying, and mapping the west – "is, I trust, done for posterity.... Those who come after us will extend the ramifications as they become acquainted with them, and fill up the canvas we begin."[201] Jefferson's plan for the mapping and settlement of the Western Territory was a way to sketch the "full contours of the nation," contours that future generations would fill in.[202] So it is not merely fortuitous that Jefferson eventually came to see the Declaration of Independence itself, its abstract principles as well as its preeminent role in the iconography of American nationhood, as doing similar work, extending nation through indefinite time and an enormous space.[203]

[198] On the importance of symbols in the creation of popular nationalism, see Lloyd Kramer, *Nationalism: Political Cultures in Europe and America, 1775–1865* (New York, 1998), 86–87.

[199] Carlton J.H. Hayes, "Nationalism as a Religion," in *Essays on Nationalism* (1926; New York, 1966), 93–125.

[200] To take just one example, while in Paris, Jefferson sent an artist to Florence for the express purpose of copying portraits of Columbus and Vespucci. It was, Jefferson later said, a matter of "some public concern that our country should not be without portraits of its first discoverers." See TJ to Joseph Delaplaine, May 3, 1814, in *PTJ, Retirement Series,* 7: 340–41. Also see Jefferson, "Plan for Establishing Uniformity in the Coinage, Weights, and Measures of the United States," July 4, 1790, in *PTJ* 16:602–675.

[201] TJ to William Dunbar, May 25, 1805, in *L&B* 11:78. Also see James P. Ronda, "A Promise of Rivers: Thomas Jefferson and the Exploration of Western Waterways," in Ronda, *Finding the West: Explorations with Lewis and Clark* (Albuquerque, 2001), 1–16. Rivers, Ronda says, would carry the "message of union and nation" to the West, "enlarging [Jefferson's] Empire for Liberty while at the same time imposing order and stability."

[202] TJ to Madison, *PTJ* 7:118–119; Jefferson, "Report on Government for Western Territory, March 1, 1784, in *PTJ* 6:603–605.

[203] Jay Fliegelman's provocative suggestion that Jefferson intended the Declaration to be read aloud simply reaffirms our sense that Jefferson was cultivating a national imagining, in this, and other instances, by a performance of nationhood. See Fliegelman, *Declaring Independence: Jefferson, Natural Language, and the Culture of Performance* (Stanford, 1993).

If he was simply the "passive auditor of the opinions of others," as he told Madison in 1823 – if his "paper of July 4, 1776" was nothing more than "the genuine effusion of the soul of our country at that time" – then Jefferson had produced a text that he assumed would continue to "command" the "assent" of all true Americans. The focus of Jefferson's final substantive letter – written as a commemoration of the Declaration of Independence – is precisely his satisfaction that the latest generation of "our fellow citizens, after half a century of experience and prosperity, continue to approve the choice we made." The "annual return" of the Fourth of July was an opportunity to "forever refresh our recollections of" the rights proclaimed in the Declaration and "an undiminished devotion to them."[204] It was through their common devotion to these "principles of '76," as Jefferson suggested to his supporters in 1801, that Americans would "learn to rally *& to recognize one another*."[205] It was never "to wound ["our English friends and Angloman fellow citizens"] that we wish to keep" the Declaration "in mind," Jefferson told Madison in 1823, though certainly it performed the act of distinguishing the one from the other. The point of remembering the Declaration was simply "to cherish the principles of the instrument in the bosoms of our own citizens."[206]

The Declaration was not only the "fundamental act of union of these States." It was also a statement of the nation's claims about itself, the memory of which would "help to nourish our devotion to this holy bond of our Union, and keep it alive and warm in our affections."[207] Even material things associated with it might become a kind of tangible reminder of those "principles of '76" that made America. He even came to imagine that the writing desk on which he wrote the Declaration might one day be "carried in the procession of our nation's birthday, as the relics of the saints are in those of the church."[208] The nation's "holy purpose" from that first moment of its birth would be "adhesion to" the "principles" of the Declaration and "a sacred determination to maintain and perpetuate them."[209] Jefferson found it "a heavenly comfort to see that these principles are yet so strongly felt" so many years later.[210]

Jefferson's Revolutionary writing thus posited a continuity between "our ancestors" of the first migration, the "one people" of the Declaration, and the

---

[204] TJ to Roger C. Weightman, June 24, 1826, in *TJW*, 1517.

[205] TJ to Fayetteville Republican Citizens, March 17, 1801, in *PTJ* 33:319, emphasis added.

[206] TJ to James Madison, August 30, 1823, in *ROL* 3:1876–1877.

[207] TJ to Dr. James Mease, September 26, 1825, in *L&B* 16:122–123; TJ to Mease, October 30, 1825, in "Notes and Queries," *Pennsylvania Magazine of History and Biography* 41 (1917), 248.

[208] TJ to Ellen Randolph Coolidge, November 14, 1825, in Betts and Bear, ed., *Family Letters*, 461–462. Jefferson, it seems, would find the pilgrimages of American families to the National Archives to venerate the "sacred" documents a worthy ritual reinforcing their commitment to founding principles. Contrast Maier, *American Scripture*.

[209] TJ to John Quincy Adams, July 18, 1826, *LC*. Also see Robert M.S. McDonald, "Thomas Jefferson's Changing Reputation as Author of the Declaration of Independence: The First Fifty Years," *JER*, 19 (Summer, 1999), 190.

[210] TJ to James Madison, August 30, 1823, in *ROL* 3:1877.

future generations that will continually reconstitute that nation in the language of the Declaration. In his Second Inaugural Address, Jefferson invoked the "favor of that Being … who led our forefathers, as Israel of old, from their native land, and planted them" in America. Nature's God had anticipated the national birth, covering "our infancy with his providence." And that same God who had filled "our riper years with his wisdom and power" would presumably lead the nation by a pillar of fire into a glorious future.[211] President John Quincy Adams, who had ridiculed Jefferson's history in the *Summary View*, nevertheless shared his sense of the continuities of "American Story." Presenting the elderly Jefferson with a facsimile of the signed Declaration, he praised the former president as well as "the country which is reaping the reward of your labours." Because Jefferson's "hand was affixed to this record of glory," the present was a "tribute of reverence and gratitude from your children, the present fathers of the land."[212] The Revolutionary moment had itself become history, and the "one people" would, Jefferson hoped, continually reverence that moment as the shared experience that gave them hope for a national future. On the one hand, in light of Jefferson's assertions, the Declaration was the culmination of a long historical process. Jefferson would also come to see it as the beginning of the nation's future. If the *Summary View* described "one people's" history, the Declaration would also explain its distinctive character and moral commitments – principles that Jefferson assumed Americans would continue to uphold if they were to continue as a people.

A good deal has been made of the American shift from historical claims made in documents like the *Summary View* to the natural rights claims made in the Declaration.[213] But, considered as a holistic project, Jefferson's rationale was to root a people in history and distinguish it from another on the basis of its own cultural and political commitments, commitments that no other people on earth could be demonstrated to hold. Americans had made a break with their European past, but not with their own past. The American past would continue to be a source of inspiration and unity to the American future, which was itself rooted in and nourished by that very process of separation from Europe. From that moment, American future began, which is why Americans would continue to remember and revere that moment as the inauguration of the American tradition.

The Declaration's assertion that "we" exist and embrace universal values prompted a lifelong project for Jefferson – a narrative, really – about who that "we" was and about how its values were to be realized in practice. The story, turned out to be more complicated than he at first imagined.

<br>

---

[211] "Second Inaugural Address," March 4, 1805, in *TJW*, 523.
[212] John Quincy Adams to TJ, June 24, 1824, *LC*.
[213] Breen, "Ideology and Nationalism;" Lynn Hunt, *Inventing Human Rights: A History* (New York, 2007), 116–126.

2

# American Woman

The Mosaic account of the creation, whether taken as divine authority, or merely historical, is full to this point, *the unity or equality of man*. The expressions admit of no controversy. "And God said. Let us make man in our own image. In the image of God created he him; male and female created he them." The distinction of sexes is pointed out, but no other distinction is even implied. If this be not divine authority, it is at least historical authority, and shows that the equality of man, so far from being a modern doctrine, is the oldest open record.

Thomas Paine, 1791[1]

However nature may by mental or physical disqualifications have marked infants and the weaker sex for the protection, rather than the direction of government, yet among the men who either pay or fight for their country, no line of right can be drawn. The exclusion of a majority of our freemen from the right of representation is merely arbitrary, and an usurpation of the minority over the majority.

Thomas Jefferson, 1824[2]

If Jefferson's Declaration, so invested in universalist language about human rights, was making particularistic claims about American nationality then what are we to make of Jefferson's vaunted cosmopolitanism? There is a way of emphasizing Jefferson's cosmopolitanism that obscures his nationalism. But juxtaposing these commitments, as if they were readily separable, is too simplistic. Jefferson's nationalism could be capacious precisely because he understood the universal to be exemplified in his nation.

Jefferson's five years (1784–1789) as American minister to the court of Louis XVI are a particular locus of historical interest surrounding this problem. It was then that he acquired an association with France that his political enemies used ad nauseam to question his patriotism. And plenty of historians

---

[1] Thomas Paine, *Rights of Man*, part one (1791) in Isaac Kramnick, ed., *The Thomas Paine Reader* (New York, 1987), 216.

[2] TJ to John Hambden Pleasants, April 19, 1824, in *L&B* 16:28.

have concurred, insisting that France turned Jefferson into a kind of internationalist, an "Apostle of European Culture." His stint in Europe, in other words, it is said, "freed [Jefferson] from provincial notions about the superiority of American life."[3] Such a reading is not so much wrong as in need of considerable qualification. To be sure, while he was in France, Jefferson's aesthetic evolved appreciably and he embraced cultural refinements that his own nation lacked, becoming an enthusiastic connoisseur of European architecture, sculpture, painting, food, clothing, and music. He also enjoyed the pleasures of the salon and the companionship of a circle of French women (and men).[4] Many of his letters from this period gush over the pleasing sociability and refined manners of French society. He was, indeed, an enthusiastic participant in the transatlantic "republic of letters" that he once described as "a great fraternity spreading over the whole earth," whose "correspondence is never interrupted by any civilized nation."[5]

"Were I to proceed to tell you how much I enjoy [French] architecture, sculpture, painting, music," Jefferson wrote Charles Bellini in September of 1785, "I should want words. It is in these arts they shine."[6] Music, which he once described as "the favorite passion of my soul," was a pleasure Jefferson particularly missed in America. In an early letter to Giovanni Fabbroni, Jefferson decried the state of music in Virginia as "deplorable barbarism" and asked Fabbroni, apparently in all earnestness, for recommendations of skilled European workers who also were accomplished musicians. These workmen presumably would build up Monticello during the day and perform on their instruments for the master's pleasure in the evening.[7] Jefferson was desperate because the lack of music in Virginia was a "deprivation ... which cannot be calculated."[8]

In Paris, too, Jefferson first viewed paintings in galleries and became an enthusiastic devotee and collector of painting and sculpture as well as fine

<hr>

[3] George Green Shackelford, *Thomas Jefferson's Travels in Europe, 1784–1789* (Baltimore, 1995), 167; Fawn M. Brodie, *Thomas Jefferson: An Intimate History* (New York, 1974), 185. Andrew Burstein offers a balanced assessment in *The Inner Jefferson: Portrait of a Grieving Optimist* (Charlottesville, 1995), 74–75; 111–115. Solid biographical treatments of this period of Jefferson's life also include Merrill D. Peterson, *Thomas Jefferson and the New Nation* (New York, 1970), 297–389; Dumas Malone, *Jefferson and the Rights of Man* (Boston, 1951), 3–237; and William Howard Adams, *The Paris Years of Thomas Jefferson* (New Haven, 1997).

[4] Adams, *Paris Years of Thomas Jefferson*, 78–122; Joseph E. Ellis, *American Sphinx: The Character of Thomas Jefferson* (New York, 1997), 72–74, 90–97; Burstein, *Inner Jefferson*, 48–49, 71–75; Douglas L. Wilson, "Thomas Jefferson's Library and the French Connection," *Eighteenth-Century Studies* 26 (Summer 1993), 676–677; Gordon S. Wood, *The Radicalism of the American Revolution* (New York, 1992), 203, 403n35.

[5] Douglas L. Wilson, "Jefferson and the Republic of Letters," in Peter S. Onuf, ed., *Jeffersonian Legacies* (Charlottesville, 1993), 50–76; "Thomas Jefferson's Library and the French Connection," 683–685; TJ to John Hollins, Feb. 19, 1809, in *L&B* 12:253.

[6] TJ to Charles Bellini, Sept. 30, 1785, *PTJ* 8:569.

[7] TJ to Giovanni Fabbroni, June 5, 1778, ibid., 2:196.

[8] TJ to Charles Bellini, Sept. 30, 1785, ibid., 8:569.

furniture and household items.⁹ Jefferson's near obsession with the art of Paris
certainly reflected his opening to a level of cultural sophistication about which
he had been partially ignorant. A "savage of the mountains of America," as he
described himself to Bellini, Jefferson was conscious of the cultural dearth of
his own country and worked hard to rectify it.¹⁰ He spent time in galleries and
became fascinated with particular pieces. He confided to Madame de Tesse that
he had fallen in love with a sculpture of Diana on his tour of southern France,
and that he gazed "whole hours at the Maison quarree, like a lover at his mis-
tress," so that the artists who worked near it likely thought him "an hypochon-
driac Englishman, about to write with a pistol the last chapter of his history."
He also confessed to having been "violently smitten with the hotel de Salm" to
which he made almost daily pilgrimage.¹¹

In his enthusiasm, Jefferson revealed some basic insecurities about the
sophistication of his own taste and the lack of cultural refinement in America.
Moved by a reproduction of a painting of Marius, Jefferson told Madame de
Tott, herself a painter, that "all Paris is running to see it, and really it appears
to me to have extraordinary merit." But he doubted his own taste and asked
her to "write me your judgement on it: it will serve to rectify my own, which
as I have told you is a bad one and needs a guide."¹² His deferential reaction to her response displayed even more clearly his feelings of inadequacy on
this relatively new subject. "The strong expression given to the countenance
of Marius," he wrote her, "had absorbed all my attention, and made me overlook the slenderness of his frame, which you justly recall to my mind as faulty
in that particular."¹³ The worldliness of Paris was enough to challenge even
Jefferson's confidence.

But, as he was quick to remind anyone who would listen, there was more to
Europe than high culture and politeness. In Jefferson's imagination, American
values and cultural practices embodied universal standards that clashed – he
discovered in Europe – with practices of other nations, practices that he took
to be "unnatural" and that heightened his skepticism about the ability of other
peoples to create enlightened societies. The overwhelming burden of Jefferson's
correspondence from his years in France, in fact, emphasized American difference from, and superiority to, the Old World, and his anxiety about the potential corrupting effect of European mores on American people and institutions.

---

⁹ Garry Wills, "The Aesthete," in *New York Review of Books*, August 12, 1993; Susan R. Stein,
  *The Worlds of Thomas Jefferson at Monticello* (New York, 1993); Adams, *Paris Years*, 83–84.
  In part, at least, all this consumption was an effort to keep up appearances. As its minister
  to France, Jefferson hoped to put forward the best face of the American diplomatic mission.
  His frequent early complaints about the lack of funds necessary to outfit himself in a respectable manner revealed some anxiety about the perception of his mission, which, he told James
  Monroe, was "the lowest and most obscure of the whole diplomatic tribe" (TJ to James Monroe,
  Nov. 11, 1784, *PTJ* 7:512).
¹⁰ TJ to Bellini, Sept. 30, 1785, ibid., 8:568.
¹¹ TJ to Madame de Tesse, March 20, 1787, ibid., 11:226.
¹² TJ to Madame de Tott, February 28, 1787, ibid., 187.
¹³ TJ to Madame de Tott, April 5, 1787, ibid., 270.

These concerns manifested themselves in many areas but in none more strik-ing than that of gender. Jefferson's correspondence from France suggests that his conception of gender and sexuality was far from tangential to his republi-canism or to his understanding of America's uniqueness. Jefferson's ideal soci-ety embraced female domesticity as part of the natural order of things – an order, he came to believe, realized only in America. The shock of his encounter with difference in France clarified this conviction and compelled Jefferson to make explicit the gendered contours and underpinnings of his nationalism.[14]

Although Jefferson's embrace of female domesticity as essential to the new republican order should not surprise any student of Revolutionary America, historians have been somewhat conflicted about Jefferson's views on gender relations, particularly his representations of women.[15] Some have identified a pattern of misogyny in Jefferson, a certain lack of comfort with women, if not worse – one scholar, for example, depicts a Jefferson full of "patriarchal rage" triggered by his mother's legal control over his property and destiny after his father's death. Another has also suggested that Jefferson's preferences for women who were "gentle, feminine, and yielding" originated with a deep hostility to his mother. Yet another describes a Jefferson fearful of women, whose uncontrolled passion and sexual aggression, he believed, threatened his masculine self-control.[16] Other scholars have demonstrated, by contrast, that, although he tended to recoil from women he considered unreserved or

[14] On the multiple and various ways gender and sexuality inform conceptions of national identity, see, among others, George Mosse, *Nationalism and Sexuality: Respectability and Abnormal Sexuality in Modern Europe* (New York, 1985); Anne McClintock, "'No Longer a Future in Heaven': Nationalism, Gender, and Race," in Geoff Eley and Ronald Grigor Suny, eds., *Becoming National: A Reader* (Oxford, 1996), 260–284; *Woman – Nation – State*, ed. Floya Anthias and Nira Yuval-Davis (New York, 1989); and Joan W. Scott, "'La Querelle Des Femmes' In the Late Twentieth Century," *New Left Review* (November–December 1997), 3–19.

[15] Jefferson was heir to an extraordinarily long patriarchal tradition in western thought. See Michele Crampe-Casnabet, "A Sampling of Eighteenth-Century Philosophy," and Natalie Zemon Davis, "Women in Politics," both in Natalie Zemon Davis and Arlette Farge, eds., *A History of Women in the West*, vol. 3, *Renaissance and Enlightenment Paradoxes* (Cambridge, MA, 1993), 315–347, 167–183; and Susan Moller Okin, *Women in Western Political Thought* (Princeton, 1979), 3–194. For the early American situation, see Linda K. Kerber, *Women of the Republic: Intellect and Ideology in Revolutionary America* (Chapel Hill, 1980); and Joan R. Gundersen, "Independence, Citizenship, and the American Revolution," *Signs* 13 (1987), 59–77.

[16] See Kenneth A. Lockridge, *On the Sources of Patriarchal Rage: The Commonplace Books of William Byrd and Thomas Jefferson and the Gendering of Power in the Eighteenth Century* (New York, 1992); Kenneth A. Lockridge, "Robert Bolling and Thomas Jefferson: Gemini Rising," *Journal of Family History*, 28 (Oct. 2003), 465–489, esp. 482–486; Kenneth A. Lockridge, "Colonial Self-Fashioning: Paradoxes and Pathologies in the Construction of Genteel Identity in Eighteenth-Century America," in Ronald Hoffman, Mechal Sobel, & Fredrika J. Teute, eds., *Through a Glass Darkly: Reflections on Personal Identity in Early America* (Chapel Hill, 1997), esp. 299–301, 324–325; and Brodie, *Thomas Jefferson*, 44. The classic account of Jefferson's fears of women as sexually aggressive and threatening to masculinity remains Winthrop Jordan, *White Over Black: American Attitudes Toward the Negro, 1550–1812* (Chapel Hill, 1968), 461–469.

aggressive, Jefferson enjoyed the company of particular women whose friendships he cultivated, women, who, in turn, generally tended to enjoy his attention as well.[17] Far from being uncomfortable in their presence, these scholars suggest, he believed they were essential to the social life that made the world of politics workable and endurable.[18] He clearly saw his wife, Martha, as a crucial (and fully engaged) figure in the salon-like world he created at Monticello, and he hardly wished for women to be ignorant or "politically uninformed."[19] Visitors to Monticello during Jefferson's retirement, for example, noted that women joined in the conversation on important topics as freely as the men, "however high the topic may be," as George Ticknor put it after an 1815 visit, and that they were clearly used to doing so.[20]

Much of the confusion originates in the simple fact that Jefferson's appreciation of salonnières coexisted with an explicit resistance to women's participation in what Lawrence Klein has called the "magisterial public sphere – the State and its related agencies and the world of office-holding they circumscribed." Exclusive attention to one or the other of these truths leads to an inbalanced reading, offering a binary juxtaposition of public and private spheres that conceals the protean nature of those concepts. The exclusion of women from the realm of state – from formal politics – did not necessarily preclude their engagement in the broader spaces understood as public in the eighteenth century.[21] So Jefferson's conception of proper gender roles afforded American women variety in behavior and visibility, though rarely, if ever, in ways that threatened male dominance of the "magisterial public sphere" or of the household.

But the point here is, in any case, to suggest that gender – wherever practiced – was more central to Jefferson's conception of American identity than we

[17] Burstein, *Inner Jefferson*, 66; Adams, *Paris Years of Thomas Jefferson*, 207, 213, 215. See also, Gisela Tauber, "Thomas Jefferson: Relationships with Women," *American Imago* 45 (1989), 431–447.

[18] Jan Lewis, "'The Blessings of Domestic Society': Thomas Jefferson's Family and the Transformation of American Politics," in Onuf, ed., *Jeffersonian Legacies*, 109–146; and Catherine Allgor, *Parlor Politics: In Which the Ladies of Washington Help Build a City and a Government* (Charlottesville, 2000), 30. A different view is Mary Ellen Scofield, "The Fatigues of His Table: The Politics of Presidential Dining During the Jefferson Administration," *JER* 26 (Fall 2006), 449–469, esp. 460–464.

[19] Jack McLaughlin, *Jefferson and Monticello: The Biography of a Builder* (New York, 1988), 177–208, esp. 178, 184; Andrew Burstein, *Jefferson's Secrets: Death and Desire at Monticello* (New York, 2005), 106, 87–90.

[20] See Alan Pell Crawford, *Twilight at Monticello: The Final Years of Thomas Jefferson* (New York, 2008), 119 and 138; G.S. Hilliard and Anna Eliot Ticknow, eds., *Life, Letters, and Journals of George Ticknow*, 2 vols. (Boston, 1876), 1:36, entry of February 7, 1815.

[21] Lawrence E. Klein, "Gender and the Public/Private Distinction in the Eighteenth Century: Some Questions about Evidence and Analytic Procedure," *Eighteenth-Century Studies* 29 (Fall 1995), 97–109, at 102; Linda Colley, *Britons: Forging the Nation* (New Haven, 1992), 244; Peter Borsay, "The Culture of Improvement," in Paul Langford, ed., *The Eighteenth-Century, 1688–1815* (Oxford, 2002), 200–201. Also see Nancy Fraser, "Rethinking the Public Sphere: A Contribution to the Critique of Actually Existing Democracy," in Craig Calhoun, ed., *Habermas and the Public Sphere* (Cambridge, 1992), 110–111.

have hitherto supposed. For, on a crucial level of significance, Jefferson's assertions about American men and women were claims about the nation itself; one of the more telling signs of national difference manifested itself, for him, in cultural expectations and practices of gender and sexuality. In France, "Jefferson the Virginian" became the American in Paris, the postcolonial nationalist who recognized in gender roles yet another manifestation of republican purity and American difference from Europe. While in France, then, Jefferson revealed the gendered foundations and boundaries of his own "imagined community" and inaugurated a long national tradition of resting American superiority on its domestic order.[22]

## CIVILIZATION, EQUALITY, AND GENDER

Jefferson first revealed his assumptions about the intersection of national identity, household economy, and gender roles in a largely overlooked passage from his *Notes on the State of Virginia*, written before he journeyed to France. In American Indian cultures, Jefferson observed, "the women are submitted to unjust drudgery." Of course, he added, this was true of "every barbarous people." Among savages, "force is law," so it was no surprise to find the "stronger sex" dominating the "weaker." In fact, Jefferson argued, it was the rule that proves the exception: "*It is civilization alone which replaces women in the enjoyment of their natural equality.*"[23]

In this brief passage, Jefferson made several claims. The most obvious is the familiar assertion that Native Americans were less advanced than Europeans in the scale of civilization. But Jefferson's critique of Native Americans came in the midst of a defense of them against a host of pseudoscientific charges that Indians were naturally inferior. So it would be a mischaracterization of Jefferson's argument here to call it a critique at all. Jefferson understood himself to be defending Indians by arguing that while they were indeed inferior, they were so only because of a deficient culture – a culture external and pliable rather than intrinsic and rigid, as some European scientists had asserted. For example, he argued, "An Indian man is small in the hand and wrist for the same reason for which a sailor is large and strong in the arms and shoulders, and a porter in the legs and thighs." Indian males, in other words, were weaker than white men because they kept themselves from hard work in the fields. Their dependence on hunting and gathering kept them "badly fed" at certain times of year and, as a consequence, rendered them less sexually active and less

[22] See Elaine Tyler May, "Cold War – Warm Hearth: Politics and the Family in Postwar America," in Steve Fraser and Gary Gerstle, eds., *The Rise and Fall of the New Deal Order, 1930–1980* (Princeton, 1989), 153–184, esp. 157–159; and Alexis de Tocqueville, *Democracy in America*, trans. George Lawrence (New York, 1966), 603.

[23] Thomas Jefferson, *Notes*, 60, emphasis added. Treatments of this passage that emphasize its "gendering" of American identity include Peter S. Onuf, *Jefferson's Empire: The Language of American Nationhood* (Charlottesville, 2000), 29–33, 46–47, 50–51; and Onuf and Leonard J. Sadosky, *Jeffersonian America* (Malden, MA, 2002), 80–123, esp. 90–91.

reproductively effective. Indian women, on the other hand, were stronger than white women because they performed hard physical labor, whereas Jefferson's ideal civilized woman did not. Indian women bore relatively few children compared to civilized women, not because they were unable to, but because of their prolonged participation in hard labor, their use of abortifacients, and the experience of "annual famine" that, Jefferson believed, dulled sexual passion.[24]

So it was artificial – historically contingent – culture, not nature, Jefferson argued, that kept Native American men weak and Native American women strong, not to mention free of bodily hair, which Jefferson also spent some time contemplating. "Were we in equal barbarism," he concluded, "our females would be equal drudges."[25] Civilization, Jefferson asserted, would change all of this – Indian men would be strong, Indian women would be domesticated, and hair would grow freely on all. "Nature," Jefferson concluded, "is the same with [Indians] as with the whites." Remove the culture, in other words, and you will discover human nature.[26]

Jefferson's second broad claim was related to the first: There was nothing natural about the subordination of women to men – at least as Jefferson understood subordination. We can read this as a liberal critique of artificial hierarchies, and that is clearly the way Jefferson intended his readers to understand this passage.[27] Civilization, he asserted, "teaches us to subdue the selfish passions, and to respect those rights in others which we value in ourselves." But, of course, a vast corpus of scholarship over the past generation has highlighted the ways in which liberalism itself can be ethnocentric, privileging as natural the ideals of a specific culture.[28] European observers of other societies in this

---

[24] Jefferson, *Notes*, 60–61.

[25] Jefferson joined a long Anglo-Virginia tradition of misunderstanding the relative value of men's and women's labor in native societies. See Suzanne Lebsock, *Virginia Women, 1600–1945: "A Share of Honour"* (Richmond, 1987), 9–10; and, especially, Theda Perdue, *Cherokee Women: Gender and Culture Change, 1700–1835* (Lincoln, 1998); and James Axtell, ed., *Indian Peoples of Eastern America: A Documentary History of the Sexes* (New York, 1981), 103–139.

[26] *Notes*, 61. See also TJ to Robert Fulton, March 17, 1810, in *L&B* 12:380–381. On "Jeffersonian" faith in the malleability of the human species and its impact on U.S. Indian policy, see Bernard W. Sheehan, *Seeds of Extinction: Jeffersonian Philanthropy and the American Indian* (New York, 1973); and Perdue, *Cherokee Women*, 62; 108–112. In the *Notes*, Jefferson tended to adopt Buffon's binary juxtapositions, *savagery* and *civilization*, as a way of differentiating white from Indian society. His discussion of "civilized" societies suggests various gradations of development. See TJ to William Ludlow, September 6, 1824, in *TJW*, 1496–1497.

[27] Onuf, *Jefferson's Empire*, 29–32.

[28] One place to begin examining the problem of liberalism's "ethnicity" is Charles Taylor, "The Politics of Recognition" in Amy Gutman, ed., *Multiculturalism and the Politics of Recognition* (Princeton, 1992), 25–73. On the relationship between women's equality and liberalism, see Catharine A. MacKinnon, *Are Women Human? And Other International Dialogues* (Cambridge, MA, 2006); and MacKinnon, *Women's Lives – Men's Laws* (Cambridge, MA, 2005), 44–57. On the complex relationship between demands for group rights, cultural respect, and the status of women, see Susan Moller Okin, *Is Multiculturalism Bad for Women?* (Princeton, 1999), 9–24; and Martha C. Nussbaum, *Women and Human Development: The Capabilities Approach* (Cambridge, 2000). For a critique of the way liberal theorists have ignored gender in their distinction between public/private, see Okin, "Gender, the Public and the Private," in David

era tended to understand difference as absence and inevitably as inferiority.[29] Jefferson followed a similar trajectory here: A culture with quite different ways of understanding proper roles for women and men must be not merely different but "barbarous." As Christopher L. Miller has suggested, such universalism makes demands that clash with its ostensibly liberal ends, proposing: "You can be equal to me when you become like me." This is ethnocentrism dressed in the guise of the universal.[30]

Because Indian women performed, or (as Jefferson imagined it) were forced into, agricultural labor, he claimed that they did not enjoy the equality of condition with men that civilized white women experienced. Here Jefferson drew on familiar eighteenth-century assumptions about women in "savage" communities. French and especially Scottish writers first refined the notion, later adopted by most American thinkers, that societies passed through several clearly discernible stages of social and economic development. The number, characteristics, and desirability of the stages varied from writer to writer, but all proposed an evolutionary progression, from what Drew R. McCoy has called "'rude' simplicity to 'civilized' complexity," and assumed that the social and economic characteristics of each stage facilitated a distinctive pattern of human behavior, transforming "manners, habits, customs, and morals" more or less predictably "as society advanced." The status of women, in particular, most philosophes agreed, improved with each successive stage of civilization and could be used as a principal barometer of a society's progress. So Jefferson's assertions about women's equality in a stage of civilization were hardly unique to him.[31]

---

Held, ed., *Political Theory Today* (Stanford, 1991), 67–90; and Elizabeth Cady Stanton in "The Solitude of Self" (1892) in Ellen Carol DuBois, ed., *Elizabeth Cady Stanton, Susan B. Anthony: Correspondence, Writings, Speeches* (New York, 1981), 246–254.

[29] Tzvetan Todorov, *The Conquest of America: The Question of the Other* (Norman, 1999), 34–50. Though see Dena Goodman, "Difference: an Enlightenment Concept," in Keith Michael Baker and Peter Hanns Reill, eds., *What's Left of Englightnment? A Postmodern Question* (Stanford, 2001), 129–147.

[30] Christopher Miller, "Unfinished Business: Colonialism in Sub-Saharan Africa and the Ideals of the French Revolution," in Joseph Klaits and Michael H. Haltzel eds., *The Global Ramification of the French Revolution* (New York, 1994), 105–126, at 116. Also see, especially, Tzvetan Todorov, *On Human Diversity: Nationalism, Racism, and Exoticism in French Thought*, trans. Catherine Porter (Cambridge, MA, 1993).

[31] Drew R. McCoy, *The Elusive Republic: Political Economy in Jeffersonian America* (Chapel Hill, 1980), 19, 21; On women's status as a barometer of civilization, see Sylvana Tomaselli, "The Enlightenment Debate on Women," *History Workshop Journal* 20 (Autumn 1985), 101–124; Paul Bowles, "John Millar, the Four Stages Theory, and Women's Position in Society," *History of Political Economy* 16 (Winter 1984), 619–638; Pat Moloney, "Savages in the Scottish Enlightenment's History of Desire," *Journal of the History of Sexuality* 14 (July 2005), 237–265; Rosemarie Zagarri, "Morals, Manners, and the Republican Mother," *American Quarterly* 44 (June 1992), 197–203; and Kerber, *Women of the Republic*, 19–27. Although he disputed Buffon's assertion that Indian deficiencies were congenital, Jefferson largely adopted Buffon's position (as well as several phrases) about the natural history of sexuality and about the effects of "civilization" on relations between the sexes. See Georges Louis Leclerc, Count de Buffon, *Histoire Naturelle*, trans. William Smellie (9 vols., Edinburgh, 1780–1785), 3:466–467. Buffon's view, incidentally, differs from that of Rousseau who described the original state of nature as

But the meaning of women's status and equality depended on the observer's assumptions about gender roles. What Jefferson meant, as we will see, was not necessarily that women in the abstract were naturally equal to men in all the ways many moderns accept, but that Indian women were denied their "natural equality" *as women* in relationship to men that women in a civilized society enjoyed. In short, they were not allowed to be domestic as white American women, ideally, were. If women were naturally domestic, it was in this capacity that they could achieve their highest potential and realize their longed-for happiness, a happiness men pursued in the "magisterial" public sphere.[32] As Jefferson later told George Washington, female exclusion from the public rights of citizenship would not merely ensure the better functioning of society as well as more harmonious relations in the family (though it was essential to both); the happiness of women themselves depended on their embrace of their proper role.[33] From Jefferson's perspective, then, domesticity was by no means an exclusion of women from their "self-evident" right to pursue happiness. Rather, it was the fulfillment of this right to enjoy the natural, a right that was, Jefferson believed, undermined in societies that allowed or forced women to practice formal politics or do "men's" work in the economic sphere.[34] Only "civilization" protected women from the oppression to which they were liable in primitive communities, affording them their "natural equality" and happiness. Unless transformed, Jefferson suggested, such unnatural arrangements would continue to keep natives beyond the pale of civilization and from incorporation into the new American nation, which alone allowed women to fulfill their natural potential.

For Jefferson, then, the "natural equality" of women as women was a signpost of civilization, which, evidentially, entailed the removal of all artificial hierarchies and shackles that prevented men and women from achieving their highest natural potential.[35] In Jefferson's view, the dawning of "civilization" would produce proper gender roles, and the practice of proper gender roles

one of primitive sexual equality, and from that of Engels who associated increasing commercialization of society with a decline in the status of women. See Joel Schwartz, *The Sexual Politics of Jean-Jacques Rousseau* (Chicago, 1984); and Paul Bowles, "Millar and Engels on the History of Women and the Family," *History of European Ideas* 12 (Issue 5, 1990), 595–610.

[32] Onuf and Sadosky, *Jeffersonian America*, 92. Also see Klein, "Gender and the Public/Private Distinction in the Eighteenth Century," 105. On these nuances in the early American Republic, see Jan E. Lewis, "Politics and the Ambivalence of the Private Sphere: Women in Early Washington, D.C.," in Donald R. Kennon, ed., *A Republic for the Ages: The United States Capitol and the Political Culture of the Early Republic* (Charlottesville, 1999), 122–151; and Jan E. Lewis, "'Of Every Age Sex & Condition': The Representation of Women in the Constitution," *JER* 15 (Autumn 1995), 359–387.

[33] TJ to Washington, Dec. 4, 1788, in *PTJ* 14:330. See also TJ to Gov. William H. Harrison, Feb. 27, 1803, in *TJW* 1118.

[34] Jefferson was not alone in defining women's equality in ways that undermined their enjoyment of legal and political rights cherished by men. See Rosemarie Zagarri, "The Rights of Man and Woman in Post-Revolutionary America," *WMQ* 55 (April 1998), 203–230.

[35] Nussbaum, *Women and Human Development*, also emphasizes the cultural limitations on women's achievement but has a more expansive view of women's potential.

would produce civilized people. Jefferson's implicit reasoning was circular: Gender roles – especially the status of women – became both sign and cause of relative standing in the hierarchy of peoples. If "civilization alone" granted women their "natural equality" and if "natural equality" for women guaranteed their domesticity, then civilization could be measured easily by the degree to which women were domesticated. The corollary might also be true: Corruption in a society might be measured, in part, by women's power and activity in the public sphere, whether this took the form of hard labor, as in Indian communities, or, as he discovered in France, political engagement and sexual license. Jefferson's underlying assumption, then, was that civilization could be identified where people expressed what he considered to be natural gender roles.

This universalist argument ultimately served the ends of Jefferson's nationalism, for only in America, he came to believe, were natural gender roles uninhibited by artificial culture. Unlike the many European writers who consciously prescribed the transformation of gender roles to conform with nature, Jefferson confidently proclaimed that the United States already provided the kind of cultural, political, and economic environment in which these natural roles could flourish. Other societies (Native and European) needed change, but Americans already practiced gender in accordance with nature's prescription. For Jefferson, then, appropriate expression of universal manhood and womanhood became part of what it meant to be an American. American masculinity and femininity, then, were both expressions of a particular national identity and the fulfillment of natural human gender roles.[36]

This assumption underlay Jefferson's frequent exhortations urging Indians to acquire "civilization" and to incorporate themselves into the new nation by correcting the twisted way they organized relations between men and women. Jefferson encouraged Indian men to take up agricultural labor and remove "the labour of the earth from the women" who had historically been tillers of the soil in Native American cultures.[37] Women would be thus "freed," as Jefferson put it, to "spin and weave and to clothe their families." No longer drudges, Indian women would literally reproduce the nation, birthing children at rates comparable to white women, thus "doubl[ing]" their numbers "every twenty years." The Indian male would become a *man* – a family farmer no longer exposed to "yearly famine," virile, industrious, and monogamous, committed to cultivation of the earth and the acquisition and improvement of property for the purpose of providing for his nuclear family, his wife and children, "whom he loves more than he does his other relations, and for whom he will work with pleasure during his life."[38] Once Indians abandoned the traditional roles

---

[36] Compare Jefferson's confidence about American practice with the contemporary analysis of French national character discussed in David A. Bell, *The Cult of the Nation in France: Inventing Nationalism, 1680–1800* (Cambridge, MA, 2001), 142, 149–151.

[37] TJ to Captain Hendrick, et al., Dec. 21, 1808, in *L&B* 16:452. See also TJ to Brothers of the Choctaw Nation, Dec. 17, 1803, in *TJW*, 559.

[38] TJ to the Chiefs of the Cherokee Nation, Jan. 10, 1806, in *TJW*, 561.

prescribed by their culture, Jefferson told the Oneida leader Captain Hendrick in 1808, "We shall all be Americans." Indians would "mix with us by marriage," and their "blood will run in our veins." If they wanted to become incorporated into Jefferson's nation as true Americans, in other words, Indians would need to undergo a radical revolution in relations between men and women.[39]

In the 1780s, when Jefferson first expressed these views about Natives, he was particularly concerned with the development of the kinds of institutions and individual characters that would sustain the new Republic. In the *Notes*, Jefferson emphasized the importance of political, cultural, and even ethnic homogeneity to the preservation of the gains made in the Revolution. For, beneath the surface of his confidence about the correspondence of America with nature's prescription was a concern that America could decline.[40] Paradoxically, America's place as "nature's nation" would require no little amount of social engineering. In addition to his advice that Indians shed their cultural distinctions, the *Notes* also contains Jefferson's clearest articulation of the need to couple emancipation of black slaves with their colonization outside the United States.[41] Less well known are Jefferson's serious misgivings about European immigration to America. In all three cases, Jefferson prized homogeneity *within* the nation. But at the same time, Jefferson was also keen to distinguish American identity from *external* "others." So it is not surprising that a sense of the crucial importance of properly expressed masculinity and femininity also informed his nationalist anxieties during his years as minister to France where the assumptions about gender described in the *Notes* colored his perceptions of French manners and where his experience, in turn, would confirm and reinforce those very assumptions.

In France, as he had among Indians back home, Jefferson wandered into a kind of "gender frontier" where his culturally specific sensibilities were confronted by gender practices that were quite literally foreign to his experience and approval.[42] As the representative American in France, Jefferson's projection of American identity was informed to a significant degree by his comparison of gender and sexuality in France and the United States. If Native Americans needed a revolution in gender relations to become "civilized," the French, too, Jefferson asserted throughout his years in Europe, needed a comparable revolution, if they ever hoped to enjoy the blessings of republican government

---

[39] TJ to Captain Hendrick, December 21, 1808, in *L&B* 16:452.

[40] Jefferson's concern reflected a widespread anxiety. See Gordon S. Wood, *Creation of the American Republic* (Chapel Hill, 1969), 97–114; and Richard L. Bushman, *The Refinement of America: Persons, Houses, Cities* (New York, 1992), 186–203. Also see TJ to William Hay, August 4, 1787, *PTJ* 12:685.

[41] *Notes*, 137–138, 83–85.

[42] I borrow this concept from Kathleen M. Brown, "Brave New Worlds: Women's and Gender History," *WMQ* (1993), 311–328; esp. 317–320; Kathleen M. Brown, *Good Wives, Nasty Wenches, Anxious Patriarchs: Gender, Race, and Power in Colonial Virginia* (Chapel Hill, 1996), 33. Also see Theda Perdue, "Columbus Meets Pocahontas in the American South," *Southern Cultures* 3 (Spring 1997), 4–21.

and of the "natural equality," which, in Jefferson's view, remained peculiar to America. Jefferson's negative assertions about Indians and Europeans, then, were also about the construction of a positive, stable, coherent American national identity. For Jefferson was doing much more than defining a masculine subject against a female other within the nation or striving to keep women in their proper place. He was articulating a normative gendered American identity that profoundly liberated both men and women to enact their natural roles. France served Jefferson as a Manichaean "other" against which American identity could assume coherence. Couched in a moralized criticism of France was Jefferson's projection of American nationhood.[43]

## "AMAZONS AND ANGELS"

In a well-known letter he mailed from France in 1785, about fourteen months into his residence there, Jefferson described for a fellow Virginian "the disadvantages of sending a[n American] youth to Europe." John Banister, Jr. had sought Jefferson's advice on a younger brother's education and Jefferson spent most his reply urging Banister to keep his brother far away from Europe. To go into much detail, Jefferson noted, "would require a volume" so he would "select a few" evils only. In England, the young innocent American male would learn "drinking, horse-racing and boxing." "These," Jefferson said, were "the peculiarities of English education." More insidious were other temptations awaiting him on the continent. The American student in Europe would acquire "a fondness for European luxury and dissipation and a contempt for the simplicity of his own country." He would become "fascinated with the privileges of the European aristocrats" and begin to view "with abhorrence the lovely equality which the poor enjoys with the rich in his own country."[44]

For Jefferson, this dangerous attraction to European aristocracy was inextricably linked with its unnatural gender practices and unbridled sexuality. French women would be the entrée into an appreciation for everything Americans ought to abhor. The young American, he believed, would be "led by the strongest of all the human passions into a spirit for female intrigue destructive of his own and others happiness, or a passion for whores destructive of his health, and in both cases learns to consider fidelity to the marriage bed as an ungentlemanly practice and inconsistent with happiness." Worst of all, perhaps, memory of "the voluptuary dress and arts of the European women" would lead him to "pit[y] and despise ... the chaste affections and simplicity of those of his own country." The young American would return "to his own

---

[43] Carroll Smith-Rosenberg, "Dis-Covering the Subject of the 'Great Constitutional Discussion,' 1786–1789," *JAH* 79 (Dec. 1992), 841–873, esp. 842–846.

[44] TJ to John Banister, Jr., Oct. 15, 1785, in *PTJ* 8:635–637. Jefferson can hardly have been unaware that horse racing, boxing, and drinking were vices associated with the Virginia gentry. Jefferson's concerns about the moral content of foreign education were not entirely unique to him. See Richard D. Brown, *The Strength of a People: The Idea of an Informed Citizenry in America, 1650–1870* (Chapel Hill, 1997), 69–74.

country, a foreigner." Jefferson apologized to Banister for this "sermon" but excused it because "the consequences of foreign education are alarming to me as an American." Banister, Jefferson assumed, was "sufficiently American to pardon me for it."[45]

Three things are immediately obvious here. First, Jefferson had not allowed his love of French wine and fine art to cloud his basic understanding of the differences between Europe and America. Second, relations between men and women, and the boundaries of acceptable behavior for both, served as a clear signifier, for Jefferson, of American identity. Third, his assertions about American gender were confident but anxious. The achievement of the *natural* was not, for him, a foreordained outcome of human societies (witness Indians and the French); it must be actively maintained. The identity he claimed would require careful tending. Gender roles were not Jefferson's only concern here, but his worries about the creeping influence of aristocracy and luxury in the Republic cannot be separated easily from the gender talk that permeated this discussion throughout his time in France. French conceptions and practice of gender and sexuality could, he feared, snag American youths abroad, threatening the domestic happiness he considered central to the reproduction of national identity.[46] The rising generation of American leaders, then, would not be those educated in Europe. Instead, political leadership would fall, Jefferson wrote, to "those who have been educated [in America], and whose manners, morals and habits are perfectly homogeneous with those of the country."[47]

Jefferson's letter, far from uncharacteristic of his correspondence from France, marked neither the first nor the last time he would dissuade Americans from sending their children to Europe. Only a few weeks after arriving in Paris, Jefferson told Charles Thomson that observation and experience had confirmed his belief that "not one good purpose on earth" could "be effected by a young gentleman's coming here." He later told his lifelong friend Eliza House Trist that although academic opportunities for her son in England might be just "as good, perhaps, as in America," it would take a vigilant chaperone "to prevent his being diverted from his studies." Accordingly, Jefferson recommended that she accompany her son to England, guarding his republican virtue in a den of temptation.[48]

Jefferson had considered bringing his nephew, Peter Carr, to France, but by August of 1785 had become, as he put it, "thoroughly cured of that Idea." As he explained to Peter's tutor: "Of all the errors which can possibly be committed in the education of youth, that of sending them to Europe is the most

---

[45] TJ to Banister, October 15, 1785, in *PTJ* 8:636–637.

[46] For reflections on these concerns, see Lewis, "'Blessings of Domestic Society'"; Jan Lewis, "The Republican Wife: Virtue and Seduction in the Early Republic," *WMQ* 44 (Oct. 1987), 689–721; Jan Ellen Lewis, *The Pursuit of Happiness: Family and Values in Jefferson's Virginia* (Cambridge, England, 1983), esp. 169–208.

[47] TJ to John Banister, Jr., Oct. 15, 1785, in *PTJ* 8:637.

[48] TJ to Charles Thomson, Nov. 11, 1784, in ibid., 635–637; TJ to Eliza House Trist, Feb. 23, 1787, ibid., 11:180–181.

fatal." Any American who removed to Europe before the age of thirty "will lose in science, in virtue, in health and in happiness, for which manners are a poor compensation, were we even to admit the hollow, unmeaning manners of Europe to be preferable to the simplicity and sincerity of our own country."[49] This was such a common theme of Jefferson's correspondence and conversation that even Nabby Adams (John and Abigail's daughter) recorded in her journal entry about an account of Paris she was reading that "Mr. Jefferson" was right to insist "that no man was fit to come abroad until 35, unless he were under some person's care."[50]

The rot of French gender practice grew more odious in explicit comparison with America's. Jefferson held up the simple pleasures of American domestic life as the standard the French could never reach. In particular, the virtue and simplicity of American women – precisely what he feared European-educated men would come to despise – marked the happiness of New World society. In sharp contrast to the "empty bustle of Paris," Jefferson described for Anne Willing Bingham – fresh from three years residence in Europe and soon to become the matron of Philadelphia's most important salon – the "tranquil pleasures of America," where "the society of your husband, the fond cares for the children, the arrangements of the house, the improvements of the grounds fill every moment with a healthy and an useful activity."[51]

Bingham, hoping to complicate Jefferson's picture, replied that although French women were indeed occupied with many frivolous activities, they were nevertheless "more accomplished" than those of America. French women, she wrote, "interfere in the politics of the Country" and "have obtained that Rank and Consideration in society, which the Sex are intitled to, and which they in vain contend for in other countries." Unlike Jefferson, Bingham felt "bound in Gratitude to admire and revere them, for asserting our Privileges."[52]

Jefferson was not impressed. Bingham's appreciation directly challenged Jefferson's vision of the meaning of female equality and betrayed what he

---

[49] TJ to Walker Maury, August 19, 1785, ibid., 8:409–410.

[50] Abigail Adams Smith, *Journal and Correspondence of Miss Adams: Daughter of John Adam, Daughter of John Adams, Second President of the United States: Written in France and England, in 1785*, ed. C.A. de Windt (New York, 1841), 48–49. Adams's journal, throughout, reveals her own ambivalence about French manners, almost certainly fueled by her mother's (which seems to have equaled Jefferson's). See Charles W. Akers, *Abigail Adams: A Revolutionary American Woman* (New York, 1997), 97–104. Also note John Quincy Adams's observation of the women of England: "There is something so fascinating in the women I meet with in this country, that it is well for me I am obliged immediately to leave it [for his mission to Holland]." Adams diary entry of October 27, 1794, in Charles Francis Adams, ed., *Memoirs of John Quincy Adams* (Philadelphia, 1874), 1:55.

[51] TJ to Anne Willing Bingham, Feb. 7, 1787, in *PTJ* 11:122–123. On Bingham's life and career, see Susan Branson, *These Fiery Frenchified Dames: Women and Political Culture in Early National Philadelphia* (Philadelphia, 2001), esp. 125–126; and David S. Shields, "The Early American Salon," *Humanities*, 29 (January/February 2008). Available: http://www.neh.gov/news/humanities/2008–01/TheEarlyAmericanSalon.html, accessed October 9, 2010.

[52] Bingham to TJ, June 1, 1787, *PTJ* 11:392–393.

considered an astonishing short-sightedness about the sources of such female behavior. Women's political activity reversed roles in a way that reinforced the worst features of European life and could, if exported to America, spell the death of republican society. To George Washington, Jefferson revealed his shock at the "influence of women in the [French] government. The manners of the nation allow them to visit, alone, all persons in office, to solicit the affairs of the husband, family, or friends." The French nation, Jefferson wrote, had "been awaked by our revolution," but "none of their plans of reform" took account of this serious problem that, Jefferson thought, would complicate the prospects for French republicanism. "Without the evidence of his own eyes," Jefferson wrote, an American would not "believe the desperate state to which things are reduced in this country from the omnipotence of an influence which, fortunately for the happiness of the sex itself, does not endeavor to extend itself in our country beyond the domestic line." The American Republic would remain safe as long as its women remained domestic. So much for Anne Bingham's admiration of French women.[53]

Jefferson's confident assertions about the American domestic order tend to mask his understanding that such an order must be maintained by the choices of individual men and women as well as by the active encouragement – and sometimes the constraint – of political, economic, and cultural institutions. As in so many other areas, what Jefferson here celebrated as a kind of spontaneous natural American order, he was not reticent about managing. American men must be kept from association with French women and the milieus of aristocracy; American women must be educated and culturally conditioned to a simple republican domesticity.[54]

Accordingly, Jefferson told his sister-in-law that his own daughter Martha, who had spent several years with him in France, would need "finishing to render her useful in her own country." "Of domestic economy," Jefferson wrote, "she can learn nothing here: yet she must learn it somewhere, as being of more solid value than every thing else."[55] In his official request for a return to

---

[53] TJ to Washington, Dec. 4, 1788, ibid., 14:330.

[54] During his tenure in France, Jefferson told Abigail Adams of "terrible" rumors that "our ladies" had begun running to excess after luxury "in the article of dress." He even appeared favorable to "the adoption of a national dress," although he worried that American women might not have "resolution enough for this." See TJ to Abigail Adams, August 30, 1787, in *AJL*, 193. Adams fed Jefferson's anxiety about American post-Revolutionary "luxery and extravagance" (which she blamed for Shays's Rebellion) even as he filled her orders for French lace, gloves, and shoes. See ibid., 168.

[55] TJ to Elizabeth Wayles Eppes, July 28, 1787, in *PTJ* 11:634. See also TJ to Martha Jefferson, March 28, 1787, ibid., 251. Martha's daughter, Ellen Randolph Coolidge, later noted that her mother's education had indeed been so deficient in household economy that she was ultimately forced "to acquire with painful conscientiousness, a knowledge of many matters certainly not taught in the Abbaye Royal de Panthemont, Faubourg Saint-Germain, Paris." Coolidge quoted in Elizabeth V. Chew, "Carrying the Keys: Women and Housekeeping at Monticello," in Damon Lee Fowler, ed., *Dining at Monticello: In Good Taste and Abundance* (Chapel Hill, 2005), 29–35, at 31.

America, Jefferson emphasized the need to attend his affairs in Virginia. But he told James Madison that the unofficial but "more cogent" reason was "the necessity of attending my daughters myself to their own country, and depositing them safely in the hands of those with whom I can safely leave them." Jefferson was concerned about his financial situation, but it seems clear that he considered the needs of his daughters just as pressing – more so, he told Madison. Among the frivolous and politicized women of France (characteristics that Jefferson tended to conflate), Martha had no example of the kind of fully realized woman she would need to be in America. Just as he feared the Europeanization of American men in France, Jefferson seemed convinced that American women brought up in Europe would be unable to be truly American wives and mothers without a crash course in domesticity.[56]

And yet, happy American homes also demanded a course of more formal education for women. Jefferson's plan for Martha's was more expansive than a course in home economics, he said, precisely because she was an American. In keeping with Benjamin Rush's stricture that "female education should be accommodated to the state of society, manners, and government of the country in which it is conducted," Jefferson prepared a "plan of reading" for Martha that was "considerably different from what I think would be most proper for her sex in any other country than America." Because Martha might marry a "blockhead" – Jefferson calculated the chances at "fourteen to one" – she would need to be prepared for the likelihood that the education of her children would "rest on her own ideas and direction without assistance." A "certain extent of reading in the graver sciences," then, should supplement the more traditional "vocational" training in dancing, needlework, and fashion, if Martha was to be a desirable marriage partner and a better mother.[57] Her education, accordingly, although different from what he would have prescribed for a son, was neither solely vocational nor academically unrespectable.[58] At a time when some reformers were calling for the elimination of outdated languages from liberal curricula, to take one example, Jefferson was encouraging fifteen-year-old Martha to work through her fifteenth-century Italian translation of Livy as "an exercise in surmounting difficulties" and claimed a desire "to see you more qualified than common."[59]

---

[56] TJ to James Madison, Nov. 18, 1788, ibid., 14:189. But, see Herbert E. Sloan, *Principle and Interest: Thomas Jefferson and the Problem of Debt* (Charlottesville, 1995), 253n12.

[57] TJ to Marquis Barbe-Marbois, Dec. 5, 1783, in *PTJ* 6:373–374; Benjamin Rush, "Thoughts Upon Female Education, Accomodated to the Present State of Society, Manners and Government in the United States of America" [1787], in Frederick Rudolph, ed., *Essays on Education in the Early Republic* (Cambridge, MA, 1965), 27.

[58] On Martha's education, see Billy Wayson, "'Considerably Different ... for Her Sex': A Reading Plan for Martha Jefferson," in Robert C. Baron and Conrad Edick Wright, eds., *The Libraries, Leadership, & Legacy of John Adams and Thomas Jefferson* (Golden, CO, 2010), 133–155, 273–279.

[59] Martha had complained that "*Titus Livius* puts me out of my wits. I can not read a word by myself." Martha Jefferson to TJ, March 25, 1787, in Edwin Morris Betts and James Adam Bear,

But everything about Martha's superior education was designed to qualify her for a good marriage and for the proper training of children, not for politics or independence.[60] And Jefferson freely dispensed instruction about how to please by attention to dress and cleanliness, which, he told eleven-year-old Martha, "I know you are a little apt to neglect." "Above all things, and at all times let your clothes be clean, whole, and properly put on." "Some ladies" believe they can neglect their appearance in the morning, he told her, but Martha must be "as cleanly and properly dressed" in the morning "as at the hours of dinner or tea." "A lady who has been seen as a sloven or slut in the morning, will never efface the impression she then made with all the dress and pageantry she can afterwards involve herself in." The crux of the matter was this: "Nothing is so disgusting to our sex as a want of cleanliness and delicacy in yours." Women were to adorn themselves and acquire taste and learning largely for domestic purposes – for the pleasing of others, particularly gentlemen.[61] "The tender breasts of ladies," Jefferson later told Angelica Schuyler Church, "were not formed for political convulsions."[62] And it was in America alone that women seemed to understand this and put it into practice.

Anne Bingham may have admired the relative independence and public activity of French women, but American women, Jefferson argued, were "too wise to wrinkle their foreheads with politics." Instead, they would be content to "soothe and calm the minds of their husbands returning from political debate." American women had the "good sense to value domestic happiness above all other, and the art to cultivate it beyond all others." It was not surprising, then, that "there is no part of the earth where so much of this is enjoyed as in America." If motherhood was "the key-stone of the arch of matrimonial happiness," and "notable" housewifery its "daily ailment," as he told Martha, "French ladies," unlike American women, had "miscalculate[d] much their own happiness" by "wander[ing] from the true field of their influence into that of politicks."[63] Jefferson explicitly linked women's embrace of natural domesticity

---

Jr., eds., *The Family Letters of Thomas Jefferson* (Columbia, MO, 1966), 33. On the translation, see *PTJ* 11:252; and Bailyn, "Boyd's Jefferson," 390–391.

[60] TJ to Nathaniel Burwell, March 14, 1818, in *TJW*, 1411–1413. Jefferson's approach to women's education was not atypical. See Kerber, *Women of the Republic*, 203–210; and Carl F. Kaestle, *Pillars of the Republic: Common Schools and American Society, 1780–1860* (New York, 1983), 27, 84–87. For the international context within which Jefferson's views on women's education should be understood, see Martine Sonnett, "A Daughter to Educate," in *Renaissance and Enlightenment Paradoxes*, 101–132. On women's education in the South, see Cynthia A. Kierner, *Beyond the Household: Women's Place in the Early South, 1700–1835* (Ithaca, 1998), 59–67, 110.

[61] TJ to Martha Jefferson, Dec. 22, 1783, in Betts and Bear, *Family Letters*, 22. Jefferson also recommended that Maria pay "pointed attention" to dress. See TJ to Maria Jefferson, Jan. 7, 1798, ibid., 151.

[62] TJ to Angelica Schuyler Church, Sept. 21, 1788, in *PTJ* 11:623; compare TJ to Martha Jefferson Randolph, May 17, 1798, in Betts and Bear, *Family Letters*.

[63] Ibid.; TJ to Martha Jefferson Randolph, Feb. 9, 1791, in Betts and Bear, *Family Letters*, 71.

with the flowering of general happiness in a society, and classified it among the distinctive attributes of the new nation.

The "gendered" nature of the language Jefferson used to describe the differences between America and France during his Paris years is striking. At no other time was he so prone to describe American identity in terms of men's and women's roles. Perhaps this was a period, as some historians have suggested, when he was particularly conscious of temptation because of his relationship with Maria Cosway and a perhaps budding attraction to Sally Hemings.[64] In addition, Jefferson's daughter Martha came of age during his Paris years, and he surely thought a good deal about her emerging role as a woman and about her potential relationships with men. On some level his idealization of American marriage and domestic life probably also reflected his intense recollection of his wife Martha, whose death just two years before his appointment to France had plunged him into deep grief and shattered the tranquility of his own family life. More generally, it is not surprising that a temporary residence in a foreign country among unfamiliar people and customs might heighten or renew an appreciation for home; Jefferson acknowledged that his views of Europe were colored by "all the prejudices of country, habit and age."[65]

But an equally compelling explanation for his increased attention to gender roles and sexuality during these years is that French practices exposed – and reinforced – his notions about the major differences between America and Europe and rekindled his efforts to keep these societies and political cultures separate. This forced Jefferson to articulate his otherwise-hidden assumptions about the connections between gender and national identity. Time and again throughout this period, Jefferson boasted that American women knew and practiced their natural roles in a way that few others did. As a consequence, then, America presented nearly universal opportunity for what he called "domestic happiness." Moreover, because "every class of people" in America was able to experience such family life, "most of its inhabitants" were blessed

---

[64] *Jefferson in Love: The Love Letters Between Thomas Jefferson and Maria Cosway*, ed. John P. Kaminski (Madison, 1999); Brodie, *Thomas Jefferson*, 199–227; Jordan, *White Over Black*, 429–481; Burstein, *Inner Jefferson*, 75–99, 106–111; Annette Gordon-Reed, *Thomas Jefferson and Sally Hemings: An American Controversy* (Charlottesville, 1997), ch. 4 and 5. Some see Jefferson's relationship with Cosway, in particular, as an experience that renders hypocritical his cautions to young men about the sexual dangers lurking abroad. It is worth noting, however, that Jefferson's characterization of her as a "lady" with "qualities and accomplishments, belonging to her sex, which might form a chapter apart for her: such as music, modesty, beauty, and that softness of disposition which is the ornament of her sex and the charm of ours" contrasts with the sexually forward, dominant, politically active French women he castigated elsewhere, and hints at Jefferson's feminine ideal. See TJ to Maria Cosway, Oct. 12, 1786, in *TJW*, 869. Annette Gordon-Reed offers a provocative and compelling suggestion that Sally Hemings could have more closely approximated "Jefferson's type." See Gordon-Reed, *Jefferson and Sally Hemings*, 184–193. For a different view, see Burstein, *Jefferson's Secrets*, esp. 154, 182.

[65] TJ to Charles Bellini, Sept. 30, 1785, in *PTJ* 8:570.

with "tranquil, permanent felicity" in the private world of the home.[66] Jefferson did not endorse a female symbol of national difference like the later French "Marianne" or the German "Germania."[67] But he did find such a signifier of American national difference in the collective virtue of its women.

Precisely because he considered chaste republican marriages and strong committed family life to be a cornerstone of a nation's strength and happiness, Jefferson considered the most dangerous and immediate snare for American youth abroad to be the temptations of French women who were, Jefferson revealed, shockingly unlike anything known in America outside of salacious novels and the imaginations of profligates.[68] Jefferson worried that the bright young men America sent to Europe would be easily swept up in tormented "intrigues of love" – which offered "only moments of extasy amidst days and months of restlessness and torment" – and would begin to find virtuous and simple American women less desirable. This could have a profoundly degenerative effect on the health of the Republic. So Jefferson took an interest in the young men who went abroad and hoped they would have the strength to keep from, as he put it, "forming a connection ... which [they] might be unwilling to shake off when it shall be proper for [them] to return to [their] own country." Jefferson was particularly anxious, he wrote, because he knew how difficult it was for a young man "to refuse it where beauty is a begging in every street."[69]

Jefferson remained unrelenting when his nephew, Peter Carr, now seventeen years old, expressed disappointment with Jefferson's insistence that Americans under thirty should not visit Europe. "I have," Carr told him, "an invincible inclination to see the world" and "mix knowledge of books with that of men."[70] Jefferson's response was sober: Travel abroad, he wrote, "makes men wiser, but less happy." Young men in particular would lose from the experience. With careful wording, Jefferson argued that "their first and most delicate passions are hackneyed on unworthy objects here, and they carry home only the dregs, insufficient to make themselves or any body else happy." They also would acquire a "habit of idleness" and "an inability to apply themselves to business." In short, Europe – and, in particular, relationships with European women – could quickly transform young republicans into aristocrats "useless to themselves and their country" – unfit for leadership or labor in the new nation. Only "in your own country," Jefferson told Carr, would the "virtues of the heart ... be

---

[66] TJ to Bingham, May 11, 1788, ibid., 13:151; TJ to Charles Bellini, Sept. 30, 1785, ibid., 8:568–569. For comparable assertions that the United States was a paradise for women and sexual equality, see Zagarri, "Morals, Manners, and the Republican Mother," 208.

[67] On the importance of symbols in the creation of popular nationalism, see Lloyd Kramer, *Nationalism: Political Cultures in Europe and America, 1775–1865* (New York, 1998), 86–87.

[68] Lewis, "The Republican Wife;" and Lewis, "'Blessings of Domestic Society.'" On the central importance of family to most nationalisms, see Kramer, *Nationalism*, 88–93.

[69] TJ to Bellini, Sept. 30, 1785, in *PTJ* 8:568–569; TJ to Thomson, Nov. 11, 1784, ibid., 7:518–519. Jefferson later reiterated "how little" such infidelity was "thought of" in France, and how difficult it might be for a man – even one "much above the common level" – to resist "the gallantries of the country." See TJ to James Monroe, Feb. 21, 1818, *LC*.

[70] Carr to TJ, April 18, 1787, in *PTJ*, 11:299.

less exposed to be weakened." Only in America would the "pursuit of knowlege ... be so little obstructed by *foreign objects*."[71] Here, indeed, was the point. Proper American character could be acquired, nourished, and developed in America only. The companionship of "foreign" women, and exposure to the mores of European men, could only derail American youths from the path to true manhood, transforming their national character into something alien.

There is more than a hint here of a sense that sexual passion threatened to breach national boundaries better left undisturbed. What would be left of uniquely American manners if its leadership class intermarried with the French aristocracy and adopted its contempt for equality and republicanism? There is more to Jefferson's anxiety about sex here than individual morality (though that, too, is an unmistakable element of his concern); his warnings from Europe parallel his fear that miscegenation between whites and blacks threatened natural racial boundaries between independent nations.[72] Dalliances with French women menaced the purity of the Republic in similar fashion, subtly threatening to sap the universal example America offered – reducing it to merely one more particularistic culture among many. If reproduction of the nation was a primary function of American women, unions between American men and French women ultimately threatened the civic bloodline precisely because French women could never hope to replicate the American woman's indispensable contribution to domestic and societal happiness.

The women of Paris spent their time "hunting pleasure in the streets, in routs and assemblies, and forg[ot] that they [had] left it behind them in their nurseries." A contrast with American women, who remained "occupied in the tender and tranquil amusements of domestic life," left only one conclusion: It was "a comparison of Amazons and Angels."[73]

GENDER AND PROSPERITY

Jefferson's praise of American women, then, slid easily into paeans to America itself, which, Jefferson argued, experienced the kind of widespread prosperity in which natural gender roles could flourish. During his tour of southern France in 1787, Jefferson linked gender behavior there to the domination of aristocracy and the resulting poverty of the masses. The overrefinement of the French aristocracy relegated the majority of French society to an economic stage akin to barbarism. Just as he had considered the position of Indian women an indication of savagery, Jefferson read in the daily involvement of French peasant

---

[71] TJ to Carr, August 10, 1787, ibid., 12:17, emphasis added.

[72] Onuf, *Jefferson's Empire*, 169, 182; and Peter S. Onuf, "Every Generation is an 'Independent Nation': Colonization, Miscegenation, and the Fate of Jefferson's Children," *WMQ* 57 (2000), 155–172.

[73] TJ to Bingham, May 11, 1788, in *PTJ* 13:152. Jefferson's views of French women and of women's essential nature were, of course, widely shared. For one interesting example, see John Quincy Adams's journal entry of February 23, 1795, in Charles Francis Adams, ed., *Memoir of John Quincy Adams* 1:81; also see entry of February 4, 1795, in ibid., 69–70.

women in agricultural labor a sign of poverty and lack of enlightened civilization. In both cases, he blamed the unnatural cultural and political structures
that made such behavior possible. In Champagne in 1787, Jefferson recoiled at
"women and children carrying heavy burthens, and labouring with the hough."
This, he knew, was "an unequivocal indication of extreme poverty." "Men in a
civilised country," he wrote, "never expose their wives and children to labour
above their force or sex, as long as their own labour can protect them from
it."[74] Virginia values informed this assertion. Most Chesapeake planters, large
and small, had long considered their independent financial support of wives –
ability to keep them from the fields – to be a badge of manhood.[75] Although
many white women had worked the fields in the early years of English settlement in Virginia, white men tended to rely exclusively on adult male labor
for fieldwork as soon as it became economically viable to do so.[76] Alexander
Hamilton's later endorsement of large-scale manufacturing in the United States
threatened to replicate precisely the arrangements Jefferson had witnessed in
Europe where the "flower of the country" were employed as "servants."[77]
Hamilton's suggestion that "women and Children" would be "rendered more
useful... by manufacturing establishments" and that the American "hus-
bandman" would "experience.. a new source of profit and support from the
increased industry of his wife and daughters" could not have been better calculated to astonish Jefferson whose farmers would never seek "profit" from
their wives by seeing them employed by owners of factories.[78] It was axiomatic
for Jefferson that men would never allow their wives to work the fields (or in
factories) unless compelled by economic dearth or perverted cultural imperative. It followed that American gender roles could also be a sign of American
economic prosperity.

By the 1780s, Jefferson believed, America had practically eradicated the kind
of poverty that necessitated the convoluted gender roles he found in Europe.
In the *Notes* he asserted confidently that "from Savannah to Portsmouth [from
the lower South to New England] you will seldom meet a beggar. In the larger

[74] *PTJ* 11:415.
[75] Allan Kulikoff, *Tobacco and Slaves: The Development of Southern Cultures in the Chesapeake* (Chapel Hill, 1986), 178.
[76] Ibid., 167; and James Horn, *Adapting to a New World: English Society in the Seventeenth-Century Chesapeake* (Chapel Hill, 1994), 265, 283. The connection between manhood, provi-
sion for families, and female domesticity was not limited to the South (or the gentry). For the development of a "plebeian cult of domesticity" among New York artisans in the early republic, see Sean Wilentz, *Chants Democratic: New York City and the Rise of the American Working Class, 1788–1850* (New York, 1984), 51, 248–250; and the nuanced assessment in Christine Stansell, *City of Women: Sex and Class in New York, 1789–1860* (Urbana and Chicago, 1987), 138–140. For the "cult of the male 'breadwinner'" among the New England middle class, see Jeanne Boydston, *Home and Work: Housework, Wages, and the Ideology of Labor in the Early Republic* (New York, 1991), 73, 153–155.
[77] TJ to James Madison, Ocotber 28, 1785, in *TJW*, 841.
[78] Hamilton, Report on Manufactures [1791], in Joanne Freeman, ed., *Hamilton: Writings* (New York, 2001), 661.

towns indeed they sometimes present themselves." But these "urban" beggars, significantly, were not Americans but "usually foreigners, who have never obtained a settlement in any parish." Americans, on the contrary, lived in a land of plenty with a government and social institutions and culture that allowed everyone to flourish. "I never yet saw a native American begging in the streets or highways," Jefferson wrote. "A subsistence is easily gained here: and if, by misfortunes, they are thrown on the charities of the world, those provided by their own country are so comfortable and so certain, that they never think of relinquishing them to become strolling beggars."[79]

Jefferson found just the opposite situation in his tours of Europe. His travel notes explicitly connected the reversal of gender roles in the European countryside with the poverty created by an aristocratic social system. As the nobility wallowed in luxury, the countryside remained pitifully backward. Here, Jefferson encountered what he considered "a great derangement in the order of things." Men here actually usurped "the offices proper for the women," becoming "shoemakers, tailors, upholsterers, staymakers, mantua makers, cooks, doorkeepers, housekeepers, housecleaners, bedmakers. They coeffe the ladies, and bring them to bed: the women therefore, to live are obliged to undertake the offices which [men] abandon." Men had taken all the professions more properly reserved for women, forcing the latter to "become porters, carters, reapers, wood cutters, sailors, lock keepers, smiters on the anvil, cultivators of the earth &c." – exactly the kind of role reversals he had noted among Indians. It was no wonder, Jefferson mused, that women who "have a little beauty," as he put it, "prefer easier courses to get their livelihood, as long as that beauty lasts." Jefferson's characterization of prostitution as a relatively easy way to earn a living may have been shortsighted (although some scholars confirm his assessment that prostitution paid better than other jobs available to women in early modern Europe), but it served his point, which was to lay bare connections between aristocracy and hardship for women.[80] "Ladies who employ men in the offices which should be reserved for their sex," Jefferson mused, "are they not bawds in effect? For every man whom they thus employ, some girl, whose place he has taken, is driven to whoredom."[81]

Jefferson's attack on aristocracy's unwitting complicity in prostitution may reflect an anxiety about the properly private – female sexuality – becoming public.[82] But Jefferson's stance was less a condemnation of individual "public women" than a liberal critique of a society or culture that could countenance or compel such activity. And his analysis, again, endorsed American uniqueness. Such sexual exploitation (not to mention immorality), Jefferson implied,

[79] *Notes*, 133. Also see TJ to Thomas Cooper, September 10, 1814, *L&B* 14:182, "we have no paupers" (and no truly wealthy, either).

[80] See Kathryn Norberg, "Prostitutes," in Davis and Farge, eds., *A History of Women in the West* 3:458–474, esp. 471–473. Jefferson would undoubtedly balk at Norberg's claim that prostitutes "were not victims" but "independent entrepreneurs who controlled their own labor."

[81] *PTJ* 11:446–447.

[82] Lynn Hunt, ed., *Eroticism and the Body Politic* (Baltimore, 1991), 10; Colley, *Britons*, 246.

would be utterly unknown in a free republican society like the United States, where all citizens were able to express natural gender roles and proper sexuality – where families, in other words, were not artificially burdened with poverty, where the agricultural labor of men was sustaining and even profitable, and where women, as a result, could be virtuous and domestic. Jefferson's critique of the exploitation of European women led him – much as did the critique of the roles of Indian women in the *Notes* – to assertions of women's essential difference from men, exaltations of domesticity, and claims for the uniqueness of American character. Anne Bingham's culturally sensitive suggestion that the manners of French women were "by no means calculated for the Meridian of America" – intended as a corrective to Jefferson – was, for him, precisely the point he intended to celebrate. America, he insisted, was "made on an improved plan." Americans were "a people at their ease."[83]

Traveling the Rhine Valley in 1788, Jefferson explicitly compared the "hard labor" of peasant women with the Indian societies he described in the *Notes*. At least Indians had an excuse: Because the men were all warriors "there remain no laborers but the women." But, whatever its origins, wherever practiced, this reversal of gender norms was "a barbarous perversion of the natural destination of the two sexes." It was "honorable … for a man … to allot … the internal employments to his female partner, and take … the external on himself." The opposite arrangement was symptomatic of deep structural imbalances, proof that the people were "not at their ease."[84]

If, as Jefferson assumed, human behaviors closely corresponded with or reflected stages of development, clearly more was involved than individual choice.[85] Jefferson valued domesticity but understood that only a certain kind of society would encourage it, making it a viable option for individuals and families. So Jefferson's concern with gender behavior was less a simple-minded moralism exhorting individual females to be virtuous than a critical analysis of the sources of national character.

In most eighteenth-century social analysis, commerce, advanced division of labor, increased and increasingly refined wants, production of luxury items, and refined manners and social graces characterized the highest stages of civilization. Despite their clear advantages over barbarism, advanced commercial societies left many thinkers ambivalent; historically, this "stage" had been accompanied by a propensity toward "superfluity and vast wealth … avarice, gross luxury, and effeminacy among the higher ranks of men."[86] Republicans like Jefferson associated this corruption with aristocracy and monarchy, which they believed manufactured artificial inequality and misery. Here was the ultimate source of the problems in the European countryside. It was the "unequal

[83] Bingham to TJ, June 1, 1787, in *PTJ* 11:392–393; TJ to Angelica Schuyler Church, Feb. 17, 1788, ibid., 12:600–601; TJ to Maria Cosway, Oct. 12, 1786, ibid., 10:448.

[84] "Notes of a Tour Through Holland and the Rhine Valley," ibid., 13:27–28; 36n29.

[85] McCoy, *Elusive Republic*, 20–21; Bell, *Cult of the Nation in France*, 143–146.

[86] McCoy, *Elusive Republic*, 19–20, 32–33, at 33.

division of property," Jefferson told Madison, that "occasions the numberless instances of wretchedness" so common throughout Europe, and particularly in France, where "the poor who cannot find work" formed "the most numerous of all classes."[87] In Europe, Jefferson echoed Voltaire, "Every man ... must be either the hammer or the anvil." "Under pretence of governing," Jefferson argued, Europeans had "divided their nations into two classes, wolves and sheep. I do not exaggerate. This is a true picture of Europe."[88] The overrefinement of the wolves, to use Jefferson's metaphor, left the sheep grossly underdeveloped and in a stage of economic life that resembled nothing so much as that of the Native Americans whom Jefferson had called "savage." Out of a total European population of twenty million, he was convinced that "there are nineteen millions more wretched, more accursed in every circumstance of human existence, than the most conspicuously wretched individual of the whole United States." Europe revealed, he claimed, "what precious blessings" Americans were "in possession of, and which no other people on earth enjoy."[89]

With European extremes bereft of the "lovely equality" Jefferson understood to be characteristic of America, it was no surprise that gender roles had wandered from nature's prescription. Jefferson's evaluation of European gender reversal, then, was ultimately a condemnation of the artificiality of aristocracy. The behavior of peasant women in the South of France, he believed, subtly acknowledged the contrived nature of their oppression. Even "while employed in dirt and drudgery," Jefferson observed, "some tag of a ribbon, some ring or bit of bracelet, earbob or necklace, or something of that kind," revealed that women were "formed by nature for attentions, not for hard labor." Even in poverty, Jefferson suggested, aspirations to natural womanhood forced their way to the surface and indicated a subtle resistance to an artificial situation. Thus was nature's plan revealed; women, Jefferson noted, were formed to be the "objects of our pleasures," not field hands.[90]

Jefferson's point here was complex, reflecting the liberal compassion for the oppressed that emerged in his discussion of Indian women in the *Notes*. But if the passage does not entirely deny women their subjectivity, it nevertheless assumes – as Jefferson did of Indian women – that they will embrace a kind of objectification as natural and entirely proper to their domestic role.[91] And it is this reduction of women to objects of respectable male pleasure that seems

---

[87] TJ to Madison, October 28, 1785, in *ROL*, 1: 390.

[88] TJ to Bellini, Sept. 30, 1785, in *PTJ* 8:568; TJ to Edward Carrington, Jan. 16, 1787, ibid., 11:49; "Traveling notes," June 3, 1788, in *TJW* 660. Somewhat ironically, Jefferson's emphasis on the lack of a middling order in France anticipated the Republican Party's critique of the American South in the 1850s. See Eric Foner, *Free Soil, Free Labor, Free Men: The Ideology of the Republican Party Before the Civil War* (Oxford, 1970), 46–48.

[89] TJ to Monroe, June 17, 1785, in *PTJ* 8:233; TJ to Trist, Aug. 18, 1785, ibid., 404; TJ to Benjamin Hawkins, Aug. 4, 1787, ibid., 11:684.

[90] Ibid., 13:27–28.

[91] For helpful reflections on the multivalent nature of this concept, see Martha C. Nussbaum, "Objectification," *Philosophy and Public Affairs* 24 (Autumn 1995), 249–291.

difficult to reconcile with Jefferson's passion for "equality" until we understand what his writing from these years tells us so forcefully: that this *was* American equality *for women*. For men, American equality removed artificial barriers to economic autonomy and political participation. For women, on the other hand, equality destroyed artificial barriers to their natural domesticity, their essential contribution to the household and their care and protection by men. In such a natural order, in contrast with Europe, no artifice would bar men and women from the way of life nature prescribed. As he scanned the globe, he found only one society in which this order was actualized: "There is no part of the earth where so much [domestic happiness] is enjoyed as in America." Love itself, he told Maria Cosway, was "felt in its sublimest degree" there.[92]

## ARISTOCRACY AND MASCULINITY

If European aristocracy made American-style "happiness" impossible for peasants and nobles alike, nobles experienced the trouble differently. In contrast with the common folk of the countryside, aristocrats spent their days, Jefferson asserted, desperately seeking escape from the ennui that dominated their lives. Jefferson's letters outlined in splendid detail the indolence, foppery, infidelity, and consequent unhappiness of the aristocracy. Aristocrats suffered from a hopeless boredom that they attempted to overcome by excessive attention to fashion, idle conversation, cardplaying, gaming, and marital infidelity.[93]

For Anne Bingham, Jefferson sketched a scathing caricature of a "typical" day in the life of a Parisian aristocratic woman:

At eleven o'clock, it is day, chez madame. The curtains are drawn. Propped on bolsters and pillows, and her head scratched into a little order, the bulletins of the sick are read, and the billets of the well. She writes to some of her acquaintance, and receives the visits of others. If the morning is not very thronged, she is able to get out and hobble round the cage of the Palais royal; but she must hobble quickly, for the coeffeur's turn is come; and a tremendous turn it is! Happy, if he does not make her arrive when dinner is half over! The torpitude of digestion a little passed, she flutters half an hour through the streets, by way of paying visits, and then to the spectacles. These finished, another half hour is devoted to dodging in and out of the doors of her very sincere friends, and away to supper. After super, cards; and after cards, bed; to rise at noon the next day, and to tread like a mill horse, the same trodden circle over again. Thus the days of life are consumed, one by one, without an object beyond the present moment; ever flying from the ennui of that, yet carrying it with us; eternally in pursuit of happiness, which keeps eternally before us. If death or bankruptcy

[92] TJ to Bingham, May 11, 1788, in *PTJ* 13:151; TJ to Cosway, May 21, 1789, ibid., 15:143.

[93] Jefferson was not alone in his characterization of French society as "frivolous and licentious." See David A. Bell, "Culture and Religion," in William Doyle, ed., *Old Regime France, 1648–1788* (New York, 2001), 101–102; Landes, *Women and the Public Sphere*; and Elizabeth Colwill, "Just Another *Citoyenne*?: Marie-Antoinette on Trial, 1790–1793," *History Workshop Journal* 28 (Autumn 1989), 63–87; but see Bell, *Cult of the Nation*, 147–152, for the variety of opinions current. For a nuanced view of the eighteenth-century salon as a serious space for the facilitation of Enlightenment, see Dena Goodman, "Enlightenment Salons: The Convergence of Female and Philosophic Ambitions," *Eighteenth-Century Studies* 22 (Spring 1989), 329–350.

happen to trip us out of the circle, it is a matter for the buz of the evening, and is completely forgotten by the next morning.[94]

This vapid squandering of time and resources in vain pursuit of pleasure was the reciprocal to the drudgery experienced by peasant women. This, too, was far from the American ideal. Jefferson in no sense advocated a life on a pedestal for American women; "domesticity" was not a euphemism for leisure.[95] The American woman would be simple, chaste, and unworldly, but never idle. Her days would be occupied by the "fond cares of the children" and husband, housekeeping, and other tasks that would "fill every moment with a healthy and an useful activity."[96] American women played a crucial role in the maintenance of household economy and the self-sufficient independence of Jefferson's ideal family farm. Although hc distinguished between the kinds of contribution men and women should make, Jefferson acknowledged and embraced the indispensable role of women in the household economy – without it, he said, "ruin follows."[97] Madame Aristocrat may "rise at noon," but there would be no sleeping in for the American wife and mother.

Jefferson claimed an industriousness and seriousness of purpose for American life, domestic and political, that he believed to be utterly lacking in France. When Louis XVI called the Assembly of Notables, Jefferson proclaimed his amazement at the adolescent way the aristocracy reacted to this "measure so capable of doing good." Indeed, "the most remarkable effect of this convention as yet is the number of puns and bon mots it has generated." These could fill more volumes than the *Encyclopedie*, he moaned. Such a puerile response convinced Jefferson that France was "incapable of any serious effort but under the word of command." French aristocrats considered everything, including politics, in light of its ability to "furnish puns and bon mots," Jefferson said, "and I pronounce that a good punster would disarm the whole nation were they ever so seriously disposed to revolt." Disgusted, Jefferson temporarily washed his hands of the French: "We may conclude that nation desperate, and in charity pray that heaven may send them good kings." Damning words from this Revolutionary enemy of monarchy.[98]

Jefferson's criticism was not directed at the salon, which he evidently appreciated as a potentially serious site for the facilitation of enlightenment, but at the broader aristocratic milieu. Jefferson could enjoy the world of the salon and critique France's aristocracy without necessary contradiction.[99]

---

[94] TJ to Bingham, Feb. 7, 1787, in *PTJ* 11:122–123.

[95] For a description of the multiple and onerous tasks assigned to women of the home, see Kulikoff, *Tobacco and Slaves*, 179–180. See also, Lebsock, *Virginia Women, 1600–1945*, 41–42.

[96] TJ to Bingham, Feb. 7, 1787, in *PTJ* 11:122–123.

[97] TJ to Nathaniel Burwell, March 14, 1818, in *TJW*, 1413.

[98] TJ to Abigail Adams, Feb. 22, 1787, in *PTJ* 11:174.

[99] Goodman, "Enlightenment Salons," 338–339. Just before Jefferson's arrival in France, Goodman suggests, "the philosophes captured the salons from the aristocracy," transforming, as Jurgen Habermas has put it, "conversation into criticism and *bon mots* into arguments."

None of this is to say, in other words, that Jefferson was not enamored by France, only that his critique was not necessarily in conflict with his appreciation. During his Paris years, as we have seen, Jefferson, was rather taken by French society and Henry Adams was not far wrong to suggest that "he seemed during his entire life to breathe with perfect satisfaction nowhere except in the liberal, literary, and scientific air of Paris."[100] There is plenty of evidence to suggest, as he himself did in his *Autobiography*, that he considered French character "preemin[ent] ... among the nations of the earth." Its people were "more benevolent" and more devoted "in their select friendships" than any other, he remembered. "Their kindness and accommodation to strangers is unparalleled." The French excelled in science, and "the politeness of the general manners, the ease and vivacity of their conversation, give a charm to their society to be found nowhere else."[101]

Jefferson repeatedly described for correspondents the "polite manners" he encountered in Paris. French civility was quite simply more pleasant than American rudeness. "I would wish [my] countrymen to adopt just so much of European politeness as to be ready [to] make all those little sacrifices of self which really render European manners amiable, and relieve society from the disagreeable scenes to which rudeness often exposes it." In France, Jefferson informed Bellini, "It seems that a man might pass a life without encountering a single rudeness."[102] As he later wrote to George Wythe, the French were "a people of the most benevolent, the most gay, and amiable character of which the human form is susceptible."[103] Jefferson contrasted French manners with those of Americans who tended, he wrote, to "terminate the most sociable meals by transforming themselves into brutes." Jefferson claimed that, in contrast, he had never seen a drunken Frenchman.[104] In this sense, Jefferson had nothing but positive things to say about the French. "I am much pleased with the people of this country," he wrote Eliza House Trist. "The roughnesses of the human mind are so thoroughly rubbed off with them that it seems as if one might glide thro' a whole life among them without a justle."[105] Or, as he told Abigail Adams, the French were "polite, self-denying, feeling, hospitable, good humoured ... and amabil[e] in every point of view."[106]

But Jefferson was no unqualified Francophile, and such admirable cultural refinement in the upper class could not right the deep inbalances and the consequent blurring of gender roles Jefferson witnessed in France. It was one thing to be polite and refined, but Jefferson believed aristocratic life cultivated and even

---

[100] Adams, *Paris Years*, 78–122. Henry Adams, *History of the United States During the Administrations of Thomas Jefferson* (New York, 1986), 100–101.
[101] *Autobiography*, in *TJW*, 98.
[102] TJ to Bellini, Sept. 30, 1785, *PTJ* 8:569.
[103] TJ to George Wythe, August 13, 1786, ibid., 10:244.
[104] TJ to Bellini, Sept. 30, 1785, ibid., 8:569.
[105] TJ to Eliza House Trist, August 18, 1785, ibid., 404; also see TJ to Madame de Corny, June 30, 1787, ibid., 11:509.
[106] TJ to Abigail Adams, June 21, 1785, ibid., 8:233.

prized a level of effeminacy in men that Jefferson found repulsive.[107] "Under the most imposing exterior," he wrote, the nobility "are the weakest and worst part of mankind."[108] Although Jefferson participated in his fair share of polite conversation with French aristocrats and enjoyed the pleasures of the salon, he distinguished between a pleasing French civility and frivolity.[109] Throughout his correspondence ran an implicit disgust about a national culture that prized politeness and wit in the salon over the industrious labor and manly democracy of American political culture. Jefferson's concern was not unique to him. This contrast between true manhood and the self-consciously elaborate, polite, and effeminate French aristocrat was a common theme in constructions of masculinity on both sides of the Atlantic in the eighteenth century.[110] Numerous French intellectuals even blamed effeminacy directly on *salonnieres* who, they said, encouraged a softness in men that transformed them "into women," as Rousseau put it.[111]

The French critique, in particular, began to pepper his own correspondence and appeared to shape his thinking about gender relations in the old regime. Jefferson repeatedly warned against the contagion among American men of what passed for "masculinity" in France and its potential for erasing a distinctive American manhood. And he seemed to pick up on the themes reiterated in contemporary French "political pornography" that characterized aristocrats as both sexually degenerate and politically corrupt. Such writing – especially that attacking the queen – multiplied and became more open after 1789, reflecting

---

[107] This chapter, focused as it is on the intersection of Jefferson's gender discourse with his nationalism (rather than biography), can only begin to hint at Jefferson's personal complications on this issue, but it seems worth noting that Jefferson's political enemies frequently charged him with effemininacy, that his friends benefitted from his easy sociability, and that his biographers have noted in him a kind of sensitivity that Henry Adams labeled "almost feminine" (Adams, *History*, 100). "He was more refined," Adams suggested, "than many women in the delicacy of his private relations." In short, "Jefferson's nature was feminine" (Adams, *History*, 220). Catherine Allgor suggests that Jefferson presided over a sort of salon in the White House where he "acted the part of the perfect lady," See Allgor, *Parlor Politics*, 33. For one brief but suggestive reading, see Frank Shuffelton, "In Different Voices: Gender in the American Republic of Letters," *Early American Literature* 25 (1990), 289–304, esp. 296–302. It seems to me, however, that Nancy Isenberg sums everything up with her suggestion that Jefferson's manners – and, by implication, his appreciation for the Parisian salon – "were an accepted part of the culture of sensibility" that was prominent in the eighteenth century, so that they were "not necessarily feminine as much as a genteel style." See Isenberg, review of Allgor, *Parlor Politics*, in *Journal of Social History* 36 (2002), 473–475, quote at 473–474.

[108] "Travelling notes," June 3, 1788, in *TJW*, 660.

[109] TJ to George Wythe, Aug. 13, 1786, in *PTJ* 10:244; TJ to Bellini, Sept. 30, 1785, ibid., 8:569; TJ to Abigail Adams, June 21, 1785, ibid., 233; and TJ to Eliza House Trist, Aug. 18, 1785, ibid., 404.

[110] Michele Cohen, "Manliness, Effeminacy and the French: Gender and the Construction of National Character in Eighteenth-Century England," in Tim Hitchcock and Michele Cohen, eds., *English Masculinities, 1660–1800* (London, 1999), 44–61; Colley, *Britons*, 251–252. For a different argument, see, Gerald Newman, *The Rise of English Nationalism: A Cultural History, 1740–1830* (New York, 1987), 17.

[111] Landes, *Women and the Public Sphere*, 70–71, 87; Goodman, "Enlightenment Salons," 336.

what Lynn Hunt has identified as "a fundamental anxiety about queenship as the most extreme form of women invading the public sphere." This analysis helps make sense of Jefferson's consistent hostility to Marie Antoinette, whom he repeatedly castigated as "haughty and bearing no contradiction," "proud, disdainful of restraint … eager in the pursuit of pleasure," an "inordinate gambl[er]," "inflexibl[y] perverse," "capricious," and "devoted to pleasure and expence," whose "breast … never knew the presence of one moral restraint." She apparently embodied, for Jefferson, most of the vices of the French aristocracy. Even worse, Jefferson asserted, the queen "had an absolute ascendancy over" the king; an "absolute sway over his weak mind, and timid virtue;" Louis XVI was "too much governed by her." Jefferson, in his 1821 *Autobiography*, claimed that instead of executing the royal couple, he "should have shut up the Queen in a Convent, putting harm out of her power, and placed the king in his station, investing him with limited powers, which I verily believe he would have honestly exercised, according to the measure of his understanding." In short, Jefferson wrote, "I have ever believed that had there been no queen, there would have been no revolution." The weak, effeminate king and the willful, ambitious, sexually depraved, and very public queen epitomized, then, the very gender reversals Jefferson understood to be ingrained in French society and went some distance, in his view, toward explaining the "crimes & calamities" of the French Revolution, "which will forever stain the pages of modern history."[112]

Even before leaving the United States, Jefferson had noted the power of women's sway over men. His own secretary, he suggested to Madison, was a potential danger precisely because "in the company of women … he loses all power over himself and becomes almost frenzied." His "good enough heart" and "an understanding somewhat better than common" was in danger of being undermined by his "too little guard over his lips" when he was around women.[113] Were the nation's vital interests secure with such a man?

Jefferson's critique of aristocratic sloth and effeminacy brings into sharper clarity the frequent admonitions against idleness he sent to his teenage daughter Martha. "Body and mind both unemployed," Jefferson told her, "our being becomes a burthen, and every object about us loathsome, even the dearest. Idleness begets ennui, ennui the hypochondria, and that a diseased body." This

---

[112] On the characterization of aristocrats as sexually and politically corrupt, see Lynn Hunt, "The Many Bodies of Marie Antoinette: Political Pornography and the Problem of the Feminine in the French Revolution," in *Eroticism and the Body Politic*, 119; Sara Maza, "The Diamond Necklace Affair Revisited (1785–1786): The Case of the Missing Queen," ibid., 68–69, 76, 82, 84; and Colwill, "Just Another *Citoyenne*?" 66–67, 69, 72. The Jefferson quotes in this paragraph are compiled from his *Autobiography*, in *TJW*, 80, 92–93; TJ to James Madison, June 20, 1787, in *PTJ* 11:482; and TJ to John Jay, Sept. 19, 1789, ibid., 15:460. Compare this assessment of the queen with President Jefferson's description of the wife of British minister Anthony Merry as "a virago" whose assertive and capricious behavior both "disturbed our harmony extremely" and threatened the "good understanding of nations" although she "ostensibly has nothing to do with them," TJ to James Monroe, Jan. 8, 1804, in *FE* 10:66–68.

[113] TJ to Madison, February 14, 1783, in Smith, ed., *ROL* 1:223.

was not the American way, he insisted. Unlike that of the effete Paris aristoc-racy, he told Martha, "it is part of the *American* character to consider nothing as desperate; to surmount every difficulty by resolution and contrivance."[114] In contrast, aristocratic French women played, simultaneously, the coquette and the politically active busybody, while elite French men concentrated their greatest efforts on refined wit, polite conversation, and sexual pleasure, usually content to leave their own public affairs to women. The opinion of "all the handsome young women" of Paris, Jefferson half joked, made "an army more powerful in France than the 200,000 men of the King."[115]

Jefferson exaggerated for effect, of course. He was intimately connected with a number of French aristocrats who were deeply concerned about the political situation, and, as we have seen, he enjoyed the serious activity of enlightened salon culture.[116] Nevertheless, compared with American men who had com-mitted their "lives, fortunes, and sacred honor" to the cause of freedom, many French men came off as unserious at best, effeminate at worst. And effeminate men could never lead a nation to greatness, or even stability. Jefferson's asser-tion in the *Summary View* that flattery was the province of "those who fear" and "not an American art" foreshadowed his later criticism of French aristo-crats sweating over the construction of puns in the salon while their country was on the edge of revolution. Men more concerned with the reception of their witticisms than the creation of stable institutions in a time of crisis could never hope to control their own sexuality and govern their wives, much less create a republic.[117]

Jefferson's early ambivalence about the French Revolution reflects his con-cern that a people, through years of bad culture, government, and political economy, could become unfit for republicanism. Jefferson worried, in turn, that aristocratic practices might impair the abilities of American youth to function effectively as men in American society on their return home. Thomas Jefferson Randolph remembered his grandfather telling the story of a young American lately returned from Europe, bewildered by a broken saddle. This

---

[114] TJ to Martha Jefferson, March 28, 1787, in *PTJ* 11:251, emphasis added. For similar admoni-tions see TJ to Martha Jefferson, May 5 and 21, 1787, ibid., 348–349 and 369–370.

[115] TJ to David Humphreys, March 18, 1789, ibid., 14:677. The spirit of this letter emphasizes Jefferson's wonder at the power of "public opinion" – "a complete revolution in this govern-ment has, within the space of two years … been effected merely by the force of public opin-ion." In other words, the point was not to denigrate women but to note how powerful a force public opinion was at the time – more powerful than the army! But in his later *Autobiography*, in (*TJW*, 62–63), Jefferson remembered that "most of the young women" were attracted to the Revolution only when revolutionary "sentiments became a matter of mode." Women, in other words, participated in Revolution only as it became the fashion or whimsy of the day, not because of genuine political commitment. See the discussion in Jennifer Tiercel Kennedy, *Signing History: The Memoirs of Benjamin Franklin, Benjamin Rush, John Adams, and Thomas Jefferson* (Ph.D. Dissertation, Yale University, 1999), 325.

[116] Sloan, *Principle and Interest*, ch. 2.

[117] Manuscript text of *A Summary View*, July 1774, in *PTJ* 1:134. Also see TJ to George Gilmer, July 5, 1775, ibid., 186.

young dandy required help to fix his saddle girth – something every American-educated man could supposedly do on his own. Jefferson told the story, according to Randolph, to reiterate his opinion that European education "made men ignorant and helpless as to the common necessities of life."[118] The story, possibly apocryphal, nevertheless effectively captures Jefferson's belief that a premature tour of Europe would hamper, if not destroy, the republican masculinity of American men. No wonder right-thinking Europeans sent their sons to America where education was, Jefferson told Abigail Adams, "more masculine … and less exposed to seduction."[119]

The critique of aristocracy and monarchy that pervaded Jefferson's correspondence from France cannot be separated from the discussion of gender and national identity woven throughout it. France had compelled Jefferson to articulate his own latent assumptions about the connections between gender, nature, equality, and national identity in ways he previously had not. In an undated draft outline for a prospective essay he entitled "On Sending American Youth to Europe," Jefferson succinctly captured his impression of gender roles in France: "Sexes have changed business."[120]

## COMPLICATIONS AND CONCLUSIONS

Jefferson's observations about French economic life, gender, and sexuality tell us more, perhaps, about his assumptions than they do about "old world" manners and mores. The same may hold true for his idealized American woman (and man). Jefferson claimed that Americans actually experienced the happiness that Europeans pursued in vain. But American realities nevertheless threatened to unravel the coherence he sought for American character, thus challenging the claims he was making – and celebrating – about American life.

Although Jefferson transcended the provincialism of the Virginia gentry in many ways, his views of gender and sexuality were nurtured in the particular cultural milieu of the elite Virginia planter aristocracy, whose masculinity was tied to both personal independence and to mastery over subordinates, including slaves.[121] Jefferson recognized the importance of slavery to his own

---

[118] Ibid., 8:412.

[119] TJ to Abigail Adams, August 30, 1787, ibid., 12:66.

[120] Ibid., 8:637–638. As he returned to the United States, entering Washington's cabinet as Secretary of State, this emphasis tapered off, never again becoming an explicit topic of extended discussion in Jefferson's correspondence. For an indication that Jefferson's worries about the corrupting effect of European gender relations on American young men diminished when he returned to the United States, see Archibald McCalester to TJ, Nov. 1, 1791, ibid., 22:253–255; and TJ to McCalester, Dec. 22, 1791, ibid., 429–430. On the subtle revelation of Jefferson's gender assumptions later, see David Waldstreicher, "Why Thomas Jefferson and African Americans Wore Their Politics on Their Sleeves: Dress and Mobilization between American Revolutions," in Jeffrey L. Pasley, Andrew W. Robertson, and Waldstreicher, eds., *Beyond the Founders: New Approaches to the Political History of the Early American Republic* (Chapel Hill, 2004), 79–103.

[121] See Lockridge, *On the Sources of Patriarchal Rage*; and Brown, *Good Wives, Nasty Wenches, Anxious Patriarchs*, 319–321.

lifestyle, but his catalog of differences between French and American domestic order remained conspicuously silent about the connections between white male independence, white female domesticity, and black slavery.[122] Unlike later proslavery theorists, Jefferson never elevated the dependence of his domestic ideal on slavery to the status of conscious principle, although on some level he must have understood how it underwrote domesticity for the white women of his class.[123] For what kept elite Virginia planters' wives from the drudgery experienced by both Indian and European peasant women was less the American political culture Jefferson prized than the conspicuous alienation of black male slaves from the "privileges of white manhood" and black females, slave and free, from their natural equality as women.[124] Class privilege hardly kept planters' wives – including Martha Jefferson – from hard labor, but it did keep them from what was understood to be men's work. And this was a privilege for whites only, although Jefferson did spare the Hemings women from fieldwork even during "the grueling weeks of the wheat harvest, when every healthy slave was drafted to bring in the crop" – a significant exception that nevertheless proves the rule, telling us more about the privileged position of the Hemings family than anything else. (Hemings males tended not to do fieldwork, either.)[125] Jefferson's concern that other slave women not be forced to perform physical labor above their capacity emerges occasionally in his writing. Such concern was rare, however, and did not seem to affect the lives of Jefferson's field hands much.[126] Slave women, unlike white women, were not candidates for natural equality. Rather, their labor, which Jefferson usually failed to acknowledge, made the very white male independence and white female domesticity Jefferson valued possible. If white women reproduced the nation, slave women reproduced the capital that silently undergirded Jefferson's domestic ideal.[127]

Slavery undermined Jefferson's claims about America, not simply because of its clash with the values he expressed in the Declaration, but also because

---

[122] For one intriguing, although only partial, exception, see TJ to Angelica Church, Nov. 27, 1793, in *PTJ* 27:449.

[123] For a brilliant discussion of the self-conscious purchase of white domesticity in the slave market, see Walter Johnson, *Soul By Soul: Life Inside the Antebellum Slave Market* (Cambridge, MA, 1999), 90–95. Jefferson was quite aware that slaveholding fostered the very kind of aristocratic behavior he so despised abroad. See *Notes*, 162–163.

[124] Brown, *Good Wives, Nasty Wenches, Anxious Patriarchs*, 185; and Jacqueline Jones, *Labor of Love, Labor of Sorrow: Black Women, Work, and the Family from Slavery to the Present* (New York, 1984), 13–29.

[125] Lucia C. Stanton, "'Those Who Labor for My Happiness': Thomas Jefferson and His Slaves," in Onuf, ed., *Jeffersonian Legacies*, 147–180, esp. 153; Kulikoff, *Tobacco and Slaves*, 167, 179. On the similarities between tasks assigned Hemings women and those Jefferson associated with white domesticity, see Gordon-Reed, *Jefferson and Sally Hemings*, 192. Even many of Martha's meticulously recorded household duties were performed by slaves. See McLaughlin, *Jefferson and Monticello*, 177–187.

[126] See, especially, TJ to William Drayton, July 30, 1787, in *PTJ* 11:647–648. See also, Stanton, "'Those Who Labor for My Happiness,'" 163.

[127] See Stanton, "'Those Who Labor for My Happiness,'" 150, 173n12.

it reinforced class divisions that Jefferson's ideal denied. Interspersed "among these rich plantations where the Negro alone is wretched," the Marquis de Chastellux wrote during travels in Virginia in the early 1780s, "one often finds miserable huts inhabited by whites, whose wane looks and ragged garments bespeak poverty." Chastellux professed astonishment at the "state of poverty in which a great number of white people live in Virginia" and blamed it on exactly the kind of aristocratic hoarding of land and resources that Jefferson later condemned in France.[128] Chastellux's assessment was hardly news to Jefferson, who had long condemned "the feudal and unnatural distinctions" that characterized Virginia landholding patterns. Jefferson's bills to abolish fee tail and primogeniture were efficacious, and Jefferson himself believed that the Revolution had destroyed artificial privilege in Virginia.[129] But slaveholding remained the key variable differentiating whites from one another in the Old Dominion.

From France, Jefferson imagined an essentially classless America, and he returned to advance a politics that was theoretically unbound by class, heading a party that made its conscious appeal to the common man. But the household economy he defined as American was not what most southern yeomen experienced. In the absence of slaves, the economic autonomy Jefferson prized for yeoman farmers tended to demand female labor, including the fieldwork Jefferson despised in Native and European societies.[130] Facing this fact would call into question much of what Jefferson had championed as exceptional about America in his correspondence from France. Ownership of slaves was largely essential to the kinds of household relations he prized – at least in Virginia – and

---

[128] Francois Jean, Marquis de Chastellux, *Travels in North America in the Years 1780, 1781, and 1782*, trans., Howard C. Rice, Jr., 2 volumes (Chapel Hill, 1963), 2:438. In an interesting letter to Chastellux, Jefferson acknowledged American "poverty" but considered it a temporary result of the Revolutionary War's "total destruction of our commerce, devastation of our country, and absence of the precious metals," rather than the structural imbalance that Chastellux emphasized. See TJ to Chastellux, Jan. 16, 1784, in *PTJ* 6:467. Chastellux's assessment is largely confirmed (although with significant regional variation) by Jackson Turner Main, "The Distribution of Property in Post-Revolutionary Virginia," *Mississippi Valley Historical Review* 41 (Sept. 1954), 241–258.

[129] Jefferson, *Autobiography*, in *TJW*, 44; TJ to John Adams, Oct. 28, 1813, in *AJL*, 389; Holly Brewer, "Entailing Aristocracy in Colonial Virginia: Ancient Feudal Restraints and Revolutionary Reform," *WMQ* 54 (April 1997), 307–346.

[130] Stephanie McCurry, *Masters of Small Worlds: Yeoman Households, Gender Relations, and the Political Culture of the Antebellum South Carolina Low Country* (New York, 1995), 79. Scholars note a decrease in the numbers of white women working Virginia's fields over the course of the eighteenth century, although such a dip is difficult to verify. See Kulikoff, *Tobacco and Slaves*, 167; and Brown, *Good Wives, Nasty Wenches, Anxious Patriarchs*, 335. See also, Lois Green Carr and Lorena S. Walsh, "The Planter's Wife: The Experience of White Women in Seventeenth-Century Maryland," *WMQ* 34 (Oct. 1977), 542–571. In contrast, Stephanie McCurry argues (based on research from the South Carolina Low Country in a slightly later period, but with broad implications for the way historians think about southern yeomen) that white women's work *in the fields* was the great unspoken truth that ensured yeoman household independence. See McCurry, *Masters of Small Worlds*, 78–85, 36, 72–75.

this was a privilege limited to a very small percentage of the population. The wealth hoarding of the French aristocracy may have kept the majority of French people in an arrested stage of underdevelopment. But Jefferson was unable or unwilling to acknowledge that the exploitation of black labor on the plantations of Virginia's elite granted privileges for its women unavailable to the majority of white families. Jefferson's idealization of women's "equality" as an American characteristic turned on his ability to ignore, or perhaps deny, the largely class- and race-based nature of the phenomenon.[131]

Jefferson's own granddaughters, facing financial turbulence, knew what Jefferson himself could not acknowledge. In 1825, Cornelia Randolph told her sister that she wished she "could do something to support myself instead of this unprofitable drudgery of keeping house here, but I suppose not until we sink entirely will it do for the granddaughters of Thomas Jefferson to take in work or keep a school."[132] Her position, Randolph understood, had been less a national characteristic than a class one; Jefferson's domestic ideal *itself* became a "drudgery" in the absence of the money that made it viable. Jefferson's exaltation of women's domesticity as uniquely or truly American, then, allowed him – in what *did* become a genuinely American pattern – to avoid acknowledging

[131] Because the 1790 census did not list a slave distribution for Virginia, it is difficult to know what percentage of white Virginia households in the late eighteenth century owned slaves. Later U.S. Census Bureau estimates, based on county records from the 1780s, concluded that in 1790, 44.9% of all Virginia families held slaves (a higher percentage than in any other state). However, Jackson Turner Main has shown that the majority of adult white men in Virginia in the 1780s were landless. Of the minority who owned land, most were slaveholders, but with great regional variation from east to west. "East of the fall line," Main estimated, "almost nine out of ten farmers owned slaves, whereas in the Piedmont some 35 per cent of the farmers were without slaves, and in the westernmost counties ... half or more of the farmers had no slaves." Those numbers suggest that even in Jefferson's Virginia many white families likely could not afford the kind of domesticity that he claimed defined America. See *A Century of Population Growth: From the First Census of the United States to the Twelfth, 1790–1900* (Washington, D.C., 1909), 135, 137–138; Lee Soltow, "Economic Inequality in the United States in the Period from 1790 to 1860," *Journal of Economic History* 31 (December 1971), 827; Main, "Distribution of Property in Post-Revolutionary Virginia," 246. Jefferson himself estimated that over half of the free adult male citizens were disqualified from voting because they lacked the property requirement. See Charles Sydnor, *Gentleman Freeholders: Political Practices in Washington's Virginia* (Chapel Hill, 1952), 37. Also see TJ to John Pleasants, April 19, 1824, in *L&B* 16:28. More recently, Richard Beeman suggests that Jefferson, Sydnor, and Main were wrong and that a very high percentage of Virginians – some 70% – met the requirements to vote and serve in the House of Burgesses: 100 acres of land or 25 acres and a house in town. See Beeman, *The Varieties of Political Experience in Eighteenth-Century America* (Philadelphia, 2004), 52, 310n.38. In any case, the point here is that Jefferson's own estimates were in conflict with his assessment of America as a classless society.

[132] Cornelia Randolph to Ellen W. Coolidge, Nov. 24, 1825, quoted in Lewis, *Pursuit of Happiness*, 148–149. For a brilliant discussion of the way Jefferson's daughter and granddaughters shaped the limited space Monticello (and its architect) afforded them for self-culture, see Elizabeth Chew, "Inhabiting the Great Man's House: Women and Space at Monticello," in Joan Hartman and Adele Seeff, eds., *Structures and Subjectivities: Attending to Early Modern Women* (Cranbury, NJ, 2007), 223–252.

"the dirty secret of class in America" and of its relationship to slavery in the South.[133] Jefferson's generalized claims for American identity, to borrow John Ashworth's words, "obscured the social power of the slaveholder, by merging him with the farmer, even as it ignored the plight of the slave."[134]

If Jefferson's middling ideal was increasingly betrayed by post-Revolutionary contradictions, Jefferson's assertions of fundamental equality for white men were nevertheless becoming dominant American mythology and, thus, ideologically hegemonic.[135] And it is against the backdrop of the ideology of male independence that the dependence of women becomes most glaring. But women's dependence was far from the troubling problem for Jefferson that it has become for historians today. To the contrary, Jefferson's views of American women were not simply the dark "underside" of his liberalism.[136] Rather, he saw American independence as profoundly *liberating* for women as well as men and characterized domesticity as the natural fulfillment of femininity – as the realm in which women could most thoroughly enjoy their "natural equality." For Jefferson, domesticity for white women was as much an achievement of the Revolution as independence for white men. In America, men and women could be what they were meant, by nature, to be. From France, Jefferson made this explicit without cynicism or any sense of conscious incongruity. He was hardly troubled by his views. In the absence of prominent alternatives in the early Republic, in fact, Jefferson considered himself progressive on the issue.

Jefferson's gender assumptions, then, should be seen as part of a liberal critique of artificial hierarchies, his defense of domesticity as a critique of the oppression of women. But – to stay on this liberal ground – this explicit champion of free thought largely ignored the oppression of enslaved women, and he rarely entertained the possibility that the logic of liberty might lead free American women to make choices challenging his domestic ideal. Rarely the explicit enemy of women's choice, Jefferson simply assumed that American women would continue to embrace their natural roles in the way that we would all, presumably, choose to drink clean water over dirty, given the option. Different choices, then, were not American, but foreign, unnatural, and, frankly, unimaginable.

Jefferson never shared the totalitarian's contempt for popular human judgment – precisely the opposite.[137] He once even described his own convictions

---


[133] John Kasson, *Rudeness and Civility: Manners in Nineteenth-Century Urban America* (New York, 1990), 67.

[134] John Ashworth, *Slavery, Capitalism, and Politics in the Antebellum Republic*, Volume 1: *Commerce and Compromise* (Cambridge, England, 1995), 22, 340. Also see Walstreicher, "Why Thomas Jefferson and African Americans Wore their Politics on their Sleeves," 85.

[135] Rowland Berthoff and John M. Murrin, "Feudalism, Communalism, and the Yeoman Freeholder: The American Revolution as a Social Accident," in Stephen G. Kurtz and James H. Hutson, eds., *Essays on the American Revolution* (Chapel Hill, 1973), 256–288; Wood, *Radicalism*.

[136] Joyce Appleby, "Jefferson and His Complex Legacy," in Onuf, ed., *Jeffersonian Legacies*, 10.

[137] Appleby, "Jefferson and His Complex Legacy," 12.

about women in public life as, at least in part, deference to popular sentiment.[138]
As his lifelong project makes clear, Jefferson consistently resisted active coercion of human thought.[139] As he told Edward Carrington, keeping popular
opinion "right" required a free press and public education of all citizens – not
an authoritarian state.[140] But we cannot ignore a certain tension in Jefferson's
thought between a sincere commitment to a human freedom limited only by
the liberty of others (a view exemplified in Jefferson's bill for religious freedom) and a sense that human happiness requires that people choose correctly.
Removal of artificial barriers, then, would result in a natural gravitation of
human beings toward particular roles, which would produce happiness for all.
But, as Isaiah Berlin pointed out in a different context, when the "sole criterion of action is happiness and unhappiness" rather than liberty, rights become
dispensable.[141] For white men, Jefferson emphasized unalienable rights, but
when he came to white women, Jefferson tended to shift his focus to natural roles and the happiness of society. American men were the happiest in the
world, Jefferson said, because they experienced more liberty than other men.
American women were the happiest in the world, on the other hand, precisely
because they conformed to their natural roles more closely than women in the
rest of the world were able or willing to. Both men and women benefited from
the peculiarly American freedom from artificial barriers to happiness. But the
natural results of such freedom were clearly different for women and men.[142]
Jefferson couched his gendered version of American happiness in terms of what
was best for all, but this is something less than liberal democracy, for women
at least.

And yet, Jefferson's "condescension was not contempt," nor was the patriarchy inherent in his ideal domestic order a cynical end in itself.[143] The larger
end was the perpetuation of the republicanism of which affectionate families

---

[138] See TJ to Albert Gallatin, Jan. 13, 1807, in *FE* 9:7.

[139] TJ to Benjamin Rush, Sept. 23, 1800, in *PTJ* 32:168.

[140] TJ to Carrington, Jan. 16, 1787, in *TJW*, 880. Also see TJ to Samuel Kercheval, July 12, 1816,
ibid., 1400; and *Report of the Commissioners for the University of Virginia*, Aug. 4, 1818,
ibid., 459–460.

[141] Rights "which nobody may impinge upon," Berlin noted, become "obstacle[s] to the transformation of society in the direction of the greatest happiness for the greatest number." See Berlin,
*Freedom and Its Betrayal: Six Enemies of Human Liberty*, ed. Henry Hardy (Princeton, 2002),
18–19. For a discussion of the broader context in which Berlin wrestled with this tension, see
Michael Ignatieff, *Isaiah Berlin: A Life* (New York, 1998), especially ch. 13 and 15. I do not
mean to suggest an equivalence between Jefferson and the sources of Berlin's concern. For a
remarkably succinct description of the contemporary situation that Berlin addressed (and which
would have horrified Jefferson), see Eric Hobsbawm's assessment of the German Democratic
Republic in *Interesting Times: A Twentieth Century Life* (New York, 2002), 149–150.

[142] For reflections on how this distinction complicated (rather than facilitated) the implemtation
of companionate marriage – another of Jefferson's ideals – see Anya Jabour, *Marriage in the
Early Republic: Elizabeth and William Wirt and the Companionate Ideal* (Baltimore, 1998),
3–6, 170.

[143] This phrase is Sean Wilentz's. See *Chants Democratic*, 249.

were the building blocks.[144] His embrace of companionate marriage and republican womanhood acknowledged women's importance to the Republic in a way that potentially threatened the distinction between public and private.[145] Moreover, Jefferson offers hints that he was not entirely oblivious to the possibility that gender hierarchy could create very different experiences of the private sphere for women and men, that the home could, in extreme cases, become an unhappy place for women, particularly in a liberal regime that valued the sanctity of the private sphere, especially the household. In notes he prepared for a 1772 divorce case, Jefferson observed that divorce "restores to women their natural right of equality" and suggested that it would be "cruel to confine Divorce or Repudiation to husband who has so many ways of rendering his domestic affairs agreeable by command or desertion, whereas wife confined & subject."[146] Many years later, Jefferson repeatedly advised his granddaughter Ann to separate from her violent husband and move to Monticello, and he seemed to hint at the need for stronger laws against domestic abuse.[147]

According to careful students of the family in the post-Revolutionary South, women rarely demanded formal equality with men in relation to the state. What many seemed to want – and occasionally demand – was a husband that fulfilled his end of the companionate bargain: love, kindness, and affection, as well as financial support. They wanted the virtuous husbands Jefferson also claimed for America.[148] So his assumptions about women's roles were not particularly peculiar. They seem glaring – even hypocritical – today in light of Jefferson's general assertions of inalienable political rights and human equality. They were less troubling to Jefferson precisely because he assumed that women's domesticity was natural.[149]

---

[144] See Peter Onuf, "Liberty to Learn," in *Thomas Jefferson: Genius of Liberty* (New York, 2000), 138–143.

[145] See Colley, *Britons*, 273–274, for an insightful look at how women exploited such an opening in Rousseau.

[146] See Frank Dewey, "Thomas Jefferson's Notes on Divorce," *WMQ* 39 (January 1982), 212–223. Because whatever right to privacy existed in early America tended to attach to families rather than to individuals, Ruth Bloch has suggested, the American liberal regime "often conceal[ed] oppression as much as combating it." Bloch, "The American Revolution, Wife Beating, and the Emergent Value of Privacy," in *Early American Studies* 5 (2007), 223–251, at 251.

[147] TJ to Wilson C. Nichols, March 8, 1819, *LC*; and Dumas Malone, *Jefferson and His Time*, vol. 6: *The Sage of Monticello* (Boston, 1981), 159–160, 298–300.

[148] Lewis, *Pursuit of Happiness*, 202; Jabour, *Marriage in the Early Republic*, 6; Michael O'Brien, *Conjectures of Order: Intellectual Life and the American South, 1810–1860* (Chapel Hill, 2004), 266. For complications of this point, suggesting that alternative conceptions of women's relationship to the state were available in the early Republic, see Kierner, *Beyond the Household*, 105–107, 163–164, 169–170; and Linda K. Kerber, "The Paradox of Women's Citizenship in the Early Republic: The Case of Martin vs. Massachusetts, 1805," *AHR* 97 (April 1992), 349–378, esp. 354–355, 371, 378.

[149] See, especially, the explicit statement in TJ to John H. Pleasants, April 19, 1824, in *FE* 12:353; and TJ to Samuel Kercheval, Sept. 5, 1816, *L&B* 15:72.

What *was* peculiar about Jefferson's gender assumptions was how crucial they were to his vision of American character. At the core of Jefferson's conception of American identity was a domestic order he understood to be both universally appropriate and uniquely American. So, in the end, Jefferson tried to keep his cosmopolitanism and his nationalism too. Other peoples, nations, and cultures could become equal to America when they became like America: hospitable to the natural equality of women.

# 3

# American Character

If it is true that our society is really capable of knowing only the quantity which we call "citizen," that it debauches its own innermost nature when it tries to deal with the quantity called "subject," then the potential scope of our system is limited; then it can extend only to people of our own kind – people who have grown up in the same peculiar spirit of independence and self-reliance, people who can accept, and enjoy, and content themselves with our institutions.

George Kennan, 1951[1]

the yeomanry of the United States are not the canaille of Paris.

Thomas Jefferson, 1815[2]

There is no special Providence for Americans.

John Adams, 1787[3]

When John Adams told Jefferson about "the stupidity with which" the people "not only become the … Dupes" of their "aristocratical" leaders "but even love to be Taken in by their Tricks," he could hardly have chosen a less receptive interlocutor.[4] But, as is often the case, Adams had put his finger on something worth considering. The source of much of our present ambivalence about Jefferson is precisely the awkward tension between our sense that he was not inclusive enough to qualify as what most of us today would be willing to call a "democrat," on the one hand, and, on the other, that he, as Adams would suggest, was, nevertheless, too naïve about the ability of ordinary white men to make wise decisions in a deliberative democracy to offer us anything useful in the way of a political theory. If Jefferson's, democratic theory was stunningly inclusive in his own day it feels shockingly exclusive in ours. If we

---

[1] *American Diplomacy, 1900–1950* (Chicago, 1951), 22.

[2] TJ to Lafayette, February 14, 1815, in *L&B* 14:252.

[3] *A Defence of the Constitutions of Government of the United States of America* (1787), in *WJA* 4:401.

[4] Adams to TJ, November 15, 1813, in *AJL*, 398.

mean, by "democracy," a government peculiarly responsive to majority sentiment, then we tend to think Jefferson incontrovertibly a democrat. If we mean, instead, that democracy must incorporate the most capacious possible effort to encourage participation without limitations on race and gender, then Jefferson looks remarkably outdated, at best, even un-American in the eyes of some critics. There are so many compelling and well-understood reasons to challenge Jefferson's long-standing association in the American imagination with our more expansive concept of "democracy" that it seems gratuitous to revisit them here. Jefferson's complicity with slavery, his mostly unchecked racism, his hostility to women's participation in high politics, and his embrace of a more traditional conception of elite leadership than any later American politics would acknowledge all provide a number of asterisks next to Jefferson's name in the record book of our democracy.[5]

Yet Jefferson's name belongs in that book, and not simply for the usually agreed-upon reasons: that his "magical" words belie his lifestyle and provide a rhetorical touchstone toward which all movements to make American democracy more inclusive have nodded.[6] What ultimately makes Jefferson a "democrat" in his day, and ours, is his willingness to trust the political and moral instincts of the American public, and, by theoretical extension, the democratic element in any properly constituted political community – however unfortunately circumscribed by race and gender his definition was – in a way that few political theorists before or since have done. By the late eighteenth century, government had long been considered "too important a matter to be entrusted to the people."[7] Yet, Jefferson seemed to share little of the distrust of the "democracy" that had characterized political theory and statesmanship over the centuries.[8] As he told William Johnson in 1823 – and he never seemed

---

[5] Perhaps the most forceful and explicit statement disassociating Jefferson from the "modern civil religion" of America remains Conor Cruise O'Brien, "Thomas Jefferson: Radical and Racist," *The Atlantic Monthly* 278 (October 1996), 53–74, and O'Brien, *The Long Affair: Thomas Jefferson and the French Revolution, 1785–1800* (Chicago, 1996), which declares Jefferson a "more suitable … patron of white supremacists" and the "most ferocious" and "militant extremists" of the far right "than of modern American liberals," (321–322). For reflections on Jefferson's declining modern reputation among professional historians, see Peter S. Onuf, "The Scholars' Jefferson," *WMQ* 50 (1993), 671–699; and Francis Cogliano, *Thomas Jefferson: Reputation and Legacy* (Charlottesville, VA, 2006).

[6] For Jefferson as magician, see Joseph Ellis, *American Sphinx: The Character of Thomas Jefferson*, 10. For Jefferson, the national (and international) significance of whose words transcend his specific historical limitations, see Joyce Appleby, "Jefferson and his Complex Legacy," in Peter S. Onuf, ed., *Jeffersonian Legacies* (Charlottesville, VA, 1993), 1–16, and Sean Wilentz, "American Historians vs. American Founding Fathers: The Details of Greatness," in *New Republic* (March 29, 2004).

[7] J.R. Pole, *The Gift of Government: Political Responsibility from the English Restoration to American Independence* (Athens, 1983), xi. Also see Richard D. Brown, *The Strength of a People: The Idea of an Informed Citizenry in America, 1650–1870* (Chapel Hill, 1996), esp. ch. 1. Even the American revolutionaries failed to agree about "who, precisely, should be informed and what, exactly," they should know (86).

[8] Traditionally used (often negatively) by political thinkers to describe direct citizen participation in government, the word *democracy* over time lost much of this original meaning and became

to tire of repeating it – the main difference between he (and his party) and the Federalists was his willingness to trust the judgment of ordinary citizens. "The cherishment of the people then was our principle, the fear and distrust of them, that of the other party."[9]

But it is precisely this repose that provokes questions about Jefferson's seriousness. When John Adams told Jefferson that the "foundation" of Jefferson's "Unbounded Popularity" was his "steady defence of democratical Principles," he certainly meant Jefferson no unqualified compliment.[10] Throughout their justly fabled correspondence, Adams suggested that Jefferson was naïve and idealistic, at best, and blessedly ignorant or utopian, at worst, with his fundamental trust in the democracy. But Adams misunderstood Jefferson, and we will, too, unless we are careful to make sense of precisely why Jefferson never really doubted the people, as Adams did, or fail to see the ways in which his trust was specific and qualified. Jefferson's embrace of "the people" may have inspired the world – and he hoped it would.[11] But, as in multiple other areas, Jefferson's commitment to universal enlightenment principles in this instance obscures his belief that only the American people were ready for self-government, freed as they were, he believed, from so many of the limitations traditional theorists had placed on the democracy (and which still applied, he feared, to most other peoples on the earth). In other words, there was, he believed, a sociological foundation for his optimism about Americans. "Popular taste," as Joyce Appleby has so nicely put it, may have been "the final arbiter for Jefferson," but the taste he valued and considered authoritative was one that demanded a certain cultivation and that reached enlightened conclusions – a cultivation that only Americans had experienced and conclusions that only Americans had reached.[12] What is perhaps most striking about Jefferson's democratic instincts

more closely associated with representative republics that were responsive to popular majorities made up of a universally enfranchised citizenry. For important reflections on the meanings of the word in the late eighteenth century, see R.R. Palmer, "Notes on the Use of the Word 'Democracy' 1789–1799," *Political Science Quarterly* 68 (June 1953), 203–226. For a critique of the imprecision with which the term has been used to describe the governments of early America, see J.R. Pole, "Historians and the Problem of Early American Democracy," *American Historical Review* 67 (April 1962), 626–646. For a discussion of the confused uses of this term in contemporary political discourse, see Fahreed Zakaria, "The Rise of Illiberal Democracy," *Foreign Affairs* (November/December 1997). For a helpful discussion of the difficulties of evaluating early American government and institutions in terms of current democratic discourse, see Alan Gibson, *Understanding the Founding: The Crucial Questions* (Lawrence, 2007), 46–90. Russell L. Hanson, "Democracy," in Terence Ball, James Farr, and Russell L. Hanson, eds., *Political Innovation and Conceptual Change* (Cambridge, 1989), 68–89, is a particularly helpful introduction. Also see Wilson Carey McWilliams's important reflections in "Democracy and the Citizen: Community, Dignity, and the Crisis of Contemporary Politics in America," in Robert A. Goldwin and William A. Schambra, eds., *How Democratic is the Constitution?* (Washington, D.C., and London, 1980), 79–101.

9 To Judge William Johnson, June 12, 1823, in *L&B* 15:442.

10 John Adams to TJ, in *AJL*, 356.

11 See TJ to John Dickinson, March 6, 1801, in *TJW*, 1084–1085.

12 Joyce Appleby, "Commercial Farming and the 'Agrarian Myth' in the Early Republic, *JAH* 68 (March 1982), 845.

is how intimately linked they were with a faith in the peculiar ability of a particular people – the American people – to arrive at truth and govern themselves. What distinguished Jefferson and the Republicans, he insisted, was their belief that Americans, "enjoying in ease and security the full fruits of their own industry, enlisted by all their interests on the side of law and order, habituated to think for themselves, and to follow their reason as their guide, would be more easily and safely governed, than with minds nourished in error, and vitiated and debased, as in Europe, by ignorance, indigence and oppression."[13] This late statement is consistent with what Jefferson suggested throughout his lifelong correspondence and public career: Only Americans seemed to be a public sufficiently enlightened to trust. In short, this is yet another case in which Jefferson's universalist commitments are fully realized, in his assessment, only by his nation, so that his timeless cosmopolitan sentiments quickly merge into a description of a historical America. When our attention is on the universal claims Jefferson makes, we miss the nationalist assumptions that animated his enthusiasm.

Long remembered as a champion of international democracy, Jefferson did, in fact, embrace a faith in the God-given capacity of human beings to live in society and govern themselves.[14] And, to be sure, Jefferson saw the American Revolution as an example to the rest of the world, and he hoped that the "ball of liberty" would continue to "roll 'round the globe." But the kind of self-government Americans enjoyed was not as easy as all that.[15] Liberty would be enjoyed by "the enlightened part" of the globe only, for "light & liberty," Jefferson told Tench Coxe, "go together."[16] The corollary of this point is that without "light" there can be no "liberty." In other words, it is impossible to speak meaningfully of liberty in the absence of capacity for sustaining and enjoying it.[17] As Jefferson noted in 1805, "the people are the only safe depositories of their own liberty," but those people "are not safe unless enlightened to a certain degree." Even American liberty would be "a short-lived possession unless the mass of the people could be informed to a certain degree."[18]

Fortunately for the survival of liberty in the world, Jefferson believed, the American people had proven themselves sufficiently enlightened to preserve

<br>

13  TJ to William Johnson, June 12, 1823, *L&B* 15:441–442, and to William Green Munford, June 18, 1799, in *TJW*, 1064–1065.

14  See, among multiple other letters, TJ to John Adams, October 14, 1816, in *AJL*, 492.

15  See, for example, TJ to John Melish, January 13, 1813, in *L&B* 13:212; and TJ to Du Pont, April 24, 1816, in Dumas Malone, ed., *Correspondence Between Thomas Jefferson and Pierre Samuel Du Pont de Nemours, 1798–1817* (Boston, 1930), 182.

16  TJ to Tench Coxe, June 1, 1795, in *FE* 8:183.

17  For a fuller exploration of this theme, see Johann N. Neem, "'To Diffuse Knowledge More Generally through the Mass of the People': Thomas Jefferson on Individual Freedom and the Distribution of Knowledge" in *Light and Liberty: Thomas Jefferson and the Power of Knowledge*, ed. Robert M. S. McDonald (Charlottesville, 2012), 47–74., and Neem, "Developing Freedom: Thomas Jefferson, the State, and Human Capability," unpublished paper in possession of the author.

18  TJ to Littleton Waller Tazewell, January 5, 1805, in *TJW*, 1149.

their own. America remained, Jefferson told the citizens of Washington, D.C., in 1809, "the sole depository of the sacred fire of freedom and self government."[19] Other nations would "be lighted up" only when and "if" they "shall ever become susceptible to its benign influence." Self-government was the human ideal, but its spread was limited to the capacity of various national communities to handle it. American democracy did not come ready-made for export.

Jefferson's optimism about democracy was rooted in his sense that the American people possessed an exceptional "spirit" that would both resist tyranny and preserve law and order, as well as a "public opinion" that could be trusted to give energy and direction to government. Jefferson was such an enthusiastic democrat, in other words, largely because he was an American nationalist.

## THE TROUBLE WITH EUROPE

Much has been made of Jefferson's support of the French Revolution. But Jefferson's enthusiasm for that event was late and short-lived.[20] Prior to 1789, he repeatedly insisted that the French were not ready for republicanism; they would do best to settle for a benevolent constitutional monarchy until they were exercised in the habits of self-government. And the convulsions that ended in The Terror and, eventually, military dictatorship, only served to confirm his initial warnings and to disappoint deeply the enthusiasm he did experience after 1789.[21] As for the Spanish-American republics, which Jefferson

[19] TJ to the Citizens of Washington, March 4, 1809, in *L&B* 16:347.

[20] Despite his brief, and undeniable, enthusiasm in the early 1790s, Jefferson later made a conscious effort to disassociate himself from the most egregious excesses of the French Revolution, associating himself with Lafayette and other moderates in his memoirs. For this insight, see Robert M.S. McDonald, "Thomas Jefferson and Historical Self-Construction: The Earth Belongs to the Living?" in *The Historian* 61 (1999), 295. My argument here is that this was not simply a posture for effect (although it was that), but reflected Jefferson's own mature assessment. On Jefferson's French Revolution, see R.R. Palmer, "The Dubious Democrat: Thomas Jefferson in Bourbon France," *Political Science Quarterly* 72 (September 1957), 388–404; Lawrence S. Kaplan, *Jefferson and France: An Essay on Politics and Political Ideas* (New Haven, CT, 1967), 27–30; 33–35; and Elkins and McKitrick, *Age of Federalism: The Early American Republic, 1788–1800* (Oxford, 1993), 314–317 and 336–354. These treatments should be read in light of the fact that for Jefferson, as Nicholas Onuf and Peter Onuf have rightly noted, "the important thing about the French Revolution was that it vindicated the principle of national self-determination," a principle Jefferson never relinquished. See Onuf and Onuf, *Nations, Markets, and War: Modern History and the American Civil War* (Charlottesville, VA, 2006), 231. For a more standard reading of Jefferson and the French Revolution, see Gordon S. Wood, *Empire of Liberty: A History of the Early Republic, 1789–1815* (New York, 2009), 179–181. It seems worth noting R.R. Palmer's suggestion that Jefferson was not offered honorary French citizenship by the National Assembly in 1792 (unlike Madison, Washington, and, yes, Hamilton) precisely because the Jacobins knew him largely as a friend of Lafayette and, thus, unlikely to be favorably disposed to their Revolution. See Palmer, *The Age of the Democratic Revolution: The Struggle*, vol. 2 (Princeton, 1970), 55.

[21] Jefferson later acknowledged that Adams's "prophecies" about the likely outcome of the French Revolution "proved truer than mine." See TJ to Adams, January 11, 1816, in *AJL*, 459.

welcomed in theory, he never once imagined that they would end in anything other than military despotisms.

The problem in France and Spanish America, as Jefferson explained again and again, was that the people there simply did not yet have the capacity for self-government. This was not a judgment about any *natural* incapacity. There was nothing inherent in the Spanish or French people that disqualified them for democracy.[22] The opposite is true. Culture, unique historical circumstances, environmental characteristics, but especially multiple generations of despotic government, and the power of the Catholic Church over the minds of the people had taken human beings created by God for freedom and self-government and rendered them incapable of running their own affairs. It was sad but true. Spanish Americans would gain independence from Spain, and Jefferson wished them well, but he was under no illusion about the possibility for self-government once Spain had fled the hemisphere. "History," he told Baron von Humboldt, "furnishes no example of a priest-ridden people maintaining a free civil government. This marks the lowest grade of ignorance, of which their civil as well as religious leaders will always avail themselves for their own purposes." In Spanish America, in other words, an elite of priests and aristocrats had for so long held a monopoly of the various forms of capital – social, cultural, and financial – that the people had been rendered incapable of engaging in democratic politics.[23]

So the Spanish-American republics "must end in military despotisms," Jefferson said. "The different castes of their inhabitants, their mutual hatreds and jealousies, their profound ignorance and bigotry, will be played off by

---

Jefferson's never-wavering identification with republican revolutionaries everywhere intensified considerably as he began to comprehend the beleaguered nature of his own Revolution on his return home. So his passion for the French Revolution ebbed and flowed with his perceived need for international reinforcement of the meaning of the republican revolution here. For an example of Jefferson's enthusiasm, see TJ to James Madison, June 29, 1792, (*ROL*, 736) in which he suggests that the Jacobins represented "the true revolution-spirit of the whole nation" and were "carrying the nation with them." Ultimately, this sense that the Revolution had the imprimatur of the French people was what seemed to legitimate the Revolution in his eyes. See TJ to Francois de Marbois, June 14, 1817, in *TJW*, 1410. The most notorious example of Jefferson's defense of the French Revolution is TJ to William Short, January 3, 1793, in *TJW*, 1003–1006.

[22] Otherwise, Jefferson's stance might be less easy to distinguish from John C. Calhoun's, that liberty "is a reward to be earned, not a blessing to be gratuitously lavished on all alike; – a reward reserved for the intelligent, the patriotic, the virtuous and deserving; – and not a boon to be bestowed on a people too ignorant, degraded and vicious, to be capable either of appreciating or enjoying it," Calhoun, *Disquisition on Government* in Ross M. Lence, ed., *Union and Liberty: The Political Philosophy of John C. Calhoun* (Indianapolis, 1992), 42. Calhoun used this theory to justify inequalities of condition (especially South Carolina slavery) within a single political community, against which he posited, it might be worth noting, Jefferson's theory of universal rights. Jefferson's point is merely that, although all are entitled to liberty, Americans have come the farthest in ability to enjoy and maintain such liberty without falling into licentiousness.

[23] See Neem, "Developing Freedom;" and Pierre Bourdieu, "The Forms of Capital" in John G. Richardson, ed., *Handbook of Theory and Research for the Sociology of Education* (New York and Westport, 1986), 241–258.

cunning leaders, and each be made the instrument of enslaving the others."[24] So the real issue was that the people had been "habituated from their infancy to passive submission of body and mind to their kings and priests," and this lethargy and submissive spirit rendered them unqualified "to think and provide for themselves." This naturally made them "instruments ... in the hands of" despots.[25] It remained to be seen "whether the blinds of bigotry, the shackles of the priesthood, and the fascinating glare of rank and wealth, give fair play to the common sense of the mass of their people, so far as to qualify them for self-government."[26] The South Americans certainly had the same right to self-government that all people possessed by nature, and all Americans should cheer their effort. "But the question is not what we wish," Jefferson insisted, "but what is practicable."[27] And it seemed clear to him that, in this case anyway, "our wishes may be stronger than our hopes."[28]

The real trouble would not be throwing off external (in this case, Spanish) tyranny. "The dangerous enemy is within their own breasts."[29] The "ignorance & bigotry of the mass" led Jefferson to "doubt their capacity to understand and to support a free government."[30] On the contrary, such "ignorance and superstition" would "chain their minds and bodies under religious and military despotism." "The degrading ignorance into which their priests and kings have sunk them, has disqualified them from the maintenance or even knowledge of their rights." So a move straight from such despotism to self-government was unthinkable. Much better, Jefferson argued again and again, for these people to "obtain freedom by degrees only; because that would by degrees bring on light and information, and qualify them to take charge of themselves

[24] TJ to Baron Alexander Von Humboldt, December 6, 1813, *L&B*, 14:21. John Adams agreed about the prospects for liberty in Roman Catholic countries. See Adams to TJ, February 3, 1821, in *AJL*, 571; Adams to TJ, May 19, 1821, ibid., 573; and Adams to TJ, August 15, 1823, ibid., 595. Jefferson and Adams encouraged each other in this conviction: see TJ to Adams, September 4, 1823, ibid., 596.

[25] TJ to Adams, September 4, 1823, in ibid., 596.

[26] TJ to Alexander von Humboldt, June 13, 1817, in *FE* 12:68.

[27] TJ to Lafayette, May 14, 1817, in *L&B* 15:117.

[28] TJ to Alexander von Humboldt, June 13, 1817, in *FE* 12:68.

[29] TJ to John Adams, May 17, 1818, in *AJL*, 524.

[30] TJ to Du Pont de Nemours, April 24, 1816, in Malone, ed., *Correspondence Between Jefferson and Du Pont*, 186. This seems also to have been largely the assessment of Bolivar who noted, less than a year before his death in 1830, that "I am ashamed to admit it, but independence is the only benefit we have gained, at the cost of everything else," cited in John Lynch, *The Spanish American Revolutions, 1808–1826* (New York, 1973), 293. See also the analysis of the role of peasant inequality in the persistent underdevelopment and authoritarianism of Latin America – in ibid., 335–347. Also compare the 1834 suggestion by Antonio Lopez de Santa Anna that Mexicans were not ready for liberty: "A hundred years to come my people will not be fit for liberty. They do not know what it is, unenlightened as they are, and under the influence of a Catholic clergy, a despotism is the proper government for them" – a convenient enough view for an enlightened despot to hold, but not one that different in its essentials from Jefferson's. Santa Anna quoted in Fred Anderson and Andrew Cayton, *The Dominion of War: Empire and Liberty in North America, 1500–2000* (New York, 2005), 264.

understandingly."[31] So, "as their sincere friend and brother," he urged, not revolution and republicanism, but "an accommodation with the mother country ... until they shall be sufficiently trained by education and habits of freedom to walk safely by themselves." Only then, Jefferson said, would they be prepared "for complete independence."[32]

This was exactly the advice Jefferson had offered the French reformers with whom he was associated in the 1780s. The French people wanted liberty, but they lacked the light necessary to maintaining it, so the best they could hope for was a constitutional monarchy. As he told Madison in 1788, "The misfortune" of the French people was "that they are not yet ripe for receiving the blessings to which they are entitled. I doubt, for instance, whether the body of the nation, if they could be consulted, would accept of a Habeas corpus law, if offered them by the king. If the Etats generaux, when they assemble, do not aim at too much, they may begin a good constitution.... If they push at much more, all may fail."[33] As late as March 1789, Jefferson registered his belief that "this nation will in the course of the present year have as full a portion of liberty, dealt out to them as the nation can bear at present, considering how uninformed the mass of their people is."[34] The French, like the South Americans, had the same rights as other peoples to self-government and liberty. Jefferson's concern was that neither of them had the necessary character, manners, and spirit to maintain those blessings. Such acquisition demanded time. But "a thousand years" of work emancipating "the minds" of Europeans "from their present ignorance & prejudices ... would not place them on that high ground on which our common people are now setting out."[35] Europe's "literati" may be "half a dozen years" ahead of Americans in science, but "the mass of the people" remained "two centuries behind ours."[36] "Ignorance, superstition, poverty, & oppression of body & mind in every form" were "so firmly settled on the mass of the people," Jefferson warned, "that their redemption from them can *never* be hoped."[37] At the time, Jefferson assumed that the ignorance of the French masses would quite simply "prevent their immediate establishment of the trial by jury."[38] His later retrospective analysis for French correspondents was a bit more hopeful, suggesting that if the French patriots had been

<hr>

[31]  TJ to John Adams, May 17, 1818, in *AJL*, 524.

[32]  TJ to Lafayette, May 14, 1817, in *L&B* 15:117; TJ to John Adams, January 22, 1821, in *AJL*, 570.

[33]  TJ to Madison, Nov. 18, 1788, *PTJ* 12:188–189. On this sentiment also see *Autobiography*, in *TJW*, 85–86; TJ to John Jay, Nov. 19, 1788, *PTJ* 12:212–213; and TJ to John Adams, November 13, 1787, *AJL*, 211–213.

[34]  TJ to David Humphreys, March 18, 1789, *PTJ* 14:677. It is worth noting that the overall tone of this letter is enthusiastic about the reformations in French political life, but it is the qualifications that stand out in comparison with his expectations for American reform.

[35]  TJ to George Wythe, August 13, 1786, in *PTJ* 10:244.

[36]  TJ to Charles Bellini, September 30, 1785, in *TJW*, 833.

[37]  TJ to George Wythe, August 13, 1786, in *PTJ* 10:244, emphasis added.

[38]  TJ to David Humphreys, March 18, 1789, ibid., 14:677.

able to secure such concessions as habeas corpus, "freedom of the press," and "trial by jury," they could "go home, and let these work on the amelioration of the condition of the people, until they should have rendered them capable of more." But, ultimately, he remained clear about the limitations French reformers faced. Liberty would not avail "an unprepared people." "Habituation," he told Lafayette, was the key, and the kind of habituation Jefferson imagined necessary for the security of self-rule demanded time: "More than a generation will be requisite." In the end, the French sought more than they were capable of handling, and the results were tragic.[39]

Looking back years later, Jefferson believed his initial instincts had been right. Having lived through Robespierre and Bonaparte, the French people were now, in 1815, back to their "ante-revolutionary condition … nearly where [they] were at the *Jeu de paume* on the 20th of June 1789."[40] The point was, Jefferson told Du Pont, "the excellence of every government is it's adaptation to the state of those to be governed by it." In other words, the worth of a government can be judged by how adequately it matches the propensities and capabilities of its people. Americans, Jefferson noted, were "constitutionally & conscientiously Democrats," so they could handle the maximum amount of liberty. Until other national peoples met this standard, their rightful share of liberty would need to be tempered by more heavy-handed government than Jefferson usually advocated.[41] If "an unprepared people" acquired freedom "by mere force or accident" (instead of through long "habituation" and "growth in the progress of reason"), they would immediately pervert their freedom into "a tyranny still, of the many, the few, or the one." The constitutional monarchy he was recommending for the French and for Latin Americans was "not the best possible government," Jefferson admitted, "but the best" such degraded peoples could "bear."[42] This is perhaps why Jefferson assumed that Louisiana, immediately

---

[39] TJ to Lafayette, February 14, 1815, in *L&B* 14:245–246.

[40] TJ to Du Pont de Nemours, February 28, 1815, and April 15, 1811, in Malone, ed., *Correspondence Between Jefferson and Du Pont*, 151, 132. For the same sentiment, see TJ to Lafayette, February 14, 1815, in *L&B* 14:245–246.

[41] TJ to Du Pont de Nemours, April 24, 1816, in Malone, ed., *Correspondence Between Jefferson and Du Pont*, 181.

[42] Ibid., 187. Jefferson recognized – and acknowledged – that the American Revolution had thrown off an external tyranny that, for all its faults, had nevertheless (largely through what Edmund Burke called "salutary and benign neglect") left Americans a heritage of liberty and a history of self-government. This is possibly why Jefferson noted during his retirement that other than the Americans, only the English people were "capable of bearing a considerable portion of liberty," precisely because of their "habits of law and order" and "almost innate" grasp "of the vital elements of free government." A reformation of government along the American "model," Jefferson argued, could be much more easily realized in England than in other parts of the world, he thought, precisely because of this character of the English people. And if they did institute a government that would "treat us with justice and equality," Jefferson declared that he would "feel with great strength the ties which bind us together, of origin, language, laws and manners." The two nations were really "natural friends and brethren," and Americans were "more interested in a fraternal connection with them than with any other nation on earth" (TJ to John Adams, November 25, 1816, in *AJL*, 497–498). It is impossible to know what

after its purchase by the United States, could not be a self-governing territory in the already established tradition of American geographical expansion (and why Jefferson saw the more traditionally imperial arrangement enacted there as less troubling than later historians have). Louisiana could be republican only when it was filled up with Americans.[43]

Even the ancient models he had long valued fell far short of Jefferson's ideal. The "good government" of republican Rome, Jefferson suggested to John Adams, was largely mythological. "When the enthusiasm however kindled by Cicero's pen and principles, subsides into cool reflection, I ask myself What was that government which the virtues of Cicero were so zealous to restore, and the ambition of Caesar to subvert?" The fact was, he argued, "they never had" any good government that might be worth restoring. Rome's people "were so demoralized and depraved as to be incapable of exercising a wholesome controul" over their government. "If Caesar had been as virtuous as he was daring and sagacious," it was doubtful he could have done much with such people. "Steeped in corruption vice and venality as the whole nation was … what could even Cicero, Cato, Brutus have done, had it been referred to them to establish a good government for their country?" The people needed deep training to understand "what is right and what wrong" and long inculcation "in habits of virtue" to "render" them "a sure basis for the structure of order and good government." But such habituation would take "a generation or two at least," and in that time multiple "Neros and Commoduses" would have arisen to "quash … the whole process." The fact was, the Roman people had "never … known to this day, and through a course of five and twenty hundred years … one single day of free and rational government."[44]

AMERICAN "SPIRIT"

Americans, by contrast, had "sucked in the principles of liberty as it were with their mother's milk."[45] American republicanism was located "not in

impression such a statement from Jefferson would have made on Alexander Hamilton, had he lived to read it, but, for his part, John Adams quickly dismissed such effusive hopes: "Britain will never be our Friend, till We are her Master" (Adams to TJ, December 16, 1816, ibid., 502). But the central point here is clear. People with long-ingrained habits of self-government and an ability to handle liberty without running into anarchy were the only ones who were realistically eligible for democracy. On this heritage of English liberty as understood in America on the eve of the Revolution, see Bernard Bailyn, *The Ideological Origins of the American Revolution* (Cambridge, MA, 1967), 66. Note also the contrast Jefferson posits in his letter to David Humphreys from Paris on the eve of Revolution, March 18, 1789, *PTJ* 14:677. The irony was that oppression awakened the French and lack thereof rendered the English complacent.

43 See Everett Sommerville Brown, *The Constitutional History of the Louisiana Purchase, 1803–1812* (Berkeley, 1920), 97–98; and James E. Scanlon, "A Sudden Conceit: Jefferson and the Louisiana Government Bill of 1804," *Louisiana History*, 9 (Spring 1968), 139–162. Also see TJ to John Breckenridge, November 24, 1803, in *FE* 10: 51–53; to DeWitt Clinton, December 2, 1803, in ibid., 55.

44 TJ to Adams, December 10, 1819, in *AJL*, 549–550.

45 TJ to Richard Price, August 7, 1785, in *FE* 4:448.

our constitution" but "in the spirit of our people." And this American spirit, Jefferson asserted in a remarkable statement, "would oblige even a despot to govern us republicanly."[46] The character of the American people, in other words, would force even tyrants to abide by republican principles if they ever hoped to govern Americans.[47]

In an earlier iteration of this view, Jefferson told William Carmichael, American minister to Spain, during a war scare in 1790, that Spain would never be able to control America's western citizens. These "could be quiet but a short time under a government so repugnant to their feelings." Even if the Spanish managed to control the American West for a time, these Americans "would communicate a spirit of Independence to those with whom they should be mixed" – the contagion of the American "spirit," in other words, would infect even the conquerors of American physical space.[48]

In Jefferson's thought, the nature of the regime and the character of its citizens were mutually constitutive and reinforcing; American republicanism was the natural fit for a people who had long enjoyed self-government. Neither the people's character nor the government was altogether plausible, or even conceivable, without the other.[49] The American people, Jefferson asserted over and again, would not long suffer a government that did not ascend from their will; nor could they abide a government inconsistent with their republican character, precisely because, as Jefferson put it, "our countrymen" had been "impressed from their cradle" with the "habit of self-government" and the principles of republicanism "so that with them it is *almost innate*."[50]

Years later, when he read John Marshall's *Life of Washington*, which praised the general for resigning his commission and refusing to "perpetuate ... his authority," Jefferson suggested that even if Washington *had* desired to translate his military authority into a political tyranny, the American people would

---

[46] TJ to Samuel Kercheval, July 12, 1816, *L&B* 15:35. For a compelling evaluation of the modern distinction between constitutions and the manners or character of a people, see Paul A. Rahe, "Between Trust and Distrust: *The Federalist* and the Emergence of Modern Republican Constitutionalism," in *1650–1850: Ideas, Aesthetics, and Inquiries in the Early Modern Era* 11 (2005), 375–406.

[47] It is instructive to compare Jefferson's assertion with Fred Anderson's discussion of the volunteerist assumptions of Massachusetts soldiers during the Seven Years' War, who more or less forced British superiors to alter their approach to dealing with enlisted men. Anderson (like Jefferson) rests a good deal of explanatory power on the freehold independence of these soldiers who, consequently, understood their relationship with superior officers as a contractual one. Anderson, *A People's Army: Massachusetts Soldiers and Society in the Seven Years' War* (Chapel Hill, 1984).

[48] TJ to William Carmichael, August 2, 1790, *PTJ* 17:114.

[49] Legitimate government had to be rooted in popular consent, yes, but popular consent, in the absence of proper cultivation, might countenance illiberal governance. This is why it is nearly impossible, in the end, to fully separate the people's character from the political architecture endorsed in Jefferson's thought. This fundamental insight – that a people's habits, mores, and experience sustained the political institutions that cultivated and enabled those very behaviors – is a key to understanding Jefferson's thought.

[50] TJ to John Breckenridge, January 29, 1800, in *L&B* 10:149, emphasis added.

never have allowed it.[51] "He who supposes it was practicable, had [Washington] wished it, knows nothing of the spirit of America, either of the people or of those who possessed their confidence."[52] And this "spirit of America," Jefferson told Madison, would strengthen with time. "The rising race [of Americans] are all republicans. We [of the revolutionary generation] were educated in royalism; no wonder if some of us retain that idolatry still. Our young people are educated in republicanism, an apostasy from that to royalism is unprecedented & impossible."[53] Just as oil and water will not mix, just as the princess will always sense the pea under the mattress, true Americans would be unable to adjust to or become complacent under despotic government. The character of Americans – not simply their institutions – would preserve the Republic.

The French Revolution had failed, by contrast, Jefferson came to believe, because it depended largely on "the mobs of the cities," a people "debased by ignorance, poverty and vice." Such people simply "could not be restrained to rational action."[54] But in America, he asserted, "the proper spirit of the people" would shape the behavior of even an "absolute Monarch" as long as "our present character remains, of order, industry and love of peace."[55] If the Roman people (or, by extension, the French) "had been, like ours, enlightened, peaceable, and really free," Jefferson argued, they might have obtained good government, too. The names of Caesar and Nero just might have remained unknown to history.[56]

When he was evaluating other societies, Jefferson could sound a good deal like Emerson's "conservative" who concludes that "the order of things is as good as the character of the population permits."[57] Only when he turned to America did he see the possibilities for what J.R. Pole has called a "politics of vigilance" that presupposed a knowledge of public affairs that legitimated the people's engagement without at the same time courting the anarchy so feared by conservatives who typically favored what Pole called a "politics of trust."[58] Jefferson's instincts were remarkably (although only relatively) conservative, then, when it came to evaluating other societies. In other words, when he looked around the world, Jefferson's analysis was not always that different from Adams's. What made him a radical democrat – the basis for his radical

---


[51] Marshall, *The Life of George Washington, Commander in Chief of the American Forces, During the War Which Established the Independence of His Country, and First President of the United States*, 5 volumes (Philadelphia, 1807), 5: 2.

[52] Jefferson's notes on the fifth volume of Marshall's *Life of Washington*, in *FE* 11:122. Charles Royster makes a similar assertion in *A Revolutionary People at War: The Continental Army and American Character* (Chapel Hill, 1979), 257.

[53] TJ to Madison, March 15, 1789, *WTJ* 5:83.

[54] TJ to John Adams, October 28, 1813, in *AJL*, 391.

[55] TJ to John Taylor, May 28, 1816, *L&B* 15:22.

[56] TJ to John Adams, December 10, 1819, in *AJL*, 549.

[57] "The Conservative," in Joel Porte, ed., *Emerson: Essays and Poems* (New York, 1996), 182.

[58] Pole, *Gift of Government*, 140. Compare Rahe's elaboration in "Between Trust and Distrust," esp. 401–404.

politics, in other words – was his evaluation of American character, which, he believed, could sustain republican institutions.

Public spirit for Jefferson essentially connoted the engagement of the American people.[59] And engagement seemed to mean two things, primarily. One, that Americans were alert and informed enough to recognize, and courageous enough to resist, tyranny when it appeared in whatever guise. Two, that Americans were devoted to constituted authority: law, order, and to preservation of their Union and system of government. These two facets of public spirit have been in tension in modern political thought, but they are complementary in Jefferson's.

Jefferson's confidence in the American people was rooted in his sense that they were exceptional. "Never was a finer canvas presented to work on than our countrymen," he effused to John Adams in 1796 in a letter in which he spelled out some of the characteristics that rendered Americans uniquely able to govern themselves. "All" Americans, he said, were "engaged in agriculture or the pursuits of honest industry, independent in their circumstances, enlightened as to their rights, and firm in their habits of order and obedience to the laws." The lesson was clear: "If ever the morals of a people could be made the basis of their own government, it is our case."[60] In America, he told Adams years later, "every one may have land to labor for himself if he chuses; or, preferring the exercise of any other industry, may exact for it such compensation as not only to afford a comfortable subsistence, but wherewith to provide for a cessation from labor in old age." It followed, Jefferson noted, that

every one, by his property, or by his satisfactory situation, is interested in the support of law and order. And such men may safely and advantageously reserve to themselves a wholesome controul over their public affairs, and a degree of freedom, which in the hands of the Canaille of the cities of Europe, would be instantly perverted to the demolition and destruction of every thing public and private. The history of the last 25 years of France, and of the last 40 years in America, nay of it's last 200 years, proves the truth of both parts of this observation.[61]

Here, and elsewhere, Jefferson made several striking claims about the United States. First is his assertion of its unique prosperity. Because of the "immensity of land" in the United States, Americans were "a people at their ease" in

---

[59] Donald Lutz confirms Jefferson's anecdotal sense of widespread engagement, quantifying an incredible level of "activist participation" in politics during the Revolutionary era. See Lutz, "Political Participation in Eighteenth-Century America," *Albany Law Review* 53 (Winter 1989), 327–355, esp. 343–345. It seems worth noting also that, for Jefferson, this American spirit also suggested a certain panache. Americans were the kind of people who would consider it a "duty to buy a copy" of a censored or "persecuted" book just to vindicate their "right to buy, and to read what [they] please." America was "a country which is afraid to read nothing, and which may be trusted with anything, so long as its reason remains unfettered by law," TJ to Monsieur N.G. Dufief, April 19, 1814, in *L&B* 14:127; and TJ to Joseph Milligan, April 6, 1816, ibid., 463.
[60] TJ to John Adams, February 28, 1796, in *AJL*, 260.
[61] TJ to John Adams, October 28, 1813, in ibid., 391.

possession of a "lovely equality," in which most families, by and large, were not artificially burdened with poverty, where the agricultural labor of men was sustaining and even profitable.[62] America was essentially a classless society, Jefferson told Thomas Cooper, with "no paupers" and very few rich.[63] All Americans worked and all maintained a comfortable competence. This generalized prosperity had important consequences, not least of which, as we will see, was a peculiar disposition in favor of law and order. But it also created a kind of rough equality that freed people up to achieve their natural human potential and to indulge their independence, following a moral sense unclouded by artificial hierarchies or crushing dependence. Two hundred years' experience with this kind of freedom rendered Americans familiar with the habits of self-government and comfortable, as well as safe, with their liberty.[64] In addition, as we have seen, American prosperity underwrote American domestic happiness, freeing men and women to enact their natural gender roles and create

[62] *Notes*, 164; TJ to Maria Cosway, October 12, 1786, in *PTJ* 10:448. Like many other observers at the time, Jefferson passed over multiple inequalities in Revolutionary America that would be glaring to later scholars, and Jefferson's confidence about the American common man was predicated, especially in Virginia to a degree that he was rarely explicit about, on the enslavement of much of the laboring class. It is worth considering whether, in the absence of slavery, the United States would have retained the classless – and superior – character that Jefferson prized; whether, in other words, common white men would remain "the yeomanry of the United States" and not rather become the "canaille of Virginia." In addition, many white men would have substantial reason to question Jefferson's characterization of their society as classless. Nevertheless, this theme of unusually widespread prosperity (especially relative to Europe) is as old as the idea of America and remains a prominent component in contemporary American exceptionalism. Certainly his observations about the relatively widespread prospects for freedom and ownership of property were not altogether imaginary. See Jack P. Greene, *The Intellectual Construction of America: Exceptionalism and Identity from 1492 to 1800* (Chapel Hill, 1993); Hannah Arendt, *On Revolution* (New York, 1965), 15–17; and David M. Potter, *People of Plenty: Economic Abundance and the American Character* (Chicago, 1954). For an effort to quantify American prosperity and social mobility in the late eighteenth century, see Jackson Turner Main, *The Social Structure of Revolutionary America* (Princeton, 1965).

[63] To Thomas Cooper, September 10, 1814, *L&B* 14:182. Also see, *Notes*, 133.

[64] It seems worth noting that these claims about the colonial period conflict with some of Jefferson's other suggestions that the Revolution had destroyed a deferential, hierarchical, and monarchical society. The historiography surrounding these competing claims is rich and no less contentious. See Jack P. Greene, *Pursuits of Happiness: The Social Development of Early Modern British Colonies and the Formation of American Culture* (Chapel Hill, 1988); Greene, *Intellectual Construction of America*; Alfred Young, "George Robert Twelves Hewes (1742–1840): A Boston Shoemaker and the Memory of the American Revolution," *WMQ* 38 (October 1981), 561–623; Holly Brewer, "Entailing Aristocracy in Colonial Virginia: 'Ancient Feudal Restraints' and Revolutionary Reform," *WMQ* (April 1997), 307–346; Jon Butler, *Becoming America: The Revolution Before 1776* (Cambridge, MA, 2001); Joyce Appleby, *Inheriting the Revolution: The First Generation of Americans* (Cambridge, MA, 2001); Gordon Wood, *The Radicalism of the American Revolution* (New York, 1991); and Richard R. Beeman, "Deference, Republicanism, and the Emergence of Popular Politics in Eighteenth-Century America," *WMQ* 49 (July 1992), 401–430. In any case, this association of America with freedom was never "merely a parochial view," as Bernard Bailyn has noted, but was "reinforced" by Enlightenment figures who identified America as the "special preserve … of virtue and liberty," Bailyn, *Ideological Origins*, 84.

the stable foundation of self-government in the republican family. In short, American circumstances had forged a people safe with the franchise and with a degree of liberty unknown in the history of the world: "men susceptible of happiness, educated in the love of order, habituated to self-government, and valuing its blessings above all price."[65]

All of these characteristics were easy to contrast with those of Europe. Because Europeans were "not at their ease," Jefferson argued, they lived degraded lives.[66] Every man in Europe, Jefferson argued, was "either the hammer or the anvil."[67] And European aristocracy created artificial hierarchies that stifled human potential and condemned the mass of society to ignorance and poverty, leaving them without a true stake in the society or any public spirit that might preserve republican government.

It seems worth noting here that the claims Jefferson was making about America were not original or unique to him, although he articulated them as well as anyone else ever did. America's association with prosperity, mild government fostering individual private pursuits of betterment and happiness, remarkable fluidity, and comparative social mobility – all of which, the narrative went, cultivated a unique character in the American people – had been part of the European conception of America from the time it first entered the "Old World's" consciousness and retained currency with many European reformers who endorsed Jefferson's sense that America actually practiced what the philosophes dreamed.[68]

Adam Smith himself gave his seal of approval to this view, admiring the American farmer "who cultivates his own land, and derives his necessary subsistence from the labour of his own family." Such a yeoman, Smith reported, considered himself "really a master, and independent of all the world." With some qualification, this was precisely the kind of condition Jefferson believed fostered the unique American spirit. In contrast, Smith noted in a familiar

---

[65] First Annual Message, December 8, 1801, in *TJW*, 503. Environmental (as opposed to historical/sociological) distinctions also shaped the American character, although the extent to which Jefferson truly embraced such influence is unclear. The climate of the United States was "more cheerful" than that of Europe, and Jefferson suggested (with a rare touch of humor) that "it is our cloudless sky which has eradicated from our constitutions all disposition to hang ourselves, which we might otherwise have inherited from our English ancestors," TJ to C.R. de C. Volney, February 8, 1805, in *TJW*, 1155.

[66] "Notes of a Tour Through Holland and the Rhine Valley," *PTJ* 13:27–28; 36, n. 29, emphasis added.

[67] TJ to Charles Bellini, September 30, 1785, *PTJ* 8:568.

[68] Greene, *Intellectual Construction of America*. Greene, in *Pursuits of Happiness*, argues that this "intellectual construction" more or less reflected American reality and that American visions of the "good life" were bound up with "unrestrained" material acquisition. Also see Greene's review of Main, *Social Structure of Revolutionary America* in *Political Science Quarterly* 81 (December 1966), 646–649, esp. 648–649 (quotation on 648). On European endorsement of Jefferson's sociology, see Louis S. Greenbaum, "Thomas Jefferson, the Paris Hospitals, and the University of Virginia," in *Eighteenth-Century Studies*, 26 (Summer 1993), 607–626, at 614–615.

passage from the *Wealth of Nations*, the laborer in Europe, where land was scarce and the division of labor had advanced to a much more considerable extent, spent his "whole life … performing a few simple operations" and consequently had "no occasion to exert his understanding or to exercise his invention in finding out expedients for removing difficulties which never occur." Such a laborer "naturally loses, therefore, the habit of such exertion, and generally becomes as stupid and ignorant as it is possible for a human creature to become. The torpor of his mind renders him, not only incapable of relishing or bearing a part in any rational conversation, but of conceiving any generous, noble, or tender sentiment, and consequently of forming any just judgment concerning many even of the ordinary duties of private life." Perhaps most damning here, from Jefferson's perspective, was that such a worker was soon rendered "altogether incapable of judging … the great and extensive interests of his country; and unless very particular pains have been taken to render him otherwise, he is equally incapable of defending his country in war."[69] Americans, by contrast, Jefferson believed, excelled in precisely these public virtues.

To be sure, Jefferson continued to have faith that liberty would eventually spread around the globe. Unlike later manifestations of it, Jefferson's American exceptionalism was not ultimately exclusive or coextensive with a desire to hoard liberty for America. But Jefferson seemed compelled by observation to consider America the only living example of the kind of society he craved for the rest of the world. In his final substantive letter,[70] he offered a ringing endorsement of the right of all peoples to self-government, a reformulation of what he had long been telling multiple correspondents – even those to whom he had expressed doubts about the ability of other contemporary peoples to handle republicanism – that one day, the world would be made of republics.[71] Adams's "prophecies" about the French Revolution might have "proved truer than mine" (even Adams underestimated the horrors, Jefferson said), but that did not, he hoped "preclude a better final result." "Opinion is power," he told Adams earlier, "and that opinion will come. Even France will yet attain representative government." But he did not expect to see this happen during his own lifetime, and he predicted that "rivers of blood may yet flow" before it was realized.[72] The broad cultural transformation that would make republics

<hr>

[69] Adam Smith, *The Wealth of Nations*, in Robert L. Heilbroner, ed., *The Essential Adam Smith* (New York, 1986), 250–251, 302. On Smith's ambivalence, see R.L. Heilbroner, "The Paradox of Progress: Decline and Decay in the Wealth of Nations," in Andrew Skinner and Thomas Wilson, eds., *Essays on Adam Smith* (Oxford, 1975). Adam Ferguson, for his part, was even more concerned than Smith about the dangers posed by commercial society and division of labor. See Richard B. Sher, "Adam Ferguson, Adam Smith, and the Problem of National Defense," in *Journal of Modern History* 61 (June 1989), 240–268.

[70] For clarification about Jefferson's truly "last" letter, see J. Jefferson Looney, "Thomas Jefferson's Last Letter," *Virginia Magazine of History and Biography* 112 (no. 2, 2004), 178–184.

[71] TJ to Roger C. Weightman, June 24, 1826, in *TJW*, 1517.

[72] TJ to John Adams, January 11, 1816, in *AJL*, 460.

possible was not to be hoped from one act of force or from wishful thinking. History, Jefferson understood, offered few shortcuts.

So the contrast between these real, but distant, hopes for the world and his confident assertions about the present character of the United States is striking. The American example was the only one encouraging Jefferson's hope that all "men" would one day "burst the chains under which monkish ignorance and superstition had persuaded them to bind themselves, and to assume the blessings and security of self-government."[73] America could act or be an example "for all mankind" precisely because "circumstances denied to others" had been "indulged to us." And only "a nation, composed of such materials, and free in all its members from distressing wants, furnishes hopeful implements for the interesting experiment of self-government."[74]

Dreams were for the future; practical politics in the present demanded an appreciation of reality. Or, as Jefferson put it to Madison, it was not "advantageous" for men to create governments when they were "acquainted with man only as they see him in their books and not in the world."[75] Government had to be tailored to fit the character of a people rather than any universal theory of man. As Jefferson told William Lee, "every people have their own particular habits, ways of thinking, manners, etc., which have grown up with them from their infancy, are become a part of their nature, and to which the regulations which are to make them happy must be accommodated." Unfortunately, Jefferson said, "no member of a foreign country can have a sufficient sympathy with these. The institutions of Lycurgeus, for example would not have suited Athens nor those of Solon Lacedaemon. The organizations of Locke were impracticable for Carolina, and those of Rousseau and Mably for Poland."[76] If the question was whether to "mould our citizens to the law, or the law to our citizens," Jefferson largely came down on the side of the latter.[77] Any fair answer to this question, he told John Quincy Adams, could not neglect the "peculiar character" of the American citizenry.[78]

Accordingly, one of Jefferson's principal critiques of the Federalists in the 1790s was that they were attempting to force on Americans a style of government ready-made for the European societies he described, but ill-suited for the American people. Part of the reason the Federalists governed with a heavy hand, hoping, Jefferson imagined, to consolidate power in the central state and create a more authoritarian system of government for America was that they did not understand "the difference between the rabble who were used as instruments" for the French revolutionaries, "and the steady & rational character of the American people, in which [they] had not sufficient confidence."

---

73 TJ to Roger C. Weightman, June 24, 1826, in *TJW*, 1517.
74 TJ to Joseph Priestley, June 19, 1802, in *L&B* 10:324.
75 TJ to Madison, August 28, 1789, in *ROL* 1:628.
76 TJ to William Lee, January 16, 1817, in *L&B* 15:100–101.
77 Even Jefferson's reformation of the laws of Virginia he described as a tearing down of traditional scaffolding unfit for a free people.
78 To John Quincy Adams, November 1, 1817, *L&B* 15:145.

"Like the rest of mankind," the Federalists were justifiably "disgusted with atrocities of the French revolution," but, unlike the Republicans, they forgot about the unique spirit of the American people.[79] The Federalists had to be resisted, Jefferson thought, precisely because they were not sufficiently well-attuned to what was special about the American people and destiny.

Early in his political career, Hamilton had suggested to John Jay what all history to that point seemed to have confirmed: "When the minds of [the people] are loosened from their attachment to ancient establishments and courses, they seem to grow giddy and are apt more or less to run into anarchy."[80] Jefferson, as we will see, did not exactly disagree with Hamilton that "a due medium" between "opposition to tyranny and oppression," on the one hand, and "a contempt and disregard of all authority," on the other, was "almost impossible among the unthinking populace."[81] The crucial difference was that his own analysis of the American people suggested that Hamilton and the Federalists were wrong about their character. Americans, unlike the French proletariat, indeed unlike most peoples of history, were not an "unthinking populace," but instead had proven themselves capable of casting off tyranny *while* resisting the impulse to licentiousness that had damned the French Revolution. The Federalist program failed to recognize this and was, thus, an inappropriate political agenda for the American republic. Accordingly, Jefferson characterized his own election to the presidency in 1800 – the defeat of the Federalist agenda – as "the resistance which our republic has opposed to a course of operation *for which it was not destined.*" His victory, he wrote, had proven "a strength of body which affords the most flattering presages of duration.... The character which our fellow citizens have displayed on this occasion gives us every thing to hope for the permanence of our government."[82]

Jefferson's critique, then, turned Federalist campaign literature on its head. Styling Jefferson's program as "Laputian" and inattentive to experience, Federalists warned against the dangers of experimentation in politics.[83] But, for Jefferson, it was the Federalists who had been ignoring American experience and had rooted their politics in a theory based on the experiences of other peoples. As a political program for Americans, then, the Federalist agenda – not the Jeffersonian – was incongruent with reality. No useful positive lessons for Americans, in fact, could be drawn from the experiences of the peoples of history. Seeking precedents for proper governance from ancient Rome, "where the government was of a heavy-handed unfeeling aristocracy, over a people ferocious, and rendered desperate by poverty and wretchedness," would be

---

[79] The "Anas," in *FE* 1:183.
[80] Hamilton to John Jay, November 26, 1775, *PAH* 1:176–177.
[81] Ibid.
[82] To James Warren, March 21, 1801, *PTJ* 33:398–399, emphasis added.
[83] See Linda Kerber, *Federalists in Dissent: Imagery and Ideology in Jeffersonian America* (Ithaca and London, 1970), esp. 1–22.

folly and "misapplied ... to a people, mild in their dispositions, patient under their trial, united for the public liberty, and affectionate to their leaders."[84]

If the ancients offered little in the way of guidance, neither did contemporaries. In light of Federalist propaganda associating Jefferson with the madness of the French Revolution, it is worth remembering that Jefferson worried lest the American people link their own experience too closely to the trajectory of the French republic. It remained crucial for Jefferson – "very material," as he put it – that the American people ("our countrymen") remain "sensible that their own character & situation are materially different from the French." Americans should "be made" to understand, he wrote, "that whatever may be the fate of republicanism" in France, "we are able to preserve it inviolate here." Because of their long experience of self-government and the conditions that had rendered their freedom meaningful and secure, Americans had the luxury (as well as the "duty & expediency") of "submitting our opinions to the will of the majority" and of waiting "with patience till they get right if they happen to be at any time wrong." Thankfully, Jefferson suggested, "our vessel is moored at such a distance, that should [the French one] blow up, ours is still safe, if we will but think so."[85]

The most salient difference between Jefferson and the Federalists, then, by Jefferson's own reckoning here, was not his "utopianism" about worldwide democracy and revolution so lampooned in Federalist campaign literature, but, rather, his sense, rooted in a sociological appraisal of their character, that Americans had, in fact, shrugged off the fetters that still bound the majority of the world's peoples – of necessity – to governments of hierarchy, deference, and force. In their attempt to govern such a people with the tools that had served rulers of the European past, Federalists, Jefferson believed, were simply out of touch (and date) with American realities.

Jefferson's Americans, then, maintained an alert "spirit of resistance" to tyranny that was uncharacteristic of the lethargic, ignorant, poverty-stricken masses in other countries. It was precisely this kind of rebellious spirit that had led young Hamilton to worry about the longevity of constituted authority in America.[86] But, for Jefferson, the American habit of "order and obedience to the laws" was not in tension with but rather the logical corollary to this spirit of resistance.[87] American "love of liberty," its "steady character," would be manifested in both the spirit of resistance to tyranny and its complement, "obedience to law, and support of the public authorities." In both, Jefferson recognized "a sure guaranty of the permanence of our republic."[88] "Love of

[84] *Notes*, 129.
[85] TJ to John Breckinridge, January 29, 1800, in *TJW*, 1075.
[86] And, if Jefferson is to be believed, the older Hamilton, too. See Report of a Conversation with Alexander Hamilton, *Anas, FE* 1:169.
[87] TJ to John Adams, February 28, 1786, in *PTJ* 28:618.
[88] Eighth Annual Message, November 8, 1808, in *TJW*, 549.

order & obedience to the laws," in fact, "considerably characterizes the citizens of the United States," Jefferson told a group of citizens from Columbia, South Carolina, who had sent their congratulations on his recent election to the presidency. It was this character that would "peaceably dissipate all combinations to subvert a constitution dictated by the wisdom & resting on the will of the people" – a succinct description of what he believed had happened in the election.[89] The American government would be, Jefferson argued, "a model for the protection of man in a state of freedom *and* order."[90]

Such a stance was de rigueur for enlightenment intellectuals. Few philosophes sought destruction of tradition for its own sake and not rather as the basis for a new stability and rational order rooted in nature rather than artificiality.[91] Throughout the Revolutionary era, good Whigs recognized that tyranny was not the only threat to liberty; licentiousness, too, was liberty's "other," the perversion of true liberty and a very real likelihood in governments responsive to the people.[92] James Wilson made the point clearly, noting that liberty could never exist without law because, "without liberty, law loses its nature and its name and becomes oppression. Without law, liberty also loses its nature and its name, and becomes licentiousness."[93] Because the two existed along a continuum, the founders, Jefferson among them, were never unconcerned about the potential threat licentiousness – that "bane of liberty" – posed to republican government, and few were hostile to George Washington's call for public education as a possible remedy that might enable the citizenry "to discriminate the spirit of liberty from that of licentiousness."[94] Although Jefferson tended to agree with Josiah Quincy, Jr., who believed it "much easier to restrain liberty from running into licentiousness than power from swelling into tyranny and oppression," he was not unaffected by concerns articulated by Tory Jonathan Sewell that "an over hasty attempt to eradicate (small tho' real evils in government)]," was to risk "subverting a good constitution."[95] After all, Jefferson's own statement in the Declaration of Independence had explicitly incorporated this warning, noting as an axiom that "governments long established should not be changed for light and transient causes." As we have seen, much of his criticism of European efforts to overthrow tyranny, justifiable though they may have been, centered around his sense that Europeans were not yet capable of

[89]  TJ to Columbia, SC, Citizens, March 23, 1801, in *PTJ* 33:409.
[90]  TJ to Thaddeus Kosciusko, February 21, 1799, *L&B* 10:115, emphasis added.
[91]  See Roy Porter, *The Creation of the Modern World: The Untold Story of the British Enlightenment* (New York, 2000), 18.
[92]  See John Phillip Reid, *The Concept of Liberty in the Age of the American Revolution* (Chicago, 1988), esp. 32–37.
[93]  James Wilson, *Lectures on Law* (1790–1791), in Kermit Hall and Mark David Hall, eds., *Collected Works of James Wilson*, 2 volumes (Indianapolis, 2007), 1:435. Note that Wilson also asserts here, like Jefferson, that "the American character ... has been eminently distinguished by the love of liberty, and the love of law" (432).
[94]  First Annual Message to Congress, January 8, 1790, in W.W. Abbot and Dorothy Twohig, eds., *Papers of George Washington, Presidential Series* (Charlottesville, VA, 1993), vol. 4:545.
[95]  Quincy and Sewell quoted in Reid, *Concept of Liberty*, 36.

stopping at the mean between the degradation born of oppression, on the one hand, and the excess of licentiousness, on the other. European immigrants to America would "bring with them the principles of the governments they leave, imbibed in their early youth," he wrote, and, "if able to throw them off, it will be in exchange for an unbounded licentiousness, passing, as is usual, from one extreme to another. It would be a miracle were they to stop precisely at the point of temperate liberty."[96] Indeed, the kind of liberty Americans were able to enjoy, Jefferson told John Adams, would, in France, "be instantly perverted to the demolition and destruction of every thing public and private."[97] Jefferson grew to be so enthusiastic about the possibilities for the maintenance of liberty in the American Republic precisely because, he believed, the dualistic American spirit he identified had equipped the American people to maintain liberty without allowing it to run – as it had in most other republics of history – into unlimited indulgence, anarchy, and, ultimately, tyranny.

Jefferson first became infatuated with this phenomenon during Shays's Rebellion. To a degree largely unremarked in the scholarly literature, Jefferson's confidence about the American experiment began with Shays's. Not his commitment to self-government, which he believed to be a natural God-given human right, but his sense that things were going to work out in the new nation. In the early 1780s, Jefferson had expressed anxiety about the ability of Americans to maintain their republics. In Query XIX of his *Notes on the State of Virginia*, Jefferson noted that it was the "manners and spirit of a people which preserve a republic in vigor."[98] But in the previous two sections, Jefferson had suggested that the "spirit of the people" might not be "an infallible, a permanent reliance." In fact, the "spirit of the times may alter, will alter. Our rulers will become corrupt, our people careless." After the Revolution, Jefferson expected things to go "down hill." Because "human nature," Jefferson noted, was "the same on every side of the Atlantic," it would not be unexpected for American political leaders to soon become enamored with the trappings of power. The people, he feared, would soon "forget themselves, but in the sole faculty of making money, and will never think of uniting to effect a due respect for their rights."[99]

If it was, in fact, the "manners and spirit of a people which preserve a republic in vigor," the next section of the *Notes* was even more frightening. It does not seem an accident that Jefferson chose the query about American "manners" to address slavery in Virginia. Much can be said (and has been written) about this short, deeply emotional passage, but what seems most striking about it in this context is how clearly Jefferson suggests that slavery more or less undermined everything he considered exceptional and superior about America. Slavery fostered and cultivated a hereditary aristocracy (with its attendant habits of tyranny), crushed rights, perverted morals, discouraged industry, and undermined

---

[96] *Notes*, 84–85.
[97] TJ to Adams, October 28, 1813, *AJL*, 391.
[98] *Notes*, 165.
[99] Ibid., 161, 121.

love of country.[100] Jefferson knew what Madison later acknowledged in private: "In proportion as slavery prevails in a State, the Government, however democratic in name, must be aristocratic in fact."[101]

Read together, these sections of the *Notes* form a depressing picture of the future of the United States – particularly in terms of developing the kind of public spirit sufficient to maintain republican government and rights. Here in the *Notes*, accordingly, Jefferson placed a good deal of hope in the efficacy of institutions to check a declining character in the public and its leaders. Because the spirit manifested during the Revolution might be temporary, and because the manners (of Virginians, anyway) were already suspect because of the very presence of slavery, institutional checks and balances seemed a proper remedy. "Better to keep the wolf out of the fold, than to trust to drawing his teeth and talons after he shall have entered." Surely "the time to guard against corruption and tyranny," then, "is before they shall have gotten hold on us."[102] Certainly it is not entirely inaccurate to suggest that Jefferson's obsession with the education of citizens and the cultivation of their moral character was rooted in his lack of "faith in institutional structures to preserve freedom."[103] But Jefferson's commitment to institutions as a check on human propensities ran deeper than this observation suggests, and, combined with his concerns that the Virginia Constitution had laid the groundwork for legislative despotism, these sections of the *Notes* suggest an early anxiety about American character that historians typically do not associate with Jefferson.[104]

Jefferson's ordinarily effusive optimism about the American future struggled, during these years, then, with a post-Revolutionary fear (shared by many) that Americans might lack the virtue requisite to the maintenance of self-government.[105] But Shays's Rebellion – which only confirmed such fears for so many American leaders – perversely appears to have done something extraordinary for Jefferson's confidence. Even as it drove most American leaders to embrace institutional checks on the public, Shays's infused Jefferson, by contrast, with a new confidence in the character of the American people and partially checked the resort to institutions he had encouraged in the *Notes*. Jefferson never lost his commitment to checks and balances or his concern that power was corrupting. On the contrary, he understood that even his "natural

---

[100] *Notes*, 162–163.

[101] "The Southern States of America, are on the same principle," Madison concluded, as "aristocracies." Madison's extraordinarily honest and revealing assessment was never published in his lifetime. See "Notes for the *National Gazette* Essays" [ca. December 19, 1791 – March 3, 1792], in *PJM* 14:163–164.

[102] *Notes*, 121.

[103] Lorraine Smith Pangle and Thomas Pangle, *The Learning of Liberty: The Educational Ideas of the American Founders* (Lawrence, 1993), 106.

[104] *Notes*, 120.

[105] See Gordon S. Wood, *The Creation of the American Republic* (Chapel Hill, 1969), 97–114, 413–425; Richard L. Bushman, *The Refinement of America: Persons, Houses, Cities* (New York, 1992), 186–203.

aristocracy" could quickly become a pack of "wolves" if left without the oversight of an attentive and enlightened public and institutional limitations on
power.[106] But he did come to think – to a degree that John Adams and many
later historians would find problematic – that the spirit of the public might
prove itself an efficacious, if not entirely sufficient, check on both tyranny from
above and anarchy from below. That such a public spirit had, in Jefferson's
view, been cultivated and sustained by institutions uniquely appropriate to the
United States suggests that the distinction scholars have posited between those
favoring institutional checks on public wickedness and those trusting public
virtue to sustain a republic may be too starkly drawn.[107] Jefferson believed in
institutions, but he gradually gained a confidence that those very institutions
might cultivate a public character that could be somewhat self-sustaining – that
might be counted on to uphold the integrity of those very institutions in turn.
Institutions and character could be mutually constitutive and reinforcing.

This insight first became prominent in his thought in the aftermath of Shays's.
John Jay's letter informing Jefferson of the turbulence in Massachusetts "really
affected me," he said. Jay told him that fear of anarchy had led many to question the capacity of republicanism to maintain security and order: The "rational and well-intentioned" and "more sober part of the people," Jay wrote, in
their quest "for Peace and Security," had even toyed with the re-establishment
of monarchy.[108] But a disarming letter from John Adams quickly restored
Jefferson's faith.[109] From then on, Jefferson seemed unconcerned, even non-
chalant about Shays's, telling some alarmed correspondents not to worry, that
"a little rebellion now and then" was a sign of public health: "I like to see the
people awake and alert."[110] He was now "persuaded," he wrote, "that the good
sense of the people will always be found to be the best army."[111]

The lesson Jefferson ultimately took from Shays's Rebellion was twofold:
one, that the American people were not lethargic but could be counted on
to sense and resist tyranny in their government; two, that the American people could be counted on to defend their republics when unlawful threats to
them appeared. This only seems paradoxical or contradictory. Jefferson never
endorsed the "motives" or methods of the insurgents, which he believed were
"founded in ignorance" and "produced acts absolutely unjustifiable." But he
insisted that the spirit of the rebels was to be cherished, even when it was dead
wrong, precisely because it would keep the government honest and good.[112]

---

[106] TJ to Edward Carrington, January 16, 1787, in *TJW*, 880–881.

[107] For a helpful corrective, see Rahe, "Between Trust and Distrust."

[108] John Jay to TJ, October 27, 1786, *PTJ* 10:488–489. On calls for the establishment of monarchy in Massachusetts, see David P. Szatmary, *Shays's Rebellion: The Making of an Agrarian
Insurrection* (Amherst, MA, 1980), 81–82.

[109] John Adams to TJ, November 30, 1786, in *PTJ* 10:557.

[110] To Abigail Adams, February 22, 1787, ibid., 11:174; To Abigail Adams, December 21, 1786,
ibid., 10:621. Also see TJ to Ezra Stiles, December 24, 1786, ibid., 10:629.

[111] TJ to Edward Carrington, January 16, 1787, ibid., 11:49.

[112] TJ to William Stephens Smith, November 13, 1787, in ibid., 12:356; TJ to Madison, January
30, 1787, ibid., 11:92. This combination of sympathy with some of the Shaysite grievances

But what Jefferson found truly encouraging about Shays's Rebellion was never the anarchy that so alarmed many of his correspondents, but that the people, in the end, had intervened to defuse it. The ultimate outcome of Shays's uprising, in fact, was "confidence in the firmness of our governments" because of the "interposition of the people themselves *on the side of government*."[113] Shays's was ultimately pacified in large part, Jefferson believed, because of the "discretion which the malcontents still preserved" – itself a telling sign of the nature of American public spirit. Similarly "tumultuous meetings" in Connecticut and New Hampshire were cut short because "the body of the people rose in support of government and obliged the malcontents to go to their homes."[114] Jefferson valued the people's attention to public affairs on both sides of the issue – the public spirit of the rebels (misinformed though it was) and the public spirit of those who supported law and order – and described both as manifestations of the American spirit.[115]

Shays's Rebellion gave Jefferson "no uneasiness" for a variety of reasons: from the vantage point of despotic Europe, a bit of resistance to authority looked positively refreshing to him – even as his location far from the events at hand distanced him from the palpable fear many of his correspondents experienced.[116] In any case, the reports he did have generally assured him that the "rebellion" was a misconceived (although somewhat justifiable) expression of discontent, rather than a full-scale assault on the constituted institutions of society.[117] "No injury was done," he noted, "in a single instance to the person or property of any one." The rebellion lasted, he said, less than twenty-four hours and ended largely because the "rebels" had enough public spirit to back off in the face of majority rejection of their proposals.[118] In Europe, much

with deploration of their methods Jefferson shared with perhaps most of the citizens of Massachusetts. See Richard D. Brown, "Shays's Rebellion and the Ratification of the Federal Constitution in Massachusetts," in Beeman, Botein, and Carter, eds., *Beyond Confederation*, 113–127, at 115.

[113] TJ to Edward Carrington, January 16, 1787, *PTJ* 11:49, emphasis added.

[114] TJ to William Carmichael, December 26, 1786, in ibid., 10:633. It is not clear that Jefferson's interpretation of the suppression of the rebellion is strictly accurate, but, as he clearly believed it to be so and reiterated it over and again, his view shaped his reading of the events. Whether we should consider Jefferson our authoritative historian of this episode is not particularly germane to the discussion here. David Szatmary argues that suppression came largely from the commercial interests and commercialized areas of the state, rather than from "the people" as a whole. See Szatmary, *Shays's Rebellion*, esp. 70–119. And Richard D. Brown notes the widespread revulsion at the Bowdin government's oppressive measures, even among the majority who were not insurrectionists. See Brown, "Shays's Rebellion and the Ratification."

[115] Compare Madison's later succinct point that in a successful republic the people "should watch over … as well as obey" the government it established. Madison, "Who are the Best Keepers of the People's Liberties?" *National Gazette*, December 22, 1792, *PJM* 14:426.

[116] TJ to James Madison, January 30, 1787, in *PTJ* 10:93.

[117] See, for example, John Adams to TJ, November 30, 1786, in ibid., 10:557.

[118] TJ to William Carmichael, December 26, 1786, in ibid., 633. On the targeted – and temperate – approach of the Shaysites, see Pauline Maier, "Popular Uprisings and Civil Authority in Eighteenth-Century America," *WMQ* 27 (January 1970), 17.

more "ferocious" insurrections occurred every few years; in Turkey, they "are the events of every day." "Compare" these bloody rebellions, he challenged Madison, with "the order, the moderation and the almost *self extinguishment* of ours."[119]

It is true that Jefferson had no real answer for Madison's concern that the rebels might simply use the next election to "promote their views under the auspices of Constitutional forms," thus becoming a despotic majority rather than a rebellious minority.[120] But Jefferson was fully aware that a people's elected legislature could become despotic: The "elective" nature of such tyranny would bring little comfort to its victims, he noted, which is why he endorsed a strict separation of powers in the 1780s.[121] He was not simpleminded on that issue. And it seems worth reiterating here that Jefferson was never sympathetic to the methods (as opposed to the suffering) of the rebels. The forcible closing of courts and violation of contract was never part of his program.[122] And Jefferson's track record on this score suggests that he agreed with Madison that stay laws were, in fact, as Madison would later put it memorably, "adverse to the rights of other citizens, or to the permanent and aggregate interests of the community."[123]

What ultimately separated Jefferson from many of his famous contemporaries, in other words, was not – as is commonly supposed – a lack of commitment

[119] To Madison, December 20, 1787, ibid., 12:442, emphasis added. Many years later, Jefferson similarly endorsed popular engagement with an appeal to "experience," challenging critics to "show me where the [American] people have done half the mischief in these forty years, that a single despot would have done in a single year; or show half the riots and rebellions, the crimes and the punishments, which have taken place in any single nation, under kingly government, during the same period," TJ to Samuel Kercheval, July 12, 1816, in *L&B* 15:35–36.

[120] Madison to TJ, April 23, 1787, in *ROL* 1:474. Also see the discussion in Wood, *Creation of the American Republic*, 412–413. The legislature attempted to undercut such a scenario by passing a "Disqualifying Act" that barred rebels from holding public office (and even voting). But Madison's fears proved to be largely unfounded, as new governor John Hancock, despite a change in tone, continued to pursue policies friendly to commercial interests (although the new legislature and Hancock himself proved much more conciliatory to the defeated rebels than the Bowdin administration). See Szatmary, *Shays's Rebellion*, 119; and Brown, "Shays's Rebellion and the Ratification," 116, 120–121.

[121] *Notes*, 120.

[122] As early as April 1786, after he and John Adams met with a delegation of British merchants to discuss prewar debts owed to them in the United States, Jefferson had written Madison that he "wish[ed] extremely" that the states would open the courts to British creditors and institute a program for repayment (See TJ to Madison, April 25, 1786, in *ROL* 1:417). Jefferson – even though deeply in debt to those very merchants – acknowledged the justice of the Paris Peace Treaty's provision that American debts be paid in full (but not that of the 5% interest demanded by British merchants), and he never balked, later, at the Constitution's protection of contract and strictures against state issues of paper money (On this subject, see, Herbert Sloan, *Principle and Interest*, esp. 32–49). Also, late in life, Jefferson noted that issues of paper and violation of contract were the only cases in which the national government had legitimate jurisdiction over conflict between citizens of a single State (see TJ to William Johnson, June 12, 1823, in *TJW*, 1475).

[123] Madison, "Number 10," in J.R. Pole, ed., The *Federalist* (Indianapolis, 2005), 48.

to strong government and order but, instead, a willingness to trust the capacity of the American people to preserve order without running headlong into anarchy. Alexander Hamilton, by contrast, was relatively unconcerned about popular lethargy – his political science assumed it, and he was not particularly anxious about it.[124] John Adams, on the other hand, did worry about it. Who else but the people could check the unbridled power of the aristocracy? But Adams was not ever able to persuade himself convincingly that the people were capable of overcoming the demagoguery that would be practiced by the aristocracy – and, indeed, Adams's solution was partially to simply run with what he believed to be human nature. As he argued in his *Discourses on Davila*, the cultivation of the aristocracy by titles and emoluments would both attract the natural craving of the aristocracy for distinction (and, thus, harness its talents for use by the state) and reinforce the natural propensity of the populace to fawn and submit to good government.[125] But partly because such an arrangement would leave the people defenseless against "these great families," Adams rested a good deal of his hope for the new republic in a strong executive (leading many, including Jefferson, to mistake him for a monarchist).[126] The point was, Adams noted, that "education, as well as religion, aristocracy, as well as democracy and monarchy, are singly, totally inadequate to the business of restraining the passions of men, of preserving a steady government, and protecting the lives, liberties, and properties of the people." Why? Because "religion, superstition, oaths, education, laws, all give way before passions, interest, and power, which can be resisted only by passions, interest, and power."[127]

What distinguished Jefferson from either Hamilton or Adams in this regard was that he, like Adams (and unlike Hamilton), valued the engagement of the people. But unlike Adams, Jefferson believed that the American people were uniquely capable of engagement while preserving order and good government. This helps explain his initial reaction to the Constitution. The Philadelphia Convention, he told William Smith (Adams's son-in-law), had been "too much impressed by the insurrection of Massachusetts: and in the spur of the moment they are setting up a kite to keep the hen-yard in order."[128] This statement has often been understood to signal Jefferson's opposition to a national state, on the one hand, and his celebration of rebellion, on the other. To be sure, in the same letter, Jefferson exclaimed: "God forbid we should ever be 20 years without such a rebellion." But if we focus on the effusion we are apt to be misled. The key word in this famous line is *such*, a word that leads us back to Jefferson's interpretation of Shays's. However misconceived, he told Smith, the whole episode demonstrated the people's engagement: both their willingness to

---

[124] See Rahe, *Republics Ancient and Modern*, 699.

[125] Adams, *Discourses on Davila*, in *WJA*, 6:243–244, 250–251.

[126] See Richard Alan Ryerson, "John Adams, Republican Monarchist: An Inquiry into the Origins of his Constitutional Thought," in Eliga Gould and Peter S. Onuf, eds., *Empire and Nation: The American Revolution in the Atlantic World* (Baltimore, 2005), 72–92.

[127] Adams, *Defence of the Constitutions of the United States*, in *WJA* 4:557–558.

[128] TJ to Smith, November 13, 1787, *PTJ* 12:355–357.

challenge to what they believed to be a threat to their liberty, and their defense of what they ultimately believed would secure it: republican government.

Popular government was, Jefferson acknowledged, subject to what he admitted to be the "evil" of "turbulence." And while it is certainly true that Jefferson feared, as he put it, quiet slavery ("quietam servitutem") more than tumultuous liberty ("periculosam libertatem"), his choice of evils was made much simpler by his conviction that American popular spirit seemed largely limited to the kind of vigilance that was "productive of good:" preventing "the degeneracy of government" and nourishing "a general attention to the public affairs."[129]

Before the Revolution, Jefferson described the Boston Tea Party in just such terms. "There are extraordinary situations which require extraordinary interposition," he wrote in 1774. "An exasperated people, who feel that they possess power, are not easily restrained within limits strictly regular." For Jefferson, this kind of popular action, under the right circumstances – "extraordinary situations" – was a positive force. And, as with Shays's, Jefferson believed, the people "out of doors" were, in this instance, remarkably restrained. The destruction of the tea was accompanied without "any other act of violence." The difference, of course, was that in the case of the Tea Party, government response was tyrannical and unrepentant, thus invoking more drastic measures on the part of the people. After all, he wrote, "if the pulse of the people shall beat calmly under this experiment [the Coercive Acts that followed the Tea Party], another and another will be tried, till the measure of despotism be filled up."[130]

But unlike the Tea Party, which had ended in revolution, Jefferson believed that Shays's had been quelled by popular defense of government and order once the people understood the truth about their situation. In other words, the spirit of resistance he so "cherish[ed]" had also, in this case, diffused the rebellion and should not, he believed, become an excuse for setting up an unnecessary check on popular spirit that was, after all, he believed, quite capable of righting itself, given adequate and accurate information. The context of Jefferson's letter to Smith – and what sets up his famous "endorsement" of Shays's Rebellion – is his concern about "lies" in the European press "about our being in anarchy." Jefferson wrote Smith to dispel these distortions (or willful misrepresentations), registering his astonishment that even Americans could have come to believe them. The only disturbance he could see was Shays's, and history had

---

[129] TJ to Madison, January 30, 1787, in *ROL* 2:461. This letter speaks in universal terms: "Rebellions" are "necessary in the political world," and "nature has formed man" for mild governments. But a close reading suggests that these declarations apply not to people living under "governments of force: as is the case in all other monarchies [excepting England] and in most of the other republics," but to those in two republics only: "England in a slight degree, and in our states in a great one." Only in America (and somewhat less so in England), in other words, had historical circumstances prepared a people capable of handling republican liberty. For further thoughts on Jefferson's placement of England in this hierarchy, see note 42 in this chapter.

[130] Thomas Jefferson, "Draft of Instructions to the Virginia Delegates in the Continental Congress" [July 1774] ("A Summary View of the Rights of British America"), in *PTJ* 1:127–128.

not produced any other "instance of rebellion so honourably conducted."[131] What kind of rebellion was Shays's? One manifesting the "spirit of resistance" to be sure, but one conducted more or less decently and in order – one that quickly disbursed upon majority rejection of its goals.[132]

This is what Jefferson found so remarkable. Theorists like Adams would continue to wrestle with complex schemes – checks and balances, powerful executive authority, and the cultivation of a hereditary aristocracy – to harness the spirit of the people without unleashing its dangerous potential for anarchy. For Jefferson, in the euphoria of the moment, the search seemed largely over by 1787. By then, he had seen enough to convince him that the American people had proven themselves capable of resisting tyranny without running headlong into unnecessary licentiousness or insurrection. What Shays's Rebellion seemed to teach Jefferson was that the American public was not indefinitely malleable by demagoguery; that it would not be building a house on sand to rest the state's foundations in the national will – at least in America where the people were independent, informed, and alert. Jefferson's excitement about this extraordinary fact is palpable. This could very well be the political discovery of the ages: a people whose very character allowed them to harness all the positive good embodied in popular vigilance while checking its tendency (throughout history) to run amok to the very destruction of popular government and the re-establishment of despotic states. Unlike "governments of force," which included even "most … republics," American governments, Jefferson seemed to suggest, *could* be "mild in their punishment of rebellions" – not "discourag[ing] them too much" – precisely because there was ultimately little to fear from such a people (at least for "honest republican governors"). In America, popular vigilance – even when it "produced" individual incidents that were "absolutely unjustifiable" – actually could be encouraged as a healing "medicine necessary for the sound health of government" or a "storm" cleansing the atmosphere, rather than suppressed for fear of its potential for destruction.

Jefferson would come to see his reading confirmed again and again. This same spirit of engagement that both animated and quelled Shays's Rebellion, as Jefferson would never tire of telling his correspondents, would later both toss the Federalists out of power in 1800 and snuff out threats to the Union during Jefferson's presidency and beyond. And, years later, when the electorate threw out most of the Fourteenth Congress in one of the biggest legislative turnovers in American history, Jefferson declared himself "highly pleased with this proof of the innate good sense, the vigilance, and the determination of the people to act for themselves." The public response was particularly compelling because

---

[131]  TJ to Smith, November 13, 1787, *PTJ* 12:355–357.

[132]  Again, Jefferson is not the best historian to consult for a paper on Shays's Rebellion. The majority of citizens of Massachusetts were neither Shaysites nor enthusiastic supporters of government policies that led to the uprising or to its suppression. The government ultimately used military force (rather than public opinion) to squash the rebellion. But Jefferson was not wrong that the entire episode rejuvenated an incredible interest and engagement in politics. For this argument and evidence, see Brown, "Shays's Rebellion and the Ratification," 120–123.

the people had been largely let down by a "silent" press and were "unled by their leaders." In other words, the American people, without any encouragement from an "enlightened" leadership or informative press, had proven themselves capable of discerning and acting in their own interest.[133] These periodical episodes of popular vigilance simply reinforced what Jefferson had told English radical Richard Price in 1785: that the happiness of American government, "wherein the people are truly the mainspring," was "that [it was] never to be despaired of." Why? Because, "when an evil becomes so glaring as to strike them generally, they arrouse themselves, and it is redressed."[134]

So Jefferson valued this "spirit of resistance," but his was hardly a precursor to Mao's "permanent revolution." What made Jefferson's response to Shays's Rebellion unusual was not his bloodlust for rebellion, but his equanimity in the face of danger to public order from the democracy. Many have considered his a naïve, even irresponsible, position, but Jefferson thought that he had very good empirical evidence to support his view, evidence that public order – which he deeply valued – was safe with Americans mobilized and engaged in political activity. Jefferson's certainty was rooted in his sense that the American "spirit" also manifested itself as a commitment to American institutions. In fact, popular vigilance was not incompatible with such a commitment. To the contrary, the United States had the "strongest Government on earth" precisely because the American citizen, "at the call of the law, would fly to the standard of the law, and would meet invasions of the public order as his own personal concern."[135] In notes he took for his first inaugural address, Jefferson expressed hope that the "distinctive mark of an American" would be that "in cases of commotion he enlists himself under no man's banner, enquires for no man's name but repairs to the standard of the laws."[136] Alexis de Tocqueville later echoed Jefferson, noting that "each individual" in America had "a personal interest in seeing to it that everyone obeys the law." Because everyone ("apart from slaves, servants, and paupers"[137]) was allowed to vote, an attack on the laws must "either change the nation's opinion or trample upon its will." In America, Tocqueville posited, "the common man has an exalted idea of political rights because he has such rights."[138] Jefferson put it more colorfully: "Where every

<hr>

133 TJ to Gallatin, June 16, 1817, ibid., 15:132. On the Fourteenth Congress, see Charles Sellers, *The Market Revolution: Jacksonian America, 1815–1848* (New York, 1991), 104–107.

134 TJ to Price, February 1, 1785, in *TJW*, 798.

135 First Inaugural Address, March 4, 1801, in *TJW*, 493. As Paul A. Rahe has noted, even Antifederalists distanced themselves from Shays: see Rahe, *Republics Ancient and Modern*, 698, 1100, n. 44. For a different view, focused on ratification in Massachusetts, see Brown, "Shays's Rebellion and the Ratification."

136 "Notes for First Inaugural Address," in *FE* 9:193.

137 Tocqueville apparently took it for granted that his readers would understand that women were not allowed the franchise.

138 Tocqueville, *Democracy in America*, trans. Arthur Goldhammer (New York, 2004), 273–277. Also see TJ to Samuel Kercheval, July 12, 1816, in *L&B* 15:37–38, and Isaac Krammnick, ed., Tocqueville, *Democracy in America*, trans. Henry Reeve (New York, 2007), 259: An American, Tocqueville wrote, can "inform you what his rights are, and by what means he exercises them; he

man ... feels that he is a participator in the government of affairs ... he will let the heart be torn out of his body sooner than his power be wrested from him by a Caesar or a Bonaparte."[139] When the law is the people's handiwork, the people will obey it and rise to defend it.

This is precisely the way Jefferson later explained the diffusion of Aaron Burr's conspiracy before it could really do any damage. The very moment Jefferson "apprised our citizens that there were traitors among them, and what was their object, they rose upon them wherever they lurked, and crushed by their own strength what would have produced the march of armies and civil war in any other country. The government which can wield the arm of the people must be the strongest possible." The lesson of the Burr Conspiracy, then, Jefferson argued, was "that we are a people capable of self-government, and worthy of it."[140] "The suppression of the late conspiracy by the hand of the people, uplifted to destroy it whenever it reared its head," Jefferson effused, "manifests their fitness for self-government, and the power of a nation, of which every individual feels that his own will is a part of the public authority."[141]

It is easy to see why the election of 1800, from Jefferson's perspective, was, although perhaps the most profound manifestation of the American spirit, not altogether an unexpected one. Throughout the 1790s, Jefferson believed, the Republic had been threatened by "a sect" designed to overturn the Revolution and lead America to monarchy. Early on, Jefferson had assumed that the Federalists were "preachers without followers" because the "people are firm and constant in their republican purity."[142] But during the war scare with France (1798–1799), the same public sent Federalist majorities to Congress. Jefferson consistently explained Federalist popularity as the temporary result of deliberate manipulation and fearmongering. Jefferson's dilemma during the 1790s was how to legitimately resist the Federalists while they seemed to have the public imprimatur; without, in other words, seeming to threaten properly constituted government itself.

Ultimately, Jefferson distinguished "between acts against the *government*, and acts against the *Oppressions of the Government*." "The latter" (acts resisting government tyranny) he insisted, "are virtues."[143] Accordingly, Jefferson

will be able to point out the customs which obtain in the political world. You will find that he is well acquainted with the rules of the administration, and that he is familiar with the mechanism of the laws. The citizen of the United States does not acquire his practical science and his positive notions from books.... *The American learns to know the laws by participating in the act of legislation; and he takes a lesson in the forms of government, from governing*" (emphasis added).

[139] TJ to Joseph C. Cabell, February 2, 1816, in *L&B* 14:422. The irony of this passage is that Jefferson's primary example of this spirit was New England's resistance to the Embargo.

[140] To Isaac Weaver, June 7, 1807, ibid., 11:220–221. For a similar, earlier, assertion, see TJ to C.W.F. Dumas, September 10, 1787, in *PTJ* 12:113.

[141] To the Representatives of the people of New Jersey in their Legislature, December 10, 1807, ibid., 16:295.

[142] TJ to Lafayette, June 16, 1792, *PTJ* 24:85.

[143] Report on A Convention with Spain, March 22, 1792, in *FE* 6:447–448. Also see Jefferson's nuanced conception of the Republican opposition in TJ to Thomas Pinckney, December 3, 1792, in *PTJ* 24:697.

rejected the Federalist charge that the Republicans were in "opposition to the government." Hamilton and others were engaging in sophistry and obfuscation, "endeavoring to turn on the government itself those censures I meant for the *enemies* of the government to wit those who want to change it into a monarchy."[144] The same people could resist government tyranny while remaining committed to a properly constituted government, and the Federalists, he believed, were disingenuous to suggest otherwise. This is one reason Jefferson counseled patience to fellow Republicans sickened by Federalist measures. Jefferson worried that Federalist behavior might energize some Republicans to actual "insurrection," but "nothing," Jefferson warned, "could be so fatal." Such, he warned (perhaps remembering Shays's Rebellion), was "not the kind of opposition the American people will permit." Outright rebellion at such a time would have an effect opposite the intentions of its enthusiasts: It "would check the progress of the public opinion and rally them round the government." Based on his reading of earlier episodes in American history, Jefferson remained willing to wait out the good sense of the people. One lesson he held on to from Shays's was that the people "may be led astray for a moment, but will soon correct themselves."[145] This was Jefferson's consistent mantra throughout the 1790s also. A little patience and the people would rally, the "reign of witches" would pass, and the Republic would be saved.[146]

Of course, this narrative depicting a spontaneous rallying of the American citizenry left out a good deal of politicking. Nevertheless, Jefferson believed that the people had responded well; his election proved once again how compatible a spirit of resistance to tyranny was with a "love of order and obedience to the laws" in America.[147] This evidence of public opinion as manifested in elections confirmed Jefferson's hopes in 1800. The election was Jefferson's evidence that he had been right: The American people really were enlightened after all; they really were able to distinguish truth from fiction and separate the Republican "wheat" from the Federalist "chaff."[148] It seemed to ratify his confidence that the American nation would always "oblige its agents to reform the principles and practices of their administration" in a manner consistent with American principles and character. American leadership would, of necessity, conform to the will of the American people.[149] Near the end of his life,

---

[144] TJ to Madison, May 9, 1791, in *ROL* 2:688, emphasis added. See Madison's elaboration of the same argument in his reply of May 12, 1791, ibid., 688–689.

[145] TJ to Edward Carrington, January 16, 1787, *PTJ* 11:49.

[146] See, among others, TJ to John Taylor, June 1, 1798, *L&B* 10:44–47; To James Lewis, Jr., May 9, 1798, in ibid., 37; To Elbridge Gerry, Jan. 26, 1799, in ibid., 80–83; To Thaddeus Kosciusko, Feb. 21, 1799, in ibid., 115–116; To Robert R. Livingston, February 28, 1799, ibid., 118–119; To Thomas Lomax, March 12, 1799, in *PTJ* 31:77–78; To William Green Munford, June 18, 1799, in *TJW*, 1065; To Priestley, January 27, 1800, in *L&B* 10:148; To Thomas Mann Randolph, Feb, 2, 1800, ibid., 151; To Rush, September 23, 1800, *PTJ* 32:167–168; To John Dickinson, March 6, 1801, in ibid., 33:196; To James Warren, March 21, 1801, in ibid., 398.

[147] TJ to Benjamin Waring, March 23, 1801, in *L&B* 10:235.

[148] TJ to John Adams, October 28, 1813, in *AJL*, 388.

[149] TJ to Elbridge Gerry, January 26, 1799, in *L&B* 10:82.

Jefferson remembered how the Federalist desire for monarchy had been, as he put it, "completely foiled by the universal spirit of the nation."[150] It was this spirit that Jefferson had counted on to preserve the Republic, and when it finally happened, he could barely contain his enthusiasm. "We can no longer say there is nothing new under the sun," he gushed to Joseph Priestley shortly after his victory. "For this whole chapter in the history of man is new. The great extent of our Republic is new. Its sparse habitation is new. The mighty wave of public opinion which has rolled over it is new." The Federalists, including President Adams himself, had nearly brought down the curtain on the American enlightenment, Jefferson suggested, pretending "to praise and encourage education" but only "the education of our ancestors," rejecting "all advances in science" and proclaiming that we could never "go beyond" those ancestors "in real science."[151] This Federalist endorsement of the past as the repository of all wisdom, Jefferson had earlier predicted to Priestley, was "not an idea which this country will endure."[152] And, indeed, the election seemed to fulfill the prophecy: The people had "recovered from delusion" with "order & good sense."[153]

Many years after the fact, John Adams ran across this letter to Priestley when it was published – to Jefferson's embarrassment – in a memoir that Adams was reading.[154] He demanded that Jefferson explain himself, playfully mocking Jefferson's effusive encomium to the "mighty wave of public opinion" in the face of near-universal evidence that such was incapable of sustaining good government. "Oh! Mr. Jefferson! What a Wave of public Opinion has rolled over the Universe? ... What 'a wave' has rolled over Christendom for 1500 years? What a Wave has rolled over France for 1500 Years supporting in Power and Glory the Dinasty of Bourbon? What a Wave supported the House of Austria? What a Wave has supported the Dinasty of Mahomet, for 1200 Years? ... What a Wave has the French Revolution spread?"[155] Adams's humor accompanies his wisdom in this correspondence, but he misunderstood Jefferson's point (and his wisdom has misled numerous historians into believing that his position accurately contrasts with Jefferson's). Jefferson did not trust the "mighty wave of public opinion" that swept over France during the Terror, or any of the other waves Adams described. He trusted the public opinion of a particular people, enlightened and uniquely suited for democratic governance. What was new "under the sun" about the election of 1800 was not that a population rose up to affect world affairs, nor even that a government had elicited popular

---

[150] To Judge William Johnson, June 12, 1823, in *L&B* 15:443. Also see TJ to Benjamin Rush, January 16, 1811: "The nation at length passed condemnation on the political principles of the federalists."

[151] TJ to Priestley, March 21, 1801, in *TJW*, 1086.

[152] TJ to Priestley, January 27, 1800, in *L&B* 10:148.

[153] TJ to Priestley, March 21, 1801, in *TJW*, 1086.

[154] See Adams to TJ, May 29, 1813, June 10, 1813, and Jefferson's somewhat embarrassed response on June 15 in *AJL*, 325–327, 331–333, along with the editorial note on page 288.

[155] Adams to TJ, June 14, 1813, in *AJL*, 330.

support, but that this American people proved itself so capable of sorting out truth from fiction, indeed, capable of governing itself. "The most pleasing novelty" of the day, Jefferson had told Priestley, was that the "mighty wave of public opinion" had "so quickly subsid[ed] over such an extent of surface to it's true level again." The Republic would last precisely because the entire episode had manifested – once again – a "strength of character in our nation" that no other political theorists in history had been able to count on.[156]

Jefferson's enthusiasm about what he later called the "Revolution of 1800" was all the greater precisely because that election confirmed what he had long claimed about the American people. For the first time in human history, Jefferson believed, the democracy had defended its rights and upheld liberty without giving in to the unbridled passion that had always doomed republics in the past. No longer, he asserted, would "the barbarians" find it a simple matter to "bring back the times … when ignorance put everything into the hands of power & priestcraft." As they had time and again, the American people had recovered "from delusion," and it was the "order & good sense displayed in this recovery" – that dual manifestation of American spirit – "which augurs well for the duration of our Republic." The election of 1800 rendered Jefferson "much better satisfied now of [the Republic's] stability than I was before it was tried."[157]

In short, as Jefferson put it to Lafayette years later, "the yeomanry of the United States are not the canaille of Paris." They were "very different materials" from the rabble of European cities. The "cement of this Union is in the heart-blood of every American," and there was no other government on earth "established on so immovable a basis."[158]

## AMERICAN EXCEPTIONALISM?

If Marx is properly considered the father of modern sociology, the Scottish writers Jefferson absorbed in his youth (not to mention their teacher, Montesquieu) were at least as sensitive to the way historical and social conditions could explain wild variations in the expression of human nature.[159] As William Robertson, famed Scottish historian, put it, "the human mind, whenever it is placed in the same situation, will, in ages the most distant, and in countries the most remote, assume the same form, and be distinguished by the same manners."[160] Jefferson did not imagine that Americans were somehow exempt

---

[156] TJ to Priestley, March 21, 1801, in *TJW*, 1086.

[157] TJ to Joseph Priestley, March 21, 1801, in *TJW*, 1085–1086. Also see a similar expression in TJ to John Tyler, June 28, 1804, in *L&B* 11:33.

[158] TJ to Lafayette, February 14, 1815, in *L&B* 14:252.

[159] See Richard B. Sher, "From Troglodytes to Americans: Montesquieu and the Scottish Enlightenment on Liberty, Virtue, and Commerce," in David Wootton, ed., *Republicanism, Liberty, and Commercial Society, 1649–1776* (Stanford, 1994), 368–402, 477–481.

[160] See David Armitage, "The New World and British Historical Thought: From Richard Hakluyt to William Robertson," in Karen Ordahl Kupperman, ed., *America in European Consciousness,*

from the laws of human nature, and he believed with many American thinkers, including Adams, that only a long habituation in the practice and experience of liberty could render a people capable of enjoying and maintaining it. What distinguished him was his belief that American social and historical experience had made a democratic American politics possible and proper. It was this peculiar arrangement of influences on American character – environment, social practices, institutions, history – that he believed had produced a character unique in human history. Perhaps, on some level, then, there was a "special providence for America" after all. It was not the nature of Americans that made them different from other peoples nurtured in the same environment. Their unique history and environment produced a unique character capable of unique political practices. All other peoples ought to share these blessings, but they would need first to share American experiences.

Jefferson often spoke in universal terms when he reflected on what he actually considered American peculiarities: "Man is a rational animal," he told William Johnson in 1823, "endowed by nature with rights, and with an innate sense of justice." Accordingly, an individual human being "could be restrained from wrong and protected in right, by moderate powers, confided to persons of his own choice, and held to their duties by dependence on his own will."[161] But here Jefferson was endorsing a kind of politics he believed possible, at that time, only in America. Federalists had been wrong precisely because they thought that a government of force was applicable in America also. But it was precisely the American exception that animated the Republican Party's prescriptions for the United States and that, in turn, limited or qualified the use of such a politics in other places, for the time being. Such a politics was appropriate in historically and socially specific places only. Reiterating a contrast he returned to again and again, Jefferson asserted that Americans had been "impressed from their cradle" with the "sacredness of [the] law" of majority rule as the "fundamental law of nature, by which alone self government can be exercised by a society." The people of France, on the other hand, were "not yet in the habit of acknoleging ... *lex majoris partis*" and had "never been in the habit of self-government." As a result, they were evidentially willing to acquiesce in minority dominance of the "Directory & council of 500." With Americans, on the other hand, Jefferson suggested, self-government was "almost innate." And it was "this single circumstance" that "may possibly decide the fate of the two nations." National fate rested on national history and the corresponding habit of a national people.[162] The presence of the past was oppressive in France but liberating in America. Jefferson could be so positive about the American future

---

*1493–1750* (Chapel Hill, 1995), 63–64. Robertson, writes Armitage, suggested that the discovery of America made modern history possible for the first time because it allowed philosophers to contemplate "humanity in the full span of its development, from rude hunter-gatherer to polite modern European" (66–67).

[161] TJ to Johnson, June 12, 1823, in *TJW*, 1470–1471.
[162] TJ to John Breckinridge, January 29, 1800, in ibid., 1074.

precisely because he thought in terms of national (rather than merely universal) histories.[163]

Everything that Jefferson said about what was possible in (and right for) America has to be understood within this context. If "human nature [was] the same on every side of the Atlantic," as Jefferson once put it, that same human nature would, he said, "be alike influenced by the same causes," causes that would prepare different peoples for the best regimes at different times.[164] America, for Jefferson, had become a place of unique possibility. This fundamental insight enabled both Jefferson's hopeful domestic politics and his realpolitik in foreign policy.

Typically associated with an endorsement of the universal rights of man (and this is not wrong, only in need of qualification), Jefferson was much more attuned to national particularities than the Federalists who, paradoxically perhaps, became the real champions of the "unity of universal human experience."[165] This was why the Federalists, Jefferson argued, in a particularly telling phrase, had worked "to recover … in practice the powers which the nation had refused" – setting themselves up as "authorities independent of [the people's] will," working to "maintain their privileged orders in splendor and idleness, to fascinate the eyes of the people, and excite in them an humble adoration and submission, as to an order of superior beings." The Federalists attempted this move to reestablish in America "the doctrines of Europe" precisely because they extrapolated from the universal human experience to that point in history without taking into account the unique experience of the United States.[166] And the American nation, Jefferson argued, rejected their politics precisely because that very experience, he believed, had prepared them for new and greater possibilities than political theorists of the past could reasonably expect from other peoples.

Jefferson began with the universal and natural rights of man, but because, as he put it, the "habits of the governed determine in a great degree what is practicable," these "*same original principles*, modified in practice according to the different habits of different nations, present governments of very

---

[163] There is a more pessimistic way to read Jefferson on this. Although it may seem counterintuitive, Jefferson's scheme assumes a profound sense of human limitations in the face of social forces that circumscribe human behavior. See the interesting suggestion in Gerald Stourzh, *Alexander Hamilton and the Idea of Republican Government* (Stanford, 1970), 177, 181. It was Hamilton, not Jefferson, who assumed that the "outstanding individual" might rise above his social circumstances.

[164] *Notes*, 121.

[165] See Joyce Appleby, "The New Republican Synthesis and the Changing Political Ideas of John Adams," *American Quarterly* 25 (1973), 578–595, quotation at 592. In this sense, Jefferson, paradoxically, was more attuned to the vicissitudes of history than the Federalists who he consistently derided as mired in the past.

[166] TJ to Justice William Johnson, June 12, 1823, in *TJW*, 1470. See also TJ to Benjamin Rush, January 16, 1811, in *PTJ, Retirement Series* 3:305: Hamilton believed "in the necessity of either force or corruption to govern men," a deplorable lack of imagination or attention to American realities, in Jefferson's view.

different aspects."[167] This goes some distance toward reconciling Jefferson's universalism (and his grounding of rights and political freedoms in nature) with his American exceptionalism (rooted, as it was, in history) and renders apparent only the tension between his Enlightenment embrace of endless progress and his understanding of the historicity of institutions and human experience. *Nation* and *history* were concepts in his thought that complicate and qualify what is too often read as his illimitable optimism about the inevitability of progress. Jefferson was never hubristic enough to assume that "the human condition will ever advance to such a state of perfection as that there shall no longer be pain or vice in the world."[168] Even American institutions, he proposed, would require modification to keep pace with the "progress of the human mind."[169] But if the human condition was, as Jefferson believed, "susceptible of much improvement, and, most of all, in matters of government and religion," it was clearly in America, Jefferson believed, that this improvement had proceeded the farthest to that point in human history, thus making other kinds of unique ventures, including a democratic politics and the prosecution of an empire of liberty rather than conquest, possible.[170] In retrospect, then, it would be difficult for Jefferson to envision the future offering any significant improvement in the fundamental design Americans had come close to perfecting, a model that would, he believed, have transformative effects on world history.

And yet, although Jefferson's America was the norm against which other nations could measure their historical development, it was, in fact, no "exception" to the laws of nature and of nations that governed other peoples; his "American exceptionalism" (if indeed that is the most accurate phrase with which to describe his position) indicates a kind of superiority, but only relative to the progress of other peoples to that point in time, not fixed and exclusive for all time.[171] America itself was not guaranteed this advanced position in the absence of the particular historical and social conditions that made it possible.

---

[167] TJ to Du Pont, January 18, 1802, in Malone, ed., *Correspondence Between Jefferson and Du Pont*, 40 (emphasis added). "The same principles reduced to forms of practice accommodated to our habits, and put into forms accommodated to the habits of the French nation," Jefferson went on to say, "would present governments very unlike each other."

[168] TJ to Du Pont, April 24, 1816, in ibid., 186. But see TJ to William Ludlow, September 6, 1824, in *TJW*, 1497: "Barbarism has, in the meantime, been receding before the steady step of amelioration; and will in time, I trust, disappear from the earth."

[169] TJ to Samuel Kercheval, July 12, 1816, in *TJW*, 1401.

[170] TJ to Du Pont, April 24, 1816, in Malone ed., *Correspondence Between Jefferson and Du Pont*, 186.

[171] See the important reflections on the nature of this problem in Daniel Rodgers, "Exceptionalism," in Anthony Molho and Gordon S. Wood, eds., *Imagined Histories: American Historians Interpret the Past* (Princeton, 1998), 21–40, esp. 22–23, and Eric Foner, "Why is there no Socialism in the United States?" in *History Workshop Journal* 17 (1984), 57–80. Also see Carl N. Degler, "In Pursuit of an American History," in *AHR* 92 (February 1987), 1–12; and Michael McGerr, "The Price of the New Transnational History," in *AHR* 96 (October 1991), 1056–1067.

American experience was partly fortuitous: The American people "could not have been so fairly put into the hands of their own common sense had they not been separated from their parent stock & kept from contamination, either from them, or the other people of the old world, by the intervention of so wide an ocean." But Americans also had had to make something out of that gift, and he saw a need for the perpetuation of those circumstances through a statecraft that would preserve union and expand territory for landed settlement as well as institute social policies conducive to the "diffusion of knowledge among the people," which was the only "sure foundation ... for the preservation of freedom and happiness."[172]

As he told Joseph Priestley, American "self-preservation" would last only "till a change of circumstances shall take place." And, although he did not consider such a change "within prospect at any definite period," such a change was, of course, theoretically possible.[173] After all, "the finest parts of the old world," he noted in the 1780s, "are now dead in a great degree, to commerce, to arts, to science, & to society." The most advanced of civilizations, in other words, which had pioneered commerce, arts, and the sciences, had simply vanished as significant shapers of world events. "Greece, Syria, Egypt & the northern coast of Africa constituted the whole world almost for the Romans, and to us they are scarcely known, scarcely accessible at all."[174] It was particularly worrisome to Jefferson near the end of his life, then, that some Americans, particularly those in the Northeast, seemed to be losing the characteristics that had made democratic politics possible in the United States – a worry that irritated his otherwise cosmic optimism throughout his career.

So America provided a legitimate and optimistic example for the rest of the world, on the one hand, but not one that was easily or accidentally attainable or perpetually sustainable without sufficient attention to character and institutions. So Jefferson had both a remarkably hopeful sense of human potentialities as well as a sober assessment of the historical conditions necessary to secure the human freedom and happiness that rightfully belonged to all but were actually enjoyed by relatively few. In short, Jefferson was optimistic that the future could be different from the past, not that it necessarily would be.[175] The source of his hope was not the inevitability of endless progress but rather the historical moment in which America

---

[172] TJ to George Wythe, August 13, 1786, in *PTJ* 10:244.

[173] TJ to Priestley, March 21, 1801, in *TJW*, 1086.

[174] TJ to John Brown, May 26, 1788, in *FE* 5:400.

[175] For an important corrective to this image of Jefferson, see also Johann Neem, "The Early Republic: Thomas Jefferson's Philosophy of History and the Future of American Christianity," in Charles Mathewes and Christopher McKnight Nichols, eds., *Prophesies of Godlessness: Predictions of America's Imminent Secularization, from the Puritans to the Present Day* (New York, 2008), 35–52, esp., 41–42. Also see Maurizio Valsania, "'Our Original Barbarism': Man vs. Nature in Thomas Jefferson's Moral Experience," *Journal of the History of Ideas* 65 (2004), 627–645.

happened to find itself and his sense that Americans so shaped by that experience could sustain its promise.

It seems worth reiterating here by way of clarification that the nation was never an end in itself in Jefferson's thought. First, as we have seen, the cultivation of national sentiment in America was legitimate, from his perspective, precisely because there alone was devotion to nation inextricably bound up with universal values, with moral concerns that transcended national boundaries.[176] Nicholas Onuf and Peter Onuf have also suggested that Jefferson actually anticipated that a world of republican nations would one day merge into a "world society" of "perpetual peace." In this sense, they argue, "the nation's [ultimate] destiny was to simply disappear." But Jefferson's geopolitical realism assured him (sadly) that such a time was not to be expected in the near future. For now, the American union of peaceful states would "prefigure" the eventual "union of all societies" but would not imagine away history and the "rivers of blood" that must flow before this end was realized. Just as "the enormities of the times" drew Jefferson away from the "tranquil pursuits of science" and into public affairs, so his reading of history and current events led him, of necessity, to a nationalist stance in a world in which America alone was the representative of universal ideals.[177] For now, then, America could live at peace only by preparing for war to secure its national destiny, bound up as it was, with that of the world. Jefferson imagined a cosmopolitan (almost utopian) future, but he lived – and practiced statesmanship – in history.[178] And this demanded a realistic assessment of America's unique role in world history and fuelled Jefferson's sense that American self-preservation would secure the world's future, or, negatively, that the "suicide" of America would be "treason against the hopes of the world."[179]

For now, Jefferson argued repeatedly, it was in America that humans were actually freed up to fulfill their natural potential for self-government. Only in America, Jefferson asserted over and again, were citizens free to assent to truth without minds clouded by generations of despotism, priestcraft, poverty, dependence, illiteracy, sophistry, and overrefinement. The American "ploughman" – that farmer who read Homer, he said – needed only the facts to make the wise decision, to assent to truth.[180] Jefferson remained convinced that in the future America was "destined to be a barrier against the returns of ignorance and barbarism." "Old Europe," he told Adams, "will have to lean on our

---

[176] For a compelling description (and endorsement) of such a nationalism, see Martha Nussbaum, "Toward a Globally Sensitive Patriotism," in *Daedalus*, 137 (Summer 2008), 78–93.

[177] TJ to Dupont, March 2, 1809, in *TJW*, 1203.

[178] See Onuf and Onuf, *Nations, Markets, and War*, 219–246, generally, but esp. 221–222, 224, 234, 241, 244–246. Also see Sophia Rosenfeld, "Citizens of Nowhere in Particular: Cosmopolitanism, Writing, and Political Engagement in Eighteenth-Century Europe," *National Identities*, 4 (2002), 25–43.

[179] TJ to John Holmes, April 22, 1820, in *TJW*, 1435.

[180] TJ to St. John de Crevecoeur, January 15, 1787, in *TJW*, 878.

shoulders, and to hobble along by our side, under the monkish trammels of priests and kings, as she can. What a colossus shall we be, when the southern continent comes up to our mark! What a stand will it secure as a ralliance for the reason and freedom of the globe!"[181]

Americans have ever after embraced Jefferson's words as a birthright, inherently applicable for all time without reference to the circumstances that he believed made American possibility unique in the eighteenth and early nineteenth centuries.[182] But he did so, it seems worth noting, not when America was the greatest industrial and the most powerful military nation in the world, but in the context of a post-Revolutionary society, precariously holding on to its existence in a world of states hostile to its success and largely indifferent to its confidence. Only because of the unique American experience he had come to appreciate could he be so confident about the American future, but not without the nagging feeling that things could go terribly wrong if those conditions themselves changed.

In 1816, Jefferson copied a fragment from a poem by Sir William Jones into a letter he wrote to John Taylor advocating democratic reforms in the Virginia Constitution. It offers a Jeffersonian response, of sorts, to Adams's skepticism and, indeed, an illuminating reply to the assumptions of modern constitutionalism – to a politics of distrust:

> What constitutes a State?
> Not high-raised battlements, or labor'd mound,
> Thick wall, or moated gate;
> Not cities proud, with spires and turrets crown'd;
> No: men, high-minded men;
> Men, who their duties know;
> But know their rights; and knowing, dare maintain.
> These constitute a State.[183]

Things would continue to go well with America, he told Taylor in the same letter, "while our present character remains." It was precisely this character, the strength of the nation, that Jefferson believed exceptional about Americans;

---

[181] TJ to Adams, August 1, 1816, in *AJL*, 484–485.

[182] Adams to TJ, July 13, 1813, in ibid., 356; See C. Vann Woodward, *The Burden of Southern History*, 169.

[183] To John Taylor, May 28, 1816, *L&B* 15:21. The poem is "An Ode In Imitation of Alcaeus" (1781). Compare the original poem by Alcaeus of Mytilene translated in Rahe, *Republics Ancient and Modern*, 30: "Neither stone blocks/ Nor ships' timbers/ Nor even the carpenter's art/ Can make a polis./ But where there are men/ Who know how to preserve themselves/ There one finds walls and a city as well." It seems worth noting that the original poem reflected the contemporary Greek understanding of the polis as, in Rahe's words, "a moral community of men permanently united as a people by a common way of life." In this sense, Rahe notes, there simply "was no Greek state," and the modern distinction between state and civil society, certainly acknowledged by Jefferson, is "inapplicable" to any assessment of the "ancient city." "As a human being," Rahe notes, "the Greek possessed no rights against the commonwealth."

precisely why his much-lauded championing of democracy, at least during his own day, tended to stop at the borders of the United States. Other peoples could have American democracy when, and only when, they became more like Americans; and Americans could remain the world's hope for the future only as long as they maintained its remarkable character and the conditions that had cultivated it.

# 4

# American Public

> The process of the politically relevant exercise and equilibration of power now takes place directly between the private bureaucracies, special-interest associations, parties, and public administration. The public as such is included only sporadically in this circuit of power, and even then it is brought in only to contribute its acclamation.
>
> Jurgen Habermas, 1962[1]

> [American prosperity] is due, in the first place, to the reflecting character of our citizens at large, who, by the weight of public opinion, influence and strengthen the public measures; it is due to the sound discretion with which they select from among themselves those to whom they confide the legislative duties; it is due to the zeal and wisdom of the characters thus selected, who lay the foundations of public happiness in wholesome laws, the execution of which alone remains for others.
>
> Thomas Jefferson, 1805[2]

Jefferson, as we have seen, assumed, with others of his enlightened generation, a sharp distinction between nature and culture. The underlying human nature was fundamentally the same; but the natural could be altered – distorted or improved – by culture. Jefferson's friend Benjamin Rush was simply articulating what most intellectuals had come to believe: "Human nature is the same in all ages and countries" and "all the differences we perceive in its characters in respect to virtue and vice, knowledge and ignorance, may be accounted for from climate, country, degrees of civilization, forms of government, or accidental causes."[3]

From this foundational assumption sprang all manner of imperatives about the amelioration of human suffering and inequalities because most of them

---

[1] Habermas, *The Structural Transformation of the Public Sphere: An Inquiry into a Category of Bourgeois Society*, 1962, trans. Thomas Burger (Cambridge, MA, 1991), 176.

[2] Jefferson, "Second Inaugural Address," March 4, 1805, in *TJW*, 521.

[3] Rush quoted in David Freeman Hawke, *Benjamin Rush: Revolutionary Gadfly* (Indianapolis and New York, 1971), 107. Also see *Notes*, 121. On the plasticity of national character in eighteenth century thought, see Douglas Bradburn, *The Citizenship Revolution: Politics and the Creation of the American Union, 1774–1804* (Charlottesville, 2009), chapter 4.

seemed to spring from artificial causes. Such a view was useful. When it served his purposes, Jefferson could denounce a particular culture (Native American or European) for degrading human nature and exalt another (Anglo-American) for facilitating the fulfillment of natural human capacities.[4] This, in fact, was what he considered particularly special about the American regime – that it had created a realm where human capabilities could reach their natural fulfillment.

But, if the American experience offered white men the opportunity to fulfill their natural capacities, it was nevertheless likely that the natural capacities of white men might differ greatly among themselves. The hope of most Jeffersonians was clearly that the elimination of artificial distinctions would allow for a kind of rough equality never before experienced in human history. It was also clear that many Americans also expected that certain kinds of distinctions would never manifest themselves in a just society.[5] Were there, then, natural inequalities that even an American regime could not root out – or that such a regime would not find desirable to eliminate?

Much as Jefferson "cherished" the people, what he most cherished about them, on one level, was their ability to choose wise leadership, and this immediately raises important questions about the relationship between a sovereign people and its representatives in government and, ultimately, about the meaning of human equality in Jefferson's thought.

Jefferson's sense that national particularities shaped national possibilities explains his prioritizing of social reforms that would perpetuate the conditions that made the American public so reliable. But it also goes a long way toward explaining his hostility to anything that he thought might undermine the ability of the American public to distinguish statesmanship from demagoguery. His twin and apparently clashing commitments – both a capacious cultivation of citizenship for broad inclusion in the American public as well as an uncompromising exclusion of various others as un-American – were thus rooted in the same nationalist soil. It is common to contrast Jefferson's proposals for black deportation and Indian cultural suicide, as well as his exclusion of political enemies as heretics, with his plans for the cultivation of the white public's capacities for democratic self-governance because they seem at such odds in our sensibilities. But, in fact, the inclusions and the exclusions, the cultivations and the deportations, are but different manifestations of a single project in his thought: perpetuating an American nationhood.

PUBLIC CAPACITY, PUBLIC CULTIVATION

If what made Americans distinctive was rooted in their social and political experience, American superiority demanded continual cultivation and

---

[4] On the protean nature of the concept in Jefferson's thought, see Charles A. Miller, *Jefferson and Nature: An Interpretation* (Baltimore, 1988).

[5] See Gordon S. Wood, *The Creation of the American Republic* (Chapel Hill, 1969); and Wood, *The Radicalism of the American Revolution* (New York, 1992).

regeneration of that experience. Jefferson, consequently, assumed an intimate relationship between the public's fitness for self-rule and the government that would facilitate the opportunities for continual cultivation of that very fitness. The educational system that Jefferson promoted as a check on government power would be funded by the public, precisely because, as Jefferson put it, "publick happiness" depended on it.[6] So the public would become competent to pass judgment on the action of government officials through a publicly funded educational system that would "illuminate ... the minds of the people at large" and "give them knowledge of facts, which history exhibiteth," so that, "possessed thereby of the experience of other ages and countries, they may be enabled to know ambition under all its shapes, and prompt to exert their natural powers to defeat its purposes."[7] In other words, if government even hinted at tyranny or corruption, the people would check it, in part, because that very government had provided them an education that had prepared them to discern tyranny when it appeared, and had fanned the flames of American spirit by securing property such that the people would be "prompt" to defend their liberties.

This circular and intimate relationship between public and government makes sense only in a self-governing republic, and Jefferson seemed to think that such a close relationship was necessary to sustain self-governance in turn. It was a fantasy to imagine "that kings, nobles, or priests are good conservators of the public happiness," for those groups had actually formed "an abandoned confederacy against the happiness of the mass of the people." They had been all too successful in Europe. France had "the finest soil upon earth," Jefferson said, as well as "the finest climate under heaven" and "the most gay and amiable character" in its people who were nevertheless "loaded with misery by kings, nobles and priests." In other words, the general lack of public spirit or ability to sustain self-government in European countries was, in Jefferson's mind, at least in part due to the utter disconnection between government and its public. Only republican governors would have an interest in strengthening the people's ability to ensure that their government never inhibited their prosperity or undermined their liberty. European monarchs and aristocrats had no interest, needless to say, in keeping the people well-informed or preparing them to be vigilant defenders of their liberties, able to spot tyranny on the distant horizon. No wonder the "mass of the people" of Europe remained "two centuries behind ours" in science.[8] "No other sure foundation can be devised," Jefferson argued, "for the preservation of freedom and happiness" than an educational system that would render "the people the safe, as they are the ultimate, guardians of their own liberty."[9]

---

[6] Jefferson's 1778 proposal is in "Bill No. 79," *PTJ* 2:526–533. For a description of its rationale, see *Notes*, 146–149; Jefferson, *Autobiography*, in *TJW*, 42–43; and TJ to George Wythe, August 13, 1786, in *PTJ* 10: 244–245.

[7] "Bill no. 79," in *PTJ* 2:526.

[8] TJ to Charles Bellini, September 30, 1785, in *TJW*, 833.

[9] TJ to George Wythe, August 13, 1786, in *PTJ* 10:244–245; *Notes*, 148.

It was an axiom of republican political theory that government "degenerates when trusted to the rulers of the people alone." Republican government was predicated on the assumption that "the people themselves" were the "only safe depositories" of government. But "to render even them safe their minds must be improved to a certain degree." If the "influence over government must be shared among all the people," public education had to be a priority. It was as chimerical to assume that people could be rendered virtuous "by any process whatever" as it was to imagine that "every tree shall be made to bear fruit, and every plant nourishment." Briers and brambles may "never become the vine and olive," Jefferson analogized, "but their asperities may be softened by culture, and their properties improved." By the same token, "the diffusion of light and education" was "the resource most to be relied on for ameliorating the condition, promoting the virtue, and advancing the happiness of man."[10]

Jefferson's inclination was always to expand rather than contract opportunities for public engagement. While it was common to imagine that "corruption" could be best "restrained by confining the right of suffrage to a few of the wealthier of the people," Jefferson insisted that it "would be more effectually restrained by an extension of that right to such numbers as would bid defiance to the means of corruption." Rather than taking limitations as a justification for circumscribing rights and liberty, Jefferson typically looked for ways to remove the limitations themselves by ameliorating public incapacity.[11] If "the ultimate powers of the society" were safe nowhere except with "the people themselves," the "remedy" for an unenlightened people, Jefferson told William Jarvis in 1820, was "not to take it from them, but to inform their discretion by education."[12]

Many people celebrate Jefferson's emphasis on limited government without paying much attention to what he thought government should do.[13] For Jefferson, one of government's primary responsibilities was the sustaining of the kind of public that would be capable of limiting government's ability to tyrannize over it. The public that remained uncultivated and uninformed was precisely the one that would overlook encroachments on its liberty and,

---

[10] "Bill no. 79," in *PTJ* 2:526; TJ to Cornelius Camden Blatchly, October 21, 1822, in *L&B* 15:399. A free press would also be an aid to an informed and engaged citizenry. See TJ to Colonel Charles Yancey, January 6, 1816, in *FE* 11:497. On the evolution of Jefferson's views of the press, see Jeffrey L. Pasley, "The Two National 'Gazettes': Newspapers and the Embodiment of American Political Parties," in *Early American Literature* 35 (2000), 51–86, esp. 64–65; as well as TJ to Mr. Pictet, Feb. 5, 1803, *L&B* 10:357.

[11] *Notes*, 148–149.

[12] TJ to William Charles Jarvis, September 28, 1820, in *L&B* 15:277–278.

[13] Jefferson's epitaph is often taken to indicate Jefferson's preference for limited government, but none of the things he lists there can happen in the absence of government. The Declaration announced the existence of a new government dedicated to rights; the statute for religious freedom was a piece of legislation that would be enacted and upheld by government power; and the University of Virginia owed its existence to extensive government enabling. On the latter, see TJ to William Short, April 13, 1820, in *L&B* 15:245.

ultimately, acquiesce in despotism. So a state that had actively funded programs to broadly distribute access to independence and enlightenment would also be the one with the most limited capacity to "pervert … power … into tyranny." The relationship between government power and public liberty was more complex in Jefferson's thought than we typically understand.

Scholars are not wrong to note Jefferson's "ambivalence about the judgment of the untutored masses," but, as we have already seen, Jefferson trusted the American people precisely because they were "measurably enlightened" and economically independent, and his reform proposals were designed to perpetuate this trustworthiness.[14] Emphasizing the elitism ignores the coherence of his plan to ensure that all American citizens would remain capable of political judgment.

This orientation is also evident in Jefferson's proposals for land reform. If general enlightenment through education was one way to cultivate capacities in the people, another was to ensure their independence by making access to land widely available. His 1776 draft constitution for the state of Virginia included a provision appropriating up to fifty acres "in full and absolute dominion" to "every person of full age neither owning nor having owned" such land precisely for the purpose of bringing those citizens to the level required for the franchise.[15] So Jefferson followed the prescriptions of James Harrington's *Oceana*, which limited citizenship to freeholders, but with this twist: Jefferson proposed using the state to create a society in which all [white male citizens] could be freeholders. This was no passing whim: He described his own work to eliminate primogeniture and entail in Virginia during the Revolution as the removal of all "the feudal and unnatural distinctions which made one member of every family rich, and all the rest poor, substituting equal partition, the best of all Agrarian laws."[16] Jefferson continued to encourage widespread ownership of property insofar as that was considered necessary for the kind of independence required of citizens of a republic. In 1806, he urged passage of a bill that anticipated the Homestead Act of 1862, granting 160 acres to citizens willing to migrate to Mississippi Territory, improve the tract, and serve in the militia for three years.[17]

In addition to promoting widespread access to land as a means of turning more citizens into property owners, Jefferson once suggested to Madison that progressive taxation – the exemption "from taxation" of everyone who fell "below a certain point," and the taxing of "higher portions of property in

---

[14] James T. Kloppenberg, "Thomas Jefferson," in Richard Wightman Fox and James T. Kloppenberg, eds., *A Companion to American Thought* (Malden, MA, 1995), 351. Dumas Malone, "Thomas Jefferson," in Edward T. James, ed., *American Plutarch* (New York, 1964), 97.

[15] Third Draft, before June 13, 1776, in *PTJ* 1:362.

[16] Jefferson, *Autobiography*, in *TJW*, 44. Jefferson was quick to say that "all this would be effected without the violation of a single natural right of any one individual." See "Bill to Enable Tenants in Fee Tail to Convey their Lands in Fee Simple," October 14, 1776, in *PTJ* 1:560–561.

[17] See Everett S. Brown, "Jefferson's Plan for a Military Colony in Orleans Territory," *Mississippi Valley Historical Review* 8 (March 1922), 373–376.

geometrical progression as they rise" – would ameliorate inequalities when the "laws of property" had been "so far extended as to violate natural right."[18]

   All of this has proven controversial among scholars, with some emphasizing the republican – or even social democratic – aspects of Jefferson's thought, and others prioritizing Jefferson's embrace of limited government, articulated best, perhaps, in his First Inaugural Address, where "good government," he tells us, is "wise and frugal," one that "shall restrain men from injuring one another, shall leave them otherwise free to regulate their own pursuits of industry and improvement, and shall not take from the mouth of labor that bread it has earned."[19] But both are prominent aspects of his thought, and we have trouble reconciling them only because they tend to be separate in ours.

Perhaps the best way to think our way through this conundrum is to remember what Johann Neem recently described as the relationship between Jefferson's ends – the securing of natural rights and individual freedom – and his means, which certainly involved the casting off of tradition and artificial hierarchy, but also often included a fairly large role for government to make individual freedom meaningful by building up the capabilities of citizens and opportunities to meaningfully fulfill them.[20] After all, in the letter to Madison cited previously, Jefferson assumed that the measures he advocated for reducing inequality – including progressive taxation and, in certain extreme cases, perhaps, the redistribution of land – were means toward the security of natural right, which he believed had been violated by "the laws of property." Jefferson never precisely delineated the point at which inequality would violate natural right, but that such a line existed for him is undeniable: He certainly witnessed its crossing in Europe, and he hoped to prevent such in the United States. After all, the spirit that made American republicanism possible was itself cultivated in the widespread access American citizens had to property, their opportunity for what he called a "comfortable subsistence" during productive years, and their accumulation of enough resources "to provide for a cessation from labor in old age." These were normative conditions for his political theory, precisely what ultimately made it possible to distinguish "the Man of these states," he told Adams, from "the Canaille of the cities of Europe."[21] These were conditions all Americans should be able to expect, in Jefferson's calculation, not luxuries for a few, and when the conditions that sustained American republicanism no longer applied, American republicanism and exceptionalism as Jefferson understood

---

[18] TJ to Madison, October 28, 1785, in *ROL* 1:390.

[19] March 4, 1801, in *TJW*, 494. Also see his Second Inaugural Address, March 4, 1805, in which Jefferson encourages the maintenance of "that state of property, equal or unequal, which results to every man from his own industry, or that of his fathers," ibid., 522.

[20] I borrow this reading entirely from Johann Neem, "Developing Freedom: Thomas Jefferson, the State, and Human Capability," unpublished paper in possession of the author. Also see Neem, " 'To Diffuse Knowledge More Generally through the Mass of the People': Thomas Jefferson on Individual Freedom and the Distribution of Knowledge," in Robert M. S. McDonald, ed., *Light and Liberty: Thomas Jefferson and the Power of Knowledge* (Charlottesville, 2012), 47–74.

[21] TJ to John Adams, October 28, 1813, in *AJL*, 391.

it would be over. If maintaining natural rights, then, was the purpose for which governments were "instituted among men," the state would continue to fulfill its role by sustaining access to opportunity. For Jefferson, government's role was never to make choices for citizens; only to make private choices genuine by cultivating judgment, opening access to markets, and ensuring that labor can enjoy its fruit. Jefferson's ends, then, demanded a much more expansive or capacious government than we typically associate with him.[22]

For Jefferson, effective government was never distinct in any measurable way from citizen participation. If a republic was, as he put it, a government "by its citizens in mass, acting directly and personally, according to rules established by the majority," the problem was that "such a government" was of necessity "restrained to very narrow limits of space and population." And the farther government gravitated from this "direct action of the citizens," the more distant it became from "a pure republic."[23] Jefferson's solution to this problem was the intensification of citizen engagement. To facilitate and ensure maximum democratic participation of citizens within their sphere of competence, Jefferson encouraged the establishment of the most local of governments – which Jefferson called "wards," or "elementary republics." It was in the wards that most citizens would become "participator[s] in the government of affairs, not merely at an election one day in the year, but every day."[24] The overwhelming majority of citizens would never serve in State government, even fewer in the national one. But "every citizen" could be "an acting member of the government ... in the offices nearest and most interesting to him" – those offices that most deeply engaged his actual life, that is, those affairs not transcending "the small, and yet numerous and interesting concerns of the neighborhood." Local government of the wards would oversee all local business and "all the matters of common interest" to the local community. With the intense citizen participation in local affairs that Jefferson was advocating here, "there shall not be a man in the State who will not be a member of some one of its councils, great or small." And this engagement would make every citizen an invested stakeholder in the affairs of government, would "attach him by his strongest feelings to the independence of his country, and its republican constitution." In Jefferson's scheme, citizenship was a tangible practice – a "feeling" of participation – and the practice of citizenship was its actualization. It was this repeated active engagement that would render the citizenry vigilant and zealous of their liberty. By such a division and sub-division of government, paradoxically, "the whole is cemented by giving to every citizen, personally, a part in the administration of the public affairs."[25]

---

[22] Again, see Neem, "Developing Freedom." But for a reading that suggests Jefferson's later hedging on this orientation, see Matthew Crow, "Print and Political Economy in Republican Constitutionalism," unpublished paper in possession of the author.

[23] TJ to John Taylor, May 28, 1816, in *TJW*, 1392–1393.

[24] TJ to Joseph C. Cabell, February 2, 1816, in *TJW*, 1380.

[25] TJ to Joseph C. Cabell, February 2, 1816, in *TJW*, 1380; TJ to Samuel Kercheval, July 12, 1816, in ibid., 1399–1400. Because the American people were informed and engaged, they could serve

Clearly, the founders were moderns in their embrace of the civilizing effects of commerce and their acceptance as axiomatic a distinction between state and civil society that the ancients would never have understood.[26] In a free society, the principle function of government was coming to be seen as the protection of private pursuits of happiness rather than the inculcation of any specific *summum bonum*: a "particular conception of the good life," as Alan Gibson has put it.[27] But we should not expect to find a twenty-first-century pluralist liberalism in eighteenth-century North America any more than we should expect to find ancient republicanism there. To be sure, Jefferson was devoted to a kind of public/private distinction that limited the access of the state to the private realm, but as a cultural nationalist who took it for granted that "the manners and spirit of a people" were what "preserve[d] a republic in vigour," Jefferson could not be indifferent to all sorts of activities and behaviors that take place in what a strictly liberal scheme could only categorize as the realm of the private.[28] The public was to give legitimacy to the state, but the state in its turn would of necessity have an interest in making the public possible, performing all sorts of functions not quite adequately captured by the liberal dichotomy.

For Jefferson, to take only one example, the most sacred site for the cultivation of citizenship seems to have been the family, theoretically the place where the state ought to have the least ability to interfere. But creating the conditions for the flourishing of the kinds of women and men that would make those families possible did seem to fall under the purview of Jefferson's state. This dynamic is clear in his late proposal for the establishment of elementary schools in which Jefferson wrestled with the problem of compulsory education. Given his commitment to education at the public expense ("the tax which will be paid for this purpose is not more than the thousandth part of what will be paid to kings, priests & nobles who will rise up among us if we leave the people in ignorance"),[29] Jefferson assumed a public obligation to encourage general enlightenment. But, he certainly noticed that this public obligation might, in certain cases, threaten to violate the sacredness of the private realm. Jefferson wondered:

is it a right or a duty in society to take care of their infant members in opposition to the will of the parent? How far does this right and duty extend? to guard the life of the infant, his property, his instruction, his morals? The Roman father was supreme in all these: we draw a line, but where? – public sentiment does not seem to have traced it precisely.[30]

on juries, deciding, in some cases, law as well as fact. TJ to L'Abbe Arnond, July 19, 1789, in *FE* 5:483–484. Also see TJ to Joseph Milligan, April 6, 1816, in *L&B* 14:466, on the public's competence to judge the propriety of new words introduced into the language.

[26] See, especially, Paul Rahe, *Republics Ancient and Modern: Classical Republicanism and the American Revolution* (Chapel Hill, 1992).

[27] Alan Gibson, *Understanding the Founding: The Crucial Questions* (Lawrence, 2007), 157.

[28] *Notes*, 165.

[29] TJ to George Wythe, August 13, 1786, in *L&B* 10:245.

[30] Elementary School Act, 1817, in *L&B* 17:424.

Jefferson concluded, on the one hand, that this private space must be protected from state interference even when private preferences ran against public good. "Good and safe government," after all, Jefferson said, "end[ed] in the administration of every man's farm by himself," an administration that simply could not be delegated to an external authority.[31] It was, he assumed, "better to tolerate the rare instance of a parent refusing to let his child be educated, than to shock the common feelings and ideas by the forcible asportation and education of the infant against the will of the father."[32]

But make no mistake, this lone parent's intransigence, traced to its logical outcome, was a threat to common good: generalized lack of public enlightenment would ensure the degeneration of the state. Jefferson was so persuaded by this, in fact, that he found intriguing a provision in the 1812 Spanish Constitution that would disenfranchise "every citizen who cannot read and write." The more Jefferson thought about this provision, the more convinced he became of its wisdom: it would "immortalize its inventors," he said, precisely because it would ensure "an enlightened people and an energetic public opinion which will control and enchain the aristocratic spirit of the government."[33]

Accordingly, in his 1817 plan guaranteeing three years of public schooling for all children, Jefferson also offered a "nudge," of sorts, going the Spanish constitution one better by stripping the citizenship of those who remained illiterate after three years of education at the public expense: "And it is declared and enacted, that no person unborn or under the age of twelve years at the passing of this act, and who is compos mentis, shall, after the age of fifteen years, be a citizen of this commonwealth until he or she can read readily in some tongue, native or acquired."[34] Jefferson described this provision as a solution to the problem of compulsory education: The proposal would "remove [a father's] objection of expense, by offering education gratis" and would "strengthen parental excitement by the disfranchisement of his child while uneducated."[35] This seems to be a fairly strong example of what Cass Sunstein and Richard Thaler have called "libertarian paternalism": the public influencing of behavior in particular directions while continuing to respect freedom of choice.[36] Jefferson rationalized his own plan in similar fashion: "Society has certainly a right to disavow him whom they offer, and are permitted to qualify for the duties of a citizen. If we do not force instruction, let us at least strengthen the motives to receive it when offered."[37] No American father, so deeply invested himself in the practices of citizenship, Jefferson assumed, would want his

---

[31] TJ To Joseph C. Cabell, February 2, 1816, *L&B* 14: 421.

[32] Elementary School Act, 1817, in *L&B* 17:424.

[33] TJ to Chevalier Luis de Onis, April 28, 1814, in *L&B* 14:129.

[34] Ibid.

[35] Ibid.

[36] See Sunstein and Thaler, "Libertarian Paternalism is not an Oxymoron," *University of Chicago Law Review* 70 (Autumn 2003), 1159–1202; and Sunstein and Thaler, *Nudge: Improving Decisions about Health, Wealth, and Happiness* (New Haven, CT, 2008).

[37] Elementary School Act, 1817, in *L&B* 17:424.

child to be excluded from them. This threat would be enough, he believed, to overcome whatever objections the father might have to public schooling, but without, it must be noted, forcing public – as opposed to private – forms of education. The balancing act here would, Jefferson believed, respect the sanctity of the family (especially the privileges and authority of the male head of household) while preserving all the public good envisioned in his education scheme: American citizens would be enlightened and free so that they, in turn, could pass on their liberty to their children.

Jefferson presumed capabilities in citizens, the maintenance of which were to a very real extent, in his view, the responsibility of government. In another context, Jefferson described the way a society could ameliorate defects in the moral sense among those unfortunate and unusual individuals without the natural instinct toward the good: "We endeavor to supply the defect by education, by appeals to reason and calculation" and "by presenting to the being so unhappily conformed, other motives to do good and to eschew evil." The "other motives" that would assist or substitute for the absent moral sense included:

the love, or the hatred, or rejection of those among whom he lives, and whose society is necessary to his happiness and even existence; demonstrations by sound calculation that honesty promotes interest in the long run; the rewards and penalties established by the laws; and ultimately the prospects of a future state of retribution for the evil as the good done while here.

Such "correctives" would to some degree replace the recently disestablished church by "exercis[ing] the functions of the moralist, the preacher, the legislator" and would "lead into a course of correct action all those whose depravity is not too profound to be eradicated."[38] Most of these would be the province of civil society, the realm outside of the state: the family, society, and even churches. But Jefferson did see a role for the state in assisting those realms, and he envisioned a role for government cultivation of public morals and even taste. From France, Jefferson designed the new Virginia capitol building for Richmond, basing the model on the Maison Carree at Nimes, which he thought "one of the most beautiful, if not the most beautiful and precious morsel of architecture left us by antiquity." When he feared that Virginia might instead construct a less expensive building on a different design, he lamented to Madison, "But how is a taste in this beautiful art to be formed in our countrymen, unless we avail ourselves of every occasion when public buildings are to be erected of presenting to them models for their study and imitation?"[39] Jefferson, who deplored the architecture of America, especially that of Virginia, which he once called "rude, misshapen piles,"[40] even "worse than in any other part of America,"[41] hoped to inculcate cultural refinement by means of public

---


[38] TJ to Thomas Law, June 13, 1814, in *L&B* 14:144.
[39] TJ to James Madison, Sept. 20, 1785, ibid., 8:535.
[40] *Notes*, 153.
[41] TJ to John Page, May 4, 1786, *PTJ* 9:445.

works. His object, as he told Madison, was "to improve the taste of my countrymen." If built according to Jefferson's specifications, the new capitol would be "an object and proof of national good taste." If not, it would be "a monument of our barbarism which will be loaded with execrations as long as it shall endure."[42]

Moreover, because Jefferson considered it a matter "of some public concern that our country should not be without portraits of its first discoverers," he had taken the trouble to send an artist to Florence to make copies of portraits of Christopher Columbus and Americus Vespucius.[43] Around the same time, he also described his original purchase of the Natural Bridge as a "public trust," which largely forbad his "selling the land," and demanded his preservation of the site from "injur[y], deface[ment], or" even from being "masked from public view."[44]

These were private purchases intended to serve a didactic public purpose, but in other places, public and private investment overlapped in more substantial ways. Jefferson urged a moderation of American drunkenness, for example, through the legislative encouragement of brewers and a reduction of import duties on wine. Jefferson hoped to see beer replace "whiskey which kills one-third of our citizens and ruins their families" and denied that a tax on wine was "merely a tax on the rich." It was also "a prohibition of its use to the middling class of our citizens, and a condemnation of them to the poison of whiskey, which is desolating their houses." Reduce the price of wine, and the legislature would thereby reduce drunkenness. "No nation is drunken where wine is cheap; and none sober, where the dearness of wine substitutes ardent spirits as the common beverage." Its general use would "carry health and comfort to a much enlarged circle."[45] Ultimately, Jefferson believed that government had a crucial role to play in shaping the kind of public he had so celebrated as unique in world history, precisely because that government was, ideally, so animated by that very public.

## AMERICAN ARISTOCRACY

Jefferson's sense of the benign and mutually reinforcing nature of the American public and government came to its fullest fruition in his particular conception of the "natural aristocracy," the leadership class that would pass the legislation that would cultivate public capacity to, in turn, find and elect it to positions of administration. One reason Jefferson despised Plato – beyond his general distaste for metaphysics ("incomprehensibilities," he called them) – was Plato's

---

[42] TJ to Madison, Sept. 20, 1785, ibid., 8:535. Also see TJ to Edmund Randolph, Sept. 20, 1785, ibid., 538.

[43] TJ to Joseph Delaplaine, May 3, 1814, in *PTJ, Retirement Series*, 7: 340–41.

[44] TJ to William Caruthers, March 15, 1815, *LC*. Also see Garry Wills, "the Aesthete," in *New York Review of Books*, August 12, 1993, 8.

[45] TJ to Charles Yancey, January 6, 1816, in *L&B* 14:380; TJ to Monsieur de Neuville, December 13, 1818, in *L&B* 15:177.

sense that political wisdom was the province of experts who should, therefore, rule those who lacked it.[46] In contrast, Jefferson argued that moral – and, by extension, political – questions could be decided as well by ploughmen as by philosophers.[47] It is true that Jefferson assumed that those ploughmen would, by and large, not have the intellectual capacity for running national affairs.[48] But they would, he believed, have the good sense to know who did have such capacity, and the wisdom to distinguish leadership from demagoguery as well as the courage to hold leaders accountable. Jefferson assumed a value to political engagement on the part of all citizens within their capacity. In other words, all Americans were to be engaged in politics even as a few only would make it their primary preoccupation, and those few would serve legitimately only insofar as they had the public imprimatur. In this way, Jefferson reconciled tensions between his competing commitments to good leadership and to popular engagement in politics. Jefferson seemed, of all the founders, the most willing to trust the people's judgment while, at the same time, accepting the common wisdom of the day that the people could be dangerous if uninformed and apathetic, and that a sustainable state required, not simply good institutions, but a superior kind of leadership as well as a citizenry that was enlightened enough to keep that leadership honest.

Jefferson's appreciation of American uniqueness in this regard helps clarify the central differences between him and John Adams in their justly famous conversation about aristocracy in America. Adams had spent the better part of his life wrestling with the problem of aristocracy and had made numerous attempts to draw Jefferson out on the issue. When his efforts finally paid off, with one of Jefferson's most memorable letters, needless to say, he found Jefferson's enthusiasm a bit amusing. Jefferson told Adams that he believed that a natural aristocracy of virtue and talent ("the most precious gift of nature for the instruction, the trusts, and government of society") could be distinguished from an artificial one of birth, wealth, and beauty. This natural aristocracy, Jefferson argued, could be cultivated in the United States where artificial restraints on true merit were removed. There was nothing particularly original about Jefferson's embrace of the concept itself: The "natural aristocracy" had a long pedigree in republican thought.[49] Beyond that, most Americans understood the need for good leadership of the most capable men but distinguished instinctually between superiority of talent, on the one hand, and inherited privilege, on the other. After all, Americans knew that nature had "sown" talent, as Jefferson put it, "as liberally among the poor as the rich" and, on some fundamental level, associated their Revolution with a freeing of this natural

---

[46] See TJ to Adams, July 5, 1814, in *AJL*, 432–433.

[47] TJ to Peter Carr, August 10, 1787, *TJW*, 902.

[48] Though they would, he once noted, have the intellectual curiosity and ability to read epic poetry. See TJ to St. John de Crevecoeur, January 15, 1787, ibid., 878.

[49] See Rahe, *Republics Ancient and Modern*, 711. Also see Jonathan Jackson, *Thoughts Upon the Political Situation of the United States of America* (Worcester, MA, 1788), 56–58.

merit from artificial exclusions rooted in birth, connection, and influence of all sorts.[50] The real question for most American founders, then, was not whether such a thing as a natural aristocracy existed but how to find and empower it in a new republican world shorn of the traditional means of cultivating leadership through patronage and inherited status.

One of the apparent Jeffersonian paradoxes is his simultaneous loathing of aristocracy and exaltation of great men. Jefferson made no secret of his scoffing at the pretensions of aristocracy: "honesty" could not "be bought with money," nor was "wisdom hereditary."[51] And his political program in Virginia, anyway, was designed, he said, as "a system by which ever fibre would be eradicated of antient or future aristocracy."[52] At the same time, admiration of true greatness was something Jefferson understood, and he never shrunk from naming his own heroes and hoping to become more like them. Jefferson, for example, was fond of listing his pantheon of greats – among them Isaac Newton. In the hierarchy of worth, even the typical natural aristocrat could not measure up to genuises like Newton, Bacon, and Locke, who, Jefferson said, ought not be "confounded at all with the herd of other great men."[53] Closer to home, Jefferson once told his grandson that he "had the good fortune to become acquainted very early with some characters of very high standing and to feel the incessant wish that I could even become what they were." To this he attributed his preservation from other "bad company" that might have rendered him "worthless to society."[54]

But Jefferson was less perplexed by this tension than some historians have been because he distinguished sharply between an artificial aristocracy of hereditary legal privilege and a "natural" one of merit and virtue. It was possible to be a member of both (at least outside of America), but what made his own heroes great was their membership in the latter category. Moreover, Jefferson grew up in a political culture that assumed that freeholders were able to recognize good leadership and elevate it to public office.[55] He seemed

---

[50] See Edmund S. Morgan, *Inventing the People: The Rise of Popular Sovereignty in England and America* (New York, 1988), esp. 286–306, Gordon Wood, *Creation of the American Republic*, 208, and *Radicalism*, generally. The Jefferson quote is from *Notes*, 148.

[51] *Notes* 119. Also see *Autobiography*, *TJW.*, 3.

[52] Ibid., 44.

[53] See TJ to John Trumbull, February 15, 1789, in *TJW*, 939–940. Also see TJ to David Rittenhouse, July 19, 1778, in *TJW*, 763. But, as Jefferson told one correspondent, Newton's natural talent did not grant him more political rights than the lowest citizen of the republic.

[54] TJ to Thomas Jefferson Randolph, November 24, 1810, in *TJW*, 1194.

[55] See, especially, Charles Sydnor, *Gentleman Freeholders: Political Practices in Washington's Virginia* (Chapel Hill, 1952); Jack P. Greene, *Political Life in Eighteenth Century Virginia* (Williamsburg, 1987); Richard Beeman, *The Varieties of Political Experience in Eighteenth-Century America* (Philadelphia, 2006), generally, but esp., 31–68; and Fred Anderson, "George Washington's Mentors," paper delivered at "Sons of the Father" conference at West Point, June 18, 2010. For an introduction to the problem of deference in early American historiography, see the forum in *Early America in Early American Studies* 3 (2005), 227–401, esp. the essays by Smolonski, Nobles, Smith, and Beeman.

to make the transition to a more democratic politics easily largely because he assumed the same of the broader American public. After all, he told Angelica Schuyler Church, America would be a refuge for the genuinely worthy people among the declining French aristocracy precisely because there "public esteem is so attached to worth, regardless of wealth."[56]

Jefferson's "natural aristocracy" can sound like a dressed-up version of colonial deference, but he typically emphasized less the superiority of the leadership (which he nevertheless did assume) than the remarkable ability of the public to find it and check its propensity toward self-aggrandizement.[57] As a nineteen-year old rising member of the Virginia gentry, Jefferson first wrestled with the problem of aristocracy and popular judgment. In a playful but revealing letter to his friend, John Page (among the earliest Jefferson letters extant) Jefferson admitted the power of what John Adams would later build an entire system of thought upon: that "the man who powders most, parfumes most, embroiders most, and talks most nonsense, is most admired." It was nevertheless true, he suggested, that "there are some who have too much good sense to esteem such monkey-like animals as these" and that such people of judgment were "the only persons whose esteem is worth a wish."[58] So, prior to the Revolution, Jefferson conceded, sadly, that celebrity was generally electable though a remnant of the good was able to see through its pretensions and recognize true merit. Not a particularly broad base upon which to build a republic. But after the Revolution, Jefferson moved gradually toward a different view: that the American public was generally capable of the kind of understanding only the select few with "good sense" possessed in countries where the masses were degraded. In the long context of western political thought, this emphasis was much more striking than any assumptions about quality leadership arising from all ranks of men in a meritocracy. After all, even in the older system, able characters like Benjamin Franklin and Alexander Hamilton rose to prominence from obscurity because socially prominent men recognized their merit and nurtured them with patronage. What was new was the extent to which Jefferson both tried to institutionalize this process through the continual cultivation of public capacity and weed out some of its capriciousness by generalizing opportunity, but, more significant, the extent to which Jefferson trusted the public (rather than individual social superiors) to recognize and elevate talent, as well

[56] TJ to Church, November 27, 1793, *TJW*, 1012–13.

[57] For examples of Jefferson's occasional ambivalence about this process, see TJ to Madison, March 5, 1795, in *ROL* 2:875, in which he decries the "low practices" of a Virginia politician that were "but too successful with the unthinking who merchandize their votes for grog." Of course, his own account book from December 5 and 9, 1768, records expenditures for drinks and cakes prior to his own election to the House of Burgesses. On this, see Dumas Malone, *Jefferson the Virginian* (Boston, 1948), 130. Jefferson, in other words, was not always above "swilling the planters with bumbo," although Charles Sydnor makes a nice distinction between purchasing votes and practicing customary hospitality. See Sydnor, *Gentlemen Freeholders*, esp. chapter 4.

[58] TJ to John Page, December 25, 1762, in *PTJ*, 1: 5.

as check its propensity toward oligarchy. The point of Jefferson's proposal for educational reform (with the exception of the University of Virginia) was never solely to cultivate the natural aristocracy. Only a handful of diamonds would be "raked from the rubbish" (as Jefferson put it) in this way, and the natural aristocrats in Virginia's traditionally dominant families would still receive education the old-fashioned way, through opportunities created by family wealth and connection, whether the public ever supported education for the mass. The real point of the program, he noted in the proposal and reiterated ever after, was to "render… the people the safe" guardians of their liberties by equipping them to recognize from a distance both tyranny and talent when they saw it, elevating the latter to leadership and destroying the former as soon as it became visible.[59]

So, the "great object" of the educational scheme he proposed to the Virginia legislature (or so he told John Adams years later) was to perpetuate the people's ability to find and choose the wisest leaders "for the trusts of government" and exclude the "Pseudalists" – the artificial aristocracy of birth and wealth (and without either talent or wisdom).[60] In other words, the education scheme was designed to ensure that the American spirit described in the previous chapter would remain alive in the future. For now (because Virginia had rejected his proposal), he argued, the "best remedy" was that "provided by all our constitutions, to leave to the citizens the free election and separation of the aristoi from the pseudo-aristoi, of the wheat from the chaff." It was possible for the people to choose poorly, but typically, he expected, they would "elect the real good and wise."[61]

For Adams this sounded a bit naïve about human nature, a bit too trusting of the aristocracy. And, naturally, he responded with a hard-headed critique of Jefferson's faith. For his part, Adams never had to trouble himself about whether "genius" or distinctions of any sort were innate or had environmental causes – a problem important to Jefferson. For Adams, distinctions would arise in spite of institutional arrangements, and the only question that really mattered was what to do about them once they emerged.

Adams was often taken to be a defender of aristocracy in his day, but he was just as convinced as Jefferson that the very success often understood to be innate or the fruit of a superior work ethic was actually the result of unequal access to privileges. In his early years, when he was struggling to distinguish himself in a world where distinction demanded access to patronage, he found the experience galling, but it called forth deep insight that helps us better understand his position and draw his starting point closer to Jefferson's. "We define Genius to be the innate Capacity," Adams noted, "and then vouchsafe this flattering Title only to Those few, who have been directed, by their birth, education and lucky accidents, to distinguish themselves in arts and sciences,

---

[59] *Notes*, 146.
[60] TJ to Adams, October 28, 1813, in *AJL*, 390.
[61] Ibid.

or in the execution of what the World calls great Affairs, instead of planting Corn, freighting Oysters, and killing Deer, the worthy employments in which most great Geniuses are engaged."[62] Adams understood just as well as Jefferson that "nature," as Jefferson put it, had "sown" genius "as liberally among the poor as the rich" and that talent would "perish without use, if not sought for and cultivated."[63] The fact was, Adams noted, native genius, "this mighty favor of Nature, of which the Poets and Orators, Philosophers and Legislators of the world, have been in all ages so proud," was not an adequate explanation for the "formation of all those Characters" of great men. "If you pick out your great Men, from Greek or Roman, and from English history, and suppose them born and bred in Eskimeaux or Caffraria, Patagonia or Lapland, no Man would imagine that any great effects from their genius would have appeared." The bottom line was, Adams quoted Edmund Waller, "the Conqueror of the world had been, But the first Wrestler on the Green."[64]

This is exactly the point Jefferson made later: So much of what has historically been taken to be innate is, in fact, the result of unequal access to advantages. Jefferson thought that in a just society – and in a relatively equal society – it would be a simpler matter to root out the artificial and allow the natural to emerge. But Adams thought the distinction Jefferson wanted to perpetuate between artificial and natural aristocrats was itself artificial. Anything that commanded "votes in society," he told Jefferson, made a man an aristocrat. Certainly that included the kind of genuine talent and virtue that Jefferson prized. But it also included many other things – wealth, beauty, and birth – that Jefferson considered artificial and unrelated to propensity for leadership.[65] If "talent" was whatever gained the admiration of the public, the crux of the matter was, once again, how to cultivate the kind of public that could recognize real merit. The problem, Adams thought, was that however much philosophers may reserve the title of "aristocrat" for "The Wise and Good," the public has always granted it as well to "the rich the beautiful and well born."[66] Adams's difference with Jefferson on this point did not make him an advocate of hereditary aristocracy (as he repeatedly insisted to Jefferson).[67] That he was

---

[62] Adams to Samuel Quincy, April 22, 1761, in *Papers of John Adams* 1:50.

[63] *Notes*, 148.

[64] Adams to Samuel Quincy, April 22, 1761, in *Papers of John Adams* 1:50.

[65] Adams to TJ, November 15, 1813, in *AJL*, 398: "Education, Wealth, Strength, Beauty, Stature, Birth, Marriage, graceful Attitudes and Motions, Gait, Air, Complexion, Physiognomy, are Talents, as well as Genius and Science and learning." Also see Adams, *Defence*, in *WJA* 4:290.

[66] Adams to TJ, September 2, 1813, in *AJL*, 371.

[67] Adams to TJ, July 29, 1791, in *AJL*, 247, 249. For an example of Adams's early hostility to aristocracy in defense of the commons, see Humphrey Ploughjogger to Philanthrop, Jan. 5, 1767, in *The Papers of John Adams*, ed., Robert J. Taylor (Cambridge, MA, 1977), 1:179, and The Earl of Clarendon to William Pym, January 27, 1766, in ibid., 169. Adams never took his observations about human nature to be an endorsement of aristocracy. As he put it in 1812 marginalia in his own *Discourses of Davila*, the truth – that Europe owed its "superiority" to its nobility – was "by no means a justification of the system of nobility in France, nor in other parts of Europe," *WJA* 4:251.

understood to be so in the 1790s and that he has garnered such a reputation over time only goes to show how effective Adams was at making himself misunderstood. Adams deplored – and feared – the inevitable tendency of the aristocracy to carve out special privileges, to make "exceptions of themselves in the laws," and to create "a simple aristocracy or oligarchy in effect" out of a nominal democracy.[68] But Adams could not ever bring himself to imagine, as Jefferson did, that the general public – as opposed to a select few – might become capable of the judgment of Jefferson's "persons whose esteem is worth a wish." And because neither nature nor society put any check on ambition (but rather encouraged it), Adams believed that a "well-ordered and well-balanced government" was the only refuge left for those who wanted to "correct" the "prejudices, passions, imaginations, and interests" of the ambitious.[69]

The difficulty for Adams's contemporary and future reputation came when he tried to describe what he meant by "well-ordered and well-balanced government." Adams's critics at the time confessed themselves stunned that he wanted to create and perpetuate the influence of an artificial nobility as one of the fundamental *orders* of society in a nation – the United States – that lacked such distinctions, a society that, at least in theory, was made of a single "order": the people. And Adams did seem to go out of his way at times to imply that republics would work best if they granted incentives and emoluments of office to "aristocrats" to entice them to serve the public; nor did he disarm his critics by referring to social "orders" in confusing ways, even as he conceded that America had few artificial distinctions as of yet.[70]

Adams's problem with Jefferson's sanguine outlook began with the incongruity he found between what ought to be and what was. "There is a voice within us," Adams noted in *Davila*, that tells us "that real merit should govern the world; and that men ought to be respected only in proportion to their talents, virtues, and services." But, Adams said, such an outcome is generally not observable in practice, and the central question was how a polity might accomplish, or at least approximate, such results in the absence of widespread judgment.

Because all human beings craved distinction, many more would seek offices that rightly belong to "real merit" than the number of people who actually deserve such honor. And most of them would end up learning, Adams thought, that they could have the honor even without the self-discipline required of true worth because the "popular voice" was just as likely to acclaim wealth, birth, and conspicuous consumption as it was to laud merit (which would be, in any case, difficult to find and, in large nations, to even discern). The public, unfortunately,

---

[68] *Defence*, in *WJA* 4:586.

[69] *Davila*, in *WJA* 6:262–263.

[70] Adams also conflated "legislature" with "aristocracy," a move almost calculated to arouse suspicion among American republicans. But this is more a function of Adams's refusal to distinguish between a natural and an artificial aristocracy than to any advocacy of hereditary leadership: The legislature, he argues, will "always be composed of members from the natural and artificial aristocratical body in every state." See *Defence*, in *WJA* 4:579–580; 395.

tended to fawn over one celebrity after another so that "the still small voice of merit," Adams said, was typically "drowned in the insolent roar of ... dupes of impudence and knavery in national elections." Because they hoped to build the state on something more "permanent" than such shifting sands, most "nations," Adams said, in an effort to ensure that at least some merit entered the public councils, had long relied on various signs "to designate honor." These included possession of land, office, or family heritage, all on the reasonable assumption that such advantages would at least afford children growing up in such circumstances the independence and education essential to actual merit. Such a system would surely reward the unworthy, but it might also produce a handful of wise characters that could run the affairs of state in a reasonable manner. In short, wise lawmakers who wanted to harness the talent of the "most illustrious" would have to reconcile themselves to something approximating a hereditary aristocracy full of wealth and pedigree and beauty.

So Adams thought it understandable, though not entirely justifiable, that nations had historically cultivated hereditary distinctions. He agreed with Jefferson that "real merit" ought to "govern the world," but he thought that Jefferson blithely ignored the central – and ultimately unanswerable – questions he himself had raised in 1790: "How shall the men of merit be discovered? How shall the proportions of merit be ascertained and graduated? Who shall be the judge?"[71]

Because humans craved distinction, Adams believed that the incentives traditionally offered to hereditary aristocrats might be the only way to attract the best of them to public service, and that little harm would be done as long as the constitution, at the same time, checked their ability to corrupt the legislature (by isolating them in a separate house).[72] For Adams, the "natural aristocracy" was "a body of men which contains the greatest collection of virtues and abilities in a free government" and could be "the brightest ornament and glory of the nation, and may always be made the greatest blessing of society," as long as it was "judiciously managed in the constitution."[73] What differentiates this outlook from Jefferson's is that Adams's aristocracy would, of necessity, include artificial "talents" too. Adams thought that a good deal of virtue and talent would accompany all the other nonsense that gave aristocrats their status. So he certainly didn't want to snuff it out. His central concern – and why institutional checks were so crucial in his scheme – was that the advantages possessed by the aristocrats (in whichever category) might actually end up giving them "more influence than reason and equity can justify."[74]

---

[71] *Davila*, Adams, ed., *Works* 6:249–250.
[72] See Adams, *Defence*, 4:397. Also see page 290 for Adams's suggestion that relegating the aristocracy to a separate house would constitute "to all honest and useful intents, an ostracism." For a slightly different (and less favorable) reading of Adams, see Joyce Appleby, "The New Republican Synthesis and the Changing Political Ideas of John Adams," *American Quarterly* 25 (1973), 578–595.
[73] Adams, *Defence*, in *WJA* 4:397.
[74] Adams, *Defence*, in *WJA* 4:398. Adams actually wrote the *Defence* largely to counter the pretensions of French thinkers who advocated a unicameral assembly, in which, he feared, there would be no counterweight to the aristocracy.

Although, in retrospect, it is clear that Adams actually sought to mitigate, rather than perpetuate, inequality, it is easy to see how he could have been mistaken at the time for an apologist for aristocracy (and monarchy) rather than its opponent. Adams's solution seemed as strange to most Americans as it did to the French admirers of the American Revolution, both of whom understood Adams to be an advocate for the perpetuation of existing "social cleavages."[75]

Adams was no friend of aristocracy – an unbridled aristocracy (his great fear) had been, he believed, the death of all republics; harnessing and defanging it was in large measure the very point of his political science. But he understood distinctions that created aristocracy to be inevitable in any society, however small, and dangerous to ignore – precisely what he thought Jefferson was doing. If Adams had lived into the age of bumper stickers, his might say: "Aristocracy happens." But it is important to recognize that, with Jefferson, Adams certainly considered any tendency to favor "the rich the beautiful and well born" over the virtuous and talented to be "Prejudice, Folly Ignorance, Baseness, Slavery, Stupidity, Adulation, Superstition." All Adams wanted Jefferson to understand was that the dangers of aristocracy could not be wished away: We may not like it, but "The Fact, in natural, moral, political and domestic History I cannot deny or dispute or question."[76]

Adams's point, then, was not that aristocracy was an unqualified good (though he did hope to harness its talents) but that lawmakers could not ignore its existence if they hoped to set up a republic that was going to last more than a handful of years. Adams could not trust, with Jefferson, that the American people would be able to elect a natural aristocracy with "warm affection and entire confidence" in "one moment" and then turn on it with "suspicion" the next."[77] Instead, he conjectured (on the basis of his study of the history of republics and his reflections on human nature) that, without proper checks on the aristocracy, the people would continue to be so blinded by confidence in

---

[75] For this argument, see, especially, R. R. Palmer, *The Age of the Democratic Revolution: A Political History of Europe and America, 1760–1800* (Princeton, 1959), vol. 1:281–282, and Joyce Appleby, "America as a Model for the Radical French Reformers of 1789," *WMQ* 39 (1982), 267–286, reprinted in Appleby, *Liberalism and Republicanism in the Historical Imagination* (Cambridge, 1992), 232–252, quote is at 251. Also see Appleby, "New Republican Synthesis and the Changing Political Ideas of John Adams," in *American Quarterly*, 25 (December 1973), 578–595; and Appleby, "The Jefferson-Adams Rupture and the First French Translation of John Adams' *Defence*," in *AHR*, 73 (April, 1968), 1084–1091. The classic account suggesting Adams's fundamental inability to grasp the exceptionalism of the new American world is in Wood, *Creation*, 567–592 (although Wood also appreciates the "relevance" of Adams's critique). Richard Alan Ryerson, "John Adams, Republican Monarchist: An Inquiry into the Origins of his Constitutional Thought," in Eliga J. Gould and Peter S. Onuf, eds., *Empire and Nation: The American Revolution in the Atlantic World* (Baltimore, 2005), 72–92 is essential. Also see C. Bradley Thompson, "John Adams and the Coming of the French Revolution," *JER* 16 (Fall 1996), 361–387, for an interesting discussion of the epistemological differences between principles in this debate, especially Adams and Condorcet. Max M. Mintz, "Condorcet's Reconsideration of America as a Model for Europe," *JER* 11 (Winter 1991), 493–506, is broadly illuminating.

[76] Adams to TJ, September 2, 1813, in *AJL*, 371–372.

[77] Adams, *Defence*, in *WJA* 4: 400.

it that the end result would be "an oligarchy," no matter how democratic the government was in form.[78] The aristocracy would always be able to sway and mislead the people (in "their thoughtless simplicity").[79] This pattern was sown in human nature and there was, Adams warned, "no special providence for Americans."[80]

Here is precisely where Jefferson and Adams parted company. Jefferson did not dispute Adams's point about special providence, exactly, but he did think that the American republic had emerged in a unique historical moment in which a fortuitous confluence of circumstances and experiences converged to create a people who could be trusted with self-government. He was under no illusions that this would, of necessity, remain true to the end of time – exactly why he hoped to perpetuate it as long as possible through education and the expansion of opportunities for Americans to maximize freedom, including expansion across space, facilitation of a free press, and maximum possible engagement on the part of the people in governance. Talent and virtue would get into public office over "wealth, birth, and beauty" only if a people was able to accurately distinguish between the two. And, of course, as we have seen, Jefferson thought he had found such a people.

If the heart of their dispute was the ability of the American people to both distinguish merit from mere celebrity, on the one hand, and to resist the influence and manipulation of the aristocracy, on the other, Jefferson, nevertheless, did not disagree with Adams that institutional checks on the aristocracy were necessary and in order. If the natural aristocracy was a great blessing – "the most precious gift of nature," he called it – Jefferson's faith in such an assemblage of talent was not blind. He knew as well as Adams that the natural aristocracy was capable of aggrandizing its power, oppressing the people, and isolating itself from public oversight.[81] But, Jefferson offered at least three solutions to such an eventuality, none of which was exclusively sufficient. First were well-ordered institutions and frequent elections that could check the ability – if not the desire – of the natural aristocrats to parlay their political power into private gain. Here, the natural aristocracy would face the people "with a recurrence of elections at such short periods as will enable [the people] to displace an unfaithful servant before the mischief he meditates may be irremediable."[82] Second, as we have already seen, based on his experience with them, he expected that the American people were alert, spirited, and informed enough to spot tyranny on the horizon well before it did much damage and check its progress. Elections here, he thought, would actually serve an oversight function, rather than simply ratifying the wishes of the elite, as Adams assumed they would. Third, sustaining the people's "confidence" essential to

[78] Ibid., 401.
[79] Ibid., 585.
[80] Ibid., 401. Also see Adams to TJ, October 9, 1787, in *AJL*, 202.
[81] See *Notes*, 120–121.
[82] TJ to Adams, October 28, 1813, in *AJL*.

the maintenance of the "public good" would require intense scrupulousness on the part of the natural aristocrats themselves, even to the point of "sacrifice."[83] Adams found Jefferson's reliance on the self-restraint of the natural aristocracy as naïve as he considered Jefferson's confidence in the people utopian. But for Jefferson, these aspects were mutually reinforcing: a leadership class that emerged from a cultivated public in a polity that valued worth would have an interest in perpetuating that public's judgment and courage. This unique combination of institutional barriers, a public spirit cultivated for vigilance and discernment, and a leadership class that prized public confidence would do more to ensure a virtuous system than anyone of them alone.

Jefferson's program sought to make whatever membranes separated the natural aristocracy from the public ever more permeable insofar as they were rooted in artificiality. What is truly remarkable about his argument to Adams is his claim that for the first time in human history the "democracy" had become so trustworthy that its opinion embraced the most advanced views of the "aristocracy" and granted an enthusiastic consent to the implementation of the ideas of the most enlightened philosophers and scientists and statesmen.[84]

Jefferson's description of his differences with Adams was close to the mark: that Adams feared the many while Jefferson trusted them. To be precise, Adams (as he tried to tell Jefferson repeatedly) feared the few but doubted the capacity of the many to check them,[85] whereas Jefferson knew that the few could become

---

[83] For one minor but significant example, President Jefferson rejected the request for a political appointment from a distant relative, noting that "the public will never be made to believe that an appointment of a relative is made on the ground of merit alone." And the ends of "public good" that the people expected of its leadership could not "be effected if it's confidence is lost." TJ to George Jefferson, March 27, 1801, in *PTJ* 33:465.

[84] This helps makes sense of why, among other things, Jefferson – wrongly, as it turns out – assumed that all Americans would eventually become Unitarians: once exposed to the truth, this was a people capable of assenting to it. See TJ to Thomas Cooper, Nov. 2, 1822, *L&B* 15:405; and to Benjamin Waterhouse, June 26, 1822, ibid., 385. For important reflections on the way Jefferson saw in Unitarianism the fulfillment of the democratic and enlightened tendencies of American Christianity, see Peter S. Onuf, "Jefferson's Religion: Priestcraft, Enlightenment, and the Republican Revolution," in Onuf, *The Mind of Thomas Jefferson* (Charlottesville, 2007), 139–168, esp. 154–159.

[85] Adams to TJ, December 6, 1787, in *AJL*, 213; Adams to TJ, October 9, 1787, ibid., 202–203. Jefferson – and this would become a pattern in their correspondence – failed to respond in both cases to what amounted to the heart of Adams's political science. The documentary record largely bears out Adams's frustrated 1791 assertion to Jefferson that they had "never had a serious conversation together that I can recollect concerning the nature of government" and that "the very transient hints that have ever passed between Us have been jocular and superficial, without ever coming to any explanation." This in spite of Adams's own candid efforts to explain himself and draw Jefferson out. See Adams to TJ, July 29, 1791, in ibid., 248–249. No wonder that when their correspondence resumed in 1812, Adams was still hoping that they could explain themselves to each other. See Adams to TJ, July 15, 1813, ibid., 358. This later correspondence can be described, on one level, as Adams's frustrated effort – again and again – to get Jefferson to truly engage his political theory. Jefferson's famous 1813 letter on the natural aristocracy is the closest Adams ever got to a fulfillment of his wish. And Jefferson, characteristically, never thoroughly responded to Adams's thoughtful critique of Jefferson's argument there.

tyrannical but believed in the ability of the many to prevent that from succeeding, or, rather, he believed that the intimate and fluid relationship between the public and its leadership would short-circuit these tendencies from both directions. The American people – even common people who did not necessarily have the wherewithal or intellectual capacity to run national affairs – Jefferson argued, did have the sense to distinguish statesmen from demagogues and to wisely evaluate the performance of elected officials and the courage to stand against them when they went astray.[86] The trick, of course, was that, while Jefferson trusted the American people, he also believed the foundation of that trust demanded perpetual cultivation.[87]

Jefferson spelled out this relationship most clearly, perhaps, in his Second Inaugural Address. All the good he has described was "due, in the first place," he said, "to the reflecting character of our citizens at large, who, by the weight of public opinion, influence and strengthen the public measures; it is due to the sound discretion with which they select from among themselves those to whom they confide the legislative duties; it is due to the zeal and wisdom of the characters thus selected, who lay the foundations of public happiness in wholesome laws."[88] What Jefferson described here was a kind of cycle in which an enlightened public opinion would shape the character of electoral politics, leading to the election of wise statesmen who would craft the kind of legislation that would sustain public happiness, cultivating enlightened public opinion and the very civil society that would simultaneously create the next generation of natural aristocrats and the public that would be able to recognize them. The natural aristocracy could defer to the wisdom of public opinion and create a legislative framework for public happiness precisely because that very public had elevated that natural aristocracy to positions of authority in the first place. The public interest would prioritize enlightened leadership; the interest of the natural aristocracy would continue to cultivate the public from whence it came. Jefferson put it clearly when he suggested that the "chief duty" of republican leaders was "to inform the minds of the people, and to follow their will," a mutually reciprocal relationship in which leadership, cultivation, and mutual deference were inextricably intertwined.[89]

---

[86] It seems worth noting that when they discussed this issue prior to 1800, their debate took place largely in the realm of theory. By 1813 (post-1800, that is), when they picked up the subject again, their prior views had been confirmed: Adams in his suspicion that the public would never be able to fully appreciate and distinguish between talent and mere celebrity; Jefferson in his hope that the American people could be trusted to do just that! Note, though, that upon Adams's election to the presidency, Jefferson told a friend that he "never thought of questioning the free exercise of the right of my fellow citizens, to marshal those whom they call into their service according to their fitness, nor ever presumed that they were not the best judges of these." See TJ to James Sullivan, February 9, 1797, in *FE*, 8: 280.

[87] Ralph Ketcham, *Presidents Above Party: The First American Presidency, 1789–1829* (Chapel Hill, 1984), 172.

[88] Jefferson, "Second Inaugural Address," March 4, 1805, in *TJW*, 521.

[89] TJ to C.W.F. Dumas, November 14, 1787, in *PTJ* 12:359–360.

So the natural aristocracy was never the exclusive object of Jefferson's greatest enthusiasm.[90] To be sure, America was remarkable, he thought, because it, more than any society on earth, located and elevated its natural aristocrats. But leadership could only go so far. Jefferson once praised Alexander I of Russia as an "exception" to the record of kings as fools "without minds."[91] But, he also noted that: "Though his means of doing good are great, yet the materials on which he is to work are refractory."[92] Effective leadership could not do without a cultivated public. The key to the American system was precisely that Americans were "well-informed" and could exercise "their own understandings" in a perfectly "unrestrained and unperverted" way. This meant that they were "in a body ... wise" and could thus "be trusted with their own government."[93] They may not be "qualified to exercise themselves the executive department, but they are qualified to name the person who shall exercise it." They may not be "qualified to legislate," but their informed wisdom would elevate "legislators" who would guard their rights. This was precisely why "we think in America that it is necessary to introduce the people into every department of government as far as they are capable of exercising it." The oversight of the people, even when not qualified for statecraft, would "ensure a long continued & honest administration of [government's] powers."[94]

The wards, Jefferson told Adams, would complete his system by opening up spaces in which ordinary people would be engaged in public administration and democratic deliberation. Because the modern extended commercial republic made participation in public affairs less and less likely – and certainly less meaningful – for the majority of citizens, Jefferson saw the wards as ground where ordinary people could practice the reasoned discourse and cooperative action that would sustain the American spirit he valued by affording those citizens at least a hint of the meaningful participation that characterized the ideal ancient Greek polis.[95] In this way, Jefferson hoped to prevent government from devolving into mere administration by a distant officialdom, precisely the kind of situation that would produce the oligarchy Adams expected. Most people were not statesmen, qualified to run the affairs of the nation, and the filtration of talent institutionalized by the machinery of the federal Constitution, as its

[90] Here, I slightly disagree with Eric Nelson's suggestion (near the end of a brilliant book) that Jefferson's "redistributionary measures" had "explicitly hierarchical ends:" to create a ruling class, a "structure in which a few elect, virtuous men rule, and all the rest are ruled." Jefferson's scheme was designed to create a fluid and mutually reinforcing relationship between public and leadership, and, in any case, the language of ruler and ruled had no place in Jefferson's thought except insofar as it served to foil his own ideal American system. See Nelson, *The Greek Tradition in Republican Thought* (Cambridge, 2006), 233.
[91] TJ to John Langdon, March 5, 1810, in *TJW*, 1222.
[92] TJ to Thomas Cooper, November 29, 1802, in *FE* 9:402.
[93] TJ to Richard Price, January 8, 1789, in *TJW*, 935; TJ to Joseph Priestly, June 19, 1802, in *FE* 9:380.
[94] TJ to L'Abbe Arnond, July 19, 1789, in *FE* 5:583.
[95] Though without its martial orientation, its ignorance of civil society, or its denial of liberal rights to individuals. On these, see Rahe, *Republics Ancient and Modern* (see, in particular, 843n4).

most thoughtful opponents understood, made it impossible for any but the natural aristocracy to hold office in the central government.[96] But all citizens, Jefferson assumed – particularly if they were the cultivated citizens of his own plan – were qualified for self-government in their own "little republics" where they would oversee "the care of their poor, their roads, police, elections, the nomination of jurors, administration of justice in small cases, [and] elementary exercises of militia."[97] Adrienne Koch rightly suggested that the wards thus performed a "dual role, checking the petty tyrants at home in the immediate community and educating and 'activizing' people in their function as vigilant and intelligent performers in the democratic rule of an extensive federated union."[98]

Jefferson's enthusiasm for the wards is often read as confirmation of his excessive localism, but Jefferson's letters on the subject suggest something very different: an emphasis on maximum citizen participation in the public affairs of their local communities – the only places where most citizens would ever realistically participate in self-governance – and a sense of the interconnectedness of the thousands of such communities as the place where the voice of the people would be gathered, ascertained, and harnessed for public good. As Jefferson told John Adams, "A general call of ward-meetings by their Wardens on the same day thro' the state would at any time produce the *genuine sense of the people* on any required point, and would enable the state to act in mass, as your people have so often done, and with so much effect, by their town meetings."[99] He was even more explicit about his admiration for the New England town as a model for his wards in a letter to Joseph Cabell in which he described how his own presidential administration and the very "foundations of the government" were "shaken under my feet by the New England townships."[100] New England taught Jefferson a lesson in democracy, or rather, confirmed his sense of the national implications of local democratic participation. What Jefferson found so compelling about this scheme was not that everyone was focused on local affairs but that a people engaged in all areas of interest to their neighborhoods would respond when national affairs intersected with their communities. The national state itself could be affected, shaped, and turned, in fact, by the voice of the people as expressed in and through the wards. This was a relationship between government and its citizens unprecedented in human history, since at least the Greek city-states, and on a scale that the Greeks could never have imagined. Because of the little republics in local communities, the nation itself was a place "where every man is a ... participator in the government of affairs, not merely at an election one day in the year, but every day."[101] This was not

<hr>

96  See, esp, Melancton Smith's speech in the New York Ratifying Convention, June 21, 1788, in Bailyn, ed., *Debate on the Constitution: Part Two*, 760–761.
97  TJ to John Adams, October 28, 1813, in *AJL*, 390.
98  Adrienne Koch, *The Philosophy of Thomas Jefferson* (Gloucester, 1957), 162.
99  TJ to Adams, October 28, 1813, in *AJL*, 390, emphasis added.
100  TJ to Joseph C. Cabell, February 2, 1816, in *L&B* 14:422.
101  Ibid.

a localism as an end but an effort to gather the "genuine sense" of a nation. The wards, Jefferson argued, would be the vehicles through which "the whole nation is thrown into energetic action, in the same direction in one instant and as one man, and becomes absolutely irresistible." This is not a vision of local democracies undermining the general government in centripetal fashion but the opposite: It was the "little republics," Jefferson said that "would be the main strength of the great one" in the sense that the national state would gain its own power from the imprimatur of the people.[102] A collection of ward sentiment, in other words, would be the way Americans would ensure that the general government had the consent of the nation.[103] So the relationship between center and periphery would be mutually reinforcing rather than antagonistic.[104] The one people of the Declaration would be rooted as members of smaller communities of consent where their voices would be collected and unified up the ladder of communities. The "power of [the] nation" would be unfathomable when "every individual feels that his own will is a part of the public authority."[105]

If public debate was to be rational, if the public was going to be able to choose wise leaders, it had to be informed, which demanded state action to create opportunity for citizens as well as transparency on the part of natural aristocrats. Jurgen Habermas, the most prominent theorist of the eighteenth-century public sphere, has argued that the widening of the public to include those without the independence conveyed by property or the education on which rational deliberation itself was "premised," undermined the capacity of the public to act as a genuine influence on what became an essentially administrative state run by bureaucrats in the service of various interests in society.[106] Such a scenario is precisely what Jefferson's various schemes were designed to avoid. He understood that the relation between the public and the state would be an intimate one, one way or the other. Either the people would be the "safe guardians of their own rights" or they would become "the instruments which can be used for their destruction."[107] Ensuring that they remained the former demanded that "they should be instructed," that they should continually have access to the means of production, and that they should have spaces for max-

---


[102] TJ to John Tyler, May 26, 1810, in *TJW*, 1227.

[103] The wards themselves would, like the New England towns, be the creation of the state governments rather than vice versa. On the origins of the New England townships, see Pauline Maier, "The Origins and Influence of Early American Local Self-Government: *Democracy in America* Reconsidered," in Martha Derthick, ed., *Dilemmas of Scale in America's Federal Democracy* (Cambridge, 2007), 63–88.

[104] See the interesting reflections about how this relationship evolved throughout American history, in David Potter, "Social Cohesion and the Crisis of Law," in Don E. Fehrenbacher, ed., *History and American Society: Essays of David M. Potter* (New York, 1973), 412.

[105] TJ to the Representatives of the people of New Jersey in their Legislature, December 10, 1807, in *L&B* 16:295.

[106] See Habermas, *Structural Transformation of the Public Sphere*, and Melton, *The Rise of the Public*, esp. 1–15.

[107] TJ to John Wyche, May 19, 1809, *LC*.

imum democratic participation. Otherwise they would become what Jefferson always warned against: "fit tools for the designs of ambition."[108]

Jefferson thought that such a scenario was avoidable for the indefinite future and it is interesting to compare his orientation with that of Alexander Hamilton who also rested his hope in the political architecture that allowed the people "to elect their most meritorious men." Hamilton, too, understood that American conditions created a "tendency" toward the elevation of "merit even from obscurity." But this tendency would last, Hamilton knew as well as Jefferson, only as long as "property continues to be pretty equally divided and a considerable share of information pervades the community." When these conditions no longer prevailed, however, when wealth became concentrated, as Hamilton expected, "virtue" – worth – would come to be "considered as only a graceful appendage of wealth, and the tendency of things will be to depart from the republican standard." Hamilton believed such results were inevitable, rooted as they were in "the real disposition of human nature": "It is a common misfortune, that awaits our state constitution, as well as all others." It may seem strange how closely the thought of his later arch-rival tracks with Jefferson's sense that contemporary American conditions offered a promise perhaps unique in human history. Where they differed – and this is not so far from Jefferson's differences with Adams – was over Hamilton's sense that a decline was inevitable, that government would devolve into administration by a more traditional aristocracy. Jefferson had a different sense of the possibilities for prolonging the kinds of conditions that encouraged the people to elevate merit to office.[109] It is little wonder that Jefferson and Madison characterized Hamilton's later tenure as Secretary of the Treasury as an exercise in "administration," rather than an effort to remain true to the Constitution or maintain the intimate relationship between the public and the state, precisely the points on which Madison later claimed that "Colonel Hamilton deserted me."[110]

Jefferson's natural aristocracy is a difficult concept for us to grasp because it is not a precise fit for our own "meritocracy," closely related though it may be. Jefferson never accepted wealth – success in the economic sphere – as a precise proxy for virtue, talent, and wisdom (the characteristics of his aristocracy) – a stance that stands in sharp contrast with the general direction of American social thought that has long justified as natural those distinctions that emerged from the unbridled marketplace and, however subtly, conferred on those the honor and power traditionally reserved for hereditary aristocracies. Jefferson never quite bought this equation, and in this sense he is a critic as well as a father of our national "American Dream" of social mobility through acquisitiveness. Jefferson's natural aristocracy would harvest republican leadership

---

[108] *Notes*, 165.

[109] All quotes from Hamilton's speech in the New York Ratifying Convention, June 21, 1788, in Bailyn, ed., *Debate over the Constitution* 2:770–771. Also see Madison's speech in the Virginia Ratifying Convention, June 20, 1788, in *PJM* 11:163.

[110] N.P. Trist, *Memoranda*, of a conversation with James Madison, September 27, 1834, in Farrand, *Records of the Federal Convention* 3:534.

from the fields of the public as the ultimate fruit of its cultivation of that public. The natural aristocracy was not a separate category that can be differentiated from and set above the public in his thought, but, rather, remained part and parcel of the most democratic projects of his imagination.

## PUBLIC OPINION

Finding the natural aristocracy turned out to be comparatively simple for Jefferson. The real problem was finding the public. Jefferson spent so much political capital identifying his views with those of the people, and so staked the legitimacy of his state on their consent, that it is a bit strange to discover that he wasn't always absolutely sure where to find them. But, then, neither did anyone else. It was no straightforward matter, particularly for Americans who assumed, as a matter of course, that government ought to approximate the will of the people. Jefferson's solutions weren't always that much clearer than any one else's in this regard, but he had wrestled with the issues for quite a long time, so that his "public" was less untheorized than it sometimes appears.

When Jefferson told William Short that public opinion was "lord of the universe,"[111] he was reiterating what had become a truism in the Anglo-American world: that public opinion shaped the character of governance and without its approbation no government could be legitimate.[112] In the absence of public approbation, government could rule only by some combination of force, corruption, and deception; with it, government had leave to exercise energy in the service of legitimate national ends. Legitimate government was "founded on opinion," and the opinions of one's "countrymen," Jefferson insisted, "constitute[d], indeed, moral facts, as important as physical ones to the attention of the public functionary."[113] Public opinion gave a kind of legitimate energy to government that political thinkers had long otherwise attributed to coercive force, and sometimes corruption.

Although Jefferson idealized and even expected the emergence of a kind of unified public opinion within a truly republican society, he did not conceptualize a "group mind," precisely, which seems largely antithetical to Jefferson's

[111] TJ to William Short, April 13, 1820, *L&B* 15:246.
[112] See David Hume, "Of the First Principles of Government," in Hume, *Essays Moral, Political, and Literary*, ed., Eugene F. Miller (Indianapolis, 1987), 32; and Edmund S. Morgan, *Inventing the People: The Rise of Popular Sovereignty in England and America* (New York, 1988). Delegates to the Continental Congress understood the central importance of rooting its authority in the sentiments of the people (even as it worked to mobilize and shape such sentiment). On this, see Jack N. Rakove, *The Beginnings of National Politics: An Interpretive History of the Continental Congress* (New York, 1979), chapters 2–3, esp. 51–52. Also see James Madison, "Public Opinion," *National Gazette*, December 19, 1791, in Jack N. Rakove, ed., *James Madison: Writings* (New York, 1999), 500–501; and Madison, "No. 49," in J.R. Pole, ed., *The Federalist* (Indianapolis, 2005), 274. See Benjamin Franklin's succinct statement of what had become a truism in British America: Franklin, speech at the Constitutional Convention, September 17, 1787, in Bailyn, ed., *The Debate on the Constitution, Part One*, 4.
[113] TJ to Nicholas Lewis, February 9, 1791, in *FE* 6:194.

appreciation of individual freedom of thought or even the biological reality of individual uniqueness. Nature's "creation," he once wrote, was not of "classes, orders, genera, species," but "of individuals."[114] On multiple occasions, Jefferson also acknowledged the legitimacy of and embraced variety in opinion in a free society, and he valued the right of individuals to resist what later generations would call group-think or "mass society."[115] If the "rights of the whole" could be "no more than the sum of the rights of individuals," as he once suggested, then the opinion of the "public" might be no more than the aggregate of the varied opinions of individuals.[116] Jefferson once defined "the people," in fact, as "the mass of *individuals* composing the society."[117]

It would seem a simple matter to contrast Jefferson with Jacobins in France, who (following Rousseau) rejected the concept of "public opinion" as too heterogeneous, untutored, prejudicial, and conflicted, in favor of a more homogeneous "public spirit" embodying the will of the nation. Jacobin "public spirit" denied the legitimacy of contrary political opinions and led to the Terror, which Jefferson deplored;[118] after all, Jefferson's "first principle of republicanism" was "that the *lex majoris parties* is the fundamental law of every society of individuals of equal rights," a principle that recognizes and even legitimizes the existence of a minority viewpoint.[119] But it is nevertheless true that Jefferson understood that significant differences in political opinion really could hurt a political community, precisely why it is not uncommon to read Jefferson categorizing political opinions different from his own as "heresy" or "blasphemy."[120] As he told one correspondent, his "catholic principle of republicanism" was the supremacy of the "will of the nation," which seems a bit more ambivalent about the sanctity of individual opinion, threatening to absorb it

---

[114] TJ to John Manners, February 22, 1814, in *L&B* 14:97. On the concept of a "group mind," see W. Phillips Davison, "Public Opinion," *International Encyclopedia of the Social Sciences*, ed., David L. Sills (New York, 1968), 13:191.

[115] See, among others, Dwight Macdonald, "A Theory of Mass Culture," *Diogenes* 3 (Summer 1953), 1–17, and, for early critiques of the concept, see Daniel Bell, "America as a Mass Society: A Critique," *Commentary* 22 (July 1956), 75–83, and Edward Shils, "The Theory of Mass Society," *Diogenes* 39 (1962), 45–66.

[116] TJ to Madison, September 6, 1789, in *ROL* 1:632.

[117] TJ to DuPont, April 24, 1816, in Dumas Malone, ed., *Correspondence Between Thomas Jefferson and Pierre Samuel Du Pont de Nemours, 1798–1817* (Boston, 1930), 182, emphasis added.

[118] On this shift, see, especially Mona Ozouf, "Public Spirit," in Francois Furet and Mona Ozouf, ed., *A Critical Dictionary of the French Revolution*, trans. Arthur Goldhammer (Cambridge, MA, 1989), 771–780. Also see Ozouf, "'Public Opinion' at the End of the Old Regime," *Journal of Modern History* 60, suppl. (September 1988), S1–S21; and Keith Baker, "Public Opinion as Political Invention," in Baker, *Inventing the French Revolution: Essays on French Political Culture in the Eighteenth Century* (Cambridge, 1990), 167–199, 337–345.

[119] TJ to Alexander von Humboldt, June 13, 1817, *L&B* 15:127. Also see Jefferson's "Opinion on the Constitutionality of the Residence Bill," July 15, 1790, in *PTJ* 17:195.

[120] For one particularly notorious example among many, see TJ to Philip Mazzei, April 24, 1796, in *TJW*, 1037. Also see, TJ to Joseph C. Cabell, February 2, 1816, ibid., 1380; and Rahe, *Republics Ancient and Modern*, 706.

into a kind of general will.[121] After all, the law of nations suggested, he noted, that "what is done by the body of a nation must be submitted to by all its members."[122] Individual acquiescence in the will of the majority, he said, allowed "the nation" to "move ... in mass in the same direction, although it may not be that which every individual thinks best."[123] Moreover, he told Madison, "Individuals are parts only of a society, subject to the laws of the whole."[124] It followed that "laws made by common consent must not be trampled on by individuals."[125] In fact, Jefferson suggested (shortly after his own election to the presidency), "the individual who differs from ["public sentiment"] ought to distrust and examine well his own opinion."[126] In natural science, Jefferson noted, "the plan of creation is inscrutable to our limited faculties," so human beings were forced to draw arbitrary lines" – systems of classification – "in order to accommodate [such] limited views."[127] In much the same way, legitimate republics were forced to evaluate public approbation by appealing to the aggregate voice of the national community.

The question of where to find that national voice or how to isolate and identify the public opinion Jefferson trusted was a difficult one in the early Republic – one Jefferson wrestled with from early on. Jefferson, like most contemporaries, had trouble knowing how to recognize the voice of the public and when and where it was legitimate for the people to register their direct influence.

To begin with, everyone agreed that government was illegitimate without explicit public sanction. To that point, one of Jefferson's central criticisms of the Virginia Constitution in the 1780s was that the body that wrote it had, of necessity, assumed its authority to do so in a revolutionary situation but had never thereafter given the public the opportunity to actively endorse its work. Indeed, with the breakdown of royal authority in the months leading up to independence, the colonial assemblies assumed that they embodied the popular voice of their particular communities (the new states). But as extralegal bodies governing and exercising authority in an extraordinary (and extraconstitutional) time of crisis, such legislatures – and other popular associations of all sorts, including town meetings, local bodies, and up to the Continental Congress and the Committees of Safety and Inspection the Congress authorized – had not yet received the imprimatur of explicit popular sanction.[128]

---

[121] Anas, in *FE* 1:249. Also see Jefferson's "mother principle" of republics in TJ to Samuel Kercheval, July 12, 1816, in *L&B* 15:33.

[122] TJ to Miami and Delaware Nations, January 8, 1803, *L&B* 16:398.

[123] TJ to the General Meeting of Correspondence of the Six Baptist Associations Represented at Chesterfield, Virginia, November 21, 1808, *L&B* 16:321.

[124] TJ to Madison, September 6, 1789, in *ROL* 1:633.

[125] To Garret Vanmeter, 1781, *PTJ* 5:566. Also see Jefferson to Miami and Deleware nations, January 8, 1803, *L&B* 16:398.

[126] TJ to William Findley, March 24, 1801, in *FE* 9:225.

[127] To John Manners, February 22, 1814, *L&B* 14:99–100.

[128] But note that such extralegal institutions and associations could be seen (and were seen by patriots) as more accurate representations of the people than "duly constituted government." In this sense, all the state governments were "voluntary associations." For this point, see Marc

Accordingly, the "conventions" created in 1775 and 1776 to temporarily replace the defunct House of Burgesses, Jefferson pointed out, could not have been vested with powers "other than those of the ordinary legislature" and did not therefore have the authority (from the people) to "pass an act transcendent to the powers of other legislatures." Nevertheless, when Congress authorized the states to form new governments "under the authority of the people" to replace "the exercise of every kind of authority under the ... crown," Virginia's "convention," like most state legislatures, drafted new constitutions.[129] Because the Virginia convention – what he called the "ordinary legislature" – had drafted Virginia's new constitution (something he denied the legislature had the "power to do"), Jefferson believed that the Virginia legislature could alter it. The constitution, then, lacked the status of fundamental law against which ordinary legislation should be measured. It was in that sense, then, potentially no better securer of liberty than the British Constitution had been.

Some argued that the people had given their tacit consent or authorization to the document because they "did not rebel against it." But mere popular "acquiescence," Jefferson insisted, was not to "be construed into a confirmation of every illegal thing done during that period;" otherwise, the people would have to "rise in rebellion" against "every unauthoritative exercise of power by the legislature" lest "their silence be construed into a surrender of that power." Jefferson invoked and endorsed Massachusetts's position that "to render a form of government unalterable by ordinary acts of assembly, the people must delegate persons with special powers" to draft such a constitution.[130] A real constitution, then, Jefferson suggested in what would soon become a general American view, was "alterable only by a special convention."[131]

Necessity, then, had dissolved the government, and necessity had justified any number of irregularities. The Virginia House of Delegates, for another example, had decided that "during the present dangerous invasion" by British forces, "forty members," rather than a majority of delegates, would provide a quorum. Jefferson admitted that "no ill is meant" by such concession to emergency: The delegates had "been moved to this by the fear of not being able to collect a house." But, Jefferson noted, even an emergency "could not authorize them to call that a house which was none."[132] Jefferson's point was that associations of citizens outside the regular operation of government had been necessary and just during the Revolution when regular authority had become ineffectual because tyrannical. As he later put it to Madison: "General associations, coextensive with the nation," were expedient "for revolutionary

Harris, "Civil Society in Post-Revolutionary America," in Gould and Onuf, eds., *Empire and Nation*, 209.

[129] See Donald S. Lutz, "The First American Constitutions," in Leonard W. Levy and Dennis J. Mahoney, eds., *The Framing and Ratification of the Constitution* (New York, 1987), 69–81.

[130] *Notes*, 121–126.

[131] See TJ to Noah Webster, December 4, 1790, *PTJ* 18:132.

[132] *Notes*, 121–126.

purposes."[133] But would such concession to the propriety of association apply when peace arrived and the people did, in fact, grant sovereign approval to constitutions for the new states?

Jefferson is often assumed to have leaned in the direction of a more radical kind of participatory democracy, and, of course, he envisioned a deeply engaged public and took explicit issue with Noah Webster's ridicule of the notion "that rulers are the servants of the people." In republics, Webster had argued, because the people vested "all the authority of the state" in elected officials, "the only legislative or constitutional act, which the people at large can with propriety exercise" was the franchise.[134]

Jefferson rejected the logic of Webster's argument that, he believed, was merely delegating "unlimited power to our ordinary governors." The "universal and almost uncontroverted position" in the United States, Jefferson insisted, was the opposite of Webster's: that "the purposes of society do not require a surrender of all our rights to our ordinary governors." On the contrary, "there are certain portions of right not necessary to enable them to carry on an effective government, and which experience has nevertheless proved they will be constantly incroaching on, if submitted to them."[135] In other words, government was supposed to be an expression of the will of the people, as Webster suggested, but, Jefferson noted, it was possible – likely, in fact – that the governors, rulers, and representatives could act contrary to this will. In other words, even the "natural aristocracy" might be tempted to legislate in its own interest, no longer truly representative. For this reason, Jefferson endorsed public vigilance and bills of right to protect the people against their representatives – solutions Webster found unnecessary and dangerous.[136] So, to this extent, Jefferson agreed with Thomas Paine that, in free societies, government could never be a contract between rulers and ruled but should always be animated, rather, by the active consent of citizens.[137]

But it would be wrong to infer from Jefferson's argument with Webster that he would necessarily endorse the right of voluntary associations of citizens to alter legislation or intervene in the ordinary operations of government. To be sure, Jefferson could never buy Webster's argument that "the will of the state

---

[133] To Madison, Feb. 25, 1822, in *ROL* 3:1837. Also see *Summary View*: "An exasperated people," Jefferson wrote in a 1774 justification of the Boston Tea Party, "are not easily restrained within limits strictly regular," in *PTJ*, 1: 127.

[134] Noah Webster, *A Collection of Essays and Fugitive Writings: On Moral, Historical, Political and Literary Subjects* (Boston, 1790) quoted in editorial note, *PTJ* 18:134.

[135] TJ to Webster, December 4, 1790, ibid., 132.

[136] Precisely because even representatives elected by the people could become "a self-dealing and oligarchic government," an "unrepresentative and self-serving officialdom," the people required protection "from self-interested government policy." See Akhil Reed Amar, *Bill of Rights: Creation and Reconstruction* (New Haven, 2000), 68.

[137] See John Keane, "Despotism and Democracy: The Origins and Development of the Distinction Between Civil Society and the State, 1750–1850," in Keane, ed., *Civil Society and the State: New European Perspectives* (London and New York, 1988), 35–71, esp. 47.

exists no where but in the resolves of its delegates."[138] But Jefferson never completely repudiated (or even explicitly addressed) Webster's argument that the "people at large" had no place to directly participate in government outside of elections. In his exchange with Webster, Jefferson merely endorsed bills of right, not the people "out of doors" interfering with the legislative process. Vigilance was one thing. Permanent revolution was another altogether, particularly when the government was properly expressing the will of the sovereign people – as would be particularly true (in Jefferson's view) after 1800. Jefferson was aware of the distinction though he never fully and clearly worked out a solution to the problem. In other words, Jefferson's position was not Webster's but was, nevertheless, less distant from Webster's than the traditional narrative would suggest.

Although Jefferson believed in the inalienable right of free political association, he did not believe that self-appointed bodies had legitimacy as registers of public opinion under the normal operation of the Constitution. Free governments respected the opinions of individuals, then, but when individuals "chuse to act in bodies," Jefferson wrote, "the organization, objects & rights of those bodies," as well as the proper organs through which such opinion was to be expressed, were all specified in the original compact – in this case, the Constitution. So committees of concerned citizens from various local communities, Jefferson argued, were literally "unknown to the Constitution;" they could not be "ordinary & habitual instruments as a part of the machinery of the Constitution," because they reflected "solely ... local views" and were "therefore incalculable" – not only the wrong place to look for expressions of public sentiment, but to some degree literally invisible to governing authorities. Local committees (or political clubs) could not legitimately express public sentiment or opinion precisely because they were interested and had particular, as opposed to general, concerns.[139] "As revolutionary instruments (when nothing but a revolution will cure the evils of the state)," Jefferson admitted, such bodies were "necessary and indispensable, and the right to use them is inalienable by the people." Nevertheless, Jefferson noted, "to admit them as ordinary & habitual instruments as a part of the machinery of the constitution, would be to change that machinery by introducing moving powers foreign to it." The Constitution, Jefferson noted, had "sanctioned" the "opinions offered by *individuals*," but what Jefferson called "the public opinion" could be properly and

---

[138] Webster to TJ, December 12, 1790, *PTJ* 18:153. Webster continued: "The election and organization of the body which is to express the will of the state, is the only power which the people and a convention can exercise, and the only power which an ordinary legislature can not."

[139] TJ to William Duane, July 24, 1803, *FE* 10:21–22. Jefferson later told William Eustis (representing a committee of "the republican citizens of Boston" at a time when the majority of Massachusetts had stopped obeying the embargo) that the will of the majority during his administration had been "governed by no local interests or jealousies." TJ to William Eustis, January 14, 1809, *L&B* 12:227–229. Here is a case where Jefferson took the approbation of the "republican citizens" of Massachusetts, although a minority there, as an expression of the will of the only "people" that matter. The views of the republicans of Massachusetts were, he believed, coincident with the will of the nation (even though a minority in a particular state).

constitutionally expressed only through the bodies the Constitution had "prescribed" to give it voice. No other body had the right to speak as if it were "the public."[140]

Accordingly, Jefferson was never altogether as enthusiastic as some later commentators have implied about what George Washington once denounced as "self-created societies." In fact, during his own presidency he told Albert Gallatin that he considered "no government safe which is under the vassalage of any self-constituted authorities, or any other authority than that of the nation, or its regular functionaries."[141] Of course, during his own presidency, he was convinced that the government was in fact operating under the "authority ... of the nation" – this had been precisely the point of Republican opposition during the 1790s. But even during Washington's presidency, Jefferson's position was less straightforward than many later histories assume. Though he was warm to the "avowed object" of the Democratic-Republican Societies – "the nourishment of the republican principles of our constitution" – he and James Madison never permitted themselves to be publicly associated in a positive way with these groups, the "misbehavior" of some of which, he acknowledged, had done damage to the cause of "popular rights." His denunciation (to Madison) of Washington's proclamation was largely concerned with the general chilling effect the proclamation might have on "freedom of discussion, the freedom of writing, printing and publishing," not necessarily an endorsement of "self-created societies" themselves.[142] And though he shared Madison's sense that in republics "the censorial power is in the people over the government, and not

[140] TJ to William Duane, July 24, 1803, *FE* 10: 21.

[141] TJ to Gallatin, December 13, 1803, *L&B* 10:438. In this letter, Jefferson was focused on ensuring that the Bank of the United States – which he considered a private monopoly – would not undermine republican government, to which, he believed, it was inherently hostile.

[142] TJ to Madison, December 28, 1794, in *ROL* 2:867. The societies themselves, it seems worth noting, were hardly anarchistic. They typically opposed violence and "repeatedly affirmed their loyalty to orderly government and the federal Constitution" (See Sean Wilentz, *The Rise of American Democracy: Jefferson to Lincoln* [New York, 2005], 56), even though they could be boisterous (see Matthew Schoenbachler, "Republicanism in the Age of Democratic Revolution: The Democratic-Republican Societies of the 1790s," in *JER* 18 (Spring 1998), 254n25). On the relationship between the societies and the elite leadership of the nascent Republican Party, see Wilentz, *Rise of American Democracy*, 59–60. It seems worth pointing out that Jefferson's interpretation of the "Whiskey Rebellion" was similar to his take on Shays's: not enthusiastic support of the aims of the insurgents, but wonder at the general good order with which their protests were lodged. None of them "according to the definitions of the law," he said, had "been any thing more than riotous" – hardly an insurrection worth the attention of a 15,000 man force. More, the people mildly allowed the force to "pass quietly" without injury even though, Jefferson asserted (somewhat implausibly), "1000 men could have cut off their whole force in a thousand places of the Alleganey." In a similar letter to James Monroe, Jefferson added "freedom of association" and even "of conversation" to the list of rights threatened by the Federalist denunciation of the Societies, suggesting that during the partisan atmosphere of the 1790s Jefferson might have been more sympathetic to a right (freedom of association) that no government in the early Republic had been willing to recognize. See TJ to James Monroe, May 26, 1795, in *PTJ* 28:359; Johann Neem, "Freedom of Association," in Paul Finkleman, ed., *The Encyclopedia of American Civil Liberties*, 4 vols. (New York, 2006), 1:634–636.

in the government over the people," the preponderance of evidence suggests that Jefferson was generally skeptical of the claims of associations to speak or act on behalf of the sovereign people.[143] Jefferson had earlier denounced the Society of the Cincinnati in terms that focused, at bottom, on the fear that a particular interest in society might inordinately influence the government in violation of the "spirit" of America's constitutions and "of the natural rights of the people."[144] And, in fact, he feared the ability of concentrated private wealth and power to pervert the operations of the state more than he seemed to fear the opposite.

This position is consistent with Jefferson's skepticism about parties, which he believed endorsed partial interests rather than the common good, and helps explain why he always insisted that the Republicans were not a party but an embodiment of the will of the people rising up to challenge the right of a minority faction to administer the state in opposition to their will.[145] The people were to have influence on public policy, yes, but no voluntary association could adequately – or safely – represent national will. There was an important distinction, Jefferson argued, "between private associations of laudable views and unimposing numbers," on the one hand, and those, on the other, "whose magnitude may rivalize and jeopardize the march of regular government." The latter may be necessary in a revolutionary situation in which the government had become tyrannical or ineffectual, precisely the case in the 1770s, Jefferson said.[146] But it would be dangerous to countenance any permanent such association in an American republic where the nation expressed its will through the regular processes of a responsive government.

---

[143] Madison, "Speech in Congress on 'Self-Created Societies,'" November 27, 1794, in *PJM* 15, 390–392.

[144] TJ to Washington, April 16, 1784, in *PTJ* 7:105–108. For the context of suspicion about the society and for Washington's own wrestling with the implications of the Cincinnati, see Minor Myers, Jr., *Liberty Without Anarchy: A History of the Society of the Cincinnati* (Charlottesville, 1983), 48–66. On Jefferson's continued concern about the society, see ibid., 72–73, 94–95, as well as the forceful statement in TJ to Madison, December 28, 1794, in *ROL* 2:867. On the concept of freedom of association in the early Republic, see Johann Neem, *Creating a Nation of Joiners: Democracy and Civil Society in Early National Massachusetts* (Cambridge, MA, 2008), 17–20, and Neem, "Freedom of Association." For provocative reflections on the relationship between voluntary societies and the public sphere in the early Republic, see John L. Brooke, "Ancient Lodges and Self-Created Societies: Voluntary Association and the Public Sphere in the Early Republic," in Ronald Hoffman and Peter J. Albert, eds., *Launching the 'Extended Republic': The Federalist Era* (Charlottesville, VA, 1996), 273–377. On the difficult/ambiguous position occupied by the Democratic-Republican Societies in the 1790s, see Schoenbachler, "Republicanism in the Age of Democratic Revolution," esp. 257–258; Albrecht Koschnik, "The Democratic Societies of Philadelphia and the Limits of the American Public Sphere, circa 1793–1795," in *WMQ* 58 (July 2001), 615–636; and Neem, *Creating a Nation of Joiners*, 43–49.

[145] See Chapter 5 in this book and Richard Hofstadter, *The Idea of a Party System: The Rise of Legitimate Opposition in the United States, 1780–1840* (Berkeley, 1969).

[146] TJ to Jedediah Morse, March 6, 1822, in *FE* 12:222. Also see Neem, *Creating a Nation of Joiners*, 34–35, and Marc Harris, "Civil Society in Post-Revolutionary America," 202.

Jefferson's public would be engaged in maximum participation in and would express its legitimate voice through government at all levels rather than through extragovernmental organizations so celebrated in American mythology. Jefferson's ward republics themselves, it is worth remembering, would be properly constituted local governments. Private power unaccountable to the American public was cause only for alarm in Jefferson's thought, and such concern is certainly at the root of his hostility to banks, which "acting by command and in phalanx, may, in a critical moment, upset the government." If government was unsafe "under the vassalage of any self-constituted authorities, or any other authority than that of the nation, or its regular functionaries," it was no wonder that Jefferson seemed particularly hostile to "the aristocracy of our monied corporations," which, he said, would "dare ... to challenge our government to a trial of strength and bid defiance to the laws of our country."[147]

Jefferson, then, shared his generation's ambivalence about incorporating, and thus legitimizing, associations of special (minority) interest, certainly, but he went further. No private association, even one with a goal consonant with the common good, Jefferson suggested, should take on itself tasks constitutionally delegated to the state. Simply as a practical matter of efficacious public policy, Jefferson wondered whether "a plan originated by a meeting of private individuals" could be "better than that prepared by the concentrated wisdom of the nation, of men not self-chosen, but clothed with the full confidence of the people?" The question was rhetorical: With a fully functioning government possessing the confidence of the people, such a voluntary association would be a "wheel within a wheel," "more likely to produce collision than aid."[148] It is not terribly surprising, then, in light of these assumptions, that when Jefferson and Madison opposed federal government policy in 1798–1799, they (secretly) presented their protest for endorsement by state legislatures and not through voluntary associations of concerned citizens, or that Jefferson believed that the voice of the nation would be expressed legitimately through the appropriate and properly constituted local organs, themselves a creation of the higher levels of government. For Jefferson, individual liberation was never in conflict with this robust vision of a nation speaking with a single "absolutely irresistible" voice. His program for "general education" would "enable every man to judge for himself what will secure or endanger his freedom" and make his participation in local government possible. Without these outlets for individual expression and learning, "no republic can maintain itself in strength."[149]

---

[147] TJ to Albert Gallatin, December 13, 1803, *L&B* 10:438; TJ to George Logan, November 12, 1816, in *FE* 12:66.

[148] See Jefferson's response to a request that he join in a voluntary association designed to shape national policy toward Indians: TJ to Madison, Feb. 25, 1822, in *ROL* 3:1837–1838, and to Jedediah Morse, March 6, 1822, *L&B* 15:356–362 (the source of the quotations). Also see Madison's calming reply to Jefferson's request for advice on this matter, in Madison to TJ, March 5, 1822, in *ROL* 3: 838–839. For a brief discussion of this episode, see Anthony F.C. Wallace, *Jefferson and the Indians: The Tragic Fate of the First Americans* (Cambridge, MA, 1999), 281–282.

[149] TJ to John Tyler, May 26, 1810, in *TJW*, 1226.

In short, Jefferson distinguished between the state and civil society, but what seems most salient in his thought was how close he assumed the two to be in a fully functioning republic. Jefferson took it for granted that the spirit of civil society should shape the character and policy of the state; this was the only thing that legitimated authority. But he also worried about the possibility that public opinion could be perverted to illiberal ends. The will of the majority was the "sacred principle" of republics, but majority will was not necessarily the same as truth. "To be rightful," Jefferson said, majority will "must be reasonable."[150] One of the most important goals of Jefferson's education proposals, as well as his advocacy of a free press, was to ensure that public opinion remain "rightful." Either way, right or wrong, public will would influence elections and shape the character of governance. The context of Jefferson's assertion that public opinion was "lord of the universe" was his concern that intolerant Presbyterians ("pant[ing] to re-establish" Calvin's "holy inquisition") might so "infuse ... the direction of public opinion" that the Virginia legislature would reject the establishment of the University of Virginia, itself an effort "to enlighten the general mind, to improve the reason of the people, and encourage them in the use of it." Nevertheless, Jefferson retained his confidence that "the liberality of this State will support this institution, and give fair play to the cultivation of reason."[151]

In other words, there would be a crucial role for public enlightenment, but Jefferson seems to have assumed that it would be reinforced largely by the very government policies that would cultivate the American public spirit we have already explored. "Interest groups" would be free to operate, and Jefferson valued the "republic of letters" in which freedom of expression and inquiry "should be freely exercised ... for the good of society."[152] But interest groups ought to have no legitimate role in policy making precisely because they could never be the public but could only represent particular interests against which the public, identified with the common good, defined itself.[153] It was in the wards – organs of government – rather than voluntary associations where "the whole nation" could be "thrown into energetic action, in the same direction in one instant and as one man."[154]

---

[150] Jefferson, "First Inaugural Address," March 4, 1801, in *TJW*, 492–493.

[151] TJ to William Short, April 13, 1820, *L&B* 15:246–247..

[152] TJ to Noah Webster, December 4, 1790, in *PTJ* 18:132.

[153] TJ to Adams, October 28, 1813, in *AJL* 390. How the public sphere of individuals is transformed into a unified and unitary subject speaking with a single voice is a problem in the historiography of the public sphere. As a number of scholars point out, this unitary voice of "everyone" is, in reality, the opinion of "a few well-placed critics" and has historically been sharply circumscribed by race, class, and gender. See Harold Mah, "Phantasies of the Public Sphere: Rethinking the Habermas of Historians," *Journal of Modern History* 7 (March 2000), 153–182, quote at 167. Mah has suggested that historians should concern themselves with the way such transformation happened. In other words, how it is that particular groups (typically white, male, and bourgeois) are able to hide their particularity and speak as a "public" with a universal voice. Also see, among others, Michael Warner, "The Mass Public and the Mass Subject," in Craig Calhoun, ed., *Habermas and the Public Sphere* (Cambridge, MA, 1992), 377–402, esp. 382.

[154] TJ to John Tyler, May 26, 1810, in *TJW*, 1227.

Of course, Jefferson also believed that democratic leaders – even in America – sometimes had to defer to public opinion even when it failed to measure up to the enlightened views of the natural aristocracy. Jefferson's deference to American public opinion held even when he disagreed with it over issues of great importance to him.[155] Jefferson took a firm stance during most political controversies, but, as he noted to Abigail Adams, "with whichever opinion the body of the nation concurs, that must prevail."[156] Jefferson tried to walk this line. In the 1780s, for example, Jefferson told several correspondents that he would prefer to avoid contact with the rest of the world – "to stand with respect to Europe precisely on the footing of China." But American leaders were not free to indulge such preferences because the American people had "a decided taste for navigation and commerce" and "have had too full a taste of the comforts furnished by the arts and manufactures to be debarred the use of them." So isolation from the rest of the world was hardly "a theory which the servants of America" (the natural aristocracy, that is) were "at liberty to follow."[157] Likewise, Jefferson noted in 1807, he differed from certain fellow Republicans not in policy but in whether it was best to "force ... the nation to take the best road," or to "let ... them take the worse, if such is their will."[158]

In his 1821 autobiography, Jefferson described his brush with popular opposition when he first offered an emancipation bill in the Virginia legislature, where he discovered that "the public mind would not yet bear the proposition, nor will it bear it even at this day."[159] Jefferson's concern for the prospect of emancipation foundered partly on his deference to white democratic sentiment. He was concerned that his scheme would, in fact, be set back if he promoted it too vigorously in the face of resistant majorities.[160] We might see this as a convenient way to evade moral responsibility for a man who both hated personal conflict and was financially dependent on slave labor. But there is a kind of democratic virtue – and, he believed, morality – in his reticence. He privately pressed younger Virginians to take up the cause and redeem the promise of the Revolution, believing that liberty and "sympathy with oppression" was the "vital spirit" of the rising generation of Americans.[161] But he also recognized "how difficult it is to move or inflect the great machine of society, how

---

[155] TJ to Francis Hopkinson, March 13, 1789, in *TJW*, 942.

[156] TJ to Abigail Adams, September 11, 1804, in *AJL*, 280.

[157] TJ to G.K. van Hogendorp, October 13, 1785, in *PTJ* 8:633; TJ to George Washington, March 15, 1784, ibid., 7:26.

[158] TJ to Thomas Cooper, July 9, 1807, *L&B* 11:266.

[159] Jefferson, *Autobiography*, in *TJW*, 44.

[160] Peter S. Onuf and Ari Helo, "Jefferson, Morality, and the Problem of Slavery," *WMQ* 60 (July 2003), 583–614. As Winthrop Jordan points out, there was quite a variety of opinion in the early Republic on slavery and black intellectual capacity. Jordan suggests that Jefferson was unique among Southerners in finding it necessary to assert suspicion of native black inferiority and that many contemporaries were sharply critical of Jefferson's assertions. In other words, Jefferson's deference to "public opinion" here was, as in many other instances, selective. See Jordan, *White Over Black: American Attitudes toward the Negro, 1550–1812* (Chapel Hill, 1968), 456–457, 441–443.

[161] See, for example, TJ to Edward Coles, August 25, 1814, in *FE* 11:416–420.

impossible to advance the notions of a whole people suddenly to ideal right"
and that Solon was right to say "that no more good must be attempted than the
nation can bear."[162] Jefferson's encouragement of Edward Coles to "become
the missionary" to Virginia, preaching emancipation not through coercion but
"insinuate[ing] & inculcat[ing] it softly but steadily, through the medium of
writing and conversation," though typically read as pusillanimous, is actually a
primer for how to change public sentiment in a republic. Once a critical mass
of support formed, Jefferson told Coles, the time would have come to "press
the proposition perseveringly until its accomplishment."

Public opinion could be wrong; its views might not always coincide with
those of the natural aristocracy. But Jefferson almost always described this
as a problem of temporary ignorance or misunderstanding, and his solution
was that the people should be cultivated, informed, and brought along to see
truth – never that they should be "forced to be free." On the contrary, Jefferson
noted in 1824, "a government held together by the bands of reason only,
requires much compromise of opinion; that things even salutary should not be
crammed down the throats of dissenting brethren, especially when they may be
put into a form to be willingly swallowed, and that a great deal of indulgence
is necessary to strengthen habits of harmony and fraternity."[163]

But the fact is, such occasions – in which the public was wrong – would be
rare, Jefferson generally assumed, because, for all the reasons we have noted,
the American public, he believed, embraced the enlightened truth that the natural aristocracy described. One reason the issue of slavery was so agonizing
to Jefferson by the end of his life was that he could never honestly assume
this coincidence between enlightened views and public opinion. The southern
slave aristocracy seemed unable to transcend its narrow interest and appeared
predisposed to resist any calls for emancipation. And, as the Missouri crisis
showed, most Northerners seemed content, Jefferson thought, to think of slavery as a southern problem to be moralized about, not an American one to be
shared and eradicated together. Neither group seemed reconciled to Jefferson's
sense of the national interest or willing to ask itself what the natural aristocracy would do. This problem was profoundly troubling for Jefferson precisely

---

[162] TJ to Walter Jones, March 31, 1801, in *L&B* 10:256; TJ to George Tucker, August 28, 1797,
in *PTJ*. This is, of course, consistent with what he had written about France and the South
American republics and only goes to show how frustrating the slave question was for him. In
most other instances, Jefferson believed he could count on the public to validate the enlightened view of the natural aristocracy. And, at least once, Jefferson dismissed the idea of women
holding public office with an argument that the public wasn't ready for such a move. In this
case, Jefferson wasn't either, he said, but it is worth noting his suggestion that public opinion
limited the options elected officials could legitimately pursue. See TJ to Albert Gallatin, January
13, 1807, in *FE* 10:339. Certainly, it was easy for Jefferson to "defer" to public sentiment
when it coincided so closely with his own attitudes (or needs), but the larger point holds: that
Jefferson sought legitimacy for his policies in public approbation, and when this was not readily forthcoming, the policies required considerable rethinking or more careful presentation.

[163] TJ to Edward Livingston, April 4, 1824, *L&B* 16:25.

because it was one of the few issues about which he could not honestly reconcile the apparent will of the people with the enlightened national interest.[164]

Jefferson's stances toward public opinion – and the concept of the public in his thought – is ripe for fuller exploration, and this brief discussion does not pretend to convey the complexities of his approaches. It was actually a considerably less complicated matter to discover who the public was *not* than to clarify precisely who and where it was.

NATION AND DIFFERENCE

If the American public was to play the historical role as the facilitator of benign republican government that Jefferson imagined for it, it would have to maintain a particular character, a character that would be cultivated and regenerated, in turn, by institutional contrivance. But the capacious emphasis on cultivating capacities always dances on the edge of exclusion, restricting democratic participation to those with whatever requirements are demanded for citizenship. When the incapacities seemed cultural, as Jefferson imagined of European peasants and American Indians, the solutions were cultural transformation and integration. But when the incapacities were natural, as Jefferson imagined of American slaves, exclusion itself seemed the proper – and natural – response. Jefferson's proposals for sustaining the existing American public through education, expansion across physical space, eradication of gross social and economic inequalities, and creating fora for maximum democratic participation and deliberation, then, were of a piece with his more notorious exclusions. Jefferson's basic stance toward difference was to eradicate it as alien. Among the community of whites, this tended generally to look forward to the eradication of artificial barriers to equality. But vis-à-vis other kinds of difference, including racial and ethnic, Jeffersonian amelioration takes on rather more sinister connotations. But the point here is that these were two aspects of the same search for a public capable of sustaining liberty.[165]

Jefferson insisted on the right of "every society" to "fix the fundamental principles of its association, and to say to all individuals, that if they contemplate pursuits beyond the limits of these principles, and involving dangers which the society chooses to avoid, they must go somewhere else for their exercise." If "we want no citizens, and still less ephemeral and pseudo-citizens, on such terms," Jefferson suggested, "we may exclude them from our territory,

---

[164] On this particular issue he had enough trouble convincing even the "natural aristocracy" of the wisdom of his own views. See, especially, Peter S. Onuf, "Every Generation Is an 'Independant Nation': Colonization, Miscegenation, and the Fate of Jefferson's Children," *WMQ* 57 (January 2000), 153–170, esp. 161–165.

[165] For a largely negative assessment of Jefferson's approach, see Thomas Bender, "New York in Theory," in Leslie Berlowitz, Denis Donoghue, and Louis Menand, eds., *America in Theory* (New York: Oxford, 1988), 53–65, especially 56–58. Also see Harold Hellenbrand, "Roads to Happiness: Rhetorical and Philosophical Design in Jefferson's *Notes*," *Early American Literature* 20 (Spring 1985), 3–23.

as we do persons infected with disease."[166] Sovereign nations could exclude as well as include. And they could exclude both those who rejected their principles through volition and, as we will see, those whose nature was incompatible with national character.

Given Jefferson's keen appreciation of the differences between the American yeomanry and Europe's "canaille," his ambivalence about the migration of Europeans to America is hardly surprising. Population growth was desirable, he suggested in the *Notes*, but the character of that population mattered more to Jefferson than quantity. So no benefit the importation of large numbers of "foreigners" might offer was worth the disadvantages involved in integrating people with remarkably different social mores and political principles into a community of citizens that already made democratic politics possible and desirable.

If the legitimacy of government was rooted in consent, as he had written in the Declaration, social harmony was crucial for its administration: "It is for the happiness of those united in society to harmonize as much as possible in matters which they must of necessity transact together." Because "every species of government has its specific principles" and because American principles were "perhaps ... more peculiar than those of any other in the universe," the character of the people was essential to its proper administration. But if the United States began importing large numbers of immigrants from "absolute monarchies," it would see an influx of people nursed in precisely the "maxims" most radically "opposed" to the principles of American civil government. These immigrants would "transmit to their children" both those principles and a strange "language." Precisely because American governments were rooted in consent, these immigrants and their descendants, Jefferson warned, "would share with us the legislation ... in proportion to their numbers." The problem was that these people would "infuse into" American laws "their spirit." This would "warp and bias" the "direction" of American legislation and "render it a heterogeneous, incoherent, distracted mass." Much safer, Jefferson argued, to await with patience America's natural population growth. This would render "our government ... more homogeneous, more peaceable, more durable." If "20 millions of republican Americans thrown all of a sudden into France" would render that nation "more turbulent, less happy, less strong," Jefferson insisted, "the addition of half a million of foreigners to our present numbers would produce a similar effect here."[167]

While in France, Jefferson got word of a "visionary scheme" hatched by a "Frenchman from Philadelphia" who hoped for a congressional grant of 400,000 acres in the Ohio River Valley for the settlement of 500 French emigrants who would remain French subjects under the scheme. Jefferson assumed that Congress would never "encourage a settlement in so large a body of strangers whose language, manners and principles were so heterogeneous to ours."[168]

[166] TJ to William H. Crawford, June 20, 1816, in *L&B* 15:28.
[167] *Notes*, 83–85.
[168] TJ to James Monroe, November 11, 1784, in *PTJ* 8:511.

Jefferson would later come to have a more favorable view of immigration, particularly in the 1790s when recent European émigrés with Republican sympathies applied for citizenship, and he was always eager to see intellectuals and "useful artificers" resettle in America.[169] But in the 1780s, Jefferson seems to have felt no assurance that European immigrants would be absorbed into an American "melting pot" or assimilated into an American cultural mold: Recent immigrants, he said, would teach their monarchical principles to their children. There is no indication that Jefferson appreciated a modern cultural pluralism or thought of immigration as a continual refreshing of American character and culture rather than a threat to what had already been achieved by the historical experience here.[170] American freedom and prosperity, in fact, originated in separation from Europe: Americans were "kept from contamination … from … the … people of the old world, by the intervention of so wide an ocean," and he considered the separation a significant advantage "to us."[171]

It would be easy to see in this warning the seeds of later immigration restriction in American history. And this rhetoric about immigrants holding on to old world values, unable to thoroughly assimilate, does prefigure our later debates over immigration.[172] But Jefferson never advocated restrictions on immigration, and his rationale does not seem to have been rooted in some kind of xenophobic fear of the "ethnicity" of the people who were to come. If they did come, immigrants would be "entitled to all the rights of citizenship," rooted as it was here in voluntary allegiance. But Jefferson warned against "inviting them by extraordinary encouragements."[173] The problem with immigration, it seems clear, was precisely its threat to what Jefferson considered unique about American political culture and character. European peasants would corrupt American character by infusing the spirit of monarchy and quiescence into the

169  See Jefferson's "First Annual Message," December 8, 1801, in *TJW*, 508; *Notes*, 85. On the politicization of debates surrounding naturalization in the 1790s, see Bradburn, *The Citizenship Revolution*.

170  On these views, see Horace Kallen, "Democracy Versus the Melting Pot," *Nation* 100 (February 18–25, 1915), 190–194, 217–220; Randolph Bourne, "Trans-National America," *Atlantic Monthly* 118 (July 1916), 86–97. Despite their significant differences, both writers resisted characterizations of American identity as the exclusive possession of an Anglo-American culture to which other groups must assimilate. For a perceptive reading of these pieces, see David A. Hollinger, *Post-Ethnic America: Beyond Multiculturalism* (New York, 1995), 79–104, esp. 92–95. For the concept of the "melting pot," see Philip Gleason, "The Melting Pot: Symbol of Fusion or Confusion," in *American Quarterly* 16 (Spring 1964), 20–46.

171  TJ to George Wythe, August 13, 1786, in *PTJ* 10:244; TJ to G.K. van Hogendorp, October 13, 1785, in *PTJ* 8:633.

172  One French reviewer of Jefferson's *Notes* was more hopeful than Jefferson that the liberty of the new world would encourage European immigrants to discard the manners with which they arrived. On the French reception of *Notes*, see Gordon S. Barker, "Unraveling the Strange History of Jefferson's 'Observations sur la Virginie,'" in *Virginia Magazine of History and Biography* 112 (2004), 134–177, at 141. Jefferson, it is worth noting, did eventually suggest that "the general character and capabilities of a citizen" might "be safely communicated to every" immigrant "manifesting a *bona fide* purpose of embarking his life and fortunes permanently with us." See Jefferson, "First Annual Message," December 8, 1801, *TJW*, 508.

173  *Notes*, 83–85.

legislation and the electoral process. These were people taught from birth to awe artificial trappings of European aristocracies. They had developed their instincts in the very state of "dependance" Jefferson denounced as antithetical to American dreams. If "dependance begets subservience and venality, suffocates the germ of virtue, and prepares fit tools for the designs of ambition," it was simply not clear that such people would be able to differentiate statesmen – the natural aristocracy – from demagogues and celebrities in the way Jefferson believed Americans could – and would have to if they wanted to maintain America's distinctive political culture.[174] The proportion of a state's "unsound to its healthy parts" could be measured by checking the ratio of dependent and independent citizens.

If this was so, it is simple to understand why Jefferson hoped to exclude the workers of European cities or the peasantry from the United States. If the American public was that which gave direction to legislation, if the American public was the only one in human history that had made democracy possible because of its vigilance and its devotion to the law (rooted, as it was, in independence), then an influx of people unprepared for it would quickly pervert it. It would be a "miracle," Jefferson said, were such people to experience sudden freedom without falling into "unbounded licentiousness."[175]

Jefferson eventually grew less uncomfortable with European immigration into the United States, and took to describing America in lofty terms as an "asylum" for "oppressed humanity," but the narrative Jefferson told about American homogeneity and its power to assimilate the other was always troubled by differences already extant within the community.[176] Even all the blank space that Jefferson imagined in the West – which had "room enough," he said, "for our descendants to the thousandth and thousandth generation"[177] – which the United States, he believed, would eventually populate,[178] was actually full of potential enemies: French and Spanish in the Floridas and Louisiana, Russians and British on the Pacific, and, not least, Indians who could either become tools of European powers hoping to disrupt American expansion or threats to American settlers.[179] Jefferson's narrative of a coherent American nationhood projected that "a people speaking the same language, governed in similar forms, & by similar laws" would eventually fill "the whole northern, if not the southern continent" and recoiled at the thought of any "blot or mixture on that surface."[180]

---

174 *Notes*, 164–165.

175 *Notes*, 85.

176 Jefferson, "First Annual Message," December 8, 1801, in *TJW*, 508.

177 Jefferson, "First Inaugural Address," March 4, 1801, in *TJW*, 494.

178 TJ to Archibald Stuart, January 25, 1786, in *TJW*, 844.

179 See Peter S. Onuf, "Jefferson, Louisiana, and American Nationhood," in Peter Kastor and Francois Weil, *Empires of the Imagination: Transatlantic Histories of the Louisiana Purchase* (Charlottesville, VA, 2009), 25; and Alan Taylor, "Jefferson's Pacific: The Science of Distant Empire, 1768–1811," in Douglas Seefeldt, Jeffrey L. Hantman, and Peter S. Onuf, eds., *Across the Continent: Jefferson, Lewis and Clark, and the Making of America* (Charlottesville, VA, 2005), 16–44.

180 TJ to James Monroe, November 24, 1801, in *TJW*, 1097.

Jefferson's quest for such pure identity was always frustrated by the challenge of difference within the nation itself, and there is a sense in which his own narrative of American nationhood, which is the subject of much of this book, was always in a kind of dialectical struggle with various problematics that would call its coherence into question. Jefferson's confident assertions about union, national identity, and character always had their frustrated counterparts in laments that questioned the future coherence of American nationhood. The most emotionally powerful passages in Jefferson's writing tend not to be projections of his famous cosmic optimism but those fraught with anxiety about the future.[181] The Union was always in danger of collapse; the republicanism of the majority always had its Federalist foil; American spirit always had its tendency to disengage in the absence of cultivation; and outsiders might undermine the homogeneity of American society. When Jefferson talked about the American public, he had in mind an entity that never existed free of challenges to its integrity from slavery, cultural difference, political heresy, and even poverty. It is possible to see, then, Jefferson's exclusions as the necessary counterpart to his more progressive reforms; they were efforts to make the American public more closely approximate the public of his assertions.

For every confident assertion about the projection of the new nation across empty space, for example, there is another in Jefferson's writing quite aware of the presence of Indians whose practices he considered incompatible with white expansion. With Indians, Jefferson continued to stress the power of American civilization to gradually erode the regressive tendencies of culture on human nature. Native Americans, Jefferson believed, were equal with whites in their capacity for knowledge and civilization, and he admired certain qualities of native society. But, if Indians were, in fact, as he suggested, "on a level with whites in the same uncultivated state," then a humane project would envision their cultural uplift.[182] Because it was their culture rather than their nature that remained incompatible with the necessary attributes of the American public, the ultimate goal of Jefferson's philanthropy toward the Indians was assimilation into American society. Jefferson saw this paternalistic approach as a generous one, but, from another perspective, it invited Indians to commit a kind of cultural suicide.

As early as 1781, on his last day as Governor of Virginia, Jefferson told Jean Baptiste Ducoigne, chief of the Kaskaskia nation that "we, like you, are Americans, born in the same land, and having the same interests."[183] And as President, Jefferson told the Mandan Nation that he wished, "as a true father

---

[181] See, for example, TJ to John Holmes, April 22, 1820, in *TJW*, 1433–1435; *Notes*, 162–163; and "Draft of the Kentucky Resolutions," October 1798, in *TJW*, 449–456. This suggestion draws its inspiration from Homi K. Bhabha, ed., *Nation and Narration* (London and New York, 1990), and, esp., Lloyd Kramer, "Nations as Texts: Literary Theory and the History of Nationalism," in *The Maryland Historian* 24 (1993), 71–82.

[182] TJ to Chastellux, June 7, 1785, in *TJW*, 801.

[183] TJ to Jean Baptiste Ducoigne, June 1, 1781, in *PTJ* 6:60.

should do, that we may all live together as one household."[184] It was part of the "natural progress of things," Jefferson assumed, that Indians and whites should "blend together … intermix, and become one people." "You will mix with us by marriage," Jefferson told various Indian leaders, "your blood will run in our veins, and will spread with us over this great island."[185] Jefferson told Benjamin Hawkins, U.S. agent to the Creek Indians, that such integration would be the "ultimate point of rest and happiness" for the natives.[186] But this generous offer of assimilation – never something he would suggest for American blacks – would come with a price. In order to become citizens of the United States, the Indians would need to give up their vast tribal lands and lifestyle of hunting and become the yeoman farmers of Jefferson's fondest hopes. In short, to become American citizens, Indians would need to cease being Indians.[187]

Jefferson appears to have believed sincerely and firmly that the advance of "civilization" among Indians would bring them happiness and relief from the burdens and inadequacies of their savagery. "I consider the business of hunting as already become insufficient to furnish clothing and subsistence to the Indians," he told Hawkins. "The promotion of agriculture therefore, and household manufacture," would be "essential in their preservation."[188] Indians could survive and become incorporated into the national community by adopting white cultural and economic practices. "Now, my children," he told one group of Indians, "if you wish to increase your numbers you must give up the deer and buffalo, live in peace, and cultivate the earth."[189] Jefferson told the Choctaw Nation of his joy on hearing that they planned "to become cultivators of the earth for the maintenance of [their] families." Such a life, he suggested, "will support [Choctaw families] better and with less labor, by raising stock and bread, and by spinning and weaving clothes, than by hunting. A little land cultivated, and a little labor, will procure more provisions than the most successful hunt; and a woman will clothe more by spinning and weaving, than a man by hunting."[190]

---

[184] TJ to the Wolf and People of the Mandan Nation, December 30, 1806, in *TJW*, 565.

[185] TJ to Captain Hendrick, The Delewares, Mohiccons, and Munries, December 21, 1808, in *L&B*, 16: 450–454 at 452.

[186] TJ to Benjamin Hawkins, February 18, 1803, in *TJW*, 1115.

[187] Bernard W. Sheehan, "American Indians," in Merrill D. Peterson, ed., *Thomas Jefferson: A Reference Biography* (New York, 1986), 399; Sheehan, *Seeds of Extinction: Jeffersonian Philanthropy and the American Indian* (New York, 1973); Wallace, *Jefferson and the Indians*.

[188] TJ to Hawkins, February 18, 1803, in *TJW*, 1115.

[189] TJ to Captain Hendrick, The Delewares, Mohiccons, and Munries, December 21, 1808, in *L&B*, 16: 450–54 at 452. Here, Jefferson described the way whites could become Indians by degenerating in the opposite direction: "If we wanted to diminish our numbers, we would give up the culture of the earth, pursue the deer and buffalo, and be always at war; this would soon reduce us to be as few as you are." On this fear as a kind of spur to Jefferson's desire to civilize the continent, see Maurizio Valsania, "'Our Original Barbarism': Man vs. Nature in Thomas Jefferson's Moral Experience," *Journal of the History of Ideas* 65 (2004), 627–645.

[190] TJ to the Brothers of the Choctaw Nation, December 17, 1803, in *TJW*, 559.

Jefferson thought that Indian women grew crops to supplement and at times supplant the game brought by men. "Nothing is so easy as to learn to cultivate the earth," he told Captain Hendrick, the Delewares, Mohiccons, and Munries. "All your women understand it." But for Jefferson, this was an insufficient, wasteful, and ultimately barbarous division of labor. Men should give up hunting, which failed to adequately provide for the needs of their families anyway, and "take the labor of the earth from the women." Once domesticated, the women would "learn to spin and weave and to clothe their families." Treated well and cared for by their farmer husbands, the women, Jefferson promised, would be able to "raise many children, [and] will double your numbers every twenty years."[191] Nearly everything Jefferson read about human history assumed the progressive development of societies from savage to barbaric to pastoral to commercial; in this light, his encouragement of Indians to take the next step toward human betterment seems remarkably benevolent.

Of course, this change of lifestyle by the Indians would serve U.S. interests also. Once the Indians began to cultivate small tracts of land, Jefferson believed, they would "perceive how useless to them are their extensive forests and will be willing to pare them off from time to time in exchange for necessaries for their farms and families."[192] Sensitive to the imperative of western expansion for the survival of the Republic, Jefferson realized that the domestication of Native Americans would facilitate white settlement of the frontier. If it was "in their interest," as he believed it was, for Indians "to cede lands at times to the U.S.," it undoubtedly would also "procure gratifications to our citizens from time to time, by new acquisitions of land."[193]

Jefferson also encouraged Native Americans to reconceptionalize their notions of property to conform with Lockean standards in which improvement of land confers ownership. To the chiefs of the Cherokee Nation Jefferson wrote, "When a man has enclosed and improved his farm, builds a good house on it and raised plentiful stocks of animals, he will wish when he dies that these things shall go to his wife and children, whom he loves more than he does his other relations, and for whom he will work with pleasure during his life." Such improvement necessitated the implementation of property rights and laws. The Indians would "find it necessary," Jefferson suggested, "to establish laws for this." After all, "when a man has property, earned by his own labor, he will not like to see another come and take it from him because he happens

<hr>

[191] TJ to Captain Hendrick, The Delewares, Mohiccons, and Munries, December 21, 1808, in *L&B*, 16: 452.

[192] TJ to Governor William H. Harrison, February 27, 1803, in *TJW*, 1118.

[193] TJ to Hawkins, February 18, 1803, in ibid., 1116. Jefferson suggested a mutuality of interest involved in Indian domestication. See, TJ to Brother Handsome Lake, November 3, 1802, in ibid., 556. One scholar has also suggested that Jefferson hoped that Indians would provide a buffer against European encroachment in North America from the Pacific Ocean, holding the land in a kind of stewardship before whites could take possession. See Jenry Morsman, "Securing America: Jefferson's Fluid Plans for the Western Perimeter," in Seefeldt, Hantman, and Onuf, eds., *Across the Continent*, 45–83.

to be stronger."[194] Native adoption of Anglo-American property laws would facilitate the peaceful blending of Indians and whites on the frontier. Once the Indians owned land in freehold tenure and mixed their labor with it, they would comprehend (and desire) laws to protect it. And whose laws were more adequately suited to such protection than those of the United States? "You will find," Jefferson wrote, "that our laws are good for this purpose; you will wish to live under them, you will unite yourselves with us, join in our great councils and form one people with us, and we shall all be Americans."[195]

On the one hand, Jefferson's counsel describes a relatively stunning inclusion of Indians in the national public. On the other, his paternalism masked what would lead to a massive expropriation of Indian land by the United States and pave the road for the Dawes General Allotment Act of 1887.[196] The Indians would become "Americans" by committing cultural suicide. The alternative, Jefferson concluded, would be forced "remov[al] beyond the Mississippi" both for their protection and for the advance of white settlement.[197] Jefferson recognized on some level the injustice of such a future. Indians were aboriginal, there was no disputing it, and they loved liberty and independence as much as whites did.[198] But, though they originally had had "no desire but to be undisturbed," they had been sadly "overwhelmed" by white settlement, "driven before it," as it were, and were "now reduced within limits too narrow for the hunter's state." Indians had no real choice, in other words, if they hoped "to maintain their place in existence." They must conform. And whites, too, had a moral obligation to help them do so: "Humanity enjoins us to teach them agriculture and the domestic arts" and "prepare them in time for that state of society, which to bodily comforts adds the improvement of the mind and morals." Consistent with that humanitarian vision, then, Jefferson claimed in his Second Inaugural Address, "We have therefore liberally furnished them with the implements of husbandry and household use." So, Jefferson quickly shifted from a kind of lament for the sad fate of Indians to an imperative: If Indians were to survive in the world they must "change their pursuits with the change of circumstances."[199]

If Indians and European peasants could become Americans via a process of casting off the culture and principles that, in Jefferson's view, distorted

---

[194] TJ to the Chiefs of the Cherokee Nation, January 10, 1806, in ibid., 561. On the conception of property that informed Jefferson's approach to Indian occupation, see Barbara Arneil, *John Locke and America: The Defence of English Colonialism* (Oxford, 1996).

[195] TJ to Captain Hendrick, The Delewares, Mohiccons, and Munries, December 21, 1808, in *L&B*, 16: 452.

[196] David Hurst Thomas, "Thomas Jefferson's Conflicted Legacy in American Archaeology," in Seefeldt, Hantman, and Onuf, eds., *Across the Continent*, 84–131, esp. 118–120.

[197] TJ to Harrison, February 27, 1803, in *TJW*, 1118.

[198] Jefferson suggested that "the red men of America" were "of greater antiquity than those of Asia," implying that Asia itself may have been populated by American Indians rather than North America populated by Asians. See *Notes on the State of Virginia*, in *TJW*, 227.

[199] TJ, "Second Inaugural Address," March 4, 1805, in *TJW*, 520–521. Note that this is no more than Jefferson expected of whites.

their human nature, Jefferson never could comprehend African Americans, by contrast, as fit subjects of assimilation into white society. Jefferson was fully aware of the hypocrisy of American slavery. No British critic of the American Revolution ever highlighted it more clearly than Jefferson did in this 1786 letter to the editor of the *Encyclopedie Methodique*: "What a stupendous, what an incomprehensible machine is man! Who can endure toil, famine, stripes, imprisonment & death itself in vindication of his own liberty, and the next moment be deaf to all those motives whose power supported him thro' his trial, and inflict on his fellow men a bondage, one hour of which is fraught with more misery than ages of that which he rose in rebellion to oppose."[200] Jefferson never denied slaves their own right of revolution, which made the American situation particularly troubling for him: Whites, he declared, were "trampl[ing] on the rights" of blacks in a country whose founding charter declared the "right of the people to alter or abolish" any government that "becomes destructive" of the "inalienable rights" of "all men."[201] It was worth considering, Jefferson said, reflecting on the slave's "disposition to theft," "whether the slave may not as justifiably take a little from one, who has taken all from him, as he may slay one who would slay him."[202] Much of Jefferson's anxiety about slavery emerges from his understanding that slave revolt – "a revolution of the wheel of fortune" – was entirely justifiable by natural right.[203] Even more troubling, perhaps, the "*religious* precepts against the violation of property were … framed for [masters] as well as" slaves.[204] God's justice, Jefferson argued, could not "sleep forever" when he contemplated the misery white Americans had inflicted on blacks. On the contrary, the liberties whites "trample[d]" were "not to be violated but with [God's] wrath." The "spirit … of the slave" was "rising from the dust," and slave revolution would be justified by the nation's creed, natural right, and God's justice. "The Almighty has no attribute which can take side with us in such a contest."[205] "A god of justice" would one day, he knew, "awaken to their distress, and by diffusing light & liberality among their oppressors, or at length by his exterminating thunder, manifest his attention to the things of this world, and that they are not left to the guidance of blind fatality."[206] Jefferson's invocation of an engaged and enraged Providence is striking here because rare. "Nature's God," typically benign and benevolent in Jefferson's thought, here suddenly and unexpectedly manifests itself in human affairs, whether by transforming white intransigence and granting repentance or by war: "exterminating thunder."

But the problem with slavery was never solely that the institution was unjust to slaves, though that was a more significant element of Jefferson's hatred of

---

[200] TJ to Jean Nicholas Demeunier, June 26, 1786, in *TJW*, 592.
[201] *Notes*, 162; Jefferson, *Autobiography*, in *TJW*, 19.
[202] *Notes*, 142.
[203] *Notes*, 163.
[204] *Notes*, 142, emphasis added.
[205] *Notes*, 162–163.
[206] TJ to Jean Nicholas Demeunier, June 26, 1786, in *TJW*, 592.

it than many commentators allow. The problem was also what slavery did to masters. It was the "unhappy influence on the manners of our people" that really undermined the coherence of the American project. Slavery cultivated, in the American citizenry, the very habits of despotism that rendered republicanism an impossible dream in Europe. The pathos of Jefferson's lament about American "manners" cannot be adequately comprehended without an appreciation of Jefferson's assumptions about American character described in Chapter 3. For if it was true that slavery turned American citizens into tyrants, then the projection of slavery across several generations would absolutely transform the sociological entity of Jefferson's hopes. "The whole commerce between master and slave is a perpetual exercise of the most boisterous passions, the most unremitting despotism on the one part, and degrading submissions on the other. *Our children see this, and learn to imitate it.*"[207] And what they imitated were manners remarkably similar to those of the European aristocracy he had so forcefully condemned as poisonous to the prospects for republicanism there.

That an American could develop "a partiality for aristocracy or monarchy," as he had warned John Banister, Jr., was perhaps the ultimate horror in Jefferson's catalogue of European influences. It was precisely in contrast to the degradations of Europe that he had first discovered "what precious blessings" his countrymen were "in possession of, and which no other people on earth enjoy."[208] The privileges of the European aristocracy were purchased at the expense of the majority of the people who endured poverty, hunger, ignorance, and psychological and emotional distress as a direct result.

It was this assessment of the stark differences between Europe and America that made Jefferson's condemnation of slavery in America so pronounced. Right here in America, children were learning to be tyrants, lording it over those weaker than themselves! "The parent storms, the child looks on, catches the lineaments of wrath, puts on the same airs in the circle of smaller slaves, gives a lose to his worst of passions, and thus nursed, educated, and daily exercised in tyranny, cannot but be stamped by it with odious peculiarities." Under "such circumstances" republican manners and morals would not long remain innate for ordinary American citizens and the sustenance of the republic would require everyone to be "a prodigy."[209]

By this light, American slavery was Jefferson's nightmare. Everything he described as a uniquely American virtue, in other words, had its exact counterpart – its precise antithesis – in the slave quarters. For every independent economically autonomous producer, there was a slave, the owned and exploited means of production, as well as a master who owned other men as if they were commodities. Jefferson's virtuous citizenry with the wherewithal to make wise decisions in deliberation with other citizens in participatory democracy was matched, on the one hand, by a "mudsill class" without political power or

---

[207] *Notes*, 162, emphasis added.
[208] TJ to James Monroe, June 17, 1785, *PTJ* 8:233.
[209] *Notes*, 162.

voice, and, on the other, by its aristocratic counterpart. The republican wife and mother and the companionate marriage – the domestic cradle of republican citizens, the site of national reproduction – was matched by a slave family without legal recognition and under constant threat of arbitrary disruption, itself the site for the reproduction of labor – of the means of production, itself. And the natural aristocracy among whites – "raked from the rubbish" by avenues recognizing merit – was matched by a more or less hereditary aristocracy of slaveowners; a republic of freemen paired with a nation of slaves with an inherited feudal status broken only by escape or deportation from the country itself. So there is a sense in which Jefferson could spin his tales of American prosperity, equality, republican virtue, and, indeed uniqueness itself (a world without exploitation or artificial hierarchy) only by ignoring the slave problem. One reason that the Missouri crisis was so troubling for him was that through it, slavery forced itself on the nation's consciousness[210] – and he saw again in that moment what he had understood clearly in the 1780s, that slavery was ultimately the doom of the nation he was making. (Jefferson was never so precise or prescient as when he heard in the debate over the Tallmadge amendments the "knell of the union.")

Even worse, in a way that Jefferson never consciously allowed but that later proslavery theorists would affirm, all of these American virtues were in a very real sense dependent on the enslavement of the nation's other.[211] Even the North was complicit.[212] So on a conscious level Jefferson understood slavery to be incompatible with republicanism and the cultivation of republican manners. But on another level slavery made many of the things Jefferson prized possible, both on a personal level and at the level of the national community. Slavery, then, was the American nightmare lurking behind the dream.

[210] Although he did explicitly note this as the one positive feature of the crisis, because it would encourage, he believed, emancipation and deportation of free blacks. See TJ to Albert Gallatin, December 26, 1820, in *FE* 12:189.

[211] For one interesting example, see *Notes*, 176. In a book praised for its condemnation of slavery, Jefferson here suggested that Virginia's future prosperity was dependent, in part, on an increase in the numbers and values of slaves – and the increased productivity that would follow. Slavery was always present for Jefferson and leaves traces on nearly everything he wrote. When Jefferson made it explicit, he condemned it. When he did not, it was nevertheless a part of his unconscious calculation. For further reflections on this general problem, see Lucinda Stanton, "Those who Labour for my Happiness," in Onuf, ed., *Jeffersonian Legacies*. For a complication of this argument, see Christa Dierksheide, "'The great improvement and civilization of that race': Jefferson and the "Amelioration" of Slavery, ca. 1770–1826," in *Early American Studies*, 6 (Spring 2008), 165–197.

[212] Jefferson insisted that Congress excised his critique of the slave trade from the Declaration of Independence out of deference to the "tender" consciences of Northerners as well as the more explicit interests of South Carolina and Georgia. "Tho' their people [in the North] have very few slaves themselves yet they had been pretty considerable carriers of them to others." See Jefferson, *Autobiography*, in *TJW*, 18. This sense of slavery as a national problem, Peter Onuf argues, is what fueled Jefferson's hostility to the Missouri Compromise, which seemed to cast the blame, and the responsibility, entirely on the South. See Onuf, *Jefferson's Empire*. Lincoln's eventual owning of the problem as "American slavery" in his Second Inaugural Address is consistent with the healing intention of that message.

This helps clarify Jefferson's characterization of slavery as the "wolf by the ear," which he could "neither hold" nor "safely let ... go." Insofar as slavery, as an injustice and as an incubator for white tyranny, was incompatible with republicanism, justice, and the American character, it demanded emancipation. But insofar as emancipation would unleash millions of the most degraded Americans for incorporation into the American public, and less explicitly, insofar as emancipation would deprive Americans of a good deal of the prosperity many of them enjoyed, emancipation itself would threaten the integrity of the national character. This is surely one reason why Jefferson's proposals for emancipation were never unaccompanied by plans for the expatriation of blacks – the expulsion of blacks from America. Jefferson's explicit argument was always that colonization would be necessary precisely because blacks and whites could not live together in the same nation, because of white racism (he is explicit about this) and white oppression of blacks (which would make blacks themselves loathe to join in any harmonious polity with whites), but also because of certain alleged black incapacities. There is no good excuse for Jefferson's tendentious and relentless accounting of these putative incapacities in *Notes*, which makes for the most cringe-inducing reading in the Jefferson oeuvre. But if we consider the slaves as a people without any experience in self-government, without habits of liberty, without even the most rudimentary education demanded of citizens in Jefferson's scheme, in short, without any of the components Jefferson considered essential for a self-governing people – utterly without the American "spirit" described in the previous chapter, a people deprived of the "amor patriae" necessary for citizenship, and in fact rendered its "enemies" by its historical experiences – then his racalist assertions become largely unnecessary as an explanation of the fundamental incompatibility of freed slaves and Jefferson's ideal America.[213] Jefferson's racism and his nationalism were fully compatible and tended to fuel each other.[214] Even without the racism, in other words, Jefferson understood slaves to possess characteristics incompatible with self-government – exactly the kinds of people, Jefferson believed, who populated Europe – people sadly fit only for governments of force and corruption, certainly not people capable of maintaining self-rule for any significant length of time – but definitely capable of undermining the Republic as it was then constituted. "Justice [was] in one scale," he wrote of the intractable dilemma; "self-preservation [was] in the other."[215]

Now the first question might be, why not cultivate those very capacities in freed slaves that Jefferson was so eager to cultivate in whites? And one answer must be that Jefferson's colonization plans do in fact contain such components, so much so that a moment of reflection suggests that they go some distance toward undermining everything he says about the allegedly natural incapacities of blacks – for if blacks can learn everything they need to govern

---

[213] *Notes*, 163.

[214] Onuf, "Jefferson, Race, and National Identity," in Onuf, *The Mind of Thomas Jefferson*, 211.

[215] TJ to John Holmes, April 16, 1820, in *TJW*, 1434.

themselves under the temporary tutelage of the United States, one of the most fundamental objections to incorporating blacks into the political community could be solved – and without the expense and hassle of transporting them to Africa. After all, Jefferson's first emancipation plan proposed that freed slave children should "be brought up, at the public expence, to tillage, arts or sciences, according to their geniuses," a plan not at all unlike (in theory) Jefferson's proposal to cull a natural aristocracy of statesmen from white children educated at the public expense who would advance to successive stages of instruction precisely according to "genius," their capacity for science.[216] Surely a "free and independent" black republic would need its statesmen and scientists as well as its husbandmen. In other words, if black capacities were cultivable through education, Jefferson's objections to their incorporation, insofar as they rest on an assertion that blacks were "inferior to the whites in the endowments both of body and mind," fall away.[217] If some blacks have a natural inclination to science and art, this would drastically amend the racist arguments that strongly hint at naturalistic explanations for the black intellectual inferiority he had witnessed. If, by contrast, Jefferson was serious in his "suggestion" in the *Notes* that "black intellectual inferiority" was, as James Oakes characterizes Jefferson's position, "beyond the reach of environmental improvement," this would, in turn, largely undo his entire colonization scheme, which would depend a good deal on black capacity for intellectual improvement and progress in the sciences and arts necessary to "render them an independent people." If blacks really were incapable of the kind of intellectual achievement necessary to statesmanship and nation building, then Jefferson's encouragement of colonization was nothing but a utopian fantasy because such a people could never maintain themselves in independence. There is no logic that can sustain all of these propositions simultaneously.[218]

Jefferson never seemed to consciously wrestle with this contradiction, possibly because not every objection Jefferson had to black citizenship could be solved by cultivating black intellectual capacities. There was still white prejudice (including his own) and black resentment, though both, one might assume, could be mitigated significantly by the cultivation of black capacities for governance described in Jefferson's plan: Whites would surely lose their prejudices when they begin to understand that black ignorance really was a result of the environment of oppression under which they had grown up, when they began to see, that is, blacks learning and doing what becomes citizens of a republic. And blacks surely would lose some of the resentment of whites inculcated by

---

[216] *Notes,* 137–138; 146. For later reiterations of this colonization proposal much less explicit about the education of freed slaves, see Jefferson, *Autobiography,* in *TJW,* 44; and TJ to Jared Sparks, February 4, 1824, in ibid., 1484–1486. The latter merely suggests "putting them to industrious occupations, until a proper age for deportation."

[217] *Notes,* 143.

[218] But see James Oakes, "Why Slaves Can't Read: The Political Significance of Jefferson's Racism," in James Gilreath, ed., *Thomas Jefferson and the Education of a Citizen* (Washington, DC, 1999), 177–192, at 181 and 348n15.

years of slavery when those very same whites emancipated and cultivated their capacities for self-governance, all with the ultimate design of incorporation into the American polity.

As most American history demonstrates, Jefferson was wrong about black resentment destroying a desire for incorporation into the American polity. But what Jefferson got right, sadly, was white prejudices that were not so easily eradicated, as he understood well because he shared them.

The incapacities Jefferson described here need not necessarily depend on the racial explanation he nevertheless resorted to in the end; he might have discussed them, as he did for the European masses he witnessed in the French countryside, with reference to an environmental or cultural rather than a natural explanation. One reason he resorted to arguments about innate inferiority may have been that the environmental explanation would have undermined a good deal of what he asserted about the uniqueness of America. Because if Americans were actually keeping a large segment of its population artificially in conditions akin to – no, worse than – those of European peasants, then everything Jefferson had said about America's greatness would need to be radically qualified and everything Jefferson considered great about America would become, on some fundamental level, dependent on keeping a full 30 percent of its population from any of its promises. Suddenly, there would be no way to trumpet America's greatness without first acknowledging its terrible weaknesses and its tragic hypocrisies.[219] If, in other words, the American republic was complicit in the artificial degradation of a people who could, if given the opportunity, achieve at the level of whites, such a scenario would be too awful to look square in the face. This is the dilemma that caught Jefferson and the one that implicated him in all sorts of rhetorical evasions.

Though he often hesitated in his condemnation of blacks ("I advance it as a suspicion only") and professed a hope of witnessing "a complete refutation of the doubts I have myself entertained and expressed on the grade of understanding allotted to them by nature," Jefferson usually dismissed proofs of black intellectual achievement as inconclusive, or worse. Phillis Wheatley, the African-American poet widely praised in Europe and the United States (George Washington and Voltaire, among others, paid their compliments), merited only disdain from Jefferson. "The compositions published under her name are below the dignity of criticism."[220]

The most famous case of Jefferson's refusal to countenance evidence of black intellectual achievement is that of the mathematician and astronomer, Benjamin Banneker.[221] Banneker, a free black from Maryland, sent Jefferson a copy of his almanac in 1791 along with a letter that mildly rebuked Jefferson

---

[219] See Edmund S. Morgan, "Slavery and Freedom: The American Paradox," in *JAH* 59 (June 1972), 5–29.

[220] *Notes*, 140.

[221] This story is told well by John Chester Miller, *The Wolf by the Ears: Thomas Jefferson and Slavery* (New York, 1977), 76–77; and in the editorial note in *PTJ* 22:52–54.

for his inconsistency on the question of liberty and slavery.[222] Jefferson's reply was courteous and hopeful, suggesting that Banneker's almanac provided proof "that nature has given to our black brethren, talents equal to those of the other colours of men, and that the appearance of a want of them is owing merely to the degraded condition of their existence both in Africa and America." He thought the almanac provided a "justification against the doubts which have been entertained of" blacks.[223] Secretary of State at the time, Jefferson employed Banneker as a surveyor in the new capital of Washington, D.C., and sent the almanac to the Marquis de Condorcet with endorsement of the author as a "very respectable Mathematician" who had produced "very elegant solutions of Geometrical problems." Banneker, Jefferson said, was also "a very worthy and respectable member of society."[224] Despite these early recommendations, Jefferson eventually abandoned Banneker, advancing the suspicion that the almanac was written with the help of white abolitionists. Banneker's letter, Jefferson later told Joel Barlow, "shows him to have had a mind of very common stature indeed."[225] Jefferson may have resented Banneker's publishing of their brief correspondence without his approval. Indeed, the perceived antislavery sentiments expressed in Jefferson's letter to Banneker drew heavily racist criticism from Southern Federalists during the presidential campaign of 1796, what the twentieth century would know as race baiting.[226] Whatever the cause of the change, it was the last time Jefferson would entertain the real possibility that blacks were potentially equal to whites in intellect.

At this point, the question is why Jefferson found it necessary to go into an extensive diatribe (in the guise of scientific research) about race. Of course, the immediate answer is that he was justifying colonization. All of the most shocking things Jefferson says are an answer to the question: "Why not retain and incorporate the blacks," surely, the easiest and certainly the least expensive course. Jefferson could be forgiven a certain failure of imagination for his nevertheless plausible answer that whites were too prejudiced to incorporate blacks and that blacks had too much dignity to simply forgive whites for years of suffering at their hands and join a political community with them.

But Jefferson went further and began to describe natural, biological, and, aesthetic differences between whites and blacks: color, beauty, and physical difference play a large role in Jefferson's argument, suggesting that the very considerations he believed should matter little when it came time to separate a "natural aristocracy" from the white public actually did matter for differentiating blacks from whites. One of his central concerns about

---

[222] Benjamin Banneker to TJ, August 19, 1791, in *PTJ* 22: 49–52.
[223] TJ to Banneker, August 30, 1791, in ibid., 97–98.
[224] TJ to Condorcet, August 30, 1791, in ibid, 98–99.
[225] TJ to Joel Barlow, October 8, 1809, in *L&B* 11:322.
[226] William Smith of South Carolina wrote, for example: "What shall we think of a secretary of state thus fraternizing with negroes ... writing them complimentary epistles, styling them his black brethren, congratulating them on the evidences of their genius, and assuring them of his good wishes for their speedy emancipation." Smith quoted in Miller, *The Wolf by the Ears*, 78.

emancipation without colonization is precisely that intermixture would stain the purity of white blood and Jefferson never let go his explicit horror of miscegenation.[227]

All of this becomes particularly complex in light of Jefferson's 1815 assertion that a certain number of crosses with whites ("two crosses with the pure white and a third with any degree of mixture, however small") would turn slaves into whites eligible for American citizenship if freed.[228] At first glance, the implication that intermixture would over the generations turn blacks into whites resembles his earlier encouragement of white-Indian marriages precisely in order to render their blood indistinguishable: "We shall all be Americans."[229] But, at its best, this was a way to solve the race problem by eliminating it, by transforming all blacks into whites. But Jefferson's imagination could never wander even this far; one of the horrors of miscegenation, for Jefferson, was that such crossing might turn out the other way: that black blood would stain – and degrade – that of whites.[230]

These passages have been thoroughly evaluated by scholars – in comparison with which my passing treatment is cursory.[231] My suggestion here is that it makes a certain kind of sense for someone who was committed to the development of a sovereign polity with a unique national character, as Jefferson was, to be less than enthusiastic about diversity.[232] The homogeneity of character and political culture that Jefferson so prized and expended so much effort cultivating in whites could never sustain the kind of transformation that he believed would be required by the "incorporat[ion] of the blacks" as blacks into the American public. Such a transformation, in his view, would go some distance toward eliminating what was distinctive about that public in world history. The tragedy, or one of them, is that the presence of slavery and the degradation of blacks, free and slave, had already gone some distance toward rendering Jefferson's imagined community a kind of fantastic dream anyway. He was aware of this, as we have seen, which is why the problem of slavery elicited the most pathetically racist as well as the most tragically lamentable passages in all of his writing. This narrative he was writing about American nationhood

---

[227] See *Notes*, 143; TJ to William Short, January 18, 1826, in *FE* 12:434; TJ to Monroe, November 24, 1801, in *TJW*, 1096–1099; and to Edward Coles, August 25, 1814, in *TJW*, 1343–1346.

[228] TJ to Francis Gray, March 4, 1815, in *L&B* 6:267–271. See Garry Wills, *Inventing America: Jefferson's Declaration of Independence* (New York, 1979), 297–298; and Annette Gordon-Reed, *The Hemingses of Monticello: An American Family* (New York, 2008), 597, 599–600. Gordon-Reed suggests that the algebraic formula was "needlessly complicated" because Jefferson's children with Sally Hemings were considered white by Virginia law.

[229] TJ to Captain Hendrick, The Delewares, Mohiccons, and Munries, December 21, 1808, in *L&B*, 16: 450–454 at 452.

[230] *Notes*, 143.

[231] For an insightful overview of the enormous literature on Jefferson and slavery, see Francis D. Cogliano, *Thomas Jefferson: Reputation and Legacy* (Charlottesville, VA, 2006), 199–229.

[232] For interesting reflections on this problem, see Stanley Fish, "Boutique Multiculturalism, or why Liberals are Incapable of Thinking about Hate Speech," in *Critical Inquiry* 23 (Winter 1997), 378–395.

tried repeatedly to rhetorically erase the "blot," but he simply could never fully eradicate the traces of the other already embedded in that narrative and that would repeatedly foil the coherence of his "American story."

Jefferson remained hopeful, however, continuing a pattern we have already witnessed: If his celebration of domesticity could, as he believed, make him a liberator of women's natural capacities, he could also read his colonization plan as a liberation of Africans, enabling them to live in freedom without the deep inequalities they would continue to experience, he argued, if they remained in the United States.[233] In light of this suggestion, his stance toward Indians, which initially appears somewhat benign, may be the more troubling. The assimilationist promise he envisioned when he encouraged Indians to become farmers and intermarry with whites had no counterpart in his discussion of black emancipation. But neither did his dream of creating space for blacks to live in independence and freedom have its counterpart in his plans for Indians who refused his offer of assimilation. Though the impulse toward homogeneity was similar in both instances ("the same world will scarcely do for them and us"), Jefferson never once suggested anything for blacks that could approach in ferocity his suggestion that Indians be "driven beyond the Missisipi" or that "the end proposed should be their extermination, or their removal beyond the lakes or Illinois River."[234]

Much of this ferocity was rooted in Jefferson's awareness that Indians who refused assimilation stood in the way of white expansion and subjugation of the continent in a way that blacks – who, it must be noted, were never afforded the same opportunity to consent – never did. If the integrity of the white public depended on the continual availability of land in the West, then that integrity, of necessity, remained crucially dependent on the assimilation of Indians.[235] Insofar as Indians refused, they remained a presence on the land and thus an impediment to the peaceful white settlement of territory. But Jefferson's frustration was also rooted, perhaps, in his sense that Indians to whom he had offered opportunity, he believed, were consciously rejecting allegiance. A volitional community rooted in consent simply cannot incorporate those who choose to remain outside. The dots finally connect back to Jefferson's concerns about the character of the very people who will continue to make America unique among nations. In this sense, Indians as Indians remained an irritant in

---

[233] Onuf, "'Every Generation Is an 'Independant Nation.'"

[234] TJ to George Rogers Clark, Dec. 25, 1780, in *PTJ* 4:237; TJ to James Madison, April 27, 1809, in *ROL* 3:1586.

[235] On the crucial dependence of Jeffersonian political economy on westward expansion see, above all, Drew R. McCoy, *The Elusive Republic: Political Economy in Jeffersonian America* (Chapel Hill, 1980). On the violence generated by white expansion into land occupied by unassimilated Indians in the Ohio Valley, see Patrick Griffin: *American Leviathan: Empire, Nation, and Revolutionary Frontier* (New York, 2007). On the violence generated by white expansion onto land occupied by even "assimilated" Indians in the Old Southwest, see Adam Rothman, *Slave Country: American Expansion and the Origins of the Deep South* (Cambridge, 2005), esp. 9–13 and ch. 4.

Jefferson's narrative precisely because they threatened to undermine much of what rendered America so exceptional in his story.

Precisely because they were so dispersed throughout the American states and among the white population, blacks were a source of considerable anxiety for Jefferson, but also one potentially susceptible to what he considered a benign solution. Because blacks were not native to the continent, or "constituent members of our society," as Edmund Randolph put it, Jefferson could fantasize about removing them and consider it part of a larger project of liberation as well as cleansing.[236] Indians, in contrast, remained a "blot" on the landscape that Jefferson, committed as he was to expansion, was likewise unwilling to "contemplate."[237] Jefferson rejected the option of moving blacks en masse beyond the Mississippi precisely because whites would one day populate that area also. In Jefferson's contemplations, then, this fantasy of extracting blacks as a unitary "blot" on American geography and body politic would be easily realized in a way the Indian problem might not. Because Indians were for Jefferson "of greater antiquity than those of Asia," they were natural to the American environment in a way that neither Africans nor Europeans were. In other words, Indians were never susceptible of the same kind of solution he proposed for blacks. Jefferson certainly threatened Indian removal, but as long as whites coveted the continent to the Pacific, there was no project that could naturally extract Indians from their native soil and colonize them elsewhere; there was simply no place for them to go. In this sense, Indians who refused his assimilation policy would become the true blot on the American dream, which is perhaps why he became less hopeful about those prospects for integration as time went on.[238]

Jefferson's faith in the capacity of the American people was rooted in his sense that human variation across societies had historical and cultural explanations. It is little wonder that he would look for ways to maintain such distinctions insofar as they depended on the continual cultivation of these capacities and the maintenance of the historical experience of the American public. It is also little wonder that he understood difference within the nation as a threat to America's place in the trajectory of history. Jefferson's national community was remarkably inclusive and progressive for whites but darkly exclusive for others. The same impulse that animated his policy of cultivating the American public also underlay his encouragement of government to eradicate difference, either by complete assimilation or deportation. It was in the American interest, Jefferson always insisted, "to preserve uninfected by contagion those peculiarities in their government & manners to which they are indebted for [the] blessings ... which no other people on earth enjoy."[239]

---

[236] "Edmund Randolph's Essay on the Revolutionary History of Virginia, 1774–1782, Continued," *Virginia Magazine of History and Biography*, 44 (January 1936), 45; Onuf, "'Every Generation Is an 'Independant Nation.'"

[237] TJ to Monroe, Nov. 24, 1801, in *TJW*, 1097.

[238] See Wallace, *Jefferson and the Indians*.

[239] TJ to James Monroe, June 17, 1785, *PTJ* 8:233.

# 5

# American State

> Faction is an adherence to interests foreign to the interests of the state.
>
> Fisher Ames, 1799[1]

> Circumstances are maturing for bringing & keeping the government in real unison with the spirit of their constituents.
>
> Thomas Jefferson, 1798[2]

> The people are now able every where to compare the principles & policy of those who have borne the name of Republicans or Democrats, with the career of the adverse party; and to see & feel that the former are as much in harmony with the spirit of the nation & the genius of the Govt as the latter was at variance with both.
>
> James Madison, 1823[3]

It was the remarkably intimate connection between the public and its leadership, between the nation and its state, that the Federalists rejected (Jefferson believed) when they demanded deference of the people to their natural betters. In his mind, the Federalists assumed the posture of an artificial aristocracy largely disconnected from the public, serving an autonomous or administrative state with its own rationale, disconnected, in other words, from the nation itself, except on election day, when the public would "contribute its acclamation," as Habermas later characterized such arrangements.[4] It did not take much imagination to interpret the Congressional Report Defending the Alien and Sedition Laws that began with a "regret that the public councils should

---

[1] "Laocoon II," *Boston Gazette*, April 1799, in Seth Ames, ed., *Works of Fisher Ames*, 2 vols. (Indianapolis, 1983), 1:197.

[2] TJ to John Taylor, November 26, 1798, *FE* 8: 482.

[3] Madison to William Eustis, May 22, 1823, in Galliard Hunt, ed., *The Writings of James Madison*, 9 vols. (New York, 1900), 9: 135.

[4] Habermas, *The Structural Transformation of the Public Sphere: An Inquiry into a Category of Bourgeois Society*, 1962, trans. Thomas Burger (Cambridge, MA, 1991), 176.

ever be invited to listen to other than expressions of respect," or the *Gazette of the United States*'s straightforward assertion that it was "patriotism to write in favor of our government" but "sedition to write against it."[5]

Jefferson's concerns about Federalist concentration of power in the central state are too frequently misread as – and this is exactly what the Federalists argued about him – an opposition to government itself. What Jefferson was really after – and what he saw Federalists consistently dismissing – was precisely what he believed the Constitution provided: a federal state system of nested authorities, from the "little republics" of the wards, through the state governments, and up to the national government, each intimately responsive to a public opinion as enlightened as any in history. It is somewhat disorienting to hear Jefferson dismissed as an opponent of government when his ideal state would render the government and its public more or less inextricable. Jefferson, who had supported the ratification of the Constitution from abroad, only gradually came to understand the Federalists of the 1790s as its opponents, but once he made this connection, he considered the only patriotic response to be a concerted effort to realign what he believed the Federalists had worked to sever: nation and state. In other words, nationhood was the central rationale of his federalism – so that what often appears to us in the guise of a traditional anti-Federalist message against consolidation was actually motived by a restorationist zeal to ensure that the state was animated by the public and not simply running off on its own. This is less Jefferson the "classical" liberal or republican than it is Jefferson the democratic state builder.

Nationalism emerged with the modern state and gave the latter its rationale and its political legitimacy in popular sovereignty. A state, by this calculus, is legitimate only if it serves a people; without a people, a state is merely an exercise of power, little different in essence from ancient despotisms.[6] Jefferson and Madison embraced one component of the modern state, as Quentin Skinner has described its evolution, but not the other; They clearly understood the state to have an existence independent of the officeholders who (temporarily) exercised its functions, running its affairs as a kind of trusteeship, but they denied that the state could ever legitimately exercise absolute or autonomous power disconnected from the people.[7] The Federalists, on the other hand, were more ambivalent about criticism of officeholders because their sense of identification

---

[5] October 10, 1798, quoted in Dumas Malone, *Jefferson and the Ordeal of Liberty* (Boston, 1962), 387.

[6] See Craig Calhoun, *Nations Matter: Culture, History, and the Cosmopolitan Dream* (London and New York, 2007), 48. From the other direction, it is this claim to political sovereignty that renders nationalism distinct from other forms of group identity. See Paul Quigley, *Shifting Grounds: Nationalism and the American South, 1848–1865* (Oxford, 2012), 11.

[7] See Skinner, *The Foundations of Modern Political Thought* (Cambridge, 1978), 1:ix–x; and esp. Skinner, "The State," in Terence Ball, James Farr, and Russell L. Hanson, ed., *Political Innovation and Conceptual Change* (Cambridge, 1989), 90–131. Also see J.R. Pole, "The Politics of the Word 'State' and its Relation to American Sovereignty," in *Parliaments, Estates and Representation* 8 (June 1988), 1–10.

between government and its functionaries was much stronger; legitimate government, in their view, could be identified more closely with rulers, who, as the properly elected representatives of the people, should be objects of respect rather than criticism. But they also assumed, or so it seemed to Jefferson and Madison, that the state might, for certain purposes, prosecute its interests without the people, except in the most minimal sense that the state remained somehow rooted in popular sovereignty. Differences over where and how that sovereignty could manifest itself and what role it would play were at the heart of the differences between the parties.

If we understand the goal of the Republican opposition as a realignment of state with nation – the argument of this chapter – we are in a better position to see the unified coherence of Jefferson's effort to reverse both the Federalist "transfer [of] all the powers of the states to [the general] government" (a goal animated by his federalism) and their work to render "the depositories of the public authority as far removed as possible [from] the controul of the people" (concerns rooted in his conception of American democracy).[8]

## "TILL ANGLOMANY ... YIELDS TO AMERICANISM"

The historical literature has tended to assume that the Democratic-Republican opposition in the 1790s was primarily animated by a fear of government and an overwhelming desire to check its power.[9] Stephen G. Kurtz captured this characterization as well as anyone in his classic book on the Adams presidency: "[T]hose who demanded the use of wider powers by the central government became known as 'Federalists,' and those who feared the growing power of the national government assumed the name 'Republican.'"[10] Rather than a fresh reading, this one simply replicates precisely the Federalists's own view of the Republican opposition as a kind of resurrection or continuation of anti-federalism itself, a characterization Jefferson himself consistently resisted. Alexander Hamilton was perhaps the first to make such a claim when he described "Mr. Jefferson," in August of 1792 as "emulous" to be "the head of a party, whose politics have constantly aimed at elevating State-power, upon the ruins of National Authority."[11] John Marshall merely reiterated the standard

---

[8] TJ to Andrew Alexander, January 5, 1801, in *PTJ* 32:398. Ernest Gellner's argument is suggestive: "Nationalism is primarily a political principle, which holds that the political and the national unit should be congruent." See Gellner, *Nations and Nationalism* (Ithaca, 1983), 1. Also see John Breuilly, "The State and Nationalism," in Montserrat Guibernau and John Hutchinson, eds., *Understanding Nationalism* (Cambridge, 2001), 32–52.

[9] See a concise statement in Max M. Edling, *A Revolution in Favor of Government: The Origins of the U.S. Constitution and the Making of the American State* (Oxford, 2003), 9.

[10] Kurtz, *The Presidency of John Adams: The Collapse of Federalism, 1795–1800* (New York, 1957), 9. For a more refined statement of this position, which emphasizes the sectional nature of the partisan conflict, see James Roger Sharp, *American Politics in the Early Republic: The New Nation in Crisis* (New Haven, 1993).

[11] "An American," No. 1, August 4, 1792, in Joanne Freeman, ed., *Hamilton: Writings* (New York, 2001), 759. Also see Hamilton to John Steele, October 15, 1792, in *PAH* 12:569.

view when, years later, in the fifth volume of his *Life of George Washington*, he suggested that after the American Revolution "the continent was divided into two great political parties, the one of which contemplated America as a nation, and laboured incessantly to invest the federal head with powers competent to the preservation of the union. The other attached itself to the state authorities, viewed all the powers of congress with jealousy; and assented reluctantly to measures which would enable the head to act, in any respect, independently of the members." Only "men of enlarged and liberal minds," Marshall went on to argue, were of the former party that considered America a nation.[12]

But insofar as it tries to capture Jefferson's position in the 1790s, such a characterization, which is generally taken to be axiomatic, is simply wrong. Jefferson never read his position as opposition to the national government, but rather to a faction that had taken control of it – a party that in its fiscal and foreign policy had begun the process of creating a state with its own rationale, divorced from the will of the nation. Of Marshall's spin Jefferson wrote: "Here begins the artful complexion he has given to the two parties, Federal and Republican. In describing the first by their views and motives, he implies an *opposition to those motives* in their opponents which is totally untrue." "The real difference" between the parties, Jefferson insisted, "consisted in their different degrees of inclination to Monarchy or Republicanism. The Federalists wished for everything which would approach our new government to a monarchy. The Republicans to preserve it essentially Republican." The response to such sinister purpose, antithetical to the public will, and not an opposition to national government or nationhood itself, as Marshall had implied, "was the true origin of the division, and remains still the essential principle of difference between the two parties."[13]

To be sure, Jefferson's rhetoric during the 1790s suggests an intense anxiety about the consolidation of all power in the central state (and the consequent diminution of the administrative significance of the state governments). Once he gained the presidency, he emphasized his reduction of taxes and of the federal bureaucracy as a hallmark of his administration. He spent his First Inaugural Address describing the ways in which government in America could be strongest if limited in its coercive power over citizens and devolved a good deal of authority to the state governments, the "surest bulwarks of our liberties," as he put it. But we are too quick to extrapolate from these facts that Jefferson's entire rationale was reduction of government power and to read such an assessment back into the 1790s. Here we are confronted with another set of facts that renders Jefferson problematic from this perspective. For it is

---

[12] Marshall, *The Life of George Washington, Commander in Chief of the American Forces, During the War which Established the Independence of His Country, and First President of the United States*, 5 volumes (Philadelphia, 1804–1807), 5:33–34. Here, Marshall was describing the confederation period that preceded the writing of the Constitution, but he clearly meant to trace these positions through the 1790s, as Jefferson himself understood. See Jefferson's notes on the fifth volume of Marshall's *Life of Washington*, FE 11:123.

[13] Ibid., emphasis added.

really not to be doubted that Jefferson's practice as president actually strengthened, rather than checked, the power of the executive and actually used the power of the state in the daily lives of citizens in ways that Hamilton could little imagine. If the major premise, then, is that Jefferson's animating principle was fear of government and a desire to limit its power, and the minor premise in the historiography is that Jefferson's practice as president often strayed from such a plan, the only logical conclusion is that Jefferson has been caught in profound contradiction or even hypocrisy. Many scholars from Federalists in opposition to Henry Adams and beyond have assumed that Jefferson's presidency is a study in unintended consequences. The best we can say, from this perspective, is that the presidency was an episode in the education of Thomas Jefferson from naïve idealist to reluctant realist and that, in spite of himself, Jefferson built a stronger state out of pragmatic compromise with his most cherished principles.[14]

But this syllogism breaks down, as all syllogisms do, if the major premise is incorrect, however slightly. To be sure, Jefferson shared – and perhaps articulated most effectively – what we can only call a traditional American ambivalence about government power. I only propose here that we slightly turn the angle of perception by suggesting that although he understood that government could be dangerous he also knew that its power was necessary to sustaining nationhood. His quarrel with the Federalists was on one level – as most historians suggest – undoubtedly about the relative locus and amount of power to be granted to the central government. But I want to stress that it was, as he saw it, fundamentally a condemnation of those who saw little need to keep government aligned with public will (at least in the intimate way Jefferson imagined it should). Jefferson's quarrel with federalism then was less about government power than about the sources and uses of that power. Jefferson's theory of relations between government and public rested on an intimacy between state and people that the Federalists denied, and it was this denial that, in Jefferson's view, animated most Federalist policy. Ultimately, then, Federalists too, were rendered un-American in his thought. The Republic would never be safe, Jefferson insisted, "till Anglomany … yields to Americanism."[15]

Federalism mattered to Jefferson, and it seemed equally clear to him that it did not matter much to the Federalists themselves. Jefferson took it as axiomatic that "the true theory of our constitution is … that the states are independent as to everything within themselves, & united as to everything respecting

---

[14] Garry Wills makes a persuasive case that some version of this is the ultimate message of Henry Adams's great *History*. See Wills, *Henry Adams and the Making of America* (New York, 2005). It also remains the centerpiece of Richard Hofstadter, "Thomas Jefferson, the Aristocrat as Democrat," in *The American Political Tradition and the Men Who Made It* (New York, 1948), 22–55. See also the succinct statement in Max Edling, "The Origin, Structure, and Development of the American Fiscal Regime, 1789–1837," in Alexander Nutzenadel and Christoph Strupp, *Taxation, State, and Civil Society in Germany and the United States from the 18th to the 20th Century* (Baden-Baden, Germany, 2007), 25–49, at 27.

[15] TJ to Volney, February 8, 1805, in *TJW*, 1158.

foreign nations." In such a scheme, the "general government may be reduced to a very simple organization, & a very unexpensive one; a few plain duties to be performed by a few servants." The Constitution, then, left "with the States all authorities which respected their own citizens only, and ... transfer[red] to the United States those which respected citizens of foreign or other states." The Constitution, then, made "us several as to ourselves, but one as to all others" and Jefferson's goal was simply "to see maintained that wholesome distribution of powers established by the constitution for the limitation of both" governments. On the one hand, American federalism was simply a practical matter. "Public servants" in a centralized republic would "be unable to administer & overlook all the details necessary for the good government of the citizens" in their local communities.[16] This is essentially what Madison meant at the Federal convention when he admitted that "the Genl. Govt. could not extend its care to all the minute objects which fall under the cognizance of the local jurisdictions" – precisely why he found it necessary to find "some middle ground" between the "individual independence of the States" and "a consolidation of the whole into one simple republic," which middle ground would "at once support a due supremacy of the national authority, and not exclude the local authorities wherever they can be subordinately useful."[17] The ultimate concern about consolidation – which, in effect, Jefferson noted, would involve the transfer of "all offices ... to Washington," was that such would render public functionaries "further withdrawn from the eyes of the people" who should, in fact, be "the ultimate arbiter" of government action in a republic. The intimate relationship between people and government required of a republic, Jefferson believed, could be maintained only by the kind of federal system created by the Constitution. From this perspective, then, the two components of Jefferson's definition of the Federalists make sense as a single system: Their "original objects," he argued, "were, 1st to warp our government more to the form and principles of monarchy, and, 2d, to weaken the barriers of the State governments as coordinate powers."[18] Consolidation, in other words, would sever the relationship between the public and the government, transforming the latter, of necessity, into one of force and corruption.

We miss Jefferson's rationale entirely if we mistake it for an antistatism for its own sake. The point was always to make government as responsive to public will as possible, but the consolidation envisioned by the Federalists, as he understood it, would essentially withdraw the offices of state from careful public oversight, turning them into sinecures, "secretly ... bought and

[16] TJ to Gideon Granger, August 13, 1800, in ibid., 1078–1079; to William Johnson, June 12, 1823, ibid., 1475.

[17] Madison, speech of June 21, 1787, in Max Farrand, ed., *Records of the Federal Convention of 1787* (New Haven, 1911), vol. 1:357; Madison to George Washington, April 16, 1787, in *PJM* 9:383, though Madison was quick to register his opinion that there was "less danger of encroachment from the Genl. Govt. than from the State Govts" and that "the mischief from encroachments would be less fatal if made by the former, than if made by the latter." See Farrand, *Records* 1:356.

[18] TJ to Justice William Johnson, June 12, 1823, in *TJW*, 1472, 1475–1476.

sold as at market." So republicanism – popular sovereignty – was intimately bound up with the form: "the salutary distribution of powers" outlined in the Constitution.[19] His opposition to the Federalists was never – as they insisted – an opposition to government or the Constitutional system itself. His opposition was, rather, to what he believed to be the major Federalist sin: that they had tried to establish an autonomous state with its own rationale. Hamilton might wonder whether republicanism was "consistent with that stability and order in Government which are essential to public strength & private security and happiness," but Jefferson's republican state would be "the strongest government on earth," as he put it, precisely because it was the attentive servant of its master: the nation.[20] Reduction or expansion of government was never Jefferson's end, only his means, and his position on the state at any one point in his long career was determined not by embrace or antipathy to government, but by his nationalism. His assessment of national will and national ends determined his position on the proper use of national energy at any point in his career.

If we keep his own priorities in mind, then, it should not come as a surprise that Jefferson in power would understand that a state realigned with the will of the nation – his interpretation of the election of 1800 – would be freed up to fulfill the nation's purposes by exercising all the constitutional power at its disposal. If these premises are correct, then the conclusion follows: Jefferson's presidency, its expansion of executive authority, its projection of national power, and even, or perhaps especially, the "darker" parts identified by Leonard Levy and other scholars, is hardly out of line with his opposition in the 1790s or with his theory of state power and federalism.[21]

In short, Jefferson believed the Federalists were attempting to govern Americans with the tools reserved for European despotisms, which assumed "that men in numerous associations cannot be restrained within the limits of order and justice, but by forces physical and moral, wielded over them by authorities independent of their will."[22] The remedy was alignment of state with the nation – and this meant a proper appreciation of American federalism, against which the Federalists (ironically), he believed, chafed. The election of 1800 in his view witnessed the nation rejecting the Federalist plan and readopting the Revolution's premises: that "the will of the nation makes the law obligatory."[23] Looking back, Jefferson summed up the entire story as he understood it: "The nation declared its will by dismissing functionaries of one principle, and electing those of another."[24] Unlike the Federalists, he believed, the Republicans would administer the state with the imprimatur of the nation.

[19] Ibid., 1472, 1476–1577.
[20] Hamilton to Edward Carrington, May 26, 1792, in Freeman, ed., *Writings*, 750; Jefferson, "First Inaugural Address," March 4, 1801, in *TJW*, 493.
[21] See Levy, *Jefferson and Civil Liberties: The Darker Side* (Cambridge, MA, 1963).
[22] TJ to William Johnson, June 12, 1823, in *FE* 12:252.
[23] TJ to Edmund Randolph, August 18, 1799, in *TJW*, 1067.
[24] TJ to Judge Spencer Roane, September 6, 1819, in *TJW*, 1425.

Historians have covered the 1790s in careful and extensive fashion, and the point here is not to exhaustively recapitulate the narrative of events or to rehash the various arguments historians have made about them. Rather, the object here is to place the 1790s in the larger sweep of Jefferson's lifelong nationalist project. This chapter does not pretend to be a history of politics in the 1790s, and it admittedly gives short shrift to Federalist thinking. Accordingly, I am not as much making an argument about the nature of the party system itself (if it was a party system) as I am about Jefferson's sense of it and the ways in which this ought to shape our interpretations of him.

Jefferson's opposition to the Federalists has been described in various ways as conforming to a preconceived set of political assumptions and ideas.[25] My argument here is less to discount the remarkable insights of this literature than to suggest that Jefferson opposed the Federalists largely because he considered their program to be un-American – as a program of governance fit for a less enlightened people than he understood the Americans to be – and because he thought it inconsistent with the principled federalism that emerged from his own reading of the Constitution. Here, Jefferson's nationalism directly impacted his politics.

Jefferson always argued that the Federalists wanted monarchy, a British constitution, and a state that, although rooted in popular sovereignty in a theoretical sense, would largely be removed from its influence in daily practice. For him, Federalists were closet monarchists working to pull the wool over the eyes of the people until the day when they could safely restore British government

---

[25] The literature on the 1790s is enormous. It is worth beginning with the debate inaugurated by Lance Banning in *The Jeffersonian Persuasion: Evolution of a Party Ideology* (Ithaca, 1978) and challenged by Joyce Appleby, *Capitalism and a New Social Order: The Republican Vision of the 1790s* (New York, 1984). For an assessment of this debate that offers significant insight of its own, see John Ashworth, "The Jeffersonians: Classical Republicans or Liberal Capitalists?" in *Journal of American Studies* 18 (1984), 425–435. See also the exchange between Banning and Appleby: Banning, "Jeffersonian Ideology Revisited: Liberal and Classical Ideas in the New American Republic," and Appleby, "Republicanism in Old and New Contexts," *WMQ* 43 (January 1986), 3–34; as well as Michael Lienesch, "Thomas Jefferson and the American Democratic Experience," 316–339; and John Murrin, "The Great Inversion, or Court Versus Country: A Comparison of the Revolution Settlements in England (1688–1721) and America (1776–1816)," in J.G.A. Pocock, ed., *Three British Revolutions: 1641, 1688, 1776* (Princeton, 1980), 368–453. Peter S. Onuf and Leonard J. Sadosky, *Jeffersonian America* (Malden, MA, 2002), 33–79, is a clear and helpful overview of the sources of Republican appeal in 1800. Good general overviews of the politics of the 1790s are Stanley Elkins and Eric McKitrick, *The Age of Federalism: The Early American Republic, 1788–1800* (Oxford University Press, 1994), and James Rogers Sharp, *American Politics in the Early Republic: The New Nation in Crisis* (New Haven, 1993); the former focused on ideology, the latter on sectionalism. Marshall Smelser, "The Federalist Period as an Age of Passion," *American Quarterly* 10 (Winter 1958), 391–419; and John R. Howe, Jr. "Republican Thought and the Political Violence of the 1790s," ibid., 19 (Summer 1967), 147–165, introduce the theme of emotion and political violence of the era and are also helpful introductions. Older surveys that remain essential are Joseph Charles, *Origins of the American Party System: Three Essays* (Chapel Hill, 1956); Richard Hofstadter, *The Idea of a Party System* (Berkeley, 1970); and Noble Cunningham, *The Jeffersonian Republicans: The Formation of Party Organization, 1789–1801* (Chapel Hill, 1957).

in America. It is a fairly simple – and simplistic – description. And a good deal of work has been done to give us a more complex picture of the Federalists.[26] But it is worth remembering that Jefferson was not privy to such scholarship, nor was he particularly invested in nuanced readings of his political opponents. Jefferson's assessment of Federalist motivations is two-dimensional (and occasionally one-dimensional). But the point is largely irrelevant to understanding Jefferson, whose position rested on this admittedly flat analysis.

Accordingly, I focus on Jefferson's claims without suggesting that I am necessarily offering a description of actual differences – my claims in this respect are circumscribed and a clear discussion of these actual differences must await further research. My point is actually much simpler: that Jefferson's own assertions about the meaning of the 1790s lend a kind of coherence to his career that focus on his accuracy as an analyst can miss. As we might expect, no one joined the discussion with a greater sense that the party battles of the decade were about the meaning of America than Thomas Jefferson.

## "A SECT WHICH IS ALL HEAD AND NO BODY"

In November 1789, Jefferson arrived in Virginia from his five-year stint in France to the hearty welcome of his county and state and to the news that Washington had appointed him the first secretary of state under the new Constitution.[27] Initially inclined to keep his current post as ambassador to France, Jefferson protested his inadequacy for the new office but accepted Washington's judgment that no one else could better perform its duties. He accepted the post in February of 1790.[28]

Jefferson had experienced frustration about the relative lack of power of the Articles of Confederation, especially with respect to his efforts to forge treaties of commerce abroad, and he looked with anticipation at the greater consolidation of the government.[29] In fact, he suggested in 1789, he "approved, from the

---

[26] See, for example, esp., Fischer, *The Revolution of American Conservatism: The Federalist Party in the Era of Jeffersonian Democracy* (New York, 1965); Linda Kerber, *Federalists in Dissent: Imagery and Ideology in Jeffersonian America* (Ithaca, 1970); James Banner, *To the Hartford Convention: The Federalists and the Origin of Party Politics in Massachusetts, 1789–1815* (New York, 1970); Ben-Atar and Oberg, eds., *Federalists Reconsidered*; and Todd Estes, *The Jay Treaty Debate, Public Opinion, And The Evolution Of Early American Political Culture* (Amherst and Boston, 2008).

[27] See the Address of Welcome by the Citizens of Albermarle, February 12, 1790, *PTJ* 16:177–178 and Jefferson's Response, 178–179; Jefferson's Reply to the Address of Welcome of the Virginia House of Delegates; Address of Welcome of the Virginia Senate and Jefferson's Response, ibid., 11–13. For Washington's appointment of Jefferson see Washington to TJ, October 13, 1789, ibid., 15:519–520; November 30, 1789 in ibid., 16:8–9; and January 21, 1790, ibid., 116–118.

[28] For Jefferson's early protests, see letters to William Short, December 14, 1789, in ibid., 16: 27–28 and to Washington, December 15 in ibid., 34–35. Jefferson accepted the position on February 14; see his letter to Washington on that day, ibid., 184.

[29] See TJ to James Monroe, August 11, 1786, ibid., 10:225; TJ to John Brown, May 26, 1788, *WTJ* 5:17–18.

first moment, of the great mass of what is in the new constitution." His only objections had been its lack of a Bill of Rights and its provision for the perpetual reeligibility of the executive. Never had he expressed disapproval of the Constitution's declaration that national law would be supreme over state law, its provisions for the national government to federalize the state militias, or its restrictions on the states, forbidding them from coining money or conducting foreign policy. The first on his list of what he approved when he first heard the news about ratification was "the *consolidation* of the government," the darkest word in the anti-Federalist lexicon. With justification, Jefferson suggested that he was "much farther from" the "Antifederalists" than from the Federalists whose company he disclaimed only because, as he put it, "I never submitted the whole system of my opinions to the creed of any party of men whatever in religion, in philosophy, in politics, or in anything else where I was capable of thinking for myself."[30] Jefferson favored a stronger national state that would be capable of collecting taxes, creating a uniform system of tariffs, and presenting a united voice in international diplomacy, and he never expressed any real qualms about the Constitution's transference of many of the fundamental attributes of sovereignty from the states to the national government. The notion that Jefferson was a closet anti-Federalist, an opponent of the stronger national government and strengthened union created by the Constitution, is simply wrong.

But what almost immediately became apparent to him as Jefferson took office was that the Constitution he had so often praised was being read in a different, and to his way of thinking, dangerous way by Hamilton, secretary of the Treasury, and some leading figures in Congress. For Jefferson, political legitimacy ascended from the people. The "good sense of the people," Jefferson wrote, had led them to transform the Articles of Confederation into the new Constitution[31] and could always be counted on to lead the operations of the government in the "right way."[32] Hamilton, it appeared to Jefferson, was trying the opposite tack – using the state to lead the people in a particular direction, despite their widespread opposition.[33]

Jefferson, who entered the government with good faith and great hopes for its future, demonstrated a willingness to compromise for the sake of the common good. When the first serious national crisis erupted over Hamilton's plan for the federal government to assume the debts of the states, Jefferson was inclined to agree with Madison that the proposal was unjust to the original holders of the debt, most of whom were Revolutionary veterans and widows and many of whom had sold their certificates of indebtedness to speculators

[30] TJ to Francis Hopkinson, March 13, 1789, in *FE* 5:456.
[31] TJ to David Humphreys, March 18, 1789, ibid., 5:89.
[32] Jefferson's Response to the Address of Welcome by the Citizens of Albermarle, February 12, 1790, *PTJ* 16:174.
[33] Madison believed that at least "four fifths of the citizens of the United States" opposed assumption. See Speech on Assumption of the State Debts, April 22, 1790, *PJM* 13:166.

on discount.[34] Like Madison and other opponents of the bill, Jefferson also worried about the fact that certain states, Virginia included, had already gone some distance toward repayment of their debts. Nevertheless, throughout the crisis, which threatened legislative impasse, Jefferson recognized the debate as one between "honest and able men" and expressed in several private letters the need for compromise.[35] "In general," he confided to George Mason, "I think it necessary to give as well as take in a government like ours."[36] In any case, a compromise on assumption would keep the United States from what Jefferson called "the greatest of all calamities, the total extinction of our credit in Europe." Compromise was connected, in Jefferson's calculation, with the "the peace and continuance of the union," for without it, American credit in Amsterdam would "burst and vanish, and the states separate to take care everyone of itself."[37] Despite his initial "aversion" to the assumption bill, a rejection of it, he now believed, would involve "something much worse."[38] For this reason, "a mutual sacrifice of opinion and interest is become the duty of every one." If "every one retains inflexibly his present opinion, there will be no bill passed at all for funding the public debts," which he favored. If Congress were to "separate without funding, there is an end of the government."[39] These hardly seem rationalizations for a program Jefferson secretly hated. Confronted by a choice between nationhood with a funded debt or disunion without it, Jefferson chose the former. It would not be the last time he would make such a choice.

Accordingly, when Hamilton approached him, "somber, haggard, and dejected beyond comparison," over the impasse created by his proposal for

---

[34] See Whitney K. Bates, "Northern Speculators and Southern State Debts: 1790," in *WMQ* 19 (January 1962), 30–48. Discussion of Hamilton's financial program can be found in numerous sources. Among the most lucid and illuminating is Stanley Elkins and Eric McKitrick, *The Age of Federalism: The Early American Republic, 1788–1800* (Oxford, 1994), 92–131. For the essential background, see Herbert Sloan, *Principle and Interest: Thomas Jefferson and the Problem of Debt* (New York, 1995), 86–201.

[35] Jefferson to David Howell, June 2, 1790, *PTJ*, 16: 553–554. Jefferson actually came to think assumption, though somewhat disagreeable in detail, was necessary from a practical standpoint. As he told John Harvie in July, just as the bill was passing the senate, the states would never have been able to pay their debts alone, most of the debts were "for the general defence as much as those contracted by Congress directly," and state creditors were demanding repayment and "might defeat the funding any part of the public debt, if theirs also were not assumed." In other words, though he at first viewed assumption "with as much aversion as any man," he had come around to seeing its necessity. "Considering it therefore as one of the cases in which mutual sacrifice and accommodation is necessary, I shall see it pass with acquiescence." Jefferson to John Harvie, July 25, 1790 ibid., 17: 271. If anyone was ideologically doctrinaire on assumption, it was Madison.

[36] Jefferson to George Mason, June 13, 1790, ibid., 16: 493; see also Jefferson to David Ramsay, ibid., 577

[37] Jefferson to James Monroe, June 20, 1790, ibid., 537.

[38] Jefferson to John Harvie, July 25, 1790, ibid., 17: 271.

[39] Jefferson to Thomas Mann Randolph, Jr., June 20, 1790, ibid., 540–541; also see Jefferson to George Gilmer, June 27, 1790, ibid., 574–575.

assumption, Jefferson suggested dinner at his home as a forum for negotiation with Madison, the leader of opposition to assumption in the House of Representatives. By bringing Hamilton and Madison together for private conversation, Jefferson hoped to carry the controversy to a solution. Thus ensued the famous dinner at which the "Compromise of 1790" – by which Madison agreed to loosen his opposition to assumption in the House and Hamilton agreed to use his influence to move the future capital to the Potomac – was forged.[40] Jefferson, though he would later claim that this incident gave him the "deepest regret," was, at the time, more than willing to work with Hamilton for the greater good of saving the Union.[41]

Jefferson even suggested that the particular dissatisfaction of Virginians and North Carolinians, among the most vehement opponents of the bill, rested in their basic anti-federalism.[42] Some of these, Patrick Henry in particular, Jefferson believed, were worried about their "speculations" in the Yazoo territory, which the power and assertion of the federal government was threatening to abort.[43] This was not the first time Jefferson had condemned remnants of anti-federalism in the conspiratorial terms he would later reserve for Federalists. Shortly after arriving home from France, Jefferson told William Short that "Antifederalism is not yet dead in this country. The gentlemen who opposed it retain a good deal of malevolence towards the new government." Patrick Henry, he believed, merely awaited an opportunity "to overturn the new constitution."[44] Jefferson always distinguished between the Republican opposition of the 1790s, which he characterized as an effort to restore government to true

---

[40] Jefferson's account is in ibid., 205–207. Accounts of the dinner and the compromise of 1790 abound. Among the best is Joseph Ellis, *Founding Brothers: The Revolutionary Generation* (New York: Vintage Books, 2002; originally published in 2000), 48–80. Also see Dumas Malone, *Jefferson and the Rights of Man* (Boston: Little, Brown, 1951), 289–305. Other important analyses of the compromise are Jacob E. Cooke, "The Compromise of 1790," *WMQ* 27 (1970) 523–545; Kenneth Bowling, "Dinner at Jefferson's: A Note on Jacob E. Cooke's 'The Compromise of 1790,'" ibid., 28 (1971), 629–648 (including Cooke's rebuttal, 640–648); and Norman K. Risjord, "The Compromise of 1790: New Evidence on the Dinner Table Bargain," ibid., 33 (1976), 309–314.

[41] Jefferson to George Washington, September 9, 1792, *PTJ*, 24: 351. It is clear that Jefferson had qualms about assumption, upon reflection in 1792, but the deep regret appears, upon close reading, to refer to his intermeddling with the legislature, and thus breaking the constitutional rule of separation between the executive and legislative powers of government, though, of course, he believed he had been "duped" into it by Hamilton. Even his later recollection in the "Anas" identifies this as Hamilton's "main object" – "the phalanx of the treasury was reinforced by additional recruits" in the legislature which "ensured him always a majority in both houses: so that the whole action of the legislature was now under the direction of the treasury." See *FE*, 1: 171–78.

[42] The Virginia House of Delegates and Senate condemned assumption as unconstitutional, a particular assessment with which Jefferson seems to have disagreed. See the text in William Waller Hening, comp., *The Statutes at Large* (Richmond, 1809–1823), 13: 234–35. Also see Richard Beeman, *The Old Dominion and the New Nation, 1788–1801* (Lexington: University Press of Kentucky, 1972), 78–79.

[43] Jefferson to Gouverneur Morris, November 26, 1790, *PTJ*, 18: 82–83.

[44] TJ to William Short, December 14, 1789, *PTJ* 16: 26.

Constitutional principles, and anti-federalism, which he viewed as an attempt to throw out the Constitution altogether.[45]

But just as he believed the old anti-Federalists were threatening the Constitution from one end, Jefferson was beginning to fear threats to it from the secretary of the Treasury, on the other. First hints of this came in Jefferson's letter to George Mason to whom he had defended assumption some eight months before. "We have among us a sect," he wrote, "who believe" that the English constitution, which Jefferson considered a "kind of Half-way-house," contains "whatever is perfect in human institutions." Jefferson still believed, he told Mason, "that the great mass of our community is untainted with these heresies," but some unnamed high officials in the government were, unfortunately, "members of th[e] sect." The opinions of the people fortunately suggested that "we have not laboured in vain, and that our experiment will still prove that men can be governed by reason," but the "sect" was worrisome. "The only corrective of what is amiss in our present government," he told Mason, "will be the augmentation of the numbers in the lower house, so as to get a more agricultural representation, which may put that interest above that of the stockjobbers."[46]

That same day, Jefferson asked Robert R. Livingston of New York whether the people of his state were as content "with the proceedings of our government, as their representatives say they are." In the South, Jefferson worried, "there is a great mass of discontent" that might, he feared, jeopardize the unity of the new nation.[47] As these letters indicate, Jefferson was beginning to think that the government was embarking on a journey away from the direction the people imagined it should go, and, in an effort to understand this popular will, he sent tentative queries to test opinions in various regions of the country.

The fundamental point was less "whether these measures be right or wrong abstractedly," Jefferson suggested, than whether sufficient "attention" was being "paid to the general opinion," which he understood to be hostile to the proposals. After all, when Jefferson was at sea returning from France, Madison had more or less warned Hamilton – then a close political ally – that public

---

[45] Jefferson's insistence that Republicans were different from anti-federalists confirms the judgment of most recent historians, that the connections between anti-Federalists and Republicans, asserted by Charles Beard in *Economic Origins of Jeffersonian Democracy*, are not so clear. Most historians seem to agree with Lance Banning, that "the Constitution's victory introduced new issues and led to a realignment that made the distinctions of the ratification contest obsolete" (Banning, *The Jeffersonian Persuasion*, 114). See also, Harry Ammon, "The Formation of the Republican Party in Virginia, 1789–1796," *Journal of Southern History* 19 (1953); Charles, *The Origins of the American Party System*; and Noble E. Cunningham, Jr., *The Jeffersonian Republicans: The Formation of Party Organization, 1789–1801* (Chapel Hill, 1957), 23, and footnotes 71 and 72. Norman K. Risjord, "The Evolution of Political Parties in Virginia, 1782–1800," *JAH* 60 (1974), 961–984, is certainly right, however, to see a connection in membership between the two parties. Almost all known Virginia anti-Federalists eventually identified with the Republican party in the end (Patrick Henry is one great exception).

[46] To George Mason, February 4, 1791, *PTJ*, 19: 241–242.

[47] To Robert Livingston, February 4, 1791, *WTJ*, 5: 277

opinion would recoil at the prospect of a funded debt and that Americans would prefer heavier taxes for the actual "discharging the debt" to a perpetual scheme in which American securities might fall largely into "the hands of foreigners." The central concern here is not that Jefferson opposed Hamilton's program, though he certainly would come to in time, but rather that Hamilton, in his view, was being less responsive to the public voice than a republican officer ought to be. As Jefferson suggested to Nicholas Lewis a few months later: "There are certainly persons in all the departments who are for driving too fast. Government being founded on opinion, the opinion of the public, even when it is wrong, ought to be respected to a certain degree."[48] The public that seemed to have Hamilton's ear, though, was not the "mass" Jefferson and Madison seemed to prioritize, but the nation's creditors. This would soon appear to the Virginians as a willful disregard for the will of the people in the service of a "monied elite" that had more in common with the foreign creditors than with ordinary Americans.[49]

To this point, Hamilton had experienced almost unqualified success in implementing his financial program, which involved shoring up the public credit by funding the $54 million national debt and assuming the $25 million debt the states had incurred during the Revolution.[50] To the chagrin of many Southerners, debt holders were concentrated among the northern merchant class, the group most inclined to put it to productive uses and thus develop the country's economy.[51] The debt – Hamilton called it "a national blessing" – would be funded through a mixture of excise taxes on domestic and imported alcohol and import taxes, 90 percent of which would come from Britain. Thus,

[48] TJ to Mason, February 4, 1791, *PTJ*, 19: 241–242; TJ to Nicholas Lewis, February 9, 1791, in *FE* 6: 194.

[49] See Madison to Hamilton, November 19, 1789, in *PJM* 12: 451; and the discussion in Sloan, *Principle and Interest*, 134–135, from which this paragraph draws. Note that Hamilton always assumed and argued that those willing to invest in American securities demonstrated the most public spirit, precisely because they were willing to trust the government to honor its promises. See Hamilton's "Report on Public Credit," January 9, 1790, in Freeman, ed., *Writings*, 534; and Hamilton to Washington, August 18, 1792, in ibid., 779: "It is a strange perversion of ideas, and as novel as it is extraordinary, that men should be deemed corrupt & criminal for becoming proprietors in the funds of their Country."

[50] I rely heavily on Elkins and Mckitrick, *Age of Federalism*, 77–131, for this and the following two paragraphs.

[51] On the transfer of southern debts to northern speculators, see Bates, "Northern Speculators and Southern State Debts," esp. the summary of findings on p. 42. Madison told Jefferson that "packet boats and expresses are sent from this place [Philadelphia] to the Southern States, to buy up the paper of all sorts which has risen in the market here.... My imagination will not attempt to set bounds to the daring depravity of the times. The stockjobbers will become the pretorian band of the Government, at once its tool and tyrant," to TJ, August 8, 1791, *ROL* 2:705–706; Jefferson wrote in the same colorful vein a few days later to Edward Rutledge, August 25, 1791, *PTJ* 22:73–74. Also see TJ to Gouverneur Morris, August 30, 1791, ibid., 104–105; and Jefferson's "Memoranda of Conversations with the President," March 1, 1792, ibid., 23:184–187.

commerce with Britain – amicable relations with the former mother country – was essential to the proper working out of Hamilton's plan.

For both Jefferson and Madison, as well as many others, especially in the South, almost every piece of Hamilton's financial puzzle produced a visceral reaction. The problem of debt ranked first. For Virginia planters, most of whom, from pre-Revolutionary times, were heavily indebted, this condition was an unmitigated evil; it would never cross their minds to call it a "blessing." Virginians, however difficult they found it in practice, wanted to pay their debts, not fund them perpetually.[52]

Many Virginians, Madison first among them, also looked on the transfer of Continental securities from war veterans and widows into the hands of an urban merchant elite (the actual effect of assumption without discrimination between original and current holders) as the height of injustice. Such concentration of capital, though, became the underlying aim of assumption. To Hamilton's way of thinking, wide dispersal of the debt would be next to useless. Widows and war veterans would never be able or inclined to use their bonds for anything productive in terms of the development of the American economy; Hamilton wanted these resources in the hands of those disposed to use them for long-term public good.

Most important, in the long run loomed the British connection. No wonder Jefferson and Madison reviled Hamilton for "Anglomania." First of all, his plan really *was* British: Hamilton modeled his program after the fiscal-military state pioneered there.[53] Perhaps even more significant, though, commerce with Britain, even subservience to a British commercial system, appeared absolutely essential to the plan. Without the revenue from the impost, the public credit would fall through the floor. As Stanley Elkins and Eric McKitrick put it, Hamilton's financial program made "an anglophile position on virtually everything … a basic component in what [he] would come to stand for ideologically." Hamilton valued the British example as a model that he hoped to translate into American superiority, but Jefferson and Madison read his appreciation as a kind of obeisance to England, the essence of what the American revolutionaries sought to escape. For Jefferson and Madison, political, economic, and moral separation from Britain had only begun with the Revolution. They had, in the works, plans to keep the separation permanent by commercial treaties with France and commercial discrimination against Britain, and by shoring up the

---

[52] Jefferson revealed a great deal about his views of debt in a brief letter to James Monroe in 1791: *PTJ* 20:235. A caricature of Hamilton's position, to be sure, but one that Jefferson believed accurate. For a brilliant look at how the problem of debt colored Jefferson's outlook, see Sloan, *Principle and Interest*. On debt among Virginia planters, see T.H. Breen, *Tobacco Culture: The Mentality of the Great Tidewater Planters on the Eve of Revolution* (Princeton, 1985). See also TJ to Nicholas Lewis, April 12, 1792, *PTJ* 23:408; to Henry Remsen, April 14, 1792, ibid., 23:426; and to Washington, May 23, 1792, ibid., 23:536–537.

[53] See John Brewer, *The Sinews of Power: War, Money, and the English State, 1688–1783* (New York, 1989), though, also see Edling, "Origin, Structure, and Development," on the specifics of the American case.

republican nature of American institutions. From this perspective, swallowing Hamilton's plan was a clear step backward into colonial dependence, and they began to fear and loathe him for it.[54] Hamilton's picture of national greatness involved deep connection with and a certain kind of imitation of Great Britain. For Jefferson, American greatness would be rooted in what differentiated its outlook and behavior from Great Britain and, as we have seen, Europe generally. This perceived clash of worldviews goes some distance toward explaining the conflict that erupted between Hamilton and Jefferson in the early 1790s.

Jefferson's and Madison's continuing efforts to levy extra duties on all nations not in commercial treaty with the United States deliberately aimed to force Britain to relax its commercial restrictions on American commerce; but they also unwittingly threatened Hamilton's domestic program. Jefferson and Madison believed that America's agricultural and staple production rendered its commerce essential to industrial Britain in a way that Britain's manufactured goods were not to the United States. British goods, exported to the United States were "luxuries" that frugal, virtuous, American republicans could forgo for a time in the interest of coercing Britain into fairer trade practices. The British, so went the logic, could not do without American essentials and would quickly crack, thus opening up the West Indies to American shipping and eliminating other restrictions on American commerce.[55] This kind of operation had precedent in the Association of 1769, with which Virginians protested the Townshend Acts. This example, in which a nonimportation agreement among Americans appeared to result in the overturning of hated legislation abroad, would provide Jefferson with a workable precedent for his future designs, as secretary of state and as president, to coerce European nations into acting in the interest of the United States by means of commercial, not military, warfare, itself a European predilection.[56] But Hamilton saw these proposals as rooted in a misconception of America's strength relative to Britain as well as anathema to his grand design; hence the logic of the later Jay Treaty. Hamilton, as Jefferson wrote James Monroe, "still thinks that these new encroachments of Gr. Brit. on our carrying trade must be met by passive obedience and nonresistance, lest any misunderstanding with them should affect our credit, or

---

[54] *Age of Federalism,* 128.

[55] For Jefferson's and Madison's views on political economy see McCoy, *Elusive Republic;* Merrill D. Peterson, "Thomas Jefferson and Commercial Policy," *WMQ;* Jefferson's "Report on the Tonnage Law," January 18, 1791, *PTJ* 18:565–570; Jefferson's "Report on the American Fisheries," February 1, 1791, ibid., 19:206–220. For the logic of discrimination see Madison, "Fashion," *National Gazette,* March 22, 1792, in *PJM* 14:257–259.

[56] Jefferson gave a brief, clear explanation of his ideas in a letter to James Innes: The United States should take measures "for forcing Gr. Britain, by a navigation act, to come forward in fair treaty, and let us substantially into her islands, as a price for the advantages in navigation and commerce which she now derives from us," March 13, 1791, *PTJ* 19:543. See also TJ to William Short, March 15, 1791, ibid., 19:570–572; to David Humphreys, March 15, 1791, ibid., 19:573; to William Carmichael, March 17, 1791, ibid., 19:574–575; to James McHenry, March 28, 1791, ibid., 19:628; to Charles Carroll, April 4, 1791, ibid., 20:100; to James Monroe, April 17, 1791, ibid., 20:234–236, among others.

the prices of our public paper."[57] This, for Jefferson, was as good as the old colonial subservience to the British navigation system. The two visions were destined for a major confrontation.

The first open clash between these worldviews came over the question of Hamilton's proposed National Bank. About the same time that Jefferson and Madison were doing all they could to persuade Congress to enact navigation laws against Britain, Congress itself, in the short session from December to March of 1791, basically ignored Jefferson's reports on the subject in favor Hamilton's proposals for a series of excise taxes and the chartering of a National Bank. Jefferson and Madison viewed the institution with suspicion for reasons rooted in policy and constitutional interpretation.[58] The latter largely boiled down to Jefferson's concern that Hamilton's liberal reading of the "general welfare" clause "would reduce the whole instrument to a single phrase, that of instituting a Congress with power to do whatever would be for the good of the United States." Jefferson assumed, in other words, that such a reading of the Constitution would effectively sever the responsibility the natural aristocracy would have to canvass and assimilate public opinion: Congress "would be[come] the sole judges of the good or evil," never a safe arrangement, in Jefferson's view.[59]

But perhaps the heart of Jefferson's and Madison's discontent with the bank was less the alleged unconstitutionality of the measure than their own growing realization that the same crowd that had participated in speculation of Continental securities and that had worked to defeat their proposals for discrimination against British shipping also were sold on Hamilton's plan for the Bank. These, mostly northern commercial interests, were wedded, they believed, to a foreign policy the overarching theme of which was to keep from upsetting the British, and to a domestic policy calculated to consolidate power in their own small circle of influence, thus driving Americans apart from one another – a threat to the unity of the nation. Jefferson and Madison, suspicious already

[57] TJ to Monroe, April 17, 1791, *PTJ* 20:235.

[58] For policy objections, see Report of Madison's speech on the Bank Bill (February 2, 1791), *Gazette of the U.S.*, February 23, 1791, in *PJM* 13:373. The story of the fight over the Bank can be found in several places, including Malone, *Jefferson and the Rights of Man*, 337–350; Benjamin B. Klubes, "The First Federal Congress and the First National Bank: A Case Study in Constitutional Interpretation," *Journal of the Early Republic* 10 (Spring 1990), 19–41; and, perhaps the best retelling, Elkins and McKitrick, *Age of Federalism*, 223–244. For the opinions of the three principals, see Madison's "Speech in Congress Opposing the National Bank," February 2, 1791, *PJM* 14:117–122; Jefferson's "Opinion on the Constitutionality of a National Bank," February 15, 1791, *PTJ* 19:275–282; and Hamilton's "Opinion on the Constitutionality of a National Bank," February 23, 1791, *PAH* 8:63–134.

[59] "Opinion on the Constitutionality of a National Bank," in *TJW*, 418. Hamilton agreed with Jefferson to this extent – and the point is often overlooked – that "no government has a right to do merely what it pleases." But the crux of his argument was that the power necessary to do whatever "has a natural relation to any of the acknowledged objects or lawful ends of the government" is implicit in the nature of sovereignty. See Hamilton's "Opinion," in Freeman, ed., *Writings*, 619.

of Hamilton's plans, began to see everywhere the influence of an "English interest" – an interest calculated, they believed, to undermine the Republic. Although Jefferson and Madison already had begun to use what Elkins and McKitrick call "tag words," or shorthand phrases that encapsulated their views of this group – "monocrats," "stock-jobbers," "tories," "speculators," "aristocrats," and the all-encompassing "anglomen" – it is at this point that these phrases became pervasive throughout their correspondence.

In the spring of 1791, Jefferson first began to connect all these dots and imagine a deliberate program on Hamilton's part to undermine the constitutional system and administer the state according to his own design. It was at a dinner Jefferson threw for the members of Washington's cabinet that Hamilton told the guests that the British government was "the most perfect government which ever existed," its corruption and its inequality – much as David Hume had suggested earlier – essential parts of that perfection.[60] It may have been an off-handed comment in the privacy of the salon, but Jefferson latched onto it and never forgot it, scribbling it down at the time and recounting it to various correspondents (even years later), including Washington, to whom he somewhat unfairly asserted that Hamilton had told him that the "constitution was a shilly shally thing of mere milk & water, which could not last, & was only good as a step to something better."[61] It seems to have brought everything together in Jefferson's mind in a way that made sense of all the shocking things that had been happening since his return from France. As Jefferson later recalled, suddenly Hamilton's rationale became clear to him: Hamilton must want "a hereditary king with a house of lords & commons, corrupted to his will, *and standing between him and the people.*"[62]

A few months later, Jefferson took note of a conversation he had with Hamilton on the nature of the government. Hamilton admitted ("tho' I do not publish it in Dan & Bersheba") that he believed that "the present govnmt is not that which will answer the ends of society, by giving stability & protection to it's rights, and that it will probably be found expedient to go into the British form." But Jefferson also recorded Hamilton's hope:

However, since we have undertaken the experiment, I am for giving it a fair course, whatever my expectns. The success indeed so far, is greater than I had expected, & therefore at present success seems more possible than it had done heretofore, & there are still other & other stages of improvement which, if the present does not succeed, may be tried, & ought

---

[60] Jefferson, "Anas," in *FE* 1:179–180. See Hume, "Of the Independency of Parliament," in Eugene F. Miller, ed., *Essays: Moral, Political, and Literary* (Indianapolis, 1985), 42–46. On the importance of this moment, I am following the suggestion of Paul Rahe in *Republics Ancient and Modern*, 682–683, but see Merrill D. Peterson, "Thomas Jefferson and Commercial Policy," in *WMQ* 22 (October 1965), at 604, for a suggestion that Hamilton's opposition to Jefferson's commercial policy of discrimination against Britain first led Jefferson to see a "system" in "Hamilton's different measures."

[61] "Notes of a Conversation with Washington at Mount Vernon," October 1, 1792, in *FE* 1:236. Also see TJ to Joel Barlow, January 24, 1810, in *PTJ Retirement Series* 2:176.

[62] "Anas," in *FE* 1:180, emphasis added.

to be tried before we give up the republican form altogether, for that mind must be really depraved which would not prefer the equality of political rights which is the foundation of pure republicanism, if it can be obtained consistently with order.

Hamilton said all this, Jefferson recalled, by way of criticism of Adams, whose writings Hamilton believed had "disturb[ed] the present order of things" by "having a tendency to weaken the present govm't," as Jefferson remembered Hamilton's argument.[63] Jefferson noted that Hamilton's statement was "more formal than usual for a private conversation between two," and assumed that he was trying "to qualify some less guarded expressions which had been dropped on former occasions." It seems a shame that Jefferson discounted Hamilton's sincerity, writing the conversation down "the moment of A.H.'s leaving the room" instead of engaging the secretary of the treasury in a deliberate discussion of policy and political theory. Jefferson, it seems, had already written Hamilton off by the summer of 1791.[64] The gist of his complaint was that Hamilton hoped to change the republican form of the Constitution into a British government (which Hamilton had explicitly denied) and to substitute administration for a government rooted in public opinion.

To be fair to Jefferson, it seems likely that Madison had already begun to share with him some of the things Hamilton had said in the Constitutional Convention where he had advocated a life appointment for the executive and the upper branch of the legislature and even indicated his desire to abolish the state governments and substitute subordinate administrative units of the national state.[65] Jefferson also had at hand a secret British report from the Committee of the Privy Council for Trade and Plantations that noted the favorable nature of American commercial policy under the Washington administration (Hamilton's rather than Jefferson's) and explicitly described the existence of *"a party"* in the Congress that was *"in favor of a connection with Great Britain"* and that could be "strengthened, as to bring about in a friendly way" a policy favorable to British interests.[66] Jefferson would eventually

---

[63] Jefferson, "Notes of a Conversn Between A. Hamilton and Th J.," August 13, 1791, in *FE* 1:184–185. Compare Hamilton to Edward Carrington, May 26, 1792, in Freeman, ed., *Writings*, 750–751: Although *"affectionately* attached to the Republican theory" and possessed of "strong hopes of the success of that theory," Hamilton nevertheless expressed "in candor" that he was "far from being without doubts" precisely because it had "yet to be determined by experience whether it be consistent with *stability* and *order* in Government which are essential to the public strength & private security and happiness." Hamilton then characterized Jefferson as a demagogue, "a man of profound ambition & violent passions," willing to exploit "the spirit of faction and anarchy," even to the death of republicanism.

[64] See a similar suggestion in Rahe, *Republics*, 684–686.

[65] For Hamilton's speech, see Farrand, *Records of the Federal Convention* 1: 282–311. The proposal re. the states begins on 287. For Jefferson's later recounting, see, *FE* 1:170; as well as TJ to George Washington, September 9, 1792, in *TJW*, 996. Hamilton himself fully acknowledged, prior to signing the document and defending it during Ratification, that "no man's ideas were more remote from the plan than his own were known to be." See Farrand, *Records* 2: 645–46.

[66] Report on the Committee of the Privy Council for Trade and Plantations, January 28, 1791, *TJP*, cited in Peterson, "Thomas Jefferson and Commercial Policy," 606.

elevate this British assessment into an unassailable truth, and, after all, here was the British government itself noting the existence of a party favorable to its interests and vowing to do everything it could to strengthen it against its American opponents.[67] It seems perfectly understandable, then, in light of all these events, that Jefferson would begin to suspect Hamilton rather than offering him the benefit of the doubt. Indeed, Jefferson would later tell Washington that Hamilton had gone some distance toward undermining his own efforts in the Department of State by meeting on his own with the British and French ministers, seeking to influence foreign policy.

The point here is that Jefferson considered Hamilton's system, aligned with the interests of British commerce and modeled after the British state, as designed to stifle rather than cultivate and conform to public opinion. The problem with Treasury's corruption of the legislature, as Jefferson understood Hamilton's design, was, he told Washington, that their votes would "no longer" be "the votes ... of the representatives of the people, but of deserters from the rights & interests of the people." Such a situation, of course, would utterly undermine the close relation between people and government, nation and state, that Jefferson assumed essential for American government. It would render unworkable the connection Jefferson understood to exist between the public and the natural aristocracy, which, under Hamilton's design, would no longer cultivate public competence but only its own interest.[68] The double tragedy here was that the corruption of the leadership would lead to the neglect of the public, ultimately rendering it incapable of guiding government through its wise counsel. The bottom line was that the legislature had begun "legislating for their own interests in opposition to those of the people."[69]

In contrast, and in an effort to ameliorate the situation, Jefferson began the opposite tack, gauging public opinion from different sections of the country and asking certain reliable people to consider joining Congress to counterbalance the influence of the mercantile interest there. Accordingly, Jefferson wrote Kentuckian James Innes in March, expressing his wish that Innes would "come forward to the federal legislature." Jefferson had "such confidence in the purity of your republicanism, that I know your efforts would go in a right direction. Zeal and talents added to the republican scale will do no harm in Congress." For now, President Washington, fortunately, remained "purely and zealously republican." His successors, on the other hand, very well might be members of the English interest. For this reason, Jefferson wrote, we "should avail ourselves of the present day to establish principles and examples which may fence us against future heresies preached now," which may be "practiced hereafter."[70]

---

[67] Jefferson never relinquished this assessment. See TJ to Henry Dearborn, June 14, 1809, *PTJ, Retirement Series* 1:279.

[68] TJ to George Washington, September 9, 1792, in *TJW*, 994–995.

[69] TJ, "Notes of Conversation with Washington," July 10, 1792, in *FE* 1:230.

[70] To James Innes, March 13, 1791, *PTJ* 19:543.

Because the opinions of Hamilton and Jefferson on the bank were in the form of memoranda to President Washington, the controversy between them on the issue remained essentially unknown to the public; because Jefferson presumably did not see Hamilton's opinion, which was written in response to Jefferson's, the full theoretical dissonance between them may have remained unknown even to him. Nevertheless, the public did not have long to wait for the first open clash between Jefferson and what he was soon calling the "sect," this time over the publication of Thomas Paine's *Rights of Man*.

Jefferson endorsed Paine's book, a response to Edmund Burke's *Reflections on the Revolution in France*, in a private letter that the American publisher included as the preface to the American edition. There, Jefferson expressed his satisfaction "that something is at length to be publickly said against the political heresies which have sprung up among us."[71] Jefferson was, by his own admission, referring to John Adams's recently published *Discourses on Davila*, which Jefferson believed revealed Adams's new preference for monarchy and aristocracy.[72] Nevertheless, as he wrote to Washington explaining the situation, he never expected to see his own letter in print. The opinion of the note was his, to be sure, but he was "sincerely mortified to be thus brought forward on the public stage."[73]

It was nevertheless true, Jefferson told Washington, that "some Anglomen" were upset about Jefferson's endorsement of Paine because it "tends to give offence to the British government." More to the point, Jefferson argued, they were afraid that Paine's book would "likely at a single stroke ... wipe out all the unconstitutional doctrines which their bell-weather Davila has been preaching."[74] To Paine himself, Jefferson said that the deeply favorable response to *Rights of Man* among the American people demonstrated that "they appear firm in their republicanism, notwithstanding the contrary hopes and assertions of a sect here, high in names, but small in numbers." The people, Jefferson told Paine, were "confirmed in their good old faith."[75] Nearly a year later, Jefferson again told Paine that "we have a sect preaching up and panting after an English constitution of king, lords, and commons, and whose heads are itching for crown, coronets and mitres. But our people, my good friend, are firm and

---

[71] *WTJ* 5:354n. There are many retellings of this story. A serviceable one, though a bit too favorable to Jefferson, is Dumas Malone, *Jefferson and the Rights of Man*, 354–359, 363–370. Also see Banning, *The Jeffersonian Persuasion*, 155–160. The best place to begin is the collection of documents under the heading "Rights of Man: The Contest of Burke and Paine in America," in *PTJ* 20:268–313.

[72] "Even since his apostacy to hereditary monarchy and nobility, tho' we differ, we differ as friends should do," To Washington, May 8, 1791, ibid., 291.

[73] "I certainly never made a secret of my being anti-monarchical, and anti-aristocratical," ibid., 292. Nevertheless, he told Adams, he was "thunderstruck with seeing it come out at the head of the pamphlet," Jefferson to Adams, July 17, 1791, ibid., 302. See also, TJ to Thomas Mann Randolph, July 3, 1791, ibid., 295–296.

[74] Ibid.

[75] TJ to Paine, July 29, 1791, ibid., 20:308–309.

unanimous in their principles of republicanism, and there is no better proof of it than that they love what you write and read it with delight."[76]

Describing the controversy over his endorsement of Paine, Jefferson told Madison that "Colo. Hamilton and Colo. Beckwith [un-official British minister to the United States] are open mouthed against me, taking it in another view, as likely to give offence to the court of London." Hamilton went further than this and claimed that the letter to Paine implicated Jefferson in "opposition to the government." But Hamilton had it backward, in Jefferson's view. Hamilton's was an attempt "to turn on the government itself those censures I meant for the enemies of the government."[77] The "anglomen," in other words, in resisting the spirit of the American Revolution, were the true opponents of the Constitution. Madison concurred with this opinion. In a particularly vehement attack on Adams, he told Jefferson that the vice president had no reason to complain about Jefferson's public statement about *Davila*. "Under a mock defence of the Republican constitutions of this Country, [Adams] attacked them with all the force he possessed.... Surely if it be innocent and decent in one servant of the public thus to write attacks against its Government, it can not be very criminal or indecent in another to patronize a written defence of the principles on which that Government is founded."[78] In other words, Adams's doctrines were the truly oppositional ones because they expressed views in direct contradistinction to the founding principles of American government and in favor of English constitutionalism, or so the Virginians believed. Jefferson would go on to formulate this explicitly: "Acts against the government" might be usurpation, but "acts against the *Oppressions of the government*" were "virtues."[79] If Jefferson and Madison's opposition was a defense of the true principles of American government and if these sentiments had the full support of the majority of the American people, it was the Federalists who were fighting the public will in defense of an antirepublican minority opinion. No wonder Jefferson described Federalism as "a sect which is all head and no body."[80]

These different perspectives erupted in a remarkable series of conversations, letters, and essays by the three principals during the spring and summer of 1792, when the clash between Hamilton and Jefferson became viciously personal and all but irreconcilable. Jefferson, who began keeping detailed records

---

[76] TJ to Paine, June 19, 1792, ibid., 312. See also Jefferson to Benjamin Vaughan, May 11, 1791, ibid., 391–392.

[77] TJ to Madison, May 9, 1791, in *ROL* 2:687–688. Jefferson linked Hamilton and Beckwith for obvious reasons. On Beckwith's American career, see Frank T. Reuter, "Petty Spy" or Effective Diplomat: The Role of George Beckwith," in *Journal of the Early Republic* 10 (Winter 1990), 471–492.

[78] Madison to TJ, May 12, 1791, ibid., 688–689. See also, Gordon Wood, *The Creation of the American Republic*, 567–593.

[79] Report on A Convention with Spain, March 22, 1792, in *FE* 6:447–448. Also see Jefferson's nuanced conception of the Republican opposition in TJ to Thomas Pinckney, December 3, 1792, in *PTJ* 24:697.

[80] TJ to Edmund Pendleton, July 24, 1791, *PTJ* 20:670. On this notion, see also Jefferson to William Short, July 28, 1791, ibid., 692–693; and to Lewis Littlepage, July 29, ibid., 703.

of conversations with Hamilton and Washington, recorded an exchange in March with the president in which he first revealed to Washington his concerns about Hamilton. Washington had expressed some dismay at the recent general "symptoms of dissatisfaction" with the government. Jefferson took the opportunity to tell Washington that "there was only a single source of these discontents" – Hamilton, who had corrupted the legislature. Many members of Congress, he said, had "feathered their nests with paper" before voting for Hamilton's financial program. This corruption, this blurring of lines between the executive and the legislative departments of government, along with Hamilton's interpretation of the Constitution, had turned this Constitution into "a very different thing from what the people thought they had submitted to." Worse, Hamilton's recent proposal for national encouragement of manufacturing was not even, like the bank, extrapolated from an "enumerated power." For Jefferson, this raised the question "whether we live under a limited or an unlimited government." Jefferson told Washington that he looked forward to the upcoming elections, which should, he hoped, "remove a great deal of the discontent" among the people.[81]

In addition to influencing the legislature, Jefferson told Washington, Hamilton had indiscreetly begun to interfere with the workings of the Department of State, revealing secret Cabinet opinions and conversations to the British minister, George Hammond, as a way to further the "English interest." Jefferson had noticed that whenever any proposal concerning Britain was made during a cabinet meeting, "Hamilton had constantly ready something which Mr. Hammond had communicated to him, which suited the subject, and proved the intimacy of their communications: insomuch that I believe he communicated to Hammond all our views and knew from him in return the views of the British court."[82] The point here, of course, is not whether Hamilton "did or didn't," but that Jefferson believed that the Treasury had corrupted the legislature elected by the people, had interfered with the diplomacy of the nation in a way that undermined its perceived interests, and remained committed to an English constitution and apparently to American subordination to English commercial dominance. Historians today understand these fears to be greatly exaggerated, but Jefferson, through these lenses, saw Hamilton's treachery everywhere.

For his part, Hamilton began to attack Jefferson, first in private correspondence and then in anonymously authored newspaper essays. Hamilton had become convinced, he wrote Edward Carrington, that "Mr. Madison cooperating with Mr. Jefferson is at the head of a faction decidedly hostile to me and

---

[81] Memoranda of Conversations with the President, March 1, 1792, ibid., 23:184–187.

[82] Memoranda of Consultations with the President, March 11–April 9, 1792, *PTJ* 23:258–264. Although Jefferson had no way of knowing it beyond a shadow of a doubt, his fears were confirmed by the British minister himself who wrote Lord Grenville regularly of conversations he had had with the Secretary of the Treasury about U.S. policy in which Hamilton revealed state secrets and even undermined Jefferson's diplomacy. Hammond wrote Grenville exactly what Jefferson believed; that Hamilton was of the "party of the English interest."

my administration, and actuated by views in my judgment subversive of the
principles of good government and dangerous to the union, peace and happiness of the Country." Hamilton was beginning to identify himself and his
financial program with the government or state in such a way that he perceived any opposition to either as designed to overturn the government. In
addition to their "womanish attachment to France and a womanish resentment
against Great Britain," Jefferson and Madison were "disposed to narrow the
Federal authority." Jefferson, Hamilton asserted, at first weakly supported the
new Constitution; but this tentative "attachment to the Government of the U
States" had "given way to something very like dislike."[83]

Jefferson's wrong-headedness failed to appreciate the dangers of weakening
the central government, Hamilton believed. In his reading, the Republicans
were the party of "National disunion, national insignificance, Public disorder and discredit." They believed, he said, that the people "erred in adopting
the present constitution." How could Jefferson remain a member of the present administration, "if he disapproves of the Government itself and thinks it
deserving of opposition?" Jefferson, Hamilton argued, desired to be "the head
of a party, whose politics have constantly aimed at elevating State-power, upon
the ruins of National Authority."[84]

It was at least as unfair for Hamilton to characterize Jefferson's position as
an endorsement of disunion, national insignificance, and public disorder as it
was for Jefferson to call Hamilton a servant of British interests and a closet
monarchist. Jefferson and Madison did not consider themselves in opposition
to American governmental institutions; they believed they were preserving them
from Hamilton's assault. The worst thing Hamilton had done, Jefferson told
Washington, was use his influence in the Treasury Department, by means of an
artificially perpetuated debt, to corrupt the legislature. This "corrupt squad-
ron" was then able to swing the vote of the entire Congress in the direction of
funding.[85] The "ultimate object" of these plans, Jefferson feared, was "to prepare the way for a change, from the present republican form of government,
to that of a monarchy, of which the English constitution is to be the model."
"The republican party," Jefferson insisted, "wish to preserve the government in
it's present form." It was the nascent Federalist Party, under the leadership of
Hamilton, not the Republicans, who wanted to overturn the government.[86] It
was Hamilton, whose "system flowed from principles adverse to liberty," who
wanted to "undermine and demolish the republic, by creating an influence of
his department over the members of the legislature."[87]

---

[83] Hamilton to Edward Carrington, May 26, 1792, *PAH* 11:426–445.
[84] Hamilton, "An American, No. 1," from the *Gazette of the United States*, August 4, 1792, in *PAH*
    12:157–164.
[85] To Washington, May 23, 1792, *PTJ* 23:536–537.
[86] To Washington, May 23, 1792, ibid., 23:537.
[87] To Washington, September 9, 1792, ibid., 24:353. However accurate Jefferson's perception
    of Hamilton's actions, it may not quite capture his motives or the propriety of his behavior.
    The Constitution places the departments of State and War under the executive, but insists that

Worse still, Jefferson feared the effects of Hamilton's policies on the Union's future. Although he could "scarcely contemplate a more incalculable evil than the breaking of the union into two or more parts," he feared that this might be the result of Hamilton's plans. Hamilton's casual (to Jefferson's mind) dismissal of the constitutional boundaries between state and federal authority, Jefferson worried, would strengthen the remaining anti-Federalists by fulfilling their earlier predictions about the consolidation of the national government. This revived anti-federalism would consequently "disarm" what Jefferson called, significantly, "the republican federalists" who supported the Constitution but opposed the direction in which certain high officials were taking it, thus leading to general dissatisfaction with the Constitution itself. It was therefore imperative, Jefferson told the president, that Washington remain in office for another term. "The confidence of the whole union is centered in you." Washington's remaining "at the helm" would dissuade people from buying into arguments for violence and secession.[88]

The Federalists hoped to brand the Republicans with the "anti-federal" label and convince the public that anti-federalism and republicanism "were the same." Nevertheless, Jefferson insisted, "those who felt themselves republicans and federalists too" were not persuaded by this "artifice."[89] For Jefferson there were three groups to keep in mind: the small band of remaining anti-federalists who opposed the Constitution from a perspective of complete state sovereignty and would be content to see the union fall apart; the Federalists, who were "a sect" that explicitly espoused the Constitution, "not as a good and sufficient thing itself, but only as a stop to an English constitution, the only thing good and sufficient in their eye;" and the Republicans who wished merely to preserve the government in its present form – a model of republican purity. The mass of the people, of course, were "firm and constant in their republican purity," so that the other parties were "preachers without followers."[90]

Treasury only report to Congress. This created an ambiguity in the function of the secretaryship that Hamilton was quick to exploit to the advantage of his vision. On this, see Freeman W. Meyer, "A Note on the Origins of the 'Hamiltonian System,'" in *WMQ* 21 (October 1964), 579–588. In any case, Hamilton appears to have been uniquely scrupulous on a personal level, as Jefferson later acknowledged (for one example, see Hamilton to Henry Lee, December 1, 1789, in Freeman, ed., *Writings*, 530). In addition, Hamilton's patronage of the "monied interest," however corrupt it looked to Virginians, was, in a way, designed to use that group in the service of the national interest. Hamilton looked on the support of the holders of financial capital as essential to national greatness, where Jefferson and Madison assumed a wider notion of the "public" that government must cultivate and respect. This contrast – between Jefferson's sense that the democratization of patronage would rally the interest and affection of all citizens in favor of national ends, and Hamilton's assumption that the government need only secure the pecuniary interest of what he once called "the rich, and the well-born" to preserve its interests – is, in many respects, perhaps the heart of their conflict. On this, see the caution of Thomas P. Govan, "The Rich, the Well-born, and Alexander Hamilton," *Mississippi Valley Historical Review* 36 (March 1950), 675–680.

[88] TJ to Washington, May 23, 1792, *PTJ*, 23:538–539.
[89] TJ to Thomas Pinckney, December 3, 1792, ibid., 24:697.
[90] TJ to Lafayette, June 16, 1792, ibid., 24:85–86.

Madison summed up early Republican thinking on the parties in his remarkable essays for the *National Gazette*, written in the winter and spring of 1791 and 1792. In December, Madison argued against the melding of the states into one government. He made a number of objections to such a scenario, among them, that without state legislatures as clearinghouses for popular opinion, the will of the people could not be as easily conveyed to national leaders. There would come a point of "universal silence and insensibility" from the people, and the government would be left to a "self directed course." But, said Madison, while a complete consolidation of government was to be deplored, a unification of the "interests and affections" of the people is much to be desired and encouraged. With such unity, the people will be able to better present a "defence of the public liberty," and the interests of the states would merge "into one harmonious interest."[91]

Hamilton, by contrast, had earlier suggested that the "tendency in the nature of things" in the federal system of the United States was for the state governments to encroach on the powers of the national one, and he worried that "the Government of the U. States will not be able to maintain itself against their influence." He hoped to "erect every fence to guard" the national government "from depredations" of the states.[92] A few months earlier, Jefferson had written Archibald Stuart that he wished "to preserve the line drawn by the federal constitution between the general and particular governments as it stands at present and to take every prudent means of preventing either from stepping over it." In contrast to Hamilton, Jefferson feared that the "nature of things" was that "incroachments of the state governments will tend to an excess of liberty which will correct itself." The encroachments of the national government, on the other hand, "will tend toward monarchy, which will fortify itself from day to day, instead of working it's own cure." Jefferson thought it proper, in the situation as it stood, to "strengthen the state governments." The federal Constitution already provided the framework for this; consequently, the Republicans needed only to preserve the Constitution as it stood. The context of this work to strengthen the states was the perceived Federalist consolidation of power in the national state rather than an abstract conception of state sovereignty, which Jefferson and Madison never shared. The states themselves would need to erect "such barriers at the constitutional line as cannot be surmounted either by themselves or by the general government."[93] The Constitution, in other words, would preserve the spheres, protecting both state and national government from the encroachment of the other.

The strengthening of the state governments was never its own rationale but was, rather, intimately connected with Jefferson and Madison's views of the

<hr>

[91] Madison, "Consolidation," *National Gazette*, December 5, 1791, in *PJM* 14:137–139.

[92] Hamilton to Edward Carrington, May 26, 1792, in *PAH* 11:443. Note that this had been Madison's view, too. For one, but only one, example, see his "Remarks in Congress on the 'Most Valuable Amendment,'" August 17, 1789, in Rakove, ed., *Writings*, 470.

[93] TJ to Stuart, December 23, 1791, *PTJ* 22:436.

proper relation between government and citizens. This is most clearly articulated, perhaps, in Madison's 1791 essay on "Public Opinion." "Public opinion," Madison wrote, "sets bounds to every government, and is the real sovereign in every free one." There were "cases," Madison insisted, "where the public opinion must be obeyed by the government." But there were others, when public opinion was "not … fixed." In these cases, public opinion "may be influenced by the government." Leaving aside the question of who was to decide when precisely the public opinion was "fixed" (perhaps the most crucial, although unanswerable, question), Madison's essay and Jefferson's writing on the wards suggest that, in their view, the proper relationship between people and government demanded the kind of federal system that the Constitution had created. For in a large consolidated state, Madison said, the "real opinion" of the country was difficult to discern and much simpler to "counterfeit."[94] In other words, the closer the relation of people to governmental institutions, the more clearly those institutions could both shape and be shaped by public will. If government was legitimate only as it obeyed the public opinion, government would be wise only when "the will of the society" was subjected "to the reason of the society."[95] And the public opinion would be wise only as government itself operated wisely on "the understanding and interest of the society."[96] So the intimate relationship between public and state, leadership and people, could be sustained only by a federal system, never by a consolidated one, and Jefferson and Madison's concern about consolidation took as much of its rationale from this conception of public opinion as it did from any kind of abstract commitment to "states' rights."

Hamilton believed that by their opposition to his plans, Jefferson and Madison were alienating the "affections and confidence of the people" from the national government and rendering it "odious." Jefferson and Madison believed, to the contrary, that the affections of the people would merge in support of the federal system if the Republicans were victorious in maintaining the Constitution intact from either the anti-Federalists or the "monocrats." In his essay, "The Union: Who Are Its Real Friends?" Madison answered his title question: "not those who study … to pervert the limited government of the Union, into a government of unlimited discretion, contrary to the will and subversive of the authority of the people." True friends of the Union were "not those, in a word, who would force on the people the melancholy duty

---

[94] Madison, "Public Opinion," in *National Gazette*, December 19, 1791, in *PJM* 14:170. My reading of these essays, and of Madison, generally, has been influenced by Colleen Sheehan, "Madison and the French Enlightenment: The Authority of Public Opinion," in *WMQ* 59 (October 2002), 925–956; and "Madison vs. Hamilton: The Battle over Republicanism and the Role of Public Opinion," in Douglas Ambrose and Robert W.T. Martin, ed., *The Many Faces of Alexander Hamilton: The Life and Legacy of America's Most Elusive Founding Father* (New York, 2006), 165–208.

[95] Madison, "Universal Peace," in *National Gazette*, January 31, 1792, in *PJM* 14:206.

[96] Madison, "Spirit of Governments," in *National Gazette*, February 18, 1792, in *PJM* 14:234.

of chusing between the loss of the Union, and the loss of what the union was meant to secure."[97]

The principle of popular sovereignty also shaped Jefferson's approach to treating foreign governments. If the authority of government ascended from the will of the people (rather than the other way around), Jefferson advised America's minister to France in late 1792, the United States ought "to acknolege any government to be rightful which is formed by the will of the nation." The French National Assembly had met for the first time in September, declared France a republic, and convicted Louis XVI of treason. Just as it had earlier recognized the monarchy as the expression of the will of the nation of France (however this may have been ascertained), so the United States must acknowledge any alteration "made by the will of the nation substantially declared."[98] Jefferson said the United States recognized the former government because it had been established "by the authority of the nation;" as a consequence, we must recognize any "other which should be established" by this same authority. Hamilton's view of this situation was different. Hamilton said the United States had recognized the monarchy "because it contained an important member of the antient, to wit the king, and wore the appearance of his consent." If the king was deposed, Hamilton argued, we might not "with safety recognize" whatever government was established in its place.[99]

Jefferson's principle has been praised as the first enunciation of America's diplomatic recognition of de facto regimes, but the significant point here is the way that the different views revolved around the relationship between state and nation. Hamilton's view was an identification of the state with its rulers rather than with nation. For Jefferson, legitimacy of state was rooted in the will of the people. "Every people," he wrote, "may establish what form of government they please and change it as they please. The will of the nation [was] the only thing essential." Jefferson called this "the Catholic principle of republicanism,"[100] and he wrote Thomas Pinckney, the American minister to Great Britain, a classic statement of it: "We certainly cannot deny to other nations that principle whereon our own government is founded, that every nation has a right to govern itself internally under what forms it pleases, and to change these forms at it's own will."[101] This principle applied to the United States as well. The "source of authority with us," Jefferson told Washington, is "the Nation." The laws of the Continental Congress "were as valid and permanent in their nature, as the laws of the new Congress." Both derived their authority "equally ... from the will of the Nation." If a question arose "whether any particular

---

[97] Madison, "The Union: Who Are Its Real Friends?" *National Gazette*, April 2, 1792, *PJM* 14:274–275.

[98] TJ to Morris, November 7, 1792, *PTJ* 24:593.

[99] "Notes on the Legitimacy of the French Government," November 18, 1792, ibid., 633.

[100] "Notes on the Legitimacy of Government," December 30, 1792, ibid., 802. Also see TJ to C.W.F. Dumas, November 14, 1787, in *PTJ* 12:359–360.

[101] TJ to Thomas Pinckney, ibid., 803; also see Jefferson to Thomas Mann Randolph, Jr., November 16, 1792, ibid., 623.

law or appointment is still in force," Jefferson argued, the question was not "whether it was pronounced by the antient or present organ," as Hamilton suggested, "but whether it has been at any time revoked by the authority of the Nation expressed by the organ competent at the time."[102]

Pressed to explain his falling out with Hamilton, Madison reportedly claimed that he "deserted Colonel Hamilton, or rather, Colonel Hamilton deserted me; in a word, the divergence between us took place – from his wishing to *administration*, or rather to administer the government ... into what he thought it ought to be; while, on my part, I endeavored to make it conform to the Constitution as understood by the Convention that produced and recommended it, and particularly by the State conventions that adopted it."[103] Madison's succinct assessment seems to correspond well with the general tenor of Jefferson's: that Hamilton, and, by extension, the Federalists, assumed that they could administer a state as if it could in many respects operate autonomously from the nation itself. The necessary and proper clause, for example, Hamilton clearly read as legitimizing action Madison and Jefferson understood to be antithetical to the original understanding of the Constitution itself. Over and above any specific policy differences – and there were plenty of those, as we have seen – Madison and Jefferson had mostly been astonished to discover that the Federalists in general, and Hamilton in particular, assumed that the state was theirs to administer largely without reference to the public will, which, in their view, was to grant legitimacy to the policies of its officers. This is not to credit Republican views with the status of historical veracity, but this reading, as well as any other explanation, suggests the essential difference between the parties as they were understood by Jefferson and Madison.

Reflecting years later on Alexander Hamilton's life and career, Jefferson admitted that his archrival possessed "acute understanding," was "disinterested, honest, and honorable in all private transactions, amiable in society, and duly valuing virtue in private life." Nevertheless, Hamilton had been "so bewitched & perverted by the British example, as to be under thoro' conviction that corruption was essential to the government of a nation."[104] This passage is often read as Jefferson's generous separation of the private from the public in his evaluation of political enemies. Jefferson could condemn Hamilton's public policy and still recognize and praise his private character. But Hamilton

---

[102] TJ to Washington, February 4, 1792, ibid., 23:100–101.

[103] N.P. Trist, *Memoranda*, of a conversation with James Madison, September 27, 1834, in Farrand, *Records of the Federal Convention* 3:534, emphasis in original. The question of Madison's consistency is a significant one in the literature. For recent discussions, see Gordon Wood, "Is there a 'James Madison Problem'?" in David Womersley, ed., *Liberty and the American Experience in the Eighteenth-Century* (Indianapolis, 2006), 425–447; Lance Banning, *The Sacred Fire of Liberty: James Madison and the Founding of the American Republic* (Ithaca, 1998); Michael Schwartz, "The Great Divergence Reconsidered: Hamilton, Madison, and U.S.–British Relations, 1783–89," in *Journal of the Early Republic* 27 (Fall 2007), 407–436. Also see Rahe, *Republics Ancient and Modern*, 1089n.82.

[104] "The Anas," February 4, 1818, in *TJW*, 671.

had become subservient to the "British example" – his fatal error – and had forged his system accordingly, a foreign system designed not for an American people but for Britain. This was the heart of Jefferson's quarrel with Hamilton: a nationalist's demand that the government and public policy coincide with the spirit and character of the people of the nation. Long seen by historians as playing the nationalist to Jefferson's parochialism, Hamilton, in Jefferson's assessment, had not been American enough for the job.

## FOREIGN POLICY OF ANGLOMANY

Despite a brief lull from the end of the Washington administration through the first months of the Adams presidency, Republican opposition continued throughout the late 1790s and, if anything, intensified well into the Adams administration. Initially, Jefferson and Madison had high hopes for the new president. Adams, Jefferson suggested, was "perhaps the only sure barrier against Hamilton's getting in," so it might be wise to come to an understanding with Adams "as to his future elections."[105] Because Adams was "detached from Hamilton," the wisest course was "to be silent till we see what turn the new administration will take."[106] Jefferson was content with the vice presidency for a variety of reasons, personal and political, and many Republicans, despite their loss in the election, also saw Adams as a welcome relief from a Washington administration they believed too much under the influence of Hamilton. Others were less sure. Madison and Thomas Paine, for example, pressed Jefferson to accept the office as a way to "keep an eye on John Adams," who, Paine predicted, would soon enough commit some "blunder" necessitating Republican opposition.[107] Adams was not long in complying with Paine's prediction.

The "blunder" was a speech Adams delivered to Congress concerning the crisis in foreign affairs; specifically the refusal of France to recognize the representative of the United States to the new republic. The French Directory had announced in March that it would no longer abide by the "free ships, free goods" provision of the Treaty of 1778, which recognized the right of neutrals to trade in noncontraband items during wartime. From this point, "any English goods found aboard American ships could be confiscated," and Americans

---

[105] TJ to Madison, January 1, 1797, *ROL* 2:953.

[106] TJ to Archibald Stuart, January 4, 1797, *PTJ* 29:253. Jefferson's sentiments in this regard appear to have been genuine. Jefferson repeatedly denied a desire to be the chief executive, even to his closest political friends, and reported respect and affection for Adams. See TJ to John Langdon, January 22, ibid., 269–270; to Elbridge Gerry, ibid., 361–364; To Adams, December 28, 1796, ibid., 235; to Madison, December 17, 1796, *ROL* 2:949–950; to Madison, January 1, 1797, ibid., 953–954. Madison and Thomas Paine pleaded with Jefferson to accept the vice presidency. See Paine to TJ, April 1, 1797, *PTJ* 29:340–344; Madison to TJ, December 19, 1796, *ROL* 2:950–951.

[107] Paine to TJ, April 1, 1797, *PTJ* 29:340–344; Madison to TJ, December 19, 1796, *ROL* 2:950–951.

serving on British ships would be treated as pirates.[108] In addition, the French Directory had snubbed Charles Cotesworth Pinckney, sent to replace James Monroe as Minister to France, and refused to deal with him as the official representative of the United States.

In response, Adams called a special session of Congress to address the French action. Adams deprecated the French challenge to American honor that, he said, indicated that the French were determined "to treat us neither as allies nor as friends, nor as a sovereign state." Worse, Adams argued, the French action was an attempt to persuade the people of the United States "that they have different affections, principles, and interests from those of their fellow-citizens whom they themselves have chosen to manage their common concerns, and thus to produce divisions fatal to our peace." In short, Adams said, "it evinces a disposition to separate the people of the United States from the Government." Adams called on Congress to establish "a permanent system of naval defense" to protect American shipping from French depredations and to create a provisional army. Only these kinds of preparations for possible war would "convince France and the world that we are not a degraded people, humiliated under a colonial spirit of fear and sense of inferiority, fitted to be the miserable instruments of foreign influence."[109]

For Jefferson, Federalist foreign policy of this stripe was merely the other half of Hamilton's domestic program. Both required a measure of dependence on and emulation of Britain that Jefferson found incompatible with American character and sovereignty. Foreign policy had been divisive in the young American Republic from the first days of the Washington administration, but the domestic financial program of Alexander Hamilton had been the principle fuel for the emergence of opposition in Washington's first term. With the increasing importance of the French Revolution for the rest of Europe and with the signing of the Jay Treaty in Washington's second term, however, foreign policy became wedded to domestic political dissension to such a degree that Republican opposition in the mid and late 1790s makes no real sense without the context of foreign affairs. Jefferson's response to these two foreign policy crises reveals a great deal about his understanding of American national interests in a dangerous world at war.

The 1794–1795 Jay Treaty, labeled by one of its most careful students the "political battleground of the founding fathers," was indeed the occasion of vehement dissention among the nation's elite and perhaps the greatest expression of popular discontent with an action of the Washington administration.[110]

---

[108] Elkins and Mckitrick, *Age of Federalism*, 552; Kurtz, *Presidency of John Adams*, 230.

[109] Adams, "Special Session Message," May 16, 1797, in James D. Richardson, ed., *A Compilation of the Messages and Papers of the Presidents, 1789–1897*, 10 volumes (Washington, D.C., 1897), 1:235.

[110] Jerald A. Combs, *The Jay Treaty: Political Battleground of the Founding Fathers* (Berkeley, 1970). On the widespread unpopularity of the treaty, see David Waldstreicher, *In the Midst of Perpetual Fetes: The Making of American Nationalism, 1776–1820* (Chapel Hill, 1997), 138–140, and *ROL* 2:885. Also see Elkins and Mckitrick, *Age of Federalism*, 375–449. A new

The treaty was intended to tie up loose ends left over from the American Revolution, such as British occupation of frontier posts in the American Northwest and the payment of American debts to British creditors held over from pre-Revolutionary days. These issues had become sources of serious contention, provoking a number of hostile incidents, including British attacks on American shipping and impressment of American sailors into the British navy.[111]

The treaty that resulted from negotiations between John Jay, then chief justice of the United States, and William Lord Grenville, British secretary for Home Affairs, is now generally recognized by historians as the most favorable treaty the United States could have extracted from the British at the time. Although it granted certain major commercial concessions to Britain, it did succeed in dislodging the British army from American territory, reducing British influence on the Indians of the Northwest, and ushering in a period of general prosperity for American merchants and shippers.[112] Nevertheless, the initial and widespread public reaction was strongly negative and portrayed the treaty as a weak capitulation to British power. The patriotic vehemence of the public response, suggesting some insecurity about the place of the United States in the world of nations, reflected this understanding. As Madison noted to James Monroe, "The first impression was universally and simultaneously against it,"[113] with Jay burned in effigy in cities up and down the seaboard. From his retirement, Jefferson said, "This monument of folly or venality is universally execrated ... from North to South."[114] The treaty "has excited a more general disgust than any public transaction since the days of our independence," creating a "burst of dissatisfaction" that had "never before appeared against any transaction."[115]

Although the most vehement public anger at the treaty eventually subsided,[116] for the leaders of the Republican opposition Jay's Treaty remained

assessment that should encourage reexamination of the treaty's problems is Lawrence Hatter, "The Jay Charter: The Laurentine Trade and the Problem of American Sovereignty in the West, 1796–1811," unpublished paper in possession of the author.

[111] On the British Order in Council of November 6, 1793, which blockaded the French West Indies and resulted in the seizure of 250 American ships by March of 1794, see Elkins and McKitrick, *Age of Federalism*, 389–391.

[112] Elkins and Mckitrick, *Age of Federalism*, 436–441. Although it is by no means clear that the treaty led to prosperity as opposed to coinciding with it.

[113] Madison to Monroe, December 20, 1795, in *PJM* 16:168.

[114] TJ to Thomas Mann Randolph, August 11, *PTJ* 28:435. Also see TJ to Mann Page, August 30, 1795 in ibid., 440–441.

[115] TJ to Philip Mazzei, September 8, 1795, in ibid., 457; TJ to James Monroe, September 6, 1795, in ibid., 449.

[116] Elkins and McKitrick assume the "initial outburst against the treaty" was "wildly emotional" and rather devoid of serious intellectual content, *Age of Federalism*, 431. Eventually, they imply, the thinking few among the mobs of opponents had their questions answered by pamphlets and articles defending the treaty and by the general prosperity ushered in its wake. This explanation, while persuasive to a point, ignores the continued use of negative assessments of Jay's Treaty in the arguments of Republican leaders and the apparent resonance of such arguments among their supporters. It also ignores serious shortcomings in the treaty that left American sovereignty vulnerable in the West. On this, see Hatter, "The Jay Charter."

tangible evidence that their interpretation of the current political situation was correct. Jefferson and Madison believed that the treaty provided demonstrable proof, as Madison heatedly told Robert R. Livingston, that the Federalist party was, in fact, "a British party, systematically aiming at an exclusive connection with the British Govert. and ready to sacrifice to that object as well the dearest interests of our commerce, as the most sacred dictates of national honor."[117] While Hamilton, in a series of essays, was defending the treaty on constitutional and economic ground, Madison excoriated Hamilton's "anglomany,"[118] and Jefferson condemned the treaty as "really nothing more than a treaty of alliance between England and the Anglomen of this country against the legislature and people of the United States."[119] Shocked about the treaty as they professed themselves to be, Jefferson and Madison had long been convinced that Hamilton's policy orientation traded national freedom of action for a colonial subservience that served the financial interest of a very small number of citizens.[120] The treaty simply confirmed their belief. Hamilton and Jay, Jefferson told Madison, were implicated "in the boldest act they ever ventured on to undermine the constitution." In short, "a bolder party-stroke was never struck."[121]

Jefferson's opposition to Jay's Treaty reflected what he called a concern for principles and for the character of American institutions and public behavior. His consistent trope was that the treaty was an affront to national honor and independence.[122] "The Anglomen have in the end got their treaty through, and so far, have triumphed over the cause of republicanism," Jefferson told Monroe, but it was at the expense of "the rights, the interest, the honor and faith of our nation," which had been "so grossly sacrificed" by a faction in "conspiracy with the enemies of their country."[123] In the face of such widespread opposition

[117] Madison to Livingston, August 10, 1795, *PJM* 16:47. James Morton Smith points out that this interpretation was also, to a degree, held by Lord Grenville, who seemed to believe that the treaty had established "a permanent union" between Great Britain and the United States. The Grenville quotation from a letter to George Hammond, November 20, 1794, is in Mary K. Bonsteel Tachau, "George Washington and the Reputation of Edmund Randolph," *JAH* 73 (June 1986), 24. See *ROL* 2:884, n. 16.

[118] Madison to an Unidentified Correspondent, August 23, 1795, *PJM* 16:56.

[119] TJ to Edward Rutledge, November 30, 1795, *PTJ* 28:542. It is important to note here that Hamilton condemned the Republicans in similar terms for their attachment to France. See Camillus [Hamilton], "The Defence," No. 1, July 22, 1795, in *PAH* 18:481–482. Also see Hamilton, "The Stand," No. 1, March 30, 1798, *New York Commercial Advertiser*, in *PAH* 21:384–386; "A French Faction," April 1798, in ibid., 452–453 (in which Hamilton asserted that the Republicans hoped to make the United States a "province of France"); and Hamilton to Washington, May 19, 1798, in ibid., 467.

[120] See Donald R. Adams, Jr., "American Neutrality and Prosperity, 1793–1808: A Reconsideration," *Journal of Economic History* 40 (December 1980), 713–737.

[121] TJ to Madison, September 21, 1795, *ROL* 2:898.

[122] Edward Rutledge told Jefferson that the opposition to the Treaty boded well for the future and suggested that "the people of America" preferred "a temporary obstruction to their Commerce, and a suspension to their progress to Wealth; to the Abandonment of national Honor," Rutledge to TJ, April 30, 1796, *PTJ* 29:92.

[123] TJ to Monroe, July 10, 1796, *PTJ* 29:147; to Madison, March 27, 1796, *ROL* 2:928.

by the people, whose "pulse," Jefferson insisted, "beat so full and in such universal unison" on this subject, the Federalists had rammed the treaty through Congress. Only by defying the will of the people, the only legitimate source of national action, and handing over sovereignty to a foreign power, had the "anglomen" come close to enacting their program.

Nevertheless, Jefferson remained optimistic. Because the Federalists, in his estimation, had no popular backing and could stand only on the "colossus of the President's merits with the people," Washington's retirement would surely "lead things into the channel of harmony between the governors and governed." Jefferson retained an abiding faith in the tendency of popular majorities, as long as they remained well-informed, to come to their senses and make correct, enlightened, republican decisions. "In the mean time," then, Jefferson counseled Monroe, "patience."[124] The upcoming election would set things right, or so he believed.

The Jay Treaty crisis illustrates the significance of foreign affairs in the domestic political battles of the new nation. Stances on the French Revolution, likewise, became such telltale barometers of party persuasion in the minds of Americans, that the parties were often known by shorthand – the "French" party or the "English" party.[125] Most Americans started with a basic appreciation of the help France had given them during the Revolution.[126] Beyond this, the leading political and military figures had developed close working relationships and even friendships with French officers stationed in the United States. When the French Third Estate declared itself the "nation" in 1789, most Americans responded enthusiastically to what they saw as a French imitation of the principles of the American Revolution. In one of its first commentaries on the news, the *Boston Gazette* proclaimed that "liberty will have another feather in her cap."[127] This was certainly how Jefferson first understood the French Revolution – as a continuation overseas of the same spirit of liberty that had been cultivated and brought to fruition in America.[128] Federalists, on the other hand, tended to view the French Revolution with increasing horror,

---

[124] TJ to Monroe, July 10, 1796, *PTJ* 29:147.

[125] On the significance of the French Revolution in the development of American political culture, see Lloyd S. Kramer, "The French Revolution and the Creation of American Political Culture," in Joseph Klaits and Michael H. Hatzel, *The Global Ramifications of the French Revolution* (Cambridge, 1994), 26–54. See also, Charles Downer Hazen, *Contemporary American Opinion of the French Revolution* (Baltimore, 1897); Gary B. Nash, "The American Clergy and the French Revolution," *WMQ*, 20 (1965), 392–412; and Elkins and Mckitrick, *Age of Federalism*, 308–311, 354–355.

[126] See, for example, Hamilton to Carrington, May 26, 1792, in Freeman, ed., *Writings*, 746; and "Memorandum on the French Revolution," ibid., 833–834.

[127] *Boston Gazette*, September 7, 1789, cited in Hazen, *Contemporary American Opinion of the French Revolution*, 142.

[128] Among multiple examples of this sentiment, see TJ to Tench Coxe, June 1, 1795, *PTJ* 28:373. For examples of a slightly different emphasis – one that suggests that the success of the French Revolution will strengthen republicanism in America, see TJ to Henry Innes, May 23, 1793, ibid., 26:100, and to Thomas Mann Randolph, Jr., June 2, 1793, ibid., 169.

fearing its propensity to anarchy and atheism. Hamilton told Washington that the Revolution had "unhinged the orderly principles of the People of this country." America, as a consequence, was itself on "the threshold of disorganization and anarchy."[129]

Although he tended to think closer commercial relations with France were in the American interest, Jefferson, for his part, never confused friendship with France with American national interest itself (a mistake Republicans regularly accused the Federalists of making in their deference to Britain).[130] Jefferson, although he did tend to be more favorably disposed toward France, insisted upon American neutrality in the war between France and Britain. Early evidence of this position came during the diplomatic mission of French minister Edmund Genet when Jefferson's efforts to steer a neutral course brought him into direct confrontation with Genet's blundering designs for a closer relationship between France and the United States than Jefferson was willing to countenance. The story is worth briefly retelling because of what it demonstrates about lines Jefferson drew.

Arriving in Charleston in April of 1793, Genet received showers of affection and good will from Americans on his journey north to the capital.[131] Jefferson's initial response to the French minister was, with that of many Americans, favorable, and he even suggested that public enthusiasm was a compensation for the Federalist administration's decided lack of it.[132] After Genet's initial presentation of his credentials and a short speech outlining his intentions, Jefferson gushed to Madison that "it is impossible for any thing to be more affectionate, more magnanimous than the purpot of his mission.... In short he offers every thing and asks nothing."[133]

This early assessment soon changed. Genet began outfitting French privateers in American ports, manned by American sailors, for the purpose of preying on British shipping. This behavior, of course, would involve the United States in a clear violation of its stated neutrality. Moreover, he acknowledged that Genet's behavior was a breach of American sovereignty.[134] Soon the secretary of state was lecturing Genet on the law of nations – "the right of every nation to prohibit acts of sovereignty from being exercised by any other within its limits" as well as the "duty of a neutral nation to prohibit such as would

---

[129] Hamilton to Washington, April 14, 1794, in *PAH* 16:270. Also see Hamilton's "Memorandum on the French Revolution" (1794) a Revolution he pronounced " a caricature of human depravity," in Freeman, ed., *Writings*, 833–836, at 835.

[130] Elkins and Mckitrick, *Age of Federalism*, 336–341. For two such accusations see Madison to TJ, September 2, 1793, *ROL* 2:815; and Monroe to TJ, September 3, 1793, *PTJ* 27:27. Republican leaders also worried that Federalists would use Republican Francophilia as an excuse to crush their opposition. See Madison to TJ, June 1, *ROL* 2:846.

[131] On Genet's mission see, especially, Elkins and McKitrick, *Age of Federalism*, 330–373. Also see, Sharp, *American Politics in the Early Republic*, 69–91; Harry Ammon, *The Genet Mission* (New York, 1973); and Joanne B. Freeman, *Affairs of Honor*, 91–99.

[132] TJ to James Madison, May 19, 1793, *ROL* 2:775.

[133] Ibid.

[134] See TJ to Madison, June 2, 1793, ibid., 778–780.

injure one of the warring parties." Genet's actions were particularly egregious because they encouraged American citizens "to commit acts contrary to the duties they owe their own country."[135]

Genet ignored repeated warnings from Jefferson about his actions – defied him, in fact – arguing that France had a natural right or at least a right by international law or by treaty with the United States to outfit privateers in American ports. He also insisted that Washington had no authority to order French privateers to depart American ports, which he had done on May 20. He apparently also threatened to go over Washington's head to appeal to the people who earlier had received him so warmly.[136] Jefferson now regretted the unfortunate choice of minister from the French republic. "Never in my opinion," he exclaimed to Madison, "was so calamitous an appointment made, as that of the present minister of F[rance] here. Hothead, all imagination, no judgment, passionate, disrespectful and even indecent towards the P[resident] in his written as well as verbal communications, talking of appeals from him to Congress, from them to the people, urging the most unreasonable and groundless propositions, and in the most dictatorial style, etc. etc. etc."[137] Jefferson assured Monroe, "I am doing every thing in my power to moderate the impetuosity of his movements, and to destroy the dangerous opinion, which has been excited in him, that the people of the US will disavow the acts of their government" on his appeal.[138] But no sooner would Jefferson's advice cool Genet down, he wrote, than "he breaks out again on the very first occasion, so as to shew that he is incapable of correcting himself."[139]

The cabinet eventually decided unanimously to ask for the recall of the French minister.[140] Washington hoped to have Genet sacked while still preserving good relations with France. Hamilton, on the other hand, hoped to exploit the situation for domestic political advantage – to discredit the French Revolution in America and link the Republican party with the French minister by revealing Genet's correspondence and defiance to the public.[141] Jefferson thought Hamilton's meddling would eliminate the possibility of maintaining good relations with France and would actually endanger American neutrality in the process.[142]

---

[135] TJ to Edmond Charles Genet, June 5, 1793, *PTJ* 26:195–196. See also TJ to Genet, June 17, 1793, ibid., 297–300.

[136] Editorial note on the Recall of Genet, *PTJ* 26:687–688.

[137] TJ to Madison, July 7, 1793, *ROL* 2:792.

[138] To Monroe, June 28, 1793, *PTJ* 26:393.

[139] To Madison, July 7, 1793, *ROL* 2:792. Also see TJ to Madison, July 14, 1793, ibid., 793 and to Monroe, July 14, 1793, *PTJ* 26:502–503.

[140] TJ to Madison, August 3, 1793, *ROL* 2:798–799, and "The Recall of Edmond Charles Genet, editorial note with documents," *PTJ* 26:685–715.

[141] Ibid., 689, and Joanne B. Freeman, *Affairs of Honor*, 93.

[142] "Hamilton and Knox have pressed an appeal to the people with an eagerness I never before saw in them," TJ to Madison, August 11, 1793, *ROL* 2:803. Despite Washington's eventual decision that Hamilton's public statement would not be necessary, the Secretary of the Treasury leaked the information anyway in an essay in a Philadelphia newspaper. See Freeman, *Affairs of Honor*, 95.

Jefferson, as insulted as Hamilton and Washington at Genet's impropriety and challenge to American sovereignty, argued that "the mass of the republican interest has no hesitation to disapprove of this intermeddling by a foreigner."[143] Jefferson was indeed concerned about the reputation of the Republicans in the wake of the Genet affair, but he also sent a strong message that the Republicans would not abide any dictation from foreign powers or breaches of American sovereignty. American interest, from his perspective, demanded maintenance of the nation's sovereignty *and* neutrality. When war with France threatened in the first months of the Adams administration, Jefferson's first concern continued to be protection of what he considered American national interests.

Accordingly, Jefferson believed Adams's special message to Congress in May 1797 was too bellicose and threatened the hard-won neutrality Americans had been trying for years to maintain. From his perspective, any movement toward war on the part of the Federalists was a more or less conscious attempt to drive Americans into further dependence on Britain by artificially stoking their fears of French invasion. Consequently, the war preparations on the part of the Congress and the Adams administration had created an environment in which any "neutral" position tended to be characterized as an undue devotion to France detrimental to American interests. "Those who have no wish but for the peace of their country, and it's independance of all foreign influence," Jefferson wrote, "have a hard struggle indeed, overwhelmed by a cry as loud and imposing as if it were true, of being under French influence." This accusation, he insisted, was "raised by a faction composed of English subjects residing among us, or such as are English in all their relations and sentiments."[144] Confirming this assessment, in Jefferson's mind, was Adams himself, who, in his special message, drew a clear line between those who would "support the Government established by their voluntary consent and appointed by their free choice" and those who instead would surrender "themselves to the direction of foreign and domestic factions, in opposition to their own Government."[145]

But Jefferson rejected this characterization of the opposition. Adams's speech and the conduct of the Federalists in general, he believed, "was turned toward war," despite the desire of the people for "a continuance of peace." This was the same unwillingness to heed the public will that had characterized Federalist policy from the beginning, Jefferson believed. Opposition to such intransigence took the rhetorical form of demanding that the nation give direction to national policy. It was hardly taking direction from the French, as the Federalists charged. Jefferson lamented that American honor and interests had been "grossly trampled on by both" England and France. War with France would damage American interest in neutral commerce and drive the nation into the English camp. "War is not the best engine for us to resort to." American "*commerce* ... if properly managed, will be a better instrument for

---

143 To Madison, August 25, 1793, *ROL* 2:811.
144 TJ to Horatio Gates, May 30, 1797, *PTJ* 29:407.
145 Adams, in Richardson, *Messages and Papers of the Presidents* 1:239.

obliging the interested nations of Europe to treat us with justice." Accordingly, Jefferson encouraged the same economic coercion to solve the French crisis that he and Madison had advocated against England earlier in the decade. Whereas the English "spoilations" on American shipping might be halted by the recent victories of Napoleon, Jefferson wrote, "I see nothing to check the depredations of the French but the natural effect they begin to produce of starving themselves by deterring us from venturing to sea with provisions."[146] Because the United States had endured England's "defiance of the laws of nations" for several years, he wrote in the summer of 1798, he thought it would be better "to continue to bear [the same] from France through the present summer" until peace came, he predicted, that winter.[147]

Jefferson assumed that the threat of war was generated solely by the warmongering of the Adams administration, which, Jefferson believed, betrayed an "ungrateful predilection … in favor of Great Britain" and took "to the very brink" of war "two nations, who love one another affectionately."[148] But his private correspondence reveals disgust with the French Directory and a toying with the prospects for commercial influence on French conduct. The true American interest was a genuine neutrality with both France and England. That had been Jefferson's position since the first news of war between France and England in 1793 and, indeed, continued to be throughout the 1790s.[149]

On the specific question of war with France, Jefferson told Polish patriot General Thaddeus Kosciusko that in event of war, "we must give up political differences of opinion, and unite as one man to defend our country."[150] And when President Adams revealed the true nature of the XYZ affair, Jefferson wrote Madison that Talleyrand's demand for a bribe from the American delegation was "unworthy of a great nation." The French had miscalculated, he

---

[146] TJ to French Strother, June 8, 1797, *PTJ* 29:425; to John Moody, June 13, 1797, ibid., 428–429; TJ to John Strode, June 14, 1797, ibid., 432; to Thomas Pickney, May 29, 1797, ibid., 405.

[147] TJ to Samuel Smith, August 22, 1798, ibid., 30:485.

[148] TJ to Aaron Burr, June 17, 1797, ibid., 29:438–439.

[149] See Jefferson's advice to Madison – who had been stuck on the constitutionality of the executive's declaration of neutrality as an interference with Congress's war power – in TJ to Madison, August 11, 1793, *ROL* 2:803. "The desire of neutrality is universal," Jefferson wrote. Accordingly, "it would place the republicans in a very unfavble. point of view with the people to be caviling about small points of propriety; and would betray a wish to find fault with the President in an instance where he will be approved by the great body of the people who consider the substance of the measure only, and not the smaller criticisms to which it is liable…. So in Congress, I believe that it will be true wisdom in the Republican party to approve unequivocally of a state of neutrality." Many historians have pointed to this letter as an example of Jefferson's political savvy, but it also surely reflects his genuine position on neutrality, as multiple private statements confirm. Compare Jefferson's sentiments with Madison's early reaction to the neutrality proclamation: Madison to TJ, June 19, 1793, ibid., 786, and TJ to Madison, June 23, 1793, ibid., 787. For an excellent discussion of the debates within Washington's cabinet over the question of neutrality, see Stuart Leibiger, *Founding Friendship: George Washington, James Madison, and the Creation of the American Republic* (Charlottesville, 1999), 169–181.

[150] TJ to Kosciusko, February 21, 1799, in *L&B* 10:115–116.

warned his friend. They had assumed that the Republicans were attached to France and to a hatred of the Federalist party, when, in reality, "the love of their country [was] their first passion."[151] "The first object of my heart," Jefferson wrote Elbridge Gerry, "is my own country.... I have not one farthing of interest, nor one fibre of attachment out of it, nor a single motive of preference of any one nation to another, but in proportion as they are more or less friendly to us."[152] Accordingly, Jefferson wrote another correspondent, the American people needed to understand "that their own character and situation are materially different from the French; and that whatever may be the fate of republicanism there, we are able to preserve it inviolate here."[153] Pierre Adet, who had replaced Genet as France's minister to the United States, and who had openly campaigned for Jefferson in the election of 1796, independently noted the limits of Jefferson's alleged Francophilia. "Jefferson," Adet wrote, "although a friend of liberty and learning, although an admirer of the effort we have made to break our bonds and dispel the cloud of ignorance which weighs down the human race, Jefferson, I say, is American and, as such, he cannot be sincerely our friend. An American is the born enemy of all the European peoples."[154]

The real problem, as Jefferson understood it and described it later, was not that French policy toward the United States was so much better than advertised, but that in the absence of Washington's restraining hand, the minority of high Federalists – "these energumeni of royalism," Jefferson called them – were now "mounted on the Car of State & *free from controul*, like Phaeton on that of the sun, drove headlong & wild, looking neither to right nor left, nor regarding anything but the objects they were driving at."[155] A clearer image of a rogue state taken by a cabal and running away from its public is difficult to imagine. Jefferson's opposition was oriented around an impulse to bring the nation back into correspondence or union with the state – the essence of the nationalist project.[156] The Republican aim, he affirmed, was "bringing and keeping the government in real unison with the spirit of their constituents."[157]

---

[151] TJ to Madison, April 6, 1798, in *ROL* 2:1034.

[152] TJ to Gerry, January 26, 1799, in *WTJ* 7:329. This letter is calculated but not insincere. Jefferson still wished the French people well, "but I have not been insensible under the atrocious depredations they have committed on our commerce."

[153] TJ to John Breckinridge, January 29, 1800, in *WTJ* 7:417–418.

[154] Adet quoted in Malone, *Jefferson and the Ordeal of Liberty*, 289–290. On Adet's career in America, see Michael F. Conlin, "The American Mission of Citizen Pierre-Auguste Adet: Revolutionary Chemistry and Diplomacy in the Early Republic," in *Pennsylvania Magazine of History and Biography* 124 (October 2000), 489–520.

[155] "Anas," in *FE* 1:181, emphasis added.

[156] See Ernst Gellner, *Nations and Nationalism* (Ithaca, 1983), 1: "Nationalism is primarily a political principle, which holds that the political and the national unit should be congruent."

[157] To Taylor, November 26, 1798, in *FE*: 8: 482; also see TJ to Madison, November 26, 1799 in *ROL* 2:1122: "Our objects, according to my ideas, should be these.... Protestations against violations of the true principles of our constitution, merely to save them."

## THE PUBLIC AND ITS STATE

In one sense, the fundamental problem faced by the first generation of national leaders under the Constitution was the question of the proper relation of the public to the state. All Americans largely understood that public will legitimated everything the government did or, rather, that nothing government did was legitimate unless ratified by popular opinion. No one in American politics denied the fundamental sovereignty of the people. What divided thinkers of various stripes was the question of how that sovereignty was to play itself out in the day-to-day operations of government in the absence of constitutional crisis. The party battles of the 1790s revolved around this problem. Conflicts over policy spilled out into the public arena, and as they did, leaders had to decide how to approach the people.[158]

Jefferson and Madison clearly believed that the approach to public opinion was one of the most crucial differences between them and the Federalists. Whether the differences were quite as substantive as they imagined is another question. Clearly there were high Federalists who demanded unthinking deference from the people and expressed utter disdain for democracy, as when Uriah Tracy suggested that the people "are vicious and love vicious men for their leaders."[159] And, as David Hackett Fisher has demonstrated, Federalists of what he calls "the old school," like Theodore Sedgwick, insisted "upon an open and habitual display of subordination" from his social inferiors and were, as a group, "deeply conscious of inequalities," hoping "to sustain a governing elite with the consent of the people, by reinforcing the deferential spirit of colonial society." Their ideals, he suggests, could be summarized in Samuel Stone's slogan: "a speaking aristocracy in the face of a silent democracy."[160]

But many other Federalists held more complex views.[161] George Washington, for example, even as he condemned the Democratic societies, declared that "no one denies the right of the people to meet occasionally, to petition for, or to remonstrance against, any Act of the Legislature." He instead condemned only the view (if anyone held it) that such petitioners could turn themselves into a "permanent body" of "Censors" and by "a stretch of arrogant presumption,"

---

[158] Precisely why a full accounting of these events – which this is not – must engage the public shaping of American political culture. For good introductions to this recent emphasis in the literature, see Simon Newman, *Parades and the Politics of the Street: Festive Culture in the Early American Republic* (Philadelphia, 1997); David Waldstreicher, *In the Midst of Perpetual Fetes*; Jeffrey Pasley, *The Tyranny of Printers*; and Pasley, Andrew Robertson, and Waldstreicher, eds., *Beyond the Founders: New Approaches to the Political History of the Early American Republic* (Chapel Hill, 2003).

[159] Tracy quoted in Fischer, *The Revolution of American Conservatism*, 23.

[160] Ibid., 14–17.

[161] See Todd Estes, "Shaping the Politics of Public Opinion: Federalists and the Jay Treaty Debate," *JER*, 20 (Fall 2000), 393–422; and "John Jay, the Concept of Deference, and the Transformation of Early American Political Culture," *The Historian* 65 (Winter 2002): 293–317.

give law to Congress.[162] Even a "Patriotic Society," such as that contemplated by his nephew, Washington warned, could become "a kind of imperium in imperio," thus undermining "deliberate, and solemn discussion by the Representatives of the people, chosen for the express purpose, and bringing with them from the different parts of the Union the sense of their Constituents."[163] After all, the fleeting "public sentiment," Washington suggested, was not the same thing as "the real voice of the people," which could "be known" only "on great occasions ... and after time has been given for cool and deliberate reflection."[164] These views are not quite so far off from Jefferson's own ambivalence about voluntary societies, as we have seen, or from his argument that the public will, "to be rightful, must be reasonable," or from Madison's sense that popular opinion needed to be subjected to the reason of the community.[165]

If Jefferson and Madison had trouble crediting their opponents with much sincerity in the matter, it is partly because the Federalists seemed to go out of their way to squelch public dissent. Nevertheless, it seems that, in retrospect, the Federalist-Republican split over the nature of the relation between state and public was, in more respects than Republicans were willing to admit, an intramural struggle among the original federalists who all assumed, as a foundational premise of republican government, that the people had to be capable of electing a wise leadership and remaining engaged with public affairs. To be sure, as we have seen, the Federalists are more than responsible for their historical reputation as encouragers of silent deference from the people. But this may credit Republicans with a bit more clarity than they actually offered about the precise way the public would relate to the government. That such a relationship was, in Jefferson's thought, to be dynamic and fluid, intimate and mutually reinforcing, does, nevertheless, I think, distinguish his thought from that of Hamilton, especially, and even Washington and Adams. It certainly made sense for members of the opposition to consider the proper relation to be more dynamic than members of the governing party were willing to countenance. It was in the Republican interest to assume that the legislation the Federalists were passing could not possibly be the fixed opinion of the public, just as it was in the Federalist interest to argue that they were the natural aristocracy that the public itself had chosen to write such legislation. In such circumstances, it is hardly surprising that Madison encouraged the people to "watch over" the government "as well as obey it."[166] And it is hardly surprising that such "rousing" of the people would elicit ambivalence or outright hostility from the Federalists.

---

[162] George Washington to Burgess Ball, September 25, 1794, in., John C. Fitzpatrick, ed., *The Writings of George Washington*, 39 vols. (Washington, DC, 1931–1944), 33:506.

[163] George Washington to Bushrod Washington, September 30, 1786, in ibid., 29:21–23; George Washington to Burgess Ball, September 25, 1794, in ibid., 33:506.

[164] George Washington to Edward Carrington, May 1, 1796, in ibid., 35:31–32.

[165] Jefferson, "First Inaugural Address." Also see Colleen A. Sheehan's brilliant essay, "Madison and the French Enlightenment: The Authority of Public Opinion," in *WMQ* 59 (October 2002), 925–956.

[166] "Who are the Best Keepers of the People's Liberties?," in *PJM* 14:426–427.

Jefferson's definition of Federalists eventually became so narrow that he was able to imagine them in handfuls as opposed to Republicans who were, as he once put it, "the nation" itself.[167] Jefferson could remain confident precisely because he never once believed that the Republicans represented anything other than the public itself. Federalists, at best, represented a minority view, and if their philosophy of government was truly embraced by only the smallest fraction of Americans, Jefferson could easily read them out of the American public.

But aside from these few "incurables," the "main body of the federalists" could be reconciled to the nation because the "great body" of them were real republicans & honest men under pure motives" who had only been deluded by Federalist fearmongering (as well as "ill conduct in France"). It was precisely because these honest Federalists returned to their senses "that we gained the victory in Nov, 1800, which we should not have gained in Nov, 1799."[168] Much like his offer of assimilation to Indians, this approach wraps an appeal to exclusion in the garb of generosity: it identifies the nation with a uniform set of ideas, deviation from which would be un-American, heretical, blasphemous.[169]

His rejection of pluralism afforded Jefferson a more hopeful outlook on the future; he had greater confidence that, once properly informed, the public's views would largely coincide with his own. This gave him a kind of comfort with an aroused populace that Federalists simply did not share. Federalists, Richard Buell points out, had "no reason to assume that" awakening the public "would spontaneously work in their favor," which was precisely why their "aggressive" efforts to "mold … public opinion" were rather more like an attempt to "instruct the people in 'truths' to which they were not naturally sympathetic." Every time Federalists tried to engage the public, then, they opened themselves to a popular politics for which their deepest instincts were ill suited.[170] "Many Federalists," Buell says, "believed that education would teach the people to respect their superiors," whereas Jefferson, on the other

[167] Jefferson to William Duane, March 28, 1811, *FE*, 11: 193. See Madison's similar description of the party conflict in Madison to William Eustis, May 22, 1823, in Hunt, ed., *Writings of James Madison*, 9: 135–37, where Madison insists that there was indeed a "deep distinction between the two parties or rather," he said, "between the mass of the Nation, and the part of it which for a time got possession of the Govt."

[168] TJ to James Monroe, March 7, 1801, in *FE* 9:202–204; TJ to Thomas Paine, March 8, 1801, in ibid., 213. Also see TJ to Henry Knox, March 27, 1801, in ibid., 237–238; TJ to Nathaniel Niles, March 22, 1801, in ibid., 220–221; and TJ to John Dickinson, March 6, 1801, in ibid., 201–202; TJ to Elbridge Gerry, March 29, 1801, in *TJW*, 1088–1090..

[169] On Federalists as "apostates" committed to "heresies," see TJ to Philip Mazzei, April 24, 1796, in *TJW*, 1037. On Federalist thinking as "blasphemy," and the predeliction of a "little selfish minority," see TJ to Joseph C. Cabell, February 2, 1816, ibid., 1380–1381.

[170] Buell, *Securing the Revolution: Ideology in American Politics, 1789–1815* (Ithaca, 1972), 123. But see 91–135, generally, for a superb discussion of this problem. Federalists, Buell writes, "were at one and the same time appealing to the people and asking them to stay out of politics" (127). Also see Elkins and McKitrick, *Age of Federalism*, ch. 15.

hand, expected that education, as we have seen, would render the people the wise judges of their republican statesmen.[171]

Jefferson externalized the vulgar (as well as the aristocrats). His canaille were in Paris; his degraded poor were in London; the only peasants he had seen, in Europe. All of which made him remarkably democratic within the nation. In Europe, the demos might be the degraded "mobs of great cities," but in America the citizens were eminently trustworthy. But the Federalists simply could not trust the American people, Jefferson believed, and this dictated their entire stance toward the republican experiment. As we have seen, Jefferson became convinced that Hamilton held out little hope for republicanism and simply assumed that American "order," too, would eventually require a government of force and corruption. No wonder Jefferson believed that "the toryism with which we struggled in '77, differed but in name from the federalism of '99, with which we struggled also."[172] Hamilton's outlook seems to have come as something of a shock to Jefferson on his return from France, but he eventually made sense of it with an assessment of Federalist behavior that came to rest in a kind of biological determinism: Their fear and contempt of the public was rooted quite as firmly in their natural "constitution" as well as their unwillingness or inability to face the fact of American uniqueness. When he described the two parties in 1795, he contrasted the Republicans – "the entire body of landholders" and the "body of labourers" – with the "Antirepublicans" (the Federalists), who included:

1. The old refugees & tories.
2. British merchants residing among us, & composing the main body of our merchants.
3. American merchants trading on British capital.
4. Speculators & Holders in the banks & public funds.
5. Officers of the federal government with some exceptions
6. Office-hunters, willing to give up principles for places.
7. Nervous persons, whose languid fibers have more analogy with a passive than active state of things.[173]

This boils the Federalists down to two categories: sufferers from pathological paranoia and those who would elevate personal gain over principle and common good. It identifies the Federalists as a minority sect – the Republicans, after all, he said, outnumbered them "500 to one" – which, at heart, hoped to use the state to serve its own interests, largely pecuniary, against the needs and interests of the nation itself. They seemed to crave the kind of governments Jefferson had witnessed in Europe "where the dignity of man is lost in arbitrary distinctions, where the many are crouched under the weight of the few" rather

---

[171] Buell, *Securing the Republic*, 122.
[172] TJ to John Langdon, March 5, 1810, in *TJW*, 1218. In *Notes*, Jefferson said that "A Tory has been properly defined to be a traitor in thought, but not in deed." See ibid., 281.
[173] Notes on Professor Ebeling's Letter of July 30, 1795, in *TJW*, 700.

than the egalitarian system envisioned by Americans where Republican leaders would "give fair play to … the republican sense of [their] constituents."[174] It ultimately came down to a battle between "aristocrats and democrats," natural categories in Jefferson's account.[175] No wonder most Federalists served in the federal government and hoped "to transfer all the powers of the states to [the general] government & all the powers of that government to it's [executive]." They were, after all, the tories of nature whose ultimate goal was to render "the depositories of the public authority as far removed as possible [from] the controul of the people."[176] Federalists, in other words, hoped to create a state independent of the people, whereas, for Jefferson, "independence" could "be trusted nowhere but with the people in mass" who were, he insisted, "inherently independent of all but moral law."[177]

So some Federalists directly benefited from British connections and Hamiltonian concentration of wealth, but many others, Jefferson said, were simply "nervous persons," somehow naturally predisposed toward fear. Federalists tended to be "by their constitutions" among those "who fear and distrust the people, and wish to draw all powers from them into the hands of the higher classes."[178] "The division of whig and tory is founded in the nature of men," Jefferson told Joel Barlow in 1802: "The weakly and nerveless, the rich and the corrupt" would naturally find "more safety and accessibility" in a government of concentrated power.[179] The "parties of whig and tory are those of nature," Jefferson insisted to Lafayette. "They exist in all countries, whether called by these names, or by those of aristocrats and democrats, *cote droite* and *cote gauche*, ultras and radicals, serviles and liberals. The sickly, weakly, timid man fears the people, and is a tory by nature," whereas "the healthy, strong and bold, cherishes them, and is formed a whig by nature."[180] These "nervous persons" could not see what Jefferson could so clearly: that the American people had been rendered capable of self-government by their unique experience and could be trusted to wisely animate public policy. The State had nothing to fear from its public, and it was only those with idiopathic fear of the people or those with darker motives who would work to sever the connection between them.

Jefferson told John Adams that "the terms of whig and tory belong to natural as well as to civil history." "They denote the temper and constitution of minds of different individuals" and "every one takes his side in favor of the many, or of the few, according to his constitution" as well as "the circumstances in which he is placed."[181] "Those of firm health and spirits," Jefferson noted, "are unwilling to cede more of their liberty than is necessary to preserve

<hr>

[174] TJ to James Monroe, July 10, 1796, in *PTJ* 29:147; TJ to in *PTJ* 10:52.
[175] TJ to Henry Lee, August 10, 1824, in *FE* 12:375.
[176] TJ to Andrew Alexander, January 5, 1801, in *PTJ* 32:398.
[177] TJ to Spencer Roane, September 6, 1819, in *FE* 12:135–138.
[178] TJ to Henry Lee, 1824, in ibid., 375.
[179] TJ to Barlow, May 3, 1802, in *FE* 9:371.
[180] TJ to Lafayette, November 4, 1823, in *L&B* 15:492.
[181] TJ to Adams, June 27, 1813, in *AJL*, 335.

order; those of feeble constitutions will wish to see one strong arm able to protect them from the many. These are the whigs and tories of nature."[182]

This assessment went some distance toward explaining, for Jefferson, why Federalists believed that Republicans were stirring up the people against their betters and why the standard posture of Federalists toward the people was a demand for deference to constituted authorities – authorities that the people had elected and therefore sanctioned. The Federalists may have awakened to a need to canvas their position before the public in the wake of the Jay Treaty, and some of them later attributed their failure in 1800 to the general ways they "neglected the cultivation of popular favor."[183] But in the 1790s, Jefferson thought, the Federalists largely addressed the public as a way to ensure its deference: The public should embrace the Jay Treaty, Federalists seemed to say, because the Federalist leadership, privy to better information and a competence not comprehensible by the people, said it was the right thing to do. So, even their efforts to acknowledge the public were grudging concession to the reality that they really did have to address a people who seemed unalterably opposed to the treaty they had negotiated among themselves. The Federalist "system" was designed, Jefferson said, "to keep up an alarm," to stoke the natural fears of those predisposed to worry and to manipulate the patriotism and anxiety of those natural republicans with less adequate information.[184] Republicans had an entirely different approach to the public that is a separate issue from the actual differences on policy, or, rather, that is even more fundamental to Jefferson and Madison than the specific issues around which their critique was oriented and around which the historiography is generally organized.[185]

The irreconcilable Federalists, in Jefferson's view, did not just offer a difference of opinion about policy that could be accommodated with candor and respect within a republican framework (the beautiful ideal among genuine Republicans). Jefferson and Madison believed that the Federalists were questioning the framework itself: that the people could govern themselves without running into anarchy. This was not a question of simple policy differences to be hashed out and compromised in deliberation. For them, it was the deliberation itself that the Federalists were questioning and attempting to eradicate.

We make a mistake to think of this as partisan politics, although some historians have taken a certain delight in showing just how partisan (in a

---

[182] TJ to Lafayette, November 4, 1823, in *L&B* 15:492.

[183] Hamilton to James Bayard, April 16–21, 1802, in *PAH* 25:606. Also see James McHenry to Oliver Wolcott, Jr., July 22, 1800, in ibid., 112–125: The Federalists "write private letters to each other," McHenry lamented, "but do nothing to give a proper direction to the public mind" or work to "prepare the mass of the people for the result they meditate in private." Also see, Fischer, *Revolution in American Conservatism*, ch. 2 and 5, for the way the younger generation of Federalists adopted populist techniques more closely associated with Republicans. On this, see, also, Alan Taylor, "From Fathers to Friends of the People: Political Personae in the Early Republic," in Ben-Atar and Oberg, eds., *Federalists Reconsidered*, 225–245.

[184] TJ to James Madison, June 21, 1798, in *ROL* 2:1061.

[185] On this see, esp., Buell, *Securing the Republic*.

modern ugly sense) the founders could be. After all, Jefferson and Madison used patronage to get rid of Federalist bureaucrats; they clandestinely set up opposition newspapers; they wrote letters to undercut politicians they disagreed with. But the great insight of Richard Hofstadter and others was that for Jefferson and Madison, the partisan politics they engaged (into which they backed out of necessity, said Jefferson) was about the rules of the game – about fundamentals.[186] Will we be a republic? Will we be an American nation? Will we have a government based on informed consent or on obedience and submission? And this, of course, comports perfectly with their own explanations at the time and in retrospect – that their opposition was about principles not politics – but about whether a republican politics was going to be allowed to exist at all, whether democratic deliberation would even take place.

Jefferson and Madison may have failed to pick up on some of the subtleties of Federalist thinking, but their explanations insist that the Republican opposition was essentially a matter of fundamentals – of keeping the state an expression of the will of the nation. We will be misled, then, if we look at the politics of the 1790s as a series of differences over a handful of economic and foreign policy issues only.

## OUTFEDERALIZING THE FEDERALISTS?

Jefferson is famous for saying that "that government is best which governs least." The problem, as we have seen, is that he never said it. To be sure, Jefferson's ambivalence about the uses to which governments were too frequently put explain why many people have assumed the phrase to be a summarization of his view of government, but, by itself, such a statement does not properly capture his views on the relationship of the state to the public. His analysis of this relation is too subtle to sustain such a reading. It is true that Jefferson sometimes expressed admiration for the lack of coercive control in Indian societies. In the absence of force, Indians seemed to experience freedom without crime simply by following their moral sense and the dictates of social mores. If it was a question of "whether no law, as among the savage Americans, or too much law, as among the civilized Europeans, submits man to the greatest evil, one who has seen both conditions of existence would pronounce it to be the last."[187] But Jefferson's juxtaposition here was a choice between evils. It might be possible, Jefferson said elsewhere, to "be ignorant and free" in a primitive state but not "in a state of civilization."[188] Jefferson lived in the latter and was hardly nostalgic for the era of "ignorance."[189] The trick for him – and in some

---

[186] In this sense, Hofstadter's late *Idea of a Party System* is clearer about the fundamental differences, at least among contemporaries, between Federalists and Republicans than is his earlier *American Political Tradition*.

[187] *Notes*, in *TJW*, 220.

[188] TJ to Colonel Charles Yancey, January 16, 1816, in *FE* 11:497.

[189] See "Report of the commissioners for the University of Virginia," August 4, 1818, in *TJW*, 461–462.

sense his lifelong project – was maintaining freedom with minimal coercion in a stage of civilization. Indians broke their societies "into small ones" because "great" ones could not "exist without government." This was an arrangement that white Americans with pretensions to national greatness were not at liberty to emulate. The ward republics of his dreams, one possible solution, would preserve the freedom while remaining intimately connected to governments at higher levels on up to the national state.

It might be more accurate to say that Jefferson wanted to Americanize the government.[190] In substance, this program turned out to be less about reduction of state power as an end than an appropriately American confinement of government at all levels to its proper constitutional sphere. This helps explain the apparent paradox of Jefferson's reduction of government in some key areas (taxation, spending, debt, and judiciary) and his dramatic expansion of it in others, particularly in the area of foreign policy.[191] So making Jefferson out to be an "antistatist" is simply not complex enough a characterization to describe either Jefferson's stance during opposition or his behavior and theory as president. It fails to make the essential distinction he did between opposition to the government and opposition to a particular administration of government. What explains his own uses of government power – which most explain only by citing apparent inconsistencies or hypocrisies – is that the realignment of state with nation freed government up to operate with legitimate energy within its respective sphere of authority.

There was no necessary incongruity between Jefferson's worries about consolidation in the domestic sphere and his augmentation of national power in the service of empire; both remained salient from the 1790s through his presidential administrations. Jefferson believed with most Federalists that the fundamental elements of sovereignty were transferred to the "general government" by the Constitution and that the national state should vigorously advance American imperial interests in the West and aggressively defend its sovereignty in relation to other states.[192] As Bethel Saler demonstrates, Jefferson resisted Federalist efforts to exercise "energetic central administration over both colonial and domestic realms." But insofar as the national state bore exclusive responsibility

---

[190] See Theodore J. Crackel, *Mr. Jefferson's Army: Political and Social Reform of the Military Establishment, 1801–1809* (New York, 1989).

[191] Whether the two were compatible is another question. It was the effort to conform state practice with Jefferson's American ideal that led to both an aggressive foreign policy (to open markets for agricultural production and to open land for settlement in the West), on the one hand, and to a reduction in ability of government to meet the contingencies that arose from such aggression, on the other. Jefferson never imagined that government should not be equipped to do its duty, but he may have failed to envision precisely what his foreign policy would cost. This is the view of many scholars, starting perhaps with Henry Adams. See the statement in Robert W. Tucker and David C. Hendrickson, *Empire of Liberty: The Statecraft of Thomas Jefferson* (New York, 1990). For a different view, see LaFeber, "Jefferson and an American Foreign Policy," in Onuf, ed., *Jeffersonian Legacies*, 370–391.

[192] See Jefferson, "Opinion on Certain Georgia Land Grants," May 3, 1790, in *PTJ* 16:406–408, for a clear (and explicit) demonstration of this belief.

for what Saler calls the "imperial" realm, Jefferson, she suggests, "was by far the greater centralizer."[193]

In other words, Jefferson's keen sense of the tensions between power and liberty, his ambivalence about the uses to which state power could be put, did not translate into the blanket hostility to government that is the hallmark of Federalist caricature.[194] What Jefferson opposed was any power unaccountable to democracy and unresponsive to and unconcerned with public opinion. Rather than mindlessly juxtaposing power and national interest, he saw their alignment as proper when wedded to national will. Within its proper constitutional sphere, Jefferson's state could fully display its energy precisely because, as he put it, "governments are republican only in proportion as they embody the will of the people and execute it."[195] States aligned with the national will had an obligation to execute public purposes.

If "the equal rights of man, and the happiness of every individual" were to remain "the only legitimate objects of government," as Jefferson described the proper ends, the means would continue to be negotiable, dependent on the inevitable change in circumstances the nation might face. After all, "the forms of government, adapted to" one "age and country" would not remain "practicable" or properly imitable in another day or place. "The circumstances of the world," Jefferson noted, "are too much changed for that."[196] As Jefferson put it to Benjamin Austin: "In so complicated a science as political economy, no one axiom can be laid down as wise and expedient for all times and circumstances, and for their contraries." It was characteristic of Jefferson to wonder whether "an opinion founded in the circumstances of" an earlier time could "be fairly applied to those of the present."[197] Jefferson's confidence in the American people to make the right choices "under the unrestrained and unperverted operation of their own understandings," implies a continual rethinking of the means by which government can best achieve national ends.[198] The next generation of Americans would be "as capable as another of taking care of itself, and of ordering its own affairs."[199] Committed to proper ends, the nation could be, with Jefferson, pragmatic with policy.

[193] Saler, "An Empire for Liberty, a State for Empire: The U.S. National State Before and After the Revolution of 1800," in James Horn, Jan Lewis, and Peter Onuf, eds., *The Revolution of 1800: Democracy, Race, and the New Republic* (Charlottesville, 2002), 360–382, quotes at 368 and 373. Also see Lawrence Hatter, "The Jay Charter," which argues that Jefferson's prosecution of the embargo closed loopholes left open by the Jay Treaty and thereby secured U.S. commercial domination of the West.

[194] See Hamilton, "An American, No. 1," from the *Gazette of the United States*, August 4, 1792, in *PAH* 12:157–164; Hamilton to Washington, May 19, 1798, in Freeman, ed., *Writings*, 467; Kerber, *Federalists in Dissent*.

[195] TJ to Samuel Kercheval, July 12, 1816, in *TJW*, 1396. See the perceptive extrapolation of the implications of this commitment in Jeremy Bailey, *Thomas Jefferson and Executive Power* (Cambridge, 2007).

[196] TJ to Adamantios Coray, October 31, 1823, *LC*.

[197] To Benjamin Austin, January 9, 1816, in *FE* 11:502–505.

[198] TJ to Joseph Priestley, June 19, 1802, *FE* 9:380.

[199] TJ to Samuel Kercheval, July 12, 1816, in *TJW*, 1397, 1401. Also see Madison's explanation in Madison to William Eustis, May 22, 1823, in Hunt, ed., *Writings of Madison*, 9: 135–136.

Alexander Hamilton knew that Jefferson would never dismantle the state; indeed, he understood that such was never Jefferson's animating rationale, no matter what he had tried tell the newspaper-reading public. During the election crisis of 1800, Hamilton told Gouverneur Morris: "If there be a man in the world I ought to hate it is Jefferson. With *Burr* I have always been personally well. But the *public good* must be paramount to every private consideration."[200] Hamilton clarified his meaning the following month to James Bayard. In his own experience with him in the cabinet, Hamilton had observed that Jefferson

was generally for a large construction of the executive authority, & not backward to act upon it in cases which coincided with his views.... I have more than once made the reflection that viewing himself as the reversioner, he was solicitous to come into possession of a Good Estate. Nor is it true that Jefferson is zealot enough to do anything in pursuance of his principles which will contravene his popularity, or his interest. He is as likely as any man I know to temporize – to calculate what will be likely to promote his own reputation and advantage; and the probable result of such a temper is the preservation of systems, though originally opposed, which being once established, could not be overturned without danger to the person who did it. To my mind a true estimate of Mr. J.'s character warrants the expectation of a temporizing rather than a violent system. That Jefferson has manifested a culpable predilection for France is certainly true; but I think it a question whether it did not proceed quite as much from her popularity among us, as from sentiment, and in proportion as that popularity is diminished his zeal will cool. Add to this that there is no fair reason to suppose him capable of being corrupted, which is a security that he will not go beyond certain limits. It is not at all improbable that under the change of circumstances Jefferson's Gallicism has considerably abated."[201]

Hamilton had pegged Jefferson as someone not wedded to particular policies so much as to a form of national greatness (actually he described a man whose craving for popularity would temper his inclination to do anything truly devastating to the public good, but it is not difficult to read into this description an appreciation of Jefferson's desire for fame, which Hamilton shared). Hamilton understood that Jefferson would not sacrifice this to some wild scheme, Federalist propaganda notwithstanding. Historian Bernard Bailyn has put the point as succinctly as anyone: "Jefferson would, if need be, jump out of a syllogism to save the major premise."[202]

If Jefferson's major premise was nationhood, many puzzles about his politics and statecraft seem solvable. Jefferson once told John B. Colvin that "saving our country" was a higher obligation than "strict observance of the written laws." Why? Because "to lose our country by a scrupulous adherence to written law, would be to lose the law itself, with life, liberty, property and all those who are enjoying them with us; *thus absurdly sacrificing the end to*

---

[200] Hamilton to Gouverneur Morris, December 26, 1800, in *PAH* 25:275, emphasis added to second phrase.
[201] Hamilton to Bayard, January 16, 1801, in *PAH* 25:319–320.
[202] Bailyn, *To Begin the World Anew: The Genius and Ambiguities of the American Founders* (New York, 2003), 47.

*the means*." Sacrificing the end to the means; this is precisely what Hamilton understood Jefferson would never do – and why he trusted Jefferson to maintain national integrity. For all the later admiration of Hamilton's statesmanship, Jefferson's assessment of the relation of means to ends in the service of national greatness sounds a good deal like Hamilton's own justification of an unscrupulous scheme to manipulate election results in New York in 1800: "It is easy to sacrifice the substantial interests of society by a strict adherence to ordinary rules."[203] Insofar as Jefferson read his election as the nation's recovery of the state, his theory would sanction the kind of energetic state that Hamilton might appreciate even if he could never fully admire the uses to which that state would be put.

[203] Hamilton to Jay, May 7, 1800, in *PAH* 24:465. Hamilton's preference for Jefferson over Burr by no means implies joy about Jefferson's election. The scheme Hamilton pushed on Jay was designed "to prevent an *Atheist* in Religion and a *Fanatic* in politics from getting possession of the helm of the State."

6

# American Union

... absolute acquiescence in the decisions of the majority, the vital principle of republics, from which is no appeal but to force ...

Thomas Jefferson, 1801[1]

The cement of this Union is in the heart-blood of every American.

Thomas Jefferson, 1815[2]

During the winter of 1860–1861, President James Buchanan, facing what would prove to be the great crisis of the Union, argued, on the one hand, that secession was illegal and unconstitutional and, on the other, that the federal government had no constitutional right to coerce the seceded states back into the Union. Even if coercion *was* constitutional, Buchanan argued, it would violate the spirit of the Union for the remaining states to make war on the others. The Union must remain alive in the affections of the people, and this could not be forced by arms.[3] Buchanan's argument paid silent homage to Jefferson's original notion of a voluntary union based on consent, affection, and interest rather than force.[4] So it seems natural to assume that Buchanan's response to

[1] "First Inaugural Address," March 4, 1801, in *TJW*, 493.

[2] TJ to Lafayette, February 14, 1815, in *TJW*, 1364.

[3] Buchanan, "Message of the President of the United States," December 3, 1860, *Congressional Globe*, 36th Congress, 2nd Session, Appendix, 1–4.

[4] On this, see, above all, Peter S. Onuf, *Jefferson's Empire: The Language of American Nationhood* (Charlottesville, 2000), especially 38, 45, and 53–146. See also, Onuf, "The Expanding Union," in David Thomas Konig, ed., *Devising Liberty: Preserving and Creating Freedom in the New American Republic* (Stanford, 1995), 50–80; and the succinct statement in James E. Lewis, Jr., *The American Union and the Problem of Neighborhood: The United States and the Collapse of the Spanish Empire, 1783–1829* (Chapel Hill, 1998), 20. Also see TJ to James Madison, December 16, 1786, and December 28, 1794, in *ROL* 1:458, 2:867; and TJ to Priestly, January 29, 1804, in *L&B* 10:447. This concept of union as rooted in affection rather than coercion, although associated with Jefferson, was hardly unique to him. See, generally, Paul C. Nagel, *One Nation Indivisible: The Union in American Thought, 1776–1861* (New York, 1964), esp. 69–103; and Rogan Kersh, *Dreams of a More Perfect Union* (Ithaca and London, 2001).

the crisis would approximate Jefferson's own, had he lived to see it. In fact, many historians go farther and suggest, with Joseph Ellis, that had he lived, "Jefferson would have gone with the Confederacy."[5]

Of course, there is no DNA test to reconcile the counterfactual problem of what Jefferson "would have" done. But Jefferson's conception of Union generally, suggests a different conclusion than the standard view: Jefferson, in fact, believed that the executive had the duty to enforce federal law throughout the Union and that the Union had a natural right to coerce seceding states and force them back into the fold.

To be sure, Jefferson occasionally spoke as if the Union was dispensable. After the Louisiana Purchase, for example, he envisioned "our sons" spreading across the continent and saw "happiness" in the Union of the "Atlantic & Missipi States." But he could understand, he suggested, if later generations saw "their interest in separation." In either case, all of the inhabitants of the continent would be "our ... descendants"; it would merely be a matter of "the elder and the younger son differing." So, "God bless them both, & keep them in union, if it be for their good, but separate them, if it be better."[6] In any case, "our confederacy" would be "the nest from which all America, North & South

[5] Ellis talk at the Massachusetts Historical Society, December 16, 2004. Available: http://www. cspanarchives.org/library/index.php?main_page=product_video_info&products_id=184902–1&highlight=184902–1. Also see Ellis, *Founding Brothers: The Revolutionary Generation* (New York, 2000), 199–200; and Cynthia A. Kierner, "Sex, Science, and Sensibility at Jefferson's Monticello," *Reviews in American History* 33 (Sept. 2005), 338: "Everything we know about Jefferson's politics suggests that in 1861 he would have cast his lot with slavery and secession under the guise of states' rights." Of course, some of Jefferson's grandsons did follow this logic out of the Union. Thomas Jefferson Randolph was a Confederate supporter, and George Wythe Randolph served briefly as the Confederate secretary of war after voting for secession at both Virginia Secession Conventions. Obviously they believed themselves to be honoring Jefferson's legacy. My point here is not so much to dispute that implied claim as to suggest that Lincoln's coercion of the seceded states has Jeffersonian roots also. Other Jefferson descendants apparently took this latter line, including his great-grandson Major Sydney Coolidge (son of Ellen Wayles Randolph Coolidge), who was killed at Chickamauga fighting for the Union, as well as four of Jefferson's grandsons through Sally Hemings who fought for the Union, two as white men and two as black. Beverly Jefferson, son of Eston Hemings, was a lieutenant colonel in the Union army, and his brother, John Wayles Jefferson was wounded at Vicksburg and Corinth. See Henry Beebee Carrington, "Winfield Scott's Visit to Columbus," *Ohio History* 19 (July 1910), 278–291, at 290; and Fawn Brodie, "Thomas Jefferson's Unknown Grandchildren: A Study in Historical Silences," *American Heritage* 27 (October 1976), 28–33 and 94–99. Another son of Ellen Wayles Coolidge, Thomas Jefferson Coolidge, spent his life as a Boston financier and supported the Union in the war during which he made a fortune speculating on commodities. See *The Autobiography of T. Jefferson Coolidge, 1831–1920* (Boston and New York, 1923). It is entirely possible, of course, that Jefferson, had he lived (itself quite a counterfactual leap), would have felt and embraced what Paul Quigley calls "the key element in the acceptance of secession and national independence for the South": "a sense of shared victimhood at the hands of a hostile North" and the felt intrusion of this "northern threat into the realm of the domestic and the personal." See Paul D.H. Quigley, "Patchwork Nation: Sources of Confederate Nationalism, 1848–1865" (Ph.D. dissertation, University of North Carolina at Chapel Hill, 2006), 17, 154. In any case, Jefferson's legacy embraces multiple (and sometimes mutually antagonistic) heirs.

[6] TJ to John C. Breckinridge, August 12, 1803, in *TJW*, 1138.

is to be peopled."[7] But none of the territory Jefferson contemplated here was yet part of the Union, so there is no live option of "disunion" in these letters. When territories in the national domain did become states, however, they would "forever remain a part of the United States of America," according to Jefferson's 1784 proposal.[8] Moreover, Jefferson more typically demonstrated (and explicitly claimed) the goal of tying the interests of American settlers in the west with those of the east. As he suggested to one friend who had removed to Kentucky in the late 1780s, he hoped "to see that country in the hands of people well disposed, who know the value of the connection between that & the Maritime states, and who wish to cultivate it," because, as he put it, "I consider their happiness as bound up together, and that every measure should be taken which may draw the bands of union tighter."[9]

But even more significant, Jefferson could entertain the idea of political separation only when the continent was peopled with Americans who shared his values.[10] He could never be so sanguine about people without those values holding any political authority in North America. "We have seldom seen neighborhood produce affection among nations," Jefferson told John C. Breckenridge in 1803. "The reverse is almost the universal truth."[11] Prospects for peace rested on the settlement of one nation only on the continent, precisely why Jefferson feared the possible separation of Americans in the West during the era prior to the acquisition of Louisiana when European powers retained an interest there (and why he could remain troubled by Burr's later effort to, as he understood it, separate the Union).[12] On the mission to purchase New Orleans (and eventually Louisiana), Jefferson told James Monroe, "depends the future destinies of this republic." If Monroe failed and the French took possession of New Orleans, Jefferson wrote, "we shall get entangled in European politics" and become "much less happy and prosperous."[13] The purchase ensured that the American continent would not replicate European strife precisely because the states that did emerge in the West would be peopled by Americans, culturally homogeneous and sharing the same republican values. In other words, nation transcended union, and Jefferson assumed on some level that ties between Americans were too organic to be broken by lone adventurers, even with the sanction of foreign governments.[14]

---

[7] TJ to Archibald Stuart, January 25, 1786, in *TJW*, 844.

[8] "Report on Government for Western Territory," in *TJW*, 377.

[9] TJ to John Brown, May 26, 1788, in *FE* 5:398. Jefferson went on to describe the opening of the Mississippi to the navigation of American settlers as a "duty of the maritime states" that they should "push … to every extremity to which they would their own right of navigating the Chesapeake, the Delaware, the Hudson or any other water."

[10] John Murrin, "The Jeffersonian Triumph and American Exceptionalism," *JER* 20 (Spring 2000), 23; Onuf, *Jefferson's Empire*, 119.

[11] TJ to John C. Breckenridge, August 12, 1803, in *L&B* 10:409.

[12] TJ to James Madison, January 30 and February 5, 1787, in *ROL* 1:461–462; Special Message to Congress on the Burr Conspiracy, January 22, 1807, in *TJW*, 532–538.

[13] TJ to Monroe, January 13, 1803, in *TJW*, 1112. Also see TJ to Robert Livingston, April 18, 1802, ibid., 1105.

[14] Special Message on the Burr Conspiracy, in *TJW*, 534.

To be sure, Jefferson's Kentucky Resolutions have been understood as giving sanction to later secession movements, and it is not always a simple matter to resolve Jefferson's views on coercion with his stance in the late 1790s when he asserted the duty of states to challenge unconstitutional policies enacted by the general government. Nevertheless, neither Jefferson's Kentucky Resolutions nor Madison's Virginia Resolutions advocated – or even broached – secession, and there were substantial qualitative differences between them and the later claims made by some New England Federalists and South Carolina nullifiers, despite the claims to Jefferson's legacy made by the latter group, especially.[15]

[15] Melvin Yazawa argues that the resolutions were attempts to diffuse secessionist sentiment by forcing Americans to reflect on the central importance/value of the Union to their happiness: "Dionysian Rhetoric and Apollonian Solutions: The Politics of Union and Disunion in the Age of Federalism," in Eliga Gould and Peter S. Onuf, eds., *Empire and Nation: The American Revolution in the Atlantic World* (Baltimore, 2005), 178–196, especially 191–196. Richard E. Ellis shows that while Jefferson and Madison "added new elements to the states' rights argument" by providing a kind of intellectual framework and legal roadmap for future attempts at nullification, their resolutions were "grounded in … majoritarian sentiment" and that later efforts that adopted the framework of protest they had constructed were for purposes "essentially antithetical to the one for which it had been used up to that time." It was the Federalists in dissent during the Republican ascendancy who first "laid bare … the disunionist tendencies that might, but also did not have to, be extrapolated from the states' rights argument." They also, along with the South Carolina nullifiers, essentially decoupled the states' rights discourse from its democratic (majoritarian) origins. Opposition to South Carolina nullification, Ellis shows, came from "nationalists" like Daniel Webster who rejected the compact theory, but, more importantly, from traditional states' rights unionists who embraced the compact theory but believed that the South Carolina doctrine "subverted the democratic assumptions that underlay the states' rights thought that had been associated with the Jeffersonian tradition" and rejected South Carolina's claim that the states were completely sovereign. Traditional states' rights thought accepted Madison's formulation in *Federalist* 39 that the American political system was "neither wholly national, nor wholly federal" but contained essential elements of each. Both Calhoun and Webster worked hard to remain faithful to Blackstone's concept of undivided sovereignty. Ellis's traditional states' righters, among whom Madison and Jefferson (and later, Andrew Jackson) were most prominent, embraced a truer federalism. See Ellis, *The Union at Risk: Jacksonian Democracy, States' Rights and the Nullification Crisis* (New York, 1986), especially 1–12; and Ellis, "The Path Not Taken: Virginia and the Supreme Court, 1789–1821," in A.E. Dick Howard and Melvin I. Urofsky, eds., *Virginia and the Constitution* (Charlottesville, 1992), 24–52, esp. 49–52. On the limited appeal of what Ellis calls the "nationalist" argument associated with Daniel Webster, see Kenneth Stampp, "The Concept of a Perpetual Union," *JAH* 65 (June 1978), 5–33. For the way Jefferson's resolutions were used in the years after his death, see Merrill D. Peterson, *The Jefferson Image in the American Mind*, second edition (Charlottesville, 1998), 36–66. The compact theory of the Union governed by the law of nations could lead to different kinds of conclusions about the nature of that union. On these connections, see Robert Shalhope, "Thomas Jefferson's Republicanism and Antebellum Southern Thought," *JSH* 42 (November 1976), 537–545; Peterson, *Jefferson Image*, 216; and Andrew C. Lenner, "John Taylor and the Origins of American Federalism," *JER* 17 (Autumn 1997), 399–423, esp. 420–422. On the expressed confusion of the South Carolina nullifiers over Madison's rejection of the connections they drew between the Principles of '98 and their own doctrine, see Keven R. Gutzman, "A Troublesome Legacy: James Madison and 'The Principles of '98'," *JER* 15 (Winter 1995), 569–589. For two examples of the too easy way scholars connect Jefferson's states' rights thought with an embrace of secession, see Cass R. Sunstein, "Constitutionalism and

Much of the way we have thought about and understood the 1790s has been distorted by our viewing that period through the lens of later events, particularly the tariff showdown of the 1830s and, especially, the secession crisis of 1860–1861.[16] It is thus crucial to read the resolutions in light of what we already know about Jefferson's conception of American nationhood and in the context of Democratic-Republican oppositional politics described in the previous chapter.

One reason Henry Adams had trouble appreciating what he considered the "energetic turn" of Jefferson's presidential administration was that his own interpretation of it rested on his assumption that the Virginia and Kentucky Resolutions – what he called "the Virginia theory" – constituted the organizing principle of Jefferson's politics from which all his behavior should be judged. And since Adams could imagine "no relation" "between the embargo and the old Virginia theory of the Constitution," he assumed that Jefferson's presidency was a study in contradiction and irony.[17] But if the previous chapter is correct, that the Jeffersonian movement, at least from Jefferson's own perspective, was primarily designed to break the hold of the autonomous state that the Federalists were creating and to realign the state with the nation, then the Kentucky Resolutions might be better read within that context.[18] After all, Adams also recognized that Jefferson's "mind shared little in common with the provincialism on which the Virginia and Kentucky Resolutions were founded," and[19] as we have seen, Jefferson imagined the American system as a unique constitutional distribution of authority between a variety of nested governments, from national to state to the ultra-local, so that his purported commitment to "states' rights" was in fact one aspect of a commitment to something larger. Insofar as that larger system was invested in his mind with the stuff of nationality, Jefferson's commitment to the rights of states within their proper sphere was part and parcel of his nationalism.

## THE KENTUCKY RESOLUTIONS AND AMERICAN FEDERALISM

The Alien and Sedition Acts, passed by the Federalist-dominated Congress during the war scare with France in the summer of 1798, together increased the period of residence required of immigrants for naturalization from five

---

Secession," *University of Chicago Law Review* 58 (Spring 1991), 657; and Forrest McDonald, *States' Rights and the Union: Imperium in Imperio, 1776–1876* (Lawrence, 2000), 40.

[16] On this broad point, and for an important corrective view, see Kevin M. Gannon, "Calculating the Value of the Union: States' Rights, Nullification, and Secession in the North, 1800–1848" (PhD dissertation, University of South Carolina, 2002); and David C. Hendrickson, *Peace Pact: The Lost World of the American Founding* (Lawrence, 2003), 154–155.

[17] Adams, *History of the United States During the Administrations of Thomas Jefferson* (New York, 1986), 1110.

[18] See Alfred H. Kelly, Winfred A. Harbison, and Herman Belz, *The American Constitution: Its Origins and Development*, 2 volumes, seventh edition (New York 1991), 1:134.

[19] Ibid., 100.

to fourteen years, the highest in American history; authorized the president to deport aliens in peacetime subject to his discretion; and, most odious to Republicans, threatened imprisonment for any statements spoken or printed against the government of the United States, the Congress, or the president.[20] Jefferson privately raged against the spirit and letter of these acts, seeing in them a design to rid the Federalists of domestic political enemies, including himself. Jefferson argued that the Alien Bill was "worthy of the eighth or ninth century," and that the acts together were "palpably in the teeth of the constitution."[21] The rationale of the bills seemed almost consciously designed to confirm precisely what Jefferson had long believed about the Federalists. Their identifying criticism with disloyalty assumed an equation of the administrative state with sovereignty and administration with legitimate rule.

Jefferson understood the primary purpose of the bills to be "the suppression of the whig presses," the expulsion of Republican leaders like the Swiss-born Albert Gallatin, and the elimination of voters among newly naturalized immigrants who tended to support Republican candidates and measures.[22] The original draft of the sedition bill, penned by Federalist Senator from Maryland, James Lloyd, described France as an enemy of the United States and prescribed the death penalty for the treason of giving the French "aid and comfort."[23] Despite what he viewed as the gutting of his original bill by "Jacobins," Lloyd expressed his hope that an eventual declaration of war with France would "enable us to lay our hands on traitors."[24] Secretary of State Timothy Pickering,

---

[20] The four laws that became known as the Alien and Sedition Acts are summarized nicely by DeConde in *The Quasi War: The Politics and Diplomacy of the Undeclared war with France, 1797–1801* (New York, 1966), 94–100. Dumas Malone's discussion of the acts in *Jefferson and the Ordeal of Liberty* (Boston, 1962), 384–394 is concise and to the point, from a perspective favorable to Republican views. The acts themselves are conveniently reprinted in James Morton Smith, *Freedom's Fetters: The Alien and Sedition Laws and American Civil Liberties* (Ithaca 1966).

[21] Peterson, *Thomas Jefferson and the New Nation*, 604; Jefferson to Madison, June 7, 1798, in *ROL* 2:1056–1057. Madison added that "the Alien bill proposed in the Senate is a monster that must forever disgrace its parents," Madison to TJ, May 20, 1798, in ibid., 1051.

[22] TJ to Madison, April 26, 1798, in ibid., 1041. Jefferson also believed the Alien Enemies Act looked to suppress resident citizens of European countries, often philosophers and scientists of liberal Enlightenment views, who remained friendly with Jefferson and sympathetic to opponents of the Federalist regime. In this regard, Jefferson worried particularly about the fate of French philosopher Volney, who had spent time with him at Monticello, and English scientist and Unitarian theologian Joseph Priestly. See Malone, *Jefferson and the Ordeal of Liberty*, 386. Volney, who fled the country before the passing of the bill, Jefferson feared, "has in truth been the principal object aimed at by the law," TJ to Madison, May 3, 1798, in *ROL* 2:1045. Also see Stephen G. Kurtz, *The Presidency of John Adams: The Collapse of Federalism, 1795–1800* (Philadelphia, 1957), 307–373; especially 313–314, 356.

[23] Malone, *Jefferson and the Ordeal of Liberty*, 387. Even many Federalists, including Hamilton, it must be noted, considered this altogether too harsh, although Hamilton himself later hoped to strengthen the bill as passed. See ibid., 390, and Kurtz, *Presidency of John Adams*, 355–356.

[24] Lloyd to Washington, July 4, 1798, in Dorothy Twohig, ed., *The Papers of George Washington, Retirement Series*, 4 volumes (Charlottesville and London, 2000), 2:375–376.

along with other cabinet ministers, attempted to stonewall eventual peace negotiations with France, and Hamilton himself left evidence that he desired to use the military force raised to fight the French to provoke and crush dissent in Republican-dominated Virginia.[25]

Whether the Federalists who passed the acts and fomented a war scare with France did so primarily to suppress domestic opposition is unclear. They can hardly be held responsible for Talleyrand's demand for bribes before negotiating with American ministers or for the martial enthusiasm among the public that resulted. But that the Federalists used the crisis to what they saw as their political advantage is probably indisputable, although such strategy certainly backfired in the end. In any case, Jefferson and Madison, not privy to much of this private maneuvering, assumed the Federalists were artificially drumming up war largely as a way to crush the Republicans.

Jefferson and Madison responded to the Alien and Sedition Acts with their own anonymous resolutions affirming what they and others believed to be the "*real laws* of our country"[26]: in defense, in other words, of the republicanism secured by the Revolution and the federalism Virginians thought they had ratified in 1788.[27]

Because Jefferson and Madison wrote from behind a veil of secrecy, historians will never know the precise nature of their consultation regarding the two sets of resolutions. Jefferson and Madison exchanged no letters between June 21 and October 26, likely fearing potential exposure and probable prosecution under the Sedition Act. This was not unfounded paranoia. During the interval between Jefferson's draft of the Kentucky Resolutions and Madison's writing of the Virginia Resolutions, for example, Matthew Lyon, congressman from Vermont, was convicted of sedition and jailed for accusing John Adams, in a private letter, of "a grasp for power, thirst for adulation and selfish avarice."[28] Jefferson and Madison seem to have met only two times during that period, once in July and again in October, so it is likely that Jefferson wrote his set of resolutions without direct consultation with Madison, who apparently did not see them until their second meeting in late October.[29] Intending them for Virginia or North Carolina,[30] Jefferson wrote his set of resolutions and entrusted them to his neighbor and member of the Virginia Senate, Wilson Cary Nicholas, who then passed them along to John Breckenridge, a former

---

[25] Hamilton to Theodore Sedgwick, February 2, 1799, *PAH* 21:453.

[26] George Nicholas quoted in James Roger Sharp, *American Politics in the Early Republic: The New Nation in Crisis* (New Haven, 1993), 201. Also see K.R. Constantine Gutzman, "The Virginia and Kentucky Resolutions Reconsidered: 'An Appeal to the *Real Laws* of Our Country,'" *JSH* 66 (August 2000), 473–496.

[27] Gutzman, ibid., 485; and, generally, Richard R. Beeman, *The Old Dominion and the New Nation, 1788–1801* (Lexington, 1982).

[28] Irving Brandt, *The Life of James Madison*, 6 volumes (Indianapolis, 1941–1961), vol. 3, *James Madison: Father of the Constitution*, 458. See the extended discussion of prosecutions under the Sedition Act in Smith, *Freedom's Fetters*.

[29] Brandt, *Life of Madison* 3:459; *ROL* 2:1069.

[30] See TJ to Wilson Cary Nicholas, October 5, 1798, *PTJ* 30:557, but also note *PTJ* 30:531–532.

neighbor of Jefferson's and member of the Kentucky legislature, who happened to be visiting Albemarle County.[31] Nicholas suggested that Breckenridge could quite likely carry them through the legislature of his state. Jefferson approved the switch and asked Nicholas to show the resolutions to Madison, from whom Jefferson said he kept "no secrets."[32] Nicholas unfortunately took sick, preventing the desired consultation with Madison before Breckenridge carried the resolves to Kentucky without explicit approval from Madison, who would wait until late October before he penned his own set of resolutions for the Virginia legislature.

In what has likely remained the most influential academic assessment ever written on the Virginia and Kentucky Resolutions, Adrienne Koch and Harry Ammon went to great lengths to demonstrate that Jefferson and Madison intended to defend civil liberties as Americans living in the wake of World War II might understand them.[33] The editors of the *William and Mary Quarterly* in fact took the very unusual (and, from the vantage point of hindsight, troublingly presentist) step of prefacing the essay with an editorial note indicating the journal's "special pleasure" in printing the article in the wake of the opposition of Southern Democrats to President Truman's stance on civil rights and their efforts to use Jefferson and Madison in their defense of the "Rights Reserved to the States."

In response, some were quick to point out that all Jefferson and Madison argued about civil liberties was that the Constitution reserved the prosecution of seditious libel to the states, with which the two founders seemed to have no quarrel. But historians have been too quick to jump to the opposite extreme, that because Jefferson and Madison were not articulating a twentieth-century, post-fourteenth-amendment defense of civil liberties, the resolutions must have been exclusively about federalism, the relation between state and national governments. But what was so troubling to Jefferson about the Alien and Sedition bills went deeper, cutting to the very heart of everything he believed unique about America. The acts essentially moved to shut down the public sphere of deliberation; they would, he believed, snuff out the American spirit by telling citizens to quietly submit to administrative rule; and they thereby undercut the intimate connection and fluid relationship between the natural aristocracy and the public of Jefferson's ideal. Yes, the resolutions were about federalism, but that is because, in their dismissal of the constitutional spheres, the Alien and Sedition Acts worked to sever the link between state and nation. The resolutions were not an abstract defense of civil liberties in the way Koch and Ammon assumed, but they were not an abstract assertion of "states' rights," either. They were a defense of American republicanism itself, and in that sense they were at heart consonant with Jefferson's democratic nationalism.

---

[31] *ROL* 2:1068.

[32] TJ to Wilson Cary Nicholas, October 5, 1798, in *PTJ* 30:557.

[33] Adrienne Koch and Harry Ammon, "The Virginia and Kentucky Resolutions: An Episode in Jefferson's and Madison's Defense of Civil Liberties," *WMQ* 5 (April 1948), 145–176.

Both sets of resolutions, Jefferson's for Kentucky and Madison's for Virginia, articulated what has come to be called the "compact theory" of the Constitution. "The Several States composing the US of America," Jefferson argued, "are not united on the principle of unlimited submission to their general government." Instead, they had formed such government "by a compact under the style and title of a Constitution for the US." The compact granted "certain definite powers" to the general government and reserved "each state to itself, the residuary mass of rights to their own self-government." Each state, he wrote, "acceded" to the compact "as a state, and is an integral party, it's co-states forming, as to itself, the other party."[34] Madison agreed that "the powers of the federal government" came "from the compact to which the states are parties" and were "limited by the plain sense and intention of the instrument constituting that compact."[35] Because the federal government was created by this compact among the states, its authority was limited by the explicit grants of power stipulated in the Constitution. All other power, in accord with the tenth amendment, was retained by the states or the people. What Jefferson and Madison understood as the main problem with the Alien and Sedition Acts, and other actions of the Federalists, was that they authorized the general or national government to exercise powers not granted to it in the compact and, in the case of the Sedition Act, powers strictly forbidden. There certainly was no suggestion in either that the states retained sovereignty outside of the compact. The only claim was that Federalists were using the national state to encroach on powers the Constitution left to the states. The onus of the Kentucky and Virginia Resolutions, then, was to delineate the compact theory and assert the essential unconstitutionality of the Alien and Sedition Acts. The duty of the states, they declared, was to "arrest … the progress of the evil" and to preserve "within their respective limits, the authorities, rights, and liberties appertaining to them."[36]

Because the compact theory later became associated with secession, these resolutions have been described as the seminal expression of the classic states' rights "doctrine," but there was a remarkable range of positions within the "states rights" camp in the early Republic, and whatever it boiled down to then has been consistently misunderstood as shorthand for hostility to central state power, a shorthand that applies more properly to "defenders" of "states' rights" in the twentieth century than it does to Jefferson and Madison, certainly.[37] Jefferson and Madison never found it necessary to formulate an ideology they

---

[34] Jefferson's Draft of the Kentucky Resolutions of 1798, *ROL* 2:1080.

[35] Madison, "Virginia Resolutions," *PJM* 17:189. See also, especially, Madison's "Report of 1800," ibid., 308–312. For a cogent discussion of the resolutions in the context of compact theory, see David Mayer, *The Constitutional Thought of Thomas Jefferson* (Charlottesville, 1994), 199–208.

[36] Madison, "Virginia Resolutions," *PJM* 17:189.

[37] Gary Gerstle, "The Resilient Power of the States Across the Long Nineteenth Century: An Inquiry into a Pattern of American Governance," in Lawrence Jacobs and Desmond King, eds., *The Unsustainable American State* (Oxford, 2009), 61–87.

called "states' rights," which renders anachronistic efforts to label their views in this way. They clearly defended state prerogatives as one facet of a larger national system of government that included central state authority in certain clearly defined spheres as well. Nothing about their theory is organically hostile to national power as such.

In his 1774 *Summary View*, Jefferson had argued that Parliament was simply another legislature in a system of polities within the British imperial system, which is why he saw Parliament's late behavior a travesty of justice: How can one legislature take it upon itself to suspend the rightful powers of another, Jefferson asked. But this is simply not the way Jefferson thought about the national government created by the Constitution. In the Kentucky Resolutions, the national legislature is a "creature of the compact," but Jefferson never pretended that it was somehow the equivalent to the state legislatures or that the state legislatures were precisely analogous to it in the way he argued about the colonial legislatures and Parliament. The national Congress was the legislature for the common whole – precisely the argument Jefferson rejected about Parliament. And this is why we don't see him making a similar argument in the Kentucky Resolutions: that the national state "has no right to exercise authority over us." His argument instead is that the national government has no constitutional right to do so in certain areas that are reserved to the state legislatures – a very different argument than he ever made for colonial relations in the British empire.

The literature on the relations between the people, the Union, and national government is vast and complex, and scholars replicate the founding generation's own contested (and even confused) sense of whether the Union preceded the states as corporate entities or whether the people of the nation or the people of the states ratified the Constitution, for example.[38] Jack Greene is right, it seems to me, to note that "the process by which the American union was formed is ... too complicated to support either a national or a compact theory of its origins" and that "what was clear throughout was that from the first Continental Congress on, the national union had involved a division of authority in which Congress and the states both exercised powers normally associated with sovereign governments."[39] The Declaration of Independence, as we have seen, announced the existence of "one people," but it also asserted the sovereignty of ... what? That people in a national capacity or thirteen sovereign states? That is a question not easily answered. Or, rather, that is a question that was not answered until 1865 at Appomattox Courthouse – an experience which has shaped our subsequent reading of the early republic. The Continental Congress had long spoken for the people of America, and the states had long deferred to

---

[38] See Stampp, "The Concept of a Perpetual Union." For a good brief introduction to the controversy among scholars, see Greene, *Peripheries and Center: Constitutional Development in the Extended Polities of the British Empire and the United States, 1607–1788* (Athens, GA, 1986), 178–180.

[39] Greene, *Peripheries and Center*, 180.

it as a kind of national body that, after all, was the only body imbued with what
Vattel defined as sovereignty: the capacity to enter into relations with other
states, a capacity that the thirteen states were explicitly denied by the Articles of
Confederation.[40] As Rufus King pointed out at the Constitutional Convention,
the states simply "did not possess the peculiar features of sovereignty. They
could not make war, nor peace, nor alliances, nor treaties." In fact, "considering them as political Beings, they were dumb, for they could not speak to
any foreign Sovereign whatever," and "they were deaf, for they could not hear
any propositions from such Sovereign."[41] When it came time to try to describe
what the Union actually was, frankly, the "founders" were as conflicted as the
historians. At the Constitutional Convention, Luther Martin was sure that independence from Britain "placed the 13 States in a state of nature towards each
other" and that "they would have remained in that state till this time, but for
the confederation." But James Wilson "could not admit the doctrine that when
the Colonies became independent of G. Britain, they became independent also
of each other." Instead, Wilson argued, the Declaration of Independence had
declared "the *United Colonies* … to be free & Independent States" thus "infer-
ring that they were independent, not *Individually* but *Unitedly*." Rufus King
objected with a middle position. The "import of the terms 'States' 'Sovereignty'
'national' 'federal,'" he said, "had been often used & applied in the discussion
inaccurately & delusively." The simple fact was, he suggested, that "if the States
… retained some portion of their sovereignty, they had certainly divested themselves of essential portions of it. If they formed a confederacy in some respects –
they formed a Nation in others."[42]

If the Constitution itself undid whatever union existed under the Confederation Congress, as Kenneth Stampp argued, its own articulation of the precise
nature of the relationship between the national and state governments was not
always entirely clear, either.[43] Madison himself acknowledged the "arduous"

[40] This reading is most clearly articulated by Jack N. Rakove, *The Beginnings of National Politics:
An Interpretative History of the Continental Congress* (New York, 1979).

[41] King, June 19, 1787, in Farrand, *Records of the Federal Convention* 1:323. Also see Elbridge
Gerry, June 29, 1787, in ibid., 467: "We never were independent States, were not such now, &
never could be even on the principles of the Confederation."

[42] All discussion from Tuesday, June 19, 1787, in Farrand, *The Records of the Federal Convention*
1: 323–324. Also see ibid., 461. Hamilton went so far as to suggest "an abolition of the States"
precisely because the problem that had plagued the British Empire was now troubling the
Union: "No boundary," Hamilton argued, "could be drawn between the national & state legislatures; that the former must therefore have indefinite authority. If it were limited at all, the
rivalship of the States would gradually subvert it" (June 19, ibid., 323). Or, as he put it a
day earlier, quite simply, "Two Sovereignties can not co-exist within the same limits" (June 18,
ibid., 287). James Read later agreed that the states "must be done away" (June 29, ibid., 463).
Compare Edmund Randolph, who, in proposing the Virginia Plan on May 29, according to
notes by Yates, described it as "a strong consolidated union, in which the idea of states should be
nearly annihilated" (ibid., 24). Jefferson, for his part, considered a prime defect in the Articles of
Confederation that it left "each state to become sovereign & independent in all things," implying that the Constitution remedied this situation. See "Anas," in *FE* 1:167.

[43] Stampp, "Concept of a Perpetual Union," esp. 7–10.

nature of the "task of marking the proper line of partition, between the authority of the general, and that of the state governments," comparing the divisions to
the "delicate shades, and minute gradiations" that separate "sense, perception,
judgment, desire, volition, memory, imagination," – boundaries, he said, that
"have eluded the most subtle investigations." "When the Almighty himself con-
descends to address mankind in their own language," Madison continued, "his
meaning, luminous as it must be, is rendered dim and doubtful, by the cloudy
medium through which it is communicated." How much more difficulty must
the collection of mere demigods at the Constitutional Convention have had in
"delineating the boundary between the federal and statue jurisdictions"?[44]

All Madison could say was that the system of government created by the
Constitution was "in strictness neither a national nor a federal constitution; but
a composition of both."[45] The Constitution of the United States, he wrote, was
neither a "single Government" nor "a mere league of Governments." It "divides
the sovereignty; the portions surrendered by the State composing the Federal
sovereignty over specified subjects; the portions retained forming the sovereignty of each over the residuary subjects within its sphere." "If sovereignty
cannot be thus divided," Madison insisted to the end of his life, "the political
system of the United States is a chimera."[46] Jefferson and Madison even found
this description something of a point of pride in a uniquely American form of
government. The federal system created by the Constitution, Madison said,
was "emphatically *sui generis*, for designating which there consequently was
no appropriate term or denomination pre-existing."[47]

If the Constitution "did not make a decisive disposition of the locus of sovereignty in the new nation," as some prominent constitutional historians argue,
then we will likely never get an answer if the question we ask is which theory of
the Constitution and Union is truer to the original intention of the founders.[48]
All we can do is examine what some theorists argued at the time and describe
how the federal system worked in practice.[49] Furthermore, our current understandings of federalism and especially of the phrase "states rights," tainted as it
is by association with secession, defense of slavery, and "massive resistance" to

[44] *Federalist* 37, in Pole, ed., *The Federalist*, 194–196.
[45] *Federalist* 39, in Pole, ed., *The Federalist*, 206–211, quotes at 211. Also see Madison to Robert
     S. Garnett, February 11, 1824, in *Letters and Other Writings of James Madison*, four vols. (New
     York, 1884, originally published Philadelphia, 1865), 3:367.
[46] Madison to Nicholas P. Trist, February 15, 1830, in ibid., 4:61.
[47] Madison to Garnett, February 11, 1824, in ibid., 3:367. Also see Jefferson's to Peregrine
     Fitzhugh, February 23, 1798, in *FE* 8:375–378.
[48] Kelly and Harbison, *The American Constitution: Its Origins and Development* (New York,
     1963), 143, quoted in Stampp, "Concept of a Perpetual Union," 12.
[49] For a recent assessment that endorses Madison's as a more accurate empirical description of the
     American system than the ideal concept of unitary sovereignty, see Jack N. Rakove, "Making
     a Hash of Sovereignty, Part I," *Green Bag* 2 (Autumn 1998), 35–44, and "Making a Hash of
     Sovereignty, Part II," *Green Bag* 3 (Autumn 1999), 51–59. Also see Jefferson's explicit endorse-
     ment of the Constitution's division of sovereignty in his letter to George Wythe, September 16,
     1787, in *PTJ* 12:128.

black equality, tends to cloud rather than illuminate the meaning of the texts themselves.[50] The compact theory set forth by Jefferson and Madison was, in some form or other, commonly understood to explain a great deal about the nature of the Union, even as the precise meaning of it was nevertheless in continual contestation until at least the end of the Civil War. Only one of the many state legislatures that explicitly condemned the Virginia and Kentucky Resolutions, for example, took issue with the basic notion of the compact.[51]

Properly understood, of course, the resolutions must also be viewed in the context of Republican opposition to Federalist policies of the 1790s and Jefferson's sense that, as we have seen, the national state was out of sync with the national will. The resolutions are only two texts out of many with which to examine widespread opposition to Federalist policies; their uniqueness may account for the excessive attention paid to them by later interpreters of this period, but it may also mislead these interpreters. Many later students of the resolutions have been quick to emphasize their theoretical underpinnings and constitutional implications. This interpretative tendency may reverse the order of importance for Jefferson and Madison at the time, who were perhaps less focused on articulating a general theory of union than they were on rectifying

[50] See, in particular, Joseph J. Ellis, *Founding Brothers*, 199–201. Ellis argues that "Jefferson's line of thought led logically to the compact theory of the Constitution eventually embraced by the Confederacy in 1861," while "Madison's arguments led toward the modern doctrine of judicial review and constitutional guarantees for free speech and freedom of the press." In short, Jefferson and Madison maintained "incompatible notions of where sovereignty resided in the American republic." But Jefferson's "thought" in the resolutions did not lead to the compact theory; it *was* the compact theory. Madison's resolutions, which also advance the same compact theory, say nothing about judicial review but instead insist on state authority to interpret the Constitution (which several states, especially in New England, specifically condemned the Virginia Resolutions for advocating). Madison later, in his fight against South Carolina nullification in the late 1820s and early 1830s, conceded judicial review as the proper arbiter in disputes between states and federal government but reserved the ultimate right of the people of the states "in their highest sovereign capacity" to interpret the Constitution in cases in which the Supreme Court or the courts generally were corrupted – a difficult and subjective situation to perceive, to say the least. For an argument that judicial review was intended by the constitutional convention and less ambiguous than scholars often assume, see Paul Rahe, "Background to *Marbury v. Madison*: The Debate Concerning Judicial Review at the Federal Convention and during the Ratification Period," in *Marbury v. Madison: 1803–2003: Un dialogue franco-américain/A French-American Dialogue*, ed. Élisabeth Zoller (Paris: Dalloz, 2003) 19–36.

[51] See the responses to Virginia of Delaware, Rhode Island, Massachusetts, New York, Connecticut, New Hampshire, and Vermont reprinted in *Resolutions of Virginia and Kentucky* (Richmond, 1826), 5–15; and the responses of Maryland, Pennsylvania, Delaware, and Connecticut to Kentucky; Maryland and Pennsylvania to Virginia; and New York to both Virginia and Kentucky reprinted in Frank Maloy Anderson, "Contemporary Opinion of the Virginia and Kentucky Resolutions, II," *AHR* 5 (December 1899), 245–249. Only Vermont's reply to Kentucky went "directly to the nature of the federal union" by arguing that "the people of the United States formed the federal constitution, and not the states, or their Legislatures." Quoted in Anderson, "Contemporary Opinion of the Virginia and Kentucky Resolutions, II," 233. Note that Vermont's reply – however in the minority – does suggest that Stampp's case might be slightly overstated.

the political wrongs of the moment.[52] What does seem clear is that the Alien and Sedition Acts seemed to confirm everything that Jefferson had suspected of the Federalists since the early 1790s: that they were administering the state with little other than a formulaic nod to public opinion, corrupting the proper role of representatives of the people, and running affairs in the interest of a minority. For playing its proper role in Jefferson's American vision – that of "exposing … the improper conduct and views of the president and Congress," as George Nicholas of Kentucky put it – the public was threatened with prosecution and jail. The perversion was that the "servants of the people" had found a way to undercut their necessary deference to "the people, their master."[53] If the resolutions contained seeds others would later use to destroy the Union (or undermine civil liberty), their initial rationale was to rescue the nation from a rogue state.[54]

In their pursuit of this goal, Madison and Jefferson appear to have been encouraging the states to act exactly as a younger Hamilton supposed they would "against invasions of the public liberty by the national authority." State "legislatures," Hamilton had written in December 1787, "will have better means of information" so that they will be able to "discover the danger at a distance … readily communicate with each other in the different states; and unite their common forces for the protection of their common liberty."[55]

Contemporary Federalist opinion nevertheless insisted that the protests of the Kentucky and Virginia legislatures indicated a dangerous dissatisfaction with the general government, an unfortunate disregard for the clear (in their minds, at least) constitutional provision of judicial review, and an insidious design to sever the Union.[56] Historians have often followed this lead and pointed to the radical nature of Jefferson's Kentucky Resolutions as indicative of disunionist, sectional tendencies. Jefferson's eighth draft resolution, in the most cited example, argues that "every state has a natural right … to nullify … all assumptions of power … which have not been delegated" by the compact.[57] Because the term "nullification" was eventually to have such a prominent place in the history of the sectional crisis that led to the Civil War, historians have

---

[52] See Peterson, *Thomas Jefferson and the New Nation*, 615.

[53] James Morton Smith, "The Grassroots Origins of the Kentucky Resolutions," *WMQ*, 27 (April 1970), 221–245, at 231.

[54] Federalists defended the constitutionality of the acts, stressed the way dissent undermined national unity and threatened national security, and argued that the alien bills did better by immigrants than the policies of other nations. But largely the Federalists seemed content to equate dissent with disloyalty and disunion. See Smith, "Grassroots Origins," 233.

[55] *Federalist* 28, in Pole, ed., *The Federalist*, 150–151.

[56] See Anderson, "Contemporary Opinion of the Virginia and Kentucky Resolutions," *AHR* 5 (October and December 1899), 45–63, 225–252; and Smith, "The Grass Roots Origins," esp. 233–234 and 243–244.

[57] Jefferson's draft of the Kentucky Resolutions can be found in *ROL* 2:1080–1084, and *PTJ* 30:536–541. The final draft of the Kentucky Resolutions as issued by the Kentucky legislature omitted Jefferson's references to nullification. The resolutions as passed are in *PTJ* 30:550–555.

centered in on the meaning and import of Jefferson's earlier use of the term. The South Carolina followers of John C. Calhoun, who gave the idea of nullification the status of a constitutional doctrine in the 1830s, wrapped themselves in Jefferson's mantle and claimed that his draft of the Kentucky Resolutions was the earliest expression of their own theory.[58]

Jefferson himself, in contrast to later interpreters, including Madison, seemed remarkably unconcerned about the theoretical implications of his use of the term and, in fact, made no recorded objection to its removal by the Kentucky legislature that passed the resolutions.[59] Even late in life, when finally acknowledging his authorship, he failed to mention his early draft and the changes the legislature made.[60] He merely accepted the resolutions as passed as his handiwork. He also praised Madison's Virginia Resolutions along with the set passed by Kentucky as together embodying the principles of the Republican party and encouraged the wide distribution of Madison's judicious Report of 1800, which explicitly represented itself as "expressions of opinion" only, "unaccompanied with any other effect than what they may produce on opinion by inciting reflection."[61] Jefferson never publicly (or privately) defended anything that distinguished his resolutions from Madison's and insofar as he talked of the resolutions at all, endorsed them as if there were no distinctions of significance.

Historians, in contrast, have made a good deal of the distinction between Jefferson's and Madison's drafts. Madison's draft states that "the states who are parties [to the compact] have the right, and are in duty bound, to *interpose* for arresting the pro(gress) of the evil, and for maintaining within their respective limits, the authorities, rights and liberties appertaining to them."[62] There is no disputing the fact that Jefferson's "nullification," unlike Madison's word

---

[58] See Joseph Ellis, *Founding Brothers*, 199–200; Sharp, *American Politics in the Early Republic*, 197–199; 201; and Drew R. McCoy, *The Last of the Fathers: James Madison and the Republican Legacy* (Cambridge, 1989), 119–170. McCoy's exceptionally fine discussion of Madison's defense of himself and of Jefferson is ambivalent, in the end, about Madison's success in rescuing the reputation of his friend from the South Carolinians and Virginians who linked their own opposition to the tariff of 1828 to Jefferson's use of the term "nullification." Also see, Gutzman, "A Troublesome Legacy."

[59] John C. Breckenridge, who sponsored the resolutions in the Kentucky legislature, apparently changed them before introducing them, transposing resolutions 8 and 9 and removing the assertion of a natural right to nullification (although he kept the phrase "declaring these acts void and of no force"). See *PTJ* 30:533, and "Resolutions Adopted by the Kentucky General Assembly," November 10, 1798, in ibid., 550–555.

[60] TJ to Mr. Nicholas, December 11, 1821, in *L&B* 15:350–352.

[61] Jefferson often coupled the resolutions. See, for example: "The principles already advanced by Virginia and Kentucky are not to be yielded in silence," TJ to Madison, August 23, 1799, in *ROL* 2:1119; TJ to James Monroe, February 6, 1800, *WTJ* 7:424. For Jefferson, it is clear, certain fundamental principles united the two sets of resolutions perhaps despite certain differences in detail. Madison's Report of 1800 is in Galliard Hunt, ed., *The Writings of James Madison*, 9 volumes cited hereafter as *WJM* (New York, 1900–1910), 9:341–406, quotation at 402.

[62] Virginia Resolutions Against the Alien and Sedition Acts, December 21, 1798, *PJM* 17:189, emphasis added.

"interposition," carries the weight of layers of subsequent historical meaning in American history.[63] It is not entirely clear, though, just what Jefferson meant by the word any more than it is clear what Madison meant by "interposition," although Madison was more precise in his later exposition of his text than Jefferson ever would be.[64] Some clarification comes from Jefferson's later assertion that the sedition law was, as he recalled, "a nullity as absolute and as palpable as if Congress had ordered us to fall down and worship a golden image."[65] This suggests that his use of the word "nullification" was closer to a statement of fact, a truism, than an incitement to any particular action.[66] In other words, his declaring the acts "unconstitutional, and therefore void" was a way of saying that the acts had no moral or constitutional legitimacy – an assertion that was not incompatible with peaceful protest.

Certainly this was the view of Republican leaders who organized the protest against the Alien and Sedition Acts in Kentucky. George Nicholas (brother to Wilson Cary) stated that because the acts were "clearly unconstitutional; as such they are void and of no effect," but "they may be declared to be so, by legal and constitutional means." He encouraged Republicans to protest but to declaim "improper opposition," which might in fact render them odious or even enemies of liberty.[67] Years later, the Kentucky legislature censured South Carolina nullification, reminding readers that the Kentucky legislature of 1798 had merely "expressed ... its firm conviction that [the Alien and Sedition bills] were unconstitutional, and therefore void. There it stopped, and that is the limit which no state should pass."[68] Madison's own later reflections on the

[63] In Madison to Joseph C. Cabell, May 31, 1830 in *Letters and Other Writings* 4:85–86; to Nicholas P. Trist, June 3, 1830, in ibid., 87; and to Edward Everett, August 20, 1830, in ibid., 106–107, Madison repeatedly insisted that Jefferson never used the term. He retracted after reading the draft (which he *had* seen in October and November 1798), but he continued to defend Jefferson, arguing that his friend did not actually draft the Kentucky Resolutions of 1799, which explicitly defended a right of nullification, and that Jefferson's use of the term was quite different from the current South Carolina doctrine : "I believe that [Jefferson] did not attach to it the idea of a constitutional right in the sense of South Carolina, but that of a natural one in cases justly appealing to it," Madison to Edward Everett, September 10, 1830, in ibid., 109–110; Madison to Trist, September 23, 1830, in ibid., 110–111; Madison to Townsend, October 18, 1831, in ibid., 198–200.

[64] Even at the end of his life, Madison was ambiguous about the precise implications of "interposition." Writing in 1835–1836 about the third Virginia Resolution, Madison conceded, "The mode of their interposition, in extraordinary cases, is left by the Resolution to the parties themselves"; Madison, "Notes on Nullification," 1835–1836, in Hunt, ed., *WJM* 9:576.

[65] TJ to Abigail Adams, July 22, 1804, in *AJL*, 275.

[66] Compare Jefferson's similar assertion in the *Notes* that: "If the present assembly pass any act, and declare it shall be irrevocable by subsequent assemblies, the declaration is merely void, and the act repealable, as other acts are," in *Notes*, 122,.

[67] Nicholas quoted in Smith, "Grassroots Origins," 231–232. All Republicans were doing, declared a writer in the Kentucky *Gazette*, was deliberating "on the conduct of their *public servants*," ibid., 234–234.

[68] Kentucky reply to South Carolina, January 27, 1830, in Herman V. Ames, ed., *State Documents on Federal Relations* (Philadelphia, 1911), 161.

Virginia Resolutions also endorse this reading. After Madison had drafted these resolutions, he sent them through Wilson Cary Nicholas to Jefferson, who then added to Madison's assertion that the acts were "unconstitutional" the clarification that they were: " ab initio – null, void and of no force, or effect." Nicholas incorporated the change in the draft introduced to the House of Delegates by John Taylor on December 10.[69] Approving a motion by Taylor, however, the House had struck the phrase from the resolutions, just before the final vote.[70] Years later, responding to questions about the origin and meaning of the excised phrase, Madison responded that he could not recall who inserted it or if he himself had written it. Nevertheless, he was "confident" that the words "must have been regarded" at the time, "only as giving accumulated emphasis to the *declaration*, that the alien & sedition acts had in the opinion of the Assembly violated the Constitution of the U.S. and not that the addition of them could annul the acts or sanction a resistance of them."[71] Indeed, Madison argued, "the words were in fact but synonymous with 'unconstitutional,'" and were removed by the delegates only to "guard against a misunderstanding of this phrase as more than declaratory of opinion, the word "unconstitutional" alone was retained, as not liable to that danger."[72] Jefferson's addition to Madison's draft, then, Madison characterized in the same way Jefferson had described his stance to Abigail Adams, as not necessarily a pronunciation of a radical new doctrine, but merely a statement of fact similar to "A equals A." "Unconstitutional," in short, meant "null, void, and of no effect" – not valid. Madison did see Jefferson's draft of the Kentucky Resolutions once at Monticello in October 1798 and again as an enclosure in Jefferson's letter to him in November.[73] At the time, Madison made no recorded comment on the phrasing, perhaps because it had already been sent to Kentucky by the time he read it in October, and had passed through the legislature (without the phrase) by the time Jefferson sent him the draft in November. But it is at least possible that he passed over it at the time because he considered it, as he said later, merely "synonimous with 'unconstitutional'" and worth clarifying only as a

---

[69] Nicholas's were in a slightly different format: "and not law, but utterly null, void and of no force or effect." See *PTJ* 30:590, editorial footnote. James Morton Smith suggests that Lyon's arrest nudged Jefferson to make this change in Madison's draft. See, *ROL* 2:1071.

[70] It is not clear who added the word "alone" to the third clause of Madison's draft of the resolutions ("to which the states *alone* are parties"); Jefferson did not request that Nicholas add the word in his letter of November 29. Taylor asked this word to be struck as well. See Taylor's motion in "Debates in the House of Delegates of Virginia," December 21, 1798, in *Resolutions of Virginia and Kentucky*, 202–203. Madison, who was visiting his wife's relatives near Richmond at the time, may have insisted on the excision, although this is not confirmable by the evidence. The editors of *PJM* suggest that it is "more likely" that John Taylor removed the phrase sometime during the debate "in deference to what he might have understood as Jefferson's original wish for a more moderate stance," 17:187–188.

[71] Madison to James Robertson, March 27, 1831, in Hunt, ed., *WJM* 9:444–445.

[72] Madison to Edward Everett, August 28, 1830, in ibid., 9:402.

[73] Brant, *James Madison: Father of the Constitution*, 461; TJ to Madison, November 17, 1798, in *ROL* 2:1079–1084.

"guard against misunderstanding of this phrase as more than declaratory of opinion."[74]

In fact, historians have made too much of the differences between Madison's and Jefferson's draft resolutions. In the end, much may boil down to a difference of style and emotion. Both sets contained clear expressions of support for the Constitution and the Union, but both qualified their support by explicitly defining the kind of Union and Constitution they were willing to support and defend.[75] Jefferson argued that the welfare of the states was not served by a transfer of "all the powers of self-government ... to a general and consolidated government, without regard to the special delegations and reservations solemnly agreed to in that compact." Such would not accomplish "the peace, happiness or prosperity of these states." As a consequence, Jefferson wrote, "this commonwealth is determined, as it doubts not its co-states are, to submit to undelegated, and consequently unlimited powers in no man, or body of men, on earth."[76]

The emotion of Jefferson's statement, however, cannot ultimately mask what amounted to the same substantive assertion in Madison's draft. Madison wrote that the General Assembly of Virginia was resolved to defend the Constitution of the United States and "*will support the government of the United States in all measures, waranted by*" the Constitution. In some senses, this is indeed "cooler" language, as some historians have asserted. But it seems clear that, turned around, Madison's declaration of devotion to the government of the United States becomes a suggestion that Virginia will not support the government in measures it considered "not warranted" by the Constitution. This seems, in the end, an oblique way of saying exactly what Jefferson said: The states in question will not support or enforce unconstitutional acts of the federal government. Madison's third paragraph makes this even more explicit and brings the two sets of resolutions even closer in tone and content. The powers of the federal government were "*no farther valid than they are authorised* by the grants enumerated in [the] compact."[77] If the Alien and Sedition Acts were, as Madison believed, unauthorized by the Constitution, they were, by his reasoning, invalid. To say that the acts were unconstitutional and, thus, on their face, "invalid" in general, may not be the same thing as saying that the acts were null and void within the boundaries of a particular state. Nevertheless, his later acknowledgment that "void and of no force" added nothing substantive to "unconstitutional" illuminates Madison's understanding of the text and suggests that the reason Madison never commented at the time on Jefferson's supposedly stronger phrase may have been because it amounted to much the same thing as his own.[78]

---

[74] Madison to Edward Everett, August 28, 1830, in Rakove, ed., *Madison: Writings* (New York, 1999), 851.

[75] *PTJ* 30:539; *PJM* 17:188–189.

[76] *ROL* 2:1082, 1084.

[77] Madison, "Virginia Resolutions," *PJM* 17:189, emphasis added.

[78] Madison to Edward Everett, August 28, 1830, in Hunt, ed., *WJM* 9:402.

Jefferson also contributed the stirring line that the Alien and Sedition Acts, "unless arrested at the threshold, necessarily drive these states into revolution and blood." But the interposition of the states against unconstitutional acts of the federal government should be undertaken, Jefferson insisted, precisely because such acts "will furnish new calumnies against republican government, and new pretexts for those who wish it to be believed that man cannot be governed but by a rod of iron."[79] As Jefferson and Madison had insisted time and again in the 1790s, republicanism itself was at stake in these contests over American political and constitutional identity. Indeed, Madison's draft maintained, it was the "duty" of the Assembly of Virginia "to watch over and oppose every infraction of those principles which constitute the only basis of [the] union, because a faithful observance of them, can alone secure its existence, and the public happiness."[80] In soberer tones than Jefferson, Madison was saying something quite similar: It was incumbent on the states to stand in the way of violations of the Constitution on the part of the federal government. If they refused this obligation, the Union and republicanism itself was doomed.

As for potential solutions, Jefferson argued that if the Congress abused its rightful powers, the "constitutional remedy" would be a "change by the people," presumably during the next election. If, on the other hand, Congress assumed a power that had not been granted it by the people in the Constitution, such as, in this case, the right to prosecute sedition, "every state has a natural right in cases not within the compact ... to *nullify* of their own authority all assumptions of power by others within their limits."[81] Madison's resolutions argued that the states were "duty bound, to *interpose* for arresting the progress of the evil, and for maintaining *within their respective limits*, the authorities, rights and liberties appertaining to them."[82] As we have seen, Madison never quite explained what he meant by "interposition," either in the resolutions or the Virginia Report of 1800, but historians have been predisposed to assume the moderation of the word, and indeed of the entire third resolution, in comparison with Jefferson's more heated statement of proposed remedies. This interpretation seems unwarranted by a close comparison of the two sets. There are indeed differences between these two statements of "action" in the resolutions. But the right of states to stand up to and render inoperative unconstitutional acts of the federal government is present in both Madison's and Jefferson's resolutions.

Writing in the 1830s, in defense of the Principles of '98 against South Carolina nullifiers, who saw Madison's and Jefferson's resolutions as the template for Calhoun's doctrine, Madison insisted that the Virginia Resolutions, anyway, had been "expressly *declaratory*." Because they "proceed[ed] from the Legislature only which was not even a party to the Constitution," they naturally

---

[79] *ROL* 2:1083.
[80] Madison, "Virginia Resolutions," *PJM* 17:189.
[81] Jefferson, "Draft of the Kentucky Resolutions," in *TJW*, 453.
[82] Madison, "Virginia Resolutions," *PJM* 17:189, emphasis added.

"could be declaratory of opinion only" rather than incitement to any particular action.[83] But such a reading is not the only plausible way of reading the original sets of resolutions which urge the states to act, either to "interpose" or to "nullify" federal law that, by its unconstitutionality (according to Madison's later understanding), was invalid anyway. In other words, there was no reason to add "interpose" or "nullify" if the only purpose was "declaratory."

On the other hand, except for the secret resolutions he sent to Kentucky, Jefferson continued to urge the remedy of declaration, deliberation, and the spread of information to the public. Given his commitment to educating the public and cultivating its judgment, and given his sense that such was one of the obligations of the natural aristocracy, it is worth thinking about the Kentucky Resolutions, too, as an effort to persuade the public at a time when other avenues were being shut down by Federalist legislation and prosecution.[84] If the American people were "essentially republican," he told John Taylor, they would be cured of any "disease of the imagination" by physicians "in the guise of a taxgatherer" and by adequate information about the nature of Federalist misrule. Accordingly, "I should be for resolving the alien & sedition laws to be against the constitution & merely void, and for addressing the other states to obtain similar declarations: and I would not do any thing at this moment which should commit us further, but reserve ourselves to shape our future measures or no measures, by the events which may happen." Of course, it is not clear what was implied by the potentially ominous, but murky, "future measures." What is transparent, however, was Jefferson's caution in the height of opposition and his belief that the American people would come to right conclusions without "action" on the part of the states.[85] Accordingly, Jefferson counseled "patience" until "the reign of witches pass[ed] over."[86]

One potentially significant difference between Madison's and Jefferson's resolutions was raised in a question Madison asked Jefferson a few days after the Virginia House of Delegates and Senate passed his set. Madison asked whether Jefferson had "ever considered thoroughly the distinction between the power of the *State* and that of the *Legislature*, on questions relating to the federal pact."[87] In the years since the Revolution, American thinkers had begun to emphasize the crucial difference between legislation and fundamental law.[88]

---

[83] Madison to James Robertson, March 27, 1831, in *WJM* 9:444–445.

[84] On this, see especially, Jeremy Bailey, *Thomas Jefferson and Executive Power* (Cambridge, 2007), esp. chapter 4.

[85] TJ to John Taylor, November 26, 1798, in *PTJ* 30:588–589.

[86] TJ To John Taylor, June 1, 1798, *WTJ* 7:265. Also see TJ to Wilson Cary Nicholas, September 5, 1799: ibid., 391. Taylor had hoped to place "the State & general government at issue" and submit "the point to the people in convention, as the only reform." Taylor saw this as a way to "attach to the real republicans, the physical power of the state," but recognized that Jefferson "disapprove[d] of pushing on at present to this ultimate effort" and deferred to his judgment. See Taylor to TJ, before December 11, 1798, in ibid., 601–602.

[87] Madison to TJ, December 29, 1798, in *ROL* 2:1085.

[88] On this transformation, see Gerald Stourzh, "Constitution: Changing Meanings of the Term from the Early Seventeenth to the Late Eighteenth Century," in Stourzh, *From Vienna to*

In the British system, as Sir Edward Coke put it, "subsequent laws nullify earlier laws which are contrary."[89] In America, legislation enacted by the elected representatives of the people was likewise liable to change by subsequent legislatures, but all legislation, Americans had come to believe, ought ultimately to conform to the fundamental law of the Constitution, ratified by the people in state constitutional conventions – what Madison called "the people in each of the States, acting in their highest sovereign capacity."[90] Many historians have read in Madison's question a critique of Jefferson's failure to make the distinction clearer in the Kentucky Resolutions.[91] If the state was indeed the "ultimate Judge of infractions," it did not thereby follow that the legislature was "the legitimate organ especially as a Convention was the organ by which the compact was made."[92] But this was less a complaint than a practical statement of fact that Jefferson never disagreed with. Both Madison's and Jefferson's resolutions use the term "State" or "States" or "commonwealth" without clearly distinguishing between the state legislature and a state in its "highest sovereign capacity." Jefferson's previous writing on the subject suggests that he would have agreed with Madison about this distinction. In his *Notes on the State of Virginia*, for example, Jefferson's major complaint about the Virginia state constitution was precisely that it had been written and approved by a state legislature rather than created by a State Constitutional Convention called for that specific purpose. This was a major flaw that exposed Virginia to the "hazard of having no fundamental rights at all." It was an "absurdity," Jefferson insisted, to think that the "ordinary legislature" could "establish an act *above the power of the ordinary legislature*."[93] Nothing in the Kentucky Resolutions suggests that Jefferson would in the long run necessarily insist that the legislature was the rightful organ to judge infractions by the federal government. Both sets of resolutions, for that matter, leave the problem unresolved.

To be sure, the draft Kentucky Resolutions, of course, actually have the state legislature declaring the Alien and Sedition Acts – federal law – "void and of no force." But, the distinction between a state and a legislature was not always one that Madison himself had made clear. For example, in his 1789 speech on constitutional amendments, in which he introduced what became the Bill of Rights, Madison made no such distinction, insisting only that "the state

---

*Chicago and Back: Essays on Intellectual History and Political Thought in Europe and America* (Chicago, 2007), 80–99.

[89] Coke quoted in *Notes*, 124.

[90] Madison to Edward Everett, August 28, 1830, in Rakove, ed., *Madison: Writings*, 843. On this distinction see Bernard Bailyn, *The Ideological Origins of the American Revolution* (Cambridge, MA, 1967), 175–198; Gordon S. Wood, *The Creation of the American Republic* (Chapel Hill, 1969), 259–389; Harry V. Jaffa, *A New Birth of Freedom: Abraham Lincoln and the Coming of the Civil War* (Lanham, 2000), 42–43; and McCoy, *The Last of the Fathers*, 134–135.

[91] See, for example, Sharp, *American Politics in the New Republic*, 199.

[92] Madison to TJ, December 29, 1798, *ROL* 2:1085.

[93] This specific critique of the Virginia constitution and the quotations in the text are in Jefferson, *Notes*, 121–125. Jefferson's full criticism of the "very capital defects" of the Virginia constitution is in 118–129.

legislatures" would "jealously and closely watch the operations of" the national "government" and would "be able to resist with more effect every assumption of power than any other power on earth can do."[94] This was, in fact, exactly what many of the seven states that responded to Virginia's Resolutions read them to say. Rhode Island, for example, arguing specifically with Madison's version, registered its opinion that "for any *state legislature* to assume that authority" to rule "on the constitutionality of any act or law of the congress of the United States" would be to usurp the rightful authority of the federal judiciary and would "hazard … an interruption of the peace of the states by civil discord, in case of a diversity of opinions among the state legislatures; each state having, in that case, no resort for vindicating its own opinion, but to the strength of its own arm."[95] Massachusetts also declared that it could not "admit the right of the State Legislatures to denounce the administration of that Government to which the people themselves, by a solemn compact, have exclusively committed their national concerns."[96] In other words, Massachusetts assumed that Madison's Virginia Resolutions were in substance suggesting – less forcefully, perhaps, but nevertheless exactly what Jefferson's Kentucky Resolutions seemed to.

If the distinction between state legislature and the state itself was not altogether clear in the original drafts, when Madison re-read the resolutions in the 1830s he made more of that "between the right of *the parties* to the Constitution and of a single *party*."[97] Jefferson's draft, it is true, seems more explicit than Madison's: "Every state," Jefferson wrote, "has a natural right in cases not within the compact (causus non foederis) to nullify of their own authority all assumptions of power by others within their limits."[98] But Madison's draft, too, argues that "the *states* who are parties thereto [the compact] have the right" and were compelled, in fact, to intervene in order to maintain "*within their respective limits*, the authorities, rights and liberties appertaining to them."[99] Madison's "states" is plural, unlike Jefferson's "every state"; but his

---

[94] Madison, "Speech in Congress Proposing Constitutional Amendments," June 8, 1789, in Rakove, ed., *Madison: Writings*, 437–452, at 449. Also see Hamilton's similar suggestion in *Federalist* 28, in Pole, ed., *The Federalist*, 150–151.

[95] "State of Rhode Island and Providence Plantations, In General Assembly," February 1799, in Smith, ed., *Resolutions of Virginia and Kentucky*, 6, emphasis added.

[96] Ibid, 7. New Hampshire, likewise, argued that "the state legislatures are not the proper tribunals to determine the constitutionality of the laws of the general government" (13). Vermont said, "It belongs not to state legislatures to decide on the constitutionality of laws made by the general government." As with most of these responses, NH and VT also placed this authority with the federal judiciary.

[97] Madison to Edward Livingston, May 8, 1830, in *Letters and Other* Writings 4:80, emphasis in original.

[98] *ROL* 2:1082. Compare Jefferson's note in the *Summary View* that the king had the "executive power in the laws of every state; but they are the laws of the particular state which he is to administer within that state, and not those of any one within the limits of another. *Every state must judge for itself* the number of armed men which they may safely trust among themselves." *PTJ* 1:134, emphasis added.

[99] Madison, "Virginia Resolutions," *PJM* 17:189, emphasis added.

addition of the word "respective" to Jefferson's "within their limits" raises the possibility that he, too, is arguing that each state will need to maintain its own sovereignty inviolable – thus suggesting that his earlier question about the distinction between state and legislature might not have been rhetorical at all.[100]

The fact is, in any case, that Jefferson remained fairly unconcerned about the theoretical detail of the resolutions, and, because he died in 1826, he had the luxury of doing so; whereas Madison lived long enough to witness the Resolutions' appropriation during the nullification controversy for purposes unwarranted, he believed by the texts. What is often overlooked in the effort to distinguish between Madison's and Jefferson's resolutions is the fact that Madison's later concern was not to separate himself from Jefferson, but to maintain that he and Jefferson were emphatically not the originators of what he called the "preposterous & anarchical pretension" of the South Carolina nullification.[101]

It seems certain that Madison was right about this on a number of levels, although not necessarily in all the ways he hoped. Despite South Carolina's claim of deference to the Principles of '98, Madison denied the "honor" they bestowed on him as the originator of their doctrine and instead spent countless hours explaining how the South Carolina nullifiers had "perverted" the meaning of the 1798 Resolutions.[102] In the first place, the Kentucky and Virginia Resolutions protested what nearly all later commentators on the issue would agree were among the most egregious assaults on civil liberties by congressional legislation in American history and a fairly clear violation of constitutional boundaries placed around the federal government. South Carolinians, by contrast, were protesting a tariff – one they considered unfair to their region – but nonetheless a policy explicitly authorized by the Constitution.[103] The comparison to 1798 seemed fairly weak to Madison. He recognized, at least by the late 1820s, that the Constitution had, by the authority to regulate commerce, granted the federal government the power to implement tariffs as a boost to domestic manufacturing. The first Congress had recognized the power as "indisputable," and all presidents had as well. Implementation of such tariffs might indeed fall more or less unequally on certain regions of the country over time, but "mere *inequality* in imposing taxes" was not "synonymous with *unconstitutionality*." Madison believed it "essential" to understand

---

[100] Madison took note of this word in an 1832 letter to Nicholas P. Trist and deplored "the pretext" it supplied for "the liberty taken with" the Virginia Resolutions by the SC nullifiers. "Could the abuse of the expression have been foreseen or suspected, the form of it would doubtless have been varied." Madison to Trist, December 23, 1832, in Hunt, ed., *WJM* 9:491.

[101] Madison to Nicholas P. Trist, December 1831, in Hunt, ed., *WJM* 9:471–472.

[102] Madison's "Notes on Nullification," 1835–1836, in ibid, 9:574.

[103] See the discussion of this controversy in William Freehling, *Prelude to Civil War: The Nullification Controversy in South Carolina, 1816–1836* (New York, 1966); and Ellis, *The Union at Risk*. On the southern experience of national tariff policy as an unjust burden, see Brian Schoen, "Calculating the Price of Union: Republican Economic Nationalism and the Origins of Southern Sectionalism, 1790–1828," in *JER*, 23 (Summer 2003), 176–206.

the "distinction ... between the usurpation of a power" not granted by the Constitution and the "abuse of a delegated power" that had been granted by the Constitution, precisely the distinction Jefferson did make in 1798. If the South Carolinians were right, that the tariff was unequally damaging to their economy, Madison suggested, they should work to change it by constitutional means of ballot and protest.[104] Until it became so oppressive "and intolerable as to justify civil war," however, such abuse, Madison insisted, "cannot be regarded as a breach of the fundamental compact."[105] "No Constitution," Madison wrote, "could be lasting without an habitual distinction between" these – "an abuse of legitimate power, and the exercise of a usurped one."[106] With the Alien and Sedition Acts in 1798, as Jefferson was at pains to make clear, Congress had not merely abused "delegated powers" but had assumed powers "which have not been delegated."[107] If the states failed to make the distinction and instead saw unconstitutionality in every unequal tax, Madison asked, "is there a State in the Union whose Constitution would be safe?"[108]

Madison did not deny that "there may be abuses so enormous as to be not only at war with the Constitution, whether Federal or State, but to strike at the foundation of the social compact itself."[109] Insofar as such cases of "oppression so iniquitous and intolerable,"[110] would "justify a dissolution of" the social compact itself,[111] Madison noted, they would justify the natural right of revolution "about which there is no theoretic controversy."[112] Such a step could be taken only for grave reasons, not "light and transient causes," as the Declaration of Independence, which announced that the thirteen colonies were availing themselves of this same right, had indicated years earlier. Jefferson's Kentucky Resolutions opposed acts he believed "so palpably against the constitution as to amount to an undisguised declaration that that compact is not meant to be the measure of the powers of the General government, but that it will proceed in the exercise, over these states, of all powers whatsoever." In Jefferson's view, this would be "seizing the rights of the states, and consolidating them in the hands of the General government, with a power assumed to bind the States, (not merely in the cases made federal [casus foederis] but) in all cases whatsoever, by laws made, not with their consent, but by others against

---

[104] This is precisely what Calhoun would later find impossible, thus necessitating the concurrent majority as a protection of minority interests. See, especially, Lacy K. Ford, "Inventing the Concurrent Majority: Madison, Calhoun, and the Problem of Majoritarianism in American Political Thought," *JSH* 60 (February 1994), 19–58; and James H. Read, *Majority Rule Versus Consensus: The Political Thought of John C. Calhoun* (Lawrence, 2009).

[105] Madison to Joseph C. Cabell, March 22, 1827, in *Letters and Other Writings* 3:571–574.

[106] Madison to Joseph C. Cabell, December 5, 1828, in Hunt, ed., *WJM* 9:327.

[107] Jefferson, draft of Kentucky Resolutions, *ROL* 2:1082.

[108] Madison to Cabell, March 22, 1827, in *Letters and Other Writings* 3:574.

[109] Madison to William Cabell Rives, January 23, 1829, in ibid., 4:8–9; see, also, Madison to C.E. Haynes, August 27, 1832, in Hunt, ed., *WJM* 9:483–484.

[110] Madison to Cabell, March 22, 1827, in ibid., 3:573.

[111] Madison to Rives, January 23, 1829, in ibid., 4:9.

[112] Madison to Daniel Webster, March 15, 1833, in ibid., 4:293.

their consent." This was not a "light and transient cause," if Jefferson was in fact right. Such a situation "would be to surrender the form of government we have chosen, and to live under one *deriving it's powers from its own will, and not from our authority*" – a surrender, indeed, to an autonomous state.[113] South Carolina's hostility to the tariff simply did not rise to the level that would justify revolution.

But the natural right of revolution was not what South Carolina was contending for. Instead, as Madison pointed out, the nullifiers held that "a single State has a *constitutional* right to arrest the execution of a law of the U.S. within its limits; that the arrest is to be presumed right and valid, and is to remain in force unless 3/4 of the States, in a Convention, shall otherwise decide."[114] Of course, Madison was at pains to make clear that Calhoun's concurrent majority was "countenanced by nothing known to have been said or done by [Jefferson]."[115] For Jefferson, in the Kentucky Resolutions of 1798, by contrast, "nullification" was a "natural right," which, as Madison later argued, applied only "to extreme cases, as alone justifying a resort to any forcible relief."[116] The "right of nullification meant by Mr. Jefferson," Madison believed, "is the natural right, which all admit to be a remedy against insupportable oppression."[117] South Carolina, Madison pointed out by way of contrast, argued nullification as a constitutional right, "the State not ceasing to avow its adherence to the Constitution."[118]

Unlike the doctrine of South Carolina, the right of revolution put the state taking such a step (and even Madison agreed that a single state could take this revolutionary leap[119]) outside of the compact, no longer adhering to the Constitution or enjoying its privileges. This was not a constitutional step, but a revolutionary one that put the state or states leaving the compact in jeopardy of being forced back into it. For, as Harry Jaffa puts it, an "appeal to natural right was a justification of the use of force *by either side* upon the other."[120] Contrasting this with South Carolina's doctrine, Madison marveled

---

[113] Jefferson, "Kentucky Resolutions," *ROL* 2:1084, emphasis added.

[114] Madison, "Notes on Nullification," 1835–1836, in Hunt, ed., *WJM* 9:573, emphasis added.

[115] Madison to Townsend, October 18, 1831, in *Letters and Other Writings* 4:199. Also see Madison to Edward Everett, September 10, 1830, in ibid, 4:109–110. In this letter, Madison reluctantly admits to Everett that Jefferson used the word "nullification" in his draft of the Kentucky Resolutions (a fact Madison had forgotten until he re-read the draft). "Still," he wrote, "I believe that he did not attach to it the idea of a constitutional right in the sense of South Carolina, but that of a natural one in cases justly appealing to it."

[116] Jefferson, "Kentucky Resolutions," *ROL* 2:1082; Madison to Townsend, October 18, 1831, in *Letters and Other Writings* 4:199.

[117] Madison, "Notes on Nullification," 1835–1836, in Hunt, *WJM* 9:589, n. 1.

[118] Ibid.

[119] "There is nothing which excludes a natural right in the States individually, more than in any portion of an individual State, suffering under palpable and insupportable wrongs, from seeking relief by resistance and revolution." Madison, "Notes on Nullification," Hunt, ed., *WJM* 9:575.

[120] Harry V. Jaffa, *A New Birth of Freedom*, 53.

at "how closely the nullifiers who make the name of Mr. Jefferson the pedestal for their colossal heresy, shut their eyes and lips, whenever his authority is ever so clearly and emphatically against them."[121]

To be sure, Jefferson did express in a private letter to Madison that Virginia should leave the Union "rather than give up the rights of self government … in which alone we see liberty, safety and happiness."[122] But "giv[ing] up the rights of self-government" is a major qualification; and Jefferson followed this with a repudiation of the notion to Wilson Cary Nicholas and an affirmation to Madison that the "objects" of the Republican party should be "a sincere cultivation of the Union" and "protestations against violations of the true principles of our constitution, merely to save them, and prevent precedent and acquiescence from being pleaded against them; but nothing to be said or done which shall look or lead to force, and give any pretext for keeping up the army."[123]

The most important distinction between Jefferson's "nullification" and South Carolina's later adaptation, however, may remain the different ways they approached majority rule.[124] Jefferson's "respect for the will of majorities, as the vital principle of Republican government," Madison argued, stood firmly against the South Carolina understanding of the Constitution.[125] The Kentucky Resolutions, and indeed the entire onus of Republican opposition, as Jefferson saw it, was a defense of majority rule and American national identity from the depredations of the Federalists, who Jefferson viewed as a minority "sect" of

[121] Madison to Nicholas P. Trist, December 23, 1832, in Hunt, ed., *WJM* 9:491. Also see Madison's "Notes on Nullification," where he decried the tendency of the Calhounites to ignore Jefferson's "repeated assertions of the federal authority, even under the articles of Confederation, to stop the commerce of a refractory state," in Marvin Meyers, ed., *The Mind of the Founder: Sources of the Political Thought of James Madison* (Hanover and London, 1981), 428–429, note 3.

[122] TJ to Madison, August 23, 1799, *ROL* 2:1119. For a similar statement also easily misconstrued, see TJ to William Branch Giles, December 26, 1825, in *TJW* 1509–1512. We should "separate from our companions," Jefferson said, "only when the sole alternatives left, are the dissolution of our Union with them, or submission to a government without limitation of powers." Jefferson's hostility to consolidation, then, did not justify Virginia's standing "to our arms, with the hot-headed Georgian." That would be "the last resource, not to be thought of until much longer and greater sufferings." After all, "if every infraction of a compact of so many parties is to be resisted at once, as a dissolution of it, none can ever be formed which would last one year." The states "should be watchful to note every material usurpation on their rights" and "protest against them" but never separate until a choice was forced. It is hard to imagine an American disagreeing with Jefferson that the Union should not legitimately harbor "a government without limitation of powers." The difficulty is knowing when the "accumulation" of evils would "overweigh that of separation." Clearly, in 1825, as he had been in 1798, Jefferson was still in the camp counseling patience rather than disunion.

[123] TJ to Wilson Cary Nicholas, September 5, 1799, in *FE* 9:79–81; TJ to Madison, November 6, 1799, in *ROL* 2:1122.

[124] For a succinct discussion of South Carolina's rejection of majority rule, see Harry L. Watson, *Andrew Jackson vs. Henry Clay: Democracy and Development in Antebellum America* (New York, 1998), 87–88. For a thorough assessment of Calhoun's thought, see Read, *Majority Rule Versus Consensus*.

[125] Madison to – – Townsend, October 18, 1831, in *Letters and Other Writings* 4:199; "Notes on Nullification," (1835–1836), Meyers, ed., *The Mind of the Founder*, 428–429, note 3.

"preachers without followers" committed to running a managerial state and to fostering English-style government in America.[126]

Instead of defending a region or a particular state interest, Jefferson remained insistent that his opposition was a defense of majority will. Jefferson was convinced that the majority of Americans were devoted to republicanism and that the character of Americans and the "American mind" would not countenance the kind of violation of its will represented in the Federalist legislation. Although temporarily deluded, "our fellow-citizens" would be brought "to their true minds" by the press and the Republican opposition.[127] Jefferson remained convinced that the "true" American mind would respond to his own fundamental assumptions. "I know my own principles to be pure, & therefore am not ashamed of them," he wrote Samuel Smith two months before drafting the Kentucky Resolutions. These principles "are the same, I am sure, with those of the great body of the American people."[128]

Of course, as we have seen, the difficulties of ascertaining public opinion on particular issues were legion compared with the sophisticated polling techniques of our day. National leaders were, in a quite literal sense, isolated from the public while in the nation's capital.[129] Jefferson, along with others in the capital, wrote countless letters to Virginia and other states in explicit effort to gain some sense of public sentiment. Often enough, Jefferson read difference of opinion as evidence of willful evil intention or, at best, ignorance on the part of the people. Some of the state responses to the Kentucky and Virginia Resolutions pointed out that "the people" the Republicans ostensibly prized had voted for the very characters who enacted the Alien and Sedition Acts.[130] Federalists also registered clear victories in the midterm elections of 1798, especially in the South, where they gained more seats in Congress then they ever would again.[131] But the point here is that Jefferson always saw his opposition as a stance for majority will against minority usurpation. Jefferson acknowledged Federalist gains and explained them as transitory effects of the XYZ affair and French attacks on American shipping. As they had done many times before, he thought, Americans would soon come to reason on this issue as well by recognizing that the Federalists were not their champions but potential destroyers of their liberties.[132]

[126] TJ to Lafayette, June 16, 1792, in *TJW*, 990.

[127] TJ to James Lewis, Jr., May 9, 1798, in *FE* 8:416–417; TJ to Colonel Nicholas Lewis, January 30, 1799 in *L&B* 10:92.

[128] TJ to Samuel Smith, August 22, 1798, ibid., 277. Also see TJ to Elbridge Gerry, January 26, 1799, ibid., 329.

[129] Joanne B. Freeman, *Affairs of Honor: National Politics in the New Republic* (New Haven, 2001), 79–80.

[130] See the statement of Massachusetts in *Resolutions of Virginia and Kentucky*, 7.

[131] John W. Kuehl, "Southern Reaction to the XYZ Affair: An Incident in the Emergence of American Nationalism," in *Register of the Kentucky Historical Society* (January 1972), 21–49; and Kuehl, "The XYZ Affair and American Nationalism: Republican Victories in the Middle Atlantic States," *Maryland Historical Magazine* 67 (Spring 1972), 1–20, esp. 4.

[132] TJ to William Duane, March 28, 1811, in *FE* 11:193, emphasis in the original.

From this perspective, the resolutions are less about localist or sectionalist aspiration than an effort to clarify the meaning of American federalism and even of American identity itself. To be sure, the Kentucky Resolutions were a defense of local control of the constitutionally mandated sphere of sovereignty designated to the states. But they constituted a states' rights in the defense of a national identity. Jefferson spelled this out in his First Inaugural Address. The state governments were "the most competent administrations for our domestic concerns and the surest bulwarks against antirepublican tendencies," but Jefferson also called for the "preservation of the General Government in its whole constitutional vigor, as the sheet anchor of our peace at home and safety abroad." These, and the other principles he outlined, would ensure that Americans would "unite with one heart and one mind." This deep unity of the people, and not the consolidation of power in the national or the state institutions of government, would make America's government "the strongest Government on earth ... the only one where every man, at the call of the law, would fly to the standard of the law, and would meet invasions of the public order as his own personal concern."[133] So "local self-rule and national unity" could be, Peter Parish suggests, deeply "interdependent."[134]

Jefferson's protest in 1798, and throughout the 1790s, was that the "equilibrium" was unbalanced by the preponderance of power in the federal government. The defense of state prerogatives in 1798 was a compensation to restore the balance in favor of the peculiarly American system of republican government and give each sphere the respect and authority due it. Jefferson's qualification in the Kentucky Resolutions that states have a natural right to nullify "in cases not within the compact," is a significant one, not often noted, suggesting that states are rightful judges only of cases that the Constitution clearly leaves to states, to cases obviously "non foederis," and leaving a wide range of cases under which states would not be proper judges of congressional legislation. For Jefferson, "an inviolable preservation of our present federal constitution" meant "preserving to the States the powers not yielded by them to the Union, & to the legislature of the Union it's constitutional share in the division of powers."[135]

The focus on the constitutional powers of the states at this time was certainly more than pragmatic, but, as Merrill Peterson noted, Jefferson had limited options: "No danger came from the states."[136] Jefferson believed the republicanism secured by the Revolution was being threatened by a faction in control

---

[133] Jefferson, "First Inaugural Address," in *TJW*, 493–494.

[134] Parish, "An Exception to Most of the Rules," *Prologue* 27 (Fall 1995), 223.

[135] TJ to Gerry, January 26, 1799, in *FE* 9:17–18.

[136] Peterson, *Thomas Jefferson and the New Nation*, 616. See also Dumas Malone, *Thomas Jefferson as Political Leader* (Berkeley, 1963), 65–67. "If he had not turned to the states for their protection at this time," Malone asks, "whither could he have turned? There would have been no point in appealing to the Supreme Court of the United States. That partisan body was no guardian of the rights of individuals, as the Supreme Court is today." For another reading, see Sharp, *American Politics in the New Republic*, 187.

of the federal government in opposition to the will of the majority of the people of the United States. Naturally, from his perspective, he appealed to the states as the parties to the compact that had created this government. Jefferson emphasized the states because he saw the federal government as exceeding its sphere. Insofar as this could be called an appeal to states' rights, it was made on behalf of what he considered a uniquely American political system threatened by efforts to transform it to a British one.

Jefferson's assertion of states' rights paradoxically expressed a national vision. When the national state became corrupted, resistance was necessary, not from sectionalist or parochial sentiment, but in defense of the national character itself. The Kentucky and Virginia Resolutions were part of a larger movement designed to bring the state back into line with the will of the people. Whether Jefferson's arguments would have, under some scenario, placed the states in open defiance of federal law or whether they opened a kind of Pandora's box of rhetoric and logic that others would use to break the Union, they remain, nevertheless, one component of a nationalist project. The resolutions, far from purely localist or sectionalist in nature, were invocations of states' rights in defense of an American identity seemingly threatened by corruption and foreign influence. With his victory, Jefferson suggested, the state had been made safe for the nation.

## COERCION AND THE LIMITS OF HARMONIOUS UNION

Reading the Kentucky Resolutions in context helps us think through the larger questions about union with which this chapter began. Jefferson's theory of union has to be combined with some understanding of his practice, which is less a function of his inconsistencies than of the ambiguous nature of the Union itself as created by the Constitution.

Jefferson's thought on the problem of union first took shape during the Confederation period, during and after the Revolution, and we need to return briefly to that period to make sense of Jefferson's qualified approval of the use of coercion against recalcitrant states. Jefferson spent a good deal of this period out of the country as American minister to France, attempting to gain commercial concessions. But he was continuously frustrated by the inability of Congress to formulate a coherent commercial policy that would make such a treaty attractive to the French (or other European powers, including the English).[137] At first, Jefferson assumed that Congress's power to enter into treaties would do the work of bringing "all the operations of commerce which are protected by [such a treaty's] stipulations ... under their jurisdiction." In other words, if Congress could preemptively enter into treaties with European powers, those treaties would do the work of "bringing all our commerce under the

---

[137] On the volitional nature of consent under the Articles of Confederation, see Christian R. Esh, "'The Sacred Cause of State Rights': Theories of Union and Sovereignty in the Antebellum North" (PhD Dissertation, University of Maryland, 2006), 40–58.

jurisdiction of Congress." Until then, he worried, "the commerce of the United states with those countries not under treaty with us" would remain "under the jurisdiction of each state separately" – precisely why, he told Adams, he desperately wanted to "enter into treaties with the other powers of Europe." For, once under the jurisdiction of Congress, Jefferson argued, "the power of the states to thwart [Congress] by their separate acts ceases."[138]

European powers were rightly skeptical of this back-door method of ensuring that the states would abide by the stipulations of any treaty, particularly given Congress's track record of collecting revenue from the states. The inability of the Confederation government to compel states to provide revenue was, in fact, one of the problems that would lead to the writing of the Constitution. But repeatedly during this period, Jefferson argued that the Confederation simply needed to act on its natural right to collect taxes, using coercive force, if necessary, to do so. "It has been so often said, as to be generally believed," he complained to Edward Carrington in 1787, "that Congress have no power by the confederation to enforce any thing, e.g., contributions of money." But, Jefferson argued, "it was not necessary to give them that power expressly; they have it by the law of nature." Jefferson explained his reasoning: "When two nations make a compact, there results to each a power of compelling the other to execute it."[139] Jefferson had made this point more explicit earlier in his commentary on Jean Nicholas Demeunier's article on the United States in the *Encyclopedie Methodique*. Congress was far from "impotent," he wrote. Whenever "two or more nations enter into compact, it is not usual for them to say what shall be done to the party who infringes it. Decency forbids this, and it is as unnecessary as indecent, because the right of compulsion naturally results to the party injured by the breach." Accordingly, "When any one state in the American Union refuses obedience to the Confederation by which they have bound themselves," he told Demeunier, "the rest have a natural right to compel them to obedience."[140] The essential point, Jefferson told Edmund Randolph, was that the Congress did not lack the "coercive powers" most people imagined "to be wanting." On the contrary, the "law of nature" quite simply gave "one party to an agreement" the authority "to compel the other to performance."[141]

---

[138]	TJ to John Adams, July 7, 1785, in *AJL*, 38–39. Compare TJ to Miami and Delaware nations, January 8, 1803, in *L&B* 16:398: "It is a rule in all countries that what is done by the body of a nation must be submitted to all its members. We have no right to alter, on a partial deputation, what we have settled by treaty with the body of the nations concerned."

[139]	TJ to Edward Carrington, August 4, 1787, in *PTJ* 11:678. Note that the editors of Jefferson's *Papers* have transcribed the word *nations*, which earlier editors rendered *parties*. See, for example, *FE* 5:319.

[140]	Answers to Demeunier's First Queries, January 24, 1786, in *PTJ* 10:19. Jefferson clearly has commercial objectives in mind here that encourage him to present a much more sanguine picture to Europeans who might be concerned about the financial stability of a trading partner. To Americans like Carrington and Monroe, Jefferson is less evasive about his frustration with the apparent inability of Congress to compel compliance of the states.

[141]	TJ to Edmund Randolph, August 3, 1787, in *PTJ* 11:672. Jefferson also seemed not to oppose congressional oversight of new states – even a degree of arbitrary oversight – in the stage of

Moreover, the Confederation was more than a mere "diplomatic assembly," he told John Adams. The "Confederation is part of the law of the land, and superior in authority to the ordinary laws, because it cannot be altered by the legislature of any one state."[142] The Congress had a role to play in maintaining the integrity of the separate states. Jefferson hoped that the Confederation Congress, for example, would hold the line against new states breaking off from old ones; otherwise, "our several states will crumble to atoms by the spirit establishing every little canton into a separate state."[143] Congress, in fact, was, he told Madison, "a good school for our young statesmen" precisely because "it gives them impressions friendly to the federal government instead of those adverse which too often take place in persons confined to the politics of their state."[144] Even before the Revolution itself, Jefferson noted that the instructions of the Virginia Convention binding their delegates to "conform to such resolutions only of the Congress as our deputies assent to" would "totally destroy ... that union of conduct in the several colonies which was *the very purpose of calling a Congress.*"[145]

Jefferson hoped that the states would comply voluntarily or respond to a kind of congressional soft power. Congress, he said, "would probably exercise long patience before they would recur to force."[146] He told George Wythe in 1787 that, "some *peaceable* means should be contrived for the federal head to enforce compliance on the part of the states."[147] His most common suggestion along these lines was the development of a navy that could patrol the coast and take "the deficiency of" any state's "contributions" to the Union out of its "commerce."[148] Bellicose as this sounds, Jefferson believed that such a naval force, he told John Adams, would "arm the Federal head with the safest of all the instruments of coercion over its delinquent members, and prevent it from

temporary government as outlined in the Ordinance of 1784 and the Northwest Ordinance of 1787. On this, see Robert F. Berkhofer, Jr., "Jefferson, the Ordinance of 1784, and the Origins of the American Territorial System," *WMQ* 29 (April 1972), 231–262, at 252–253 and 256–258. Jefferson even proposed (as a milder alternative to Madison's proposed congressional veto over state legislation) the establishment of a federal court of appeals on questions of concern to the Union as a whole. If a state court upheld a state violation of a national treaty, for example, Jefferson said, "an appeal to a federal court sets all to rights" because such a treaty would, of course, "control ... the state law." Jefferson saw this as a corrective to Madison's veto because Congress would be able to "watch and restrain" the proposed federal court, whereas no such oversight would accompany a congressional veto power. Jefferson endorsed such a plan even while acknowledging the potential for federal "encroach[ment] on the jurisdiction of the state courts." See TJ to Madison, June 20, 1787, in *PTJ* 11:480–481.

142  TJ to John Adams, February 23, 1787, in *AJL*, 174.
143  TJ to Richard Henry Lee, July 12, 1785, in *LC*.
144  TJ to Madison, April 25 and 30, 1784, in *ROL* 1:309.
145  "Observations by Jefferson" on the "Instructions of the Virginia Convention," August 1774, in *PTJ* 1:143, emphasis added.
146  TJ "Answers to Demeunier's First Queries," January 24, 1786, in *TJW*, 578.
147  TJ to Wythe, September 16, 1787, in *PTJ* 12:128–129, emphasis added.
148  TJ to Carrington, August 4, 1787, ibid., 11:678. A "single frigate" would do the trick, Jefferson thought: "Compulsion was never so easy as in our case."

using what would be less safe."[149] Earlier, when Adams had argued for negotiation and payment of tribute to the Barbary states, Jefferson argued for war and saw the enhanced coercive power of the Congress as one of the side benefits of outfitting a naval force to fight the pirates in the Mediterranean.[150] To be sure, Jefferson remained concerned about the wisdom of giving such coercive power to the "federal head," which is why he advocated naval rather than military force. Americans, he told James Monroe, had less need to fear a national coercive force "on ... the water" than "any other element," because a naval instrument would be, he told Demeunier, "more easy, less dangerous to liberty, and less likely to produce much bloodshed."[151] And he remained convinced that Congress was right to wait "to the last extremities before it ... execute[d] any of it's powers which are disagreeable."[152]

But apparently he feared the inability of Congress to compel "delinquent members" more than he worried about the negative consequences of arming it with such authority. Recounting these dilemmas in his 1821 *Autobiography*, Jefferson remembered that "the fundamental defect of the Confederation was that Congress was not authorized to act immediately on the people, and by its own officers. Their power was only requisitory, and these requisitions were addressed to the several legislatures, to be by them carried into execution, without other coercion than the moral principle of duty" – a moral claim that was, Jefferson believed, not always sufficient.[153] Jefferson's argument later, and at the time, was not altogether different from Hamilton's 1782 suggestion that "the great danger has been shown" (by the experience of the Confederation) "to be" that the Congress "will not have power enough to defend itself and preserve the Union," and "not," rather, "that it will ever become formidable to the general liberty."[154]

Accordingly, Jefferson told James Monroe: "There never will be money in the treasury till the confederacy shows it's teeth. The states must see the rod; perhaps it must be felt by some one of them. I am persuaded all of them would rejoice to see every one obliged to furnish it's contributions.... Every national citizen must wish to see an effective instrument of coercion."[155] If one party to the compact failed to meet its obligations or broke the compact in some way, in other words, the other party could compel it by force to fulfill its responsibilities. In his clearest statement of this view, Jefferson told Edmund Randolph that "a delinquent State makes itself a party against the rest of the confeder-

---

[149] TJ to John Adams, July 11, 1786, in *AJL*, 142.

[150] Adams to TJ, July 3, 1786, ibid., 138–139.

[151] TJ to Monroe, August 11, 1786, in *PTJ* 10:225; "Answers to Demeunier's First Queries," January 24, 1786, in ibid., 19.

[152] TJ to Edward Carrington, August 4, 1787, in *PTJ* 11:678–679.

[153] *Autobiography*, in *TJW*, 71.

[154] "The Continentalist," No. 6, July 4, 1782, in Freeman, ed., *Hamilton Writings*, 117.

[155] TJ to Monroe, August 11, 1786, in *PTJ* 10:225. Note that Boyd transcribed as *national* what Paul L. Ford rendered *rational*. See *FE* 5:150.

acy" and that the offended party had a natural right to force this delinquent to do its duty.[156]

Jefferson's argument here anticipated Madison's in *Federalist* 40, defending the Philadelphia Convention's decision to make ratification contingent on the approval of nine states only instead of all thirteen. All Americans, Madison suggested, understood "the absurdity of subjecting the fate of twelve states, to the perverseness or corruption of a thirteenth." The demand for unanimity meant that one small state could derail the entire process; a situation, Madison suggested sardonically, in which an "inflexible opposition given by a *majority* of one sixtieth of the people of America," could overrule "the voice of twelve states comprising fifty-nine sixtieths of the people."[157]

By way of contrast, it is worth remembering Jefferson's absolutely inflexible devotion to majority rule as the sine qua non of republican government and his reflexive distrust of minority factions in possession of public authority.[158] As Jefferson told William Eustis in 1809, "the fundamental principle of" the "common government" of "sister States" is "that the will of the majority is to prevail."[159] Because the "executive & legislative authorities are the choice of

---

[156] TJ to Edmund Randolph, August 3, 1787, in *PTJ* 11:672. Jefferson used the same language to describe the later Union in his Kentucky Resolutions: Each state "acceded" to the compact "as a state, and is an integral party, it's co-states forming, as to itself, the other party," *ROL* 2:1080. In light of his earlier arguments about the nature of the compact, the implication, at least, is that Jefferson understood that Kentucky's resolutions would expose it to the legitimate oversight of the rest of the Union – in other words, that Kentucky was making itself vulnerable to the criticism of the other states, or even in jeopardy of coercion by other states (unless those states decide to forebear). Madison later insisted that it was "inseparable from the nature of a compact, that there is as much right on one side to expound it, and to insist on its fulfilment according to that exposition, as there is on the other so to expound it as to furnish a release from it; and that an attempt to annul it by one of the parties may present to the other an option of acquiescing in the annulment, or of preventing it." Madison to Nicholas P. Trist, February 15, 1830, in *Letters and Other Writings* 4:64. Also see Madison to Trist, December 23, 1832, in *WJM* 9:490: "The essential difference between a free government and Governments not free, is that the former is founded in compact, the parties to which are mutually and equally bound by it. Neither of them therefore can have a greater right to break off from the bargain, than the other or others have to hold them to it." Also see Madison to C.E. Haynes, August 27, 1832, in ibid., 483. Harry Jaffa's reading of some of these letters has influenced my understanding of this aspect Jefferson's thought on the compact. See especially, "Partly Federal, Partly National: On the Political Theory of the American Civil War," in Jaffa, *The Conditions of Freedom: Essays in Political Philosophy* (Baltimore and London, 1975), 161–183. See also, Jaffa, *A New Birth of Freedom*, 53.

[157] Madison, *Federalist* 40, in J.R. Pole, ed., *The Federalist* (Indianapolis, 2005), 216. Compare Abraham Lincoln: "By what principle of original right is it that one-fiftieth or one-ninetieth of a great nation, by calling themselves a State, have the right to break up and ruin that nation as a matter of original principle?" "Speech from the Balcony of the Bates House at Indianapolis, Indiana," February 11, 1861, in Roy P. Basler, ed., *The Collected Works of Abraham Lincoln*, 9 volumes (New Brunswick, NJ, 1953–1955), 4:196.

[158] Madison to − − Townsend, October 18, 1831, in *Letters and Other Writings* 4:199; "Notes on Nullification," (1835–1836), in Meyers, ed., *Mind of the Founder*, 428–429, note 3.

[159] TJ to Eustis, January 14, 1809, *FE* 11:86. Jefferson assured Eustis that the "will [of the majority] has been governed by no local interests or jealousies" during the recent crisis of Embargo, which, he said, was "a legitimate and honest exercise of the will and wisdom of the whole."

the nation, & possess the nation's confidence," he told William Duane, "it is the duty of the minority to acquiesce & conform" to "measures ... approved by the majority."[160] Rule of the majority – "absolute acquiescence in" its "decisions" – is "the vital principle of republics," and force is "the vital principle and immediate parent of despotism," Jefferson wrote in his First Inaugural Address.[161] But the two – majority rule and force – were not ultimately incompatible. In fact, there is a sense in which they are inseparable. Failure to acquiesce in the will of the majority, Jefferson continued, is an "appeal to force" that must be addressed in some way by the majority. Or, as he put it to Alexander von Humboldt in 1817, the will of the majority even "of a single vote" must be "as sacred as if unanimous" and that "this law once disregarded, no other remains but that of force, which ends necessarily in military despotism."[162] This is not terribly different from Lincoln's later reading of this problem: "If the minority will not acquiesce, the majority must, or the government must cease. There is no other alternative; for continuing the government, is acquiescence on one side or the other."[163]

Minority rejection of majority will, Jefferson believed, was fundamentally a rejection of the principle of equality on which affectionate union was based. It was a claim for distinction and preference over other equal bodies – states or individuals.[164] As Jefferson told Henry Dearborn in 1815, one problem with Massachusetts was that it overestimated its own significance or value in the Union relative to other States. This could be corrected by a humble appreciation that "her Southern brethren are somewhat on a par with her in wisdom, in information, in patriotism, in bravery, and even in honesty." Massachusetts "would really be great, if she did not think herself the whole."[165]

But minority refusal to acquiesce in the will of the majority was more than merely insulting or arrogant. It also was a recipe for chaos. The pursuance of independent policies by some states jeopardized the security of the others by threatening union with a potential unraveling of the federal system. Lincoln, of course, argued in his First Inaugural Address that "the central idea of secession, is the essence of anarchy," but he was hardly the first to make this connection.[166] The federalist defense of the Constitution, for one example, had rested to a considerable degree on the frightening assertion that the alternative to

---

[160] TJ to William Duane, April 30, 1811, in *PTJ, Retirement Series* 3:592. Ambiguity surrounded discussion of the specific nature of the obligations of the constituent parts of the Union. See Kersh, *Dreams of a More Perfect Union*, 96. But on the general duty of the minority to acquiesce in majority will, Jefferson was remarkably consistent.

[161] "First Inaugural Address," March 4, 1801, in *PTJ* 33:151.

[162] TJ to von Humboldt, June 13, 1817, in *FE* 12:68–69.

[163] Lincoln, "First Inaugural Address," in Basler, ed., *Collected Works* 4:267.

[164] See Onuf, *Jefferson's Empire*, 142; and Andrew C. Lenner, "John Taylor and the Origins of American Federalism," *JER* 17 (Autumn 1997), 422.

[165] TJ to Dearborn, March 17, 1815, in *L&B* 14:289. Also see TJ to Thomas Ritchie, January 21, 1816, *LC*, which criticizes New England for "arrogating an ascendancy over the rest of the Union" (this in matters of religion).

[166] Lincoln, "First Inaugural Address," in Basler, ed., *Collected Works* 4:268.

union was anarchy.[167] But it was Jefferson who perhaps most clearly articulated the view that Lincoln would later echo – that the alternative to union was not peaceable coexistence of neighboring confederacies, but genuine Balkanization *avant la lettre* and unending crisis. If "each state" was "sovereign and independent in all things," he reflected in 1818, they all "would be eternally at war with each other, & would become at length the mere partisans & satellites of the leading powers of Europe."[168] National existence, it followed, depended on union. Secession, then, was madness, he told John Taylor, who had advocated the merger of Virginia and North Carolina into a separate confederacy. Jefferson, counseling patience, outlined the evils of secession:

If on a temporary superiority of the one party, the other is to resort to a scission of the union, no federal government can ever exist. If to rid ourselves of the present rule of Massachusetts & Connecticut we break the union, will the evil stop there? Suppose the N. England States alone cut off, will our natures be changed? Are we not men still to the south of that, & with all the passions of men? Immediately we shall see a Pennsylvania & a Virginia party arise in the residuary confederacy, and the public mind will be distracted with the same party spirit. What a game too will the one party have in their hands by eternally threatening the other that unless they do so & so, they will join their Northern neighbors. If we reduce our union to Virginia & N. Carolina, immediately the conflict will be established between the representatives of these two states, and they will end by breaking into their simple units.... Who can say what would be the evils of a scission and when & where they would end?[169]

Secession – anarchy at home – would weaken America's example to the world that "a government so modeled as to rest continually on the will of the whole society, is a practicable government."[170] More to the point, Jefferson repeatedly

---

[167] On this, see especially Alexander Hamilton's first few contributions to *The Federalist* as well as two remarkable essays by Peter S. Onuf, "Anarchy and the Crisis of the Union," in Ronald Hoffman, Peter Albert, and Herman Belz, eds., *"To Form a More Perfect Union": The Critical Ideas of the Constitution* (Charlottesville, VA, 1992), 272–302; and "State Sovereignty and the Making of the Constitution," in Terence Ball and J.G.A. Pocock, eds., *Conceptual Change and the Constitution* (Lawrence, 1988), 78–98. Also see Richard H. Kohn, "The Constitution and National Security: The Intent of the Framers," in Richard H. Kohn, ed., *The United States Military Under the Constitution of the United States, 1789–1989* (New York, 1991), 64–65; and David C. Hendrickson, *Peace Pact.* Of course, for anti-Federalists, disunion was less a threat than that posed by a consolidated national government that would inevitably, they believed, favor one state or region over others. Anti-Federalists turned out to be men of great faith – in the propensity of republics to coexist in harmony in the absence of coercion – after all. But note that even Federalists generally described the proposed system as a federal one rather than a consolidated national government, relying on interest rather than force to hold the states together. See Hendrickson, *Peace Pact,* 12–13.

[168] *The Anas,* February 4, 1818, in *FE* 1:167.

[169] TJ to Taylor, June 4, 1798, in *PTJ* 30:388–389. Also see TJ to James Ogilvie, August 4, 1811, in *L&B* 8:70–71. As far as I have seen, Jefferson never once suggested that a state could peaceably leave the Union in opposition to the will of its sister states, a stance even the staunchest defenders of states rights rejected prior to the 1830s. See, for example, Thomas Ritchie, Richmond *Enquirer,* November 1, 1814.

[170] TJ to Richard Rush, October 20, 1820, *L&B* 15:283–284. Jefferson went on to predict that any separation of states would be "for a short term only; two or three years' trial will bring

suggested, only union would ensure "internal peace, and a political system of our own, independent of that of Europe."[171] The very existence of the independent nation and the republicanism it represented, then, rested in large part on union, and Jefferson was under no illusions about "the miseries which would follow a separation of the States." Without union, in short, America would become Europe, imitating its "eternal and wasting wars" and "the abject oppression and degradation to which" its people were subject.[172]

Jefferson's argument about the natural right of coercion in a compact largely took shape during the Confederation period. But it seems clear that these reflections shaped his view of the Union created by the Constitution and provide the framework within which we should consider his views of that Union. Many years later, in 1818, Jefferson amended his earlier assertions, classifying the Articles of Confederation with those mere "treaties of alliance" that tend to be "insufficient" to "enforce compliance with their mutual stipulations." This concession – that in spite of the natural right of parties to a compact or the dictates of international law, the Confederation had, in fact, proven unable to compel the obligations of delinquent states and for all practical purposes left "each state to become sovereign & independent in all things" – implies a contrast with the Federal Constitution and suggests that, in Jefferson's view, the later compact did in fact represent a transformation in the nature of the relationship between the states and granted the new Union a kind of coercive power beyond that which he had claimed for the Articles.[173]

Jefferson was explicit about the transfer of sovereignty from states to the general government in his 1790 opinion on Georgia's land grants to the Yazoo companies. Any society "taking possession of a vacant country" had a natural right to occupy and thus "appropriate to themselves" land that had been "common." If that land was not "altogether vacant," but was "thinly occupied by another nation" the right of the indigenous people "forms an exception to that of the new-comers." But the newcomers did have the "right of preemption," which essentially meant that they could purchase the right from the Indians or acquire it by war; "for even war," Jefferson said, "may sometimes give a just title." During the Confederation period, when Georgia was sovereign in this respect, Georgia had, by the "law of nations," the means to acquire and grant native land. But by the Constitution, Jefferson argued, they had "completely ceded both [of the means of acquisition] to the general government." Consequently, Georgia could never "convey" to another (the Yazoo companies) "what she had not herself, that is, the means of acquiring. For these they must come to the general government, in whose hands," Jefferson insisted, such means had "been wisely deposited for the purposes both of peace

them back, like quarrelling lovers to renewed embraces, and increased affections. The experiment of separation would soon prove to both that they had mutually miscalculated their best interests."

[171] *The Anas*, February 4, 1818, in *FE* 1:167.
[172] TJ to James Ogilvie, August 4, 1811, in *L&B* 13:70.
[173] *The Anas*, February 4, 1818, in *FE* 1:167.

and justice," precisely why he believed that "the right of the general government" was, in this case, "to be maintained."[174] Clearly, with the Constitution, relations between the states and the national government had been altered in significant ways.

To be sure, Jefferson's ideal was harmonious union based on affection and interest; the necessity of coercion indicated a failure on some level of this ideal. For this reason, Jefferson suggested that "respect and friendship should ... mark the conduct of the general towards the particular governments" and "time and colour given them to tread back their steps, before coercion is held up to their view."[175] But the very suggestion of "coercion" here indicates the general government's right to implement it, in Jefferson's view, if such generous and delicate handling of the passions of states was not effective.

Again, this is not to question that Jefferson's entire project recoiled at the thought of coercion of individuals, states, or nations. As he told George III in the *Summary View*, "force cannot give right," and in his own First Inaugural Address he called force "the vital principle and immediate parent of despotism."[176] After the Revolution, Jefferson told Madison that new states in the West would remain united with the original union only as the Confederation managed "their interests honestly and for their own good.... A forced connection is neither our interest nor within our power."[177] This sensibility also informed Jefferson's view of relations between individuals, including marriage partners. It would be "cruel," he once noted in a set of reflections on divorce, "to continue by violence an union made at first by mutual love, but now dissolved by hatred." "No partnership," he suggested, "can oblige continuance in contradiction to it's end and design."[178] Even war with foreign nations was to be a last resort: "Those peaceable coercions which are in the power of every nation, if undertaken in concert and in time of peace, are more likely [than force] to produce the desired effect."[179]

Perhaps the clearest statement of Jefferson's horror of coercion comes in his Statute of Religious Freedom:

All attempts to influence [the human mind] by temporal punishments, or burthens, or by civil incapacitations, tend only to beget habits of hypocrisy and meanness, and are a departure from the plan of the holy author of our religion, who being lord both of body and

---

[174] "Opinion on Certain Georgia Land Grants," May 3, 1790, in *PTJ* 16:407.

[175] Ibid., 408. Consider the approach Jefferson advocates here with his view of the Missouri Compromise as described in Onuf, "Every Generation Is an 'Independant Nation': Colonization, Miscegenation, and the Fate of Jefferson's Children," *WMQ*, 57 (January 2000), 153–170; and Onuf, *Jefferson's Empire*, ch. 4.

[176] *Summary View*, in *PTJ* 1:134 (first quotation); "First Inaugural Address," in ibid., 33:151 (second quotation).

[177] TJ to Madison, December 16, 1786, in *ROL* 1:458.

[178] Frank L. Dewey, "Thomas Jefferson's Notes on Divorce," *WMQ* 39 (January 1982), 212–233, quotes at 216 and 218. Dewey suggests that Jefferson drafted these notes between May 1771 and December 1772.

[179] TJ to Robert R. Livingston, September 9, 1801, in *L&B* 10:281–282. On this point also see Reginald Stuart, *The Half-Way Pacifist: Thomas Jefferson's View of War* (Toronto, 1979).

mind, yet chose not to propagate it by coercions on either, as was in his Almighty power to do, but to exalt it by its influence on reason alone.[180]

Confirming the general ideal, late in life, Jefferson wrote Richard Rush in 1820: "A government of reason is better than one of force."[181]

It is no simplistic dismissal of his ideal, however, to suggest that Jefferson was well aware that claims to sovereignty must at some point be backed up, by force, if necessary – that, as James Sheehan has put it recently: "States can survive only as long as they retain the ability to keep on making claims."[182] As Governor of Virginia, for example, Jefferson expressed his associationist ideal – "it is inconsistent with the spirit of our Laws and Constitution to force tender consciences" – in the midst of a proclamation whose very purpose was to compel citizens of Virginia to choose sides in the war and fulfill "the duties they owe to their Country while remaining in it."[183] Suggestive, too, are distinctions Jefferson made between "a separate state," "a county of a state," and "*a mere voluntary association*, as those of the quakers, Dunkars, Menonists." Only the latter did Jefferson explicitly shield from coercion: "If merely a voluntary association, the submission of it's members will be merely voluntary also; as no act of coercion would be permitted by the general law." A county, on the other hand, "must be subject to those [laws] of the state of which it is a part." States presumably, by implication, would also maintain an obligation to the Union, enforceable by violence, if it came to that.[184] Coercion, then, was less a violation of Jefferson's concept of union than a natural, although undesirable, part of it.[185]

Ultimately, as David Hendrickson has noted in another context, the "proposition that America could not [or should not] be governed by force" was for Jefferson no proof "that it could be governed *without* force."[186] In other words, force, perhaps paradoxically, was latent in the very concept of union. In any

---

[180] Jefferson's draft "Bill for Establishing Religious Freedom," in *TJW*, 346.

[181] TJ to Rush, October 20, 1820, *L&B* 15:284. This letter, nevertheless, does display Jefferson's full awareness of the tensions between this ideal and the potential need for coercion. Gerald Stourzh offers a concise and compelling statement of the tension between this kind of ideal – government by reason, cooperation, and love rather than force – and the unfortunate necessity of coercion. See *Benjamin Franklin and American Foreign Policy*, 2nd ed. (Chicago, 1969), 1.

[182] James J. Sheehan, "The Problem of Sovereignty in European History," *AHR* 111 (February 2006), 3.

[183] "Proclamation Concerning Paroles, by His Excellency, Thomas Jefferson, Esqr., Governor of the Commonwealth of Virginia," January 19, 1781, in *PTJ* 4:403–404.

[184] TJ to William Lee, January 16, 1817, *L&B* 15:101–102.

[185] Jefferson understood implicitly what Reinhold Niebuhr later criticized interwar liberals for forgetting: "While no state can maintain its unity purely by coercion neither can it preserve itself without coercion." This "coercive factor" may remain latent in societies with an institutional commitment to justice, so that it "becomes apparent only in moments of crisis," but, for all that, coercion is "never absent." Reinhold Niebuhr, *Moral Man and Immoral Society: A Study in Ethics and Politics* (Louisville, KY, 2001), 3–4.

[186] From Hendrickson's description of Edmund Burke's opposition to Britain's prosecution of the American Revolution. *Peace Pact*, 91.

case, the received wisdom that Jefferson simply refused to acknowledge any tension between the spiritual appeal of union and the potential necessity of coercion is unfounded.[187] Even marriage, which Jefferson was loath to continue by force, was, he admitted, more complicated than it first had seemed. "When 2 have become joint traders for life," he noted by way of illustration, "neither can take his stock out without consent of other." Even if "both consent," Jefferson suggested, it would be "impolitic to allow divorce on consent of parties." If the meaning of "impolitic" here is somewhat ambiguous, the clear implication is that there is something problematic or troubling about allowing divorce even by mutual consent.[188] Compacts between nations, were likewise "obligatory on them by the same moral law which obliges individuals to observe their compacts." Circumstances may "excuse … non-performance" of obligations, when, for example, the fulfillment "becomes impossible" or "self-destructive," in which case "the law of self-preservation overrules the laws of obligation to others." But nothing in the law of Nature or of Nations permitted annulment of obligations merely because their performance becomes "dangerous, useless, or disagreeable." To be sure, Jefferson acknowledged, violation of compact may become permissible "under certain degrees of *danger*," but, such danger, Jefferson argued, "must be imminent, & the degree great." Otherwise, the "obligation is not suspended." It was never "the *possibility of danger*, which absolves a party from his contract: for that possibility always exists, & in every case." The failure of one nation to comply with compact without "just cause or compensation" was, in fact, Jefferson suggested, "a cause of war."[189]

Much has been made of Jefferson's embrace of Shays's Rebellion, but Jefferson (comfortably distant in France) celebrated only the vigilance and public spiritedness of the American people. As we have seen, he never endorsed the "motives" or methods of the insurgents. These, he admitted, were "founded in ignorance"[190] and "produced acts absolutely unjustifiable."[191] Significantly, Jefferson never once suggested that Massachusetts was wrong to suppress the rebellion. On the contrary, his most frequent statement about Shays's,

---

[187] See, for example, Nagel, *One Nation Indivisible*, 98.

[188] Dewey, "Thomas Jefferson's Notes on Divorce," 218. Compare this statement with Lincoln's argument that true "lovers of the Union" understood that preservation of the Union might require "coercion or invasion" of a state. Otherwise, "the means for the preservation of the Union" would be "of a very thin and airy character" and "the Union, as a family relation," Lincoln suggested, "would not be anything like a regular marriage at all, but only as a sort of free-love arrangement … to be maintained on what that sect calls passionate attraction," Speech at Indianapolis, Indiana, February 11, 1861, in Basler, ed., *Collected Works* 4:195. Contrast with John Quincy Adams to William Vans Murray, April 7, 1801 (in the context of concern that Jefferson and Burr might "mean to dissolve the Union"): "I love the Union as I love my wife. But if my wife would ask and insist upon a separation, she should have it, though it broke my heart," in Worthington Chauncey Ford, ed., *Writings of John Quincy Adams*, 7 vols. (New York, 1913) 2:525–526.

[189] Opinion on the French Treaties, April 28, 1793, in *TJW*, 422–434.

[190] TJ to William Stephens Smith, November 13, 1787, in *PTJ* 12:356.

[191] TJ to James Madison, January 30, 1787, in ibid., 11:92.

outside of the often-cited celebration of the American "spirit of resistance to government"[192] and "general attention to the public affairs," was a hope that the government would be "mild in [its] punishment of rebellions" – not that the rebellions would succeed.[193] The only sure "remedy" for such turbulence was to "reclaim" the people by "enlightening them,"[194] disabusing them of false information, "set[ting] them right as to facts, pardon[ing] and pacify[ing] them."[195] To be sure, these were not the "virgorus [sic] measures to quell and suppress" Shays's that Abigail Adams endorsed, but they were a way of carefully defusing a misguided and ignorant resistance to civil government in a way that would not also crush the spiritedness Jefferson valued.[196]

Jefferson's endorsement of the people's attention to public affairs, on both sides of the issue, was never a suggestion that the appropriate government should not take action to pacify rebellion. Patience, transparency, and education were the weapons Jefferson preferred to Abigail Adams's "broadsword" and "Light horse," but both were motivated by desire to quell discontent.[197] So Jefferson's endorsement of the "spirit of resistance" in this case is not terribly helpful in predicting what Jefferson might do in the face of a more serious challenge to republican institutions or to the Union, which he never imagined under existential threat by Shays's Rebellion.

In the Kentucky Resolutions, Jefferson called the national government a "creature of the compact" – not an original party to it. There is a tendency on the part of historians to associate this compact theory of the Constitution, which Jefferson articulated, with a kind of "take it or leave it" view of the Union. This tendency is not altogether misplaced. Subsequent conflicts would taint the "states' rights" doctrine with the stain of disunion.[198] But, as Jefferson told William Eustis in 1809, the Union – "the spirit of concord with her sister States" – had "placed us under that national government, which constitutes the safety of every part, by uniting for its protection the powers of the whole." The national government, in other words, might have been the "creature of the compact," but it was an umbrella of protection for that very compact, emerging out of the Union and remaining an indispensable part of it, rather than a separate entity to be ignored or discarded at pleasure. Jefferson suggested, in

---

[192] TJ to Abigail Adams, February 22, 1787, in ibid., 174.
[193] TJ to James Madison, January 30, 1787, in ibid., 92–93.
[194] TJ to Edward Carrington, January 16, 1787, in ibid., 11:49.
[195] TJ to William Stephens Smith, November 13, 1787, in ibid., 12:356.
[196] Abigail Adams to TJ, January 29, 1787, in ibid., 11:86.
[197] ibid., 87.
[198] In 1811, for example, Massachusetts Federalist Josiah Quincy asked the House, "Is there a moral principle of public law better settled, or more conformable to the plainest suggestions of reason, than that the violation of a contract by one of the parties may be considered as exempting the other from its obligations?" For Quincy, disunion was less problematic than violation of minority interests. Union "grows out of the affections," and when those affections wane, the Union has no moral value that can compel allegiance. Edmund Quincy, *Life of Josiah Quincy of Massachusetts* (Boston, 1868), 210, 212.

fact, that the national government was the instrument through which the states were to act in their relations with one another.[199]

In any case, there is nothing inherent in the compact theory or in strict construction of the constitution that precludes vigorous enforcement of federal law or an energetic national government. On the contrary, it is precisely as a function of such theory or constitutional construction that Jefferson (and later Jackson) prosecuted federal power to its fullest scope – because he believed that within its clearly prescribed sphere, the federal government should energetically do its duty. Historians have tended to think of strict construction or compact theory as limiting what government can do. Of course, this is an important function of American constitutionalism, and the warmest advocates of compact theory feared unbridled central power most. Strict construction was designed above all to check national consolidation.[200] But the Constitution also grants considerable energy to government within more or less well-defined limits.[201] In Jefferson's hands, the compact theory and strict construction also legitimated those powers that were granted to the national government.[202]

State limitation or encroachment on the legitimately prescribed power of the national government, then, would be just as much a violation of the Constitution as national government usurpation of powers granted by the Constitution to the states. Accordingly, when Joseph C. Cabell asked Jefferson in 1814 "whether States can add any qualifications to those which the Constitution has prescribed for their members of Congress," Jefferson's reflexive answer was "no." For a state to "add new qualifications to those of the Constitution, would be as much an alteration as to detract from them."[203]

---

[199] TJ to Doctor William Eustis, January 14, 1809, *FE* 11:84. Also see Jefferson's Answers to Demeunier's First Queries, January 24, 1786, *PTJ* 10:19, in which Jefferson argues that when a delinquent state makes itself an enemy of its sister states, the other states act on it through the institution of Congress.

[200] This is true of certain Virginia theorists like John Taylor, for whom "the law of nations applied ... not as a prop for the federal government but as an impediment to its actions." See Lenner, "John Taylor and American Federalism," 412.

[201] See the helpful discussion in Richard B. Bernstein, "*The Federalist* on Energetic Government, 1787–1788," in Stephen L. Schechter, ed., *Roots of the Republic: American Founding Documents Interpreted* (Madison, 1990), 335–354; and in Daniel Farber, *Lincoln's Constitution* (Chicago, 2003), 33–44. Also see Kohn, "The Constitution and National Security," 74. On Jackson's handling of the nullification crisis, see Richard B. Latner, "The Nullification Crisis and Republican Subversion," *JSH* 43 (February 1977), 19–38. On Jefferson's federalism, see David N. Mayer, "'Necessary and Proper': West Point and Jefferson's Constitutionalism," in Robert M.S. McDonald, ed., *Thomas Jefferson's Military Academy: Founding West Point* (Charlottesville, 2004), 57–58, 60. A nuanced and compelling case for the overall consistency of Jefferson's constitutionalism (theory and practice) is Mayer, *The Constitutional Thought of Thomas Jefferson* (Charlottesville, 1994), esp. 185–256.

[202] Even Taylor, for example, "supported assertion of federal power under limited and carefully defined circumstances," Lenner, "John Taylor and American Federalism," 415.

[203] TJ to Joseph C. Cabell, January 31, 1814, in *L&B* 14:82–84. Jefferson went on to reconsider his position, eventually concluding that states likely could add such qualifications not explicitly reserved to the nation by the Constitution, but the point rests that each sphere had its rightful

Jefferson's First Inaugural Address, rightly remembered as a celebration of limited government, illustrates this point as well as any document in the Jefferson archive. Here, Jefferson laid out what he considered to be "the essential principles of our government," one of which was "the support of the state governments in all their rights, as the most competent administrations for our domestic concerns and the surest bulwarks against anti-republican tendencies."[204] Another of Jefferson's "essential principles" was "the preservation of the General government in its whole constitutional vigor, as the sheet anchor of our peace at home, and safety abroad."[205] Strict construction of a Jeffersonian variety, then, did limit federal power, but it also realized the full scope of federal power within those limits strictly prescribed. This is why Jefferson and Jackson (and Madison for that matter) found it necessary to call for constitutional amendments for national programs of internal improvements, on the one hand, but remained unafraid to enforce the embargo or squash nullification, on the other. All were committed to states' rights, to strict construction, and to limited government, but all nevertheless vigorously enforced federal law and even expanded federal power in certain areas. It would be simplistic to dismiss such a stance as contradictory or hypocritical.

As Jefferson explained in a fascinating letter from early in 1798, the state governments and the central government were "like the planets revolving round their common Sun, acting & acted upon according to their respective weights & distances." In its ideal form, Jefferson believed, such a system would "produce that beautiful equilibrium on which our Constitution is founded" and would provide the world an example of a government ordered to "a degree of perfection unexampled but in the planetary system itself." The goal of "the enlightened statesman" would be "to preserve the weight & influence of every part, as too much given to any member of it would destroy the general equilibrium." The point here, as it seems to have been in the First Inaugural Address, was that each of the "planets" has its appropriate "weight & influence" and to grant too much of either to "any member" would in fact wreck the system. This was a prescription for both limits and energy within the prescribed spheres.[206]

---

grant of power that was not to be violated and that Jefferson took *both* seriously. In cases like these, Jefferson reminded Cabell, "caution requires us not to be too confident, and that we admit this to be one of the doubtful questions on which honest men may differ with the purest motives." In fact, he said, in cases "where the line of demarcation between the powers of the General and the State governments was doubtful or indistinctly drawn, it would be prudent and praiseworthy in both parties never to approach it but under the most urgent necessity."

[204] Jefferson, "First Inaugural Address," in *PTJ* 33:150. Compare with Hamilton's assertion of a similar point in *Federalist* 28: "It may safely be received as an axiom in our political system, that the state governments will in all possible contingencies afford complete security against invasions of the public liberty by the national authority," in Pole, ed., *The Federalist*, 150.

[205] Jefferson, "First Inaugural Address," in *PTJ* 33:150.

[206] TJ to Peregrine Fitzhugh, February 23, 1798, in *PTJ* 30:130. Jefferson's metaphor diagrams Madison's claim in *Federalist* 39 that the U.S. Constitution was "neither wholly *national*, nor wholly *federal*" but "a composition of both." See Pole, ed., *The Federalist*, 211. The planetary metaphor for the federal system seems to have first been used by John Dickenson (as well as

Interestingly, few understood Jefferson's orientation better than Alexander Hamilton. In the *Federalist*, Hamilton had pointed out that force was a necessary component of the new national government, arguing that "the idea of governing at all times by the simple force of law ... has no place but in the reveries of those political doctors, whose sagacity disdains the admonitions of experimental instruction."[207] But Jefferson, Hamilton knew, was not nearly such a "wavering" or "whimsical" dreamer as Federalist pamphlet literature suggested.[208] Hamilton was quick to separate campaign rhetoric from reality during the election crisis of 1801, urging fellow Federalists to understand that Jefferson was far from "an enemy to the power of the Executive" and predicting, rightly it would turn out, that Jefferson would prove himself (as he had in the past) in favor of "a large construction of the Executive authority and not backward to act upon it in cases which coincided with his views."[209] Jefferson largely fulfilled Hamilton's prophecy, leading many historians from Jefferson's day to our own to construe his presidency as a fundamental contradiction. But, as Hamilton himself understood, the paradox was more apparent than real.

Jefferson, Hamilton knew, was not the Peter Pan of much current historical writing, unable to grow up and translate his adolescent longing "for a world in which all behavior was voluntary and therefore all coercion unnecessary" into mature and effective governance.[210] As his presidential career

James Wilson and Madison) in the Federal Convention. See James Madison, *Notes of Debates in the Federal Convention of 1787* (New York, 1987), 84, 88–89.

[207] Hamilton, *Federalist* 28, in Pole, ed., *The Federalist*, 148.

[208] For important reflections on this literature, see Jeffrey L. Pasley, "Politics and the Misadventures of Thomas Jefferson's Modern Reputation: A Review Essay," *JSH* 72 (November 2006), 871–908, esp., 879–881.

[209] Hamilton to James A. Bayard, January 16, 1801, in *PAH* 25:319–320. Hamilton's suggestion ran counter to the concern of many other Federalists, that Jefferson would dismantle executive authority if elected and, in the words of John Marshall, "embody himself in the House of Representatives," thus "weakening the office of the President" (a claim Hamilton explicitly rejected). Marshall quoted in Gary J. Schmitt, "Thomas Jefferson and the Presidency," in Thomas Cronin, ed., *Inventing the American Presidency* (Lawrence, 1989), 326–346, at 329. Hamilton's perspicacious view also seems to counter Jefferson's own admission that he was "not a friend to a very energetic government," TJ to Madison, December 20, 1787, in *ROL* 1:514. Close inspection of this letter, however, reveals that Jefferson was referring to a government without clear boundaries, objecting particularly to the lack of a bill of rights and to the lack of term limits for the executive in the proposed Constitution that Madison had outlined for him. Nothing in this traditionally expressed Whig view precludes energetic government *within a clearly defined sphere of power* – precisely how Jefferson understood the system the Constitution enacted. Indeed, Jefferson's primary objection to the Sedition Act of 1798 was that the national legislature had, with this act, taken on itself powers to criminalize printing, which the Constitution had "expressly" taken "out of their coercion" – powers outside its rightful sphere. TJ to Madison, June 7, 1798, in ibid., 2:1056.

[210] Joseph J. Ellis, *American Sphinx: The Character of Thomas Jefferson* (New York, 1996), 59. For similar reflections on Jefferson's preference for what Ellis calls "a wholly voluntary world," see ibid., 120, 136. Jefferson could be quite supportive of energetic government that pursued ends he believed were warranted. Convinced that Madison's tonnage bill (which discriminated against British trade) would pass the House, for example, Jefferson happily described it as "a

illustrates, Jefferson was hardly under the illusion that union could survive
without energy in government. His own rhetoric describing the Revolution as
a destruction of artificial barriers to "consensual ties of affection, principle, and
common interest" often made union seem natural and spontaneous.[211] But this
rhetoric tended to mask the "critical role of the state in the progress of settlement and development," and Jefferson's own sense that "the very idea of the
nation implies enormous force."[212] As Peter Onuf has put it, "the paradox of
expansion in Jeffersonian America was that a supposedly spontaneous, natural
process depended so crucially on the exercise of state power."[213] If construction
and maintenance of the republican legacy embodied in union required so much
governance, we could hardly expect Jefferson to meet threats to union with
philosophical hand-wringing.

And he did not. During the crisis that unfolded during the Burr Conspiracy
(which Walter LaFeber calls "the last important attempt to create an independent empire in the North American West"[214]), Jefferson consulted Madison
about whether the executive had the authority to use regular troops in cases
of domestic insurrection.[215] When Madison told him that he did not, Jefferson
promptly drafted a remedial bill "authorizing the employment of the land and
naval forces of the US in cases of insurrection" in all cases where the president is authorized to use militia "to suppress such insurrection or to cause the
laws to be duly executed."[216] To be sure, Jefferson hoped that local authorities
would suppress the plot and counted on the loyalty and republicanism of the
inhabitants of the western states. And after the plot failed, the lesson Jefferson
took from it was that government was strongest when "every man feels himself a part" of it – the message of the First Inaugural Address. It proved, too,
"the importance of preserving to the State authorities all that vigor which the
Constitution foresaw would be necessary, not only for their own safety, but
for that of the whole." The "hand of the people" had "given the mortal blow

> mark of energy in our government, in a case where I believe it cannot be parried," TJ to Thomas
> Mann Randolph, May 30, 1790, *PTJ* 16:450. Jefferson's endorsement of national "energy" to
> characterize a measure that was both decidedly un-Hamiltonian and opposed to the short-
> term interests of southern planters seems ironic only because of a historiography that tends to
> equate energy with Hamilton and the opposite with Jefferson.

[211] Peter S. Onuf, "Thomas Jefferson, Federalist," in Peter S. Onuf, *The Mind of Thomas Jefferson*
(Charlottesville, 2007), 94.

[212] Peter S. Onuf, "The Revolution of 1803," in ibid., 107.

[213] Peter S. Onuf, "Thomas Jefferson and the Expanding Union," ibid., 116.

[214] Walter LaFeber, "Jefferson and an American Foreign Policy," in Onuf, ed., *Jeffersonian Legacies*
(Charlottesville, 1993), 382.

[215] See Dumas Malone, *Jefferson the President: Second Term, 1805–1809* (Boston, 1974), 253.

[216] TJ to John Dawson, December 19, 1806, *LC*. Jefferson then told Dawson to rewrite the bill
and burn the letter because he was "very unwilling to meddle personally with the [debaits?] or
the proceedings of the legislature" (although, of course, he was doing just that here!). Jefferson
also suggested such a bill in his Sixth Annual Message to Congress, December 2, 1806, in *TJW*
526–527. The Ninth Congress passed this bill in March of 1807 under the title: "An Act authorizing the employment of the land and naval forces of the United States, in cases of insurrections," *Annals of Congress*, 9th Cong., 2 Sess., 1286 (March 3, 1807).

to a conspiracy which, in other countries, would have called for an appeal to armies."[217] Federal force, then, might seem unnecessary in a union of such harmony and affection.[218]

But if the people of Ohio and Kentucky and Louisiana did not come through, Jefferson was prepared for Burr. In his Sixth Annual Message, Jefferson, as if echoing Hamilton, reminded Congress that a benign government directed by the will of the people made "insurrection or enterprise on the public peace or authority" nearly unimaginable. Nevertheless, Jefferson remained unwilling to trust such "moral restraints only" and praised the wisdom of laws that "provided punishments for these crimes when committed." But even this seemed insufficient to deal with a conspiracy of such magnitude. Accordingly, Jefferson encouraged Congress to pass laws giving him the power to prevent even the "commission" of such crimes. As much as Jefferson trusted the magnetism of affection and interest to hold the Union together, then, he nevertheless considered a kind of preemptive suppression of "insurrection" a legitimate function of the national government.[219]

The letters he sent reflecting on the conspiracy likewise suggest his willingness to fall back on federal force if necessary. Jefferson told Charles Clay that Burr's plans were "effectually crippled by the activity of Ohio" but that "if he is able to descend the river with any means we are sufficiently prepared at New Orleans."[220] In addition to proving the strength of the government in the affections of the people, the Burr conspiracy also proved a "wholesome lesson too to our citizens, of the necessary obedience to their government."[221] So the crushing of the conspiracy turned out to be both evidence of the people's attachment to the government and a warning that the people had better obey it; evidence both of local ability to crush threats to public safety and of the willingness of the federal government to step in if states failed in their duty.

The same dual lesson applied to Jefferson's enforcement of the embargo, which precipitated not only widespread violation of federal law but also called for secession from the Union among some Massachusetts leaders.[222] Throughout the crisis, Jefferson remained committed to enforcement of federal law. He continued to rely on local enforcement – even when proclaiming the Lake Champlain region to be in a state of insurrection, for example, Jefferson initially encouraged the governor of New York to use state militia to put it

---

[217] TJ to Governor Edward Tiffin of Ohio, February 2, 1807, in *L&B* 11:146–147.

[218] Largely the message of TJ to Lafayette, July 14, 1807, in ibid., 278–279, and to DuPont de Nemours, July 14, 1807, ibid., 274–276. For important reflections on the lessons Jefferson drew from the Burr Conspiracy, emphasizing the benign nature of the government's response, see Onuf, *Jefferson's Empire*, 133–135.

[219] Sixth Annual Message, December 2, 1806, in *TJW*, 526–527.

[220] TJ to Rev. Charles Clay, January 11, 1807, *FE* 10:339.

[221] TJ to Governor W.C.C. Claiborne, February 3, 1807, in *L&B* 11:150–151.

[222] In addition to the appropriate pages in Malone, *Jefferson the President: Second Term* (especially 583–657) and Peterson, *Thomas Jefferson and the New Nation*, see especially Gannon, "Calculating the Value of the Union," 67–122.

down.[223] And, as he did during the Burr crisis, Jefferson counted on republican majorities to suppress the insurgencies of minorities, hoping, for example, that Republicans (and loyal Federalists) in Massachusetts would rally against "mob law" and "crush it in embryo."[224] But Jefferson eventually sent regulars to the Canadian border in New York and told his Secretary of War that "on the first symptom of an open opposition to the laws by force" in Massachusetts, he should "fly to the scene" and "take direction of the public authority on the spot."[225] He expected the people to rally in support of the "public authority."[226] But he also thought that it might prove necessary at some point to institute martial law in Boston and crush the opposition by use of the regular army.[227] And when Albert Gallatin, Jefferson's secretary of the Treasury (who was responsible for much of the enforcement), suggested that the success of the embargo would demand granting the president "the most arbitrary powers," Jefferson agreed: Congress, he said, "should legalize all *means* which may be necessary to obtain its *end*."[228]

As Jefferson told Massachusetts Governor James Sullivan, he trusted the "character" of the good people of his state to suppress violations of the embargo,

---

[223] Peterson, *Thomas Jefferson and the New Nation*, 891. See Jefferson's Proclamation, April 19, 1808, *LC*, in which he "require[d] and command[ed] all officers having authority civil or military, and all other persons civil or military who shall be found within the vicinage of such insurrections ... by all the means in their power by force of arms or otherwise to quell and subdue such insurrections ..."

[224] TJ to Gallatin, August 19, 1808, in *L&B* 12:138. Among many other expressions of this sentiment, see the later letter Jefferson sent Horatio G. Spafford, March 17, 1814, ibid., 14:120: "I see our safety in the extent of our confederacy, and in the probability that in the proportion of that the sound parts will always be sufficient to crush local poisons."

[225] TJ to Henry Dearborn, August 9, 1808, in *L&B* 12:119 (first and second quotations); TJ to Gallatin, August 19, 1808, in ibid., 138 (third quotation). These soldiers were part of an expansion of 6,000 troops that Jefferson had requested and Congress had granted. On the debate surrounding this expansion (and with predictably gleeful attention to the irony), see Adams, *History of the United States in the Administrations of Thomas Jefferson*, 1071–1077.

[226] TJ to Gallatin, August 19, 1808, in *L&B* 12:137–138; and to Robert Smith, August 9, 1808, *LC*. Jerry M. Cooper points out that "no president has imposed martial law when interposing force in a civil disorder during peacetime," so that Jefferson's suggestion here would have been, if enacted, more expansive than Washington's suppression of the Whiskey Rebellion. See Cooper, "Federal Military Intervention in Domestic Disorders," in Kohn, ed., *The United States Military Under the Constitution*, 133. On Jefferson's views of the latter crisis, see Jefferson to Madison, December 28, 1794 in *ROL* 2:867–868, which condemns the response as incommensurate with the cause. Jefferson does not argue that Washington would not have been justified in his action had the Whiskey Rebels participated in "anything more than riotous" behavior "according to definitions of the law." It is worth noting that Jefferson's (and Madison's) main concern was Washington's partisan effort to blame the "democratic societies" for the "rebellion" – an association both denied – and thus crack down on "freedom of discussion, the freedom of writing, printing and publishing." In other words, Jefferson's reaction was not an blanket condemnation of the national use of force in genuine cases of insurrection.

[227] TJ to Henry Dearborn, August 9, 1808, in *L&B* 12:119; and TJ to the Secretary of the Navy, August 9, 1808, ibid., 121.

[228] Gallatin to TJ, July 29, 1808, in Henry Adams, ed., *The Writings of Albert Gallatin*, 3 vols. (Philadelphia, 1879), 1:399; TJ to Gallatin, August 11, 1808, in *FE* 11:41.

but the laws passed "by the general government" authorized the president "to have the embargo strictly observed, for the general good; and we are sworn to execute the laws."[229] In fact, it was the sacrifice of the people – their own devotion to the laws – that invigorated Jefferson's eagerness to enforce those laws. As he put it to South Carolina Governor Charles Pinckney: "Our good citizens having submitted to such sacrifices under the present experiment, I am determined to exert every power the law has vested in me for its rigorous fulfillment."[230]

Jefferson even declared himself willing to go beyond the law, claiming executive prerogative to preserve the nation. "The feelings of human nature revolt," Jefferson wrote in 1774, "against the supposition of a state so situated as that it may not in any emergency provide against dangers which perhaps threaten immediate ruin."[231] "Self-preservation is paramount to all law," he told a correspondent in 1808. "There are extreme cases where the laws become inadequate even to their own preservation."[232] In these cases, he later elaborated, those "who accept of great charges" will "risk themselves on great occasions, when the safety of the nation, or some of it's very high interests are at stake."[233] This claim to an executive prerogative outside of the Constitution forces the president, somewhat paradoxically, to make himself vulnerable to the people even as he goes beyond their explicit grant of authority – to "throw himself," as Jefferson put it, "on the justice of his country" for the purposes of national self-preservation.[234] State defiance of legitimate national authority would require

[229] TJ to Governor James Sullivan, August 12, 1808, in *L&B* 12:129. This appeal to his oath of office seems to anticipate Lincoln's similar argument during the secession crisis: "*You* have no oath registered in Heaven to destroy the government, while *I* shall have the most solemn one to 'preserve, protect and defend' it." "First Inaugural Address," in Basler, ed., *Collected Works*, 4:271. See also Lincoln to Albert G. Hodges, April 4, 1864, ibid., 7:281–282.

[230] TJ to Pinckney, July 18, 1808, in *L&B* 12:104.

[231] Jefferson, ms. draft of *Summary View*, in *PTJ* 1:132. Nearly ninety years later, Lincoln would echo this sentiment: "It is safe to assert that no government proper, ever had a provision in its organic law for its own termination." Lincoln, "First Inaugural Address," March 4, 1861, in Fehrenbacher, ed., *Lincoln: Speeches and Writings, 1859–1865*, 217.

[232] TJ to Doctor James Brown, October 27, 1808, *L&B* 12:183. Even here, however, Jefferson falls back on the vigilance of the people. During the Burr conspiracy, Jefferson claimed: "I never entertained one moment's fear," and "I as little fear foreign invasion" (184).

[233] TJ to John B. Colvin, September 20, 1810, in *PTJ, Retirement Series*, 3:101. Also see TJ to John C. Breckinridge, August 12, 1803, in *L&B* 10:411, which describes a similar prerogative for the legislature during the crisis over the purchase of Louisiana and offers a nice illustration of the process as "the case of a guardian, investing the money of his ward in purchasing an important adjacent territory."

[234] TJ to John B. Colvin, September 20, 1810, in *PTJ, Retirement Series*, 3:101. On this point, see Jeremy David Bailey, "Executive Prerogative and the 'Good Officer' in Thomas Jefferson's Letter to John B. Colvin," *Presidential Studies Quarterly* 34 (December 2004), 732–754, at 749; and Paul A. Rahe, "Thomas Jefferson's Machiavellian Political Science," *Review of Politics* 57 (Summer 1995), 449–481, esp. 462–468, which emphasizes the way Locke and Jefferson both understood that executive prerogative must be accompanied by the people's right of resistance and the executive's ultimate accountability to the people. Also see Lincoln to Erastus Corning and Others, June 12, 1863, in Fehrenbacher, ed., *Lincoln: Speeches and Writings, 1859–1865*, 454–463; and "Reply to the Ohio Democratic Convention," June 29, 1863, ibid., 465–470.

executive enforcement of the law; separatist plans for "division of the Union" might demand something more. In any case, for Jefferson, the right of self-preservation – the first law of nature and of nations – applied to internal threats to national existence as well as external. Jefferson's embrace of the prerogative suggests both the crucial significance of union in his statecraft and the lengths to which he was willing to go to preserve it.

After retiring from office, Jefferson followed the War of 1812 from Monticello but with great interest and increasing alarm. The war, which Samuel Eliot Morison labeled (in 1970!) "the most unpopular war that this country has ever waged," saw widespread opposition in New England, including continued smuggling, refusal to aid the war effort, attempts on the part of Governor Caleb Strong of Massachusetts to establish a separate peace with Great Britain, and repeated calls for secession from the Union, culminating with the infamous Hartford Convention late in the war.[235]

Even before the war, Jefferson worried – not without reason – about the loyalty of New England, telling Henry Dearborn that he feared the "possibility of a separate treaty between [England] and your Essex men." Jefferson did not broach the subject of coercion here, relying instead (as was his wont) on the "majority" of Republicans in Massachusetts to "save us from this trial." But he also noted that this "majority" would be "entitled to" unspecified "aid" to snuff out such a conspiracy.[236] In another prewar reflection on the nature of the Union, Jefferson examined the possibility that disunion was latent in the federal system of "seventeen distinct states." Even if a "single state" was engulfed by despotism (not likely, in Jefferson's estimation), "sixteen others, spread over a country of two thousand miles diameter, rise up on every side, ready organized, for deliberation by a constitutional legislature, & for action by their Governor, constitutionally the commander of the militia of the state." Local discontent, Jefferson argued in an echo of *Federalist* 10, would not "spread to such an extent as to be able to face the sound parts of so extensive an Union." If it did so spread, the discontented could become the majority – "the regular government" – where they would control Congress and "redress their own grievances by laws peaceably and constitutionally passed." The very organization of the Union, then, should, without need of coercion, prevent secession. But the underlying implication remained clear: One discontented state would make itself the enemy of the other sixteen. So, even in his most sanguine moments, Jefferson hinted that the suppression of secession by force was a necessary, although of course extraordinary and undesirable, implication of his conception of the Union.[237]

[235] Morison, "Dissent in the War of 1812," in Morison, Frederick Merk, and Frank Freidel, *Dissent in Three American Wars* (Cambridge, MA, 1970), 3–31, at 3 and 31; Gannon, "Calculating the Value of the Union," 123–190.
[236] TJ to Dearborn, August 14, 1811, in *L&B* 13:73.
[237] TJ to A.C.V.C Destutt De Tracy, January 26, 1811, *PTJ, Retirement Series*, 3:337–338. It is no accident that Jefferson was batting this around with Destutt who had published a commentary on Montesquieu's *Spirit of the Laws* that Jefferson had translated and published. Long before,

Just days before the U.S. declaration of war in 1812, Jefferson told his old friend Elbridge Gerry that although the purposes of the "English faction" in Massachusetts were unclear, if it sought rebellion and disunion, "it ought to be met at once." While the national government "should be slow" to jump to conclusions, it "should" also, nevertheless, "put forth its whole might … to suppress" such a scheme. If the minority demanded to govern the majority on threat of disunion, then, such an "anti-republican" threat should be met with force. Again, Jefferson counted on what he believed to be the republican majority in Massachusetts to put down such schemes. But if they needed the "aid of their brethren of the other States" to bring "the rebellious to their feet," they should have it. The goal, Jefferson argued, was always repentance and reconciliation – the re-union of Massachusetts and Virginia would allow Jefferson to "say with old Simeon, 'Lord, now lettest thou thy servant depart in peace, for mine eyes have seen thy salvation.'"[238] But the outside possibility that the sister states, through the instrument of the national government, would need to use force to compel Massachusetts to remain in the Union is fairly clearly an open one here.[239]

Jefferson, in his imagination, was always able to count on a majority of citizens of the nation (or in a particular state) to support union and republican government. In 1785, in contrast with some of his other less hopeful statements from the Confederation period, he told English radical Richard Price that the American motto was "nil desperandum" over the question of union. Congress might not have explicit authority to enforce union now, he said, but as soon as "two States commit hostilities on each other … the hand of the Union will be lifted up and interposed, and the people will themselves demand a general concession to Congress of means to prevent similar mischiefs." The American people, in other words, were reflexively unionist and were willing to enlarge the powers of Congress to see "peace among the

Jefferson had copied into his commonplace book Montesquieu's reflections on the possible outcomes of insurrections in confederated republics. "Should a popular insurrection happen in one of the confederate states," Montesquieu had written, "the others are able to quell it. Should abuses creep into one part, they are reformed by those that remain sound." See David Carrithers, "Montesquieu, Jefferson and the Fundamentals of Eighteenth-Century Republican Theory," in *The French-American Review* 6 (Fall 1982), 160–188, quote at 180. See also TJ to Horatio G. Spafford, March 17, 1814, in *L&B* 14:120.

[238] TJ to Elbridge Gerry, June 11, 1812, *FE* 11:256–258.

[239] To this point, Jefferson had largely considered the disaffection and potential secession of single states only; although a case can be made for his concern about the entire region of New England, his fears of a state breaking off usually focused on Massachusetts. What made the later Missouri crisis so frightening to him, among other things, was its stark division of the Union into two large sectional interests – the scenario that Lincoln faced in 1861. How Jefferson projected to deal with this kind of situation is unclear. He largely despaired at the time. Jefferson understood the crisis in partisan terms, even as he feared the sectional consequences. In other words, he did not necessarily understand himself to be defending a "Southern" position when he resisted the Tallmadge Amendments. See the important discussion of Jefferson's response to the Missouri crisis as a threat to his ideal expanding harmonious union in Onuf, *Jefferson's Empire*, 127–129, 137–146.

States" enforced.[240] Later, under the Constitution, he nearly always blamed secessionist sentiment on the work of an English conspiracy and/or of "a few base & cunning leaders." Almost without exception, he fell back on this faith, even in his darkest moments.[241] He simply assumed that the good people of Massachusetts, for example, were true republicans and would, as such, subordinate their material interests for the good of the Republic. This may have been wishful thinking, but it was also extraordinarily magnanimous. As long as a majority, even of those with different ideological views, remained committed to Union – and Jefferson believed this to be true of most Federalists – the Union itself was safe. As Jefferson explained to Destutt de Tracy, when the discontented became the majority, they could redress their grievances within the framework outlined in the Constitution. Until then, the majority would always squelch any attempts to destroy the Union because the majority always had an interest in maintaining it. Jefferson's point anticipates Lincoln's 1856 question: "A majority will never dissolve the Union. Can a minority do it?"[242] Implied is a reminder to disaffected minorities that

[240] TJ to Richard Price, February 1, 1785, in *PTJ* 7:631.

[241] TJ to David Bailie Warden, December 29, 1813, in Sigmund Diamond, "Some Jefferson Letters," *Mississippi Valley Historical Review* 28 (September 1941), 232. Among multiple others in this vein, see TJ to Lafayette, February 14, 1815, in *FE* 11:461; and the interesting letter to John Melish, January 13, 1813, in *L&B* 13:206–210 in which Jefferson divided the population of New England into ideological sections, and insisted that separatist elements were only a minority faction of a minority party there. It is worth noting that Lincoln made the same argument about the seceded states in 1861: "It may well be questioned whether there is, today, a majority of the legally qualified voters of any State, except perhaps South Carolina, in favor of disunion. There is much reason to believe that the Union men are the majority in many, if not in every other one, of the so-called seceded States. The contrary has not been demonstrated in any one of them," and in some of them, Lincoln suggested, "Union men" were forced at the point of bayonets to "vote against the Union." See "Message to Congress in Special Session," July 4, 1861, in Basler, ed., *Collected Works*, 4:437. Lincoln admonished the discontented secessionists to wait patiently until the next election when they could, if they gained a majority, vote him out and someone more to their liking in. "Why should there not be a patient confidence in the ultimate justice of the people," he asked. See "First Inaugural Address," March 4, 1861, ibid., 270.

[242] Lincoln, "Speech at Kalamazoo, Michigan," August 27, 1856, in Basler, ed., *Collected Works* 2:366. Note that Madison, much less sanguine than Jefferson, understood that it was more than possible for minorities to "possess such a superiority of pecuniary resources, of military talents and experience, or of secret succors from foreign powers" that would render their power, although illegitimate, more substantial and effective than that of a majority. Even when majorities formed "illicit combinations for purposes of violence" within a single state, Madison said, "the federal authority" had an obligation "to support the state authority." *Federalist* 43, in Pole, ed., *The Federalist*, 238–239. Lincoln later contemplated – no, actually witnessed – the latter case, suggesting that the "constitutional obligation of the United States to guaranty to every State in the Union a republican form of government" applied to cases "wherein the element within a state, favorable to republican government, in the Union, may be too feeble for an opposite and hostile element external to, *or even within the State*," a scenario Jefferson usually dismissed as unthinkable. See "Annual Message to Congress," December 8, 1863, in Fehrenbacher, ed., *Lincoln: Speeches and Writings, 1859–1865*, 551–552, emphasis added. Hamilton, like Jefferson, appeared more optimistic about the ability of majorities to suppress domestic insurrections of minorities in "a small part of a state." See Hamilton, *Federalist* 28, in *The Federalist*, 148.

secession is a revolutionary right to be fought for, not granted, and of the right of the majority to suppress any rebellion posed by such a minority, as well as a thinly veiled threat that a majority would likely always be sufficient to suppress minority rebellion. Like Lincoln, who actually faced the kind of crisis that only haunted Jefferson's nightmares, Jefferson recognized the right of the unionist democratic majority to preserve itself.

Throughout the War of 1812, Jefferson repeatedly discussed the possibility that Massachusetts would secede from the Union.[243] He often dismissed such worries because he considered secession so quixotic or preposterous. "The defection of Massachusetts," he wrote, would be "a disagreeable circumstance, but not a dangerous one." Jefferson rhetorically dismissed anxiety primarily because "their own people will put down these factionists as soon as they see the real object of their opposition" – disunion and alliance with England.[244] But he also believed that separation would never last because Massachusetts needed its "sister States" if it was to survive. If Massachusetts seceded, Jefferson told James Martin, one option would be to "let them go." But he could contemplate this option only because it was so remote. Even if it could find a way to leave, Massachusetts would never last on its own – if affection wouldn't keep it in the Union, economic interest would force it to come back. It was also possible that war would break out between Massachusetts and the Union and in this case "it would be a contest of one against fifteen" (can a minority do it?). Even if Massachusetts did leave, then, disunion "would be corrected by an early and humiliating return to the Union." Often, it seems, Jefferson dismissed any real danger of disunion simply by imagining that such a thing could never happen.[245]

The ubiquity of such reflections in Jefferson's correspondence – and there are many – and the simple fact that no formal secession crisis ever erupted in Jefferson's day, make it easy to overlook or dismiss Jefferson's implied commitment to keeping the Union together – by force if necessary. But such implication is there, if we care to look. As he told Demeunier in 1786, a formal statement of the "right of compulsion" was unnecessary – it was implied by the compact itself.[246] That Jefferson bent over backward to effect (and imagine) reconciliation without resort to force is testimony to his dreams and forbearance, and to

[243] Kevin Gannon describes just how deeply this sentiment was seeded in Massachusetts – suggesting that Jefferson was actually too optimistic about majority unionist sentiment there. Gannon sees states' rights rhetoric and sentiment for secession as a grassroots phenomenon in New England with a long history that began with Jefferson's election in 1800. See Gannon, "Calculating the Value of the Union," especially 123–190, and David Hackett Fisher, "The Myth of the Essex Junto," in *WMQ*, 3rd series, 21 (April 1964), 191–235, which also emphasizes the moderating influence of the leadership at the Hartford Convention – precisely the group Jefferson believed to be a radical minority. It appears, from Gannon's work, that Jefferson had a much more democratically approved crisis (within the state) on his hands than he imagined.

[244] TJ to William Short, November 28, 1814, in *L&B* 14:217–218.

[245] TJ to James Martin, September 20, 1813, ibid., 13:382–383. Peter Onuf notes that Jefferson "externalized all threats to the Union," and he emphasizes Jefferson's faith in "the Union's durability in a time of crisis," *Jefferson's Empire*, 128, 130.

[246] "Answers to Demeunier's First Queries," January 24, 1786, in *PTJ* 10:19.

his firm confidence in the American spirit, not proof that at some point coercion would not become an option for him.[247]

Of course, all of this may beg the question of whether Massachusetts had some legal or constitutional "right" to leave the Union if it desired. But Jefferson tended to lean away from this abstract question and toward the practical one of how to respond to such a scenario – and his answers suggest that whatever "right" Massachusetts had to leave was matched by an equal right of the other states to force it to stay.

Revisiting his own metaphor of the Union as a planetary system, Jefferson told John Melish in the last days of the War of 1812 that it might at some point become necessary to "reduce ... by impulse instead of attraction, a sister planet into its orbit." As Jefferson acknowledged, this was changing the meaning of the original metaphor and such coercion would "be as new in our political as in the planetary system." Falling back on his old hope, Jefferson suggested that "the operation" would be "painful rather than difficult" because the "sound part of our wandering star [Massachusetts] will probably, by its own internal energies, keep the unsound within its course." There are multiple ways of reading this somewhat confusing letter, but it seems clear that Jefferson was acknowledging a scenario in which a majority in Massachusetts might prefer disunion, in which case it might become necessary for the union to compel a state to remain in the system against its will. This would not be the ideal – and it would be, as Jefferson put it: "a new chapter in our history."[248] But sometimes human societies, Jefferson wrote in a different context, were

---

[247] Attention to Lincoln's description of "coercion" and "invasion" as mere "enforcement of the laws of the United States" seems not inappropriate here. See his "Speech at Indianapolis, Indiana," February 11, 1861, in Basler, ed., *Collected Works* 4:195. Compare with TJ to Governor James Sullivan, August 12, 1808, in *L&B* 12:129: "We are sworn to execute the laws." It seems worth noting, also that shortly after he left the presidency, Jefferson endorsed Madison's threat of national force against Pennsylvania, which was resisting enforcement of the Supreme Court's decision in *United States v. Peters*. Jefferson reassured Madison that there had never "been any difference at all in our political principles, or any sensible one in our views of the public interests." Jefferson's only concern, he said, was the defiant "spirit manifested by the" Pennsylvania militiamen who had been arrested by a federal marshal for resistance to federal law. Jefferson professed to being "much mortified" at the Philadelphia parades celebrating their release. See TJ to Madison, May 22, 1809, in *ROL* 3:1588–1589. On the controversy, see Kenneth W. Treacy, "The Olmstead Case, 1778–1809," *Western Political Quarterly* 10 (September 1957), 675–691; and Gary D. Rowe, "Constitutionalism in the Streets," *Southern California Law Review* 78 (January 2005), 401–457. The most succinct discussion of the complicated story is William O. Douglas, "Interposition and the Peters Case, 1778–1809," *Stanford Law Review* 9 (December 1956), 3–12.

[248] TJ to John Melish, December 10, 1814, in *L&B* 14:219–221. It was possible, too, Jefferson worried, that Massachusetts secessionist leaders might call in "a foreign power" that would force the rest of the Union "to meet it but so much the nearer, and with a more overwhelming force." As Jefferson speculated around the same time, the "federalists will then call in the English army, the republicans ours, and it will only be a transfer of the scene of war from Canada to Massachusetts." "But," falling back on his faith in the republican majority, Jefferson declared, "It will not come to this," TJ to William Short, November 28, 1814, ibid., 217–218.

"compelled ... to choose a great evil in order to ward off a greater."[249] Coercion is not by any means entirely incompatible with any principle Jefferson had espoused before – particularly with his often-expressed devotion to the Union and his description of the catastrophes that would follow its demise.[250] If attempted secession was quelled by a republican majority within the offending state itself, this was all to the good (and to be expected). But if not, the sister states would come to the aid of the unionists there and crush the rebellion. The goal was always repentance, reconciliation, and avoidance of civil war, but there is nothing in the compact theory or in Jefferson's ideal of affectionate union that precludes coercive action on the part of sister states. In fact, it seems to be a natural implied component of Jefferson's theory of union.[251]

This admittedly brief and tentative exploration suggests that Jefferson was willing to enforce federal law in the face of opposition by state and local authorities, that he believed the Union was empowered to coerce a seceding state, and that he claimed executive prerogative in cases of national self-preservation or even of national interest. This was hardly Buchanan's position in 1860 and appears much closer to Lincoln's. None of this is meant to imply that Jefferson and Lincoln embraced similar theories of union. They did not. It is meant to suggest that our reflexive assumption that Jefferson's approach to *disunion* would have approximated Buchanan's or even that of the fire-eaters needs careful reconsideration. The argument here should not be misread as a reciprocal assertion that Jefferson would not have "gone with the Confederacy" but, rather, as a call for historians to reconsider our reflexive tendency to assume this counterfactual.

If we look at Jefferson's political career in its entirety, then, we see a kind of alternation between fear of the potentially negative consequences of centralized power, on the one hand, and a fear of national weakness and dissolution, on the other. During the Revolution, Jefferson joined other Americans in his resistance to arbitrary metropolitan authority. But during the Confederation period, Jefferson saw the greatest threat to American interests and liberty in the inability of Congress to compel member states to perform their obligations. During the 1790s, on the other hand, Jefferson understood the Federalists in charge of the national state to be exercising authority unauthorized by the original compact. The correction for this would be a restoration of the proper constitutional role of the state governments. During his presidency and the

---

[249] Ibid., 213.

[250] For three examples among many, see TJ to George Washington, May 23, 1792, in *PTJ* 23:538–539; TJ to Robert Wright, April 3, 1809 in *PTJ, Retirement Series*, 1:107; and TJ to James Ogilvie, August 4, 1811, in *L&B* 13:70–71.

[251] This is especially the case if secession is understood (as Jefferson seemed to understand it) as an insult to democratic majorities and to the sacrifices of the people and an elevation of one state above the others – a self-indulgence the opposite of Jefferson's ideal in both politics and in marriage, both of which required mutual sacrifices to preserve affection and harmony. See TJ to Thomas Jefferson Randolph, November 24, 1808; and to Maria Jefferson Eppes, January 7, 1798, in Edwin Morris Betts and James Adam Bear, Jr., eds., *The Family Letters of Thomas Jefferson* (Columbia, MO, 1966), 362–365, 151.

Republican ascendancy, however, Jefferson saw various threats to majority rule and to the legitimate powers granted to the national state posed by outlying states.

To be sure, in nearly every case, Jefferson's approaches to these crises were simplified by the fact that the threats he perceived came largely from his ideological enemies.[252] But we need not assume his approach disingenuous or cynical simply because we understand it, in retrospect, to be rooted in partisanship. Jefferson's partisan interests aligned with his idealistic nationalism and democratic faith. When threats to union came from his ideological allies, Jefferson tended to counsel patience. But, of course, Jefferson rarely saw threats to union from his allies, partly because he simply understood his partisan opponents to be the true ideological enemies of the Republic, and because in his lifetime more genuine threats to union really did come from Federalists and wayward Republicans like Burr than from southern defenders of "states' rights."[253] In any case, there is a kind of logic to Jefferson's career that a simple dismissal as hypocrisy cannot recover. Jefferson's ideal union rooted in harmony, affection, and interest was inextricably interwoven throughout his public career with a commitment to preserving the American nation and its republican promise – a commitment that sometimes demanded energetic government and might require coercive force. The republican promise so central to Jefferson's conception of the national meaning could not be separated in any clean way from the Union and the federal system of government through which Americans expressed their will. It is not necessary to claim that Jefferson made a fetish of the Union to acknowledge that he nevertheless understood its inextricability from America's promise and that for him the creation of union implied the right and duty of the majority to keep it.

---

[252] This is perhaps a way of paraphrasing what Jean Yarborough has said of American federalism generally: that it "has always been primarily a *political* issue rather than a legal issue – since the Constitution's silence on the powers reserved to the states allows considerable flexibility in distributing power between the states and the national framers," Yarborough, "Rethinking 'The Federalist's View of Federalism,'" *Publius* 15 (Winter 1985), 32. Also see Charles Warren's succinct dismissal of states' rights thought in American history as always aligned with the "economic and social interests" of its proponents: *The Supreme Court in United States History*, 2 vols., new and revised ed. (Boston, 1926), 1:388; and, of course, the classic statement in Arthur M. Schlesinger, "The State Rights Fetish," in *New Viewpoints in American History* (New York, 1922), 220–244: "The state rights doctrine has never had any real vitality independent of vast social, economic, or political significance. The group advocating state rights at any period have sought its shelter in much the same spirit that a western pioneer seeks his storm-shelter when a tornado is raging" (243). But see Ellis, "The Path Not Taken," and Mayer, *Constitutional Thought of Thomas Jefferson*, for compelling studies of certain strands of states' rights thought as principled, nuanced, and relevant.

[253] See Kevin Gannon, "Escaping 'Mr. Jefferson's Plan of Destruction': New England Federalists and the Idea of a Northern Confederacy, 1803–1804," in *JER* 21 (Autumn 2001), 413–443; and Schoen, "Calculating the Price of Union."

# Epilogue

## *America's Jefferson*

> Dear old Jefferson! ... We discuss him by the day together, just as though he were alive. We can fight about him as ardently as ever.
>
> Henry Adams, 1877[1]

> The historical sense involves a perception, not only of the pastness of the past, but of its presence.
>
> T.S. Eliot, 1932[2]

> In truth, there was no Jeffersonian solution. There were Jeffersonian sentiments.
>
> Merrill Peterson, 1960[3]

A central assumption of this book has been that Jefferson isn't exactly "ours." The thought that animated his politics was forged in a world we have lost and cannot be seamlessly assimilated to our own time or recovered pure for implementation today. Historians tend to consider presumptuous any "unjustified familiarity" with the past and see their work as, to some degree, an operation to rescue the truth about the past from the mythologies of memory, about which they remain "perpetually suspicious."[4] Memory, especially national memory, perhaps, establishes an unbroken flow of past to present; history, through the process of contextualization, insists on the disconnection. Historians are justifiably less confident than they used to be that they can examine the past as if in an antiseptic laboratory, uncontaminated by present political commitment or the "accumulated meanings" the past has acquired in the process

---


[1] Henry Adams to Hugh Blair Grigsby, October 9, 1877 in J.C. Levenson, et al., eds., *The Letters of Henry Adams*, 6 vols. (Cambridge, MA, 1982), 2:322–323.

[2] Eliot, "Tradition and the Individual Talent," in Eliot, *Selected Essays, 1917–1932* (New York, 1932), 4.

[3] Merrill D. Peterson, *The Jefferson Image in the American Mind* (New York, 1960), 78.

[4] Drew McCoy, *The Elusive Republic: Political Economy in Jeffersonian America* (Chapel Hill, 1980), 5; Pierre Nora, "Between Memory and History: Les Lieux de Memoire," *Representations* 26 (Spring 1989), 7.

of interpretation.[5] But, however much the historical treatment of Jefferson's thought in the body of this book assumes that a full understanding of Jefferson must situate him in a time and place unfamiliar to us, the national memory of Jefferson continues to crave his wisdom for our own time; it cares less about the meaning of the past in its age than it does about the past's intersection with the concerns of the present.[6]

An exploration of this problem might be out of place in a book with a different focus, but a historian of Jefferson's conception of nationhood cannot help but notice the ways in which the nation's collective attempt to remain true to Jefferson confirms and reaffirms his own insistence that the nation was and would remain the tender of the "vestal flame" of republicanism. Jefferson, like all thinkers and actors and ideas from the past, has two lives: one embedded in context and time – the Jefferson the historian is pledged to recover; the other, transcendent, timeless, mythological, relevant. Both are real; both are worthy of the historian's attention. We have examined Jefferson's America. It seems not at all improper to reflect for a moment on America's Jefferson.

Jefferson is the American logos. It fell to him to call us into being as "a people," distinct from other peoples, a sociological entity moving through time into an

---

[5] David Harlan, *The Degradation of American History* (Chicago, 1997), 10. Perhaps the most perceptive description I have read of this problem is in Richard Hofstadter, *The American Political Tradition* (New York, 1948), xxxviii–xxxix: "Later generations, finding certain broad resemblances between their own problems and those of an earlier age, will implicitly take sides with the campaigners of former years; historians, who can hardly be quite free of partisanship, reconstruct the original conflict from the surviving ideas that seem most intelligible in the light of current experience and current conviction. Hence the issues of the twentieth century are still debated in the language of Jefferson's time, and our histories of the Jefferson era are likewise influenced by twentieth-century preconceptions that both Jefferson and his opponents might have found strange."

[6] See Eva de Valk, "The Pearl Divers: Hannah Arendt, Walter Benjamin, and the Demands of History," *Krisis* (2010, Issue 1), 36–47. The critic, Walter Benjamin noted, was free to focus on the "truth content" of a work even when the "subject matter" within which the truth was embedded has "come apart" from it during the "afterlife" of the work itself. The critic "is concerned only with the enigma of the flame itself," while the mere "commentator" on the work is left to study "wood and ashes." "Thus," Benjamin explains, "the critic inquires about the truth whose living flame goes on burning over the heavy logs of the past and the light ashes of life gone by." See Hannah Arendt, "Introduction," in Walter Benjamin, *Illuminations* (New York, 1968), 5. If historians are the commentators of our national past, sifting through the wood and ashes to discover the origins of the fire and track its influence, the nation as interpretative community is the critic "concerned" with "the flame itself" which remains alive as long as it is remembered. The national interpretative community, then, is in a sense the tender of the "vestal flame" that Jefferson described to Madison in 1826 (TJ to Madison, February 17, 1826, in *TJW*, 1514; also see *Notes*, 165, where Jefferson says that the "sacred fire" is kept "alive" in the "breasts" of American citizens). The image was appropriate because fire, Jefferson noted, was "expansible over all space, without lessening [its] density in any point," and in this sense was like an idea – not "susceptible … of exclusive property." For "the moment it is divulged, it forces itself into the possession of every one, and the receiver cannot dispossess himself of it." And "he who receives an idea from me, receives instruction himself without lessening mine; as he who lights his taper at mine, receives light without darkening me." (TJ to Isaac McPherson, August 13, 1813, in *TJW*, 1291).

indefinite future – and committed to a set of cultural values associated with human rights and equality. If the Declaration we celebrate was really the assertion of the Continental Congress[7] – Jefferson himself called it the act of a "public body" to which he had "no personal claim"[8] – there is nevertheless so much in the text that is idiosyncratic to him, and seemingly unnecessary to the task at hand, that it is hard to imagine anyone else writing it in the same way.[9] And insofar as we continue to express our national intentions and ideals in his language, he remains central to the nation's continuing narrative about itself, and we, thus, remain his heirs.

With a modesty that approaches ostentation, all Jefferson claimed to have done in the Declaration was express the "American mind."[10] And this is a kind of trick he plays on historians who want to demonstrate, by de-mythologizing and contextualizing that moment, that Jefferson was really much less central to the founding project – even to the Declaration itself – than he or we tend to think. Because what has kept Jefferson central to our national discourse then and now is precisely that Jefferson's words resonated with the disembodied (and thus transcendent) American mind. They were words, he said, calculated to "command ... assent." But only "a people" that already agreed with him could assent to the claims he made in the Declaration. So the assent itself calls into being a people whose "mind" the Declaration was merely expressing, assuming precisely what had yet to be established (and proven).[11] And as long as we continue to imagine ourselves as a people using his language, as long as everything we do is justified in his words, "we" confirm or make real Jefferson's original assumption and establish precisely the continuity with him that he desired; so we remain both his imagined community and the community that imagines, the community that remembers him. His most enduring legacy, then, is that the nation considers itself his heir, and it is in this assent that we continually reconstitute the nation in his words.

If it is true that we will find Jefferson, as Gordon Wood suggests, "wherever we Americans have struggled over what kind of people we are," then Jefferson's ultimate significance clearly transcends the deeply contextualized readings of

---

[7] Making Jefferson the draftsman rather than the author of the Declaration is the burden of Pauline Maier, *American Scripture: Making the Declaration of Independence* (New York, 1997). Distinguishing Jefferson's draft from the congressional revisions is the central organizing principle of Garry Wills, *Inventing America: Jefferson's Declaration of Independence*. Also see John Phillip Reid, "The Irrelevance of the Declaration," in Hendrik Hartog, ed., *Law in the American Revolution and the Revolution in the Law* (New York, 1981), 46–89.

[8] TJ to John Campbell, September 30, 1809, in *PTJ, Retirement Series* 1:486–487. Campbell had proposed compiling a "complete Edition of [Jefferson's] different writings." See Campbell to TJ, July 29, 1809, in ibid., 385.

[9] David Armitage, *The Declaration of Independence: A Global History* (Cambridge, MA, 2007); Wills, *Inventing America*; Calhoun, "Speech on the Oregon Bill," June 27, 1848, in Clyde N. Wilson, ed., *Papers of John C. Calhoun*, 28 vols. (Columbia, 1958–2003) 25:535, 537–538; Lincoln to Henry Pierce, April 6, 1859, in Basler, ed., *Collected Works of Lincoln* 3:376.

[10] TJ to Henry Lee, May 8, 1825, in *L&B* 16:118.

[11] Jacques Derrida, "Declarations of Independence," in *New Political Science* 15 (1986), 7–15.

his life and thought offered by historians.[12] When Jefferson claimed that he had expressed the American mind, he meant that all Americans intuited what he wrote so that their experience of reading would be not that of revelation but of confirmation or affirmation. It would be an experience of unification because it premises that all Americans reading it will come to an awareness of common (collective) values, values that all Americans – "of whom I too am one," realize its readers – share and around which they can rally as one people with a common cause. In this sense, Jefferson speaks not so much to a "candid world" as to a national interpretative community where "the only proof of membership is fellowship," as Stanley Fish puts it: "The nod of recognition from someone in the same community, someone who says to you what neither of us could ever prove to a third party: 'we know.'"[13]

As Michael Zuckert has suggested, Jefferson did not assert that these truths are self-evident. He simply told the world that Americans believed them to be so: "*We* hold these truths."[14] Others should hold them, too, and one day would, Jefferson believed, but in 1776, Jefferson claimed only that Americans were the one people on earth who did not need to be convinced. The "principles of '76," then, as Jefferson suggested to his supporters in 1801, would "forever form a point of union round which we shall learn to rally *& to recognize one another*."[15] His little "paper of July 4, 1776," Jefferson told one correspondent, was nothing more than "the genuine effusion of the soul of our country at that time."[16] And what was truly gratifying about the fiftieth anniversary of the Declaration, he wrote in his final substantive letter, was the unbroken public reaffirmation of that initial effusion – "that our fellow citizens, after half a century of experience and prosperity, continue to approve the choice we made."[17] So the people are never mere spectators in Jefferson's account of the Revolution, which is never simply the work of a handful of great men. The people had been roused by events, he said. They had "met generally, with anxiety & alarm in their countenances"; they had taken matters into their own hands, acted out their "exasperat[ion]," followed their heart's

---

[12] Gordon S. Wood, "The Trials and Tribulations of Thomas Jefferson," in Peter S. Onuf, ed., *Jeffersonian Legacies* (Charlottesville, VA, 1993), 395–417, at 399; Jan Ellen Lewis and Peter S. Onuf, "American Synecdoche: Thomas Jefferson as Image, Icon, Character, and Self," in *AHR* 103 (1998), 125–136.

[13] I take my notion of "interpretative communities" from Stanley Fish, *Is There a Text in This Class?: The Authority of Interpretative Communities* (Cambridge, MA, 1988), esp. 147–173, quote at 173. Also see Benedict Anderson, *Imagined Communities: Reflections on the Origin and Spread of Nationalism* (London, 2006).

[14] Michael Zuckert, *The Natural Rights Republic: Studies in the Foundation of the American Political Tradition* (South Bend, 1996), 42–46.

[15] TJ to Fayetteville Republican Citizens, March 17, 1801, in *PTJ* 33:319, emphasis added.

[16] TJ to Dr. James Mease, September 26, 1825, in *L&B* 16:122–123.

[17] TJ to Roger C. Weightman, June 24, 1826, in *TJW*, 1517. Also see TJ to James Madison, August 30, 1823, in Smith, ed., *ROL* 3:1877: "It is a heavenly comfort to see that these principles are yet so strongly felt."

"pulsations," and "saved our country."[18] The people's engagement and self-constitution rather than the text is what is to be celebrated; the Declaration itself had been "their work."[19] Its "sentiments were of all America."[20] In claiming merely to lend effective literary expression to those sentiments – to being "a passive auditor of the opinions of others"[21] – Jefferson capaciously endorses the social history of the Revolution favored by those historians who want to reduce Jefferson's role to that of a decent draftsman. So Jefferson, in the end, has the last word, so to speak, and slips away from the de-mythologizers precisely by agreeing with them.

At the Monticello conference surrounding the 250th anniversary of Jefferson's birth, Joyce Appleby offered one of the greatest one-liners ever penned about Jefferson: Jefferson's greatest legacy, she said, was his hostility to legacies.[22] The point has undoubted resonance, nicely encapsulating Jefferson's dream of ridding the future of all artificial encumbrance from any shackles from the past. The living generation, he said, would be sovereign.[23] But, strictly speaking, it isn't quite right. Jefferson was noticeably and explicitly concerned about linking posterity with the Revolution and its achievements of which he had been, as he once put it, an "instrument." He clearly cared what he handed to future generations and what those future generations would think of him, and, however final the break he imagined between the European past and the American future, he assumed a continuity between that Revolutionary moment and the American posterity whose very freedom was rooted in that moment. Like the other founding "fathers," Jefferson had a "personal stake" in the creation of a stable Republic that would bless future generations – his own immortality depended on it, particularly if his hero Francis Bacon was right, that founding a commonwealth was the greatest thing a man could accomplish in this life and that which would be most likely to ensure his lasting fame.[24] Freeing the future paradoxically tied posterity irrevocably to the achievements of the Revolutionary past and, implicitly, to his own image.

[18] *Autobiography*, in *TJW*, 9; ms. text of *A Summary View*, July 1774, in *PTJ* 1:127; TJ to Maria Cosway, October 12, 1786, in *PTJ* 10:451.
[19] TJ to John Binns, August 31, 1819, *LC*.
[20] TJ to Joseph Delaplaine, April 12, 1817, *LC*.
[21] TJ to Madison, August 30, 1823, in *ROL* 3:1876.
[22] Joyce Appleby, "Jefferson and his Complex Legacy" in Onuf, ed., *Jeffersonian Legacies*, 1–16, at 2.
[23] TJ to James Madison, September 6, 1789, *PTJ* 15:393.
[24] Douglass Adair, "Fame and the Founding Fathers," in Trevor Colbourn, ed., *Fame and the Founding Fathers: Essays by Douglass Adair* (New York, 1974), 3–36, at 24. On Jefferson's respect for the interconnectedness of generations, see Peter S. Onuf, "Liberty to Learn," in Onuf, *The Mind of Thomas Jefferson* (Charlottesville, VA, 2007), 169–178. Another irony: although the "Jeffersonian" has often been read as a proxy for possessive individualism and ambivalence about the state, the historical Jefferson's fame rests precisely on his public service in the halls of state and in a self-proclaimed subordination of his private pursuit of happiness to a very public engagement in the service of posterity.

Although he was not widely known as the author of the Declaration of Independence until the late 1790s,[25] and though he typically disavowed any originality to the claims he made about the American people in his draft, Jefferson eventually took to calling July 4th "our nation's birthday," celebrating it instead of his own[26] and hoping that icons and relics of that day's achievement would "help to nourish our devotion to this holy bond of our Union, and keep it alive and warm in our affections."[27] Even the writing desk on which he wrote the Declaration – the material stuff of nationhood – would accumulate significance in the nation's embrace and might one day, he imagined, be "carried in the procession of our nation's birthday, as the relics of the saints are in those of the church."[28] His epitaph finally asserted authorship – rather than mere draftsmanship – of the Declaration and, by extension, authorship of the national meaning or, by some lights, the nation itself.

Jefferson would undoubtedly be pleased to discover, then, that when we argue about who we are, we never question the basic premise: that "we" exist – that we continue to be that "people" Jefferson described in the Declaration's first sentence. The "it-ness" of the nation is assumed, and this may, in the end, be Jefferson's most enduring legacy – not his alone, to be sure, but one he had the privilege of speaking into existence because of what John Adams called the "peculiar felicity" of his pen and which, as a result, will always be associated with Jefferson rather than, say, Adams, to the latter's lasting chagrin.[29]

Jefferson's character flaws have long troubled his image in the popular imagination.[30] And the Jefferson paradox, notes Francis D. Cogliano, continues to be that the more we learn about Jefferson – by studying the copious materials he so carefully gathered, precisely because he wanted future generations to

[25] On the growing public awareness of Jefferson's link to the Declaration, see Robert M.S. McDonald, "Thomas Jefferson's Changing Reputation as Author of the Declaration of Independence: The First Fifty Years," in *JER* 19 (Summer 1999), 169–195. Also see Philip F. Detweiler, "The Changing Reputation of the Declaration of Independence: The First Fifty Years," *WMQ*, 3rd Series, 19 (October 1962), 557–574. But also see "A Fourth of July Tribute to Jefferson," July 4, 1789, in *PTJ* 15:239–241.

[26] Margaret Bayard Smith, *The First Forty Years of Washington Society*, Galliard Hunt, ed. (New York, 1906), 398.

[27] TJ to Dr. James Mease, September 26, 1825, in *L&B* 16:122–123. This is in response to Mease's request for information about the house in which Jefferson had written the Declaration. See "Notes and Queries," *Pennsylvania Magazine of History and Biography* 41 (1917), 247–248. Jefferson remained interested enough in Mease's project – it had "excited my curiosity," he wrote – to write him again in October wondering "whether my recollections were such as to enable you to find out the house." To Mease, October 30, 1825, in ibid., 248.

[28] TJ to Ellen Randolph Coolidge, November 14, 1825, in Edwin Morris Betts and James Adam Bear, Jr., eds., *The Family Letters of Thomas Jefferson* (Charlottesville, 1986. Originally published: Columbia, MO, 1966), 461–462.

[29] Adams to Timothy Pickering, August 6, 1822, in *WJA* 2:514; Adams to Rush, June 21, 1811: "The Declaration of Independence I always considered as a theatrical show. Jefferson ran away with all the stage effect of that ... and all the glory of it."

[30] Peterson, *Jefferson Image*, 112.

remember him as the "apostle of liberty" – the less he seems to live up to the image he hoped to preserve.[31] But Jefferson's legacy does not rest fully on his own character or the vicissitudes of his reputation. In fact, Jefferson's legacy is precisely what has made it possible to critique Jefferson's own flaws. Jefferson's legacy can stand up to the criticism of Jefferson's character because Jefferson's character is never its true home.

Jefferson took particular pains to craft an image of himself that future generations would embrace in admiration and even love.[32] But he also seemed to understand intuitively Aristotle's notion that the "condition of descendants" would "affect" the meaning and significance of "their ancestors," so that both the successes and failures of future generations would shape the "honors or dishonors" of a person long dead.[33] Or, as the writer of the Book of Hebrews put it, ancestors, without posterity, could "not be made perfect." In other words, Jefferson understood that his own reputation rested on the future well-being of his descendants. Their happiness – and very existence – would ensure his own continuing relevance. Jefferson wanted to be remembered as the founder of a nation and as a champion of human freedom, a destroyer of all artificial distinctions and a freer of the human spirit to a natural liberty so that when Americans celebrated their liberty and prosperity they would rarely fail to remember his own work.

So much of Jefferson's life's work is in this direction that our celebrating him as the liberator of the human spirit is not misplaced. In his very first public paper of note, in 1774, Jefferson exposed the artificiality of the way "chance, not choice" had placed men in different societies so that the vicissitudes of life, so often taken to be "natural" predictors of legitimate allegiance, actually violated natural human right. British conceptions of political obligation assumed that subjectship was rooted in that very "chance" that Jefferson described.[34] But Jefferson exposed the artificialness of chance and instead championed "choice," thus presaging a career that marshaled the claims of nature against the limits of artificiality.[35] When it came time to describe his life's work in his *Autobiography* – which he hoped would shape his image for posterity – Jefferson gave pride of place to his reforms in the laws of Virginia, characterizing the most important four, in intention at least (two were not passed) as a "system by which every fibre would be eradicated of antient or future

[31] Francis D. Cogliano, *Thomas Jefferson: Reputation and Legacy* (Charlottesville, 2006); and "'Thomas Jefferson is Looking Down on You, and He's Dissatisfied!': The Thomas Jefferson Paradox," paper delivered June 27, 2009, in Charlottesville at the conference on "John Adams and Thomas Jefferson: Libraries, Leadership, and Legacy," in possession of the author.

[32] Cogliano, *Thomas Jefferson: Reputation and Legacy*; Jennifer Tiercel Kennedy, *Signing History: The Memoirs of Benjamin Franklin, Benjamin Rush, John Adams, and Thomas Jefferson* (PhD Dissertation, Yale University, 1999), 249–340.

[33] Aristotle, *Nicomachean Ethics*, trans. and ed. Terence Irwin, 2nd ed. (Indianapolis and Cambridge, 1999), 13.

[34] James H. Kettner, *The Development of American Citizenship, 1608–1870* (Chapel Hill, 1979).

[35] TJ, ms. text of *A Summary View*, PTJ 1:121.

aristocracy; and a foundation laid for a government truly republican." The distinctions drawn by aristocratic laws were "unnatural" ones, and if there was anything Jefferson hated it was an artificial barrier to freedom.[36]

The stance is clear in his crusade against primogeniture, which perpetuated the "unequal life chances that resulted from the lottery of birth order."[37] The laws abolishing primogeniture and entail, "drawn by myself," Jefferson told John Adams, had, he claimed, "laid the axe to the root of Pseudo-aristocracy" as opposed to the "natural aristocracy" he endorsed.[38] When a fellow legislator, hoping to preserve primogeniture, "proposed we should adopt the Hebrew principle, and give a double portion to the elder son," it was characteristic of Jefferson to "observe ... that if the eldest son could eat twice as much, or do double work, it might be a *natural* evidence of his right to a double portion; but being on a par in his powers & wants, with his brothers and sisters, he should be on a par also in the partition of the other members."[39] The most important bill "by far," Jefferson said, was that for the "general diffusion of knowledge" – a system of schools for "the common people" funded at the "common expense of all" – precisely because in the absence of widespread education "kings, priests and nobles" would "rise up among us," thereby eradicating that natural freedom and happiness that Americans would otherwise enjoy.[40] Even the celebrated act establishing Religious Freedom had as one purpose "put[ting] down the aristocracy of the clergy" by restoring "to the citizen the freedom of the mind."[41]

But one of the four bills Jefferson emphasized was not quite like the others, at least not in the eyes of posterity. The bill, also not passed, was for the emancipation of Virginia's slaves. In his *Autobiography*, Jefferson made a good deal of it, blaming its failure on an immature "public mind," unable at present to "bear the proposition," thus making Jefferson's proposal heroic by contrast, which in many ways it was. But the artificiality of slavery – in need of eradication – quickly ran into what Jefferson more or less took to be natural racial differences between whites and blacks. Nature demanded emancipation: "Nothing is more certainly written in the book of fate that these people are to be free." But nature also demanded colonization: "Nor is it less certain that

---


[36] *Autobiography*, in *TJW*, 44.

[37] Mark Kishlansky, *A Monarchy Transformed: Britain, 1603–1714* (New York, 1996), 12. Kishlansky cites a contemporary complaint that primogeniture was a system that "if it did not drown all the kittens but one, threw all but one into the water."

[38] TJ to Adams, October 28, 1813, in *AJL*, 389. Also see Holly Brewer, "Entailing Aristocracy in Colonial Virginia: 'Ancient Feudal Restraints' and Revolutionary Reform," *WMQ* (April 1997), 307–346.

[39] *Autobiography*, in *TJW*, 39, emphasis added.

[40] Bill No. 79, *PTJ* 2:526–533; TJ to George Wythe, August 13, 1786, in *PTJ* 10:244–245. Jefferson later blamed the failure of this bill on the fact that it "would throw on wealth the education of the poor," a "burthen" the "more wealthy class" proved "unwilling to incur." See *Autobiography*, in *TJW*, 43.

[41] TJ to Adams, October 28, 1813, in *AJL*, 390.

the two races, equally free, cannot live in the same government. Nature, habit, opinion has drawn indelible lines of distinction between them."[42]

What was artificial was, by definition, amenable to change, but once Jefferson decided that something was natural – women's domesticity, for another example – there wasn't very much anyone could do about it, and heaven help you if you happened to be *naturally* inferior because "natural rights" would not. Where Jefferson took something to be a natural difference, there was little hope for its improvement. What remains particularly troubling about the section on race in the *Notes* is the way he seems to read black intellectual inferiority as innate, and therefore theoretically incapable of amelioration.[43]

To be sure, Jefferson's colonization scheme does depend on the cultivation "at the public expense" of black statesmen, artisans, and farmers, "according to their geniussus," thus implicitly assuming the existence of a black natural aristocracy that would make black freedom and independence real and meaningful wherever it was established.[44] But it is never clear that such could ever rise to the level of whites, in his view, and it is simply not possible to get around Jefferson's racial hierarchy, offered as "a suspicion only" in the *Notes* but apparently never modified. Miscegenation, he wrote in 1814, "produces a degradation to which no lover of his country, no lover of excellence in the human character can innocently consent."[45] Preserving "the blood of [the] master" from the "staining" of sex between blacks and whites remained one of his central rationale for colonization, which, he wrote as late as 1826, was still "greatly preferable to the mixture of colour here, to this I have great aversion."[46] Jefferson reportedly told an English visitor to Monticello in 1807 that the "Negro race" was "as far inferior to the rest of mankind as the mule is to the horse, and [was] made to carry burthens,"[47] and he suggested in 1814 that American slaves were "better fed ... warmer clothed, and labor less than the journeymen or day-laborers of England" and were, unlike British soldiers and seamen (likewise subject to "bodily coercion"), guaranteed "the certainty" that "at the end of their career, when age and accident shall have rendered them unequal to labor" they "will never want." Jefferson was quick to anticipate misunderstanding here: "Do not mistake me. I am not advocating slavery."[48] But it is not altogether difficult to see in Jefferson's various statements the seeds of the proslavery ideology that would enchant southern intellectuals shortly


[42] *Autobiography*, in *TJW*, 44.

[43] See James Oakes, "Why Slaves Can't Read: The Political Significance of Jefferson's Racism," in James Gilreath, ed., *Thomas Jefferson and the Education of a Citizen* (Washington, D.C., 1999), 177–192.

[44] *Notes on the State of Virginia*, in *TJW*, 265.

[45] TJ to Edward Coles, August 25, 1814, in *TJW*, 1345.

[46] *Notes*, in *TJW*, 270; TJ to William Short, January 18, 1826, *LC*.

[47] Sir Augustus John Foster Bart, *Jeffersonian America: Notes on the United States of America Collected in the Years 1805-6-7 and 11-12*, Richard Beale Davis, ed. (Westport, CT, 1980), 149.

[48] TJ to Thomas Cooper, September 10, 1814, in *L&B* 14:183.

after Jefferson's death. Minus James Henry Hammond's celebratory spin (and this is a crucial difference), all the elements of Hammond's 1858 "mudsill" speech in the U.S. Senate are already present in Jefferson's thinking: the critique of free wage labor, the assumption of racial hierarchy, and the hints of a paternalistic relationship between master and slave that transcended the cash nexus. Jefferson's lifelong antipathy to slavery is clear and persuasive and not in dispute here. John Quincy Adams was right to point out that Jefferson "was above that execrable sophistry … which would make of slavery the cornerstone to the temple of liberty. He saw the gross inconsistency between the principles of the Declaration of Independence and the fact of negro slavery."[49] That inconsistency is precisely why proslavery theorists cast Jefferson aside as useless – or worse – to their cause (George Fitzhugh read the Declaration as a collection of "powder-cask abstractions," and John C. Calhoun said "there is not a word of truth in it").[50] But Jefferson remained caught, throughout his public life, between this genuine revulsion at slavery on the one hand – it is difficult to think of a more emotionally powerful passage in his writing than the critique of slavery in Query 18 of the *Notes* – and his racialist thinking on the other – it is difficult to think of a more nakedly racist statement in his writing than Query 14 of the same text. Winthrop Jordan calls the latter passage "the most intense, extensive, and extreme formulation of anti-Negro 'thought' offered by any American in the thirty years after the Revolution,"[51] and black abolitionist David Walker decried it as "as great a barrier to our emancipation as any thing that has ever been advanced against us."[52] The statements about race raised objections even among Jefferson's contemporaries. Charles Thomson, whose advice Jefferson had sought, encouraged him to excise them because, he said, they "might seem to justify slavery."[53] But by 1814, Jefferson had already "ceased to think" much about emancipation – a problem for the

[49] Adams, journal entry for January 27, 1831, in Charles Francis Adams, ed., *Memoirs of John Quincy Adams*, 12 vols. (Philadelphia, 1874–1877) 8:299–300.

[50] Peterson, *Jefferson Image*, 169; Calhoun's "Speech on the Oregon Bill," June 27, 1848, in Wilson, ed., *Papers of Calhoun* 25:534. Calhoun ended his speech lamenting precisely what Lincoln appreciated about the Declaration's statement of human equality: that "in the process of time it began to germinate, and produce its poisonous fruits. It had strong hold on the mind of Mr. Jefferson, the author of that document, which caused him to take an utterly false view of the subordinate relation of the black to the white race in the South, and to hold, in consequence, that the latter, though utterly unqualified to possess liberty, were as fully entitled to both liberty and equality as the former, and that to deprive them of it was unjust and immoral" (537–538). Also see Henry Cleveland, *Alexander H. Stephens, in Public and Private: With Letters and Speeches, Before, During, and Since the War* (Philadelphia and Chicago, 1866), 126, 721.

[51] Winthrop Jordan, *White Over Black: American Attitudes Toward the Negro, 1550–1812* (Chapel Hill, 1968), 481. Jordan notes that the passage elicited harsh criticism from egalitarians in his own day. See ibid., 441–444, 450, 516.

[52] Walker, *David Walker's Appeal*, ed., Sean Wilentz (New York, 1995), 27.

[53] Douglas L. Wilson, "The Evolution of Jefferson's 'Notes on the State of Virginia,'" *The Virginia Magazine of History and Biography* 112 (2004), 98–133, at 124. It is worth noting that John Adams considered the "passages upon slavery" to be "worth diamonds." See Adams to TJ, May 22, 1785, in *AJL*, 21.

next generation, he said.[54] But the next generation, in the South, at least, would connect all these elements by dropping entirely Jefferson's hostility to slavery. It was only in the North that Jefferson's Declaration would become a "stumbling block" on the issue of slavery.[55] In the South, Jefferson was remembered as the author of the Kentucky Resolutions, and there his Declaration emphasized state equality in the Union and the consent of the governed.[56] The tragedy is that both were right; and the result was civil war.

Combine all this with the equally troubling suggestion made by an increasing phalanx of historians that Jefferson's actual antislavery credentials or zeal waned after 1784, and the picture we have in the wake of the civil rights movement, when this literature first emerged, is of Jefferson as a kind of father to the go-it-slow southern liberals castigated in King's "Letter from a Birmingham Jail," at best, and to the race-baiting White Citizens' Councils at worst.[57] If the nation had, by the 1960s, begun to read into the very meaning of the Declaration's liberty and happiness a vision of racial equality, Jefferson's reputation as the "apostle of freedom" was bound to suffer as a result of all these fresh and disturbing revelations from the letters and documents he had so carefully preserved for posterity. The problem of slavery became – and remains since the 1960s – "the most contentious and morally challenging aspect of Jefferson scholarship" and the most fundamental challenge to the national memory of the man.[58] Even the Sally Hemings "problem" suddenly had less to do with the original critics' horrors of miscegenation (which it could remain as long as Jefferson's antislavery credentials were secure) than its highlighting of Jefferson's hypocrisy as a slavemaster. As John Hope Franklin put it starkly in the 1990s: "I think that it doesn't really matter whether he slept with her or not. He could have. After all, he owned her. She was subject to his exploitation in every conceivable way."[59]

Particularly unsettling is the simple, but generally overlooked, fact that many of the things we most admire about Jefferson and take to be more or less unproblematic in his list of accomplishments depended in fundamental ways on what we consider today to be his deepest failings.[60] Would there even be a

---

[54] TJ to Edward Coles, August 25, 1814, in *TJW*, 1345; TJ to Short, January 18, 1826, *LC*.

[55] Lincoln to Henry Pierce, April 6, 1859, in Basler, ed., *Collected Works of Lincoln* 3:374–376.

[56] William Cooper, "Jefferson Davis and the Meaning of the War," in Cooper, *Jefferson Davis and the Civil War Era* (Baton Rouge, 2008), 91–100, esp. 93–95; Paul Quigley, "Independence Day Dilemmas in the American South, 1848–1865," in *JSH* 75 (May 2009), 235–266.

[57] William Cohen, "Thomas Jefferson and the Problem of Slavery," in *JAH* 56 (1969), 503–526; Paul Finkleman, "Jefferson and Slavery: 'Treason Against the Hopes of the World,'" in Onuf, ed., *Jeffersonian Legacies*, 181–221; Gary B. Nash, and Graham Russell Gao Hodges, *Friends of Liberty: Thomas Jefferson, Tadeusz Kǒ̇ciuszko, and Agrippa Hull: A Tale of Three Patriots, Two Revolutions, and a Tragic Betrayal of Freedom in the New Nation* (New York, 2008); Cogliano, *Thomas Jefferson: Reputation and Legacy*, 199–229.

[58] Cogliano, *Thomas Jefferson: Reputation and Legacy*, 200.

[59] John Hope Franklin, Interview for *Thomas Jefferson: A Film by Ken Burns* (1996). Available: http://www.pbs.org/jefferson/archives/interviews/frame.htm (June 16, 2010).

[60] Lucinda Stanton, "'Those Who Labor for My Happiness': Thomas Jefferson and his Slaves," in Onuf, ed., *Jeffersonian Legacies*, 147–180.

Monticello to visit today if his architectural genius had been denied the slave labor necessary to put his plans into execution? (The same could be asked of the University of Virginia.) Would the Library of Congress exist had not Jefferson been willing to go into debt to purchase such a collection in the first place – a debt that also, in the end, encouraged him to sell the books to Congress? One thing is clear and striking when you stop to reflect on it: Jefferson– we can say this unequivocally – simply would not have been in Philadelphia in 1776 as a member of the Virginia delegation to Congress had he not been a prominent member of Virginia's planter class, a fundamental prerequisite of which was the ownership of substantial numbers of slaves to work its fields. The Declaration itself, then, was made possible by the very institution it, in theory, most despised. Historian John Ashworth even suggests that Jefferson's very egalitarianism – his "cherishment" of common whites, as he once put it – was possible only because the planter class exploited the labor of slaves rather than ordinary white men.[61]

But if Jefferson's reputation waned in the scholarship written in the wake of the civil rights movement, the very fact that Martin Luther King, Jr., called America to live out the "true meaning of its creed" by citing the Declaration's assertion of equality meant that Jefferson would continue to be relevant to discussions of the national meaning if only because his words – which had clearly clashed so often with his practice – still called us to our better selves even as they condemned our – and his – hypocrisy.

From the moment the words were on the page, the Declaration rendered multitudes of Americans uneasy about slavery and has made Americans ever since uncomfortable with artificial inequalities of all sorts. Like T.S. Eliot's magi, Americans could remain "no longer at ease here, in the old dispensation." From that moment, even slaves espied liberation in and asserted claims in the language of the Declaration however limited the willingness of their masters, Jefferson included, to fully extend that radical potential in their direction.[62] The language of the Declaration, as Mia Bay puts it, provided a "'lingua franca' that could express [black] aspirations for liberty" that predated the Revolution.[63] But it was a *lingua franca* that many whites understood as well, precisely why opponents of slavery – of all varieties – appealed to it. The power

---

[61] Ashworth, *Slavery, Capitalism, and Politics in the Antebellum Republic*, vol. 1: *Commerce and Compromise* (Cambridge, 1995), 23; Edmund S. Morgan, "Slavery and Freedom: The American Paradox," in *JAH* 59 (June 1972), 5–29.

[62] T.H. Breen, "Making History: The Force of Public Opinion and the Last Years of Slavery in Revolutionary Massachusetts," in Ronald Hoffman, Mechal Sobel, and Fredrika J. Teute, eds., *Through a Glass Darkly: Reflections on Personal Identity in Early America* (Chapel Hill, 1997), 67–95; Douglas Egerton, "Gabriel's Conspiracy and the Election of 1800," *JSH* 56 (May 1990), 191–214.

[63] Mia Bay, "'See Your Declaration Americans!!!': Abolitionism, Americanism, and the Revolutionary Tradition in Free Black Politics," in Michael Kazin & Joseph A. McCartin, eds., *Americanism: New Perspectives on the History of an Ideal* (Chapel Hill, 2006, 25–52, at 27.

of Frederick Douglass's critique of American slavery rested, to a great degree, on the contrast the Declaration's promise of equality offered to American practice: "What to the slave is the Fourth of July?" was a question that, like the Declaration itself, could be instantly understood by the interpretative community that was America.[64]

But only retroactively. In theory, Americans had but to "see" their Declaration, and "understand" their "own language," Walker suggested, to make things right.[65] But eradicating slavery was not quite as simple as it sounds on paper: It took a civil war that claimed more than 600,000 lives to even begin to reconcile Jefferson's claims in the Declaration with America's practice.[66] It was hardly a rhetorical exercise. The trap Jefferson found himself in – that between holding the wolf's ear and letting him go – was never simply rooted in his racial fears alone but also in his understanding that slaves were legal property: "Actual property has been lawfully vested in that form," he lamented, "and who can lawfully take it from the possessors?"[67] Either compensation or violation of that right would be necessary, and disunion was a likely consequence. Ending slavery, in other words, demanded a social revolution and a government confiscation of property the likes of which the world would not see again, perhaps, until the Russian Revolution. But the Declaration, in Lincoln's reading of it, at Gettysburg and elsewhere, allowed the nation to make the transition sound more or less seamless. We have always described even our most radical social transformations as a kind of natural or logical fulfillment of Jefferson's words.

So the Declaration has continued to perform crucial work for our national meaning and significance. And what the Declaration has always done is offer America an escape hatch from moral degradation. Its alchemy is in turning America's rot into an aberration, not intrinsic to the national fabric but an alien growth (Lincoln himself called slavery a "cancer" on the body politic),

---

[64] Frederick Douglass, "What to the Slave is the Fourth of July," extract from an oration at Rochester, July 5, 1852, in Douglass, "My Bondage and My Freedom," in Henry Louis Gates, Jr., ed., *Douglass, Autobiographies* (New York, 1994), 431–435. Compare Lincoln's post-Kansas-Nebraska lament that "the fourth of July has not quite dwindled away; it is still a great day – *for burning fire-crackers!!!*" Lincoln to George Robertson, August 15, 1855, in Don E. Fehrenbacher, ed., *Lincoln: Speeches and Writings, 1832–1858* (New York, 1989), 359. Lincoln's Declaration, it seems worth noting here, was the cornerstone of a civic nationalism that theoretically transcended all ethnic division, connecting, by its "electric cord," descendants of the founding fathers and recent immigrants with no "blood ... connection" to the Revolutionary generation but who, nevertheless, could claim the Declaration as "the father of all moral principle in them" just "as though they were blood of the blood and flesh of the flesh of the men who wrote that Declaration." Lincoln, "Speech at Chicago, Illinois," July 10, 1858, in ibid., 456.

[65] Walker, *David Walker's Appeal*, 74–75.

[66] See Charles Francis Adams to His Son, July 4, 1862, in Worthington Chauncey Ford, ed., *A Cycle of Adams Letters, 1861–1865* 1 (Boston and New York, 1920), 162.

[67] TJ to Jared Sparks, February 4, 1824, in *TJW*, 1485; TJ to Edward Everett, April 6, 1826, *L&B* 16:162–163. This was, of course, precisely the problem Lincoln faced, too, which is why emancipation came in the form of an executive order – a war measure by the commander in chief.

and therefore redeemable and theoretically curable. The nation could "purify" itself, as Lincoln said, in the "blood of the Revolution" by "re-adopt[ing] the Declaration of Independence."[68] It could wash off the stain and become itself again. Scholars have shown that this reading is not quite right – that our racial tensions and ascriptive hierarchies are in fact part of the very fabric of American history and ideology.[69] But what we have from Jefferson, nevertheless, is a way to escape from nihilism, from utter cynicism. It long ago did the work of imagining and making a nation; now the Declaration's message is ultimately a message of redemption, allowing that nation to tell the world and itself: "This is not who we are! Look, instead, at what Jefferson tells us we are." Not a single significant and successful reform movement in American history has approached America's problems via any other route than the one that leads *back* to Jefferson's initial claims about us as a people. All of them call America to live up to the American promise rooted in the Declaration, which we have always tended to read as a challenge to fulfill the "better angels of our nature" and a hope that we in fact have better angels.

And to do this we don't necessarily have to fall all over ourselves about Jefferson himself. It is not necessary to evade what Herbert Croly called "difficult and novel political and economic problems" by substituting shouts of "'Hurrah for Jefferson!'"[70] To paraphrase Richard Rorty: What matters for posterity is less that Jefferson lived up to the image he projected than whether we continue to find the image itself worthy of emulation and adoption.[71] Jefferson's sins do not absolve his "children" of the obligation to harvest and accumulate the fragments from his legacy that will, "in the fulness of time," take on new meaning and significance when applied to conundrums he could not have envisioned.[72] So, the process of conscious renegotiation – striving for understanding (rather than the passive and instinctual embrace of form) – is not antithetical to Jefferson's purposes but their very fulfillment. If we fail to continually arrest our "degeneracy" and renew our commitment to Jefferson's claims, Lincoln said, we might as well move to "some country where they make no pretence of loving liberty – to Russia, for instance, where despotism can be taken pure, and without the base alloy of hypocracy."[73]

It is not really possible to get away from Jefferson as long as we continue to argue about who we are and what we mean. Even if we did decide to throw Jefferson out of the pantheon and level his memorial to the ground, we would

---

[68] Lincoln, Speech at Peoria, IL, October 16, 1854, in Basler, ed., *Collected Works of Lincoln* 2:276.

[69] Rogers Smith, "Beyond Tocqueville, Myrdal, and Hartz," in *American Political Science Review* 87 (September 1993), 549–566; and Smith, *Civic Ideals: Conflicting Visions of Citizenship in U.S. History* (New Haven, 1997).

[70] Peterson, *Jefferson Image*, 352.

[71] Richard Rorty, *Contingency, Irony, and Solidarity* (Cambridge, 1989), 79–80.

[72] TJ to John Tyler, May 26, 1810, in *TJW*, 1227.

[73] Lincoln to Joshua Speed, August 24, 1855, in Fehrenbacher, ed., *Lincoln: Speeches and Writings, 1852–1858*, 363..

do so because he wasn't American enough for us and the standard we would use to judge his Americanness would be his own creed.

Jefferson's legacy is a contested one because even though we all use his same words, we don't all mean the same thing by them.[74] Take the phrase, "pursuit of happiness," for example, a phrase so ubiquitous in our society that we can barely grasp its radical implications in the eighteenth century. The U.S. National Soccer team bus at the 2010 World Cup was emblazoned with a variant of it: "Life, Liberty, and the Pursuit of Victory!"[75] The *Splenda* packet in our coffee room at work reads, "Life, Liberty, and the Pursuit of Sweetness." And Cadillac advertises its monstrosity, the Escalade, surely among the least socially friendly vehicles on the road, with the slogan: "Life, Liberty, and the Pursuit." Because, after all, the ad tells us, "life is High School ... with money," and staying one step ahead of "the cool kids" now involves buying the Escalade.[76] Jefferson's revolutionary statement of fundamental rights, then, descends every day into a slogan more appropriate for the consumer society we have become.

But commercial exploitation of the language of the Revolution goes back to the Revolution itself. The house where Jefferson wrote the Declaration – which he hoped might one day become a republican shrine "nourish[ing]" the memory of the Revolution and keeping the Union "warm in our affections" – became a men's clothing store that called itself "BIRTH-PLACE OF LIBERTY" and advertised its wares with reference to Jefferson's "Glorious Declaration of our Unalienable Rights, Among which are Life, Liberty and Genteel Garments."[77] And why not? After all, one way to read that problematic phrase is, of course, as an affirmation or validation of the pleasures of the private sphere – surely one of the most enduring legacies of the enlightenment – and certainly one not foreign to Jefferson's own lifestyle.[78] But, although Jefferson identified the people's happiness as one of the "ends" legitimate government should "effect,"[79] the precise meaning of "the pursuit of happiness" has eluded us, with some emphasizing "pursuit" (as in *opportunity*) and others "happiness" (as in *realization* and *enjoyment*). Still others note that a true enlightenment (and Jeffersonian) concept of happiness cannot be divorced from a commitment to the public good, that benevolence to others – not heedless pursuit of self-indulgence – is the only source of genuine happiness and well-being, and that a government

---

74 Eric Foner, *The Story of American Freedom* (New York, 1999).

75 Ronald Blum, "U.S. Team Protected by Stone Walls, Barbed Wire," Associated Press, June 1, 2010. Available: http://nbcsports.msnbc.com/id/37436087/ns/sports-soccer/ (June 12, 2010).

76 Cadillac – Graduate commercial. Available: http://www.splendad.com/ads/show/2144-Cadillac-Graduate (June 12, 2010).

77 Jay Fliegelman, *Declaring Independence: Jefferson, Natural Language, and the Culture of Performance* (Stanford, 1993),196–200.

78 Roy Porter, "Material Pleasures in the Consumer Society," in Porter and Marie Mulvey Roberts, *Pleasure in the Eighteenth Century* (New York, 1996), 19–35; Porter, *The Creation of the Modern World: The Untold Story of the British Enlightenment* (New York, 2000), 258–275.

79 "Original Rough Draught," in *PTJ* 1:423–424.

interested in cultivating individual happiness must make some provision for the commons.[80] One of the only other places Jefferson used the phrase was as a critique of a vapid self-indulgence, a longing for unworthy objects: "Thus the days of life are consumed, one by one, without an object beyond the present moment; ever flying from the ennui of that, yet carrying it with us; eternally in pursuit of happiness, which keeps eternally before us."[81] Surely this is no general sanction of the pursuit itself but raises fundamental questions about that which is worth pursuing. It turns out to not be quite as "self-evident" as Jefferson claimed, after all.[82]

Our collective memory of Jefferson has always been contested precisely because his words (which to this day give us our collective sense of self) are themselves so contestable. This has made it possible for both Franklin Roosevelt and Ronald Reagan, for both Abraham Lincoln and Jefferson Davis, for right libertarians and left social democrats to claim Jefferson's mantle without any of them sounding altogether deluded.

What preserves us from anarchy or nihilism – from making every man his own Jefferson – is Jefferson's concept of the nation as the interpretative community, a community of remembrance that both constitutes and embodies as well as continually contests its own mythologies. Whatever Jefferson thought and hoped the nation was or would become is largely in our hands now. The imperative of continual reaffirmation and the self-critique involved in reexamination is deeply embedded in the Declaration itself. Robert Frost nicely captured Jefferson's approach when he noted that Jefferson's "hard mystery" would "trouble us a thousand years." "Each age," Frost said, "will have to reconsider it."[83] This is not far from Jefferson's own endorsement of the sovereignty of the living generation. As Jefferson put it in 1816:

Laws and institutions must go hand in hand with the progress of the human mind. As that becomes more developed, more enlightened, as new discoveries are made, new truths disclosed, and manners and opinions change with the change of circumstances, institutions must advance also, and keep pace with the times. We might as well require a man to wear still the coat which fitted him when a boy as civilized society to remain ever under the regimen of their barbarous ancestors.[84]

Memory and continual renegotiation seem to bear Jefferson's imprimatur as the sites where the truest meaning of the past resides. "Our children," he told John Tyler in 1810, "will be as wise as we are, and will establish in the fulness

---

[80] For an extended argument along these lines see Wills, *Inventing America.*
[81] Jefferson to Anne Willing Bingham, Feb. 7, 1787, in *PTJ* 11:122–123.
[82] Arthur M. Schlesinger, "The Lost Meaning of 'The Pursuit of Happiness,'" in *WMQ* 21 (1964), 325–327; Robert Darnton, "The Pursuit of Happiness: Voltaire and Jefferson," in *George Washington's False Teeth: An Unconventional Guide to the Eighteenth Century* (New York, 2003), 89–106.
[83] Robert Frost, "The Black Cottage," from *North of Boston* (1915), in Richard Poirier and Mark Richardson, eds., Frost, *Collected Poems, Prose, & Plays* (New York, 1995), 59–62, at 60.
[84] TJ to Samuel Kercheval, July 12, 1816, in *TJW*, 1401.

of time those things not yet ripe for establishment. So be it."[85] If the historian's ossification can render Jefferson irrelevant, memory continually reaffirms his presence and his present significance. It is not history, then, but active memory that recovers or, rather, makes the past speak to the present.

"It was a great thing to go so far," Jefferson wrote of Locke's *Letter on Toleration*, "but where he stopped short, we may go on." Likewise, Jefferson never expected that the nation would stop where the founders themselves did.[86] "The question we ask ourselves," Woodrow Wilson insisted, "is not, How would Jefferson have pursued [his "objects" or ends] in his day? But How shall we pursue them in ours?" It was "the spirit, not the tenents of the man by which he rules us from his urn."[87] Jefferson's "objects," as Wilson called them, were *prima facie* correct, he assumed, but twentieth-century citizens of an industrial power might need to explore fresh approaches to realizing them. Government for Jefferson, claimed Franklin Roosevelt, "might be either a refuge and a help or a threat and a danger, depending on the circumstances." Jefferson, Roosevelt argued, "did not deceive himself with outward forms."[88] In contrast, Ronald Reagan later tried appropriating Jefferson's legacy for his own attempt to reduce the scope of the federal government, aspiring to become, in the words of one admirer, "the Last Jeffersonian" by applying "Jefferson's ideas about small government and individual liberty to a post-industrial democracy"[89] – precisely what Progressives and New Dealers assumed impossible. The latter were at pains to stay right with Jefferson but could do so only by jettisoning what was taken to be Jefferson's philosophy of limited government and by arguing that a static Jeffersonianism would only serve conservative – even reactionary – ends; that a rigid adherence to the letter of Jefferson's eighteenth-century words was apt to undermine his spirit.[90]

Continual rethinking the meaning of Jefferson's words has long offered us different Jeffersons. Most recently, some scholars have tentatively suggested that Jefferson's decades-long relationship with Sally Hemings, if true, might in fact go some distance toward mitigating his harshest words about racial mixing and make Jefferson, in a particularly ironic move, one father of the multicultural and multiracial nation that America has become but that his words explicitly disavowed. In a 1998 editorial in the *New York Times* just after the news broke that DNA testing had linked a Jefferson male to one of Sally

---

[85] TJ to John Tyler, May 26, 1810, *TJW*, 1277.

[86] "Notes on Locke and Shaftesbury," *PTJ* 1:548.

[87] Jeffrey Lee Sedgwick, "Jeffersonianism in the Progressive Era," in Gary L. McDowell and Sharon L. Noble, eds., *Reason and Republicanism: Thomas Jefferson's Legacy of Liberty* (Lanham, MD, 1997), 189–204, at 202.

[88] Roosevelt, Address at the Commonwealth Club, San Francisco, September 23, 1932, in Samuel I. Rosenman, ed., *The Public Papers and Addresses of Franklin D. Roosevelt*. Volume 1, *The Genesis of the New Deal, 1928–1932* (New York, 1938), 745.

[89] Steven Greffenius, *The Last Jeffersonian: Ronald Reagan and Radical Democracy* (Salt Lake City, 2001), 30.

[90] Peterson, *Jefferson Image*, 330–376.

Hemings's children, Orlando Patterson confessed: "Today, I feel less alienated from him, as I suspect will most African-Americans eventually. He is part of the family, a family with a ghastly, contradictory past, to be sure, but a family nonetheless."[91] Clarence Walker, likewise, suggested that "sexual encounters between blacks and whites did occur at Monticello and are as much a part of the Jeffersonian legacy as the Declaration of Independence."[92] There certainly are dissenters from this view who continue, like John Hope Franklin, to emphasize the constraints under which Hemings operated. For example, newspaper columnist DeWayne Wickham argued that thinking of the Hemings-Jefferson relationship as a love story serves largely to protect Jefferson from being remembered as a rapist.[93] Annette Gordon-Reed rightly notes that "it will probably be left to novelists, playwrights, and poets ... to get at the ultimate meaning of this story."[94] But what is particularly interesting about this newest reading among some historians also is the way it reverses typical patterns of exonerating Jefferson. The nation has long looked to Jefferson's stirring words to locate some mitigation of his behavior. These scholars instead see the possibility that in his actual behavior there might be a way to unravel his most devastating words on the issue of race and reconcile the multicultural nation to its past. This is not the only and may not be the best way to read this particular issue, in the end, but it does serve as a particularly compelling example of the way we continually rethink Jefferson and consider the fortunes of his own reputation as bound up in some fundamental way to our national image.

So Jefferson himself is continually remade as we remake ourselves in his words, and now, perhaps, in his deeds as well.


Legacies are two-way streets. It is possible for an heir to squander an inheritance. Especially when legacies are unencumbered, as Jefferson's surely are, they can be tricky things, malleable by heirs for good or ill without much regard for the original wishes of the testator (precisely why aristocrats entailed their estates). The unencumbered nature of Jefferson's legacy is perhaps the ultimate expression of his faith in American posterity. American republicanism was to be found not in institutions or constitutions, Jefferson said, "but merely in the spirit of our people." The American spirit he witnessed in his day

---

[91] Orlando Patterson, "Jefferson, the Contradiction," *New York Times*, November 2, 1998. Available: http://www.nytimes.com/1998/11/02/opinion/jefferson-the-contradiction.html (June 16, 2010).

[92] Clarence Walker, "Denial is not a River in Egypt," in Onuf and Lewis, *Sally Hemings and Thomas Jefferson: History, Memory, and Civic Culture* (Charlottesville, 1999), 187–198, at 195; Rhys Isaac, "Monticello Stories Old and New," in ibid., 114–126, at 124; Annette Gordon-Reed, " 'The Memories of a Few Negroes': Rescuing America's Future at Monticello," in ibid., 236–254, esp. 245–248.

[93] DeWayne Wickham, "Hemings, Jefferson: No Free Will, No Love," *USA Today*, February 1, 2000, 15A.

[94] Gordon-Reed, "The Memories of a Few Negroes," 251.

reassured him that the next generation would be "as capable as another of taking care of itself, and of ordering its own affairs."[95]

Jefferson left us with a distinctive stance toward inequalities – not necessarily a guidebook for implementation, but a consistent willingness to see so much of what all previous history had characterized as natural as, in fact, artificial. Obviously, as we have seen, there were tragic limits to this stance. But it was characteristic of Jefferson to seek out the social and cultural construction of most barriers to equality rather than simply assume that they were legitimate bases for inequalities. And where he spied an artificial inequality, he generally sought ways to ameliorate it.

As we have seen, Jefferson was never content to rest with a mere declaration of rights or a procedural liberty – crucial as he believed such to be – but moved to mitigate the harshest inequalities by cultivating capabilities in citizens that would, over time, effect a more even distribution of property and power.[96] Jefferson saw less tension between liberty and equality than later generations have, and he never fetishized "negative" liberty as somehow fully distinguishable from its "positive" variants.[97] He seemed to intuit what Amartya Sen has suggested: that "the affirmation of human rights is a call to action – a call for social change – and it must not be hostage to a pre-existing feasibility."[98]

Consequently, Jefferson's stance toward artificiality and inequality has long given sanction to movements the historical Jefferson balked at in his time. When black feminist Anna Julia Cooper encouraged Americans in 1893 to see "race, color, sex, and condition ... as accidents, and not the substance of life," for example, she did so in the name of what she called "the universal title of humanity to life, liberty, and the pursuit of happiness," using Jefferson's standard to question what even he had considered natural barriers to equality.[99] If Jefferson's liberalism fell short in his day, we should hesitate to call it bankrupt or exhausted. If many feminists would later rely on Jefferson's language of equal rights, others wielded his conception of women's difference to expand,

---

[95] TJ to Samuel Kercheval, July 12, 1816, in *TJW*, 1397, 1401.

[96] Neem, "Developing Freedom: Thomas Jefferson, the State, and Human Capability," unpublished paper in possession of the author; Neem, "'To Diffuse Knowledge More Generally through the Mass of the People': Thomas Jefferson on Individual Freedom and the Distribution of Knowledge" in *Light and Liberty: Thomas Jefferson and the Power of Knowledge*, ed. Robert M. S. McDonald (Charlottesville, 2012), 47–74; Michael Hardt, "Jefferson and Democracy," *American Quarterly* (2007), 41–78; Brewer, "Entailing Aristocracy in Virginia."

[97] Steven Lukes, "Liberty and Equality: Must they Conflict?" in David Held, ed., *Political Theory Today* (Stanford, 1991), 48–66.

[98] Amartya Sen, "The Power of a Declaration," *New Republic*, February 4, 2009, 30–32.

[99] Cooper quoted in Robin D.G. Kelley, "Looking Extremely Backward: Why the Enlightenment Will Only Lead Us into the Dark," in *Yo' Mama's Disfunktional! Fighting the Culture Wars in Urban America* (Boston, 1997), 103–124, at 112. Note that Kelley himself argues that Jeffersonian universalism does not offer "a truly emancipatory vision" (124) even as many of his examples, like Cooper, call not for the abandonment of it but for its full working out and ultimate fulfillment.

rather than restrict, women's political activity.[100] By this route, too, Jefferson's ideal gender order became classified – in fine Jeffersonian fashion – as yet another *artificial* barrier to social equality in America.[101]

As Jefferson's heirs, we should ask ourselves whether we are less willing than he was to face the likely consequences of creating something so modest as equality of opportunity. It costs us nothing to denounce antebellum slavery today, but it might require a good deal of moral courage and a lot more beside to afford all Americans an equal shot at pursuing happiness in this era of deepening economic inequalities and continuing racial caste.[102] Documenting Jefferson's failures has become a fairly simple – almost routine – matter, but we might rather consider our own in light of his remarkable vision for posterity. Jefferson was brave to trust us to carry his legacy. Was he warranted in so doing?

I have emphasized the nationalist implications of Jefferson's Declaration, but, from the beginning, the Declaration raised the question of how far to widen the circle of "we." It took some two-hundred years of conflict waged with explicit reference to the Declaration before the circle could substantively include even all Americans. The international claims against the United States in reference to the Declaration were likewise powerful as early as 1776. The North Ministry's pamphleteer could not pass up the opportunity to catch the Americans in hypocrisy for charging King George with inciting "domestic insurrection" in the colonies. "Is it for them to say, that it is tyranny to bid a slave be free" when it was "their boast that they have taken up arms in support of their own self-evident truths?" Who were Americans "to complain of the offer of freedom held out to these wretched beings? of the offer of reinstating them in that equality, which, in this very paper, is declared to be the gift of God to all?"[103] In the 1840s, Charles Dickens wondered how Congress could abide the slave trade in Washington, D.C., without turning the Declaration of Independence ("gilded, framed, and glazed," as it was) "towards the wall" in shame. And he sardonically referred to one master of slaves as "the champion of Life, Liberty, and the Pursuit of happiness, who had bought them."[104] Foreign

---

[100] See the "Declaration of Sentiments" at the 1848 Women's Rights Convention in Seneca Falls, NY, reprinted in Kathryn Kish Sklar, *Women's Rights Emerges Within the Antislavery Movement, 1830–1870* (Boston, 2000), 175–178, and, esp., Abby Price, "Address," (1850), ibid., 181. See Ellen Carol DuBois, "The Limitations of Sisterhood: Elizabeth Cady Stanton and Division in the American Suffrage Movement, 1875–1902," in Barbara J. Harris and JoAnn K. McNamara, eds., *Women and the Structure of Society* (Durham, 1984), 160–169.

[101] Berthoff and Murrin, "Feudalism, Communalism, and the Yeoman Freeholder: The American Revolution Considered as a Social Accident," in Stephen G. Kurtz and James H. Hutson, eds., *Essays on the American Revolution* (Chapel Hill, 1973), 282.

[102] U.S. Department of Commerce, *Middle Class in America* (January 2010); Richard Wilkinson and Kate Pickett, The *Spirit Level: Why Greater Equality Makes Societies Stronger* (New York, 2009); Michelle Anderson, *The New Jim Crow: Mass Incarceration in an Age of Colorblindness* (New York, 2010).

[103] John Lind, *An Answer to the Declaration of the American Congress* (London, 1776), 106–107.

[104] Dickens, *American Notes*, ed. Christopher Lasch (Greenwich, CT, 1961), 141, 158.

visitors and observers have long measured American behavior in the world by the Declaration's claims so that even expressions of "anti-Americanism" abroad can become reminders of those claims, evoking backhanded admiration of American values.[105] Certainly, on the other hand, plenty of non-Americans have taken inspiration from Jefferson's words and have not seen a need to hold American citizenship to lay claim to the assertions of rights in paragraph two of the Declaration. Mikhail Gorbachev claimed to have been inspired by Jefferson while a student at The University of Moscow and to have learned from him that "without a profound democratization of our society any reform in it would be doomed to fail," thus turning Jefferson into a kind of parent (or grandfather) of Glasnost and the ultimate victor in the Cold War.[106]

But beyond this kind of appropriation, Jefferson's enlightenment cosmopolitanism imagined a day – far distant, perhaps, but nevertheless on the horizon – when the world would be populated by republics and all humanity would be joined together in a community of the enlightened, free, and happy.[107] There really is a sense in which, as Henry Adams put it, "Jefferson aspired beyond the ambition of a nationality, and embraced in his view the whole future of man."[108] Even his deep admiration for Jesus's "system of morality" as the "most sublime and benevolent code of morals which has ever been offered to man"[109] was rooted in his appreciation of its success in "inculcating universal philanthropy, not only to kindred and friends, to neighbors and countrymen, but to all mankind, gathering into one family, under the bonds of love, charity, peace, common wants, and common aids."[110] As if to confirm such a reading, Jefferson's final letter asserted the Declaration of Independence's centrality to the struggle for republicanism around the world: "May it be to the world ... the signal of arousing men to burst the chains under which monkish ignorance and superstition had persuaded them to bind themselves." The "light from our West," he told John Adams, "seems to have spread and illuminated the very engines employed to extinguish it" by giving "them a glimmering of their rights and their power."[111]

Nevertheless, as I have tried to suggest here, although Jefferson believed that the existence of rights did not depend on legislation, he also understood that

[105] Alan McPherson, "Americanism Against American Empire," in Michael Kazin & Joseph A. McCartin, eds., *Americanism: New Perspectives on the History of an Ideal* (Chapel Hill, 2006), 169–191, at 171–172.

[106] Norio Akashi, "Thomas Jefferson's Legacy in an International and a National Context: A Reinterpretation," in *The Japanese Journal of American Studies* 6 (1995), 31–45, at 33 and 37.

[107] Nicholas G. Onuf and Peter S. Onuf, *Nations, Markets, and War: Modern History and the American Civil War* (Charlottesville, 2006), 219–246.

[108] Henry Adams, *History of the United States*, 100–101.

[109] TJ to Joseph Priestley, April 9, 1803, in Dickinson W. Adams, ed., *Jefferson's Extracts from the Gospels*, in *Papers of Thomas Jefferson*, 2nd Series (Princeton, 1983), 328; to John Adams, October 12, 1813, ibid., 352.

[110] Syllabus of the doctrines of Jesus, April 21, 1803, in ibid., 334.

[111] TJ to John Adams, January 11, 1816, in *AJL*, 460.

the realization of rights did, and that legislation was the province of states.[112] The Declaration announced the emergence of a new state in the international system of states[113] but also asserted that this particular state would be committed to human rights. The nationalist implications of the Declaration, then – and this is remarkably Jeffersonian – were, in his view, less in tension with than the fulfillment of universal human rights claims. There is, consequently, nothing necessarily parochial about this strongly national vision. As long as there is a United States that continues to affirm and uphold and expand and extend its initial claims of human rights in its actual legislation and practice, it will remain the heir of Jefferson's legacy, which will die, it seems to me, only when "we" no longer embrace it.

Finally, on the other hand, Jefferson's limitations and failures, uncovered by the most recent scholarship, offer us an opportunity to check our own tendency to hubris by highlighting the many ways we have always failed to live up to Jefferson's claims about us. Jefferson's legacy is replete with irony, and he could be a poor prophet. He assumed that his promotion of religious freedom would turn the United States into a Unitarian nation. Instead, it ushered in an explosion of evangelical Christianity, the likes of which the world has arguably never seen before or since. His purchase of Louisiana, which he believed would secure the nation's expansion in harmonious union, ended up spreading slavery across the continent and leading, indirectly, to Civil War (not to mention the dispossession of American Indians, not entirely unintentional). His celebration of economic autonomy and his tendency to see monopoly as the result of artificial alliances between government and economic privilege largely missed the way class and concentration of wealth would emerge from the logic and practice of the free market itself.[114] His rhetoric of limited government and his celebration of the virtues of the private sphere have been brandished to impoverish the public sphere he long served and to leave ordinary Americans (his particular concern) without much in the way of protection from private power through long swaths of American history. His natural aristocracy of talent and virtue has tended over time – just as John Adams warned him it would – to perpetuate itself, passing on its advantages to its children who compete in a marketplace that often simply reinforces already existing power relations. And his nationalist vision – which embraced the cosmopolitanism of the "republic of letters" – has often become insular and self-congratulatory, satisfied and bombastic.[115] Jefferson's intentions rarely turned out quite like he hoped, which is at least one reason tracing his legacy is so complex a task: Should we judge him by the intentions or by outcomes (if, that is, we can even link the outcomes

[112]  Hannah Arendt, *On Revolution* (New York, 1963), 147.
[113]  Armitage, *The Declaration of Independence.*
[114]  Christopher Lasch, "The Jeffersonian Legacy," in Lally Weymouth, ed., *Thomas Jefferson: The Man, His World, His Influence* (New York, 1973), 229–245, at 232.
[115]  See Simon Schama, "The Unloved American," *New Yorker*, March 10, 2003, 34–39; and Anatol Lieven, *America Right or Wrong: An Anatomy of American Nationalism* (Oxford, 2004).

to his intentions with any pretension to accuracy)?[116] It seems fair to say, as Michael Lee Andrews does say, that "the modern United States can plausibly be viewed as both the realization and the abandonment of the original Jeffersonian vision."[117]

If we combine all these unintended consequences with Jefferson's inability to solve the problem of slavery and with his failures in personal finance, Jefferson offers us an opportunity to stare America's limitations in the face. Instead of rejecting Jefferson's sins as somehow not American enough for us, on the one hand, or merely celebrating him by ignoring his failings, on the other, we might want to consider this historiographical moment (which has been largely negative for Jefferson's reputation) as an opportunity to chasten our tendency to self-congratulation and find the moral courage to face our own limitations. Instead of defending Jefferson so we can celebrate him once again, we might embrace his complexity as a way of adjusting our conception of ourselves as a nation which, as Christopher Hitchens has put it, has both "upheld great values and principles" and "committed gross wrongs and crimes."[118]

C. Vann Woodward held out the hope in the mid-twentieth century that the southern experience of tragedy and defeat might, as he put it, "provide some immunity to the illusions and myths of American nationalism."[119] However elusive that hope proved, the decline in Jefferson's reputation offers us a similar opportunity today. Jefferson fully expected – or hoped – that future generations would find solutions to problems he characterized as blocked by "the public mind" in his own day.[120] But it is not possible to hope without a good sense of how limited our abilities have always been to resolve the most difficult kinds of inequalities, because "hope that is seen is not hope." The founders cannot solve our problems because they couldn't even solve their own. And we cannot simply wish these limitations away by ignoring them or by congratulating ourselves about how far we have come.

This is not to make Jefferson himself a tragedian, but the full story of his life and career, hard won by the painstaking work of historians, grants us an opportunity to read Jefferson as offering us both a source of hope as well as a contemplation of irony and even tragedy. And if our collective memory can reach this stage, if it can squarely face the tragedy of our limits at the same time that it cultivates appreciation for our accomplishments, then it will actually

---

[116] See Jack Rakove, "Our Jefferson," in Onuf and Lewis, *Sally Hemings and Thomas Jefferson,* 233–234.

[117] Michael Lee Andrews, *Thomas Jefferson and the Endless Republic: Liberty, Nature and the Flight from Authority* (Ph.D. Dissertation, Tulane University, 2005), 2.

[118] Christopher Hitchens, *Thomas Jefferson: Author of America* (New York, 2005), 186.

[119] C. Vann Woodward, *The Burden of Southern History* (New York, 1960), 13, 168–169; Tennant McWilliams, *The New South Faces the World: Foreign Affairs and the Southern Sense of Self, 1877–1950* (Baton Rouge, 1988), esp. 1–15.

[120] Jefferson, *Autobiography*, in *TJW*, 44; TJ to Edward Coles, August 25, 1814, in *TJW*, 1344; Ari Helo and Peter S. Onuf, "Jefferson, Morality, and the Problem of Slavery," in *WMQ* 60 (June 2003), 583–614.

be a mythology in tune with the complexities of history and would achieve something extraordinary: a national mythos that served history rather than the other way around.

For in the end, Jefferson failed to live up to our highest values, which he articulated in the moment that gave the nation its birth. And it is in both the depths of his failures and in the height of his aspirations that he perhaps reminds us most of ourselves.

# Index

CPSIA information can be obtained at www.ICGtesting.com
Printed in the USA
LVOW06s2157011215

464906LV00003B/195/P